PSYCHOLOGY: A SYSTEMATIC INTRODUCTION

PSYCHOLOGY: A SYSTEMATIC INTRODUCTION

WILLIAM R. THOMPSON
Professor of Psychology
Queen's University

RICHARD C. DeBOLD
Professor of Psychology
Long Island University

McGraw-Hill Book Company

NEW YORK   ST. LOUIS   SAN FRANCISCO   DÜSSELDORF
LONDON   MEXICO   PANAMA   SYDNEY   TORONTO

**PSYCHOLOGY:
A SYSTEMATIC INTRODUCTION**

Copyright © 1971 by McGraw-Hill, Inc. All rights reserved. Printed in the United States of America. No part of this publication may be reproduced, stored in a retrieval system, or transmitted, in any form or by any means, electronic, mechanical, photocopying, recording, or otherwise, without the prior written permission of the publisher.

Library of Congress Catalog Card Number 76-109256
64429

1 2 3 4 5 6 7 8 9 0   VHVH   7 9 8 7 6 5 4 3 2 1 0

This book was set in News Gothic by Monotype Composition Company, Inc., and printed on permanent paper and bound by Von Hoffmann Press, Inc. The designer was Edward Zytko; the drawings were done by James Stone, Engineering-Drafting Company. The editors were Walter Maytham and Helen Greenberg. Stuart Levine supervised the production.

PREFACE

To date, there have been two major ways of presenting psychology to the beginner. The more common may be called data-oriented. Psychology is surveyed under a number of empirical topic headings, such as learning, thinking, perception, and motivation. This method emphasizes the facts issuing from mainly contemporary studies rather than the theoretical frameworks within which, and because of which, such studies were initially generated. The advantage of this approach lies in its breadth and variety. Its major disadvantages lies in its failure to show the student why certain kinds of investigations are carried out. Psychology is thus presented as a vast collection of often disconnected empirical facts. It is significant, we think, that the student who chooses to major in psychology will probably never again take a course that presents the field as a unified whole.

This brings us to a consideration of the second approach, which is far less common but nevertheless strongly favored by some teachers. According to this approach, a commitment is made to a particular theoretical framework; this model is then used to explain as many empirical aspects of psychology as its limits can encompass. One of the best-known texts of this kind has adopted a neobehaviorist position, another, a physiological point of view; a third has selected "choice" and "organization" for its major themes. The impact of this method lies in its demonstrating the immense power of a carefully articulated theory. Once given a few key laws or axioms—concerning, for example, reinforcement, brain connections, or signal detection—the student may find that he can account for a variety of phenomena and also that he is able to formulate new hypotheses and designs appropriate for testing them.

Undoubtedly, such an approach has great educational merit. But its equally great fault lies in its narrowness. The present state of psychology, for better or worse, is such that no single approach can be regarded as characterizing psychology more "truly" than another. Thus, many clinical psychologists are *not* prepared at the present time to embrace a behaviorist, or stimulus-response, position. Likewise, most experimentalists, however kindly they may feel toward psychoanalysis, probably do not find it a useful way of thinking about the problems that are their immediate concern. Again, about models of behavior based on properties of brain function, many are indifferent.

This text attempts to steer a middle course between the two alternatives outlined above. It strongly affirms the value of using a theoretical approach, but not at the expense of breadth. Psychology is presented in terms of six major approaches, each with its own historical and philosophical underpinnings, emphasis on certain kinds of data, methodology, and separate unique style. Each separate system, precisely because of its narrowness of focus, stresses certain limited kinds of psychological data. The six systems together provide a more panoramic vista of the whole field.

To present psychology in this way, we believe, is to show it as it actually exists. Few psychologists would be willing to trace their intellectual ancestry to the pallid theoretical axioms that underlie an eclectic approach. Many, however, would be willing to acknowledge a debt to Freud, Hull, Lashley, Lewin, Koffka or Spearman—in a negative if not in a positive sense.

This brings us to an important point. We have structured this book around the major ideas from which psychology has emerged. In so doing, it has been necessary to lay considerable emphasis on the thinkers whose deep commitments encouraged the blazing of new intellectual trails. Such men as those mentioned above can hardly be ignored. Their unique styles and personalities are woven into the fabric of psychology. Yet, it is the ideas on which they dwelt that are of greatest importance. The concept of unconscious mental processes does not belong to Freud alone. Although he was most responsible for shaping this idea into a useful probe with which to explore human personality, many before him, in many fields, nurtured it.

Consequently, we have tried to strike a suitable balance between an emphasis on ideas and an emphasis on men. Some sections stress one more than the other. For example, in the areas of personality theory, perception, and learning, the debt to particular individuals seems greater than it does in the field of biological and social psychology. But whatever the failings of our particular emphases may be, we fully acknowledge that both men and ideas are important.

It is likewise true that our emphasis on particular lines of thought varies a good deal between sections. This is partly a matter of individual choice and taste. Our presentation is not intended to be exhaustive but rather to cover some conceptualizations that we feel have been seminal in a particular area. Thus we do not wish to give the impression, to take two examples, that the psychology of personality is today dominated by Freudian notions or that contemporary work in perception as a Gestalt orientation. We have stressed these approaches because they have been important in the historical development of the two fields and because they are intrinsically interesting.

But this is by no means a text only on the history of psychology or systems of psychology. We also wish to present some empirical facts or laws—to the extent that we possess them—not only those that have stood the test of time but also some that have been recently uncovered. Such facts are usually gathered within the framework of a theory, which may be very narrow or very broad. But in the end, it is the framework which makes the fact significant for a researcher and, we hope, understandable to the beginning student. The fact, in turn, "tests" the theory and tells us whether it is sensible and logical.

Many readers may feel that we have overemphasized history and theory at the expense of facts. This may well be true. It is most difficult in a work of this size to do justice to all three areas. Our main commitment has been to the presentation of some of the great systems of thought in psychology; consequently, we have not attempted to include as much up-to-date empirical data as is contained in most introductory texts. However, we feel that the student who has been properly equipped with some conceptual tools of theory will be much better able to assimilate additional facts provided by other sources.

One final point. There are often debates as to whether a beginning course should have a "professional" or a "general" or "liberal arts" orientation. The present approach makes this Hobson's choice unnecessary. Each of the book's seven sections deals, at a simpler and more general level, with the material usually covered in advanced psychology courses. In this sense, the book has a professional orientation. But the mode of presentation heavily emphasizes philosophy, history, and related disciplines, and to this extent it should serve at least some of the needs of the general student.

WILLIAM R. THOMPSON
RICHARD C. DeBOLD

CONTENTS

PREFACE

ONE PSYCHOLOGY: ITS NATURE AND METHODS
PROLOGUE   2

chapter 1 The Nature of Psychology   4

Definition of Psychology   4
Relation of Psychology to Other Disciplines and to Society   8
The Present Status of Psychology   14

chapter 2 Psychology and the Problem of Inference: Statistics   18

Drawing Conclusions in Psychology   18
Basic Statistics   19
Statistical Versus Clinical Prediction   29

CONCLUSION: THE PLAN OF THE BOOK   30

TWO PSYCHOANALYSIS AND THEORIES OF PERSONALITY
PROLOGUE 34

chapter 3 Basic Notions and Method of Psychoanalytic Theory 36
The Background 36
Basic Notions 37
Three Methodological Postulates 38

chapter 4 The Topography and Structure of Personality 42
The Topography of Personality 42
The Collective Unconscious 54
Structure of Personality 55

chapter 5 The Dynamics and Economics of Personality 59
Dynamics 59
Economics 68

chapter 6 The Development of Personality 74
The Stages of Development 74
Other Views of Development 85

CONCLUSION 86

THREE MODELS OF SOCIAL BEHAVIOR
PROLOGUE 92

chapter 7 The Nature of Social Psychology 95
Fundamentals 95
Social Motivation 99

chapter 8 Social Experience: Perception and Attitude 109
Social Perception 109
Attitudes and Cognitive Organization 117
Attitudes, Cognitive Structure, and Balance 122

chapter 9   Social Influence: Communication in Social Situations   130
- The Nature of Communication   130
- Communication in Small Groups   135
- The Role Concept   143
- Culture and Society   148

CONCLUSION   150

FOUR   APPROACHES TO THE PROBLEMS OF PERCEIVING AND KNOWING
PROLOGUE   154

chapter 10   The Problem of Perception   157
- The Phenomenological Method and the Categories of Experience   157
- Historical Background   159
- The Nature of the Units: Wholes and Parts   162
- The Tonic System: The Response Side   164

chapter 11   The Phenomena of Perception   165
- The Basic Articulation of the Visual Field   165
- The Three Dimensional World   179
- Perceptual Constancy   185

chapter 12   Extending the Study of Perception   191
- Sensory-tonic Theory   191
- Attitudes, Motives and Drives: Their Effect on Perception   193
- Development of Perception   198
- The Outer Limits of Perception   204
- Beyond Perception   206

CONCLUSION   207

FIVE   BEHAVIORISTIC MODELS IN PSYCHOLOGY
PROLOGUE   212

chapter 13   The Development of Theories of the Learning Process   216
- Early Approaches to the Study of the Learning Process   216

The Definition of Learning 231
Factors Which Are Important in Learning Ability 232

chapter 14 Important Issues in the Study of the Learning Process 234

The Formalization of Learning Theory 234
What Is the Major Law of Learning? 248
Summary 258

chapter 15 Verbal Behavior and Language 259

Associative Networks 259
Syntactic Structures: The Analysis of Language and Cognition 261
The Role of Meaningfulness in Verbal Learning 265
Short-term Memory 270

CONCLUSION 274

SIX BIOLOGICAL MODELS

PROLOGUE 278

chapter 16 Behavior Genetics 280

Basic Mechanisms of Heredity 281
Chromosomal Events and Behavior 286
Human Biometrical Genetics 288
The Genetics of Animal Behavior: Artificial Populations 294

chapter 17 Animal Behavior 300

The Concept of Adaptation: Ecological Behaviorism 300
The Search for General Laws of Learning: Comparative Behaviorism 304
The Analysis of Instinctive Behavior: Ethology 310

chapter 18 Physiological Psychology I: The Central Nervous System and Behavior 319

The Central Hypothesis and Methods of Physiological Psychology 319
The Geography of the Brain 320
Input and Output Systems of the Brain 321
Information Storage: Search for the Engram 325
The Physiology of Motivation 331

chapter 19 **Physiological Psychology II: Chemical Systems and Behavior** 339
  Internal Biochemical Systems   339
  Neurochemical Basis of Intelligence   349
  Exogenous Chemical Compounds and Behavior   352

  CONCLUSION   356

SEVEN INDIVIDUAL DIFFERENCES: THEIR MEASUREMENT AND MEANING
  PROLOGUE   362

chapter 20 **Scales and the Measurement of Individual Differences**   366
  Scaling   366
  Psychological Testing   370

chapter 21 **Examples of Tests: Their Usefulness**   387
  Types of Tests   387
  The Usefulness of Psychometric Procedures: Criticisms   395

chapter 22 **Tests and Psychological Traits**   399
  Response Sets and Response Styles   399
  Factor-analytic Methods   403
  The Fruits of Factor Analysis   407
  Creativity   412

  CONCLUSION   419

Epilogue **THE SEARCH FOR UNITY**   422
  Theory Building   422
  Psychology and Society   425

  NAME INDEX   427

  SUBJECT INDEX   435

SECTION ONE
PSYCHOLOGY: ITS NATURE AND ITS METHODS

"You can destroy meaning wholesale by reducing everything to its uninterpreted particulars. By paralyzing our urge to subordinate one thing to another, we can eliminate all subsidiary awareness of things in terms of others and create an atomized, totally depersonalized universe."

(Polanyi, 1958, p. 199)

PROLOGUE

On Friday, November 22, 1963, at 12:31 P.M. Central standard time, John Fitzgerald Kennedy, thirty-fifth President of the United States, was shot to death in Dallas, Texas, allegedly by Lee Harvey Oswald. At about 11:20 A.M. the next day, Oswald was himself killed, in the full sight of many witnesses and photographers as well as millions of television viewers, by Jack Ruby, a nightclub and striptease-joint entrepreneur.

Although this was only one of many assassinations in history and was the third assassination of an American President, it stands out from the rest on many counts. In the eyes of most people all over the world, John Kennedy possessed an unusual attractiveness—a youthfulness and gaiety of spirit coupled with a maturity of outlook and strength of purpose rarely to be found in a man of only forty-six years. The qualities of greatness contrasted sharply with the pointlessness of his death and the apparently trivial motive that directed the assassin to contrive it. And the entry of apparently underworld characters onto the scene, to say nothing of an array of Texas law enforcers who might have been cast in an inverted Mack Sennett movie, could only inspire, in any reasonable observer, emotions of outrage and disgust.

In this drama, we see a gamut of psychological problems being run. Supposing Lee Harvey was the assassin, what quirk of mind might have led him to such a shocking act? Was he deranged? According to his mother—"a mother in history," as she has tagged herself—he was not. As she described her son (as taped by Jean Stafford):

> He had a stamp collection . . . and he loved to play Monopoly which is a thinking game. So was stamps. He had a stamp collection. He loved to play chess, he was a very good chess player. And anything like that. So he was really a very busy little boy, and I don't see anything abnormal about any part of his life [Stafford, 1965, p. 19].

Had he, in Mrs. Oswald's eyes, done something bad? *Apparently she did not think so.* On the contrary, she regarded him as an "unsung hero" who had made a major contribution to history and petitioned to have her son buried at Arlington, in the same cemetery where the victim was laid to rest. This seems a strange point of view to many of us. Was the alleged assassin's mother also a deviant from the normal? And, if so, did she impart deviancy to her son through training or through the heritage of genes she had passed on to him?

There are many similar problems of a psychological nature that could be explored. All of them relate to the makeup of human personality, its formation by learning and by biological factors, and the way it is reflected in particular kinds of behavior.

There are other, more sociological kinds of questions highlighted by the Kennedy assassination, questions about which people have wondered. For example, it has been asserted by some that such an event could have occurred only in Dallas, with its climate of antagonism to the Kennedy administration, its dislike of his civil rights programs, and its distrust of "Northerners." Is there any truth in this? Can a whole city in any sense be held responsible for the action of one of its members? Was the assassin merely the focusing point of a violent social force? And how is it that many people—besides Mrs. Oswald—perceived Lee Harvey not as a villain or a madman but as a saint? What is it in society that allows people to view the same event so differently?

The field of psychology is devoted to analyzing just such problems. It is about people: how they think, how they learn, create, and remember; how they are alike and how they are different; how they relate to each other, why they love and why they hate, why thy marry, why they go to war; why some of them are Leonardos and Mozarts, why others are Neros and Hitlers, why the extraordinary person *is* the extraordinary person, and, especially, why the ordinary person is the ordinary person.

Every reader of this book will perhaps have his special problem and his special interest. Some, probably, will wonder sadly why they are not as popular as they might wish to be—why other people do not seek them out and surround them at parties. Others may worry because they feel they cannot think quickly and remember adequately. And still others who have a close friend—or, even more, those who are married—may wonder what it is that makes the moments of magic or of disaster occur so commonly between two persons who see a great deal of each other.

All these are problems to whose solution psychology is directed. They are partly practical, but they are also basic issues in the sense that perhaps all of us who contemplate them do so not merely in order to find quick and easy solutions but rather because we find them to be of such interest in themselves that we can hardly avoid having a deep concern and curiosity about them. Long ago, Aristotle, the great Greek philosopher and student of Plato, asserted that man, by nature, desires to know, and a thinker of the eighteenth century, Alexander Pope, said that the proper study of mankind is man.

This book is dedicated to these assertions. As people, our natural curiosity and wonder starts with ourselves and gradually extends to the world around us. With ourselves as the subjects for our study, we do not need the impulsion of utility to spur us on to try to discover the rules by which we operate. For most of us, the contemplation and management of our own lives evoke our primary interest.

How shall we go about this task? In attempting to find the solution to any problem, order and discipline and the past are needed. Not all of us can think logically and directively, and few of us are so original and creative that the problems about human behavior that we consider and the provisional solutions that we reach about them have not been thought of and reached before by other persons, great and small, who preceded us in history. The past does have its uses. And as Santayana, the Harvard philosopher and aesthetician, once said, those who do not know the past are condemned to live it again.

In this book we will make extensive reference to the past, that is, to the historical development of ideas in psychology and to the cultural setting from which they emerged. The reason is that, in our opinion, history is much more important to psychology than it is to other fields of science, especially, for example, physics, in which being up to date is of much greater importance than perusal of the past. Occasionally in physics there occurs a major shift in direction—a breakthrough such as those made by Newton or Copernicus or Einstein; but by and large, progress in the field is linear and sequential. Psychology, perhaps because it is a young science, perhaps because it has a character radically different from physics, does not move forward in the same way. As in literature and philosophy, the array of ideas built up in the past, by being looked at again and again, may yield to us fresh insights that have a value and relevance to the contemporary scene. A Princeton psychologist, Julian Jaynes, has dramatized the differences as follows:

> Physics is like a mountain: roped together by a common asceticism of mathematical method, the upward direction, through blizzard, mist or searing sun, is always certain, though the paths are not. The problem of each new generation is easy: rope on, test the pitons, follow the leader, look for better lay-backs and footholds to the heights. A source book in its history is a simple and inspiring matter; it is ledge to ledge upward....
>
> Psychology is so different!... it is less like a mountain than a huge entangled forest in full shining summer, so easy to walk through on certain levels, that anyone can and everyone does. The student's problem is a frantic one: he must shift for himself. It is directions he is looking for, not height. And the direction out of the forest is unknown, perhaps non-existent, nor is it even certain that that is what he is meant to do [Jaynes, 1966, p. 94].

This book is intended to help the student of psychology find such directions. The authors feel strongly that this can best be accomplished by demonstrating how ideas in the past have gradually unfolded into current theorizing and experimentation. In this way we hope to be better able to present a true picture of what psychology is like.

CHAPTER 1
THE NATURE OF PSYCHOLOGY

The purpose of this book is to present the basic ideas and facts of modern scientific psychology. In doing this, we will give priority to an examination of the ideas or theoretical conceptions that influence the way psychologists work and that guide their choice of what kinds of facts to look for and how to look for them. Behind every psychological study lie certain assumptions about the nature of behavior and what aspects of it are important to study. Sometimes these assumptions are quite explicit; at other times, they are only implicit. A decision regarding what is worth examining experimentally may be made on the basis of largely personal motives, or it may be made on the basis of a judgment that it would add to and enlarge on some particular body of ideas shared by others working in the field.

Because psychology has such an immediate relevance to human affairs, it is much more likely than the other sciences to be understood at only a very superficial level, or, in other words, to be misunderstood. Because we observe the behavior of other people every day of our lives, it is easy for us to convince ourselves that we can understand it perfectly. Misconceptions are further reinforced by the many aphorisms and proverbs handed down from generation to generation. For example, we are told, "Too many cooks spoil the broth," a phrase which implies a negative relationship between size of a group and its efficiency. On the other hand, an almost contrary notion is contained in the proverb "More hands make light work."

Popular psychology is represented by a multitude of such neat and simple assertions. It is consequently a good deal harder for the psychologist than for scientists in other fields to face his subject matter objectively and without prejudice.

In the ensuing chapters, therefore, we will attempt to make explicit the basic premises that comprise different theoretical approaches to the study of psychology and that constitute the reasons for doing certain experiments. Let us first discuss the nature of the field, its methodology, and its relationship to other disciplines.

DEFINITION OF PSYCHOLOGY

Our first task is to define psychology, that is to say, to delineate the subject matter of the field, and to describe the methodology it characteristically employs. Like many disciplines, psychology has its origin with the ancient Greeks. Plato and Aristotle, for example, about the fourth century B.C., wrote treatises on human psychology which they regarded as the study of the soul. In fact, this is what the word meant in its original Greek form (*psyche logos*). Today, psychology is usually defined as the *science of the behavior of man and lower animals*. Since all parts of this definition are important, each will be discussed separately in detail.

Psychology as a Science

A science may most simply be defined as a *sys-

tematic collection of empirical facts. It is never merely a collection of facts, but rather of facts which are integrated or ordered systematically in some way. This *ordering, or organizing, function of science* is its *theoretical aspect*. The empirical aspect of science concerns the gathering of those facts or data that theory has designated as important. The number of "facts" that might be gathered is infinite. Science must therefore set out some criteria that allow a restriction of our choice to practical limits. We must decide first what to look at and next how to look at it. The scientist does this by formulating a theory. Thus in a sense a theory is simply the rationalized decision as to what will be looked at and how to look. It is the actual looking that constitutes an experiment. An experiment is a special kind of experience—as Ronald Fisher has called it, "experience carefully planned in advance and designed to form a secure basis for new knowledge" [Fisher, 1937]. In an experiment, the scientist simply observes reality, not haphazardly, but in a manner he has so planned that he can be certain of observing what he wishes to observe and of being able to relate that particular observation to previous observations. A histologist's observation of a section of brain tissue is an experiment, at least in a very broad sense. The measurement of the activity level of rats following the administration of a drug (e.g., a tranquilizer) is similarly an experiment.

In such cases, the scientist, in order to interpret what he sees, must also observe a *control group*, that is, another group of animals which has not been given the drug and which is then observed under identical conditions. Without such a comparison, the experiment can yield only limited and ambiguous information. In the first experiment with the brain section, the same applies, though in a more subtle fashion. Suppose the histologist finds that a section taken from the visual centers of the brain has so many cells of a certain kind per cubic centimeter. What could make this observation *significant* would be if tissue from a different part, for example, the auditory centers, were known to have a different number or kind of cells. This other section supplies the control in the sense of telling us what is unique about the first observation.

The crucial point is that no inference can be made from an experiment unless an exact comparison can be made between one observation in which a special condition is present and another observation in which the same condition is absent. This is the essence of scientific experiment and is well summed up in the dictum of the philosopher John Stuart Mill (1893) that to know "A" we must know "Not-A." To know the effects of a drug on activity, we must know what activity is like with no drugs.

At an even more abstract level, this is a principle broadly embodied in the philosophy of Hegel. According to his principle of dialectic, the isolated thought, fact, or individual thesis achieves full realization only by being contrasted with its own negation (antithesis). Out of the conjunction of thesis and antithesis comes synthesis. On a common-sense level, we might say this: the average American sees no significance in the fact that most men go to work and most women mind the children at home. Only when this behavior is seen in contrast to the habits of another culture—the Tchambuli, for example, in which women work and men follow supposedly "feminine" pursuits—does it assume some significance and importance. What is usual is often unusual or interesting when viewed in a broader frame of reference. Indeed, it is perhaps the main purpose of higher education to confront the student with ideas and points of view that contrast with those he is used to, so that he may better understand his accepted values.

The procedure of isolating our observations by planning so that we may make inferences from them marks psychology as a science. Common sense, with which psychology is often loosely identified by the layman and even by other scientists, does not involve controlled observations, and, as a consequence, its inferences are often wrong, even though its observations may be correct. The old notion that all redheaded people have a fiery temper, for example, is probably not true. The idea is not intrinsically ridiculous, however, since morphological characteristics, such as body build, do, in fact, often relate to personality traits. But it is a conclusion that has been drawn without regard to proper control groups, that is, groups not having red hair, observed for amount of temper under similar conditions, in relation to the redheaded group.

Though often inaccurate, however, common sense

cannot be lightly dismissed. Many of the aphorisms and maxims handed down to us by cultural tradition are the results of observations which at least loosely involve control groups. Such a proverb, for example, as "Blood will tell" does, as we shall see later, turn out to be true. Heredity *is* important in the determination of physical and psychological characters. People presumably reached this conclusion by noting that children's behavior was more like that of their real parents than was the behavior of other children (e.g., foster children) reared in approximately the same environment. Broadly speaking, there is often a difference only of degree between such an observation and a formal experimental one carried out under highly controlled conditions.

Consequently, we may expect to find that frequently commonsense conclusions do actually agree with those of science. Often they do not, but the amount of agreement is sufficient to make us wary of deliberate attempts in psychology to "disprove the obvious." Being esoteric has no intrinsic value. On the contrary, in any area of science it is often the most obvious propositions that turn out to be the most fruitful in making scientific progress. It is clear that objects fall to the ground, but it took Newton to realize the vast significance of this simple and obvious fact and to develop the enormous theoretical potentialities implicit in it. In psychology, we often deal directly with what seems obvious, since we are working on a subject matter that is so dominant in human experience. This fact is neither good nor bad in itself. What counts is how we use what is obvious in constructing a logical and coherent picture of behavior. We can do this only by ignoring common sense, neither affirming nor denying it, and working strictly according to the rules of science and logic. Whitehead has put the matter aptly. He says:

> ... Science is rooted in what I have just called the whole apparatus of commonsense thought. That is the datum *from* which it starts, and to which it must recur. We may speculate, if it amuses us, on other beings in other planets who have arranged analogous experiences according to an entirely different conceptual code—namely, who have directed their attention to different relations between their various experiences. But the task is too complex, too gigantic, to be revised in its main outlines. You may polish up common sense, you may contradict it in detail, you may surprise it. But ultimately your whole task is to satisfy it [Whitehead, 1929, pp. 159–160].

The Meaning of Behavior

The datum of scientific psychology, it has been stated, is behavior. This is not as simple as it sounds. In the first place, *there are many levels of behavior*, ranging from the simple, stereotyped movements of the amoeba to the complex and variable dynamics of a student trying to pass an examination, from the twitch of a single muscle fiber to the progress of a businessman seeking a corporation vice-presidency. How do we properly limit the boundaries of the subject matter so as to present some kind of unified front? Should we study only human behavior and exclude that of animals? Should we include physiological processes or restrict ourselves only to acts or movements?

There is no simple solution to this problem. Many levels of behavior are studied by psychologists. Some prefer to work at very *microscopic* levels and to look, for example, at neural processes in the brain; others prefer to examine more *macroscopic* acts such as the running of an animal to food down a straightway; while still others like to study even more macroscopic behavior, such as the complex reactions of a person to his social milieu. All these approaches have contributions to make, and none is intrinsically more scientific than another. Without exception, they all have this in common: they study the acts or movements of an organism, insofar as these acts or movements bear some relation to the *whole organism* or to some general organismic state. A physiologist may be interested in a muscle twitch per se, just to learn about muscles—a perfectly legitimate interest. A psychologist, however, would be interested in a muscle twitch only insofar as it related to a learning process, an emotional state, or some other such variable. The phrase "whole organism," it must be admitted, is difficult to define theoretically, and the differences between the operations of the physiologist and those of the psychologist often seem very slight. In practice, the distinction is usually clearer, and we need not attempt to examine it any more closely at this time. If psychology sometimes comes close to physiology or vice versa, it is probably to the benefit of each.

A second point of great importance is that acts or movements or behaviors are *processes that are stretched out over time*. They refer essentially to the changes in states of an organic system from one point in time to another. Psychology cannot really ask questions about the *structure* of behavior as physics asks about the structure of matter or of an atom. Rather, it asks about the changes that have occurred in an organism over time. For example, we expose a person to a poem once and find he recalls a tenth of it. We expose him to it six more times and find he recalls all of it. His behavior has changed, in other words, and it is in such a change that psychology is primarily interested. Similarly, if we give two persons a problem—for example, an intelligence test item—and ask them to solve it, we may find that initially neither one can do so, but that at the end of five minutes one has emerged with the answer and the other has not. The difference between these two individuals in respect to their changes in state represents the crucial problem for the psychologist. Another way of stating this is to say that psychology is concerned with the storage properties of organisms as these are reflected in behavior. This brings us to the third point.

Behavior itself is overt, but its causes may be hidden from direct observation. Such phenomena as thoughts, feelings, or emotions are unobservables in themselves and are only inferred from some behavior actually observed. Nonetheless, they cannot be ignored by psychology. In fact, it is true that most psychologists are less interested in what is happening outside than in what is happening inside the organism. Certainly, behavior is the primary datum. But it is those processes behind overt acts that really represent the main interest of most psychologists. For example, even in everyday life, it is not so much the thousands of different ways a person may express anger that are worth studying, but rather the nature and properties of the general underlying state which we call an emotion.

In some ways, it is no more true to say that a psychologist studies behavior primarily than it is to say that a physicist studies pointer readings or a geneticist studies flower colors and other morphological characteristics. Behavior, pointer readings, and flower colors are all primary, immediate data and, as such, may be observed by anyone who cares to do so. They are public. But they represent only the first step in the scientific endeavor. Having observed, we must order and organize the observables by means of hypothesized concepts or dimensions which are usually, at least at first, themselves unobservable. Genes, the basic units of heredity, for example, have been very useful constructs to geneticists even though they have only recently been seen directly. The same applied not so long ago to the atoms and moelcules of physicists. So also with the "emotions," "personality traits," "habits," and "cognitions" of psychologists. We do not see these directly but infer them from regularities in behavior.

In a limited sense, then, it is accurate to say that psychologists are interested in studying the *mind* so long as the term "mind" is taken to mean simply those inner processes hypothesized to explain the uniformities that underlie the outer behavior being observed. As will become clear in the following chapters, psychologists differ considerably in the extent to which they are willing to use hypothetical constructs. Psychoanalytic thinkers have used them freely. Others, such as behaviorists, have tended to use them sparingly and economically.

A fourth point about behavior is that it *varies in type*. Traditionally, it is common to think in terms of such categories as intelligence, temperament and emotion, learning, motivation, thinking and reasoning, creativity, and others. This is essentially a problem of taxonomy, or classification. Just as biology finds it essential to group individual animals into species, genera, and families, so psychology must also order different types of behavior into logical or meaningful categories. The classes mentioned above are not necessarily the best we can find. Any one of them can be broken down further. For example, at a fairly broad or macroscopic level, we may designate many forms of behavior that relate to a general dimension of intelligence: solving analogies, doing arithmetical problems, vocabulary, understanding word meanings, verbal fluency, ability to abstract, and others all may be regarded as falling into this general category. Thus an important problem for the psychologist is that of deciding what are the basic categories of behavior that underlie the almost infinite number of particular acts of which organisms are capable. One branch of psychology—factor analysis—as we shall see later (cf. Section Seven) has been directed mainly to this problem.

Human and Animal Subjects

The last part of the definition of psychology given earlier states that psychology studies both human beings and lower animals. It is essential at this point to explain the reasons for including lower animals, since many people still find this surprising. They wonder why a psychologist should spend his time watching rats in a maze, for example, or observing the social behavior of chickens, when there are so many pressing human problems that might be studied directly with more profit.

One reason is the same one that explains why chemists and physicists carry out experiments in a highly abstract setting in a laboratory rather than in nature. They do this in order to be able to isolate the variables they wish to observe. All their complicated apparatus is used in an effort to simplify, since the simple is a much more fruitful starting point for discovering basic laws. Armed with such laws, we can then attempt to explain the complex. In the case of lower animals and man, the theory of evolution indicates rather strongly that at least some of the differences between higher and lower organisms are differences of degree only. Thus, any laws of behavior that can be established with, let us say, a cat or a rat should also hold for higher animals within limits set by additional complicating factors. This is not to say that the psychology of a rat is in every way like that of a human being. There are many differences that cannot be glossed over. Nonetheless, there are enough similarities in respect to the way the rat develops, the way it learns and explores, the structure of its nervous system, and its physiology that make it a feasible subject for psychologists to use.

In addition to its greater simplicity, an animal like the rat has practical advantages. It is cheap to maintain, breeds quickly, and can be manipulated in ways in which a human being cannot. Sometimes, of course, a more complex species like the monkey or the dog will be more valuable; at other times, a very simple organism like the planarian, or flatworm. Choice of what kind of animal we use depends on the type of problem being studied and the facilities that are available to the experimenter. The value of animal subjects for scientific research in general has been enormous. Most of genetics is founded on breeding experiments using the fruitfly. Much of our fundamental information about cancer has been learned through the study of mice. Psychology is certainly no exception to this rule. It is not that the psychologist is particularly an animal lover. Animals are merely one means by which he attempts to solve problems and to establish basic laws.

Another important reason for studying animals lies simply in the fact that they are, in themselves, interesting and useful. It is by no means forbidden to the scientist to spend his life observing, let us say, gorillas just because this species fascinates him, any more than it is forbidden to the artist to reproduce on canvas his experience of the world. Furthermore, the animal kingdom represents a huge natural resource for man's use. We could hardly get along without the many domestic species we presently cultivate. Cattle, poultry, horses, sheep, and many others are of such economic value to us that the task of maintaining these optimally and extending their usage is of great importance. For example, it is likely that in the near future increasing attention will be given to the many species that occupy our oceans and lakes. Underwater farming may well become a highly developed specialty before very long, and this will make necessary a thorough knowledge of the habits and behaviors of marine species.

RELATION OF PSYCHOLOGY TO OTHER DISCIPLINES AND TO SOCIETY

Psychology studies such a diversity of problems that it is difficult to set exact limits indicating where it stops and where some other disciplines begin. A psychologist may, for example, be interested in studying artistic or creative behavior. If he does so, he will have to be familiar with art and art history. Again, he may wish to investigate the way behavior traits are transmitted genetically from parent to offspring. To do this effectively, he must know something of biology and genetics. The psychologist today must have great versatility and, depending on the problem he wishes to study, be able to range into philosophy, biology, mathematics, literature, and many other fields of knowledge. In this breadth that psychology possesses it has certainly a beauty all its own; however, diversity by itself can represent merely confusion if not properly ordered in some manner. We do not need to limit the scope of psychology in any way. We should, in fact, capitalize on it. But we must also recognize that the need for systematization is that much greater. To develop this theme more fully, we will examine the relations of psychology to particular disciplines.

Psychology and Other Sciences

Properly speaking, psychology may be classified as one of the *life sciences*. It stands midway between biology at one end of a continuum and sociology at the other end. This continuum relates roughly to the complexity dimension mentioned earlier in defining behavior. As it merges with biology, psychology focuses on the cellular, biochemical, or genetic determinants of behavior. As it merges with sociology, it comes to be concerned with behavior as influenced by such factors as group membership, cultural values, and other social variables. In the hypothetical center of the continuum, we find pure psychology, the study of behavior as such. It is not true that psychology is only a part of biology unless this field is taken in a very broad sense, nor is it valid to classify psychology exclusively as one of the social sciences, since it may study behavior without any direct reference to social variables. It extends into both areas and profits enormously by its association with them. But psychology is also a unique and autonomous discipline with which we can study such behaviors as learning, thinking, or emoting without reference to variables outside these processes themselves.

As we have already indicated, this breadth is a feature of psychology that makes it particularly interesting, though equally one that makes difficult any attempt to achieve unity of method and terminology. We will discuss this point fully later on, since it is crucial to understanding the approach taken in this book. For the time being, we may simply note that psychologists work on many different kinds of problems, and there is no a priori reason to prefer one type of problem over another. The notion, fashionable among many lay and professional people, that the more microscopic the units studied, the more "scientific" the investigation has no logical validity. Validity, truth, and explanatory power are not necessarily properties of the small.

Particularly in respect to its methods, psychology also has relationships to physics and mathematics, just as do biology and physiology. Psychology borrows from the methods of physics and mathematics and also sometimes the ideas or models behind these methods. The use of mathematical techniques, especially statistics, is highly developed in psychology. In fact, it is usually impossible to investigate a psychological problem adequately without knowledge of statistics. Results are seldom so clear-cut that absolute statements can be made. We must generally resort to qualified conclusions. *Usually*, individuals react to frustration by aggression. *Usually*, individuals learn faster if they take rest periods. The adverb "usually" is expressed in science by means of probability values. Instead of "usually," we may say, "The chances are only one in a thousand that an individual will *not* react to frustration by aggression," or "only one in a hundred that he will *not* learn faster with rest periods than without them." As many thinkers have indicated, we live in an uncertain universe. Man and living organisms are certainly not exceptions to this rule. The use of probability statistics enables us, paradoxically, to state the degree of uncertainty with some certainty.

Similarly, some branches of the applied physical sciences, notably electrical engineering, are extremely useful to psychologists. To obtain exact repeatable observations, the psychologist must frequently resort to the use of complex electrical equipment. For example, a problem may involve the relation between reading speed and number of eye movements. Obviously, while reading speed may be easily gauged with an ordinary stopwatch, the measurement of number of eye movements presents a serious difficulty and can be done accurately only by means of special instrumentation.

In the use of such techniques, it sometimes happens that the investigator becomes a slave to a method. It is a human failing to become so enamored of an elegant branch of mathematics one has mastered or so attached to a complex piece of machinery one has built that one may restrict one's interest only to those problems that can be handled with these techniques. We must emphasize strongly that the problem is much more important than the method. A very costly machine may give trivial results. As one psychologist has pointed out (Maslow, 1954), it is crucial that psychology be "problem-centered" rather than "means-centered" if it is to make significant advances. It is ironic that psychology is often estimated as less scientific and less important than other sciences because its methods are not as sophisticated as those of other, better established disciplines. Certainly, its techniques are often crude and inexact, but this is because its problems are highly complex and often of first rank in importance. It is doubtful if we will solve the pressing questions of war and peace by referral to physics or chemistry. This brings us to the next point.

We have stated that psychology uses some of the methods of mathematics and physics. Directly and indirectly, they have also provided for psychology many ideas and theoretical models. A simple example is the recent approach to the study of brain processes in terms of electronic computers. A brain is not exactly the same as an electronic computer, of course, but the two do have enough properties in common so that our knowledge of the one can aid our knowledge of the other. Similarly, the concept of field force in psychology is borrowed from the concept of electrical field in physics. Many other examples could be given, some of which will appear in later chapters. Of course, psychology should be cautious about ideas taken from other sciences, particularly the physical sciences. Inorganic matter is not the same as organic, and the differences are as important as the similarities. It is necessary to assess carefully the merits and usefulness of theoretical models drawn from other fields before using them. Their premature application can often lead the researcher up blind alleys.

Psychology, Philosophy, and the Humanities

Not very long ago, most psychology departments were not autonomous but were simply subdivisions of philosophy departments. This is still true in some universities and colleges. The reason for this tie with philosophy lies partly in the history and partly in the nature of psychology. As indicated at the beginning of the chapter, psychology was, for ancient Greek and medieval thinkers, the study of the soul. After René Descartes' equation of soul with thought in the seventeenth century, it came to be regarded as the study of mind. The British empiricist philosophers, such as Locke, Mill, Berkeley, and Hume, were essentially psychologists in the sense that they directed their main efforts to describing introspectively—that is, empirically—mind, or the process of knowing. Both idealism and phenomenology (the study of the world as it is perceived by man) were further expressions of the same trend in philosophy and, in effect, set the stage for the laboratory psychology of Germany in the late nineteenth century. With such a history, psychology came to be out of step with the other sciences, which had taken matter rather than mind as a starting point.

Finding themselves thus on the wrong side of the fence, as it were, as the result of an unfortunate historical accident, many psychologists reacted late but vigorously, rejected traditional philosophy, and identified with the extreme wing of scientific positivism. In such a reaction, they perhaps went too far. Psychology does not need to be ultrascientific and to emulate physics or chemistry. Just as it can capitalize on its diversity of subject matter, so also can psychology capitalize on its intimate connections with philosophy. Ideas, if properly articulated, do have consequences. The most recondite notions of philosophy can be often explicated into science and even eventually into popular thought. Some of the most important advances in science have come from scientists who have grasped such ideas in their full implications.

Much the same applies as far as psychology's relationship to the other branches of the humanities—art, literature, and history. As a science dealing with the nature of man, psychology has much to offer the humanities. Likewise, the humanities in turn can suggest to psychology interesting hypotheses about human behavior. Again, they should never be confused. The penetrating intuitions of a Dostoevski or a Shakespeare have no scientific value as such, and of course, were never intended to have any. They may, however, point up the limitations of those ideas being used by the psychologist and may even be taken as starting points for new systematic approaches to the scientific study of man.

It is worth noting that in the close relation it bears to humanities, psychology has a unique position among the sciences and because of this it also may be better suited to close the "gap" between scientists and humanists. One psychologist, Sigmund Koch, in 1961 made a strong case for such a "bridge function" of psychology and the behavioral sciences. Of all the disciplines man has delineated, perhaps psychology most of all attempts to ask the large, important, and epic questions and to answer them in a precise empirical way. Such questions relate immediately to psychology and the behavioral sciences.

Psychology and Life

What we have just said does not mean that psychology should be tied to the practical. Science, by its very nature, must proceed without regard to the "here and now" character that defines the useful. What is useful to us may not be useful to others. What is useful today may not be useful tomorrow. To choose only problems whose solution will be useful is to follow far too narrow a course. Ideas and theories and not the demands of the moment should dictate the direction of pure scientific endeavor. It is true that the need of society can hasten the progress of research, but it cannot start it if the scientific ideas are not already there. If necessity is the mother of invention, scientific theory is the father. A good example in psychology is given by the rapid development in the field of mental testing in the United States to meet the demands of selective service in World War I. At this time, it became necessary to obtain quickly efficient means of predicting the abilities of men. The need was met by numerous psychologists who directed their efforts to the problem. But these efforts were effective only because of the theoretical advances already made in this branch of psychology previous to the war. Applied science is precisely an application to a local problem of the theoretical principles in science achieved in an independent manner. Without such principles, no useful application is possible. Poincaré, in *The Foundations of Science*, has expressed this point of view succinctly:

> One need only open one's eyes to see that the conquests of industry which have enriched so many practical men would never have seen the light if those practical men alone had existed, and if they had not been preceded by unselfish devotees who died poor, who never thought of utility and yet had a guide far other than caprice [Poincaré, 1913, p. 363].

Not utility, not caprice guides the scientist. He can be guided only by the structure of scientific thought built up gradually through the years. This is not a counsel of pessimism. Science, even when proceeding in apparently useless ways, often turns out to be useful. Sir Alexander Fleming's observations of bread mold gave us penicillin. Einstein's theory of relativity gave us atomic power. The isolation of radium by the Curies gave us x-ray. It is difficult to predict the practical implications that an apparently impractical observation may have. All we can do is put faith in science and basic research. One fundamental discovery may produce a thousand useful applications.

All that has been said above applies to psychology just as it does to the other sciences. Human behavior and social problems are experienced so immediately by the layman that he finds it difficult to envisage a discipline dealing with this same behavior but independently of the practical questions which he considers important. As we observed before, psychology as a science proceeds apart from common sense. Similarly, as a pure science it can ignore the practical while still having faith that its basic findings will eventually bring many practical benefits to society. The psychologist is quite justified if he attempts to discover the basic laws of learning by observing not human beings in the classroom but rats in the laboratory. He is not being perverse. He is merely following the usual path of science.

As it turns out, the kinds of research in psychology (and in all science) and the kinds of problems considered important by society do coincide to a great degree, although they may often seem remote from each other. The reason for this lies simply in the fact that the points of view of science and of practical society are derived from the same broad philosophic premises. In the United States, for example, a philosophy that stressed the value of the individual and the importance of the useful not only oriented psychology to do research on mental testing (individual differences) and learning but also produced a political and social climate that would consider the solutions to such problems useful. Similarly, the growing humanism of the late nineteenth century and early twentieth century produced research on mental illness as well as a society that thought this to be useful. Consequently, we need not worry too much about the supposed "ivory tower" quality of science. Even in some of its most obscure activities, it is often still working in parallel to the rest of society.

At the same time, much of psychological research is directedly oriented to practical problems. Examples 1–1 and 1–2 are of such a character. Note, however, that each of them involves standard procedures and concepts that are already well established in the discipline.

Example 1–1 *Psychological causes and effect of television viewing (Maccoby, 1954)*

The discovery of television and the realization of its tremendous potential as a social force for good or evil have led thoughtful people to wonder about some of the consequences of excessive or even moderate television viewing, particularly on children. Many parents among the more educated classes think it necessary to ration the number of shows their children may watch, on the reasonable assumption that too much exposure to the "idiot box," with its thousands of platitudinous commercial messages and prosaic plots, will produce passivity, loss of initiative, and a general brainwashing. Such parents often have a contempt for those families who spend many of their leisure hours glued to their sets and attribute to them a lack of intelligence and sheeplike personality characteristics. We thus have generated two essential hypotheses capable of test, the first dealing with the deleterious effects of television watching, the second with the already extant personality structure of those who tend to watch a great deal.

Many psychologists have worked on these problems. The usual method has been to try to contrast children who watch a great deal with those who watch a little, not only in respect to the personality characteristics that presumably are initially responsible for this difference, but also in respect to the outcomes of differential watching time when initial differences are equated or held constant. It should be emphasized that there are many problems in this kind of research. Television viewing is apt to be correlated with many other factors, and it may often be these that produce some difference. For example, it might be that permissive rearing conditions go with a higher rate of viewing. Were some differences to be found between high-viewing and low-viewing children, these might be due primarily

Table 1-1 Relation between amount of time spent viewing television and parental disciplinary practices

	Upper-middle class, hr per day	Upper-lower class, hr per day
Level of obedience demanded:		
Low	1.2	1.6
Moderate	1.4	1.7
Very high	1.6	1.6
Extent of use of physical punishment (e.g., spanking):		
Seldom or never	1.2	1.5
Occasional	1.4	1.5
Fairly often	1.4	1.7
Often	1.5	1.8
Mother-child affectional relationship:		
Extremely warm	1.1	1.2
Quite warm	1.4	1.7
Matter-of-fact	1.4	1.5
Cold	1.6	1.7

to parental rearing practices rather than to amount of viewing. In the studies that have been done, most of these kinds of loopholes have been controlled.

One well-known study was done by Eleanor Maccoby (1954). Her purpose was to provide some answers as to why children watch television in the first place—a very large and important question. To this end, she interviewed in the greater Boston area about four hundred mothers, each of whom had a child in kindergarten (about 5½ years old). She rated mothers according to the severity of the discipline they imposed on their children and obtained an estimate of the number of hours each child engaged in viewing television. A sample of her results is shown in Table 1–1.

At least two important conclusions can be drawn from these results. First, it is clear that the upper-middle-class children who come from good business and professional homes watch less than upper-lower-class children from skilled or semiskilled workers' families. Secondly, within the upper-middle-class homes only, there does appear to be a definite relation between severity of discipline and amount of television viewing. This would suggest that television is used by the child as a means of escape from a rather unpleasant and frustrating kind of existence. Such a solution might be expected, in turn, to aggravate the problems rather than to solve them. This possibility is given some credence by data obtained in another large-scale study in England (Himmelweit, Oppenheim, & Vince, 1958). A comparison made between adolescent girls whose families had television and those whose families did not showed that the former were much more anxious than the latter about their competence to deal with the problems of adulthood, such as leaving home, marriage, and work. Suitable controls indicated that these effects were not simply correlated with some family factors that resulted in buying a television set independently of watching it but were apparently a direct result of viewing programs that typically emphasized the difficulties of adult life.

The conclusions we have presented are only a few of those arrived at by researchers on the causes and effects of television viewing. They illustrate, however, what can be done by applying research methods in this field. Important practical problems continually crop up in any society, and many of these can be examined only by the techniques of the behavioral scientist. Let us look at another example in a totally different area.

Example 1–2 *Sonar in the blind (Supa, Cotzin, & Dallenbach, 1944)*

One of the greatest problems with which blind people must deal is moving in space and avoiding obstacles. A striking fact is that some individuals can do this better than others, some so well, in fact, that they give the impression of having some kind of extravisual sense—sometimes called "facial vision"—that enables them somehow to "see" things in their path. Donald Griffin, a Harvard biologist who has done a great deal of work on "sonar" systems in bats and other animals and has written two excellent books on the subject (1958, 1959), cites (1958) a description of the remarkable skill of one blind individual as given by his physician in 1909.

Martin was a native of New York City and had been blind for nine years. He was of a fearless and impetuous disposition, and went about over the city without a guide. He passed up, down, and across great thoroughfares frequently and only a few times collided with a bicycle, which vehicle he detested. I was with him on occasions when I marvelled at the perfect freedom with which he walked crowded streets, showing not the slightest timidity, and requiring no aid whatever from me. . . .

I was amazed to see him cross Broadway at 14th Street with perfect ease, and imagine my astonishment when he shied around some timbers which had been set up across the sidewalk to prop the wall of a building undergoing repairs. He got on and off street cars without betraying his blindness. He used no cane, nor did he feel his way with his hands. Had I not known that he was actually blind, I would have thought that he was feigning.

I asked him how he knew his way and avoided collisions, and he invariably told me that he did not know. He seemed to be guided by what I shall term miraculous instinct superinduced by a subconscious mental condition.

Such cases as this have been noted by many other writers well before the twentieth century, one of the first being Diderot in 1749. Various theories have been suggested to account for the phenomenon, including touch, temperature sensation, a "sixth" sense, and even the existence of little "eyes" under the skin. The major explanation, however, has been in terms of hearing. This was given added cogency because of the extensive work being done on echolocation in bats, starting with Spallanzani's experiments in 1793.

Not until 1940, however, were any really decisive conclusions reached, when a blind graduate student of K. M. Dallenbach at Cornell started with a normal colleague to work on the problem. These two students, Supa and Cotzin (Supa, Cotzin, & Dallenbach, 1944), used two blindfolded normal subjects and two blind subjects—one of whom was one of the experimenters—in a series of ten studies. Their basic procedure was to require their subjects to walk, one at a time, along a 60-foot hallway into which had been introduced at randomly chosen points a large fiberboard screen. It was the task of all subjects to report when they first detected the screen. The task was performed under normal conditions initially, a variety of modifications being gradually introduced to refine the conclusions.

Basically, they found that all four subjects could

tell where the obstacle was at some distance away, this being greater for the two blind individuals than for the two blindfolded normal subjects. The former never ran into the screen, and they were able to sense its presence, in one case from as far as 18 feet away. The normal individuals, on the other hand, repeatedly ran into the obstacle during the initial series of trials but eventually learned to do so infrequently. These results are shown in Table 1–2.

The other experiments showed that stimulation of the face or exposed areas by air currents or sound waves was not important but that aural stimulation was crucial. Furthermore, high-frequency pitch (about 10,000 cps) rather than loudness changes were responsible for the detection of obstacles. These interesting findings have recently been confirmed and extended by Rice (1967), who has shown that blind people can discriminate even between objects of different shapes or sizes by means of self-generated sounds. Apparently man is not so very far away from bats and porpoises in his skill with sonar sensing.

The practical importance of such work is obvious. Armed with facts of the kind outlined, we can turn our efforts to improving this skill of obstacle detection in the blind by means of both training and mechanical amplifying devices. Some possibilities are discussed by Griffin (1958).

Our two examples should demonstrate to the reader something of the way in which the behavioral sciences have useful and sometimes unusual applications to everyday life. Psychology is used in numerous other ways. Industry and business make use of ability and aptitude tests to screen and select personnel and questionnaire and interview methods to aid them in market research. Mental hospitals today almost always employ a staff of trained clinical psychologists to aid in research on mental illness and in its diagnosis and treatment. Especially in wartime, the military has made intensive use of psychologists to try to answer such questions as, When is propaganda most effective? How do rumors spread? Under what conditions is an enemy combat unit most likely to surrender?

Having discussed the definition and scope of psychology, we turn to a discussion of its present intellectual structure as a discipline.

Table 1-2 Perception of obstacles by two blind subjects and two blindfolded normal subjects (Supa, Cotzin, & Dallenbach, 1944)

	Blind subjects		Normal subjects	
	E. S.	M. S.	P. C.	J. D.
Series 1:				
P*	18.04	6.36	2.12	0.98
A†	0.52	0.54	0.56	0.56
R‡	0	0	15	19
Series 2:				
P*	—	6.08	2.58	0.93
A†	—	0.56	0.68	0.77
R‡	—	0	6	1

* P = distance of screen when first perceived.
† A = appraisal of where screen was without actually touching it.
‡ R = running into wall.

THE PRESENT STATUS OF PSYCHOLOGY

In the foregoing discussions, we have indicated the general nature of psychology as a science, the character of the subject matter it studies, and its broad relations to other fields of human activity. In the remainder of this chapter, we will attempt to analyze psychology more deeply, especially in some of its unique features, and show the main directions it now appears to be taking.

Historically, psychology started out as a branch of philosophy—mental philosophy, or the study of mind. In 1879, the first laboratory of empirical scientific psychology was founded by Wilhelm Wundt at Leipzig in Germany. Like his forerunners, Wundt studied mind, or, more narrowly, consciousness, but in an experimental, or inductive, rather than in a philosophic, or deductive, way. The special technique he used was introspection—not, however, the casual variety all of us engage in now and then, but a very exacting kind of introspection which called for a high degree of training. It may sound strange to think of anyone's regarding such a technique as strictly scientific or empirical, but Wundt did. He thought of introspection much as an anatomist studying a section of tissue might think of his microscope. Just as the anatomist, by his special instrument, could come to describe the minute structure of tissue, so the psychologist might, with his special method, Wundt felt, come to describe the structure and dimensions of consciousness under various conditions.

Whatever its merits—and it has some as a means of formulating hypotheses—introspection failed, simply because the information it yielded was not public information. If one researcher claimed his consciousness was made up of four main parts, no one could definitely say his observations were right or wrong. Only he could look into his own mind. Because of this ambiguity of method, many differences of opinion arose, and around each a "school" of psychology was formed. For this reason, the psychology of this period is often referred to as the "old schools" psychology. Each school had its own faithful adherents, and each thought it had the absolute truth. Some time later, just after the turn of the century, several major developments took place. In Germany and in Austria, Gestalt psychology and psychoanalysis started; in France and England the study of individual differences and testing gained momentum; in the United States behaviorism became popular; and in the U.S.S.R. Pavlovian psychology arose. Although these systems to a large extent were in agreement in that each studied different aspects of behavior, there was and still is some competition among them.

This situation tends to have one of two results: As one alternative, we find that many psychologists prefer to affiliate themselves closely with a single approach. Thus one may be a behaviorist, a Gestalt psychologist, or a Freudian and confine one's theoretical and empirical activities to the framework provided by that system. Such a position is not too different from that taken by the European schools of psychology of the nineteenth century. The second alternative, which has perhaps become more popular since the 1930s, is eclecticism. In theory, the eclectic attempts to take the best from available points of view and to discard what is judged to be inadequate. In practice, this turns out to be rather difficult to do, and what tends to be immediately lost is the unique style provided by each particular system; and the choice of what is retained may be made on the basis of superficial, methodological criteria, such as whether it is "useful" or "interesting."

These two approaches permeate the field of psychology today. Their main effect has been to generate much confusion and some doubt in the minds of laymen and other scientists as to what psychology is really all about. Those who adhere to one point of view give the impression that the field is a very narrow one which ignores many important problems that should not be ignored. Clearly, people rightly have some difficulty in understanding, for example, how a behavioristically oriented psychologist working only with rats can believe he is going to fully explain human social interaction, mental illness, and creativity or, likewise, how a psychoanalyst is going to deal with perception. On the other hand, eclecticism may often convey shallowness and naïveté. Obviously, this problem must be faced squarely. To understand its dimensions more fully, the following analogy may be useful:

Let us suppose a curator wishes to start an art museum. His goal is to familiarize the public with painting. He can do this in several different ways, assuming limited resources: First, he can pick only the works of a particular period and of a particular country, or even of a single painter and use these to represent the whole field. It is obvious that such a representation would be inadequate in one sense; in another sense, however, the very intensity of the exposure, narrow as it would be, would still produce some benefits. Something of the way in which painters work would be revealed, general notions of the use of color and composition, and, of course, a great deal about that particular painter's approach to his art.

A second possibility for our curator would be simply to pick a sample of paintings representing as many periods and as many countries as possible. The "best" from each would be chosen according to some criteria, for example, the degree to which a work had stood the test of time or was highly esteemed by experts. This would give a good representation of the field but not one in depth. A person viewing such a collection might be impressed by the variety of styles and techniques but perhaps be disturbed by the apparent lack of order and rationale.

The third option would be to collect paintings that would serve as samples showing development of the major ideas of the field of art—its intellectual structure, so to speak. This would illustrate the *reasons* behind such movements as expressionism, cubism, and surrealism. It would show why some paintings that might look foolish to a layman could still be judged to be good by experts if they represented an ingenious explication of some major idea. And it would further suggest to the viewer, if he was clever enough, new and untried possibilities that were, in a sense, predicted by extant trends.

Now all three of these methods of representing the field of art to a newcomer are legitimate, but it is the third that can give the clearest picture, and also the most economical one. It is precisely the same with psychology. We have a number of different major theories, each with its own special ideas and often its own special language and techniques. Each has much to offer if rightly understood. To be properly professional, rather than merely an amateur, a psychologist must master these different points of view and realize not merely the limitations of each but the power that each has in generating new ideas and new research. To develop this notion, let us turn back to a deeper consideration of the two phases of science, namely, theory and experiment.

We have stated that no experiment can be done in any scientific field without involving some explicit or implicit assumptions. The focused experience that defines research is by nature selective. We cannot attend to all aspects of the world at once, and by choosing to look at some rather than others or to look at some in a particular order, we thereby make an implicit statement about what we consider important. In this sense, a theory always initially involves an evaluation, not in terms of right or wrong, good or bad, but rather in terms of the potential fruitfulness of the problem for research. An investigator may observe, for example, that reward is an important factor in producing efficient learning. The more the reward, the better the learning. This simple statement can be expanded almost indefinitely in many directions, all having to do with how reward operates to promote learning.

The world is complex and may be examined from a great many different points of view. An object like a tree, for example, may be looked on as a member of the elm genus, as a roosting place for birds, as a system of chemical compounds, or as a subject of aesthetic feeling. Each of these views is valid, each is a kind of primitive theory, and each leads to different kinds of activity. Looking on the tree as a member of the elm genus leads to problems of taxonomy, or classification; looking on it as a roosting place for birds may lead to work on how birds carry seeds away from the tree to aid in its reproduction; looking on it as a system of chemical compounds will lead to biochemical analysis; viewing it aesthetically may result in a poem. Reality will probably never be fully knowable by empirical science. We cannot comprehend it in one sweep, but only gradually, by examining one side at a time.

A science like physics does exactly this, and in this respect, at least, can serve as a useful model for psychology. It has theories of gases, theories of light, theories of electricity, and theories of atoms. All these are useful and add to knowledge of matter. It would be very silly, however, to argue that one of these was "more physics" than another. A competent physicist can use any of them depending on the problem he is facing. And by knowing each thoroughly (and only if he does know each thoroughly), he can occasionally unite two theories or models together in one broader theory. This is not to say that different theories cannot contradict each other. They often do, and when they do, a decision as to which is valid is reached by means of experimental test. But just as often, theories are concerned with quite different aspects of their basic subject matter, and preference for one over the other is mainly a question of taste.

The same applies to psychology. Since it deals with behavior of organisms, a subject matter even more complex than that of physics, it has many points of view. But to a large extent, these deal with different aspects of behavior. It is ironic that those who have had enough determination and intelligence to develop a new point of view have sometimes tended to be monolithic and religiously fervent in promoting it as the true faith. Perhaps this is due to the philosophic background of psychology. Perhaps it relates to the peculiar psychology of human beings. Whatever the case, we must always beware of prophets in science. As J. Arthur Thomson once said, "A theory in science is a policy, not a creed." Thus, one should be wholly committed to the full appreciation and understanding of any particular theory in science, but not to embracing it to the exclusion of all other theories.

What criteria do we use for choosing to work on one theory rather than another? There are three main ones: The first is its *logical coherence*. To an extent, a theory is "true" if its axioms or propositions do not contradict each other. This is not as simple as it sounds. Contradiction may sometimes be only implicit, or implied, rather than explicit, so that part of the task of theory building is to make all aspects of the theory as explicit as possible.

The second criterion is the *correspondence* of a theory to reality, or, more narrowly, to experiment. That is to say, a theory is "true" if it can generate hypotheses that stand the test of observation. Thus, a theory which predicts that parent-child relationships in the fourth or fifth year of life are crucial in producing a certain kind of personality must not also contain contrary propositions and must be amenable to necessary modifications if it is found by observation that the particular empirical statement has only limited validity.

The third criterion lies simply in the *fruitfulness* of the theory. It seems to turn out that some theories generate research and some do not. Whitehead was not far wrong when he said, "The importance of a proposition lies not so much in whether it is true, but whether it is interesting" [Whitehead, 1929]. It is difficult to say whether this depends on the degree to which the theory is explicable, the degree to which it meets some kind of rising need in the scientific community, or the personal idiosyncratic appeal that the theory will have on other scientists. Probably all these factors play a role. In any case, this is a most important criterion. To some extent the first two criteria can be employed only if the third has already been met. If nobody is willing to analyze a theory and test its predictions, we cannot say much about its coherence or its empirical value. It is partly on the basis of this "fruitfulness" criterion that we have chosen the particular approaches with which this book will deal. The reader will undoubtedly find some more immediately appealing than others. He should try, however, to suspend such spontaneous biases and apply the first two criteria in order to make a proper judgment.

CHAPTER 2
PSYCHOLOGY AND THE PROBLEM OF INFERENCE: STATISTICS

DRAWING CONCLUSIONS IN PSYCHOLOGY

As a science, psychology may be expected to share, with such disciplines as physics, chemistry, and biology, a commitment to certain basic methodological principles. The main principle, of course, is contained in the notion that the subject matter with which it deals—the behavior of organisms—can be understood in terms of certain regularities which are empirically observable and which can be established as laws.

Now in some of the sciences, especially physics, location and specification of relevant variables has become so precise that once the experimental situation is set up—and this may itself take years—a very exact test of a prediction is possible. Furthermore, we may expect that any repetition of the experiment will produce the same result. In psychology the same applies, logically speaking, but in practice, psychological variables are difficult to define exactly, as are also the conditions under which they are observed. They are also often difficult to control properly. Thus in Example 1-1, it is clear that one of the major variables being examined—namely, television viewing—is one that can be measured in very many ways: for example, number of hours as reported by parents or by the children themselves, number of discrete programs watched, and number of hours the set is on. But all these may be subject to error. Watching is a complex business, and it might be assumed that much of so-called viewing time is spent in side activities, ranging from daydreaming to conversation with peers. Furthermore, it is likely that different individuals will "watch" in different ways—some intently, some casually, some with deep emotional involvement, others with no such involvement.

As a consequence, when we study a variable of this kind, we must be sure to do so in a manner broad enough to encompass all such possibilities. Psychology does this mainly by observing many subjects and making a clear allowance for the differences that occur between them. The conclusion—whatever it may be—is then couched in terms of a probabilistic rather than absolute statement. Thus inference in psychology is usually based on statistical operations. It is consequently necessary at this point to elaborate on their usage in psychology and to give examples of some of the major statistical operations that are most commonly used to handle behavioral data.

Perhaps the most essential notion in the use of statistics is contained in what is commonly called the *null hypothesis*. This states that the relationships or differences found between variables or between groups are due to chance. It is accepted or rejected depending on some standard criterion—this having to do with the calculated incidence of such differences or relationships on a purely chance basis. If the incidence is extremely low—say, one in a thousand—then we usually reject the null hypothesis and conclude that the effects are systematic, or real. This may seem like a curiously inverted way of doing things, but it is actually the only real method by which we can establish scientifically respectable conclusions. It is a common human failing to find "significance" in events which are due purely to chance. For example, a European may form a strong opinion about all Americans on the basis of observing one American tourist. The likelihood of drawing a valid conclusion on the basis of a sample of one is extremely limited. Nonetheless, it is often very hard for people to resist drawing a conclusion in this way, particularly in their less rational moments.

One of the most fundamental facts about living things, in respect to both their physical and behavioral characteristics, is that they show *variation*. Darwin saw this clearly and was impressed by it enough to make it a basic premise in his theory of evolution. Without variation, natural selection cannot act. Mendel gave us, in his gene concept, the physiological basis for such variation. In the 46 chromosomes of human beings are carried enough different genetic components to yield, in their permutations and combinations, many more different individuals than there are atoms in the universe—approximately $10^{2,400,000,000}$ (Dobzhansky, 1962). Except for identical twin births, the chances of two individuals' being exactly alike are therefore extremely small. Consequently, if we wish to make generalizations about human or animal behavior, we are faced with a difficult task indeed.

In the first place, we can deal in practice only with those individuals who are actually living and must assume that twentieth-century man in his general makeup will not be too different from, say third-century man or sixtieth-century man. In the second place, practical considerations prevent us from testing all individuals present in the world at any given time. We can thus deal with only relatively small *samples* of individuals and hope these will represent the entire *universe* of human beings. Our goals may, of course, be more modest. If we are interested in the impact of racial integration on the personality of black third graders in Georgia, we can much more easily obtain a representative sample with which to work. The more universal we wish our generalization about human beings to be, the more difficult our task and the more shaky our conclusions will be. As we shall see in Section II, Freud made many universal statements about human behavior, but he was, in fact, speaking about his experience with a relatively small sample of nineteenth-century Viennese neurotics. It was soon evident, especially from the work of anthropologists, that his inferences had a more limited validity than he thought.

If the caution we must have in making generalizations about universal human behavior from our observations of a small sample of individuals applies in the science of psychology, it applies even more in the case of the inferences of the layman. When making some assertion about behavior on the basis of the evidence at hand, the psychologist is often faced with counterarguments by laymen citing some individual they know who, in their opinion, has behaved differently from the rule. For example, we might say that there seems to be a close connection between poverty and delinquency. It is very easy for someone to say in reply to this that he has known many people from demonstrably poor backgrounds who have turned out admirably and, in fact, can attribute their success precisely to their initial lack of privilege. There is no real answer to such an objection. Most rules about behavior are not absolute, because individuals are different. Variation is a fundamental fact about behavioral characters, and we can talk about them sensibly only if we recognize this fact.

BASIC STATISTICS

Consider the hypothetical data in Figure 2–1, based on the above example. Two populations are given, A and B, one from poor homes and the

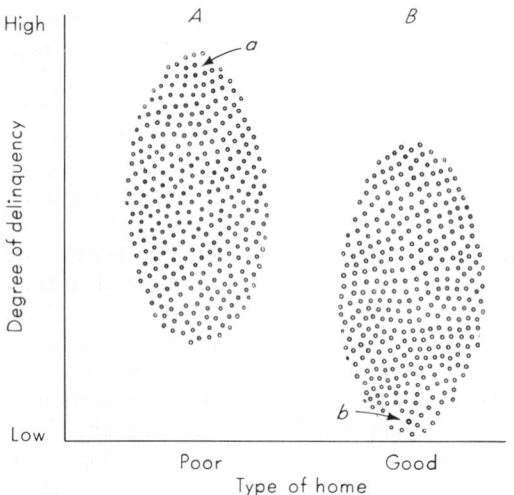

FIG. 2-1 Hypothetical scatter plot showing relation between socioeconomic level of home and degree of delinquency.

other from good homes. The "goodness" of the home, let us say, is defined in terms of social characteristics such as income level, size of dwelling, and neighborhood. On the vertical axis, or ordinate, is drawn a scale showing degree of delinquency from low to high. Each dot in populations A and B represents a single individual. Thus the figure shows the relationship between poorness of home background and degree of delinquency.

Two major features of the plot should be noticed: The first one—which we have already emphasized—is that both the populations show variation regardless of what kind of homebackground they have. Some people from good homes are delinquent, and some from poor homes are not. The second point is that the maximal density of dots, or individuals, occurs above a different point on the abscissa for group A as compared with group B. Notice that if we selected only the two individuals a and b, we might falsely infer an almost absolute connection between delinquency and home background.

The names given to these two important characteristics of the data are *dispersion* and *central tendency*. They represent the two most basic *statistical parameters* that are used to describe a population. The actual calculations we perform on the two groups yield *estimates* of these population parameters. They are only estimates because the groups are not identical with, but only representative of, the populations from which they were drawn. Thus when we wish to say something about a group in respect to some characteristic—in this case people from good or poor homes in respect to delinquent behavior—we do so in terms of the dispersion and central tendency. According to the hypothetical data, we can say that *most* of the individuals in group A show a higher level of delinquency than *most* of the individuals in group B. On the other hand—and this statement tempers the first—each group is rather variable, with the result that a good many people from good homes are in fact very delinquent and a good many people from poor homes are not at all delinquent.

It can safely be stated that the major portion of the statistics used in psychology are based on the notions of central tendency and dispersion. By using these according to various rules set down by statisticians, we are able to make inferences about behavior, that is, draw conclusions about it, which have a stated level of probability of being true. We could, to return to our example, conclude that the chance of a child from a poor home becoming a delinquent is *significantly* greater than that of a child coming from a good home. In more exact statistical terms, we might say (subject to calculation) that a difference between the averages of the two groups as large as that found between our hypothetical samples (if drawn from the same population) would occur *by chance* only once in a hundred such observations. This would be ground for rejecting the notion that the observed difference was simply due to the play of chance and for concluding that there was indeed a real association between poverty and delinquency.

Central Tendency

In the foregoing discussion, the reader may have noticed that we used the notion of central tendency in two ways. We spoke, in reference to the plot in Figure 2-1, of density of points, or individuals, around some particular score—in this case, degree of delinquency. This represents one measure of central tendency called the *mode*, which is accordingly defined as that score, on some measure, obtained by the largest number of individuals in the group. If asked to describe a group of associates, our reply that "*most of them* are very nice" is an implicit use of the mode. Taking the two arrays of scores in part a of Table 2–1, we see that in group A the score 16 is the mode and in group B the score 26 is the mode, since these are the scores obtained by the largest numbers of individuals in each respective group (20 individuals in group A and 18 in group B). The mode thus represents one quick way of saying in terms of a single number what a group is like.

The second measure of central tendency that is commonly used is the *median*. This is defined as the score which divides the population in half. Thus in part b of Table 2–1, the medians are 10 in group A and 14 in group B, since the individuals in each group getting these scores exceed three other individuals with lower scores and are exceeded by three with higher. When several individuals share scores, calculating the median becomes more complicated, though the principle is the same.

Notice that with both the median and the mode we do not need to be able to *add* scores. Thus we may state that for the population of a country the mode is the possession of blond hair, without any assumption about the additivity of hair pigment. It is obvious that black hair and red hair cannot be added, but one can say that more people possess one kind than the other; similarly with the median. We can rank persons in a class according to ability without assuming that the gap between the first and second is equal to the gap between the second and third. In an Olympic track event the first three places receive a share of the honors only according to their rank and not according to the time each took to cross the finish line. In a field of fifteen, the individual in eighth place would be at the median regardless of his clocked time.

It is not the same with the mean or average, the most commonly used—and, in fact, the most statistically useful—measure of central tendency. As probably every reader already knows, the mean is simply the sum of scores obtained by all individuals in the group divided by the number of these individuals. More exactly, it is a number so chosen that the deviations between it and every individual score in the sample are at a minimum. In this sense, the mean must be the number that reflects, in the best possible way, what all numbers of the group are like. It is written as follows:

$$\bar{X} = \frac{\Sigma X}{N}$$

Table 2–1 Measures of central tendency

a. Mode

Score	Number of individuals with that score — Group A	Group B
2	0	0
6	0	0
8	1	0
10	4	0
12	6	0
14	8	0
16	20	2
18	10	6
20	6	7
22	4	10
24	1	12
26	0	18
28	0	16
30	0	14
32	0	12
34	0	6
36	0	2
	Mode = 16	Mode = 26

b. Median

Group A (7 individual scores)	Group B (7 individual scores)
2	8
4	10
8	12
10	14
12	16
14	18
16	20
Median = 10	Median = 14

c. Mean

Group A (7 individual scores)	Group B (7 individual scores)
2	8
4	10
8	12
10	14
12	16
14	18
16	20
$\Sigma = 66$	$\Sigma = 98$
$N = 7$	$N = 7$
$\bar{X} = 9.43$	$\bar{X} = 14.00$

NOTE: Σ = sum of all scores; N = number of individuals in sample; $\bar{X}$ = mean.

Table 2-2 Divergence of mode, median, and mean in a single group

Score	No. of individuals
1	100
4	80
6	60
200	8
300	2

Mode = 1.00
Median = 1.42
Mean = 11.92

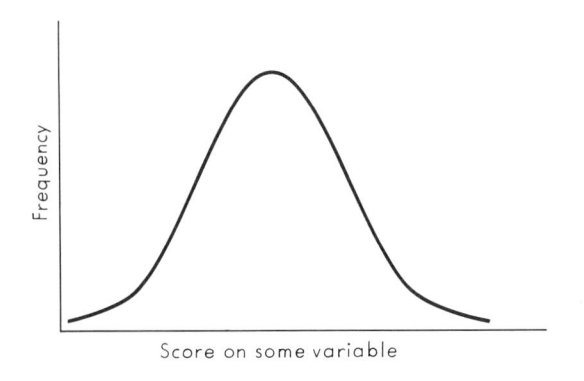

FIG. 2–2 Normal curve distribution.

Examples are again given in part c of Table 2–1. In making such a calculation, we do assume additivity of our measure—that is to say, that $1 - 0 = 2 - 1 = 3 - 2 = 4 - 3 = \cdots = k - n$. Without the validity of this assumption, we could not add and therefore could not calculate the mean, as in the case of hair color. It would make no sense to talk about the average hair color of a group, unless this character could be translated into some quantitative measure whose numerical values could be added.

These three measures of central tendency all tell us something about the characteristics of a whole group, for example, that it is bright or dull, athletic or nonathletic, or social or nonsocial. Each one gives a slightly different picture, and, in some cases, the three may diverge quite widely. An example is given in Table 2–2. In fact, in only one kind of group will they always be identical. This is a group made up of scores distributed symmetrically, as, for example, according to a *normal curve*. This bell-shaped distribution, depicted in Figure 2–2, is often found in nature for many characteristics, such as height and weight. It has a number of interesting properties, one of which is the identity of mode, median, and mean.

In cases where the mean, mode, and median are not identical, the mean is most generally preferred, since it is easy to calculate and is precisely defined. However, if the sample contains one or a few very atypical individuals—for example, as in the following: 2, 4, 8, 10, 500—then the median yields a fairer estimate of what the group as a whole is like. Finally, if we are dealing with simple frequency counts for some categorical variable—for example, letter grades such as A, B, C, D—then the mode is the statistic that must be used.

Variability

The second major property of a group of scores is their variability. We add information if we say of a class which on the whole is rather average in ability that it nevertheless contains some very bright and some very dull individuals. A statement of this kind refers essentially to the notion of *variance*. This is defined as the average amount by which individuals in the group deviate from the mean, or average. Sometimes the arithmetic average is used—called the *average deviation*. Statisticians find, however, that the square root of the average of deviations squared is a more useful measure from their standpoint. Table 2–3 shows the formula for the variance and *standard deviation*, which is simply the square root of the variance. The calculation of these for a set of scores is also given. The result for the standard deviation, for which the symbol σ is often used, is a figure of 20, which tallies with what a quick inspection of the distribution would indicate. There are three numbers greater than the mean of 40, and these are at equal intervals (10) from each other. The middle of these is 60—that is, 20 higher than the mean. The same applies to the numbers below the mean—20 is the middle one and deviates by 20 from the mean. Thus we can see almost immediately that the standard deviation would be about 20.

If we have, for two sets of group scores, their respective means and variances, we are able to com-

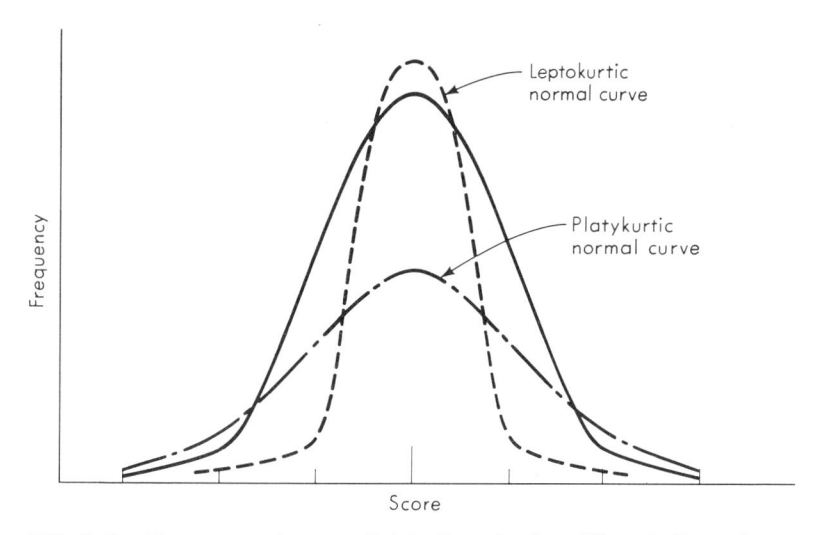

FIG. 2–3 Three normal curve distributions having different dispersions.

pare them in ways that are immediately useful. For example, a grade school teacher may be faced one year with a class whose mean IQ is 120 points with a standard deviation of 5; the next year, she may have a group with the same mean IQ but with a standard deviation of 15. It is obvious that her methods of teaching, the type of curriculum she presents, and the speed with which she takes her pupils along will have to be quite different from the first year to the second, and armed with this statistical information beforehand she can gear her preparations accordingly.

Normal Distributions

Given a normal distribution of scores, the standard deviation gives us much more information about the relation of scores with each other and with other sets of scores taken on the same or on different individuals. This brings us to a very important property of normal distributions. As with any smooth curve, we can write for the so-called normal curve a general equation that states how changes in the values along one axis accompany changes along the other axis. In the case of the normal distribution, we plot frequencies on the ordinate, or Y axis, and score for some measure (e.g., height, weight, intelligence) on the abscissa, or X axis. Three examples are shown in Figure 2–3. All are normal curves, but the variability is low in the case of the *leptokurtic* distribution (*leptos* = thin) and high in the case of the *platykurtic* distribution (*platus* = flat). Nonetheless, they share the property of symmetry and have their inflection points in common. Because of this, they belong to the same "family" of curves to which the general equation applies. Now one of the constants in this equation is the standard deviation, which in the case of any

Table 2-3 The variance and standard deviation

Score (X)	$X - \overline{X} = x$	x^2
10	−30	900
20	−20	400
30	−10	100
40	0	0
50	+10	100
60	+20	400
70	+30	900
$\Sigma X = 280$		$\Sigma x^2 = 2,800$
$N = 7$		
$\dfrac{\Sigma X}{N} = \overline{X} = 40$		

$$\Sigma x^2 = 2,800$$

$$\text{Variance} = \sigma^2 = \frac{\Sigma x^2}{N}$$

$$\text{Standard deviation} = \sigma = \sqrt{\frac{\Sigma x^2}{N}}$$

$$\text{Therefore } \sigma^2 = \frac{2,800}{7} = 400$$

$$\text{Standard deviation} = \sigma = \sqrt{400} = 20$$

particular curve is a fixed number. It must then be that the standard deviation bears an orderly relation to changes in frequency. Look at the example in Figure 2–4. The mean is 40 and the standard deviation is 10. The distance between a score of 10 and 20 is 10, or one standard deviation. On the Y axis, this corresponds to a change in frequency of 20 to 100, or 80. The same distance, however, 20 to 30—also one standard deviation—corresponds to a frequency change of from 100 to 750, or a change of 650. In the normal curve distribution, there are exact rules governing the changes of frequency that occur with differences in score. The rules are indicated in Table 2–4. They have several important consequences.

One is that given an individual's score and the mean and standard deviation of the distribution, we can immediately state the percentage of other individuals' scores in the group which his score exceeds or which exceeds his. This is a much more meaningful interpretation of a score than simply its raw value. A mark on a test of 80 made by one subject in a group whose average is 60 tells us something, but not as much as it does when stated in terms of standard deviation units and the proportion of other individuals who have higher or lower marks.

A second useful consequence of the relation between standard deviation and score in the normal curve is that it allows us to compare scores by the same individual in different tests or measures. Two scores of 80 may mean quite different levels of performance. In one test, 80 may be only one standard deviation above the mean and in the other three standard deviations above the mean. Obviously, the score represents a much better performance in the latter test. There are available a number of ways of transforming raw scores so that they directly reflect this meaning. The most common is the so-called Z score. Specifically, this expresses a person's performance score in terms of how much he deviates (number of standard deviation units) from the mean of the group. It is written as follows:

$$Z = \frac{|X - \bar{X}|}{\sigma}$$

(The vertical bars indicate that the direction of the difference—i.e., negative or positive—is to be ignored.)

Table 2-4 Score distribution in the normal curve as a function of standard deviation

A score that deviates from the mean by a standard deviation (σ) of:	Lies below approximately this percent of the whole population:
−3	99
−2	98
−1	84
+1	16
+2	2
+3	1

We now turn to perhaps the most important consequence of the relation we are considering. This has to do with the basic problem of making valid inferences.

Inference and Significance Levels

Our example in Figure 2–1 depicted individuals from good homes as showing a lower mean level of delinquency than children from poor homes. Properties of the variance in normally distributed groups allow us to state to what extent such an obtained difference could occur by chance. We already know that individuals in a group vary. But it is also true that the means for groups or samples from the same population vary. If we took 1,000 groups from good homes, we would not obtain the same mean level of delinquency for all of them. Instead the 1,000 means would show variation and be distributed according to a normal curve form. The same would apply if we took a corresponding number of groups from poor homes. The variation or standard deviation of such distribution of means is known as the *standard error of the mean,* and it can be estimated, for statistical reasons, by using

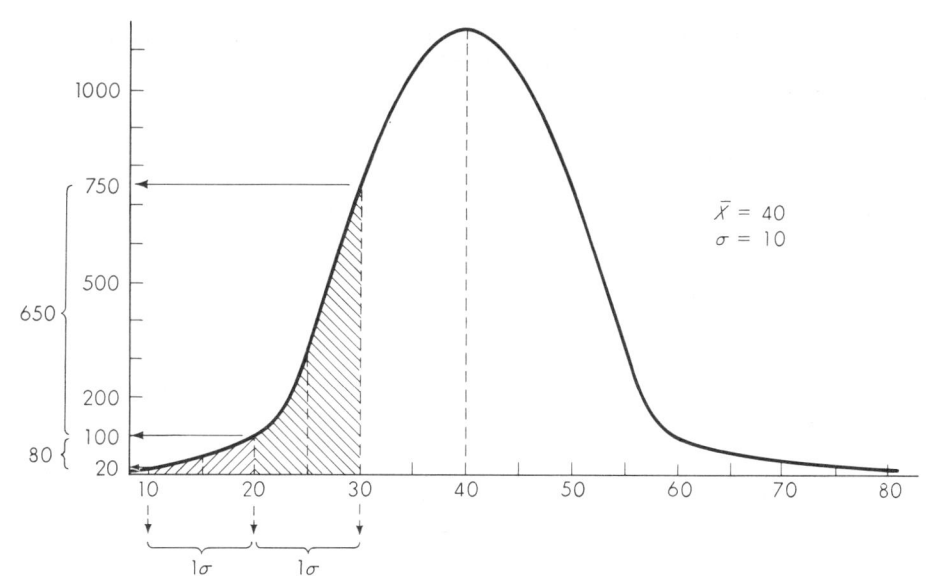

FIG. 2–4 Relation between frequency (Y axis) and standard deviation (X axis) in a normal curve distribution.

the information we have on only one group. The estimate turns out to be as follows:

$$\sigma_M = \frac{\sigma}{\sqrt{N-1}}$$

where σ_M = standard error of the mean
σ = standard deviation of the single sample being studied
N = number of individuals in the single sample

To go a step further, application of this formula to actual data tells us how much fluctuation we could expect between means from a large number of additional groups. For example, if our standard deviation were 10 and the number in the group were 101, then

$$\sigma_M = \frac{10}{\sqrt{101-1}} = 1.0$$

With a mean of 40, this would mean that we could expect to obtain quite frequently, on any other groups we took, means between 39 and 41. To be more exact, we could expect this to happen as frequently as 68 percent of the time. Groups with means as low as 35 or as high as 45, however, would be most unusual, since their means would be five standard deviations away from the initial observed mean, a very infrequent result indeed in any normal distribution of scores. For these reasons, if a group from a poor home does have a mean score of 45 or higher, we have grounds for supposing that it shows a level of delinquency that would be most unlikely among groups from good homes—so unlikely, in fact, that we must conclude that poverty and not chance produced this difference. By applying certain statistical formulas we can state the probability value of obtaining such a difference by chance, that is, its *significance level*. Generally speaking, a difference which could occur by chance five times (or less) out of a hundred— the 5 percent level—is accepted as *not* being due to chance. In such a case, we reject the null hypothesis.

A full explanation of the treatment of differences between group means is beyond the scope of this book. Our discussion is intended only to present the general ideas behind statistical inference. A concrete application is presented in Example 2–1.

Example 2–1 *The significance of differences between groups*

Let us suppose that the instructor of a large class in psychology wishes to find out whether there is any relationship between the seating position of a student in the lecture room and performance on the subject matter being taught. A reasonable hypothesis might be that those closer to the front tend to perform better, not only because audibility and perhaps social influence decrease with distance, but also because those who choose to sit in front are often more highly motivated to listen to the lecturer and to learn the course material. Note that the very general way in which the empirical relation is stated can readily be put into more precise terms. It is likely, for example, that the curve describing it is not a simple straight line but rather of an exponential form—that is, one that shows gradually increasing deceleration until it becomes rather flat. This would mean that relative seating position of all those sitting fairly close should make a large difference in performance but that the differences between rows toward the back should not be very great. There are other possibilities, of course, and the reasonableness of any particular one will depend on the kind of theory held concerning the relation between social influence and physical distance. As a starting point, however, it is perfectly acceptable simply to suppose that those farther away are different from those closer to the lecturer.

Testing this notion involves simply picking the two groups most separated in terms of distance, e.g., individuals in the first five rows versus individuals in the last five rows, and comparing them on some measure of performance. In statistical terms, we would formulate the hypothesis in *null* terms—that is, we would make the hypothesis that no differences exist between the two groups and then see if this can be rejected.

Let us suppose that the experiment is carried out and that the following data emerge:

Performance scores

Group 1 (at front)	Group 2 (at back)
72	55
65	71
80	60
63	61
57	52
78	46
69	68
55	50
75	73
56	64

The sums of scores of group 1 and group 2 can be written as follows:

$\Sigma X_1 = 670$
$\Sigma X_2 = 600$

Their respective means are

$$\bar{X}_1 = \frac{\Sigma X_1}{N_1} = \frac{670}{10} = 67.0$$
$$\bar{X}_2 = \frac{\Sigma X_2}{N_2} = \frac{600}{10} = 60.0$$

Clearly, the means differ by quite a large amount. The question, however, is whether this difference is significant, i.e., whether we can reject the null hypothesis that a difference of this size could be due to chance. The procedure used is as follows:

1. We first compute for each group the standard error of its mean.

For group 1:

X_1	$X - \bar{X}_1 = x_1$	x_1^2
72	+5	25
65	−2	4
80	+13	169
63	−4	16
57	−10	100
78	+11	121
69	+2	4
55	−12	144
75	+12	144
56	−11	121
		$\Sigma x_1^2 = 848$

$$\sigma_1^2 = \frac{848}{10} = 84.8$$
$$\sigma_1 = 9.21$$
$$\sigma_{M_1} = \frac{9.21}{\sqrt{10-1}} = 3.07$$

Likewise for group 2:

X_2	$X - \bar{X}_2 = x_2$	x_2^2
55	−15	225
71	+11	121
60	0	0
61	+1	1
52	−8	64
46	−14	196
68	+8	64
50	−10	100
73	+13	169
64	+4	16
		$\Sigma x_2^2 = 956$

$$\sigma_2^2 = \frac{956}{10} = 95.6$$

$$\sigma_2 = 9.78$$

$$\sigma_{M_2} = \frac{9.78}{\sqrt{10-1}} = 3.26$$

2. We are now in a position to estimate, by means of a given formula, another statistic known as the standard error of the difference between means. This formula is as follows:

$$\sigma_{M_D} = \sqrt{\sigma_{M_1}^2 + \sigma_{M_2}^2}$$

In our example, this works out to be

$$\sigma_{M_D} = \sqrt{9.42 + 10.63} = \sqrt{20.05}$$

$$\sigma_{M_D} = 4.47$$

3. The obtained difference between our group means was, in fact, $67 - 60 = 7$. We thus find that it is not a great deal larger than the standard error of mean differences. What the latter describes is essentially the variance of the distribution of difference between the means of many groups we might select randomly from the same population. Thus if we picked from our lecture hall pairs of groups of ten without regard to any variables and compared their means, we would find fairly large differences sometimes, small ones in other cases. How does the difference we obtained when we did choose groups differing in respect to a systematic variable compare with such chance differences? We make such a comparison by means of the so-called t test. This involves the equation

$$t = \frac{\overline{X}_1 - \overline{X}_2}{\sigma_{M_D}}$$

In our present case, this works out to be

$$t = \frac{7}{4.47} = 1.56$$

4. To interpret the t value, we must refer again to the properties of the normal curve. The t ratio tells us, in fact, how much bigger the observed difference is than the standard deviation of differences. It will be recalled that the distance between one standard deviation below the mean and one standard deviation above the mean takes in about 68 percent of cases in a normal distribution. That is, values outside this range will occur by chance only about 32 percent of the time. Likewise, in the foregoing example, only about 14 percent of values occur outside the range $\overline{X} - 1.56\sigma$ and $\overline{X} + 1.56\sigma$. Statistical tables have been made up which tell us immediately the likelihood of any standard deviation score. We find that when the t ratio is as great as 2, it can occur by chance only 5 times in 100. In our example, the difference we found could occur, however, as often as 14 times in 100. Consequently, it is not uncommon enough to allow us to reject the null hypothesis that the difference between the groups is due to chance. Thus we have not found that students seated in the front of the lecture hall are significantly different in performance from those seated in the rear.

Correlation

The final application of the notion of variance in normal distributions is in respect to the comparison of different scores made by the same individual on two or more tests. Such a comparison is made by means of the *correlation coefficient*, a statistic which describes the extent to which two measures covary. Thus height and weight correlate, or covary, fairly strongly, in that taller people tend, on the average, to be heavier. On the other hand, intelligence and weight probably do not covary—that is, they tend to show a zero correlation. Figure 2–5 shows three hypothetical examples or correlation: high positive, high negative, and zero. Note that the second of these could be made positive simply by reversing the sign on one axis. Direction of relation is unimportant in covariation, or correlation; only the size of the relation is crucial, and this may vary from -1.0 to $+1.0$. Thus a correlation of $-.9$ does not mean lack of relationship; on the contrary, it means a relationship as strong as that given by a correlation of $+.90$. The formula for the correlation coefficient is as follows:

$$r = \frac{\Sigma xy}{N\sigma_x\sigma_y}$$

where $r =$ correlation coefficient
$\Sigma xy =$ sum of products of deviation scores, that is, deviations of X scores from $\overline{X}$ and Y scores from $\overline{Y}$
$x = (X - \overline{X})$
$y = (Y - \overline{Y})$.
$N =$ number of individuals in each group; N_x must equal N_y
$\sigma_x =$ standard deviation of X scores.
$\sigma_y =$ standard deviation of Y scores.

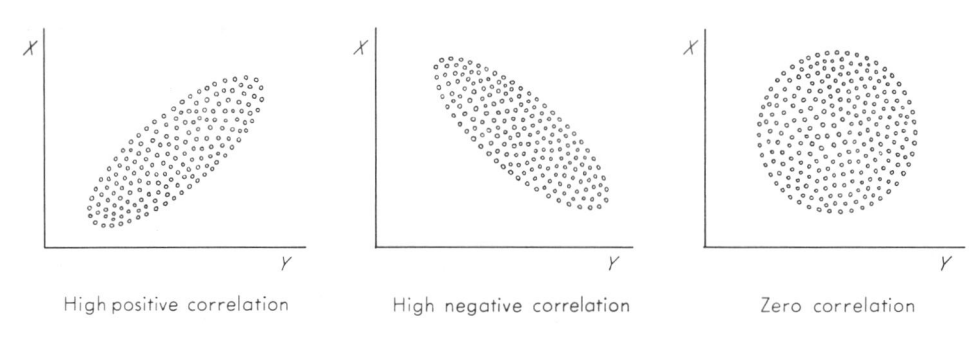

FIG. 2–5 Scatter plots for high positive, high negative, and zero correlations between two variables, X and Y.

One part of the formula, $\Sigma xy/N$, is known as the covariance, or σxy. The reader will recognize that it is quite similar to the formula for the variance discussed above—that is, $\Sigma x^2/N$. The only difference is the inclusion of y scores in the numerator. The logic of the statistic is as follows: a strong positive association will occur when high negative deviation scores on the x variable go with high negative deviation scores on the y variable and when high positive deviation scores on the x variable go with high positive deviation scores on the y variable. A strong negative association will occur when high positive deviation scores on one variable go with high negative deviation scores on the other variable. The covariance will be at a maximum when deviation scores obtained by individuals on the two variables are approximately equal. When the standard deviations σ_x, σ_y are added to the denominator of the covariance formula, we have the correlation coefficient. What this addition accomplishes is to transform simple deviation scores $(X - \overline{X}$ and $Y - \overline{Y})$ into *standard deviation* scores $\frac{X - \overline{X}}{\sigma_x}$ and $\frac{Y - \overline{Y}}{\sigma_y}$.

That the maximum correlation can be $+1.0$ or -1.0 can be readily seen if we consider two sets of identical scores. In this case, we can substitute in the equation as follows: since the deviation of any X score from its mean, $X - \overline{X}$, will equal the deviation of the Y score from its mean, $Y - \overline{Y}$, then

$$\Sigma xy = \Sigma xx = \Sigma x^2$$
and
$$\sigma_x^2 = \sigma_y^2$$

Then
$$r = \frac{\Sigma xy}{N\sigma_x\sigma_y} = \frac{\Sigma x^2}{N\sigma_x^2}$$
$$\frac{\Sigma x^2}{N\sigma_x^2} = \frac{\Sigma x^2}{N(\Sigma x^2/N)} = \frac{\Sigma x^2}{\Sigma x^2} = 1.0$$

The same will apply in the case of a correlation of -1.0 except that any deviation $(X - \overline{X})$ will equal the deviation $-(Y - \overline{Y})$; that is, $y = -x$. Hence
$$\Sigma xy = -\Sigma x^2$$
Then
$$r = \frac{\Sigma xy}{N\sigma_x\sigma_y} = \frac{-\Sigma x^2}{N\sigma_x^2} = \frac{-\Sigma x^2}{\Sigma x^2} = -1.0$$

As the orders of the two arrays depart from each other, the correlation approaches zero, meaning complete absence of relation between the two variables. Most correlations actually found, of course, usually have values somewhere in between. The problem that faces us, then, is the same as that discussed earlier of determining whether the observed difference between two means is real and significant or not. What size of correlation is real or significant? Again, there are statistical tests that supply this information. These have to do with the *standard error of correlation*, and comparison of the observed correlation with its standard error tells us whether the former could readily have been obtained by chance or not.

The correlation coefficient is the basic statistic for one important area in psychology—namely, psychometrics. The correlation not only gives us information as to the accuracy and repeatability of our measurements of a trait by means of a psychological test—*test reliability*—but also tells us whether our tests are really measuring what we want them to measure—the problem of *test validity*. The correlation tells us, furthermore, the kinds and strengths of relationships that exist between many different tests. By using a technique known as *factor analysis*, we can pull out from a set, or matrix, of intercorrelations between a large number of tests those common elements, or *factors*, which are responsible for all the covariations in the matrix. As we shall show in Chapter 22, there are many who believe that these factors represent the basic units of personality and intelligence.

STATISTICAL VERSUS CLINICAL PREDICTION

The main point emerging from the discussion above is that inference in psychology is usually based on statistics and probability theory. The data we gather are very complex in the sense that there are many variables that operate—many more variables than we can exactly control. Thus, psychology is not, for the most part, like classical physics, in which experimental findings are highly reliable and can usually be stated in exact mathematical terms. This does not, however, make psychology any less a science. It employs basically the same general methods as physics and follows the same quest for empirical truth.

There is some disagreement, however, about the usefulness of statistical methods in psychology. It was because of this that we stated in the previous paragraph that psychological inference is *usually* based on statistics and probability theory. Practicing clinicians do not measure or experiment and yet apparently achieve some success in drawing general conclusions about behavior as well as in helping individual people. Their judgments tend to be intuitive, global, and fluid. That is to say, their assessment of a person is often made in terms that are not fully explicit and may be based on a consideration of all the person's behavior; it may often be highly conditional on circumstances as well as on the person's capacity to change. An amusing catalog of the manner in which the statistician and clinician characterize each other in less friendly moments has been made by Meehl (1954) and is reproduced in Table 2–5 (Meehl, 1954, p. 4).

Suppose we attempt to predict whether an entering college student will be graduated at the end of four years. The psychometric approach would be to administer to him several tests already known through pretesting to have a good correlation with academic success. If he received a high score, we might say that his chances of getting through were eight out of ten. A clinically oriented counselor, however, would probably not be very satisfied with such a straightforward probabilistic statement. He would prefer to interview the student closely and formulate his prediction, not in terms of a single score, but in terms of a semiliterary description of his intellectual and personal assets and liabilities. He might say something like this:

John strikes me on first meeting as a quiet and reserved boy. He does not initiate much information, and his responses to questions are brief though always to the point. He appears to have a keen analytical mind with leanings toward the exact sciences and, in fact, shows some impatience toward philosophic speculation. He is the oldest of five in a middle-class family and perhaps because of this has a strong motivation to succeed. His chief drawbacks—and these may hurt his chances—are his lack of receptiveness to the ideas of others and his initial unwillingness to allow others to share his. He is obviously sensitive about this lack of capacity to relate, and one or two unfortunate incidents could easily discourage him. Careful handling by his instructors is called for, and, provided he gets this, he should have no trouble in completing his degree.

Such an assessment appears to contrast rather strikingly with a set of psychometric scores. Yet basically the same kind of logic is followed. All the characteristics used by the interviewer in his description are potentially measurable and could be correlated with the criterion. Furthermore, the conditional quality of the interviewer's judgment is little different in principle from the probabilistic statement of the psychometrician. What the counselor has done essentially, as one writer has pointed out (Meehl, 1954), has been to jump ahead of the data and methods actually available, to focus on several dimensions he considers to be important to academic success, and then to make a rough assessment of the student in terms of these. In a sense, the clinical method is more creative than the statistical but also less exact and certain. They can obviously supplement each other very usefully, as we will illustrate in the next chapter.

Table 2-5 Mutual characterizations of clinical and experimental psychologists (Meehl, 1954)

	Clinicians are	Experimentalists are
Clinicians say:	Dynamic, global, meaningful, holistic, subtle, sympathetic, configural, patterned, organized, rich, deep, genuine, sensitive, real, sophisticated, living, concrete, natural, true to life, understanding	Mechanical, atomistic, additive, cut-and-dried, artificial, arbitrary, unreal, incomplete, dead, pedantic, fractionated, trivial, forced, static, superficial, rigid, sterile, academic, oversimplified, pseudoscientific, blind
Experimentalists say:	Mystical, transcendent, metaphysical, supermundane, vague, hazy, subjective, unscientific, unreliable, crude, private, unverifiable, qualitative, primitive, prescientific, sloppy, uncontrolled, careless, verbalistic, intuitive, muddleheaded	Operational, communicable, verifiable, public, objective, reliable, behavioral, testable, rigorous, scientific, precise, careful, trustworthy, experimental, quantitative, down-to-earth, hardheaded, empirical, mathematical, sound

The reader should not get the impression from this contrast between statistical and clinical prediction that the former is always very neat and orderly. Much of science, as it is actually done in the laboratory, is surprisingly haphazard and tentative. In fact, a too strict adherence to designing neat experiments and trying to formulate very exact hypotheses can often produce sterile and trivial results. Many fundamental discoveries in science have been made in a quite accidental and unexpected manner. Furthermore, the tactics of the clinician have the striking advantage of allowing observation in depth of the behavior of a subject as it goes on over a considerable span of time. Some researchers doing work on basic problems—for example, on learning in animals—have argued that this approach can be powerfully applied in this context, provided a manageable piece of behavior can be isolated for study. The use of the bar press by rats in the experiments of Skinner and his colleagues and students constitutes the best example of such a piece of behavior. The rate of emission of the response is recorded continuously over time, and changes in rates as a function of different variables are noted. With such observations, statistics turn out to be largely irrelevant.

The discussion above will serve to introduce to the reader the manner in which inferences are made in psychology. At this stage, the particular statistical formulas and their derivations have no great importance. What are important, however, are the ideas that lie behind them. In the examples set out in subsequent chapters, frequent references will be made to the statistical significance of differences or relationships, and it is crucial that the meaning of these expressions here be properly understood.

CONCLUSION: THE PLAN OF THE BOOK

Psychology is presented here in terms of six major approaches, or theories, about the behavior of man and lower animals. They should not be regarded as formalized models, but rather as sets of commitments to some rather broad principles considered to be crucial to the understanding of mind and behavior. Each has its own style and methodology and to a large extent its own historical background and philosophic underpinnings. It will also become immediately clear that each approach tends to deal primarily with certain kinds of empirical problems to the exclusion of others, although there is still some overlap in this respect. In the authors' opinion, this fairly represents what psychology is like. Any psychologist operating as a professional makes explicit or implicit commitments to certain ideas which he feels have great explanatory power for his purposes, and it is these ideas which form the basis for the six approaches we are presenting here. In order of presentation they are as follows:

Section Two:	Psychoanalysis and theories of personality
Section Three:	Models of social behavior
Section Four:	Approaches to the problems of perceiving and knowing
Section Five:	Behavioristic models in psychology
Section Six:	Biological models
Section Seven:	Individual differences: their measurement and meaning

These approaches will be examined from three points of view, namely, their coherence as theories, their empirical validity, and their fruitfulness. Each one will be presented in terms of propositions about behavior, and each proposition will be examined in the light of relevant empirical data where this is possible. Thus, if we indicate that Freud states as a proposition that "early environment is important for later behavior," we will try to present some scientific evidence (both clinical and laboratory) that bears out this proposition. In proceeding from theory to data in this manner, we will also try to point up the different methods used (for example, the use of projective tests), and their validity and general usefulness.

The approach taken here may appear to be pluralistic. However, it is not. One theory may not be as "good" as another according to the three criteria outlined above. And, in any case, most of them are concerned with quite different aspects of the behavior of organisms. We will attempt to assess each as we go along, and also, by means of cross references, to indicate where convergences between different approaches occur.

To compare theories, we must first distinguish them, and this means close attention to the terminology and methods of each. When learning, for example, the behavioristic viewpoint, we must be prepared to enter totally into that framework, much as if we wanted to learn something about Japan, we would need to learn the Japanese language thoroughly and imbue ourselves in Japanese culture, though not so completely that we lost our own identity. It will be of considerable aid to the student if he attempts to translate as he goes along some everyday problems into the language of each model. Science is largely a game of detection. To solve problems we must use different theories to their limits. We also must be flexible enough to shift from one to the other. The crass police inspector with his single all-purpose theory never solves the crime, nor does the amateur with his happy common sense.

In a short epilogue, we will consider the possibility of unity between different approaches and the general philosophic position that can be said to underlie the point of view represented by this book.

One last word of caution: As a science, psychology must necessarily analyze and simplify from the complex totality that comprises any human being. It is this which we encounter and with which we must deal in our everyday lives, not the highly abstract models of psychology. And consequently, the latter may appear to many readers to be inept, insufficient, and often even offensive. We must emphasize here that there is no necessary opposition between these two views. The treatment of a person, during the duration of an experiment, as a statistic—a mere number in a series—does not imply a commitment, on the part of the experimenter, to such a point of view in general. There is much about man that is mysterious and arcane, and it is no concession to obscurantism to admit this, while to deny it does nothing to promote the worth of psychology as a science. We may thus end this section with two quotations, disparate in intent but equally valid in reflecting our position:

> What a piece of work is a man! How noble in reason: how infinite in faculties, in form and moving, how express and admirable, in action how like an angel, in apprehension how like a god! the beauty of the world the paragon of animals! [William Shakespeare, *Hamlet*, act II, scene 2].

and from a contemporary philosopher:

> However acute our awareness may be of the rich variety of human experience, and however great our concern over the dangers of using the fruits of science to obstruct the development of human individuality, it is not likely that our best interests would be served by stopping objective inquiry into the various conditions determining the existence of human traits and actions, and thus shutting the door to the progressive liberation from illusion that comes from the knowledge achieved by such inquiry [Nagel 1961, p. 606].

SECTION ONE: REFERENCES

DOBZHANSKY, T. *Mankind evolving: The evolution of the human species.* New Haven, Conn.: Yale University Press, 1962.

FISHER, SIR R. A. *The design of experiments.* London: Oliver & Boyd, 1937.

GRIFFIN, D. R. *Listening in the dark.* New Haven, Conn.: Yale University Press, 1958.

GRIFFIN, D. R. *Echoes of bats and men.* London: Heinemann, 1959.

HIMMELWEIT, H. T., OPPENHEIM, A. N., & VINCE, P. *Television and the child: An empirical study of the effect of television on the young.* London: Oxford University Press, 1958.

JAYNES, J. The routes of science. *American Scientist*, 1966, **54**, 94–102.

KOCH, S. Psychological science versus the science-humanism antinomy: Intimations of a significant science of man. *American Psychologist,* 1961, **16,** 629–639.

MACCOBY, E. E. Why do children watch television? *Public Opinion Quarterly,* 1954, **18,** 239–244.

MASLOW, A. H. *Motivation and personality.* New York: Harper, 1954.

MEEHL, P. E. *Clinical vs. statistical prediction: A theoretical analysis and a review of the evidence.* Minneapolis: University of Minnesota Press, 1954.

MILL, J. S. *A system of logic: Ratiocinative and inductive.* London: Longmans, 1893.

NAGEL, E. *The structure of science.* New York: Harcourt, Brace & World, 1961.

POINCARÉ, H. *The foundations of science.* New York: The Science Press, 1913.

POLANYI, M. *Personal knowledge: Towards a post-critical philosophy.* London: Routledge, 1958.

RICE, C. E. Human echo perception. *Science,* 1967, **155,** 656–664.

STAFFORD, J. *A mother in history.* New York: Farrar, Straus & Giroux, 1965.

SUPA, M., COTZIN, M., & DALLENBACH, K. M. "Facial vision": The perception of obstacles by the blind. *American Journal of Psychology,* 1944, **57,** 133–183.

WHITEHEAD, A. N. *Process and reality.* Cambridge, Mass.: Harvard University Press, 1929.

WHITEHEAD, A. N. *The aims of education and other essays.* London: Williams & Norgate, 1932.

SECTION TWO
PSYCHOANALYSIS AND THEORIES OF PERSONALITY

"But mere separateness and uniqueness are not the psychologist's chief concern. Wasps and mice, trees and stones possess this elementary distinction. In addition to separateness and uniqueness a human being displays psychological individuality, an amazingly complex organization comprising his distinctive habits of thought and expression, his attitudes, traits and interests, and his own peculiar philosophy of life. It is the total manifold psycho-physical individuality, commonly referred to as personality, that engages the attention of the psychologist."

(Allport, 1937, p. 24)

PROLOGUE

A few years ago, a grand jury in Indiana indicted, for first degree murder, a divorced mother, Mrs. Baniszewski, three of her six children, and two of their friends. The victim was sixteen-year-old Sylvia Likens, the attractive daughter of some neighbors who had come to board with the Baniszewskis while her parents were traveling on the Midwest Fair circuit. Although her relationship with this family was initially quite normal, it soon started to assume a bizarre and dreadful character. Reprimands for actual or imagined offenses became more and more frequent and more and more severe, and these came to be imposed on Sylvia not just by Mrs. Baniszewski but also by the children—two boys and a girl and their two friends. Punishment gradually gave way to torture. Mere slappings turned into whippings with a heavy belt and blows on the head with a paddle or a broom handle. Confinement to her room was followed by incarceration in a dirty basement with the family's two dogs. Finally, her captors climaxed their adventure in sadism by branding Sylvia with a heated needle on her lower abdomen with the words "I'm a prostitute and proud of it" in inch-high letters. A few days later, following further torturing, Sylvia entered a period of profound apathy and finally died.

What could have provoked such an incredible display of calculated sadism? Were all those involved insane? This seems unlikely in any usual sense, since all of them had apparently been leading, up to that point, fairly normal lives. Can we put it down to simply a symptom of the "troubled" society we live in? This is again very doubtful. The history of man shows us no shortage of horror and cruelty, and every age has had its indignant commentators on its evils. The inscription on an ancient Assyrian tablet reads:

Our earth is degenerate in these latter days; bribery and corruption are common; children no longer obey their parents; every man wants to write a book, and the end of the world is evidently approaching.

Whether writing books is a form of degeneracy we might question. But it is certainly clear that human society has always had at least as much corruption and hate as nobility and love. Must we then conclude that in all of us, for some reason, lie hidden impulses to the kind of bestiality released in Mrs. Baniszewski? Are all of us "normal" people really so normal? Some have thought not. The great French thinker Blaise Pascal remarked: "Men are by nature so mad, that not to be mad is itself a form of madness" (Pascal, 1960, p. 414). As we shall indicate shortly, this thought was later shared by Freud and many of his disciples.

Let us look at a more directly clinical example drawn from an actual psychoanalytic case study reported by a psychoanalyst—Robert Lindner (1955). The subject is Laura—"The girl who couldn't stop eating." Her problem is dramatically described by Lindner as follows:

Laura had two faces. The one I saw that morning was hideous. Swollen like a balloon at the point of bursting, it was a caricature of a face, the eye lost in pockets of sallow flesh and shining feverishly with a sick glow, the nose buried between bulging cheeks splattered with blemishes, the chin an oily shadow mocking human contour; and somewhere in this mass of fat a crazy-angled carmined hole was her mouth.

Her appearance astonished and disgusted me. The revulsion I felt could not be hidden. Observing it, she screamed her agonized self-loathing.

"Look at me, you son-of-a-bitch," she cried. "Look at me and vomit! Yes—it's me—Laura. Don't you recognize me? Now you see what I've been talking about all these weeks—while you've been sitting back here doing nothing, saying nothing. Not even listening when I've begged and begged you for help. Look at me!"

"Lie down, please," I said, "and tell me about it."

A cracked laugh, short and rasping, came from her hidden mouth. The piglike eyes raised to some unseen auditor above, while clenched fists went up in a gesture of wrath.

"Tell him about it! Tell him about it! What the hell do you think I've been telling you about all this time!"

"Listen, Laura," I said more firmly, "Stop yelling and lie down"—and I turned away from her toward the chair behind the couch. But before I could move, she grabbed my arm and swung me around to face her. I felt her nails bite through my coat and dig into the skin beneath. Her grip was like a vise.

She thrust her face toward mine. Close up, it was a huge, rotting wart. Her breath was foul as she expelled it in a hoarse, passionate whisper.

"No," she said, "I'm not going to lie down. I'm going to stand here in front of you and make you look at me—make you look at me as I have to look at myself. You want me to lie down so you won't have to see me. Well, I won't do it. I'm going to stand here forever!" She shook me. "Well," she said. "Say something—go on, tell me what you're thinking. I'm loathsome aren't I? Disgusting, say it! Say it!" Then suddenly her grasp loosened. Collapsing, she fell to the floor. "O, God," she whimpered, "please help me, please . . . , please. . . ."

Laura's compulsion was not a steady craving for excessive amounts of food. Rather it was a series of episodic and unpredictable frenzies during which she had a compelling need to fill up a hole or emptiness she felt to be inside her. She would then literally eat herself into a state of unconsciousness and subsequently sleep off the effect for as long as two days.

Bizarre behavior indeed, perhaps beyond the experience of most of us. Yet, it occurs in human beings and has an explanation. We will not indicate what this might be in Laura's case. At so early a point in our discussion, this would be premature. We only ask the reader to return to the case of Laura after he has mastered the content of this section.

Most people, of course, do not show such deviant forms of behavior. Most of us have our quirks and problems but still manage to get along fairly well in society. Furthermore, a few of us may be blessed in being unusually stable and happy. The study of personality is as much concerned with these normal people as with the Lauras and the Baniszewskis. In fact one prominent psychologist, Abraham Maslow, has argued that we can learn a great deal more from looking at the very healthy than we can from looking at the very ill. Perhaps the major difficulty lies in locating such persons. Unhappiness and deviancy are much more visible than happiness and normalcy. In addition, these latter qualities are easily confused with success, achievement, or prosperity, but it should be obvious that they are not the same thing. The saying that money cannot buy happiness is trite but nonetheless true; as a TV personality once remarked, "Money only allows us to live miserably in comfort."

In any case though much of personality study has grown out of a psychiatric tradition with its medical orientation toward sickness, a good deal has had rather different origins and has been concerned with normal or unusually healthy subjects.

CHAPTER 3
BASIC NOTIONS AND METHOD OF PSYCHOANALYTIC THEORY

THE BACKGROUND

Whether Pascal's view about the madness of mankind is true or not, there is no question that the more startling forms of deviant behavior attract our concern and attention and perhaps for this reason offer to us a method of uncovering the secrets of human personality. It is historically true that much of the study of so-called normal personality grew out of psychiatry and psychoanalysis, whose main preoccupation was with the mentally sick. Let us examine in broad perspective some of this history.

Eighteenth- and nineteenth-century France was a place of turbulence and unrest. The "old regime" paved the way to the revolution of 1789, not so much by its tyranny, which was evident enough, as by the inefficiency of its tyranny and the debauchery and confusion in the court of Louis XVI. This careless permissiveness allowed new ideas to grow. One of the major ones espoused by the philosopher Jean Jacques Rousseau was this: "Man is born free and everywhere he is in irons." This idea, good in itself, was, in a sense, qualified not only by the sentimentality of the man generating it but also by the savagery and political opportunism of the man chiefly responsible for translating it into a framework of action: Robespierre. The rallying call of the revolution, "Liberty, equality, fraternity," came to be a cry of vengeance and destruction, a preface and epilogue to the guillotine, rather than an appeal to reason, justice, and love.

Nevertheless, there were some to whom these words signified not a political revolution but a revolution of the mind and heart of man, a new humanism whose major thrust would be the giving of comfort and understanding to one's fellow man. Philippe Pinel was a man of such persuasions, and it was mainly due to his selfless efforts that modern psychiatry emerged. It is a profound commentary on the period that this man was born only five years after another famous figure—the Marquis de Sade. If Pinel reflected all that was good in contemporary French outlook, it might well be said that de Sade, in his writings, reflected all that was corrupt. Each in their own way, however, was concerned with the well-being of man.

As well as being a medical writer of great influence, Pinel was an activist. He was appointed in 1793 by the Commune to the Bicêtre, a notorious Paris mental hospital, where his first official act was to have the chains and fetters removed from the inmates, many of whom had worn them for as long as forty years. The ameliorative effect was usually instantaneous. A simply remedy, but one which many persons do not accept wholeheartedly even today. To them, mental illness is a moral inadequacy; punishment, not kindness, should be its due.

Pinel's humanism was coupled with a typically Gallic disposition to bring to the phenomenon of mental illness the illumination of reason and understanding. How many distinct syndromes could be recognized? How did each originate? What therapeutic measures could be used? These were the kinds of basic questions to whose solution Pinel dedicated his life. All European psychiatry followed his lead.

Into this tradition of rationalism a somewhat mystical note was injected during the 1770s by the hypnotist Franz Anton Mesmer. Though the formal schools that grew out of his influence—Nancy and Salpêtrière—were conventional enough, his volatile and quixotic personality did much to lend a little magic to this notion of healing. Hypnotism is still a mysterious phenomenon. In the eighteenth and nineteenth centuries, presented by Mesmer in the framework of a cabalistic and hocus-pocus theory, it was much more so. But it did sometimes produce therapeutic results.

Supporting Mesmer's general orientation were the naturalistic and romantic literary figures Zola, de Maupassant, and Marcel Proust, the symbolists, plus the quasi-scientific literature on sexuality of Krafft-Ebing, Forel, and Havelock Ellis. All these combined to create a focus on the hidden side of civilized man—his sexual and destructive impulses, his secret loves and hates, which until that time had figured little in any serious attempts to understand the human personality and its workings.

The intellectual stage was thus set for one of the greatest minds of our century, Sigmund Freud. Born in Freiberg, Moravia, on May 6, 1856, he gave his life wholly and passionately to the problem of comprehending man. Gregory Zilboorg in his beautifully incisive history of medical psychology (Zilboorg & Henry, 1941) writes of him as follows:

> Freud would appear almost strikingly a kindly shadow of the past, the last representative of the Renaissance and the humanism which wanted man free, which studied man and his humanisms, which wished him well in his frailty and admired him in his greatness.

Not all students of psychology would agree with such a view. Nonetheless, for better or for worse, Freud's impact was enormous. Out of his thinking have emerged many psychological theories of personality. The validity of these theories and those of Freud himself must be judged in terms of empirical evidence. This we will try to present fairly. We wish only to emphasize, in concluding this historical excursion, that, in our opinion, mankind would have been poorer without Freud. His death in 1939 coincided with the outbreak of World War II—a year that began a period when mankind was to give up its humanity.

BASIC NOTIONS

Perhaps the most basic idea underlying all psychoanalytic theories is that a major part of human mental process is unconscious, and this part plays a crucial role in determining behavior. True, we can usually give conscious reasons for most of our actions, and these appear to be sensibly related to our behavior in a one-to-one way: one action, one reason. Freud's great insight, based on his observations of normal and abnormal people, was to recognize that the situation is never this simple. Behind any human action lie many motives or determinations. These vary in importance and in the degree to which they enter our awareness. Further, they may be opposed by negative determinations that impel us in other directions. Many of these motives, both positive and negative, are performed literally for childish reasons.

Thus mind has at least three important characteristics: First, it is *structured* in various ways; for example, some of it is conscious, but much of it is unconscious. Second, it is *dynamic,* in the sense that what is going on in one part may interact or even conflict with what is going on in another. Third, it has a *developmental history* and stores through memory processes the residuals of its early experience with the world. Most psychoanalytic models and personality theories have been primarily concerned with the explication of these three fundamental notions. We will use them here to form the organization of this section.

Freud himself arrived at these ideas not only from his studies of mentally ill patients in his clinic but also from a careful analysis of such normal everyday occurrences as dreams, slips of the tongue, acts of forgetfulness, social customs, and even literature. In all these, he found strong evidence of unconscious determination. Not only were there often very important unconscious reasons for acts which also had obvious conscious causes, but there were usually unconscious determinants lying behind behavior which, to all appearances, had no reason at all. A deliberate action like smoking a cigarette may be motivated not only by a conscious desire to relax or relieve tension or be part of the gang, as most of us, in fact, view it, but also by unconscious desires, for example, to put objects into our mouths—a remnant of an infantile need for sucking pleasure. Similarly, an "accidental" action, like knocking over a glass of water, may result not simply from clumsiness but, on the contrary, from a well-coordinated attempt to satisfy an unconscious need for attention.

The possibility of unconscious motives for all actions, even the most trivial ones, was explicated at length by Freud and his followers. The conception of an unconscious is the cornerstone of all psychoanalytic thinking. Actually, the general idea was not new with Freud. Such philosophers as Aristotle, Nietzsche, and Hartmann had used or implied such a notion before, and, in the nineteenth century, many writers such as Blake, Coleridge, Proust, and particularly the French symbolists, had begun to turn more and more to man's unconscious (cf. Whyte, 1960).

It is a special tribute to the genius of Freud, however, that he was able to take the concept, hold it up to the light of rational inquiry, and develop it as a valuable explanatory construct in concrete cases. By reference to an unconscious, psychology became able to make sense out of a whole range of human behavioral phenomena that before had escaped rational interpretation. As we shall see shortly, Freud's investigations of the unconscious in man led him into strange and bizarre intellectual worlds. His formulations were in many ways offensive both to the common sense of contemporary laymen and to the ideas of nineteenth-century psychology, whose primary subject of study was consciousness. To state that man's consciousness was relatively unimportant was certainly a radical step. In this respect, Freud was not overestimating his discoveries when he wrote:

> Humanity has in the course of time had to endure from the hands of science two great outrages upon its naïve self-love. The first was when it realized that our earth was not the centre of the universe, but only a tiny speck in a world-system of a magnitude hardly conceivable; this is associated in our minds with the name of Copernicus, although Alexandrian doctrines taught something very similar. The second was when biological research robbed man of his peculiar privilege of having been specially created, and relegated him to a descent from the animal world, implying an ineradicable animal nature in him: this transvaluation has been accomplished in our own time upon the instigation of Charles Darwin and Wallace and their predecessors, and not without the most opposition from their contemporaries. But man's craving for grandiosity is now suffering the third and most bitter blow from present day psychological research which is endeavouring to prove to the "ego" of each one of us that he is not even master in his own house, but that he must remain content with the merest scrap of information about what is going on unconsciously in his own mind [Freud, 1935, p. 252].

As the founder of psychoanalysis, Freud was also undoubtedly the father of many theories of personality of academic psychology. In fact, most workers in this field have focused in one way or another on the three broad dimensions of mind to which we referred above, though they have not always agreed with Freud's particular formulations. In addition, most of them have tended to share his orientation toward the methodological assumptions which we must make when we attempt to dissect man's personality. Before attempting to explain the Freudian position and its offshoots, it is necessary to discuss this problem of method.

THREE METHODOLOGICAL POSTULATES

Order in Man

This postulate states that man's behavior is essentially orderly and that this order can be discovered by means of scientific investigation. The notion is basic to all scientific psychology and is by no means unique to psychoanalytic psychology. However, Freud was among the first to commit himself to it. Like many of his contemporaries, he felt that the idea of free will was quite incompatible with scientific determinism and that if man really had free will, then he could not possibly be studied scientifically. Actually this was a limited conception of the nature of freedom. Even those actions which we intuitively regard as free have reasons behind them—that is, they are not due to chance. Consequently, they may still be regarded as orderly and therefore amenable to scientific inquiry. "Freedom" lies not in lack of determination but in self-determination. One contemporary psychologist, O. H. Mowrer, perhaps put his finger on the heart of the problem when he stated in reference to "freedom":

> It does not imply caprice or lawlessness. Instead, in its most profound meaning, it implies the *capacity to change*, when circumstances change and old actions need to be replaced by new ones. Inanimate objects, like stones, are the least free, most bound, fixed. If you tap a rock with a hammer, it may "change" in the sense of flaking or cracking but it will not change in the sense of becoming more or less resistant to our blows; much less will it change its "behavior" in the sense of "going away" or "fighting back" as opposed to "staying put" and thus subject continually to our assault [Mowrer, 1953, pp. 67–68].

This is the broader meaning of free will as it has been traditionally defined, though it is a view that many nineteenth-century scientists failed to see. As a matter of fact, Freud himself did allow for some indetermination in man. This is reflected in his belief that although *postdictions* could often be made about an individual, *predictions* usually could not be. That is to say, he felt it was easier to make sense out of what a patient had already done than to say how he would behave some time in the future.

The Validity of the Clinical Method

It is true to say that the psychoanalytic model is based almost entirely on observations of patients in the clinic, rather than on carefully controlled experiments in the laboratory. This fact has led many psychologists to question the general validity of the theory. However, as we have indicated in Section I, the differences between the clinic and the laboratory are largely a matter of degree. Both are committed to empiricism; that is to say, both involve experience, and both involve a certain amount of planning and control. The clinician does not record all of his patients' behavior but only those salient features which he has already planned to study. The more advanced his theory is, the more planned will his observations be. As Freud developed his ideas about personality, for example, he became more and more interested in trying to find out about the patient's early experiences rather than his contemporary behavior. In addition, he became more aware of the importance of sexuality, of the person's relations with his parents and with the analyst. This restriction of experience to certain chosen dimensions is what is meant by planning, and it is analogous to the kind of planning that goes into an elaborate laboratory experiment.

Also, there is at least an implicit mode of control involved in the clinical situation. The inference, for example, of a link between a particular type of early parent-child relationship and homosexuality is made not only on the basis of regular occurrence of the two together but also on the basis of their being absent together. In the clinic, the data that allow such a conclusion are not gathered neatly at one time but are accumulated gradually as different kinds of patients come for treatment. In a way, the clinician carries around his control group in his head or on some kind of written cumulative record.

This does not mean that the clinical method can arrive at conclusions with the same certainty as does science. There is little question that the amount of control we can impose on an observation in the laboratory is much greater. Nevertheless, it is unrealistic to suppose that the clinical enterprise is therefore useless. What usually emerges from clinical experience is a set of *heuristics or general rules* for dealing with or helping other people. Because these rules are seldom based on established scientific conclusions, they must always be regarded as provisional and not as absolute. They are much like those we would use in playing a chess game. Here, we make moves largely on the basis of general principles that have been found by chess players to be useful; for example, "gain control of the center of the board"; "move the queen frequently"; "guard the king."

The problem of understanding people in a clinical setting is very much the same. From the standpoint of science, it is an unsatisfactory means of reaching firm conclusions, but it is a way of generating hunches which can then be tested in the laboratory in a controlled manner. As it turns out, the concepts emerging from psychoanalytic practice have been very productive of research in personality. This does not mean, however, that psychoanalysis itself is a scientific system. It is not and should not be judged on this basis alone.

The Continuity of Normal and Abnormal

One of Freud's basic hypotheses was that there is only a difference of degree between normal people and neurotics and psychotics. He saw for example, distinct similarities between the dream processes of normal people and the language and thought of the severely mentally ill, between the little ritualistic acts of normal people and the exaggerated obsessional behavior of neurotics. In Freudian thinking, normal persons were at one end of a continuum, psychotics at the other end, and neurotics in the middle. Normality was a rare blessing realized by only very few people indeed. The average person, or most people, would probably fall somewhere between normal and neurotic—neither completely sick nor completely healthy. This fairly represents Freud's view, which, it must be admitted, was a rather pessimistic one. However, it did allow him and his followers to use observations obtained in the clinic with abnormal people as support for a general theory of personality which would cover normal behavior as well.

The psychoanalytic model has often been criticized for doing this. Some writers have maintained that the personality of a sick person is radically different from that of a healthy one, so that very few generalizations from one to the other are possible. Certainly, much of psychoanalytic theory sounds old enough so that the layman feels it cannot possibly apply to him. There is something to be said for this popular point of view. It is likely that many purely somatic diseases, for example, leukemia, encephalitis, and cancer, are either present or not. By definition, they are simply not found in normal people. It would be very risky to develop a theory or description of normal lung function on the basis of study only of cancerous lungs. Similarly, it may also be risky to draw inferences about the normal personality from what we know about the abnormal personality.

We thus have two theories about the relation between the normal and abnormal, one stating that the two are categorically different, the other stating that they are different only in degree. Both of them rest, of course, on the premise that there are in fact normal as well as abnormal people in the world. Although this seems self-evident, a few psychoanalytically oriented writers, including Freud himself, especially toward the end of his career, have actually thought that perhaps no one at all is really normal and that civilization itself is sick. Such a view is perhaps extreme, but it does point up a second problem that exists for both theories: the distribution of normal and abnormal people in any population. A number of possibilities are open. Some of these are illustrated in Figure 3–1.

Consideration of these points of view may appear to be of academic interest only. Actually, each has outcomes or explications of considerable importance. For example, if we maintain that abnormal and normal are categorically distinct, then obviously we should be very careful not to generalize from what we find out about one class to the other class. Conversely, if we believe in the essential continuity between them, we may legitimately generalize from one class to the other. In fact, we may find it especially profitable to work on the abnormal, since the distortion and exaggerations of personality that exist there may better reveal what the normal is like. This is often true in the other sciences, in astronomy, for example, where a relatively rare event like the passage of a certain celestial body or a solar eclipse may furnish a large amount of information of basic and general value.

Evidently, then, these problems are real ones. It is of value to know whether there is continuity between the normal and abnormal personality and what the incidence of each is in any given population. Unfortunately, it is not possible to provide any definite answers, mainly because of the difficulty of deciding on diagnostic dimensions. Usually, reliance must be placed on fairly loose criteria, for example, whether a person goes to a psychiatrist for help or is able to function adequately in society.

It should be recognized also that the application of these criteria is not an easy matter. How well a person can function in a society depends not only on his own status but also on the status of the society itself. In other words mental health is at

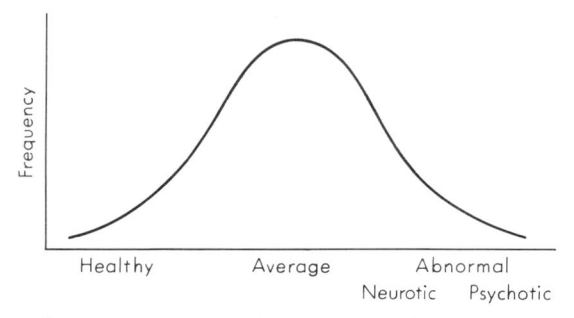

(a) Most people are fairly normal, a few are very abnormal, and a few very normal. Normality here means healthy, not average.

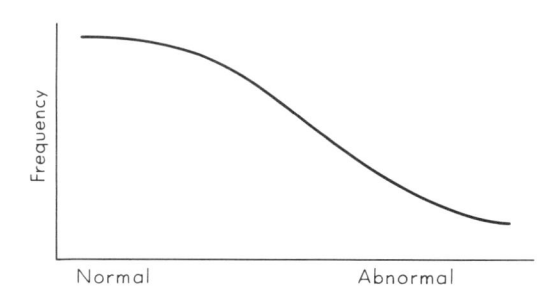

(b) Continuity between normal and abnormal. Most people are normal, fewer are abnormal. Normal here can mean what most people are like, or, if one is an optimist, healthy also.

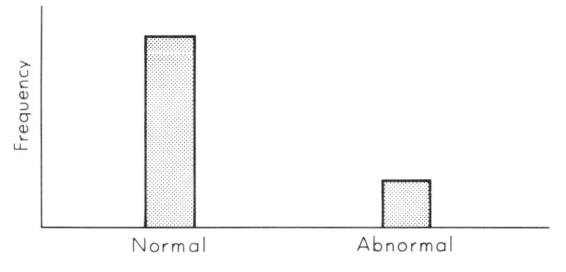

(c) No continuity between normal and abnormal. People are either sick or well. Most of them are well.

FIG. 3–1 a,b,c Hypothetical distributions of normal and abnormal individuals in the population.

least to some extent relative to the society or culture in which it is being assessed. One influential writer—Thomas Szasz (1961)—has in fact suggested that the idea of mental illness is a myth and represents simply a judgment made about certain individuals whose beliefs, values, and behavior do not happen to fit with those of most individuals in the culture. This is an extreme point of view. Nonetheless, it is certainly true that society distrusts and fears people who are different; those who are too different it may be ready to categorize as insane.

Whatever the actual truth of the matter, psychoanalytic psychology makes the assumption of a continuity between normal and abnormal. Hence it generalizes from findings obtained with patients in a clinic to the average person in everyday life. In point of fact, psychoanalytic treatment, from the patient's standpoint, is a highly rigorous intellectual exercise and cannot be applied readily to the severely ill. The theoretical inferences drawn by Freud about human personality were based on the study of individuals who could at least get by reasonably well in society. Consequently, no great strain is placed on the rules of generalization.

Armed with the above methodological principles, Freud and his followers attempted to draw up the rules governing the behavior of man. We will consider his work under the three broad headings to which we have referred above: (1) the structure and topography of personality, (2) the dynamics of personality, (3) the development of personality. Within each of these chapters, we will show the ways in which original Freudian doctrine has been modified and its ideas countered by different ones and the culmination of this dialectic in contemporary approaches to the study of personality.

CHAPTER 4

THE TOPOGRAPHY AND STRUCTURE OF PERSONALITY

We must recognize first that the unconscious is not a thing or a place but a construct, or theoretical conception, postulated to account for certain empirical observations. As we indicated in the first part of this section, Freud was by no means the first person to make such observations or to use the term "unconscious." However, he was the first to explore them empirically and to examine their theoretical and practical implications. The results of his work in these directions have been of enormous importance both to the discipline of psychology and to the treatment of many forms of mental illness. We will first look at the evidence that led Freud to his notion of an unconscious, then follow the historical development of his thinking about the structure of personality.

THE TOPOGRAPHY OF PERSONALITY

Like a country, personality can be charted along certain dimensions, and just as geographers may use longitude, latitude, and elevation, so many psychoanalytic thinkers use consciousness. In the Freudian scheme, the topography of personality is divided into three parts, the conscious, the preconscious, and the unconscious. Their relationships are shown in Figure 4–1.

In the first place, the drawing indicates that personality has three parts; it is not homogeneous. A better way of stating this is to say that three separate constructs are necessary to explain or account for all aspects of personality. The conscious, it will be noted, grades into the preconscious without any definite boundary between them. This is implicit in the idea that whereas the conscious represents immediate actual awareness, the preconscious is only potential awareness. That is to say, the preconscious refers to ideas, images, or wishes that can be recalled or recollected even though they do not occupy awareness at a particular time. On the other hand, there is a fairly sharp boundary surrounding the unconscious proper. This schematically represents the fact that the contents of the unconscious (i.e., unconscious ideas, images, and wishes) are not normally available to consciousness.

The unconscious does have an indirect relation to conscious behaviors, however, in this sense: according to Freud and others, the unconscious has a greater importance in determining behavior than either the preconscious or conscious. For this rea-

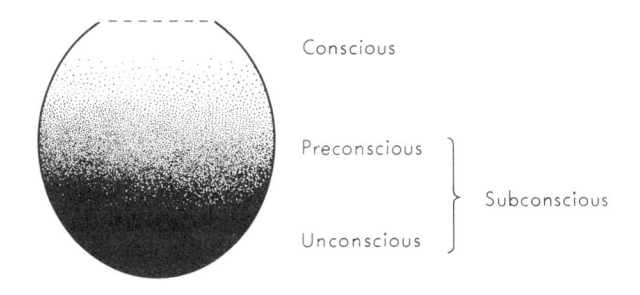

FIG. 4–1 Schematic drawing of the structure of personality according to Freud.

son, he compared personality to an iceberg, four-fifths of which lies below the surface. Such determination, of course, varies with the behavior and with the person. Some acts will be fully conscious; others, less so. Similarly, a person after analysis, we hope, will be more aware of himself and his motives than before analysis.

A final aspect of the schema is locus. Although in the diagram the preconscious is placed between the conscious and unconscious, according to the notion that there is a gradation between the three, the preconscious does not actually separate the other two in any dynamic sense. That is to say, events that occur in consciousness can directly affect the unconscious without having first to pass through the preconscious. For example, the sight of a teacher who resembles a parent may evoke in a child immediate unconscious feelings of hostility. But these same feelings may act directly on consciousness to produce antagonistic behavior.

Such is the basic topography of personality. Much has yet to be added to give even a little of its full richness and complexity, but at least these few basic premises give us a starting point.

It should be noted that not all psychologists would agree that these kinds of constructions are necessary or desirable. It is a fact, certainly, that all we can actually have direct contact with in other persons is their overt behavior, and it can be cogently argued that to go very far beyond this is to enter a realm that is so speculative as to be beyond the scope of experimental science. A number of psychologists, particularly Hans Eysenck (1952b; Eysenck & Rachman 1965) and Joseph Wolpe (1964) have argued strongly for this position, not only in respect to the analysis of normal and abnormal personality, but also in respect to any therapeutic measures that may be undertaken with patients. Thus their *behavior therapy* entails practical techniques for controlling or changing behavior of any sort that is considered by society or by its possessor to be undesirable. This is attempted without recourse to the kinds of concepts that Freud and others have considered necessary. The reader must in the end decide for himself how valuable they are. To aid in such a decision we turn now to some of the kinds of evidence from which Freud derived his notions about the topography and structure of personality.

Freud drew mainly on three sources of information in his study of personality and the unconscious. These were (1) dreams, (2) psychopathology of everyday life, (3) wit and humor. Most of the data he collected was clinical, but to some of his clinical findings we can add some experimental evidence obtained by others. Let us now look at each of these three areas of study in turn, presenting Freud's evidence followed by empirical data relating to these aspects of the basic topography of personality.

Dreams

It is astonishing that although many of us (perhaps all of us) spend a large part of our lives engaged in dreaming, very little systematic effort was devoted to the study of dreams before Freud. It is one of his major contributions to have recognized their importance for the study of man. In therapy, Freud made extensive use of dream analysis, and from his case studies he was able to describe a basic property of dreams that pointed to the existence of unconscious processes in man. This basic property is simply that *a dream has a hidden coherence and meaning underlying its apparent absurdity*. Such a statement implies that dreams have two levels, or types of "content," a *manifest content*, which we can often recall, and a *latent content*, of which we are usually unaware. Most of us can remember at least parts of our dreams, and these parts at least are conscious. Many of the remembered elements can be referred to happenings of the previous day, to external stimuli such as a twisted blanket or a cold room, or to internal stimuli such as a stomach ache or a headache. A good many studies have been done on the relation between dreams and these kinds of stimuli (Ramsey, 1953), and some of the relevant findings are summarized in Table 4–1.

These data show something of the range of events that can affect dreaming and its content. Psychoanalysts are aware of these facts but accord them little importance in understanding the deeper aspects of personality.

As already stated, behind the manifest content which the dreamer recalls in all its confusion and disconnectedness lies the latent content—a direct representation of the unconscious. As Freud put it:

> The dream as remembered is not the real thing at all, but a distorted substitute which, by calling up other substitute ideas, provides us with a means of approaching the thought proper, of bringing into consciousness the unconscious thoughts underlying the dream. [Freud, 1935, p. 103].

Two important characteristics of the latent content can be noted: (1) *The latent content itself as well as its relation to the manifest content is usually unconscious.* (2) *The latent content is difficult to uncover and, in fact, can usually be uncovered only by means of special techniques, such as free association or psychoanalysis.* Even with these, the patient often actively *resists* recalling significant associations with manifest dream elements. This is another way of saying that the boundary between the unconscious and conscious is rather impermeable. Dreams also have many other properties arising from the latent content and its relationship with the manifest content.

According to analytic theory, a second basic property of dreams is that they have a *purpose*. They are not static or accidental flights of ideas but serve definite goals. The two main goals they serve are, first, *to guard sleep* and, second, *to express or fulfill as far as possible repressed or unconscious wishes.* These together constitute the basic dynamic of dreams. What evidence suggests the validity of such a hypothesis? In the simplest case, we find that physical needs like thirst and hunger if acute enough are often fulfilled in a dream. Thus we may dream of eating or drinking to repletion, thereby allowing sleep to continue undisturbed even in the face of physiological tensions that would otherwise wake us up. The same applies in the case of psychological tension or anxiety.

Table 4-1 Properties of manifest content of dreams (Ramsey, 1953)

Variable	Summary findings
Type of imagery	Visual, auditory, dermal, gustatory, olfactory.
Speed of dreams	About the same as in waking life.
Incidence and frequency of dreams	No period during night when dreams do not occur, though some subjects report dreaming more frequently at some time of night rather than others.
Personality of dreamer	Slight evidence that young adults recall more dreams than children or the aged. More intelligent persons appear to dream more. No consistent sex differences. Slight evidence that anxious subjects dream more frequently.
Content of dreams	Similar to elements in previous day's experiences.
External stimulation of dreams	Stimuli such as odors, music, etc., occurring during sleep often tend to be incorporated into the dream. Hormones and drugs also appear to affect dream content.

Example 4–1 *A child's dream (Freud, 1935, p. 114)*

A little girl three and a quarter years old went for her first trip on the lake. When they came to land, she did not wish to leave the boat and cried bitterly, the time on the water had evidently gone too quickly for her. Next morning she said: "Last night I was sailing on the lake."

In this dream the wish fulfillment is transparently clear. The little girl, upset at not being allowed to stay on the lake, fulfilled her wish during sleep. We might also infer that, by so doing, she slept more readily than she would have otherwise, since it is fair to suppose that the tension occasioned by the wish might have kept her awake.

Here is a more complex adult dream:

Example 4–2 *An adult's dream (Freud, 1935, p. 114)*

An adult male patient of Freud's dreamed the following dream:

I am walking in front of my house with a lady on my arm. Here a closed carriage is waiting; a man steps up to me, shows me his authorization as a police officer, and requests me to follow him. I ask only for time in which to arrange my affairs.

At first sight, the dream appears to represent anything but a wish fulfillment. It is most unlikely that the patient really wished to be arrested. However, closer analysis yielded the following: the patient was having an affair with a married woman and had spent the previous night with her. His main fear was that she might become pregnant and thus reveal their illicit relationship. To avoid this he had been practicing a form of birth control—coitus interruptus. Questioning indicated that his arrest in the dream was on the charge of *infanticide*, an act associated in the patient's mind not only with the killing of an infant but with the prevention of insemination by some method of birth control, such as coitus interruptus. Consequently, by his dream the young man fulfilled his wish to avoid having his mistress bear a child by him and at the same time symbolically punished himself for his immorality by having himself arrested.

Again the dynamics of this second dream fit well with the Freudian hypothesis. We can assume that the gnawing fear on the part of the patient that his mistress might conceive would certainly tend to keep him from sleeping. This fear, or wish that this event would not occur, was assuaged by a dream of infanticide. This, in turn, might itself have disturbed him enough to wake him up but for the fact that he allowed payment for the crime to be made by his arrest, thus satisfying his conscience. In this highly complex manner, sleep was preserved and a wish satisfied. It may be added that further analysis also revealed a further fulfillment of a repressed infantile wish concerning infanticide and coitus interruptus. Many dreams do, like this one, involve wish fulfillment at several topographic levels.

A third basic property of dreams, evident in the second case given above and in most adult dreams, is the operation of what Freud called at first the *dream censor*. This is a construct hypothesized to explain the fact that the wish fulfillments in dreams are seldom represented directly and openly but only indirectly and symbolically. We have seen that there is rarely any obvious relation between the manifest and latent content and their connection can be made explicit only by close analysis. Why should this be? Why should the wishes of the patient be disguised by some obscure symbolism that can be interpreted only with great difficulty?

The answer Freud gives to these questions is that part of our personality actively resists the expression of unconscious infantile wishes because of their completely antisocial quality. Direct representation of them in a dream would occasion unpleasant feelings of guilt, horror, and anxiety. Consequently, if such wishes are to have any fulfillment, they must be so disguised as to escape notice by the censor and slide by it undetected. They are disguised by means of symbols according to fairly definite rules, some of which are described below. The dream is thus like a novel, a play, or a movie which is allowed public release by a censoring organization provided it guards its language and action rather carefully. Terms which merely suggest, hint at, or symbolize immorality can be accepted. Those which are too blatant have to be altered.

The two purposes of the dream, to guard sleep and fulfill hidden wishes, can thus be accomplished only in a manner that is acceptable to the censor. In this formulation is contained the basic theory of personality structure formulated by Freud. It should be noted that the theory is a *dynamic* one in the sense that the dream is the resultant of a number of active counterforces. As we shall see shortly, the consequences of such a theory are many and important.

Freud's basic analysis of dreams has not been accepted by everyone. One important critic, Calvin Hall (1953), has argued against the notion of a censor on the ground that only in some dreams does the wish appear in disguised form. In others, it appears quite openly. For example, the same person may on one occasion dream of flying or climbing, commonly regarded as symbolizing sexual intercourse, and on another occasion dream directly of intercourse in a quite undisguised manner. If this is true, how can we support the notion of a censor that demands translation of an immoral wish into some symbolic disguise?

At least two answers to this question are possible: In the first place, we can modify the notion of censor. For example, we might suppose that the strength, or power, of counterforces originating from the censor varies according to certain conditions. It is possible that deeper sleep may so reduce their strength that the wish is allowed more direct expression. There is no direct evidence supporting this, but it is entirely possible and could be examined experimentally. Likewise, the components of the dream to which the censor objects may also vary. Freud described a case of one patient who dreamed he was sleeping with an unknown girl. This girl turned out to represent the wife of his best friend. Here, there was no masking of the act of intercourse but only of the partner. Such a case somewhat undercuts Hall's argument.

The second answer, proposed by Hall, is to underplay the notion of a censor in dream formation and to stress instead the idea or *representability*. According to this theory, dreams have mainly a *cognitive* function; that is to say, they are simply pictorialized thinking—mental dramas in which all feelings, thoughts, and attitudes, no matter how abstract, are portrayed in terms of images.

Thus the value of studying dreams, according to Hall, is not so much in demonstrating the importance of sexual and aggressive impulses and their control by a censor; rather it lies in the fact that they can tell us how a person views himself and his environment. For example, one individual may conceive of sexuality in terms of symbols of energy and power; another, in terms of symbols of gentleness, warmth, and peace. Obviously, the two personalities are very different.

The final set of characteristics of dreams relates to the rules governing the translation of latent wishes into manifest content. These rules make up the *dreamwork*. The major ones are as follows:

CONDENSATION Usually, the manifest content is a précis, or brief summary, of the latent content by which a great many ideas are condensed into a few. For example, a dream of a thirty-seven-year-old patient involved a dark, swarthy assailant named Charles who attacked him with a number of sharp weapons. As it turned out, Charles in the dream was a combination of two dentists named Charles Stuart, the other Stuart Rankings. Both these figures were associated by the patient with pain and unpleasantness and were condensed into a single symbol of evil. It is interesting also that, in this dream, the patient succeeded in overcoming Charles in a most violent manner, thus clearly satisfying an aggressive wish. It is also of importance that his painful experience with one of the dentists had occurred twenty-eight years prior to the dream and had been completely forgotten by him (cf. Dalbiez, 1941).

DISPLACEMENT This mechanism involves the transfer of a feeling or attitude from its proper object to another that is associated with the first in some way. For example, a female patient dreamed that she was strangling a little white dog. By means of free association, it turned out that the little white dog was associated in her mind with her sister-in-law, whom she disliked intensely and whom she described as very short and of remarkably pale complexion. As we shall see later, displacement is a mechanism that occurs not only in dreams but also in waking life.

DRAMATIZATION AND SYMBOLIZATION As stressed by Hall, the dream is a kind of pictorial thinking. By dramatization, abstractions are translated into concrete, plastic forms. For example, happiness may be represented by a sunny flower garden, full of birds and humming insects; sadness, by a cold, winter landscape. Many of the arts are, of course, replete with examples of how the abstract is translated into the concrete. According to Freud, this involves a regressive element. Symbolization is very similar to dramatization. Perhaps the main difference lies in the universality of the symbols used. Dramatization tends to be more individual; symbolization, more universal. It is not possible, of course, to give a complete list of symbols that always have unequivocal meaning. A great deal depends on the culture and on the particular individual. However, a partial list taken from Freud is shown in Table 4–2. It will be noted that most of them are frankly sexual. This does not mean, as Freud himself pointed out many times, that all dreams are sexual in character. It does indicate, however, that sexual wishes are usually very important, not only in dreams but in the whole makeup of man.

SECONDARY ELABORATION A final mechanism in the dreamwork involves the imposition of some superficial logic and order on the dream, so that it more closely accords to conscious waking thought. Interestingly enough, this may make the dream harder rather than easier for the analyst to interpret, since he may be drawn away from its real or unconscious meaning.

Freud's analysis of dreams was based on clinical case studies. However, some attempts have been made to validate his ideas in more controlled situations. Example 4–3 is an illustration of these.

Example 4–3 *Experimental analysis of dreams (Farber & Fisher, 1943)*

The purpose of the study was to supply experimental confirmation of Freudian dream theory by objective methods. The subjects were college students, male and female, between eighteen and twenty-one years of age. They were of average ability, had no special talents, and had no knowledge of the psychoanalytic theory of dreams. Two approaches to the problem were used, one being concerned with translation of dreams and the other with production of dreams.

DREAM TRANSLATION The subjects were hypnotized and, while under hypnosis, were presented with dreams which they were asked to translate. Results showed that in spite of their naïveté regarding Freudian psychology the subjects could readily translate dreams into psychoanalytic terminology. Two examples are as follows:

An eighteen-year-old girl was told under hypnosis: "Dreams have meaning. Now that you are asleep you will be better able to understand them. A girl dreamed that she was packing her trunk when a big snake crawled into it. She was terrified and ran out of the room. What do you think the dream means?"

Almost before the question was finished, the subject blushed, hesitated a second, then said, "Well, I guess she was afraid of being seduced. The snake would be the man's sex organ and the trunk hers." As a control method, she was questioned later in a waking state about the dream. No comparable statement could be obtained from her.

Several female subjects were told this dream: "A boy was sitting at his desk studying when the waste basket caught on fire. He ran and got a pitcher of water and put the fire out." Their immediate response was: "Oh, he wet his bed" or "He should have gone to the bathroom."

EXPERIMENTAL PRODUCTION OF DREAMS The subjects were told under deep hypnosis, "I am going to recall an experience that happened to you some time ago. You have probably forgotten it, but as I describe it, you will remember it in all its details." The experience was then described, after which the subject was told: "A dream will come to you. Raise your right hand when the dream begins, and lower it when the dream is finished." After one or two minutes of dreaming, the subject was asked to relate his dream.

The dreams produced in this way appeared to show many of the relationships between latent and manifest content as described by psychoanalytic theory. The protocols were as follows:

1. A young woman was told, "When you were a little girl, you wet your bed, and when you awoke in the morning your mother scolded you." The subject then dreamed that she told a lie, which made her parents so angry that they spanked her. In her first account she omitted to say what the substance of the lie was. Only after considerable questioning by the experimenters and evasion on her part did she state that she had lied about risking being "*run over* in order to go to the *A & P.*" (Note the amusing instance of unconscious punning here.)

Table 4–2 Some common dream symbols and their meaning

Symbol	Meaning
King, queen, or royal persons	Parents
Elongated objects, sticks, umbrellas, sharp weapons, neckties, etc.	Male sexual organ
Small boxes, cavities, cupboards, ovens, blossoms, flowers, jewelry	Female sexual organ
Mounting steep inclines, ladders	Sexual act
Falling	Anxiety feelings
Swimming	Bed wetting (urethral eroticism)
Sliding, gliding	Masturbation, or autoeroticism

NOTE: For a good account of some of the rules involved in symbolization and dramatization, see Hall (1953). Notice how many of the symbols listed are also used in slang expressions.

2. To investigate the symbolization of the female breast, a male subject was given the following dream stimulus: "One day you were walking down the street in one of the poorer sections of town, and you happened to see a young woman sitting on the steps nursing an infant. Her breast was exposed, and you could see the baby take the nipple in its mouth and suck at it." His dream was: "I came to the corner where there was an old rundown store.... I went in to look for a magazine called *Famous Fantastic Mysteries.* I saw fruit—apples and oranges—and tobacco and candy. They did not have the magazines, so I bought some pipe tobacco and went out. I took the Mount Pleasant streetcar and rode to the top of a tall hill; it was flat on top; the other side was steep. It was the end of the car line. I got off and stood on the edge and looked down."

Under hypnosis, the dream picture of the hill was as follows:

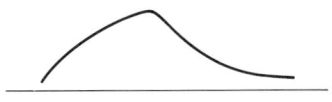

It should be emphasized, of course, that observations such as these were made on a rather few subjects only and may hence show results that are atypical for the whole population. Furthermore, it is not impossible for them to have picked up some Freudian psychology informally, simply by exposure to the culture, even though they never actually studied it. Consequently we should be cautious about accepting them completely. As far as they go, however, they do seem to bear out the Freudian theory of dreams. Not only do they demonstrate the division between manifest and latent content, but also they show that the latter is largely inaccessible except under special conditions. They further shed a good deal of light on some of the dream mechanisms, particularly dramatization and symbolization.

A more exacting series of studies initiated by Kleitman and his associates at the University of Chicago on the general nature of sleep and wakefulness has recently yielded some interesting data. Kleitman was certainly not operating within the theoretical framework of Freud, but nonetheless some of the findings from his laboratory bear indirectly on the ideas of psychoanalytic psychology. A few highlights are given in Example 4–4.

Example 4–4 *The relation of dreams to sleep (cf. Dement, 1965)*

The series of studies done by Kleitman, Dement, and their colleagues concerned the association between sleep characteristics and dreaming. Using many adult subjects, these investigators established, first of all, that dreams were always accompanied by rapid eye movements (REMs). This was done by recording the electric impulses which arise from the muscles that control movement of the eyeball. Such movements produce bursts of electric discharges of muscle potentials. If the subject is awakened while these are occurring, he usually reports that he has just been dreaming. If he is awakened at times when REMs are not occurring, on the other hand, he more commonly reports no dreaming. Why there should be such an association is not clear. Presumably, the dream produces the REMs rather than vice versa, or possibly some third factor, for example, a burst of central nervous activity, produces both.

Armed with this technique, Kleitman, Dement, and others have reported a number of interesting findings:

1. We do not dream all night, but periodically, usually about four or five times. The occurrence of dreams coincides with phases of light sleep as opposed to deep sleep. Light sleep is sometimes called *paradoxical sleep,* since it is a condition in which the subject, though behaviorally asleep, still shows many physiological signs of wakefulness, for example, a waking electroencephalogram (EEG) record, REMs, and gross bodily movements. This coincidence is shown in Figure 4–2.

Depth of sleep is indicated by type of brain wave as measured by an EEG—slower, larger waves being associated with deeper sleep. The initial dream starts after about 1½ hours of sleep and averages 9 minutes' duration. It is followed by another period of sleep before the next dream, which is 19 minutes on the average. Then more sleep occurs, punctuated by two more dream periods of 24 and 28 minutes respectively. Thus we spend about 18 to 20 percent of our sleep dreaming and dream more in the second half of the sleep period than in the first.

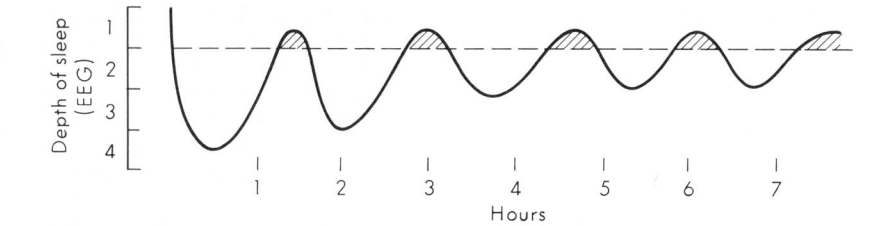

FIG. 4–2 The relation between dreaming and depth of sleep. The shaded portions represent dream periods. (*Dement & Wolpert, 1958*)

These observations appear to fit quite well with some of the speculations of Freud. He did, in fact, state (Freud, 1953, p. 79): "Dreams seem thus to be an intermediate condition between sleeping and waking," and also [1953, p. 82] "Dreams are the reaction to a stimulus disturbing sleep."

It is clear from Dement and Wolpert's (1958) graph that sleep becomes lighter *before* the occurrence of the dream and becomes deeper *following* the dream. This presumably means that *some other factors* must be tending to awaken the sleeper. Perhaps, in some sense, the dream does guard against this contingency.

2. Dream recall seldom occurs unless the subject awakens during or shortly after the dream. The amount of recall is directly related to the time elapsing between the end of the dream and the time of awakening. This would presumably mean that most of the dreams we normally recall are those that occurred just before we wake up in the morning, unless we awoke in the middle of the night. Such a finding has little bearing on the Freudian view of dreams. It might suggest, however, that some of the dream distortion, or dreamwork, may go on during the process of recall of the dream rather than (or as well as) during the actual dreaming. If true, this would not contradict but only refine psychoanalytic theory.

3. Dement found that *depriving* subjects of dreaming had drastic effects on their behavior. This condition was accomplished simply by waking up the volunteer subjects every time REMs commenced. The immediate effect of this was that dreaming started at progressively shorter and shorter intervals as the experiment proceeded. When dream deprivation was carried out over four or five nights and subjects were then allowed five nights of undisturbed sleep, they showed as much as a 50 percent increase in dream time. In addition, subjects showed a number of psychological disturbances. These included anxiety, irritability, difficulty in concentrating, and a heightened tendency to have transient hallucinations in response to a rapidly flickering light. Several subjects showed a marked increase in appetite. Controls who had been awakened an equal number of times but only between dreams showed none of these disturbances nor any changes in dream production.

This finding seems to agree with Freud's emphasis on the dynamic function of dreams—that is to say, their property of fulfilling wishes which, if unfulfilled, would wake up the sleeper. The data described do not directly prove this assertion but do show that if the sleeper is not allowed some expression of whatever mentation is occurring in him, then psychological disturbance ensues. It should be mentioned at this point that some repetitions of the dream-deprivation experiment have not yielded the same results (e.g., Kales et al., 1964). It is not entirely clear what factors were responsible for the disagreement or whether Dement's data are spurious or dependent on rather special conditions. Further work will no doubt give us more answers.

In general, the studies of Kleitman and Dement show some interesting agreements with (though not proof of) the Freudian theory of dreams. They have also opened up an area of experimental investigation that has long been refractory to the efforts of scientists.

Psychopathology of Everyday Life

It may seem strange that the ordinary everyday life of the average person should involve anything pathological, but this was Freud's view. Not only in our dreaming life, but also in many phases of our waking life, we come close to mental illness. This makes some sense when we consider that if a hospitalized schizophrenic may not be able to remember his own name or the name of his doctor, even the nonhospitalized average person often fails to remember the name of a person he knows quite well and, to that extent, is, at the moment, not so very different. The schizophrenic may forget how to dress, but the normal person often forgets to take his umbrella with him when he leaves the house of a friend. The difference is one of degree but not of principle. It was a stroke of genius on the part of Freud to see that these curious little isolated acts might have great importance in understanding personality in general and the unconscious in particular.

The basic mechanism involved in errors, slips of the tongue, and acts of forgetfulness is one at which we have already hinted in our discussion of dreams. We saw that the unconscious contains wishes which demand expression but that this is usually blocked by the censor. This blocking is known as *repression*. It is of great relevance here. For Freud, these acts represented repressed or partially repressed unconscious or preconscious wishes. Let us consider two examples.

Example 4–5 *A symptomatic act (Freud, 1938, pp. 136–137)*

> I happened to be present when an elderly couple related to me partook of their supper. The lady had stomach trouble and was forced to follow a strict diet. A roast was put before the husband, and he requested his wife, who was not allowed to partake of the food, to give him the mustard. The wife opened the closet and took out the small bottle of stomach drops, and placed it on the table before her husband.
>
> Between the band-shaped mustard glass and the small drop bottle, there was naturally no similarity through which the mishandling could be explained; yet the wife only noticed the mistake after her husband laughingly called her attention to it. The sense of the symptomatic action needs no explanation.

Another category includes those actions which should occur but do not. The forgotten name, the lost pair of gloves, the missed appointment are examples. Here is an illustration cited by Dalbiez.

Example 4–6 *A "failed act" (Dalbiez, 1941, Vol. 1, p. 21)*

> Dr. Frink [a contemporary of Freud] was the guest of a family whom he knew intimately. While husband, wife and guest were reading in silence, the mistress of the house suddenly interrupted with the question, "Who wrote *Paradise Lost?* Was it Dante?" Her husband told her that she was mixing up the authors of *Paradise Lost* and of the *Inferno*. All then went on with their reading. Shortly afterwards, the husband went out. The young woman turned to Frink and asked him to explain a very disagreeable feeling from which she had been suffering for some time. She felt an unreasoning hatred for all young men with fair hair and blue eyes. Several of her husband's friends were of this type and their visits always embarrassed her. She was aware of nothing in their behavior that justified this feeling, but she could neither free herself from it nor explain it.
>
> Frink asked her to fix her attention on the type of man in question and to say everything that came to her mind. She spoke first of a fair-haired man whom both she and Frink knew slightly, then of another whom she knew no better. After a moment's silence, she began to laugh, blushed and said with some hesitation, "I just now thought of someone else." Frink, who had certain suspicions, asked her, "And towards this man you felt no aversion?" She admitted that Frink had guessed right and gave him the following information which explained both her aversion for fair-haired men, and her forgetting the name of the author of *Paradise Lost*. The man in question was her first cousin. He was a very handsome young man, with fair hair and blue eyes. When she was sixteen years old, she had been much in love with him, but because of their relationship, and because he was ten years older than she, she had fought against her feelings, and tried to drive them from her mind. The complex, which had become largely unconscious, had not thereby been destroyed. When she married, she had destroyed the photographs of her admirers, but, as if by chance, she had "forgotten" to destroy that of her cousin. The aversion of fair-haired men was a compensatory reaction, a "reinsurance" against the return of the repressed love. Consciously she had wanted to forget the cousin, and thought she had succeeded; unconsciously she loved him still, as was shown by the incident of the photograph. Her forgetting of the name of the author of *Paradise Lost* was due to a perfectly understandable repression, for the cousin's name was Milton.

This theory of active, or dynamic, forgetting does not explain all forgetting, as Freud himself pointed out. In Section V we will cover a number of other theories which deal with similar phenomena. But there is no doubting the legitimacy of the Freudian explanation for at least some of our memory losses.

A final question concerns the possibility of experimentally demonstrating everyday psychopathology. We saw that this could be done with dreams. Can it be done with slips, errors, and lapses of memory? The answer is yes, as shown in the following example:

Example 4–7 *Experimental demonstration of the psychopathology of everyday life (Erikson, 1939)*

The problem was to supply experimental confirmation of the Freudian theories of the psychopathology of everyday life. A single subject, naïve as to the purpose of the experiment, was tested. The experiment consisted of two phases.

UNCONSCIOUS DETERMINANTS OF THE CASUAL CONTENT OF CONVERSATION The subject was instructed under hypnosis that when he awoke (1) he would notice one of the experimenters, Dr. D., searching vainly through his pockets for a pack of cigarettes, (2) he then would proffer his own pack, and (3) Dr. D. absentmindedly would forget to return the cigarettes, whereupon the subject would feel very eager to recover them, because he had no others. He was further told that (4) he would be too courteous to ask for his cigarettes either directly or indirectly but that (5) he would engage in a conversation that would *cover any topic* except cigarettes, although at the time he would have a strong desire to get his cigarettes back.

The subject clearly indicated through his conversation his now repressed desire for cigarettes, after Dr. D. had absconded with his pack. The protocol goes as follows:

He [the subject] began chatting casually, wandering from one topic to another, always mentioning in some indirect but relevant fashion the word "smoking." For example, he talked about a boat on the bay at New Haven, commenting on the fact that the sight of water always made him thirsty, as did *smoking*. He then told a story about how the dromedary got one hump and the *camel* got two. Next he told a tale of Syrian folklore in which again a *camel* played a role . . . and asked what he would like to do, he commented on the pleasant weather and said there was nothing more glorious than paddling in a canoe or floating at ease on the water, *smoking*.

Lapsus Linguae AND UNCONSCIOUS IRONY The subject was hypnotized and told that, when he awoke, Dr. D. would engage him in a long and boring conservation from which he would like to disengage himself, but would be too polite to do in an obvious manner. He was then awakened, and Dr. D. began.

Although the subject appeared to be politely attentive, Dr. D. would occasionally say, "Perhaps you're not interested." The subject would reply with excessive emphasis, "Oh, yes, certainly, I'm very much interested." Now and then he would interrupt Dr. D., trying to pin him down to some definite point for discussion, but each time this effort was evaded. At length the subject began casually to observe an open door. Finally, he interrupted Dr. D., saying, "Excuse me, I feel an awful draft," and got up to close the door. As he did so, he was asked what he was doing. He replied, "The air seems to be awfully hot ["hot air"]; I thought I would shut off the draft." When the hypnotist pretended not to understand and asked him what he was doing, the subject replied, "Why I just shut the bore." His remark was then repeated by the hypnotist for the benefit of those in the audience who had not heard it. When the subject heard his statement given as "shutting the bore," he started visibly, seemed tremendously embarrassed, and with much urgency turned to Dr. D., saying, "Did I say that? I didn't mean that. I just meant I closed the door." He was very apologetic in his whole manner and bearing.

These cases, plus eight others not given here, seem to bear out the Freudian analysis of slips and errors and unconscious motivation. Since the results are based only on a single subject and obtained under rather special conditions (hypnosis), we should be wary of their scientific value and generality. Nonetheless, they are highly suggestive and indicate that the psychopathology of everyday life can be studied experimentally.

Wit and Humor

One of Freud's early works following *Interpretation of Dreams* and *Psychopathology of Everyday Life* was *Wit and Its Relation to the Unconscious*. In this, Freud looked closely at yet another area of activity to which man not only devotes a good deal of his time but also attaches considerable importance. People enjoy jokes, humor, and comedy, as is clearly evidenced by the great respect accorded to witty persons and entertainers. Why is this? Is such activity (or the principles that underlie it) exclusively humorous? What purposes or functions does it serve? Like any other natural phenomenon, wit requires an explanation.

Freud's observations of wit led him to divide it into two main categories: harmless wit and tendentious wit (i.e., wit with a tendency or a purpose). The second of these represented wit that aimed at liberating repressed impulses in a form that was at least to some degree socially acceptable. The first, however, although it apparently did not serve repressed tendencies, did yield a playful pleasure merely by the sheer unfettered activity of the psychic apparatus. Before going further, let us look at two examples given by Freud himself:

Example 4-8 *Wit and the unconscious (Freud, 1938)*

TENDENTIOUS WIT

> Wendell Phillips, according to a recent biography by Dr. Lorenzo Sears, was on one occasion lecturing in Ohio, and while on a railroad journey to keep one of his appointments met in a car a number of clergymen returning from some sort of convention. One of the ministers, feeling called upon to approach Mr. Phillips, asked him, "Are you Mr. Phillips?" "I am, Sir." "Are you trying to free the Niggers?" "Yes, Sir; I am an abolitionist." "Well, why do you preach your doctrine up here? Why don't you go over into Kentucky?" "Excuse me, are you a preacher?" "I am, Sir." "Are you trying to save souls from Hell?" "Yes, Sir, that's my business." "Well, why don't you go there?" [p. 698]

Here the witticism (perhaps funnier in Freud's day than now) is used in the service of hostile aggression. Mr. Phillips, being a man of culture, could not allow himself to aggress too directly against the offensive minister. By recourse to wit, however, he was able to express his inner feelings in a socially acceptable manner. The reader will undoubtedly be able to think of many examples of his own. Most instances of irony, sarcasm, and cynicism come under this category.

HARMLESS WIT

> A man who was addicted to drink supported himself in a small city by private teaching. His vice gradually became known and he lost most of his pupils in consequence. A friend of his took it upon himself to admonish him to reform. "Look here," he said, "You could have the best pupils in town if only you would give up drinking. Why not do it?" "What are you talking about" was the indignant reply. "I am teaching in order to be able to drink. Shall I give up drinking in order to get pupils?" [p. 660].

This little joke, though it illustrates harmless wit, does also contain tendentious elements. It may, in fact, be difficult to find an example of wit that does not. The two types do certainly involve the same kinds of mechanism and, according to Freud, are ultimately aimed at the same goal. Let us go into his analysis a little more fully.

Wit is in many ways like dreamwork and involves many of the same mechanisms, such as substitution, displacement, punning, and condensation. Furthermore, tendentious wit, also like the dream, represents a compromise between satisfaction of hidden wishes and the demands of social pressure. In ordinary waking conditions, however, these wishes can be satisfied only in such indirect and subtle ways (since the opposition of social forces is stronger in waking life) that the pleasure to be gained from the partial satisfaction is very small indeed. A little sip of water may help to satisfy a thirsty man but does not fully do the job. To explain the compelling quality of wit, Freud suggested an additional aspect which made the enterprise of wit worth the trouble. This lay in the *play element* of wit—the relaxation of the effort we usually must make in dealing seriously with reality. The principle of "economy of psychic effort" is the central and main purpose of wit and humor, both harmless and tendentious. In this respect, it is unlike the dream, whose primary purpose is to cope with unconscious needs and thus to guard against pain. Wit serves primarily to acquire positive pleasure—it is a kind of safety valve in the machinery of the psyche. The dream is a more serious business and serves primarily to ensure absence of pain.

The problem of wit is a difficult one to attack

experimentally. However, some attempts have been made. We will report here the results of some studies on the Freudian theory of wit done by Levine and Redlich and some of their colleagues.

Example 4–9 *Experimental analysis of wit and humor (Levine & Redlich, 1955)*

The investigators outlined the Freudian theory of wit as follows:

The appreciation of humor is a result of a sudden release of inhibited wishes associated with the theme of the humor. Like dreamwork, joke work allows expression of instincts oblique enough to be acceptable to the superego. The emotion that accompanies this release is generally felt as pleasant—we find something funny, and we smile or laugh. Like the dream, the joke is cathartic. However, two other outcomes are predictable from Freudian theory, and it is mainly with these that the investigators were concerned.

We often find that a person, instead of laughing, may respond to a joke or humorous situation either with indifference or with anxiety. This may be for several reasons: (1) There may be no conflict over expression of the need; hence the person does not find the joke very funny. (2) The needs involved may be very deeply repressed, so that the person does not "get" the point. (3) There may be very rigid ego control, so that the person understands the joke but is too embarrassed to laugh. In these latter two cases, there is what Levine and Redlich call a "scotomatization" of the joke—that is to say, the production of a blind spot (scotoma) about something funny. The implication is, of course, that the person has the intelligence to get the joke and does so all too clearly but refuses to acknowledge that he does.

To examine the psychoanalytic theory of humor, the investigators first constructed a test which they called the Mirth Response Test (MRT). This consists of thirty-one cartoons taken from a number of popular magazines. The reliability of this test was found to be high ($r = .8$). The test involves three steps: (1) *free expression*, in which each subject is shown each cartoon and observed for his response to it—that is, whether he expresses complete indifference, expresses hostility, smiles, or laughs; (2) *sorting*, in which the subject is asked to sort the cartoons on a scale of humorousness; (3) *inquiry*, in which the experimenter tries to explore with the subject his reactions to the cartoons.

Levine and Redlich used this test on over a hundred mentally ill hospital patients, some mental defectives, and some normal controls. They found twice as many negative responses were obtained from the mentally ill groups as from any of the other groups. Laughing and smiling at the jokes occurred half as frequently. They ascribed this result to a lack of apprehension on the part of the mentally ill subjects, this being dependent both on intellectual and on emotional factors. In Freudian terms, this meant that scotomatization had occurred. Anxiety about the needs and wishes being revealed in the cartoons thus produced either a failure to see the point of a joke or else strong negative reactions to it.

The results are in agreement with Freudian theory, though they are by no means conclusive. Lack of suitable controls allow other interpretations. For example, it is likely that the mentally ill group were simply less expressive in general and not responsive to jokes as such. Their relationship with the tester may also have been much less satisfactory than it was for the other groups. However, the experiment represents a very interesting wedge into the problem. The following are two protocols from Levine and Redlich:

1. A highly intelligent sophisticated scientist, head of a University department, was shown a cartoon in which an office administrator approaches the "suggestions" box. Beneath the box is a bottle marked "poison." The scientist could not understand the cartoon. When the bottle of poison was pointed out to him as a clue to the meaning of the joke, he was surprised to see the poison label, though it was most prominently displayed. He was then able to understand that someone had placed the poison there as a suggestion to the boss to take it. Even after he understood the cartoon, the scientist did not consider it funny.

    The scientist revealed later that he had fears of being either too hostile or too lenient to his fellow workers and was deeply concerned over whether he was loved or hated. Scotomatization occurred for a joke which dealt directly with these anxieties.

2. A young male patient who had anxieties over homosexual and voyeuristic impulses (sexual gratification

from "looking") was shown a cartoon by Peter Arno of a young woman stripped to the waist sitting before a physician who looks puzzled. The nipples of her breasts are turned inward in such a way as to give them a cross-eyed look. The doctor says to the girl, "Have you tried an oculist?" The patient responded to this cartoon with embarrassment and disgust, exclaiming, "I don't like this . . . it's filthy . . . just sex, just plain dirty. He has got her disrobed . . . it's pure sex. I never did get a kick out of a dirty joke." When the cross-eyed breasts were pointed out to him, he still failed to comprehend.

Our brief resumé hardly does justice to Freud's lengthy and brilliant analysis of wit and the unconscious. However, it does contain the main ideas. What can these add to our knowledge of the unconscious? From a scientific standpoint, perhaps very little. The information gathered by Freud is almost completely anecdotal and has considerably less cogency than the clinical data he used in interpreting dreams or the psychopathology of everyday life. At the same time, it is suggestive, in a number of ways. In the first place, it points up another mode in which the unconscious can express itself in normal waking life. In the second place, it suggests a hypothesis rather different from that found in most of his writings, namely, that not all man's behavior is dedicated to instinctual gratification nor is it all aimed at avoidance of pain and discomfort. In wit and art we see activity aimed at sheer expression for its own sake with positive delight or pleasure as its main aim.

Freud later looked beyond the pleasure principle. In *Wit and the Unconscious*, he looks beyond the nirvana, or quiescence, principle. Positive evidence for this point of view that man finds pleasure in activity itself and not merely activity aimed at producing rest is not directly available from the clinic. There are some experiments, however, from the laboratory which suggests the operation of such a principle, one which applies to animals as well as to man. Since we will be discussing these experiments in another context (cf. Chapter 5), we will not present them here.

A final point as to the relevance to our theme of wit is made in the following quotation from a noted psychoanalyst, A. A. Brill:

Wit is the best safety valve modern man has evolved; the more civilization, the more repression, the more need there is for wit. Only relatively civilized people have a sense of humor. The child and the true primitive show no good mechanisms. The child like the savage is still natural and frank. When the child begins to dream, which shows that repressive forces are already at work, he also shows the beginnings of a sense of humor [Brill, 1938, p. 2].

The three types of phenomena, dreams, slips and errors, and wit, described above, have yielded some valuable information about the unconscious. It is clear that this relatively obscure part of personality is of great importance in determining much of our behavior. We have further seen that the unconscious is not just a passive state but a dynamic force—that is, a force spontaneously pushing for expression; it seems to have its own kinds of processes, which do not follow the ordinary rules of logical thought; it is infantile in the sense that it somehow contains the residues of infantile wishes, which it strives to satisfy; and finally the forces of the unconscious are opposed by counterforces in other parts of the personality, so that the behavioral outcome is usually some kind of compromise between these two sets of opposing forces. The many ways in which the forces of the unconscious are handled in such compromises constitute an interesting chapter in psychoanalytic theory with which we will deal later.

THE COLLECTIVE UNCONSCIOUS

Out of Freud's analysis of the topography of personality grew his notions about its structure. At this point, however, we digress a little from Freud to consider an alternative treatment of the unconscious put forward by another great thinker—initially a colleague and exponent of Freud and later an opponent—Carl Gustav Jung (see Jacobi, 1951).

Though Freud regarded the unconscious as containing in it the primitive residuals of man's long history and evolution, he did not stress this aspect. Jung, however, posited, in addition to the *personal, or individual, unconscious*, which analysts usually accept, a *collective unconscious* which is suprapersonal and contains the basic mental elements common to all mankind. It is the receptacle of all racial and ancestral memories and supplies the broad framework within which individuals think and act. The basic memories themselves Jung called *archetypes*. These may be likened to channels in the mind along which thoughts must flow. Just as we inevitably deal with the physical world in terms of categories of space and time, so also we deal with our social world in terms of such archetypal categories as God, father and mother figures, forces of evil, forces of good, and salvation.

According to Jung, man did not invent God; rather, man by reason of his inherited makeup is a "God-believing" creature. He is careful not to infer from this, however, that God is a fiction; that we must have a God because we are human and must think in this way neither proves nor disproves the actual existence of a God. People not only see the world through the spectacles of archetypes; they may also become identified with them. In Jungian terms, Adolf Hitler was a good example of a person dominated completely by the hero and the demon archetypes, and, likewise, deep in the unconscious of the German people were archaic dispositions highly responsive to such a figure.

The main sources of evidence for which Jung advanced the existence of archetypes were mythology, alchemy, witchcraft, and all the strange and bizarre writings and fringe activities of mankind that covertly accompany the march of rational civilization. One example of an archetype is shown in Figure 4-3.

In addition, Jung and his followers have claimed that archetypes appear in the spontaneous drawings and in the dreams of patients in analysis. Whether such instances are occasioned by the unconscious influence of the analyst is unknown. In any case, many people find the notion of archetypes useful, not only for the understanding of patients but for the purposes of literary and artistic criticism. They are difficult concepts which, at first sight, may appear to be nonsensical, but closer investigation of them, particularly through careful reading of the writings of Jung, will reveal their subtlety and force.

THE STRUCTURE OF PERSONALITY

Why we draw a distinction between topography and structure may puzzle the reader at this point. Perhaps the best way to explain this is by showing how Freud came to it. The reader will recall from our discussion of dreams the concept of a "censor" which tries to hold back, or repress, the forces of the

FIG. 4-3 Example of a Jungian archetype: Rosicrucian symbol. (*Jacobi, 1951*)

unconscious. Although this can be opposed to the unconscious in one sense, in another it cannot, since its operation also appears to be unconscious. That is to say, it tends to act automatically without awareness on the part of the person. In therapy, we find often that a patient seems actively to *resist* any expression of unconscious, a resistance which naturally makes it very difficult for the analyst to be of help. Such resistance is not intentional. The patient consciously wants to be helped and tries to cooperate as well as he can with the analyst. In such a case, we see the operation of a force that is blocking expression of the unconscious and *yet is unconscious itself*. This seeming contradiction led Freud to reconsider his formulation of personality. In the new scheme, the three parts of the psyche with which we have dealt until now—the conscious, preconscious, and unconscious—are supplemented by three new constructs, the ego, the superego, and the id. This is done as indicated in Table 4-3.

We shall see that the new scheme describing the structure of personality turns out to be a useful one in explaining many facts. Let us now look at each of the constituent parts in more detail.

Table 4-3 Approximate relation between topography and structure

Topography	Structure
Conscious processes	Ego
Preconscious processes (accessible to voluntary awareness)	
Unconscious processes (inaccessible to voluntary awareness)	Repressing—superego (censor) Repressed—id

Id

The id is a construct that refers to all primitive and infantile impulses and instinctual needs. By definition, these processes are unconscious. Developmentally, in the human organism the id occurs first. It is not only the source of energy, or drives, but also the source out of which are differentiated the ego and superego.

In the beginning, the infant is presumably entirely id. He has a number of physiological needs whose presence produces tension or discomfort and whose satisfaction produces pleasure and quiescence. The id is dedicated to the pleasure principle, not to morals or reality. Its only goal is full and immediate satisfaction of these needs. We may infer on the basis of analysis of dreams of young children and of the free associations of adult patients that these physiological tensions have some kind of mental representations. That is to say, an infant is not only hungry in a somatic sense but in some mental sense as well. The exact nature of this kind of mentation is not known, but it is presumed to be very primitive, timeless, and illogical. Because it is the first kind of mental activity in which human beings engage, it is called *primary process*.

The idea that such somatic needs as hunger and thirst should have mental counterparts in the infant may be hard to believe, but it makes sense if we remember that the infant does have a central nervous system which is linked to the viscera. The mind of the infant is certainly a mysterious thing, but there can be hardly any doubt, that, physiologically speaking, it has the basic equipment for mentation, however primitive a form this takes. We will discuss this further when we consider the biological correlates of behavior.

Ego

The second province of personality, the ego, is largely the same as the conscious, though parts of it may be unconscious or preconscious. It is essentially that part of the id (i.e., the whole organism in infancy) that has come into contact with reality; in Freud's words, it is "that part of the id which has been modified by the first influence of the external world acting through the perceptual-conscious [Freud, 1927]." This rather complex statement means simply that the id, which initially is the infant personality in its entirety, comes into contact with a reality, and this reality modifies part of it. These modified parts, which have to do with the outside world as well as internal bodily states, constitute the ego. In this respect, although the ego is in some ways the organizing or synthesizing force in personality, it is, for Freud, a passive agent "at the service of three harsh masters" these being the id, the external world, and the superego. To draw a rough analogy: the ego is not like a business executive who settles with a firm hand disputes between his employees; rather, it is like an office boy who tries his best to please the often contradictory demands of several bosses. Just as the office boy is forced into making all kinds of compromises if he wants to keep his job, so the ego must also make use of various tricks and compromises if it is to survive. When the strain is too great, the ego breaks down and we have mental illness.

To accomplish its task, the ego makes use of reason, logic, and thinking. It is by contact of the organism with the real world that these processes develop secondarily. Hence the functions of the ego are known as *secondary* processes. Insofar as they attempt to bring the personality into a correspondence with the outside world, their main concern is with reality. Thus we say that the ego is governed by the *reality principle*. It should be noted that although such processes develop secondarily, they are, for Freud and others, biologically built into the organism. That is to say, they are there *potentially* in the beginning, even though their emergence or maturation depends on certain experiential events. Without contact with the world, we would presumably never learn to think in logical or "realistic" terms.

Although Freud did not really develop the concept of ego as an autonomous, positive force, he did

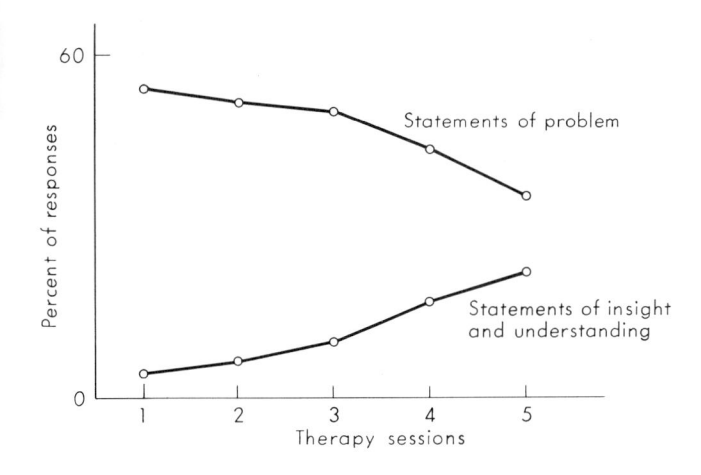

FIG. 4–4 Incidence of statements reflecting "improvement" in successive therapy sessions. (*Seeman, 1949*)

place on it his hopes for the sanity of human beings. Indeed much of his therapy involved replacing id (unconscious) by ego (conscious). Psychological health was thus largely a function of ego strength. Perhaps for this reason, many theorists who followed Freud have attempted to formulate the functions of the ego more carefully. Anna Freud, Freud's daughter, was one of the first to do this in her book *The Ego and the Mechanisms of Defence* (1946). Other theorists with similar views have been Horney, Sullivan, Hartmann, and more recently Maslow and Carl Rogers. All these writers are more optimistic than Freud in that they stress the inner potentialities for health that the ego possesses.

An outcome of this point of view has been a tendency to focus, in therapy, for example, somewhat less on the meaning assumed to lie *behind* what a patient says and thinks and more on manifest characteristics taken at their face value. Thus, according to the ideas of Carl Rogers, the therapist attempts only to provide a situation in which the patient is free to find a conscious solution to the problem that is bothering him. His ensuing overt intellectual struggles are given far more importance and emphasis than they would be in a Freudian analysis. To illustrate the difference, let us examine the data in Figure 4–4. These were gathered by Seeman (1949), a colleague of Rogers. As shown, they represent a plot of the number of times a patient makes statements about his problem during therapy. This might be, for example, an inability to get along with women. As therapy progresses, these occur with less frequency. Statements signifying insights into its causes show a corresponding increase.

A Rogerian, or an ego psychologist, would take such data as prima facie evidence of improvement. Such a conclusion would be based directly on the assumption that conscious speech arising from the ego to a large extent reflects a "true" state of affairs. What goes on in the ego is important, so that if a patient says, "I feel I am getting better," it is ground for optimism. In the Freudian scheme, however, such statements would not be taken at their face value and would be assumed to reflect or *mask* real feelings at deeper levels of personality. Thus, both therapy and methods of assessing its success depend heavily on the view we take about the structure of personality.

Superego

The third part of personality in Freud's scheme is the superego. This construct is used to describe those forces, themselves unconscious, which oppose the forces of the id. It is the same as the dream censor, which necessitates disguising infantile erotic wishes before they can be expressed. It includes those forces which cause us to hide hostility behind a witticism instead of expressing it openly or to develop elaborate customs and rituals for coping with sexual impulses. Freud came to see that what we ordinarily know as the *conscience* is, in fact, the same as the censor.

Because of its often unrealistic (or idealistic) character, he called it ego ideal, or superego. Its operation can most clearly be seen in pathology. For example, in the disease known as melancholia, the patient is literally his own worst enemy and suffers extreme guilt for the slightest and most trivial faults. Often such guilt ends in suicide—that is, destruction of the ego. Though most of us do not experience such extreme feelings, it is equally true that all of us do undergo so-called pangs of conscience which may cause us considerable discomfort.

Like the id, the superego is also largely irrational and unconscious. An overzealous prosecutor, it demands immediate punishment of any transgression and cannot tolerate immoral wishes or impulses. In this respect, it is sometimes differentiated from the classic concept of conscience as a *rational* moral force (cf. Mailloux, 1955). As we shall see later in more detail, the superego is a precipitate of the ego, its repressing part, whose formation depends on development and on the long period of dependence of children on their parents. The child, at a certain age, takes in, or *introjects*, the moral authority of the parents (particularly the father). The superego is thus a kind of internalized parent substitute, or surrogate, which continues to reward and punish the ego much in the same way as the parents did originally. It is ironical, as we might deduce, that the stronger the superego, the more moral the person will be but also the more guilt he will suffer.

We said that the superego not only punishes but also rewards. In this respect, the superego serves as a positive force which can give us a pleasant glow of *pride* when we do something good. Thus both pride and guilt are functions of the superego, whose ambivalence in this respect directly reflects the ambivalent manner in which most parents treat their children.

This tripartite structure of personality has considerable significance for understanding many kinds of behavior. It must be understood that although none of the three parts is static or fixed, the initial character of each as it is determined early in life is critical. We will offer some reasons for this basic proposition later on. For the time being, we can merely state that because of their early formation, they color all human actions. This is true for dreams, slips, wit, and other phenomena we have already considered. In this respect, ego, id, and superego turn out to be useful constructs. They can serve as conceptual tools to handle a great variety of psychological problems.

CHAPTER 5
THE DYNAMICS AND ECONOMICS OF PERSONALITY

So far we have considered personality as a static entity. We have seen that it can be described in terms of parts, both topographical and structural, which bear certain relationships to one another. Clearly, however, the organism is not a static entity like a stone or a piece of wood but has dynamic characteristics. That is to say, it has in it intrinsic forces which operate on the environment as well as on one another. It is likely that few organisms are completely at the mercy of environmental events. Somehow they generate their own power, which they channel into various modes of action. Another way of putting this is to say that in an organism there is a disproportionality between the amount of physical energy acting on it and the amount of energy involved in any resulting organic movement but that for inorganic objects there is an exact proportionality as specified by physics. Thus it would take a great deal of physical energy to move an object weighing, say, 120 pounds. However, the slight amount of sound energy emitted by a crying child may be quite capable of galvanizing its mother into action.

Dynamics deals with the nature of the forces in personality and the source from which they derive their energy. The two key energy concepts here are *libido* and *instinct*. What is called *economics* deals with the manner in which these forces can be handled and distributed in respect to the different regions of personality and channeled into the environment. The ways by which this is accomplished are called *defense mechanisms*.

DYNAMICS

Libido

To the primary source of energy in organisms Freud gave the name libido. Since it is present very early in life (before birth) and since, as we have seen, the neonate at birth and for a short time after is undifferentiated id, then libido must in some way be coordinate with id. Personality is like a developing country in which the sources of labor and wealth proceed from the regions that are just settled to those that are settled later on. The libido is thus simply a descriptive term referring to that energy underlying all physiological needs in the id. Discharge of these needs is pleasurable. Nondischarge is painful or unpleasurable.

As used by Freud, libidinal energy is of a *sexual*

character, but only in a very broad sense. Sexuality is not identical with genitality but is an attribute of other functions, in particular ingesting and excreting. Freud observed, in a very important essay ("Instincts and Their Vicissitudes," 1915), that in the so-called sex perversions, sexual pleasure could be gained through means other than conventional genital contact. From this he inferred that genital pleasure was only one mode of a broader sexual pleasure which found many means of fulfillment—not only in the perversions, but also in such everyday acts as eating, drinking, smoking, and excreting. Freud defined libidinal energy as being sexual only insofar as this term referred to the general tension underlying all bodily needs.

Although libido is presumably linked to biological processes, that is, to basic drives, it is still a psychological construct, so we can assign to it some properties that would be difficult to envisage purely at a biological level. The main such property assigned to libido by Freud is *fluidity*, or *mobility*. That is to say, libido can become "invested" in, or attached to, either the personality itself and the various regions which comprise it or, on the other hand, mental representations of animate and inanimate objects in the environment. Biologically, of course, this may not make very much sense, but psychologically it is a useful way of talking about persons and their relations to environment. The attachments of libido to objects or parts of the personality Freud called *cathexes*. The number of such cathexes that may be formed by the person in a lifetime is, of course, almost limitless. Generally speaking, it is characteristic that earlier ones, occurring before id and ego are differentiated, are oriented entirely inward, toward the person himself. The libidinal energy so invested is called *narcissistic libido*. Later on, with the development of ego and superego, libido comes to be cathected to objects or individuals in the environment. Such libido is called *object libido*.

Instincts

In general, the term "instinct" refers to the mode in which energy can be channeled. By way of analogy, we might conceive of energy as represented by a river and instinct as the bed or channel that determines its direction and rate of flow. Thus instinct is merely a classificatory device to enable us to describe behavior in more economical terms. According to psychoanalytic theory, instincts have four main properties: (1) aim, (2) object, (3) source, (4) drive (or impetus). The *aim* of the instinct is satisfaction, or diminution of the tension which the energy behind it, pushing for release, generates. The *object* refers to any of those objects or persons in the outside world that are instrumental in its satisfaction. Its *source* is simply the energy that generates it, and its *drive* is roughly the quantity of energy it possesses at any particular time. In these respects, human instincts are rather different from animal instincts as understood by a number of contemporary naturalists (cf. Chapter 16). The latter refer mostly to so-called fixed action patterns as illustrated for example, in the courtship behavior of birds. Human beings do not generally show such stereotyped responses that are automatically triggered or released by specific stimuli.

Freud's thoughts on the subject of instincts changed considerably over the years, and his final theoretical position was rather different from his initial one. We can demarcate three main stages in the evolution of his thinking. These are presented here not only because of their historical interest but also because each one is based on different kinds of clinical data and hence is important in its own right.

Initially, Freud felt that all human motives and strivings could be subdivided into two main classes of instincts: the *sex instincts* and the *ego instincts*. Sex instincts include all those types of human behavior that are concerned with satisfying organic tensions and are aimed ultimately at the preservation of race or species. The source of this set of instincts is libido, and their object, strictly speaking, is a partner of opposite sex. However, as indicated already, so-called normal procreative sexuality is only one expression of the sex instincts. The sexual drive is not originally (in infancy) focused on the genitals but successively fixates on a number of other anatomical areas. Furthermore, its object is not always another person of opposite sex. Sometimes sexual activity, as in homosexuality, involves two people of the same sex, or it may involve one person and some animal or object which has sexual significance. Consequently, the Freudian meaning of sex is much broader than the conventional meaning. Genital sexuality is merely a special case of a much broader kind of drive, though, for some psychoanalytic thinkers, it may be prototypic in the sense that it is the fullest and most normal mode of sexuality.

The evidence for supposing that the sexual drive, even in its broader sense, underlies so much of human activity is largely clinical. Again and again, Freud and other analysts have found that even some of the most "innocent" (i.e., nonsexual-appearing) wishes and behavior of patients really cloak strong sexual wishes. Certainly, there is no gainsaying the power of sex for human beings. We can see it around us every day in illustrations, advertisements, motion pictures, best-selling novels, and the arts. Equally, we can infer its strength from the strength of the defenses created against its too direct expression by different elements in the community.

On the other hand, we must be cautious about supposing, as Freud did for a time, that sex is everything. Other classifications of human motives are possible—ones which take so-called higher needs (e.g., achievement, curiosity, religion) as autonomous and quite independent of physiological drives. Freud himself did, in fact, make some allowance for this possibility by opposing the sexual instincts with another set, namely, the ego instincts.

The ego instincts have as their aim preservation of self. They included for Freud only behavior directed to achievement, and mastery over the environment. Insofar as Freud did little to develop an exact formulation of the ego instincts, we need not discuss them further. However, by designating them he did anticipate a good deal of the thinking of later workers who gave much more emphasis to the ego.

In the second stage of the development of his instinct theory, Freud gave up the ego instincts as a separate group of drives. In a classic essay entitled "On Narcissism" (1914), he developed the view that even activity apparently directed to self-preservation may be basically sexual in character. That is to say, the self may, in a sense, be loved erotically as simply another sexual object, as, in the classical myth, the beautiful youth Narcissus fell in love with his own image reflected in water.

The original love of self that is typical of all young children who have not yet clearly differentiated themselves from the world Freud called *primary narcissism*. The phrase "His Majesty, the baby" aptly described it. A later return or regression to this self-love in the grown-up who is unable to make satisfactory attachments to other people is called *secondary narcissism*. The two often operate in complex ways, side by side. One example, is the charming but exaggerated love parents bear their children. Freud described this as follows:

> They are impelled to ascribe to the child all manner of perfections which sober observation would not confirm, to glance over and forget all his shortcomings—a tendency with which, indeed, the denial of childish sexuality is connected. Moreover, they are inclined to suspend in the child's favour the operation of all those cultural acquirements which their own narcissism has been forced to respect, and to renew in his person the claim for privileges which were long ago given up by themselves. The child shall have things better than his parents; he shall not be subject to the necessities which they have recognized as dominating life. Illness, death, renunciation of enjoyment, restriction on his own will, are not able to touch him; the laws of nature, like those of society, are to be abrogated in his favour. . . .
>
> Parental love, which is so touching, and at bottom so childish, is nothing but parental narcissism born again and, transformed though it be into object-love, it reveals its former character infallibly [Freud, 1925, pp. 48–49].

Thus the primary narcissism of the child is fed and complemented by the secondary narcissism of the parents, who identify with him. Likewise, the parental narcissism is given further strength and reinforcement by the narcissism of the child.

This rather peculiar relationship, Freud thought, also may occur between some men and women. One of the kinds of women most attractive to men is the narcissistic type. Men love her precisely because she loves herself and loves to be loved. That such a relationship mirrors the child-parent one is easily seen in the infantile terms of endearment often used by men to describe a woman they love.

Whether all human relationships have such a narcissistic component is problematical. The implication, on the part of Freud, is that they need not. Whatever the case, the degree of narcissism they involve represents an important and worthwhile dimension for exploration.

The third and final stage of Freud's thinking about instincts is the most complex and perhaps the least acceptable to other psychoanalytic writers. Having collapsed the initial pair of instincts into one (the sex instincts), he came to the view that another category was needed. These he called the *death instincts,* or thanatos, and opposed them to the *life instincts,* or eros.

The death instincts were postulated by Freud to account for some facts he observed clinically as well as in the world around him. One of these facts was simply that there existed in the world a great deal of aggression and hate. Wars, riots, murder, lynching—all give evidence of some basic destructive impulse in human beings. This appeared clinically in the form of sadism and masochism, the desires to hurt and to be hurt. Another fact he observed was the tendency of human beings to return to or repeat previous experiences even when these were not pleasurable. This *repetition compulsion,* as Freud called it, could be recognized in the dreams of soldiers who had been traumatized in World War I. In these dreams, they continually relived their traumatic experiences. This could hardly be regarded as pleasurable and hence could not be attributed to the service of the life instincts. Rather it was done in service of a drive to resume an earlier state. Taking a rather large speculative leap, Freud concluded that there must be a basic drive in man pulling him back to the state of inorganic matter from which he originally came. This end state is, of course, death. Hence, the designation *death instincts.*

Aggression against other people is, then, a manifestation of the death instincts projected outward. Sometimes, in the case of defense against attack, aggression operates in service of life, in the sense that the true end of the death instincts is a *natural* rather than an accidental death. Thus the behavior of man might be viewed as a kind of dialectic between two forces which may oppose but can also complement each other. Although Freud was not clear as to the source of energy lying behind the death instinct, he did feel that it was not libido.

What is the validity of this final formulation of Freud? Do human beings really possess these two broad kinds of determinations? We cannot really answer such a question exactly. However, we can say that his formulation is useful in explaining or describing much of human behavior and to that extent has value. Human beings show affection and love, and they do hate and act aggressively. Furthermore, they appear to generate love and hate spontaneously rather than to react passively with them to appropriate stimuli. Perhaps the main problem with Freudian instincts is that they explain too much to be useful. Because of this, a number of writers have attempted to offer more refined analyses of human motivation.

Motives and Needs

Though Freud's instinct theory has some cogency, many psychologists and psychoanalysts have felt that man is more than simply an animal and that it is a distortion of his nature to derive all his higher and nobler motives from primitive biological instincts. As part of the trend toward emphasizing the importance of the ego as against the id, many have also suggested *autonomous systems of motives and needs* pertaining to the ego and quite independent of our primitive biological nature. Such theorists as Hartmann, Kris, Lowenstein, Anna Freud, Rogers, Murray, and Allport, to mention only a few, have been of this persuasion (cf. Munroe, 1955). Although we cannot discuss the views of all these, it would do an injustice to the topic of personality dynamics and motivation which we are discussing not to present some of these ideas. Henry Murray and Carl Rogers can serve as examples. Again, no attempt will be made to present their complete personality theories, but only their motivational concepts and some of the research that has come out of these.

One of Murray's main contributions to the study of personality was to suggest a classification of motives. Once we depart from the Freudian view that all secondary or higher motives are derivative from primary biological ones, we are faced with the task of boiling down all the innumerable acts of man to a list of a manageable size. Murray attempted to do this in his book *Explorations in Personality.* His basic unit is a "need," defined as "an organic potential or readiness to respond in a certain way under certain given conditions [Murray, 1938, p. 61]." Although a need is not fixedly associated with certain behavior patterns, it may tend to become so in time. For example, a *need aggression* may become characteristically satisfied by bullying or sarcasm.

In other words, a need refers to a set or push

Table 5-1 Man's basic needs, according to H. A. Murray (1938)

Viscerogenic:

Air	Defecation
Water	Harmavoidance
Food	Nonavoidance
Sex	Heatavoidance
Lactation	Coldavoidance
Urination	Sentience

Psychogenic:

Acquisition	Gain possession, take things
Conservance	Collect, repair, protect things
Order	Arrange, organize, be tidy, neat
Retention	Retain possession of things, be frugal, miserly
Construction	Organize, build
Superiority	Have power over people, ideas, things, gain approval, high status
Achievement	Overcome obstacles, exercise power, strive to do something difficult as well and as quickly as possible
Recognition	Excite praise and recognition, demand respect
Exhibition	Attract attention to self
Infavoidance	Avoid failure, shame, ridicule
Defendance	Defend self against shame or belittlement, resist probing
Counteraction	Overcome defeat by striving, defend honor
Dominance	Influence or control others, persuade, dictate, direct
Deference	Admire and follow superior
Similance	Imitate or emulate, agree, believe
Autonomy	Resist influence or aversion; defy authority and seek freedom
Contrarience	Act differently from others; hold unconventional views
Aggression	Assault or injure, harm, belittle, punish, blame
Abasement	Surrender; comply and accept punishment; apologize, self-depreciate
Blamavoidance	Avoid blame or punishment by inhibiting a social impulse
Affiliation	Form friendships and associations; cooperate, love, join groups
Rejection	Snub, ignore, or exclude; remain aloof and indifferent
Nurturance	Nourish, aid, protect, sympathize
Succorance	Seek aid, protection, dependence
Play	Relax, amuse self; have fun; be merry
Cognizance	Explore, ask questions, be curious, look, listen, seek knowledge
Exposition	Demonstrate, give information, explain, lecture

behind some segment or class of behavior, a motive force that demands appropriate satisfaction. Murray lists twenty-eight such needs. Some he calls primary, or viscerogenic. These are the basic physiological needs, such as hunger, sex, and thirst. The others are secondary, or psychogenic. A complete list of both classes is given in Table 5-1.

To these needs, Murray has assigned various properties. One is *periodicity*. That is to say, needs vary in strength over time, now waning, now waxing. Another property involves the interrelation of one need with others. Thus needs may be (1) *fused* when one action satisfies several needs as in the case of a concert pianist who gets money (need acquisition) and acclaim (need exhibition); (2) *subsidiated* to others, as when a boy works hard (need achievement) to please his parents (need succorance); (3) *contrefacted*, or succeeded in time by their opposite: a need dominance may be followed by a need deference; (4) *conflicted*, when two needs conflict, as when a man hesitates to act (need exhibition) because of fear (need infavoidance); (5) *integrated*, when several needs may be unified.

In respect to their manifestation, needs may be

(1) conscious or unconscious and (2) objectified, semiobjectified, or subjectified. Their degree of consciousness is given by whether a subject can recognize their presence or not. Their objectivity, on the other hand, is related to their overtness. Thus a person with a high need achievement may work very hard at his business (objectified), enjoy playing the role of "the conquering hero" in plays (semiobjectified), or daydream about being a hero or a general (subjectified). The subject, of course, may be quite conscious or completely unconscious of what these manifestations represent.

This, in broad outline, is Murray's essential treatment of motivation. Obviously, it raises many questions, few of which have yet been answered exactly. However, the general concept of *need* has been useful in a number of different ways.

One of these relates to the assessment of personality. If we are to describe personality in terms of needs, we should have some way of measuring them. Murray developed a method called the Thematic Apperception Test (TAT). This test consists of a set of pictures varying in degree of abstractness (one is a blank card) about each of which the subject is asked to tell a story. It is assumed that he *projects* his own pattern of needs into the story he tells, particularly that relating to the hero or heroine of the story. His stories are recorded and scored in a more or less exact manner on this basis.

Murray's need system has led to a good deal of fruitful research on human motivation. An example of an important research program is that carried out by David McClelland and his associates on one particular need—need achievement.

McClelland has taken the rather epic view that this particular need is a key to the whole progress of Western civilization. The great technological strides of the industrial revolution, the masterpieces of European art, and the pioneering of America—all these he has attributed, at least partly, to the strength of this need in Western peoples. His essential contribution has been to develop criteria for measuring it and then to look for relationships between strength of need achievement and other variables. The manner in which it is measured is illustrated in Example 5–1.

Example 5–1 *Protocols of a higher achiever and nonachiever using a projective test (McClelland et al., 1953)*

Four pictures are given to the subjects, who are asked to compose a story about each. The second picture (considered here) is shown in Figure 5–1. The following protocol is that of a higher achiever:

A student in a classroom is listening to a teacher explain the contents of a book which lies before the student. He is very interested in the subject.

He has passed through all the preceding school years and is an intelligent boy. He entered the classroom with his fellows and is now listening to the teacher.

He is trying to understand the subject which is new to him. The teacher also is trying his best to make the students understand.

The student will understand the subject and will go out of the class happy about his success in grasping it. He will be a success in life [McClelland et al., 1953, case 20–2].

The score this story received was +5. Compare it with this one:

The student is in the process of thinking over some incident or incidents which have occurred recently or remotely in his past. Some action in sight which turned the key which unlocked memories provided the impetus for the situation.

In trying to recapture these actions through memories, he is seeing some actions in the past—vividly.

He will sooner or later come out of his daydream and completely forget about this for the moment [McClelland et al., 1953, case 7–2].

This story was obviously much lower in its achievement orientation. It was scored −1 for need achievement.

One of the more interesting aspects of McClelland's work has been the experimental manipulation of need achievement. This is rather rarely done in the area of personality testing. McClelland has shown that a person's score on his test can be pushed higher simply by giving him instructions that are strongly "achievement-oriented." This point is demonstrated by the data in Example 5–2.

Example 5–2 *Experimental manipulation of achievement (McClelland et al., 1953)*

The method of "arousing" the achievement motive was by means of instructional cues. Unlike hunger and other biological drives, this need has not been found to vary in any simple way with degree of deprivation—that is, with successful performance

FIG. 5–1 A card used to measure need achievement. (*McClelland et al., 1953*)

or failure. Three types of instructions were given to college students. These were (1) *relaxed conditions:* subjects were told that the task of telling about the pictures was not important and the experimenters were just casually trying out some new ideas; (2) *neutral conditions:* the procedure was presented as a serious business and the subjects told they should cooperate fully; no indication was given, however, that their answers would be measuring any particular psychological abilities; (3) *achievement-oriented condition:* subjects were told that the test had been used to select Washington administrators and officer candidates for OCS in World War II, that it measured general intelligence, ability to organize material, and, in general, leadership qualities. It was further indicated that the test was being given to them at the time to determine which of them possessed such characteristics.

Following these instructions, all three groups were given a short paper-and-pencil test and then the pictures. Results from thirty-nine subjects for each condition in two scoring categories of achievement need are shown in Figure 5–2. It is clear that those working under the achievement-oriented instructions showed much higher scores. The differences were, in fact, statistically significant. Thus need achievement is capable of experimental manipulation.

McClelland has related the achievement need to many variables—personality traits, child-rearing practices, ethnic origins, academic success, and

FIG. 5-2 Effects of achievement-oriented instructions versus neutral or relaxed ones on two measures of need achievement. (*McClelland et al., 1953*)

others. Some of his and his colleagues' work has been summarized in several books (e.g., McClelland et al., 1953; McClelland, 1961). One example is given below.

Example 5-3 *Need achievement in ancient Greece (McClelland, 1961)*

The purpose of the study was to demonstrate the influence of the achievement need in determining the economic growth and decline of ancient Greece. The thematic material used for measuring the need consisted of representative writings such as prose, poetry, funeral orations, and exhortations from three historical periods in ancient Greece, 900–475 B.C., 475–362 B.C., and 362–100 B.C. These were scored much in the same way as that used for the original TAT pictures, for example, number of achievement images and themes, future references, and amount of affect related to success or failure outcomes. A general achievement score could then be given to each period. In the second step of the research, a measure of economic prosperity was taken, this being size of geographical trading area. Plotting the two curves together against time, we get the result shown in Figure 5-3. Note that the two curves are out of phase. Economic development is low initially, but its rise in the second period is foreshadowed by the high achievement level in the first period. Likewise, the decline of need achievement predicts the later economic decline.

In all fairness, it must be emphasized that much of the work on the achievement need and others such as need affiliation and need aggression has been more concrete and limited in scope. The "Greek" study may be a little rich for the blood of a great many psychologists. Nevertheless, McClelland has made an application of its essential principles to economic development in India. He and his colleagues offered to interested Indians a short intensive course designed to step up achievement needs. According to his reports, this "injection of entrepreneurialism" had remarkable effects. McClelland has even suggested that if conducted on a wide scale, it had the potential of increasing the economic prosperity of the whole country (McClelland, 1965).

This notion has interesting consequences. If any need can be so changed, then we perhaps are not stuck with the personality we have. If we desire more affiliativeness or more curiosity or more dominance, then presumably we should be able to have it by going through an appropriate program like that used in the case of need achievement.

Self-actualization

Need psychology has provided a rather useful

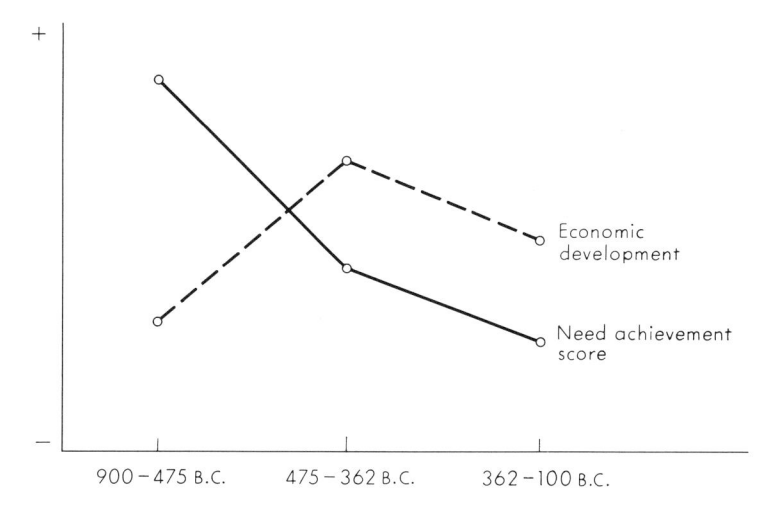

FIG. 5–3 Need achievement and economic development in ancient Greece. (*McClelland, 1961*)

framework for dealing empirically with motivation. Clinicians, however, who are less willing to dissect personality in this fashion, have tended to be more interested in some general motivational principles that reflect the patient's progress in therapy and his well-being in all aspects of his daily life. For this reason, many of them, starting with Carl Jung, have postulated a need for *self-actualization*, whose end is the fulfillment of all potentials and an integrated and balanced personality. Unlike Freud's life instinct this master need is not dedicated to peace and absence of pain, but rather to growth and creative change. As the reader may easily imagine, such a notion is conceptually rather comfortable and perhaps even useful in an open and unstructured clinical setting, but it is difficult to handle empirically. Carl Rogers, one of the foremost of those stressing the reality and importance of self-actualization, has been more successful than most in developing empirical approaches to its assessment. The following represents an example of such work at the counseling center in Chicago:

Example 5–4 *Improvement of self-perception during therapy (Butler & Haigh, 1954)*

It is always a difficult matter to judge the success of therapy. One psychologist, Hans Eysenck (1952a), has claimed, on the basis of a survey, that the rate of spontaneous cures is as high as, or even higher than, the rate of cure under psychoanalytic therapy. Most clinicians would not agree with his conclusions, but it is certainly true that judgment about the success of therapy can be a highly subjective matter. Rogers and his associates were among the first to take steps to remedy this by assessing the total personality before, during, and after therapy. They have used many techniques. The one to be reported here, called Q-technique, was developed mainly by William Stephenson (1953). It consists essentially of having a person rate a large number of traits for their *importance* in his personality. For example, he may say that for him impulsiveness is a key trait and that depressiveness is of no significance whatsoever. This can be done for the actual personality the person thinks he has and also for the personality he would ideally like to have. The relationship (i.e., correlation) between these two ratings yields a measure of the extent to which the person is integrated and content—in other words, a measure that starts to get at self-actualization. Table 5–2 shows the average relationship as given by correlation coefficients taken on twenty-five patients before counseling, immediately after termination of the session, and six to twelve months later.

The results indicate fairly clearly a degree of improvement which seems relatively permanent, and this improvement is in respect to the whole personality. In this sense, it appears to reflect an alteration brought about by some fundamental motivational change which we might refer to the self-actualization principle.

Many other experiments have been done by Rogers' group on the effects of therapy on person-

Table 5-2 Self-ideal relationship as a function of therapy

	Average correlation between self and ideal (25 cases)
Precounseling	−.01
Postcounseling	.36
Follow-up (6–12 months)	.32

ality. The main point to be made here, however, relates only to the motivational principle that Rogers, Jung, and others have hypothesized.

ECONOMICS

As already indicated, the economics of personality deals with the different ways energy arising from instinctual sources can be handled and distributed in respect to the person and his environment. As one writer (Munroe, 1955) has indicated, a consideration of this problem of economics simply deals with "how personality works." In the balance of the present chapter we have brought together in brief form most of the information we have gained so far.

According to Freud, instincts originate in the id. The aim of the id is the complete and immediate satisfaction of its needs. This can be achieved, however, only if the demands of reality and the demands of the superego allow it. Reality may exert concrete physical constraints against instinct satisfaction. For example, a tribesman in a primitive hunting community must work hard to obtain food. Likewise, the superego, which borrows energy from the id, puts up internal barriers, or countercathexes, against the satisfaction of id impulses. Clearly, then, the ego must work to resolve these possible conflicts to avoid a breakdown of personality, just as an arbitration board must work to settle a labor-management dispute in order to save the country from economic collapse. In personality, those conflicts are felt as tensions, or *anxiety*. The ego attempts to reduce this anxiety by means of a number of standard techniques called *defenses*, or *defense mechanisms*.

Obviously, there are many individual differences in the form that these defenses will take. No two people are quite alike. Nonetheless, classifications are possible, and a number have been suggested by various writers. Since we do not intend this to be an exhaustive presentation, we will look at only a few of the more important ones. We will also consider some experimental studies that have bearing on them.

Repression

We have already referred to this mechanism several times and have stated that it is a key concept in psychoanalytic theory. It refers essentially to two processes:

1. *Primal repression,* which is a withholding from consciousness of material that would be painful if it became conscious. Id impulses striving for expression set off danger signals felt as anxiety. These activate repression automatically and unconsciously.

2. *Afterexpulsion,* or repression proper. This is the pushing back into the unconscious of those conscious ideas or mental processes that have been associated with the repressed impulse. The forgetting of names, slips of the tongue, and other psychopathological phenomena of everyday life involve such repression. Since repressed impulses and materials continually exert pressure against the countercathexes holding them back, they often "return," or slip out, in various symptomatic acts. According to Freud, much of the forgetting of childhood events, especially pregenital sexual urges, is due to repression occurring around the ages of five to six (the Oedipal stage).

As will become clear later, repression is a basic mechanism in the sense that it is involved in almost all the other common defenses. Perhaps for this reason, much experimental work has been done on it (Zeller, 1950). These studies do not, of course, attempt to "prove" it. We already know from observed case studies that it does exist. What they really aim to do is to gain experimental control over it so that it can be evoked in a subject at the will of the experimenter. If this can be done successfully, then the researcher can start uncovering the essential dimensions of repression in a precise and scientific way. The following is one of the better examples of studies done on the problem:

Example 5–5 *Repression in an experimental setting (Keet, 1948)*

The purpose of the study was primarily to compare the effectiveness of several forms of therapy in a counseling situation. One method, called the *interpretive,* involved interpretation by the counselor of areas of difficulty the subject was having. In the other—the *expressive*—the patient was merely called upon to express his feelings and attitudes about the area of difficulty. Repression entered the picture incidentally but was a crucial variable in the study.

College students were used as subjects. The experiment consisted of four parts:

Phase A. By means of an association test, areas of difficulty were picked out for each subject. Words were spoken to the subject who had to give another word in response, for example, "cat—dog," "mother—father," and so forth. Emotion-arousing words were revealed by a number of indices as follows: *blocking,* that is, no association given by the subject to the stimulus word; *long reaction time,* a slower than average response to a particular word; *clang associations,* for example, "book—look."

Phase B. Subjects were requested to learn material which contained one of the traumatic words. Performance on this learning task was compared with performance on a neutral learning task.

Phase C. Therapy, either expressive or interpretive, was given.

Phase D. Subjects were required to learn another set of words, of equivalent difficulty, again containing a traumatic word.

Results were as follows: In phase B, subjects found it harder to learn material containing a traumatic word than neutral material. This itself indicated some kind of repression. In addition, therapy, particularly the interpretive method, was fairly successful in eliminating the difficulty of learning traumatic words. Thus we find that words connected with areas of initial tension tend to be forgotten easily (afterexpulsion). Further therapeutic reduction of the tension relating to them lifts the repression to some degree and allows them to be recalled more readily.

This demonstration is by no means complete, but it is highly suggestive and could well be followed up along various lines.

Reaction Formation

This mechanism defends against the expression of an impulse by exaggerating an opposite tendency. The story "The Fox and the Grapes," from which we have the expression "sour grapes," involves this mechanism. Repression is crucially involved, but because of the strength of the wish an additional safeguard is added. The chief symptom of reaction formation lies in the excessive and exaggerated behavior forms adopted. Overpoliteness often masks unconscious hostility. Extreme and meticulous tidiness often masks a strong desire to be messy and disorderly. Strong puritanical feelings about sex may hide equally strong sexual wishes. Sometimes direct expression of the impulse alternates with its opposite, as illustrated by the following case:

Example 5-6 *Reaction formation (Munroe, 1955)*

Mildred, a college student, was referred for psychotherapy because she was failing in her studies in spite of adequate intelligence. Teacher accounts of her were quite contradictory. One claimed she was overconscientious and meticulous; another, that she was inexcusably careless and messy. Inspection of her notebooks confirmed both reports. General messiness was interspersed with areas of perfect neatness and orderliness. Mildred's room paralleled her notebook. One bureau drawer was perfectly arranged. In another, there was a disarray of clean and soiled clothes plus a pen and papers and books hastily thrown together.

This case is perhaps extreme, but we can all probably think of people who behave in a similar manner. Reaction formation is often encouraged unwittingly in children by parents and educators who force the child to adopt meticulous habits of order and cleanliness in order to guard against "dirtiness."

Projection

In the New Testament, Christ was referring to the possibility of projection on the part of the Pharisees when he said, "He that is without sin among you, let him first cast a stone...." The hostile person can always find hostility in others. The latent homosexual sees homosexuality everywhere around him. Any strong attribution of an undesirable trait by one person to another probably involves some degree of projection. The following hypothetical case will illustrate:

Example 5–7 *Projection*

John is a college athlete and plays varsity football. He is an amiable if aggressive personality and is somewhat vain about his physical development. He is very masculine in his outlook and likes nothing better than "an evening with the boys" but is gruff and shy in the company of women. The favorite targets for his contempt are nonathletes, most of whom he dismisses as effeminate.

Later on after successfully completing his undergraduate degree, John gets a good job in a small business company. He marries but finds to his dismay that he is impotent. Psychiatric examination later reveals that John has never previously attempted any sexual advances to girls he has taken out and has always felt, in fact, a slight revulsion for women. His failure in sexual relations is, then, due to a latent homosexuality—quite unknown to himself—which he tends to project to others who appeared physically to be less masculine than himself.

On the experimental side, one study by Sears (1936) is worth noting:

Example 5–8 *Experimental study of projection (Sears, 1936)*

Sears used college students as subjects. He gave them a list of traits such as orderliness, obstinacy, and stinginess on which to rate themselves and their fellows. The difference between each person's rating of himself and the average rating given him by everyone else he took as a measure of insight. What he found was that persons high in a trait but also lacking insight into this fact were more likely to attribute the trait to other people. For example, an individual whom other people considered to be very bashful but who did not think of himself in this way tended to think that everyone was bashful. Interestingly enough, projection for positive as well as negative traits was found; for example, those who were noted as generous but who did not consider themselves to be so tended to see others as generous. This somewhat contradicts the classic Freudian position in which only undesirable attributes are projected and suggests the phenomenon may have a broader meaning than that usually given to it.

Fixation and Regression

These two mechanisms are usually considered together, since they are complementary. As we shall see in the section on development, they are both crucial to the understanding of psychosexual development. *Fixation* refers to the arrest in development of some psychological process. For example, excessive worry on the part of the parents about toilet training may cause their child to become excessively preoccupied with it; because success in this area of behavior produces great reduction in tension (parental approval), the child fixates on it as a habitual mode of relieving anxiety. *Regression* refers simply to the tendency of a personality to return to some earlier form of fixated behavior because of present stress. Thus an adult in whom there has occurred some fixation at the anal level (to do with toilet training) might react to some stress by becoming constipated, if earlier in his life the act of withholding feces, in the sense of not soiling himself, met with strong parental approval. We will now look first at a brief case study and then at some experimental work on fixation and regression.

Example 5–9 *Regression (Fenichel, 1946)*

Mild regressive behavior is very commonly seen in everyday life. The common habit of nail biting under frustrating circumstances signifies a temporary regression to a previously fixated form of oral-sadistic behavior. At a more complex level, tics may mean the same thing. Fenichel (1946) cites two relevant cases: the first of these—a hysterical patient—had been trained "never to show his emotions." His facial tic, which appeared in tense situations, represented the mimetic expression of a suppressed crying of which he was quite unaware. Actually, he had a tendency to cry rather easily, and the tic acted as a protection against such regressive behavior.

The second case, on the other hand, was of a tic that represented an intended but forbidden laughter at the patient's father. Here there had occurred fixation at the particular stage of development during which the basic relationship with parents is established—the Oedipal period. The patient's personality, when under stress, tended to regress to this level.

A good deal of experimental work has been done on fixation and regression. The two studies given below can serve as examples.

Example 5–10 *Fixation and frustration in the white rat (Maier, 1949)*

One of the first to demonstrate abnormal fixation in the laboratory was N. R. F. Maier (1949). His work was done with rats on a so-called Lashley jumping stand, shown in Figure 5–4. The rat is made to become hungry and then taught to jump toward one "window" covered with a card to get food. If it chooses the correct one, the card simply falls back, and the animal gets its food. If the wrong one is chosen, however, the card remains stationary, causing the rat to fall into the net below. This acts as a "punishment," or "negative reinforcement." Under such circumstances, most rats learn eventually to discriminate the cues and jump correctly.

Following this, the task is suddenly made impossible by not rewarding the same choice consistently. In addition, the animal is forced to jump by directing an air blast at his rear or giving it a sharp rap on the tail. Under such highly frustrating conditions, Maier found that his subjects would adopt stereotyped habits of jumping—for example, always to the left side. Even if this window was kept permanently closed and the other left permanently open, the fixated rat continued (for as many as 200 trials) to perform the same stereotyped response. In contrast, normally trained animals had no difficulty in shifting from one card to another, or from one side to the other. Because the response habits produced by the frustration were so resistant to change and also so maladaptive, Maier referred to them as *abnormal fixations*.

There have been numerous repetitions of Maier's experiment and also a number of attempts to refute his theoretical explanation of his data. Basically, the conclusion that frustration produces fixation seems to stand up well.

Obviously children are not rats. But there seems little doubt that they are often put into similar situations by the inconsistent rearing practices of parents and that they may respond in roughly the same way the rat does. Suppose, for example, a

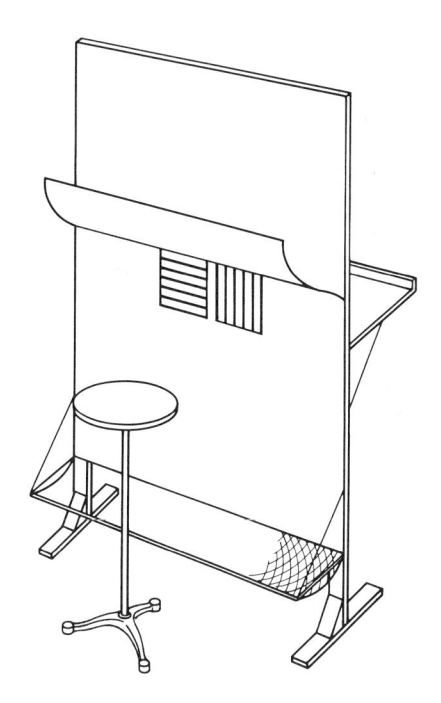

FIG. 5–4 Lashley jumping stand. (*Lashley, 1930*)

little boy of about seven is fond of taking a Teddy bear to bed with him. The parents may alternatively regard this behavior as cute and lovable and hence reward it and, at other times, view it as immature and unmasculine and hence punish it. We might not be too surprised to find the boy giving up all attempts to tackle this unsolvable problem and fixating firmly on cuddling his Teddy bear. The very common attraction young children often develop for old baby blankets may be produced in the same way. Furthermore, the way more thoughtful mothers often break the habit, namely, by slowly directing the child away from the blanket (for example, by cutting it down gradually in size until it is quite small), is very similar to that found by Maier to be successful with fixated rats. Gently pushing the rat to jump at the correct side was effective in most cases.

Example 5–11 *Frustration and regression in young children (Barker, Dembo, & Lewin, 1941)*

The experimenters made up a scale or measure of "play constructiveness" to yield a "play age" in monthly units. This was then applied to a group of thirty nursery school children who were rated on the scale. Later on, each child was given some attractive new toy to play with for a short period, following which the old toys were substituted for the new without any explanations. Only a screen separated the child from the new toys, so that they were completely visible though inaccessible. The result of this frustration was a sharp drop in constructiveness of play—on the average, a loss equivalent of 17.3 months of mental age. Such behaviors were observed as stuttering, crying and whimpering, smashing old toys, thumb sucking, or complete apathy. Barker, Dembo, and Lewin have preferred to call this change "primitivation" rather than regressive behavior.

Displacement

By this mechanism an impulse is directed from its proper object to a substitute. This is a fairly common type of behavior, but it may take very subtle and complex forms. For example, concern about the genitals may be displaced to the nose or some other part of the body; it may be displaced to some object, such as shoes. There is no end to the possibilities for such substitutions. Let us look at a concrete case (Munroe, 1955).

Example 5–12 *A case of displacement (Munroe, 1955)*

Sydney was a college student who came for treatment because he had failed college despite a very high intelligence and a good high school record. The parents were especially surprised, since he was a model boy at home and full of promises for reform and showed a sincere desire to succeed. The college dean, however, told a different story. The boy was careless about attending lectures, and impudent and rebellious toward all college authorities.

Gradually it came out that Sydney had a strong unconscious hostility to his parents, especially his father. Under the stress of a new environment plus a belated adolescent concern with sex, the boy's attitude to his father came out, but it was displaced from its original object to a new one, namely, the college dean. The displacement was made the more readily in view of the fact that the boy's father was an alumnus of the same college.

A number of experiments might be cited to illustrate displacement. Perhaps more than any of the other mechanisms, it can be related to the behavioristic theories of learning, which we will discuss in Section V. Here is an example:

Example 5–13 *Experimental study of displacement (Miller, 1939)*

The goal of this study was the demonstration of the phenomenon of displacement of aggression in white rats. Pairs of rats were given electric shock in a box. Fighting between them (standing on hind paws and "boxing") was reinforced by turning off the current only when they assumed a belligerent posture. To test for displacement, a celluloid doll was later substituted for the partner rat. Would fighting behavior then be directed to the new object?

The data indicated clearly that, in the absence of the original object to which it had been previously directed, aggression was displaced to the new object—the doll. If both a partner rat and a doll were present, the doll was ignored.

This experiment indicated that aggressive responses do become generalized to new stimuli. Strictly speaking, however, true displacement would be demonstrated only if fighting was directed to the doll after the subject had been punished for aggression to the original object, that is, the partner animal. Though this has not been tried in this context, there are available enough data from similar experiments to predict that it probably would happen.

Sublimation

Sublimation is sometimes classified as a defense mechanism, since it is, in a sense, simply another way of handling the distribution of energy in personality. However, it is not strictly a *defense*, inasmuch as it represents the *normal*, or *healthy*, mode of reaction and is not elicited by anxiety. We might also add that it is a most complex process and is not well understood. The conventional defenses are more easily identified and occur more frequently in a clinical setting.

Sublimation, unlike the defense mechanism, does not involve repression. No countercathexes are used to inhibit the original impulse. Instead, the aim and object of the impulse are transformed in such a way that the resultant behavior is not only desexualized but also culturally valuable. Perhaps we would be going beyond Freud to suggest that the energy normally utilized by instinct functions is taken over to support ego functions, but this would generally seem to be the case. To make this clear we can compare more sublimated with less sublimated behavior in two hypothetical cases:

Example 5–14 *Sublimation*

We have two surgeons. One appears almost to relish recommending and performing operations. He does these with meticulous care and skill and is usually highly successful. However, he does seem to prefer an operation when perhaps less drastic measures might be feasible. We find, in addition, that he tends to be cold and sarcastic with those under him and tyrannical at home. The second surgeon is like the first except that he avoids the excesses of the first. He is conservative about operating, does not insist on order when it is irrelevant, and obviously gains satisfaction in operating mainly insofar as it is a means of saving a life or regaining the health of the patient. He does not obtain any "secondary gains" from his vocation, as does the first surgeon.

The difference is a subtle one and is perhaps more readily experienced than read about, but it is nonetheless real and represents what we mean by saying that in sublimation both instinctual aims and objects are transformed.

It is clear that different people may engage in different professional or cultural activities for quite different reasons. Two artists, poets, doctors, philosophers, or mystics may behave in almost exactly the same way. But their motivations and satisfactions may be entirely different, a fact that may become apparent only under special conditions, for example, stress or hardship.

Character and Personality

Character and personality are also sometimes regarded as defenses against anxiety. Used in this sense the terms have the special meaning of *habitual modes of response*. Character here does *not* mean "moral forcefulness," and personality does *not* mean the total psyche in the sense in which we have used it before, nor does it mean personality in the "life of the party" sense.

As used here, the meanings of these terms are more readily available to what is often called "clinical insight" than to experimental analysis. In character defense, the ego and its mental functions may be thought of as constituting a kind of armor that is very hard to penetrate by means of psychotherapy. The juvenile delinquent represents a good example of this. Here we have a complex mode of behaving that ramifies in all directions. The delinquent may steal, do bodily harm to people, rebel against authority, and feel quite justified in all three types of behavior. He may strongly resist any form of treatment and explain his actions in a highly rational way as due to certain very real environmental pressures, such as a broken home, a "tough" neighborhood, or poverty. There is a certain unity in his behavior that allows us to collect it under one heading, namely, character, and this character is clearly a complex defense against deep anxieties. In such a case, we speak of a character disorder. Precisely because the defenses involved are so numerous, so well-worked out, and so tied to reality, they are very difficult to penetrate. Consequently, Freud himself doubted very much that character disorders were amenable to psychoanalytic therapy. Yet, today, they are probably one of the most common forms of mental illness and represent a pressing social problem.

CHAPTER 6

THE DEVELOPMENT OF PERSONALITY

Although they elaborate it in different ways, most psychoanalytically oriented writers and many contemporary personality theorists agree on this major postulate: *environmental influences during early development are crucial in forming the basis of personality.* This is to say, if a personality is assessed at some time in adulthood, we can say that its special characteristics are due more to causal agencies that occurred earlier in life than to agencies that occurred later.

This proposition is by no means as obvious as it sounds. Later events might be more important than earlier, or, possibly, they might have the same value, other things being equal. Certainly, when this postulate was first presented by Freud on the basis of his clinical experience, it was regarded with some surprise by the lay and scientific world. The idea that any of the "sensible" acts of a grown-up person could be permeated through and through by motives left over from the first years of life was hardly credible to most people. Today, the weight of clinical and experimental evidence strongly supports Freud's idea. We still do not know, however, exactly why it should be so, though we shall explore some possibilities later on. First let us look at the story of development as Freud outlined it.

The basic concepts involved in the psychoanalytic theory of development are *stages, fixation,* and *regression* (Munroe, 1955). That is to say, first, Freud looked on development as being made up of a number of main stages, or *critical periods*, rather than as a simple, continuous process. Secondly, he thought that *arrests,* or *fixations,* occurring for specifiable reasons at some stages could produce permanent effects on personality. Third, he hypothesized that under the pressure of some stress, the adult personality would return psychologically, or *regress,* to a fixated stage. Freud's notion of development may thus be characterized as *epigenetic,* in the sense that emphasis is placed on the interaction between maturational and environmental factors in determining personality.

THE STAGES OF DEVELOPMENT

Prenatal and Paranatal Stages

Although Freud did not concern himself very much with influences occurring before birth, other psychoanalysts, notably Greenacre (1941) and Fodor (1949), have suggested that they are most important. Certainly, we know from a great deal of experimental work in embryology that the fetus is not completely protected from external forces and that the effects of many such forces acting on the mother are in fact transmitted to the fetus via the maternal-fetal blood exchange across the placenta. Granting the fact that prenatal influences can occur, there seem to be two possibilities about the nature of these influences. One is that ideas, aptitudes, and needs can be transferred from mother to fetus. The evidence for such a view is negligible. There are no neural connections between mother and fetus, and the physiological makeup of the fetus is probably not equipped for complex ideation. Consequently, we may discount this theory. The second possibility, suggested by Greenacre, is simply that a characteristic level of emotional response may be set by prenatal influences on the fetus. This view is today supported by experimental data. Maternal stress during pregnancy can produce changes in the fetus, and these changes appear postnatally in the form of altered emotional responsiveness. Following are two supportive experiments, one with animals, the other with human beings.

Example 6–1 *The effects of prenatal maternal anxiety on behavior of offspring (Thompson et al., 1962)*

The writers' purpose was to discover whether emotional stress undergone by mother rats during pregnancy could affect the emotional behavior of the offspring. Ten female and ten male rats were used as parents. Sixty offspring from these matings were tested later. Five of the female rats (experimental) were trained to make a certain reaction to avoid an electric shock signaled by a buzzer. The reaction was to press a catch to open a door which led to a nonshock compartment. When this task had become well-established, these five females were mated to the males. At the same time, the five control animals were also mated to the same males.

As soon as the experimental females were known to be pregnant, they were subjected several times daily to the buzzer which before had signaled shock and were not allowed to make the avoidance response. No shock was given. It was assumed that the buzzer would arouse anxiety (because of previous association with shock) and that this anxiety could not be reduced or alleviated, because the normal way they did this before (the avoidance response) was blocked. Hence, a generalized state of anxiety should be activated. To avoid affecting the fetus directly, no shocks were given during pregnancy. This procedure was followed until the females gave birth to their litters. During the same period, control females went through their gestation period normally. Cross fostering was used to control for postnatal influences. That is to say, some offspring born of experimental mothers were reared by normal mothers, and some offspring of normal mothers were reared by experimental mothers. This procedure is crucial in any study of this kind.

When the offspring from these matings reached about 40 days of age, they were given two tests of emotional reactivity. One of these involved mainly the amount of activity in an open-field apparatus (a fairly large box, open at the top). The other involved the length of time it took an animal to leave its home cage and go down an open 3-foot runway to food. Both tests were repeated at about 140 days of age. On these two tests, statistically significant differences were found between offspring from stressed mothers and offspring from normal mothers. These data are shown in Table 6–1. High scores on the first test and low scores on the second test indicate low emotionality.

It seems clear from these data that some maternal influences do occur, that stress or emotion undergone by the mother during pregnancy can affect offspring temperament. Subsequent experiments by the same writers and others have in the main supported this conclusion, though they have also revealed new complications. For example, depending on how severe the stress is and when it occurs, the offspring may be more emotional or *less* emotional. It seems that in some ways mild stress has "good" effects in the sense of producing offspring that are more intelligent and more stable than untreated controls. Too severe stress produces just the opposite result.

Table 6–1 The effects of prenatal maternal stress on offspring emotion in rats

	Open field (activity level)		Runway (latency)	
	Age 40 days	Age 140 days	Age 40 days	Age 140 days
Experimental offspring	86.0	114.5	23.7	11.6
Control offspring	134.5	162.3	11.8	6.2

The above experiment has no exact parallels in studies on human beings. However, one investigator, Pasamanick, with his collaborators has obtained data which show an association between some physical stresses of pregnancy and labor and behavior disorders in offspring resulting from these pregnancies.

Example 6–2 *Pregnancy stress and behavior disorders (Pasamanick et al., 1956)*

The purpose of this study was to demonstrate an association between difficulties incurred by mothers during pregnancy and incidence of behavior disorders in their offspring. The experimenters collected 1,151 cases of children under sixteen years of age having behavior disorders for which they had been referred to a clinic for counseling or psychotherapy. Nine hundred and two normal controls were also used. The two groups were matched as to age, sex, socioeconomic background, and other variables. Experimentals (subjects with disorders) were compared with controls in respect to medical data relating to pregnancy experience of mothers. The results of the survey are set out in Table 6–2.

The data indicate that physical difficulties or stress during pregnancy do appear to be significantly associated with behavior disorders in children. So far, we do not know to what extent postnatal factors are also at work in producing such an association. That is to say, it is possible that a mother may behave quite differently to her baby either because of her changed physiological state or because she resents the child who caused her the trouble. These possibilities have not been closely examined.

The two experiments suggest that prenatal experiences can definitely have effects on personality that persist for some time. Obviously, we still have a great deal more to find out in this connection.

Paranatal variables, that is, those connected with the actual process of birth itself, have also been the subject of speculation. One analyst, Otto Rank, has claimed that birth is a serious traumatic experience of which the infant is actually aware at an ideational level. That is to say, for the infant, birth has meaning and represents a separation from the mother

Table 6-2 Percentage of complications of pregnancy among mothers of children with behavior disorders and mothers of normal controls

	White	Nonwhite
Behavior disorder cases	3.6	8.6
Normal controls	2.8	6.6

whose womb he has blissfully enjoyed for several months. This kind of idea has little basis in fact, since, as we have already pointed out, such ideation is undoubtedly beyond the capacity of the neonate. At the same time, however, it is true that the act of birth is regarded by all persons as an important event and many myths surround it. Freud's own idea was simply that birth brings about strong stimulation of an organism hitherto largely protected from it and that this experience may produce increased sensitivity to any kind of stress later on.

Polymorphous Perverse Stage

For the newborn infant, according to Freud, the world is probably confused, unstructured, and meaningless. Not only is he rather undifferentiated from the world in his own mind, lacking as he does the awareness than an adult has of a sharp distinction between himself and reality, but he is all id, and as such his mental activity can be described as *primary process*. Images and ideas are associated without regard to logic and primarily according to their close occurrence together in time and space. Important among such primary associations is the one between the mother and comfort or release from unpleasant stimulation such as hunger. Because the mother is so crucial in this regard, the infant is thought to establish with her a *primary identification*, in the sense that he comes to regard her as part of himself.

We may infer the importance of primary identification with the mother from observing what happens to the infant when the normally close contact it usually has with the mother is for some reason not established. The example following bears directly on this point, though it does not tell us much about the nature of the process of primary identification itself.

Example 6–3 *Importance for the neonate of contact with the mother (Ribble, 1944)*

Margaret Ribble, a pediatrician, opened up a new field in psychology when she reported her findings on neonates who had been separated from their mothers at birth for reasons of health. In a large percentage of the more than six hundred cases studied, she observed a general "wasting away" characterized by passivity, abnormal physiological responsiveness, excessive vomiting and crying, and sometimes coma and death. She called this syndrome *marasmus*. Though her results were reported by her in rather a casual form, there seems to be no doubt that early maternal separation can have very drastic effects on the health of the child. Another pediatrician, René Spitz, has reported essentially the same findings.

Many psychologists, however, have quarreled with Ribble's explanation of the phenomenon in terms of an alleged "physiological instability" of infants and their consequent need for a "love object" (cf. Pinneau, 1950). Actually these are both moot points. The young infant is certainly unstable in many ways in that it reacts inefficiently to stresses and shows a good deal of unevenness of physiological functioning (cf. Wolstenholm, 1961). Furthermore, although at birth it cannot need a love object in the adult sense, it probably does need contact comfort of the kind supplied by a mother holding and cuddling it. It is now a well-documented fact that young rats and mice which are given special handling or stimulation beyond what they would normally get from their mother show faster growth, greater resistance to stress, and often less emotionality. Consequently, we may conclude that the affection a mother usually gives her newborn baby is functionally valuable to him, not because the mother is being "nice" to him, but rather because a by-product of affection is stimulation, which does have a direct value.

To document this important point a little more fully our next example presents some of the large amount of work done on the effects of handling in rats.

Example 6–4 *Effects of early stimulation on behavior and development of young rats and mice (Weininger, 1953; Denenberg, 1966)*

Weininger designed this study to explore the effects of early "mothering" on the later behavior of rats. He gave to half of the animals, shortly after weaning (twenty-one to twenty-five days), special artificial "mothering" by removing them once a day from the home cage and stroking them for a short period. During this time, the controls (nonhandled) were left alone. Later on, at an adult age, all animals were given various tests designed to measure emotionality and resistance to stress. These included amount of activity in a small arena, weight, and internal damage following the severe stress involved in being strapped down to a board for forty-eight hours without food and water. Results showed that, in terms of the test given, handled animals proved to be considerably less emotional than nonhandled rats and were more resistant to stress. Not only did they show less internal physiological damage as a result of the restraint and deprivation, but also more of them tended to survive it.

Weininger's original data have been replicated and extended by many other workers, notably Levine (1962) and Denenberg (1966). It is thus a well-established conclusion that stimulation early in life tends to produce faster development, less emotionality, and greater stress resistance. The type of stimulation is irrelevant. Heat, cold, electric shocks, handling, or vibrating are about equivalent. Beyond a certain intensity, however, the opposite holds true. Too much stimulation has as adverse effects as too little. This conclusion is documented by data of Denenberg and Karas (1960) shown in Figure 6–1. The graph shows that no handling at all and a great deal of handling (one to twenty days) produced less avoidance learning, that is, the ability to avoid shock whose onset is signaled by a stimulus. The moderately handled groups behaved optimally in this situation. Thus lack of extra stimulation and strong stimulation paradoxically have equivalent effects with the measure used. This is not to say, of course, that all the behavior changes they produce are going to be the same. It is unreasonable to suppose that such radically different treatments do not at some point produce effects that are also very different.

The human and animal studies thus agree in their conclusions and together give support to Freud's conception of the infant-mother relation in the earliest part of life. Without any doubt, the mother is most important to the welfare of her baby at this

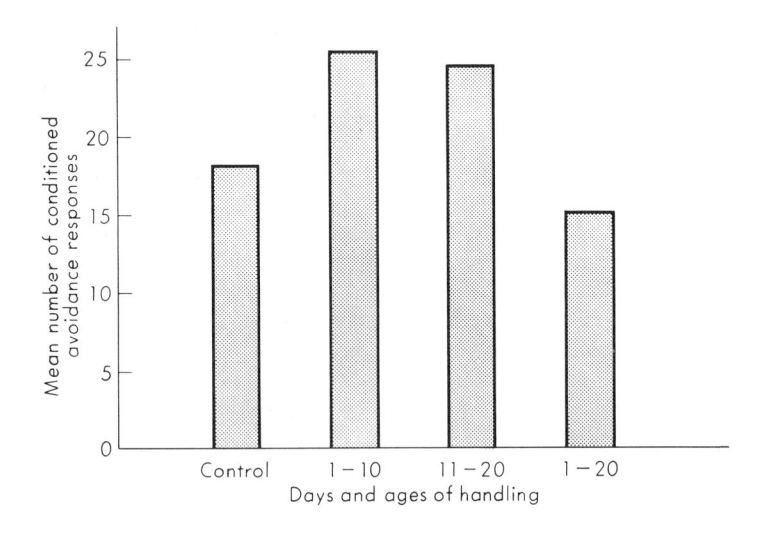

FIG. 6–1 Relation between amount of stimulation in infancy and later behavior (avoidance conditioning). (*Denenberg & Karas, 1960*)

age, insofar as she simply provides sensory stimulation. From a Freudian viewpoint, this is quite reasonable. The infant's sexuality is polymorphous—that is, distributed all over his body. Gross bodily stimulation gained by contact with his mother is both pleasurable and useful.

As the child grows older, his psychosexual energy, according to Freud, starts to focus, or concentrate, on various bodily regions. The first of these is the oral region—lips, mouth, and oral cavity.

The Oral Stage: Birth to Two or Three Years

The newborn child during a large portion of its waking hours is engaged in sucking. In fact, it does rather little else besides sleeping and eating, though, as we have just seen, it also likes and needs gross stimulation. Because of this preoccupation with eating and sucking, according to Freud, libido becomes focalized on the mouth as a main erotic zone. This is not to say that the oral period totally replaces the polymorphous period. The two obviously overlap and are similar in that both involve autoerotic satisfaction. But the oral phase has another specific aim, namely, incorporation of objects in the outside world which can in this way be made part of the individual. Finally, with the eruption of teeth another aim is added, the destruction of objects or expression of hostility by biting. Thus we have three types of orality, *pleasure sucking*, *oral incorporativeness*, and *oral sadism*. It is likely that these phases succeed each other in time.

It is probably in this period of life that the child starts forming some basic concept of relationships with others. Gradually, he learns a distinction between self and other (the mother), though he may regard the latter as in some sense belonging to him. In the oral-sadistic stage, he develops and learns to deal with *ambivalence,* that is, the simultaneous love and hate of the same object.

During the oral stage, the ego thus gradually starts to emerge, and secondary process replaces primary process as a mode of adjustment to a world that is now perceived as being real and external to the person. Some writers, notably Melanie Klein (1932), have claimed that such development starts to take place much earlier, and though this is considered doubtful by orthodox Freudians, it is a view that has considerable cogency. All that is basically needed for the germination of ego forces is the perception by the child of something which is distinct from himself that gives pleasure when it is there but which often may be absent when he wants it or may be removed when he is enjoying it. It is easy to see that certain objects in the world fulfill these conditions, notably the mother's breast. The child's relationship with this object or part object Klein has felt to be critical in later social relationships.

The notion basic to the postulation of an oral period is that libido, before unfocused and hence polymorphous, now concentrates on the oral region.

Things to do with the mouth then become pleasurable or erogenous. We may therefore ask, What is the evidence for oral eroticism? Much of it is, of course, clinical. In the course of psychoanalytic treatment, patients do in fact produce fantasy material of a clearly oral character. Furthermore, we find a great deal of oral eroticism (kissing, for example) acting as a prelude to sexual relations. Some sexual perversions are frankly oral in nature, for example, kissing or touching with the mouth the partner's genitals. As Freud pointed out, these perversions are common in the unions of quite normal married people and hence are not abnormal in a statistical sense at any rate. In addition, as we have already indicated, babies and many adults, for that matter, show obvious pleasure in oral activity. They suck pencils, their fingers, or any available objects for prolonged periods, quite independently of whether they are hungry or not. It is perhaps due only to the puritanism of our society that there occurred in the 1920s such a vigorous antagonism to the use of the pacifier in quieting infants.

Adult oral reactions as described above are certainly very common indeed. How is it that they persist for such a long time? The answer of psychoanalytic theory is that fixations have occurred at the oral level, due to either *excessive indulgence* or *frustration*, and that under the pressure of later anxiety, the personality regresses in part to that level. When many such oral fixations are woven together in a coherent way, we have what is called the *oral character*, that is, a person who uses predominantly oral modes of defenses against anxiety. Some examples of these modes are excessive talking, smoking, eating, and even sarcasm or wit.

As we have already indicated, orality can be fixated due to excessive frustration and/or overindulgence. Some experimental data bearing on this point have been collected by David Levy (1934).

Example 6-5 *Frustration and oral fixations (Levy, 1934)*

This study demonstrates the importance of a sucking drive in young puppies and examines some consequences of the frustration of this drive. The experimental group of puppies was allowed to suck from milk bottles with a large hole in the nipple, so they could satisfy hunger quickly with a minimum of sucking. The control animals sucked from bottles whose nipples had a small hole, thus necessitating a great deal of sucking to obtain a small amount of milk. In a later comparison between the experimentals and controls it was found that experimentals did much more body sucking and chewing of any available materials between meals than controls. The data thus indicated that besides a need to ingest food, dogs and perhaps all mammals also need a certain amount of nonnutritional oral gratification. If not satisfied when food is ingested, the oral drive will be satisfied in other ways irrespective of hunger.

The Anal Stage: One to Three Years

In the second major stage of psychosexual development, psychoanalytic theorists have hypothesized that libido focuses on the anal region. Three points may be made in this connection: first, the child and most adults probably obtain pleasure from urinating and defecating, though due to repression society does not generally accept these functions as sources of pleasure; second, learning control over these functions is one important way by which the child gains real mastery over himself and his environment; third, excreta are, in a sense, the first products that originate from the child, that he creates, as it were; he might therefore be expected to have some preoccupation with them. These three points add up to an important conclusion: that during this phase, the ego starts to develop strongly, since for the first time the child is made aware of his power over the environment and his potentiality for manipulation of objects.

It may sound incredible that such a lowly function as elimination could have an important part of determining personality, but it is true that most societies, especially the more advanced ones, place tremendous emphasis on toilet training. We find continual debate about how soon it should start and what methods should be used to cope with it. This concern is more than simply hygienic, since it appears in societies where general level and knowledge of hygiene is low, as among the Comanche Indians and the Tanala of Madagascar (Orlansky, 1949). In Western society, lack of training does not, in fact, seriously interfere with hygiene, due to the availability of other measures, such as diapers. Hence we can conclude only that the anal period is important because of its emotional aspects, which operate in the adult as much as they do in the child. In fact, many mothers use toilet training as a kind of yardstick by which to compare each other's success as mothers.

Again, anality appears importantly in much of our literature and culture. Chaucer and Swift are very good examples of writers who lifted, as it were, the veil of repression on anal function. Anal themes in literature have been discussed exhaustively by Brown (1959). Finally, it has been quite usual in some periods and in some countries to punish criminals by "purging" them, thus symbolically forcing them to "give up" what they had stolen or what they believed in. Fascist Italy before World War II commonly adopted this practice.

In classical psychoanalytic theory, the anal phase is divided into two phases, the first *"expulsive,"* the second *"retentive."* Each of these can have an *erotic* and a *sadistic* component. That is, both expelling and retaining functions can be enjoyable to the child, and, likewise, he can use either function as a means of influencing or even hurting his parents, by doing one when he is supposed to do the other. Thus, the act of excretion and its products in the prelogical mind of the child come to have a strong symbolic value and to stand for a great many other things. Fixations at this level are consequently thought to produce particular character traits such as parsimony, obstinacy (holding back), pedantry (giving forth), excessive neatness and orderliness (dislike of dirt). An equation is commonly made between feces and money, since in the infantile mind both are objects of value that may be given out or retained.

It should again be emphasized that we are talking about children. Most adults will find ridiculous and rather horrifying such a hypothesized connection between money and excretion. Yet if it is accepted that some notion of what is *valuable* originates in childhood and that the first things that can be considered valuable by the child may be his own feces, then it is plausible that there may be some connection.

The Phallic Stage: Three to Five Years

Starting some time around the third year and perhaps maximally in the fourth libidinal energy focuses on the genital zone. During this time an increasing interest in sex and sex play can be observed among children. Boys and girls start to obtain enjoyment from genital manipulation and pleasure in observation of other's genitals (voyeurism) or in showing off their own (exhibitionism). Boys and girls realize they are different from each other and different from the opposite sex parent. The consequences of this fact we will examine shortly. First let us look at some of the evidence for the phallic phase of development.

In general, the evidence is again largely clinical. Thus data from psychiatric case studies involving childhood memories do seem to point to the existence of such a period, and, in addition, most parents, if they look without prejudice at the children around this age, will certainly agree that there is a great deal of interest in genitals. One of the few more controlled studies on this topic, by Isaacs (1933), appears to support this conclusion. Mothers asked about the frequency of questions from their children between two and five years named the origin of babies and physical sex differences as the most frequent category.

Fixations at the phallic stage produce certain special constellations of character traits. The child at this age is autoerotic and narcissistic. He loves and admires his own body, likes to exhibit it, and also likes to investigate the bodies and sexuality of others. Consequently, a fixation at the phallic level might be expected to be represented in the adult character by traits like boastfulness, vanity, exhibitionism (as in acting), and "peeping tomism" (the burlesque house patron). It is likely that the frank sexuality manifested in teen-age dance fads and also in the reaction of this age level to their current singing idols represent a temporary regression to the phallic stage.

Another important feature of the phallic stage is that it introduces the next phase of development and the so-called *castration complex.* The genitals acquire a high value at this age. Consequently the child may come to place a value on his own and fear for their loss. In the case of the boys, this *castration fear* is encouraged by at least two factors: first, by the fact that some individuals, that is, girls, have apparently lost theirs, and, second, by the tendency of many parents to threaten him directly with their loss as a punishment for touching or manipulating them. In girls, on the other hand, we would logically expect the castration complex to have a different meaning in view of the different anatomical character of the female genitals. The girl observes she does not have something that a boy does and, as a consequence, feels she is, in a sense, incomplete. In the Freudian scheme, this notion lies at the basis of feminine psychology. We will return to this point shortly.

The Oedipal Stage: Four to Five Years

The Oedipal phase emerges out of the phallic period. Generally speaking, it concerns the relation of the child with the parents. The name of the complex derives from a play by Sophocles, *Oedipus Rex*, in which the hero Oedipus "accidentally" kills his father, the king, and "unintentionally" marries his mother, Jocasta. Since the situation is not quite the same for boys as for girls, we will consider each separately.

In boys, according to Freud, there develops a rivalry with the father for sexual possesion of the mother. The term "sexual" must, of course, be understood in a broad sense and, at this age, cannot have the same meaning for the child that it has for the adult. However, in some sense, the boy regards his mother as an object appropriate to the satisfaction of his own phallic eroticism and looks on the father as a barrier to this satisfaction. It is certainly true that in many cultures, any eroticism previously experienced by the child will have been more connected with the mother than with the father. She has held him, nursed him, probably played a large part in his toilet training, and perhaps answered his questions concerning phallic functioning. Furthermore, she is different from him sexually and as such an object of some interest. Consequently, it is not too surprising that some kind of sexual cathexis should be formed between the young boy and his mother and that his father should be regarded as an outsider or rival to this bond.

It is also likely that the parents themselves, due to remnants of their own Oedipal conflicts, directly contribute to the situation. Many mothers do, in fact, tend to "seduce" their male children, and many fathers tend to resent this "spoiling" and to show aggressive behavior to the boy. For example, the father may treat his son with contempt and deride him as a "mamma's boy." This imputation of femininity to a male child is itself a kind of symbolic castration. At the other end of the scale, the father may simply threaten actual castration, which, because of his larger size and strength, he would be theoretically capable of carrying out.

The Oedipal drama normally closes as a result of such castration anxiety. The male child comes to feel that he must give up his attachment to the mother if he is not to suffer dire consequences. As a substitute for his loss, he *introjects* the parental image, particularly that of his father, and represses all sexuality. It is this *identification* with the father by introjection of his moral values that is the basis for superego formation. It should be noted that the superego has two sides, a positive and a negative, corresponding to the emotions of pride and guilt, respectively. From now on, the child can literally be pleased with himself when he does right and ashamed of himself when he does wrong. Presumably, before the formation of the superego, the child feels for his actions no such emotions that tell him what he should do and what he should not do. He may, however, experience *shame*. This is a negative feeling consequent on an act publicly disapproved or derided by others. Guilt, by contrast, does not need the overt disapproval of others.

In general outline, the Oedipal situation and superego formation in girls resemble those in boys but differ in some important details. According to Freud, the primary feature of the castration complex in girls is envy of maleness—called, in psychoanalytic terminology, *penis envy*. That is, girls, because of the anatomical character of their sexual organs, feel that they lack something that is highly valued, which they perhaps have had taken away or removed at an earlier date. This supposed feeling of inferiority is often regarded as being responsible for a *masculine protest*—that is, aspiration to male characteristics—that may appear in women. Evidence for the existence of penis envy in young girls is again largely clinical. The few attempts at controlled studies that have been done on the subject are ambiguous. Assuming the validity of the Freudian claim, however, let us look at its consequences.

Unlike the male complex, which ends the Oedipal situation and represses sexuality, the female castration complex initiates the Oedipal relation. Having already apparently been castrated, the girl attempts to compensate for her loss by the wish to have a baby or some symbolic counterpart by the father. As a consequence, the girl transfers to the father the love that she, like the boy, formerly held toward the mother. She now comes to regard the mother as a rival for her father's affection. In the normal course of events, she then gradually introjects the feminine character traits of her mother as a way of becoming a proper love object for her father. It should be noted that because the Oedipal situation of the girl is not sharply ended by the castration complex, as it is in the boy, there is less reason for her to give it up. This means, in turn, that identification and superego formation will be less complete in the girl than in the boy. For this reason, according to Freud, the female character is typically less moral, more impulsive, more governed by emotion as compared with the male character.

Freud's analysis of the female character has not appealed to many prominent women writers, notably Simone de Beauvoir (1953) and Betty Friedan (1963). They feel that Freud, who was part of the strongly masculine culture of nineteenth-century Vienna and who himself was somewhat maladjusted in respect to sexuality, offered a biased and typically "male" account of feminine psychology. Yet, at the same time, if we assume Freud's analysis was correct, the outcomes of a deficient superego formation are not all bad. Indeed, the Freudian superego can be a stifling and constricting influence, so that while males may well be more "socialized," they may be correspondingly less empathic to the needs of others and less sensitive to individual social relationships (cf. Section III).

The Latent Period: Five to Twelve Years

With the close of the Oedipal situation, the latent period commences. This phase of psychosexual development is called latent precisely because sexuality, repressed by the superego, remains dormant until puberty. Boys during this age become very masculine and shun the company of girls, whom they now start to despise. Any kind of sex play in which they indulge is autoerotic or homosexual. Girls, as might logically be predicted from their Oedipal situation, are not nearly as clannish and homosexual as boys, in whom they still show an interest. Just as a matter of casual observation, the anti-boy attitude of girls during the latent period seems to be more a *reaction* to the basic unfriendliness of boys, rather than a genuine, spontaneous feeling. Girls are often eager to participate in boys' games if allowed to do so, but the reverse is seldom if ever true. Toward puberty, the physiological changes that occur force a resurgence of sexuality, which commences to appear again in the often curious, sporadic modes characteristic of adolescent culture. These changes mark the beginning of the final stage of psychosexual development—the genital stage.

The evidence for the existence of the latent period is somewhat shaky. The surveys that have been made show little evidence for a real decline in sexual interest. There seems little doubt that boys turn away from female company during this time, but this may be heavily conditioned by culture. In Europe and most of the West, male sports and activities are instituted soon after the age of six, and from these girls are necessarily excluded. But the situation does not apply in all societies, for example, among the Trobriand Islanders studied by Malinowski (1927). For these people, sex becomes increasingly direct and overt as the children get older. The same seems to be true of many other cultures.

The Genital Stage: Twelve Years and Over

Normal genitality is the end goal of psychosexual development. Libidinal energy is now again focused in the genital areas, and what remains is directed, in a desexualized form, through sublimation, toward various kinds of socially acceptable activities. In the ideal case, pregenital eroticism is now subordinated as forepleasure to the act of intercourse and eventual orgasm, rather than existing in its own right. The degree to which genitality is abnormal, however, is determined by the degree to which fixations have occurred at an earlier phase of psychosexual development.

To conclude this section, we will present two pieces of evidence bearing on the Freudian theory of development as a whole. One is a popular fairy tale; the other, an experimental study. Each in its own way gives some support to Freud's theory.

Example 6–6 *The psychoanalytic interpretation of Snow White (Brown, 1940)*

The Story

Snow White is a beautiful child princess whose widowed father has taken a second wife. The second wife is the "fairest lady in the land" and is possessed of a magic mirror which convinces her of this. As Snow White grows a little older, however, the mirror warns the stepmother that Snow White will soon become more beautiful than she. This excites the Queen's envy, and she plans to have Snow White done away with. She gives Snow White into the hands of a huntsman, commanding him to kill the child. Snow White prevails upon the huntsman, however, to free her in the woods, where she is taken care of by seven little dwarfs who work underground. The stepmother learns from the mirror of Snow White's continued existence with the dwarfs and again tries to kill her. After several unsuccessful attempts, she succeeds, not in killing Snow White, but in putting her into a comatose state. The dwarfs, however, keep Snow White in a beautiful coffin for seven years. She does not die but remains in a deep unconscious sleep. At the end of seven years, the wicked Queen is dead, and the fairy prince comes with a sword with which he opens the casket and takes Snow White to be his bride.

The Analysis

The story is clearly an Oedipal theme, involving rivalry between daughter and mother. The mother's narcissism (mirror) does not permit a rival, so she decides to kill Snow White. By means of a huntsman (probably symbolic of a masculine castrating figure) she represses (puts to sleep) Snow White for the time of the latency period from age five to twelve (seven years in a coffin, seven dwarfs working "underground"). Female sexuality, at the end of this "underground" period, is reawakened by a prince bearing a sword (male sexual organ). Thus, normal genitality is achieved.

Various details of the story also fit such an interpretation. For example, a stepmother rather than a real mother is cast as the villain to avoid the guilt that would arise from attributing such hostility to a real mother. The threat of "cutting Snow White's heart out" by the huntsman is symbolic of castration, and Snow White's bargaining with the huntsman to live in the forest if he spares her represents the Oedipal contract of reducing sexuality to avoid punishment. The fact that several visits by the Queen (disguised as a witch) were necessary symbolized the fact that the solution of the female Oedipal complex is not sudden but gradual.

Many other fairy tales and myths can be analyzed in the same manner. Good examples can be found by the interested student in the journal *The American Imago*. It must be noted that these kinds of material do not *prove* the validity of psychoanalysis, but they do lend considerable weight to its cogency by showing how the same basic motives and forces appear in the general experiences of people as expressed in folktales and legends. This is presumably why the latter have such universal appeal and persist for such a long time. The following is an experimental study of psychosexual development:

Example 6–7 *A study of the psychoanalytic theory of psychosexual development (Blum, 1949)*

For the purpose of exploring psychosexual development, a special test was evolved by Gerald Blum. This consisted of twelve pictures, or cartoons, which portray the adventures of a dog named Blacky and his relationships with Mama, Papa, and Tippy, a sibling of unspecified age and sex. Each cartoon is so chosen as to depict either a phase of psychosexual development or a type of relationship during development. It was assumed, as with other tests of this type, that the subject would project, into his interpretation of each card, his own unconscious feeling, attitudes, and fixations. Dogs were used, rather than people, to minimize the possibility that defenses might be raised against revealing true impulses. On the other hand, Blum felt that due to the impact of Disney cartoons on the general population, subjects could still freely identify with dog figures, especially at the kind of infantile level that was being explored. The kind of situation depicted in one Blacky card is shown abstractly in Figure 6–2.

College students acted as subjects. Each was asked to tell a spontaneous story about each picture. Following this, each was asked a series of direct multiple-choice or short-answer questions relating to the dimension depicted in the particular picture. A third type of question, a picture preference, was also obtained. Subjects were finally scored for three possible degrees of disturbance on

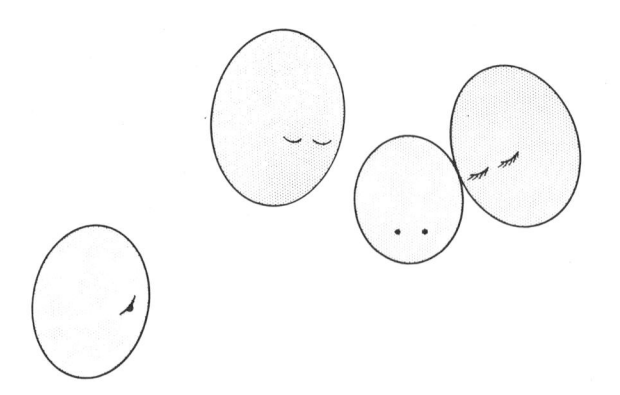

FIG. 6–2 An example of the kind of situation depicted in the Blacky test. (*Blum, 1949*)

every dimension involved, for example, oral eroticism or anal retentiveness.

The validity of a test is the degree to which it measures what it is supposed to measure. The Blacky pictures have been validated in a number of ways. One of these has been to see whether the test can actually predict a kind of mental illness known to have roots in certain kinds of early experiences. For example, as predictable from psychoanalytic theory, paranoid schizophrenics show, in comparison to controls, more evidence of oral eroticism, oral sadism, and anal retentiveness. Such a relationship was in fact found in the test. Similar agreement between the test data and psychoanalytic theory was found in regard to stutterers, peptic ulcer cases, and sexual offenders. These results were taken as compelling evidence that the test really does assess disturbances in psychosexual development. Let us now look at some of the concrete findings.

These are presented in terms of two main dimensions: (1) sex differences in psychosexual development as revealed by the test compared with those postulated by psychoanalytic theory, and (2) interrelationships of those psychoanalytic dimensions which the tests are aimed at exploring. Taking *oral sadism* as an example of the first dimension, we will first present protocols of stories for a cartoon representing strong or weak for this characteristic. This is a picture of Blacky "worrying" a dog collar. The collar is marked "Mama." Scoring is according to predetermined standards.

STRONG

Seems like Blacky has a matricidal desire. Of course, maybe he can't read, and just likes to chew and shake things. Maybe he has a fierce temper or something. Then again, maybe he's hungry, and mad because Mama isn't there to feed him.

NOT STRONG

Blacky is playful and has gotten Mama's collar away from her. She's having a wonderful time pretending it's an inanimate object, and she must fight with it so as to make it be quiet. The fierce look is fooling nobody but Blacky.

According to psychoanalytic theory as exposited by Freud himself and a leading neofreudian, Otto Fenichel, oral sadism is more prevalent in girls, specifically in reference to the mother. The Blacky test gives empirical support to this assertion. Thus significantly more females than males give the third answer in the three alternative answers to the following question:

What will Blacky do next with Mama's collar?
1. Get tired of it and leave it on the ground.
2. Return it to Mama.
3. Angrily chew it to shreds.

Besides this area, in thirteen others, males differ significantly from females. Of the fourteen, seven differences are specifically predicted by classical psychoanalytic theory. Two are predicted by inference, and five are not predicted. Blum concludes that this is good agreement, and attributes the five unpredicted differences simply to the incompleteness of psychoanalytic theory in respect to sex differences.

The second dimension, dealing with the coherence of the syntax of psychoanalytic theory, also yields a positive conclusion. An example of this is the hypothesized relation between oral eroticism and castration anxiety. Males with strong oral fixations fear castration more than others, the reason being that the oral function of biting comes to be associated with biting off and hence castration. On the Blacky test, the two indications of oral eroticism and castration anxiety show, in fact, a statistically significant correlation ($r = .35$, $p < .05$).

Blum examined eighteen such relationships predicted by psychoanalytic theory. Of these eighteen, eight were clearly found in the Blacky test. The latter also showed six relationships which could be inferred from the writings of Freud and Fenichel and three not predictable from theory. Again Blum concludes that the Blacky test provides good support for the psychoanalytic theory of development.

The experimentally minded reader will find the evidence presented in the two examples above rather slim. The myth of Snow White is obviously open to many different interpretations, of which the Freudian is only one, and it could likewise be argued that the Blacky test is so constructed as to be already biased toward agreement with psychoanalytic theory. This may be true. Yet, as we indicated in Chapter 1, the coherence of a point of view is one important criterion of its worth, as is also its fruitfulness in generating future thought and research. On these two counts at least, the examples we have given are worth something. It would certainly be useful, however, if the empirical side of the Freudian theory of development could be more closely examined than it has been to date.

OTHER VIEWS OF DEVELOPMENT

As might be expected, there have been many views about development divergent from Freud. We have already referred briefly to the position of Melanie Klein, whose main contribution was to push back to an earlier period of life the stage when events crucial for the formation of social attitudes occur. It was this stress on the importance of the very early age levels that led to a movement in psychoanalysis devoted to the understanding and analysis of young children. Though Freud himself was initially responsible for an emphasis on early experience, he himself did not observe children, and his famous analysis of Hans was carried out mostly through the boy's father.

His daughter, Anna, however, attached great importance to the direct observation of children. To deal directly with them is difficult because of their immaturity in language, and as a consequence there had to be worked out special techniques and methods allowing communication between the analyst and the young subject. These are the so-called *play techniques*. They largely dispense with the need for verbal exchange and focus instead on the manner in which the child manipulates toys representing elements of his home situation, for example, father, mother, sister, and brother dolls. The ways these are treated in play are taken by the analyst as reflecting the child's view of his world.

It must be noted, of course, that these methods are of little use below a certain age. Klein and her followers emphasize the first years of life. At such a young age, whatever unconscious fantasies the baby may have are not readily observable by any methods, and Klein's speculations about them must be considered to be no more than speculations with no appreciable empirical evidence to back them up.

Another psychoanalytically oriented writer to offer a theory of development is Erik H. Erikson. A penetrating scholar of several fields, including history, philosophy, anthropology, and psychiatry, Erikson extended in unique and interesting ways Freud's notion of childhood (Erikson, 1950). His essential contribution has been to broaden Freud's categories of psychosexual development by making a distinction between what he calls *zones, modes,* and *modalities.* The zone is the anatomical focus of libido at a particular time—the mouth, the anal region, or the genitals. The mode is the manner in which it may be used. For example, the mouth may be used to take in food, or *incorporate,* or it may be used in an *eliminative* manner as in spitting out something already taken in. The modality is the category of human existence of which a mode is the original prototype. Thus incorporation by biting is the kind of primitive behavior out of which develop later on the modality of "taking aggressively." Holding food or the nipple in the mouth—the retentive mode—produces the modality of "holding on to" and accompanying character traits of stubbornness and greediness.

We cannot present Erikson's theory of infantile development in detail. A simplified summary is presented in Table 6–3. This shows the zones along one axis and along the other axis the modes associated with a particular zone. Notice that during the phallic and genital stages male and female separate as indicated in the table.

The most important point to notice about Erikson's theory is that it greatly elaborates and extends the idea that simple habits established early can form the basis for many forms of later behavior. The baby who for various reasons needs to "root"

Table 6-3 Erikson's theory of development up to adulthood (Erikson, 1950)

Age (Years)	Zone	Major mode	Major modalities	Major problem
0–1	Oral	Incorporative Incorporative (biting)	Giving and getting	Trust vs. mistrust
1–2	Anal-urethral	Retentive Eliminative	Holding on Letting go	Autonomy vs. shame and doubt
3–5	Phallic	Intrusive (Male)	Aggression Curiosity	Initiative vs. guilt
Puberty	Genital	Inclusive (Female)	Grasping Dependence	Identity vs. role confusion
Adulthood		Generative intrusive and generative inclusive	Sharing, not sharing	

and intrude or push into his mother's breast to obtain nourishment will then form a basic habit of oral intrusiveness. This may later mean that he interrupts others, verbally attacks them, or becomes a skilled debater. All we need to accept is the proposition that early modes of action—because they occur early— form the basis of later social modalities.

Erikson is only one of a great many theorists. He does stand out, however, as a man who brought to the subject of human development a wealth of knowledge and scholarship and gave to Freud's ideas a reasonableness that did much to remove the bizarre quality they hold for many lay people. Others who have also made outstanding contributions along the same lines are Harry Stack Sullivan, Erich Fromm, Otto Rank, and Karen Horney, to mention a few. The interested reader may consult the works of these writers directly or refer to such sources as Blum (1953), Munroe (1955), and Fenichel (1946). There is little question that the topic of development is the heart and soul of psychoanalytic psychology and, in fact, of personality theory in general. As we shall see in other chapters, it is also of great importance to the other approaches examined in this book; for all living things, whatever their structure and makeup, simple or complex, show development. Freud was one of the first to give real acknowledgment to this fact.

CONCLUSION

It is a difficult task to make a final assessment of the approach to psychology taken in this section. By at least two of the criteria we are using, namely, logical coherence and empirical validity, most of the theories discussed—and this includes especially that of Freud himself—must be judged to be weak. There is no question that many of the terms commonly used in the areas of psychoanalysis and personality are so vaguely defined that it is hardly possible to find agreement on their precise meanings. Furthermore, many of the hypotheses they involve are difficult, if not impossible, to test. Can we really know what the "superego" is, or "self-actualization"? Can they be measured in any real sense? What is repression really? Is it possible to analyze such a concept in a manner rigorous enough to satisfy experimental science? The answer to all these questions is probably no. Demonstration of the validity of psychoanalytic hypotheses to a point where any guesswork or looseness of interpretation is ruled out is perhaps not possible.

Yet in spite of this, there is no doubt that the impact of Freud's ideas has been enormous. By the third criterion of fruitfulness there can hardly be any doubt that the psychoanalytic framework comes out very well indeed. Somehow, in spite of its casualness of definition and observation, it has acutely specified characteristics of human beings that stand out as salient in the experience of all thoughtful persons. Because of this, its concepts penetrate a great many contemporary theories of personality as well as the experimental study of personality variables.

Thus, though perhaps the majority of workers in the field today would probably shy away from the label "Freudian," it is nevertheless true that they still freely employ and empirically study notions about human behavior that derive from the psychoanalytic framework, for example, concepts like "conflict," "anxiety," "self-esteem," "ego strength," and "defensive behavior." A cursory inspection of almost any journal dealing with the area of personality will confirm this. For better or for worse, it is a fact that Freud has had and continues to have a strong influence on modern ideas about personality. He is not, of course, alone. Others from different traditions, especially the behavioristic and the psychometric, have also contributed a great deal. These will be discussed later.

SECTION TWO: REFERENCES

ALLPORT, G. W. *Personality: A psychological interpretation.* New York: Holt, 1937.

BARKER, R., DEMBO, T., & LEWIN, K. Frustration and regression: An experiment with young children. *University of Iowa Studies in Child Welfare,* 1941, **18** (1). 1–314.

BLUM, G. S. A study of the psychoanalytic theory of psychosexual development. *Genetic Psychology Monographs,* 1949, **39**, 3–99.

BLUM, G. S. *Psychoanalytic theories of personality.* New York: McGraw-Hill, 1953.

BRILL, A. A. (Trans. and Ed.) *The basic writings of Sigmund Freud,* New York: Random House, 1938. Introduction.

BROWN, J. F. *The psychodynamics of abnormal behavior.* New York: McGraw-Hill, 1940.

BROWN, N. O. *Life against death: The psychoanalytical meaning of history.* Middletown, Conn., Wesleyan University Press, 1959.

BUTLER, J. M., & HAIGH, G. V. Changes in the relation between self-concepts and ideal concepts consequent upon client-centered counseling. In C. R. Rogers & R. F. Dymond (Eds.), *Psychotherapy and personality change.* Chicago: University of Chicago Press, 1954.

DALBIEZ, R. *Psychoanalytical method and the doctrine of Freud.* London: Longmans, 1941.

DE BEAUVOIR, S. *The second sex.* New York: Knopf, 1953.

DEMENT, W. C. An essay on dreams: The role of physiology in understanding their nature. In T. W. Newcomb (Ed.), *New directions in psychology. Vol. II.* New York: Holt, 1965.

DEMENT, W., & WOLPERT, E. A. The relation of eye movements, body motility, and external stimuli to dream content. *Journal of Experimental Psychology,* 1958, **55**, 543–553.

DENENBERG, V. H. Animal studies on developmental determinants of behavioral adaptability. In O. J. Harvey (Ed.), *Experience, structure and adaptability.* New York: Springer, 1966.

DENENBERG, V. H., & KARAS, G. G. Interactive effects of age to duration of infantile experience on adult learning. *Psychological Reports,* 1960, **7**, 313–322.

ERICKSON, M. H. Experimental demonstrations of the psychopathology of everyday life. *Psychoanalytic Quarterly,* 1939, **8**, 338–353.

ERIKSON, E. H. *Childhood and society.* New York: Norton, 1950.

EYSENCK, H. J. The effects of psychotherapy: An evaluation. *Journal of Consulting Psychology,* 1952, **16**, 319–324. (a)

EYSENCK, H. J. *The scientific study of personality.* London: Routledge, 1952. (b)

EYSENCK, H. J., & RACHMAN, S. (Eds.) *The causes and cures of neurosis: An introduction to modern behaviour therapy based on learning theory and the principles of conditioning.* London: Routledge, 1965.

FARBER, L. H., & FISHER, C. An experimental approach to dream psychology through the use of hypnosis. *Psychoanalytic Quarterly,* 1943, **12**, 202–216.

FENICHEL, O. *The psychoanalytic theory of neurosis.* New York: Norton, 1946.

FODOR, N. *The search for the beloved.* New York: Hermitage, 1949.

FREUD, A. *The ego and the mechanisms of defence.* New York: International Universities Press, 1946.

FREUD, S. Instincts and their vicissitudes. In *Collected Papers of . . .* Vol. IV. London: Hogarth, 1925.

FREUD, S. On narcissism: An introduction. In L.

Woolf & Virginia Woolf (Eds.), *Collected Papers of* . . . London: Hogarth, 1925. Vol. IV, pp. 30–59.

FREUD, S. *The ego and the id.* London: Hogarth, 1927.

FREUD, S. *A general introduction to psychoanalysis.* New York: Liveright, 1935.

FREUD, S. (Collected writings) In A. A. Brill (Trans. and Ed.), *The basic writings of Sigmund Freud.* New York: Random House, 1938.

FREUD, S. The interpretation of dreams. In J. Strachey (Trans. and Ed.), *The complete psychological works of Sigmund Freud.* Vol. IV. London: Hogarth, 1953.

FRIEDAN, B. *The feminine mystique.* New York: Norton, 1963.

GREENACRE, P. The predisposition to anxiety. *Psychoanalytic Quarterly,* 1941, **10**, 66–94, 610–638.

HALL, C. S. *The meaning of dreams.* New York: Harper, 1953.

ISSACS, S. *Social development in young children.* London: Routledge, 1933.

JACOBI, J. The psychology of C. G. Jung: An introduction with illustrations. London: Routledge, 1951.

KALES, A., HOEDEMAKER, F. S., JACOBSEN, A., & LICHTENSTEIN, E., Dream deprivation: an experimental reappraisal, *Nature,* 1964, **204**, 1337–1338.

KEET, C. D. Two verbal techniques in a miniature counselling situation. *Psychological Monographs,* 1948, **62** (Whole No. 294).

KLEIN, M. *The psychoanalysis of children.* London: Hogarth, 1932.

LASHLEY, K. The mechanism of vision: I. A method for rapid analysis of pattern-vision in the rat. *Journal of Genetic Psychology,* 1930, **37**, 453–460.

LEVINE, J., & REDLICH, F. C. Some factors in the failure to understand humor. *Psychoanalytic Quarterly,* 1955, **24**, 560–572.

LEVINE, S. Psychophysiological effects of infantile stimulation. In E. L. Bliss (Ed.), *Roots of behavior.* New York: Harper, 1962.

LEVY, D. Experiments on the sucking reflex and social behavior of dogs. *American Journal of Orthpsychiatry,* 1934, **4**, 203–224.

LINDNER, R. M. *The fifty-minute hour.* New York: Holt, 1955.

MAIER, N. R. F. *Frustration: The study of behavior without a goal.* New York: McGraw-Hill, 1949.

MAILLOUX, N. The contribution of clinical research to personality theory. *Canadian Journal of Psychology,* 1955, **9**, 133–143.

MALINOWSKI, B. *Sex and repression in savage society.* New York: Harcourt, Brace, 1927.

McCLELLAND, D. C. *The achieving society.* Princeton, N.J.: Van Nostrand, 1961.

McCLELLAND, D. C. Toward a theory of motive acquisition. *American Psychologist,* 1965, **20**, 321–333.

McCLELLAND, D. C., et al. *The achievement motive.* New York: Appleton-Century-Crofts, 1953.

MILLER, N. E. Experiments relating Freudian displacement to generalization conditioning. *Psychological Bulletin,* 1939, **36**, 516–517.

MOWRER, O. H. Freedom and responsibility: A psychological analysis. *Journal of Legal Education,* 1953, **6**, 60–78.

MUNROE, R. L. *Schools of psychoanalytic thought: An exposition, critique, and attempt at integration.* New York: Dryden Press, 1955.

MURRAY, H. A. et al. *Explorations in personality: A clinical and experimental study of fifty men of college age, by the workers at the Harvard psychological clinic.* New York: Oxford University Press, 1938.

ORSLANSKY, H. Infant care and personality. *Psychological Bulletin,* 1949, **46**, 1–48.

PASAMANICK, B., ROGERS, M. E., & LILIENFELD, A. M. Pregnancy experience and the development of behavior disorder in children. *American Journal of Psychiatry,* 1956, **112**, 613–618.

PASCAL, B. *Pensées.* New York: Dutton, 1960.

PINNEAU, S. A critique on the articles by Margaret Ribble. *Child Development,* 1950, **21**, 203–228.

RAMSEY, G. V. Studies of dreaming. *Psychological Bulletin,* 1953, **50**, 432–455.

RIBBLE, M. A. Infantile experience in relation to personality development. In J. McV. Hunt (Ed.), *Personality and the behavior disorders.* Vol. 2. New York: Ronald Press, 1944.

SEARS, R. R. Experimental studies of projection: I. Attribution of traits. *Journal of Social Psychology,* 1936, **7**, 151–163.

SEEMAN, J. The process of nondirective therapy. *Journal of Consulting Psychology,* 1949, **13**, 157–168.

STEPHENSON, W. *The study of behavior: Q-technique and its methodology.* Chicago: University of Chicago Press, 1953.

SZASZ, T. S. *The myth of mental illness: Foundations of a theory of personal conduct.* New York: Harper, 1961.

THOMPSON, W. R., WATSON, J., & CHARLESWORTH, W. R. The effects of prenatal maternal stress on offspring behavior in rats. *Psychological Monographs,* 1962, **76** (Whole No. 557).

WEININGER, O. Mortality of albino rats under stress as a function of early handling. *Canadian Journal of Psychology,* 1953, **7**, 111–114.

WHYTE, L. L. *The unconscious before Freud.* New York: Basic Books, 1960.

WOLPE, J., SALTER, A., & REYNA, L. J. *The conditioning therapeutics: The challenge in psychotherapy.* New York: Holt, 1964.

WOLSTENHOLME, G. E. W., & O'CONNOR, M. *Somatic stability in the newborn.* Ciba Foundation Symposium. Boston: Little, Brown, 1961.

ZELLER, A. F. An experimental analogue of repression. I. Historical summary. *Psychological Bulletin,* 1950, **47**, 39–51.

ZILBOORG, G., & HENRY, G. W. *A history of medical psychology.* New York: Norton, 1941.

SECTION THREE
MODELS OF SOCIAL BEHAVIOR

"...It is evident that psychological operations of a distinctive form occur at the level where men interact and that these cannot be reduced to the generalities of instinct or habit. Between the general properties of individuals and sociological products, such as language and institutions, there lies a range of processes, today largely unknown, which constitute the core of social psychology. Failure to realize their distinctive character dulls appreciation of what is specific to the events occurring between persons and groups and of the special qualities of social facts. Instinct and habit doctrines are an attempt to derive social facts from conditions that lack the reality of a social field, or an attempt to short-circuit the need to study the processes that intervene between individuals and the facts of society."

(Asch, 1952, p. 164)

"The vast proportion of all individuals who are born into any society, always and whatever the idiosyncrasies of its institutions, assume, as we have seen, the behavior dictated by that society. This fact is always interpreted by the carriers of that culture as being due to the fact that their particular institutions reflect an ultimate and universal sanity. The actual reason is quite different. Most people are shaped to the form of their culture *because of the enormous malleability of their original endowment. They are plastic to the molding force of the society into which they are born."*

(Benedict, 1959, p. 235)

PROLOGUE

The two passages which we have quoted to open this section embody two fundamental propositions upon which are built most of social psychology and its close relatives sociology and social anthropology. The first, as stated by Solomon Asch, is simply that man is fundamentally a social being, in the sense that, with rare exceptions, he lives with his fellows, with whom he interacts and communicates. Some thinkers have indeed asserted that to be human is to be social—that a nonsocial person is a contradiction in terms. Aristotle was one of the first to think this way. "Social," as used here, does not, of course, mean friendly or outgoing; rather it means capable of interaction with other people and of orientation toward the world partly in terms of the orientation of others. The second, as stated by Benedict, is that human personality is, at birth, effectively a *tabula rasa*—an empty slate—on which a culture makes its particular imprint. Thus, we can observe that people are influenced by the society in which they grow up, though the notion that they have initially no propensities or direction is only hypothetical.

Freud, as we said in Section Two, obviously laid stress on these ideas. Although he took as his starting point the individual, he recognized clearly the part played by the strong social forces of the family. The superego was, in fact, the residue of all previous social interactions introjected by the person. In this, he was reflecting a view widespread among European nineteenth-century philosophers. Though the two propositions are simple, as we have stated them, the intellectual background from which they emerged is rather complex. We will sketch it briefly.

One of the most important figures in nineteenth-century thought—perhaps the most significant from the standpoint of the development of social psychology—was Georg Wilhelm Friedrich Hegel, who wrote and taught in Germany around the turn of the eighteenth century. Whereas previously the focus of interest in philosophy had been the individual and his destiny, now it became the group spirit, or idea common to all individuals and transcending them as a more concrete reality. The idea of the group as a *concrete* entity is difficult to understand, and we cannot even attempt to do justice to the subtle reasoning of Hegel. At a very simple level, however, perhaps the following example will make the point clearer: If we wish to understand an individual and his behavior, we can examine his group memberships. The fact that he is an ex-fraternity man, a member of the Alpine Club, and a diplomat tells us a good deal about him right away. We could obviously add many other such terms to our description, each one serving to make more precise our comprehension of him. Since all of them represent supraindividual categories, to the extent that we use them we are subordinating the individual as a focus of explanation. We are explaining him instead in terms of the "other," that is, in terms of the group.

The fact that we can do this, of course, does not at first sight seem to imply any concreteness for the group concept. We usually reserve the term "concrete" for some solid object like a chair or a person. Yet, what does it really mean? One common meaning is "real," or "tangible," something we can actually touch or feel. Yet the derivation of "concrete" is from the Latin word *concrescere* meaning "to grow together." Thus, more exactly, it refers to a collection of parts that demonstrate by their activity some kind of unity. After all, any object like a book is regarded by us as concrete, not so much from the fact that we can sense it, but rather from the inference or perception of its unity. When we pick it up, it does not suddenly fall into a million pieces. If it did, we might hesitate to call it concrete any longer.

So also with a group. We cannot touch or see a group, though we can see and touch its individual members. But then we can only touch or see one part of a book or a tree at one time. Admittedly, we can move such objects physically, and they respond as units, and we can hardly do this with a group. But in a broader sense, the principle of a common response of parts to some force impinging on them and of unity of spontaneous activity (in the case of a living thing) does certainly apply to a social group. A public insult to a country's leader or flag, for example, will evoke the same wrathful reaction in millions of its citizens. Likewise, the members of a lynch mob will share common feelings, thoughts, and actions.

Furthermore, it is usually true that certain defining characteristics of a group remain constant quite independently of turnover in its membership. The student body and faculty of a university change every year, yet the character of the institution itself, its general politics, its traditions, its academic orientation, remain about the same—or, if they do not, obey laws of change that transcend the individual members. Consequently, there is justification for regarding the group as something concrete—or at least concrete enough to be the subject of conceptual and empirical study.

This notion that the group is all-important was not seen by Hegel especially, nor by his contemporary Johann Gottlieb Fichte, as a bad thing, but rather as good. Only by participation in the slow evolution of the group spirit through history could the individual fulfill himself. Nonetheless, it is regarded as being responsible for the evolution of Marxian communism and for the nationalism of Germany culminating in the extreme statism of Hitler with its slogan *"Du bist nicht; dein Volk ist alles."* (You are nothing; your nation is everything.)

In contrast to this point of view, consider the remarks of John Stuart Mill, a British philosopher of the same period as Hegel: "The only freedom which deserves the name is that of pursuing our own good in our own way, so long as we do not attempt to deprive others of theirs, or impede their efforts to obtain it [Mill, 1865]." For Mill, the happiness of the private individual was paramount, and the main purpose of the state was to protect it. The orientation here, and in most of British philosophy at the time, was highly individualistic and empirical. It was sharply different from the idealism of German philosophy with its stress on powerful historical forces beyond the control of any single individual. The two movements both shared, however, a deep concern for the management of political systems. It was the view of most thinkers at this time that rules could be formulated about the workings of society and that social ills could be remedied, if only sufficient thought were given to these problems.

One of the most influential spokesmen for this last point of view was the French scholar Auguste Comte. He explicitly laid the groundwork for an empirical science of society which he labeled *La morale positive*—positive, or scientific, morality. This combination of down-to-earth British empiricism coupled with a Hegelian emphasis on the group concept represented the beginnings of the science of sociology; and it is no accident that Emile Durkheim, Gabriel Tarde, and Gustav Le Bon—the first real sociologists—were also Frenchmen.

We may now summarize the major philosophic commitments from which social psychology eventually emerged. They are as follows:

1. The social interactions of human beings are of prime importance and are capable of being managed on a rational basis.
2. The concept of a group is not empty of meaning but one capable of being examined by both philosophical and empirical methods.
3. The self-fulfillment of the individual comes through his membership in the group. He is, in all ways, strongly influenced by it.
4. Empirical or positivistic methods may give better results than philosophic speculation.

Against such an intellectual backdrop grew the three related sciences of sociology, social anthropology, and social psychology. All of them shared a common concern with the study of social behavior and of cultural influences on the individual and with the use of empirical method. Social anthropology came mainly from England. It combined the orientations outlined above with a strong interest in individual differences in human beings in different regions of the world. The latter focus was a natural result of Darwin's theory of evolution with its two key concepts of *variation* and *natural selection*. It is of significance that a British anthropological expedition to the Torres Strait in 1898 enlisted the aid of several psychologists, one of whom was William McDougall, writer of the first major text in social psychology. It was later to be revised twice. Sociology, on the other hand, was predominantly French in origin. Comte's dream of formulating scientifically the rules for moral conduct involved the study of both biological and cultural man. The latter was essentially sociology—the scientific study of society. Comte himself did not do very much directly in the way of sociological work, but he may certainly be regarded as the founder of this discipline.

Social psychology, with which we are mainly concerned here, has very complex origins. Certainly, it could hardly have emerged without the broad philosophic ideas which we have briefly discussed above. More immediately we can find its formal beginnings as a separate discipline in several different countries. As we have already mentioned, McDougall, in England, wrote one of the first textbooks. Comte, in France, anticipated it to a considerable degree in his proposed *morale positive*. In Germany, the man regarded as the founder of modern experimental psychology, Wilhelm Wundt, devoted the latter part of his career to writing about "folk," or social, psychology. American workers contributed something by their insistence on the experimental approach to social behavior. Such diversity of origins is clearly reflected in the character of modern social psychology today. It studies all sorts of problems, some very practical, such as the nature and origins of prejudice or the qualities of leadership, and some quite theoretical, such as the structure of attitudes or the nature of conformity behavior. It utilizes concepts from behavioristic psychology, psychoanalytic theory, and Gestalt psychology. Some workers in the field focus primarily on the social individual, others on the group as a whole.

Because it does appear to be such a mixture of different types of data, methods, and points of view, many scholars have considered social psychology to be simply applied general psychology. They have argued, in other words, that to understand man's social behavior and the behavior of groups, large or small, we first need to achieve a thorough knowledge of the individual—the way he learns, thinks, and generally copes with his environment—and then simply extend this to the special case of social behavior. One might lay down, for example, the laws that govern the learning of a maze. These we would then apply to the interactions between persons, and we should be able to predict, within limits, how an individual learns about, or gets to know, another individual—that is, how he socializes. If this view were held by all social psychologists, there would be little point in our devoting special chapters to it. In point of fact, many social psychologists not only disagree strongly with it but go to the other extreme of asserting that because man is a social animal, he cannot be studied properly as an individual, in which case the tables are turned and the psychology of the individual becomes a special application of social psychology.

Both these positions are too extreme. Certainly not all psychology is social psychology, but, on the other hand, social psychology is not just applied general psychology. Precisely because it is a unique discipline, a particular intellectual stream in psychological thought, we have devoted a special section to it. This uniqueness requires further explanation. So far, we have indicated only in very general fashion the main ideas in the field and their philosophical origins. We will try to dissect them in order to point up more precisely the nature of social psychology. To say that man is social, in the sense that he interacts continuously with his fellows and that he is shaped by the culture in which he lives, is not to say very much. We must probe further into the meaning of the terms "social" and "social interaction" and try to uncover their basic dimensions. The problem at first may seem disarmingly simple. In fact, it requires a rather profound analysis, and the attempts that have been made have also set the whole style and character of the field.

CHAPTER 7
THE NATURE OF SOCIAL PSYCHOLOGY

FUNDAMENTALS

In this chapter, we will consider two basic problems. The first concerns the essential nature of the data of social psychology and the approach taken to obtain it. We know already roughly what we are dealing with, namely, the interactions that go on between different individuals. But social psychologists have tried to specify the term "social interaction" a good deal more closely. They have attempted not only to delineate the different dimensions of a social act but also to show in what ways it differs from a nonsocial interaction—that is, one occurring between a person and the inanimate environment. The second problem we will discuss concerns the reasons for our being sociable in the first place. We know that most persons are sociable. How do they get that way? Several positions bearing on this question will be outlined.

Social Reality

We have stated that man is social because we see him interacting with other human beings. This sounds obvious enough, yet it is no answer to the problem of defining social behavior. Men interact with their physical environment as well. Is this also social behavior? Most people would probably wish to separate the two classes of interactions, reserving the word "social" exclusively for the first. We do not react to a stone or a tree or even to a beautiful painting as we do to a friend, to a wife, or to a husband. Certain characteristics of an animate being make it vastly different from an inanimate object, and hence the way a human being interacts with one is correspondingly different from the way he interacts with the other.

The specification of these differences has comprised for social psychologists a problem that lies at the very core of their discipline. Cogent analyses of it have been made by Fritz Heider (1944), by Solomon Asch (1952), and by Krech and Crutchfield (1948). They have stated the question to be answered as follows: How does our experience of "person objects" differ from our experience of "object objects"? The fact that they choose the term "experience" rather than "behavior" is of great importance, but first let us consider the interaction problem. What are the differences between persons and objects, or more broadly, between the social world and the object world? Asch gives this answer:

First, unlike objects, persons alone respond to *us*. Objects do not greet us, they do not blame or praise us, they do not love or hate us. They respond to our actions, not to us; they are not aware of our presence. The mirror reflects, but it does not see us; only another person can be a true mirror for a human. For it is only persons who can answer us with feeling and understanding, with irritation or admiration, with assistance or competition. (It may be objected that things do, under certain conditions, take on some rudimentary characteristics of persons. Things may appear kind or malevolent, mysterious and inhabited by powerful spirits. Their capacity for delighting and threatening may appear as the expression of personality. When this is so, it remains a fact that the psychological events occur only on one side. In any case, the full qualities of personhood are concentrated in humans and should be studied where they occur in pronounced form.)

The paramount fact about human interactions is that they are happenings that are *psychologically represented* in *each* of the participants. In our relation to an object, perceiving, thinking and feeling take place on one side, whereas in relations between persons these processes take place on both sides and in dependence upon one another [Asch, 1952, p. 141].

If persons have special characteristics that make them different from objects, we may rightly ask what they are. Krech and Crutchfield (1948), two workers in the same theoretical tradition as Asch, have listed six attributes with which persons are richly endowed. These are *mobility, capriciousness, unpredictability, reciprocal sensitivity, causality,* and *power qualities.* All these are readily understandable except perhaps the last two. These mean, respectively, the ability to initiate action spontaneously, rather than merely to react, and the capability of providing the other person with rewards and punishments.

Obviously, as these writers and Asch have suggested, we often attribute such qualities also to inanimate objects, particularly those of a certain kind and especially those over which we have little control. Clouds, storms, and winds are all good examples. Witness the common practice of designating hurricanes and typhoons by a feminine name. Because we cannot do much in the way of predicting what they will do and where they will go—much less control them—we tend to perceive them as diabolic female agents, capricious, impulsive, and whimsical in their destruction. Indeed, primitive man endowed most of his world with such properties. The sun, the moon and stars, the rivers and oceans, and all of nature were animate and to be placated, feared, and often worshiped. There are some grounds for arguing that this kind of experience is a precursor to, or more fundamental than, that experienced with physical objects as objects. Not only early man but also children live in an animated world. The kind of knowledge with which physics deals may therefore be a secondary achievement that came only with great difficulty. History seems to support this idea.

A qualification to this notion should, however, be mentioned. Margaret Mead (1953) in her field study of the Manus of the Admiralty Islands off the northeast coast of New Guinea did not find such animism to be characteristic of the children of this culture. She says:

> So where we give the moon sex and speak of her as "she," the Manus language, which makes no distinction between he, she, and it, all of which are "third person singular," gives no personalizing suggestion. Nor are verbs which apply to persons applied to the moon. The moon "shines," but it never smiles, hides, marches, flirts, peeps, approves; it never "looks down sadly," or "turns away its face." All the impetus to personalization which our rich allusive language suggests to a child is absent.
>
> I couldn't even persuade children to cast the blame upon inanimate objects. To my remarks, "It's a bad canoe to float away," the children would reply, "Popoli forgot to tie it up" or "Popoli didn't tie it fast enough." This suggests that this "natural" tendency in our children is really taught them by their parents [Mead, 1953, p. 83].

Consequently, we must be a little cautious in regard to the generalizations we make about the priority in ontogeny of animistic thinking. Anthropological data do not prove the opposite—indeed, it is possible that the Manus culture exerts a suppressive influence on what really is a natural tendency—but they do not give to this notion strong positive support.

Causality and Persons

One of the most crucial properties pertaining to persons is what was previously called "loci of causality." Persons are agents who do things to one another and act on the world. They are not simply reactors. The general idea of causality has been given a good deal of attention by psychologists, as we shall see. It is also, however, a very old problem which a long succession of philosophers have attacked. Two sharply contrasting views were those of the eighteenth-century Scottish philosopher David Hume and his German contemporary Immanuel Kant. Prior to Hume, the relation of cause and effect as a universal principle of reason had been taken for granted. Certainly, in the Western world, at least, everybody tacitly accepted the notion that for every effect there was a cause and every cause had an effect. It was Hume who first questioned this. In his treatise "An Enquiry concerning Human Understanding" he said:

> I shall venture to affirm as a general proposition, which admits of no exception, that the knowledge of this relation is not, in any instance attained by reasonings *a priori;* but arises entirely from experience, when we find that any particular objects are constantly conjoined with each other [Hume, 1939, p. 599].

Thus we learn to think in terms of causal principles. It is not in the nature of things. All we actually see in the world are associations in time and space. B follows A, and under certain circumstances we may say that therefore A caused B. But this is only a construction on the basis of past experience.

If Hume's argument was correct, it seemed to many, including Kant, that the whole foundation of science rested on a very shaky basis, in fact, in the end, on no more than an article of faith.

Kant's solution to this quandary was one which influenced deeply a great many thinkers following him. Roughly speaking, it was as follows: he conceived of the mind not as a kind of reflecting mirror which passively takes in and records the outside world but as an active agency which transforms the objects of its knowledge according to certain inborn categories. One might compare the mind to a machine press which stamps out, from a sheet of metal, pieces of a triangular shape. The idea of nontriangularity would then be beyond the capability of such a machine. So also with the Kantian mind, which stamped onto reality its imprint of causality. Cause and effect were then part of the basic stuff of mind.

Skipping now from the eighteenth century to the twentieth century, we find among some European schools of psychology, particularly the gestaltists and others of this tradition, a viewpoint about causality very similar to that of Kant. For them, the idea of causality was taken to be an experience or impression that occurs immediately in our perception of the world. It is a property of mind to grasp the world in this way.

Several psychologists, particularly Fritz Heider, however, went beyond Kant in making a distinction concerning this category that Kant did not come to directly. This was the distinction to which we have already referred between causal relations among *objects* and those among *agents*. In the former case, according to Heider (1944), we do not see causal efficacy originating in the object that produces change in the other. Rather we tend to project back from it to more remote causes. Thus a stone that falls from a cliff and hits our car as it passes below is not regarded as the ultimate step in the causal chain. Rather, we tend to think of other prior factors that caused the stone to be dislodged—wind, rain, temperature, and so on. However, were we to see a person throwing down the stone at our car, we would undoubtedly be ready to place responsibility at his door without looking further. In other words, we would regard him as a locus of causality, a free agent, in fact a kind of "prime mover."

Thus perception of persons is different from perception of objects. The relation between a person and his action is not causal in the same sense as that between one phenomenon and another. The concepts involved in the first case—those represented by such words as "ought," "can," or "will" —are usually not applicable to objects.

Consideration of the problem from the point of view of twentieth-century experimental psychology has grown directly out of this philosophic tradition. The workers perhaps most important in this regard, have been Jean Piaget, Albert Michotte, and Fritz Heider. All these have agreed, in effect, that the perception of causality in its most general sense, as including relations both between objects and between persons, is a fact of our experience. Piaget (1930) has further suggested that children in early life gradually build up an idea of themselves as actors, or originators of action, and this schema they then use to order events in the outside world. Michotte and Heider, on the other hand, have taken the slightly different position that the experience of causality is immediately given in our perception, given the right spatiotemporal conditions, and is not significantly influenced by factors of experience.

Not all psychologists would agree with these notions. In fact, the majority would probably be more sympathetic to an associationist point of view. We have presented the views of Piaget, Michotte, and Heider not as being necessarily true but as profound enough to lead to a good deal of very interesting theoretical and experimental work on the problem of how causality is perceived, whether it is learned or innate, and how our perception of it varies for persons as against objects. We will shortly examine a sample of this work.

Our final consideration in this introductory section on the nature of social psychology concerns the general stance taken by the field to the problem of what kinds of data are collected and the method of collecting them.

Experience and Behavior

In stating how the basic problem of social interaction was formulated, we used the term "experience." How does a person *experience* other people as opposed to inanimate objects, or nonpeople? The stress on experience as opposed to behavior is a critical feature of the mainstream of social psychology. We emphasized previously the strong influence of European philosophy in the development of the field. We may now make more explicit one aspect of this influence, which is precisely its focus on cognition and experience as against only observable behavior.

A key figure in the theoretical development of social psychology was Kurt Lewin, a student of Wertheimer, one of the founders of Gestalt psychology. Formally, he is known as a *field theorist*, and by the term "field," or "psychological" or "phenomenal field," is meant *the experience of a person in some given situation—social or otherwise*. In this view, interest is directed not so much to the overt behavior of individuals engaging in social interaction but rather to the attitudes, cognitions, and expectations that these acts may reflect. The same behavior patterns of two people may be generated by two quite different experiences. An approach made to another person may, for example, signify friendliness, or it may mean aggression. Only by a careful exploration of the person's cognitive structure and the balance of the elements that comprise it can we really understand social behavior. We study not responses to the world but responses to the world as the person *perceives* it.

Today, this "cognitive" approach, though certainly not the only viewpoint in the field, clearly dominates the style of social psychology. This does not mean that behavior is ignored. We must always start from observables. But for cognitive theorists, the really interesting variables lie behind these. Thus, it is regarded as quite permissible to begin by making certain assumptions about mind or experience and then setting up experiments to test these, rather than starting with behavioral changes and never going far beyond a description of them.

For example, a central postulate in the study of social attitudes and how they change, has been that their component parts tend to strike a *balance,* or *symmetry*. Many workers have designed studies that test predictions about behavior in particular situations, *given* the validity of this a priori concept about the human mind. The dramatic conflict favored by writers of a loved person doing some act we cannot condone provides a simple illustration. The imbalance produced by such a situation calls for radical restructuring of attitudes either to the person or to the act, or to both, *assuming imbalance is a state not tolerated by the mind*. We will later review a number of experiments elaborating on this point.

Dimensions of the Social Act

This chapter commenced with the empirical proposition that man was a highly social animal. Many thinkers through the ages have wondered *why* this should be so and, in answering the question, have suggested certain fundamental processes at work. Before examining these, it is necessary to analyze more closely than we have done so far the exact meaning of "social." For it is a complex term that has a number of connotations, and unless these are clearly delineated, we cannot properly understand the progress of empirical work in social psychology.

The first meaning of "social" is *the ability to socialize or interact with other agents as opposed to physical objects*. The ability to socialize or be socially sensitive is quite independent of the form a particular social act may take. The second definition of "social" has to do with *the type of act performed;* for example, an interaction may be friendly, aggressive, jealous, or suspicious. Such terms designate the content of a social act. Third, a social act may be defined in terms of *its conformity or nonconformity to some set of norms or values laid down by the social group.* This conformity can apply to the broad orientations we hold toward (1) certain classes of objects or persons, or (2) certain positions called for by the social structure. These two types of orientation have to do respectively with *attitudes* and *roles.* Thus we may be social insofar as during a war we share with others of our country a negative attitude to the enemy or in normal times we may have a positive attitude to cricket if we are British, or to baseball if we are American, or to ice hockey if we are Canadian.

Role is a more complicated concept, and we will elaborate it in some detail later in this section. For the time being, we can state it this way: most societies are made up of a great number of institutionalized positions, for example, doctor, politician, mother, or father. Occupying these positions entails certain kinds of behavior demanded by society. Likewise, society expects other individuals to behave toward these positions in certain ways. To the extent that we conform to these demands and expectations we are being social, according to our third meaning of the term.

These are the major dimensions of a social act. It is obviously not something very simple. Before going into the kinds of research concerned with each of its aspects, we will first look at an example to see how it may be broken up.

Consider the social relationship between men and women. In the first place, each sex may treat the other as a person and agent or else as an object. The prostitute offers herself essentially as an object that can be purchased for money like any other commodity. Certain popular magazines appear to advocate as an ethic for men a "playboy" attitude of detachment and "coolness" to women. According to this, a female is to be treated as a means to enjoyment only—never as another person with whom some give and take is possible and desirable.

Second, quite independently of whether it is social in the above sense or not, the relation between the two sexes may be also friendly or aggressive, tender or savage, loving or hateful. Two aggressive persons may have a highly satisfactory union, as may two gentle ones or, for that matter, as may two who are quite opposite but have the ability to attune their actions to the perceived needs of the other. The same applies to any kind of behavior involving person-to-person relations. The dimension we are discussing supplies the quality, or coloring, to the raw stuff of social behavior.

Third, the interactions between men and women may be so governed by social sanctions that they vary very little in form between individual members of a culture. The manners of courtship of the sixteenth-century French nobleman, for example, were prescribed by a set of rules very different from those governing the behavior of present-day North American teen-agers. It would be a mistake to think, however, that the intricacy or strength of the impositions were less in one case than the other. Society has not become much less demanding in the conformity it expects, particularly in matters of sexuality—though to those who grow up within a particular cultural matrix its regulations always appear less obvious. This aspect of the social act—its conformingness—is largely independent of the two other meanings we have discussed. The study of conformity behavior and of the manner in which the group generates it in the individual constitutes an interesting line of research in social psychology.

Having offered an analysis of the meaning of social behavior and given brief examples of its various aspects, we will now go into the basic problem of *why and how man is social in the first place.* Is he born that way, or does he learn it? Are different people social to a different degree? Are animals truly social? These and many other interesting problems suggest themselves. In discussing them, we will refer to the dimensions of social behavior designated above.

SOCIAL MOTIVATION

Instincts

Whether one stresses the individuality or the sociability of man, it is certainly true that most men live in society and prefer to do so rather than live alone in isolation from their fellow human beings. More than this, people show *concern* for each other and often assimilate each other's moods, feelings, attitudes, beliefs, and behavior. Such facts as these have suggested to some that man is innately gregarious—much like a social insect which cannot function properly outside the colony and actively seeks members of its own kind. One of the first social psychologists to put forward such a view was William McDougall. In his textbook, he listed twelve instincts, of which the gregarious instinct was one (McDougall, 1908). Other theorists inclined to this point of view were William James, H. C. Warren, and E. L. Thorndike.

The instinct doctrine was a useful step in the theoretical progress of the behavioral sciences insofar as it offered a convenient classificatory system of behavior, but from the standpoint of motivation it explained very little. The properties that usually define an instinct in lower animals are largely missing in human beings; consequently, to refer, for example, to man's tendency to like fighting as an "instinct of pugnaciousness" is to say little more than that he tends to engage in fighting behavior. It does add something, however, and this is the attribution to the behavior of the property of innateness or of minimal dependence on learning. Indeed, the *nature-nurture controversy* has been going on for many years, and although it has ceased to be regarded as a matter for intense argument, it is still being usefully studied in experimental terms. From the standpoint of social psychology, however, the bland notion that instincts lie behind social interaction has, for the most part, not offered many research possibilities. For this reason, McDougall's position has not enjoyed popularity for a good many years.

A more fruitful approach to the problem of the innateness of behavior is represented by the recent line of work done on instinctive behavior by biologists and psychologists belonging to a school of thought called *ethology*. Instead of drawing up lists of instincts to cover all the manifest activities of man and lower animals, the ethologists have focused on the actual behaviors rather than the drives supposedly lying behind them. They have tried to analyze and dissect out the units of an instinctive act and isolate the environmental stimuli that will elicit it. This orientation has led to much vigorous and productive work.

To highlight the contrast between the old and newer approaches to instinct, consider the simple case of a herring gull incubating an egg. Such behavior would formerly have been referred simply to a maternal, or brooding, instinct and dismissed summarily. Recently, however, many workers, led by Niko Tinbergen, have been inquiring into the circumstances that produce incubation behavior and the kinds of stimuli that set it off. Once the problem is stated in this way, some interesting questions are raised. For example, we may wonder whether the sea gull will incubate any egg, say, a square one. As it turns out, she will not. But she will, on the other hand, incubate a very large oval egg—say, an ostrich egg—and, furthermore, will do so with more "enthusiasm" than she normally shows with her own eggs. Hence we know that size and shape are important, and, in addition, we speak of the very large egg as a supernormal stimulus.

This ethologic point of view has been extended along some lines that have relevance to our present topic of social motivation. One such extension has to do with a form of human behavior that might well be regarded—if one took McDougall's point of view—as reflecting the gregarious instinct. This is the *smiling response*. It would seem that all normal human beings smile or at least are capable of smiling. Many think that some animals can also smile. Be this as it may, it is a rather definite and significant fact from the standpoint of social psychology that a smiling response can be elicited in very young infants from the age of about five weeks by certain kinds of situations. Two points should be emphasized about this fact: first, the eliciting situations tend to be quite specific—a baby does not smile at anybody for no reason; and, second, the smile may be viewed as a causal factor in the beginnings of social behavior. Parents and others whose features produce or release the smile are themselves attracted by it and pushed into communicative situations with the baby.

The smiling response does show some of the properties of instincts. Some data bearing on this are presented in Example 7–1. They were gathered by J. A. Ambrose at the Unit of Child Development Research of the Tavistock Institute in London.

Example 7–1 *The smiling response in infants (Ambrose, 1961)*

It has been well known for some time that a human face can evoke a smile in very young infants.

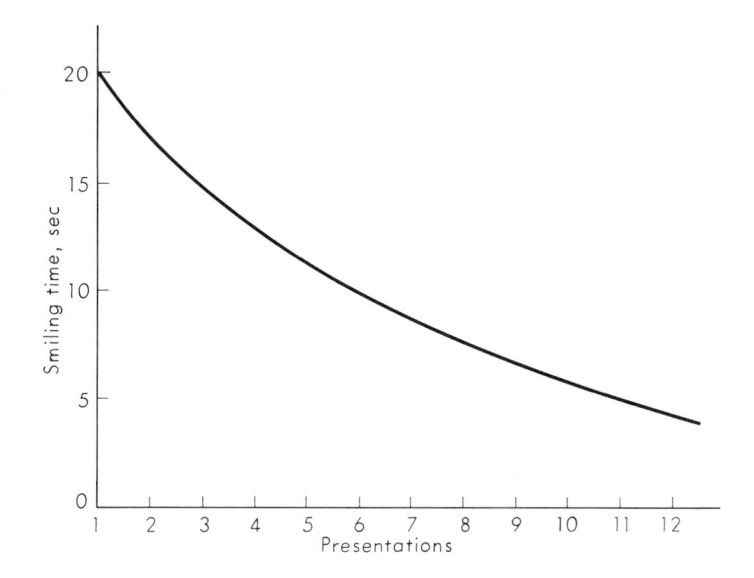

FIG. 7–1 Habituation of the smiling response. (*Ambrose, 1961*)

Spitz and Wolf (1946) were perhaps the first to show this. Ambrose has extended this work by studying the manner in which smiling changes over time. Most instinctive acts, for example, "mobbing" behavior of small birds when shown a stuffed predator, show a decline in strength if the stimulus that releases them is presented a number of times. This diminution is commonly known as *habituation*. After a rest period, however, it will reappear strongly. As it turns out, the smiling response also wanes in strength if the face eliciting it in the first place continuously reappears. Figure 7–1 shows a typical curve illustrating this fact.

Given a rest following habituation, the smile recovers to its initial strength. Thus, it does seem to bear a close resemblance to what we would call an instinctive act. Additional information obtained by Ambrose and a coworker indicated that in institutionalized or orphanage children, the average smiling time per trial rose with age to a peak at about seventeen to twenty weeks. Resistance to habituation was also higher at this time. In home-reared infants, however, the peak age of smiling comes considerably earlier, at about twelve weeks. In either case, it is likely that the decline after the peak is due to the acquisition by the child of voluntary control over his smile, which he can now display or hold back at will, depending on whether the stimulus person is a stranger or a friend, on whether he is someone to be loved or someone to be feared, or on simply the child's own feelings at the time.

It is doubtful whether human infants show any other forms of complex behavior that approach an instinct so closely as the smiling response. This is not to say that they do not possess other complex drives, but most of these, if not all, involve a good deal of variability in the way they are manifested; for example, the hunger drive is universal, but there is not just one single way of ingesting nutritive substances, nor are the acts of eating and drinking triggered automatically as the smile appears to be. The smile seems to be a rather universal kind of behavior in human beings, analogous to the fixed action patterns of lower animals and having great social significance.

Learning

Allowing that certain aspects of social motivation may be innate, we must also consider the possibility that a good deal of it is learned. Thus a second type of explanation for man's motivation to be social is based on the notion that built up gradually are habits based on the so-called primary drives having to do with self-preservation and sex. If a rat or cat is made hungry and given food only in the goal box of a maze, he will learn how to get there quickly and with few errors. A number of theorists, particularly of the behaviorist school, have used this formula to explain the socialization of the child. It is certainly a fact that in his early life the child gets hungry and thirsty and subsequently is fed by his mother. Accordingly, as he develops, he not only learns to like his mother because of her association with food, but he also learns that certain responses of which he is capable, for example, crying, smiling, and general bodily activity, will "produce" results. They will make food—and his mother—appear. The reduction in tension that ensues then cements or *reinforces* these associations. In this way, he will have learned the rudiments of social behavior—a liking for others and an ability to communicate with or at least influence them.

The next step in becoming socialized is to learn to copy the behavior of others, or match one's behavior with that of older models. Originally, many thinkers considered *imitation* to be the major force that held society together. For the French sociologist Gabriel Tarde, for example, "Society was imitation." For the biologist C. L. Morgan, imitation arose from a constitutional bias innate in human beings. More contemporary workers, however, have considered it to be simply another learned social habit of the kind we described above. Two men who have made the strongest case for this are Miller and Dollard in their now classic work called *Social Learning and Imitation* (1941). Written at Yale in the days of the great learning theorist Clark Hull, the book attempts to demonstrate that imitative behavior is a habit learned on the basis of reinforcement or reward. Let us look at an example of their work.

Example 7-2 *Experimental production of imitative behavior (Miller & Dollard, 1941)*

Miller and Dollard, as behaviorists, deal directly with *imitative behavior* rather than with any cognitive dispositions that might lie behind it. They define two classes: *matched-dependent behavior*, in which only the leader is able to read the relevant environmental cues that signal the availability of a reward whereas the follower is not, and *copying*, in which the copier slowly brings his own responses into agreement with those of a model. Most of the experimental work reported by Miller and Dollard deals with the first of these.

They use as an illustration of matched dependent-behavior the following case (p. 93):

> Two children . . . were playing in their bedroom, which was adjacent to the family kitchen. The kitchen opened upon a back stairway. It was six o'clock in the evening, the hour when father usually returned home, bearing candy for the two children. While playing in the bedroom, Jim heard a footfall on the stairs; it was the familiar sound of father's return. The younger child, however, had not identified this critical cue. Jim ran to the kitchen to be on hand when father came in the back door. Bobby happened on this occasion to be running in the direction of the kitchen and behind Jim. On many other occasions, probably hundreds, he had not happened to run when Jim did. He had, for instance, remained sitting, continued playing with the top, run to the window instead of the door, and the like; but on this occasion he was running behind his brother. Upon reaching the kitchen, Jim got his candy and Bobby his.

> On subsequent nights with similar conditions, the younger child ran more frequently at the mere sight of his older brother running. When he ran, he received candy. Eventually the behavior, under pressure of continued reward, became highly stabilized, and the younger child would run when the older ran, not only in this situation but in many others where time and place stimuli were different. He had learned in this one respect to *imitate* his older brother, but he had not learned to run at the sound of his father's footfall.

Miller and Dollard then proceed to fit the behavior of the two children into these paradigms:

Imitator (Bobby):

Drive	Appetite for candy
Cue	Leg twinkle of brother
Response	Running
Reward	Eating candy

Leader (Jim):

Drive	Appetite for candy
Cue	Father's footfall
Response	Running
Reward	Eating candy

Taken together, the two paradigms comprise this schema:

Complete paradigm of matched-dependent behavior

	Leader	Imitator
Drive	Appetite for candy	Appetite for candy
Cue	Father's footfall	Leg twinkle of a leader
Response	Running {dependent, matched}	Running
Reward	Eating candy	Eating candy

Using this paradigm, Miller and Dollard attempted to set up experimental demonstrations of imitation in rats and in children. Here are two examples:

The apparatus used was a simple elevated T-maze as shown in Figure 7–2. A group of hungry rats was taught to go consistently either to a white or to a black card to find a food reward. Members of this group were referred to as the "leader" rats. When performance of these animals was highly reliable, naïve, untrained "follower" rats were allowed to observe them as they ran on the maze. One group of follower rats was rewarded when they made the same turn as the leader; if they went the opposite way, they received no reward. For another group of followers, the situation was reversed—that is, they were rewarded when they went the opposite way from the leaders and not rewarded for going the same way. This procedure was carried on for twelve days. On two final days, new leaders were used to check on whether followers had really been imitating the behavior of their leaders or reacting to the black and white cards themselves. The new leaders had been trained *only to turn in a certain direction*—some to the right, some to the left—and to ignore the colors of the cards.

Results obtained from the study were incisive. The follower group learned to follow more and more with succeeding trials, and the nonfollowers learned more and more to take the turn opposite to that taken by the leaders. Figure 7–3 summarizes these data. Differences on the twelfth day were highly significant statistically, their probability of occurrence by chance being less than one in a thousand. Since they were maintained in the trials given on days 13 and 14 with *new* leaders, we can conclude that the follower rats were really using the leaders

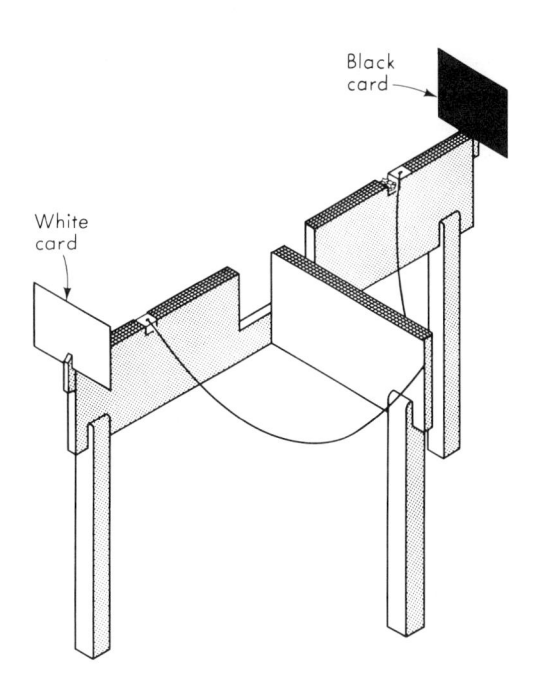

FIG. 7–2 Apparatus used to study imitative behavior in rats. (*Miller & Dollard, 1941*)

as cues and not the cards themselves.

Miller and Dollard completed three other experimental variations of this study. They concluded cautiously that rats can be taught to imitate, or can learn matched-dependent behavior, though they admitted that their own data did not preclude the possibility that following tendencies have some innate basis. Indeed, if rats are anything like chicks in their behavior propensities, it may well be that they have a genetic disposition, cemented by early learning, to follow any moving object to which they are first exposed. The slight upward inclination of the curve for nonimitators over the first three days (cf. Figure 7–3) indicates some immediate tendency to follow that becomes inhibited on ensuing trials.

Miller and Dollard also did some studies with children. The basic setup was analogous to that used in the rat experiment. It is depicted in Figure 7–4. Forty-two first-grade children were used, twenty being chosen as imitators, twenty as nonimitators, and two as leaders. Procedure was as follows: A leader was trained to go always to a box to which the

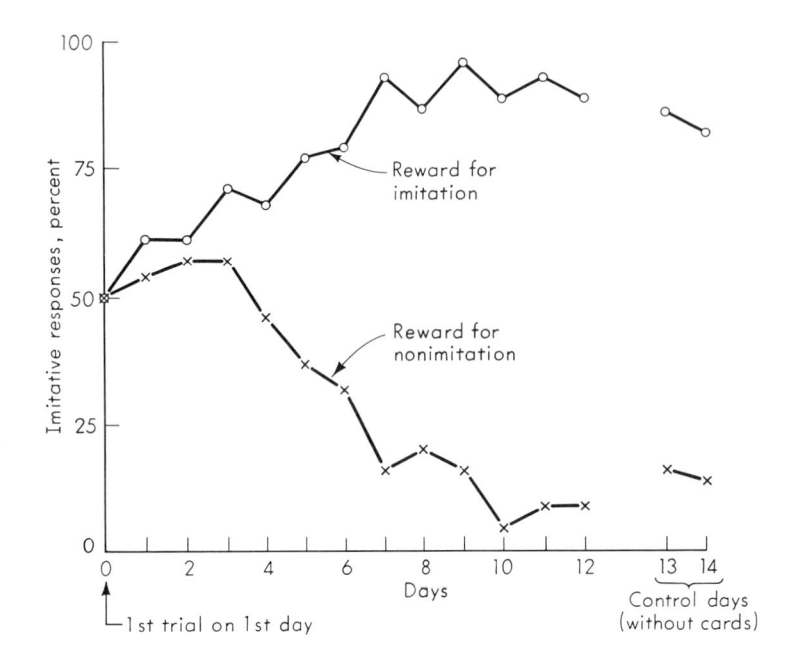

FIG. 7-3 Learning of imitative and nonimitative responses by rats. (*Miller & Dollard, 1941*)

experimenter pointed. If he did this correctly, he was rewarded by finding candy in the box. The situation was so arranged that the followers could not see the experimenter pointing, nor could they see whether the leader had obtained candy or not. After a leader had been well trained, followers were started. Together, they were told to stand at the starting position and then given these verbal instructions: "Here are two boxes, there and there. Here is a piece of candy. You are to find the candy. He [the leader] gets the first turn. Then you get a turn. If you don't find it the first time, you will get another turn."

The leader was given his turn and then the dependent subject. If he made a wrong choice, he was not allowed to go to the other box but had to wait for the next trial. For the imitative group, reward was given for choosing the box chosen by the leader, the opposite being done for nonimitators. Results are shown in Figure 7-5. It is clear that the initial behavior of the follower is in the direction of not imitating. Presumably, this is due to an already established set not to expect a reward in a place already searched by another individual. In the later trials, however, the differences between

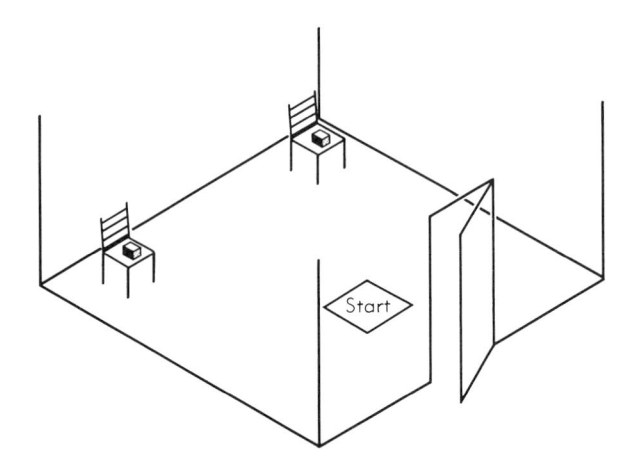

FIG. 7-4 Setup for studying imitation learning in children. (*Miller & Dollard, 1941*)

imitators and nonimitators is striking. All in the first group match their behavior to that of the leader, and all in the second do the opposite.

A second experiment showed that if a new situation was used, involving four boxes, the tendency to

104 MODELS OF SOCIAL BEHAVIOR

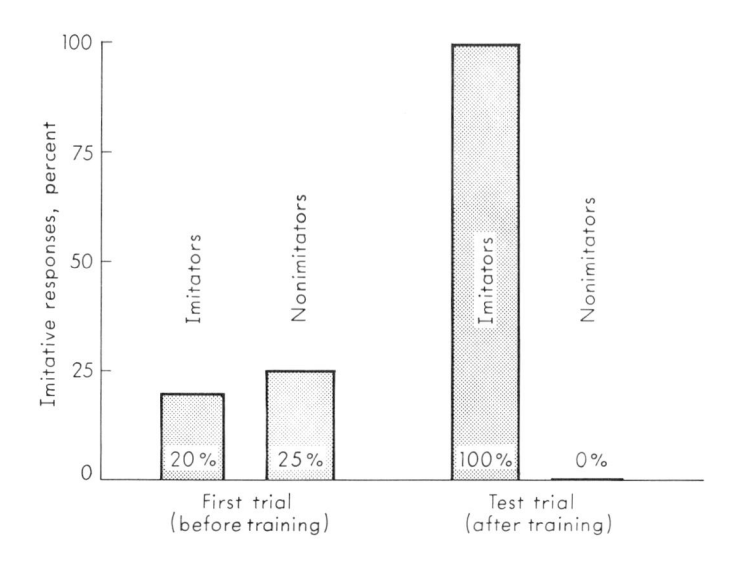

FIG. 7–5 Learning of imitative and nonimitative responses by children. (*Miller & Dollard, 1941*)

imitate generalized immediately. Thus the writers concluded that their data on children agreed with those they obtained in rats. Matched-dependent behavior can be quickly learned by rewarding the appropriate responses and will *then generalize* to new situations.

These classic experiments have led to a line of research and theorizing on imitation, modeling, and identification. The original paradigm of Miller and Dollard has been greatly extended, for example, to include those evident cases where the imitator makes no overt response initially but still learns a similar behavior or those in which the behavior of the follower is modified *vicariously* or *empathically* through rewards given only to the leader or model. To give the reader a "feel" for the kind of work now being done on imitation and the learned components in social behavior, we present a single example of some work by Bandura and his colleagues at Stanford University.

Example 7–3 *Vicarious reinforcement in imitation learning (Bandura & Walters, 1963)*

Children were asked to watch a film in which models exhibited novel aggressive responses—hitting a punching bag or knocking down a large inflated plastic doll. In some cases, the model was shown as being severely punished for such behavior; in other cases, he was generously rewarded with approval and food reinforcement. In a third condition, no effects attached to the aggression.

After the film, the children were given the opportunity to imitate the behavior seen in the film. Results are shown in Figure 7–6. Children who had seen the aggression of the model punished performed significantly fewer such responses than children in either of the other two groups. Boys were, in general, more imitative than girls—a conclusion somewhat in line with Freud's theorizing about sex differences in acculturation and superego formation, though this may have been equally due to greater aggressiveness on the part of the boys. Finally, if the children were offered rewards for imitating, differences in results under the three conditions were substantially reduced.

One interesting hypothesis suggested by Bandura and Walters on the basis of the data collected on imitation learning is that *any* pleasure or satisfaction associated with the action of a model may produce a disposition to copy the behavior of the model, as, for example, when the parents show attention to a child while he is watching a socially deviant character on a TV show. Such attention may simply be in terms of the parental comments or explanations—nonetheless they can serve as reinforcement for a disposition to imitate later the undesirable behavior of the model.

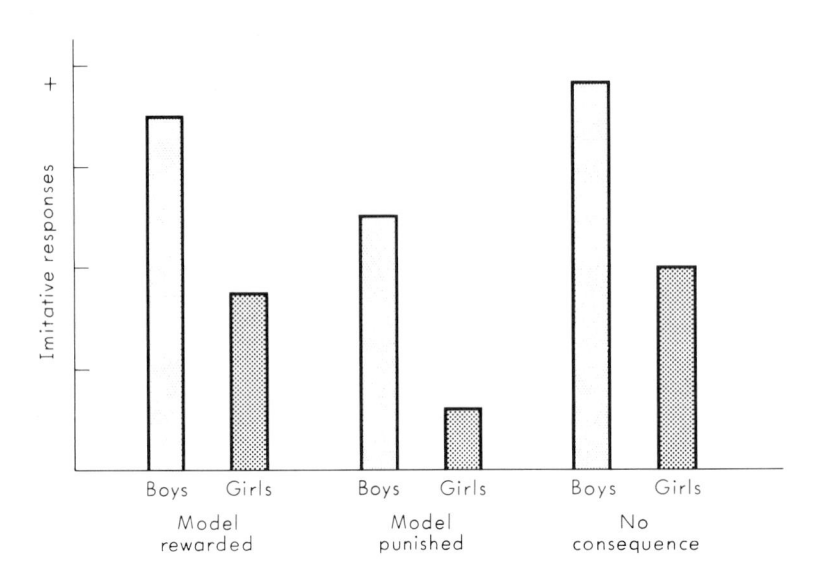

FIG. 7-6 Imitation of aggressive responses following observation of a model. The model's behavior is followed by reward or punishment or leads to no consequences. (*Baidura & Walters* [*modified*], *1963*)

It must be noted in passing that the more recent work stemming historically from the behavioristic model of Miller and Dollard has been much more cognitively oriented inasmuch as it takes account of identification with models by followers without the latter's making immediate overt responses and of the importance of how the followers perceive the model.

We can summarize by saying that the above theory of social motivation takes *learning* as the key to understanding why man is social. It does not assume that man or lower animals are innately gregarious or imitate their fellows instinctively but insists they have to acquire these dispositions gradually on the basis of reinforcements of various kinds.

Contact Needs

There are other needs, however, besides those we usually designate as primary biological drives. One of the most relevant to our discussion is one which one psychologist, Harry F. Harlow, has called "contact comfort." The existence of such a drive is suggested not only by the vigor with which young animals pursue it but also by the harmful effects that ensue on their not having it. Like the drives for food, water, and the rest, this one seems to be innate or at least is present at birth. But, unlike them, it is one that is directly concerned with social interaction. There is no doubt that a child learns to imitate and thus to be social in one of the senses in which we defined the term, namely, being like others or conforming to some institutionalized behavior patterns, but it is possible that through the physical contact he is compelled to seek from the first days of his life, the infant gets practice, at a very primitive level indeed, in the complex business of social reciprocity—that is, the business of *attuning his own actions to those of another.*

In using the term "practice," we are not implying that learning is necessarily involved, though it may well be. All we wish to emphasize is that in the simple action of a mother's holding a baby an almost continuous flow of minute physical adjustments on the part of both is involved and that this may well be the forerunner of all the complex forms of social interactions that occur later on—including those at the verbal level.

Why should such adjustments be made by the mother and by the child? At a commonsense level, we might suppose they are made because one of the two is in an uncomfortable position. Certainly no baby likes to be held with his head down, nor does a mother care to have an elbow in her mouth. These are, of course, extreme examples, but they are only exaggerations of the minor uncomfortable asymmetries which each member of the pair constantly tries to correct. Since the notion of symmetry, or balance, is a most important one in understanding the working of social behavior, it will be discussed later in some detail, but first we will present some of Harlow's data on the nature of the drive for contact comfort and the effects of being deprived of it.

In exploring this interesting but neglected area of affectional behavior, Harlow used the technique of depriving young rhesus monkeys of their proper mothers and substituting surrogates of varying similarity. It was found that, especially in fear situations, the real mother was most often preferred, after which came the terry-cloth mother. Hard wire mothers were not regarded by infant monkeys as much of a substitute for the real thing. Presumably, this was because of the unyielding physical characteristics, which did not permit any possibility of reciprocity. A hard physical object is thus, in a sense, the prototype of a nonsocial being.

Beyond their immediate preference behavior, infant monkeys reared without a real mother do badly later on in life and make neither good mates nor good mothers. They are not merely aggressive and bad-tempered but appear to be also incapable of the primitive kind of reciprocity to which we referred in our first definition of the term "social." With no opportunity for expression early in life through normal exposure to social situations, the particular skills involved in mating and mothering appear to atrophy and wither (Harlow, 1962).

Such a conclusion applies also to human beings. In Chapter 6, we presented evidence obtained by Margaret Ribble and others to show how important mothering is for the normal development of young children. Part of this must be due simply to the gross sensory stimulation the mother supplies by fondling the child, but another part may well involve the kind of primitive social exchange that we have been discussing.

Balance and Symmetry

The notion of balance and the notion of homeostasis have a good deal in common. Each implies that organisms tend to seek—automatically or voluntarily—a steady state. However, the first, as it appears in Gestalt psychology and its descendants, focuses on the cognitive or perceptual counterparts of tension management. Homeostasis, as propounded originally by Walter B. Cannon and taken up later by many behaviorists in psychology—notably Clark Hull—is oriented toward physiological mechanisms and primary drives.

The concept of balance asserts as a primary axiom that the component parts of the mind have a natural tendency to maintain, in relation to one another, *maximum congruity*, or *simplicity*. We will see many examples of this in Section Four, where the nature of perception of objects is discussed. Here we wish to discuss balance in the context of social psychology, to which the perception of persons and the interactions between them are more relevant.

The first point to emphasize is that the property of balancing is usually considered to be neither innate nor learned. The categories of nature and nurture do not apply here any more than they apply to the equilibrium of physical systems, for example, the solar system, or the atom. One of the more interesting aspects of mind, of course, is its capacity to break existing balances with the reception of new information from the environment and establish new ones.

A second point is that the tendency to maintain balanced states supplies, as it were, a motivating force. When our thoughts, attitudes, or personal relations are in an unbalanced state, we take steps to correct the situation. For example, an assertion made to many Americans that their President secretly favored the segregation of races would be quite disturbing. They could strike a new balance in several ways: one might be to formulate a new opinion of the President; another, to conclude that segregation might not be a bad course of action after all; and a third way might be simply to dismiss the assertion as unbelievable. Similarly, it often happens in the course of our social relationships that one of our best friends behaves in a manner we consider displeasing. Again, this produces in us an incongruity which motivates us to action, either overt or covert.

Our third point is one which we have already mentioned but which we now state again: the balancing of perception or cognition involved in social relationships—that is, person perception—follows somewhat different rules from those involved in the perception of objects. Persons have, at least in our perception of them (and their perception of us), a degree of indeterminateness not shared by things. The result of this is that the process of establishing any kind of balance in a social relationship is bound to be a very changing and fluid one compared with that between a person and an inanimate object. Nonetheless, the general principle should apply in both cases. After all, the tendency toward balance or symmetry that seems to be a property of man's perception—whether of objects or agents—represents another *class* of explanation of the evident fact that human beings are social—not the only one, as we have tried to make clear in our discussion of social motivation. However, it is perhaps the one on which the mainstream of workers in this field have focused their research and theorizing.

The four categories just discussed—instinct, learning, contact needs, and balance each provide a slightly different conceptual framework for studying social motivation. Undoubtedly no single one of them has a complete monopoly on the truth. Each simply represents a particular way of thinking about and researching the problem of why human beings (and many species of lower animals) have a motivation to interact socially with one another.

CHAPTER 8
SOCIAL EXPERIENCE: PERCEPTION AND ATTITUDE

This chapter is devoted to a consideration of two major concepts studied in social psychology, namely, perception and attitude. Both of these can and have been considered in reference to the world of inanimate objects. Here, however, we will be dealing mainly with social perception, that is, our immediate experience of other persons, and with social attitudes, that is, our orientations toward other people involving enduring feelings and beliefs about them.

SOCIAL PERCEPTION

Section Two dealt mainly with Freud's theory of personality. The material it covered may seem to have little to do with the subject now under discussion, but in point of fact, Freud, like many others who have speculated about human behavior, was at least implicitly concerned with the problem of social perception. After all, it was, in the end, the manner in which a person saw reality that really mattered. Objective circumstances might be favorable, but wealth, position in society, and a family counted for nothing if a person perceived these as unpleasant liabilities. The same applied in the case of childhood events. If a patient thought he had suffered severe trauma, it mattered little if he really had or not. What did matter was his belief that he had. This is a problem with which any therapist has to deal.

Freud himself never attempted to set out the rules that govern the way human beings perceive the world and each other. But his tacit emphasis on perception—the world as perceived by a patient, or the patient's phenomenal world—stems from the same European philosophic tradition out of which also grew Gestalt psychology with its stress on experience and perception.

We have already discussed one postulate about perception: the principle that the component parts of a perception or a cognition tend to strike a kind of balance, or symmetry, between each other and that this balance is as simple as prevailing conditions allow. Look at the simple line drawing in Figure 8–1. We tend immediately to see a cube projected back in space, even though the drawing is, of course, flat. Why should this be so? The explanation offered by Gestalt psychologists is that a cube is simpler, more symmetrical, and better balanced than the complex six-sided figure the lines constitute when seen as flat. Because it is simpler and requires less work for the mind to manage, it is the three-dimensional cube that is perceived.

A second property of perception, implicit in the one just discussed, is that *it tends to occur in terms of wholes which have properties independ-*

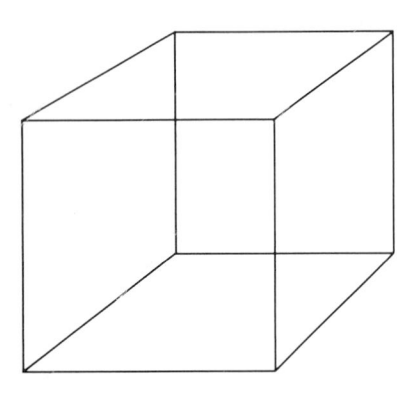

FIG. 8–1 It is difficult to see this drawing as anything but a cube projecting backward in space.

ent of the properties of the individual parts. A melody, for example, can readily be recognized whatever the key in which it is played. Not the absolute values of the individual notes but the relations between them are important. It is this property, of course, that allows us to speak of balance, congruity, or symmetry. These terms refer precisely to the *quality of relationship* that holds between different component parts of a percept or cognition. If our thoughts about a person or object could be isolated from each other, we would never have any conflicts and tensions about them. It would not then seem at all anomalous to have a friend who was deeply religious and at the same time a murderer. But, in fact, such a situation would make most of us feel troubled, and we would take steps of some kind to reduce the anxiety we felt by rearranging our cognitions.

A final property of perception to be mentioned here is that it can be readily influenced by extraneous events. Our emotions and feelings, for example, can change the way we see the world. The word "see" is used here advisedly, quite in its literal sense. Basic characteristics of size and shape, as well as meaning and value, can be grossly distorted by such simple physiological conditions as being hungry or thirsty. Needs and values, in other words, do affect perception (cf. Section Four).

These three tendencies of perception—to see the world in terms of groupings, or units, to strike some kind of balance between the elements comprising a unit, and, finally, its susceptibility to disturbance by external forces—have been studied a good deal.

In this chapter, we are concerned with the experience or perception by people of each other. As we have already indicated, this is fundamental to what we have called social reality. How we communicate and interact with fellow human beings is strongly determined by how we experience them. Consequently, we now consider some experimental data on the subject of person perception. Since the notion of causality is so fundamental to our experience of persons as against things, we start with some of the work done on this topic. The two studies which we will discuss, carried out by Michotte and by Heider, respectively, were largely descriptive in character. Nevertheless, they did set the stage for further work on this problem.

Example 8–1 *Experimental work on the perception of causality (Michotte, 1963)*

In 1956 there first appeared the English translation, by T. R. Miles and Elaine Miles of Oxford, of Michotte's work on the perception of causality originally published in more abbreviated form in 1946. The volume contains 102 brief experiments. All are concerned with variations of two basic effects, called by Michotte the "launching" effect and the "entraining" effect. One apparatus used is ingeniously simple. Called the *disk method*, it involves a wheel rotating behind a screen in which a small aperture has been cut. On the wheel are placed two disks, and on each disk a black or red line is drawn. These components are shown in Figure 8–2. When the wheel is rotated, the subject sees in the screen aperture two small squares, one black and one red. Depending on the angles at which the lines are drawn in relation to the axis, each square will move at a certain speed or remain stationary. The time at which each starts to move and the constancy of the speed of each can likewise be arranged.

Because of limitations of this apparatus, a second method, the *projection method*, was also used. Since this was simply a rather more flexible cinematic version of the first, we need not describe here its detailed components.

With those apparatuses, the two situations of launching and entraining were as follows: In the first, object 1, the black squares, moves toward object 2, the gray square, 40 mm to the right in the center of the slit. As object 1 contacts 2, it stops,

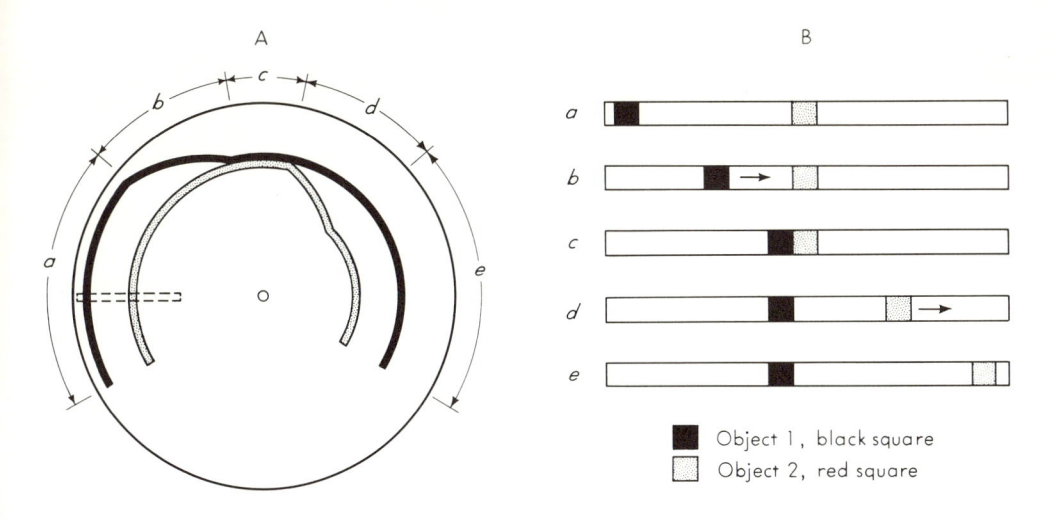

FIG. 8-2 Michotte's apparatus for studying perception of causality.
A. The wheel is rotated behind a panel (outlined in the figure). This causes the lines to move together or separately in various combinations and at various speeds.
B. The situation which the subject sees. (*Krech & Crutchfield, 1948*)

and 2 starts to move either at the same speed or at a speed lower than that of 1. The clear impression of observers is that the black square causes 2 to move, or *launches* it.

The second situation differs only in that 1, after contacting 2, does not stop but continues in motion contiguously with 2. The squares thus form a moving bicolored rectangle. Here, subjects almost unanimously get the impression that 1 is carrying 2 along, or *entraining* it.

The 100 short studies that follow these two prototypic ones specify the exact spatial and temporal conditions under which these effects are experienced. Together they offer some proof that human beings, when circumstances are right, do have an immediate perception of causality.

More to the point of our present discussion are some of the qualitative aspects of the two experimental situations. In a number of cases, certain combinations of movement produced in observers a compelling impression of human or animal activity. Since Heider's studies deal specifically with this aspect of perception, it is necessary to mention only one example from Michotte.

Only a single object is presented, this consisting of a rectangle 10 mm in length at the extreme left of the aperture. In the first phase of this experiment, the right end of the rectangle elongates toward the right until its whole length is 42 mm. At this point, the left end contracts to the right, while the right end is held stationary until the original length of 10 mm is reinstated. The whole cycle is then repeated two or more times.

The response of the subjects may best be stated in Michotte's own words:

> After they have watched for a moment what is happening in the slit in the apparatus, they generally show great surprise and without any prompting they say "Caterpillar" or "Worm." Indeed, the impression of animal locomotion is startling; one literally sees an animal crawling or creeping and it is genuinely an object *which moves of its own accord* [Michotte, 1963, p. 185; italics in the original].

"Swimming" or "pursuit" movements can be similarly produced in perception.

These results seem to indicate that two kinds of causality are indeed part of our experience: one, the mechanical causality of physical objects, and the other, the spontaneous activity of live beings; and

111   SOCIAL EXPERIENCE: PERCEPTION AND ATTITUDE

we may accept this distinction independently of whether we accept the immediacy of these impressions or not. A fuller exploration of the characteristics of the second class was made in an experiment by Heider and Simmel at Smith College in 1944.

Example 8–2 *Perception of causality (Heider & Simmel, 1944)*

In this study, Heider, with a colleague, Marianne Simmel, undertook to examine experimentally what they called "apparent behavior." This term designates those kinds of actions experienced by subjects as arising from inanimate stimuli moving in a certain way, for example, the "caterpillar" movements seen in Michotte's experiments.

The method consisted of asking subjects to describe the events in short motion-picture sequence depicting two triangles, T and t, and a disk, or circle c, moving around, into, and out of a partly enclosed space. The components of the situation are shown in Figure 8–3. The action was divided into twelve scenes. Two examples are as follows:

1. T chases c within the house; t moves along the outside of the house toward the door.
2. t opens the door, c moves out of the house, and t and c close the door.

These verbal descriptions are, of course, not made available to subjects. All they saw was the actual film. They were given different instructions in two experiments. In the first, they were required simply to write down what happened in the picture, and in the second they were asked to answer a short questionnaire consisting of ten questions framed in frankly anthropomorphic terms. For example, question 4 asked, "Why did the two triangles fight?"

In experiment 1, only one out of thirty-four subjects answered in purely geometric terms. All the others gave descriptions in terms of animate beings. One began as follows: "A man has planned to meet a girl, and the girl comes along with another man. The first man tells the second to go; the second tells the first, and he shakes his head." The story continued in the same vein.

In experiment 2, the same kinds of results were obtained. Subjects had no difficulty in ascribing personality characteristics to any of the figures.

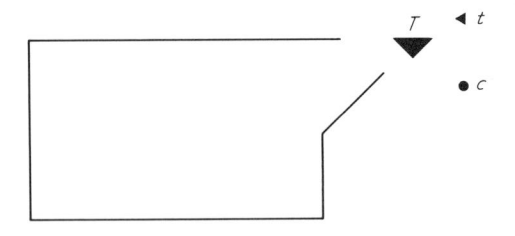

FIG. 8–3 The components of the animated cartoon used by Heider and Simmel to study the perception of causality. (*Heider & Simmel, 1944*)

Thus T was described by thirty-five out of thirty-six subjects as very aggressive, warlike, pugnacious, angry, and a bully. Other queries elicited similar categories of answers.

Heider and Simmel, after analyzing their results, concluded that under conditions in which there was *attribution of movement origin* to objects there occurred the experience of animated, emotional behavior. Depending on the quality and sequence of their movements, stimuli were seen as being angry, sorrowful, blameworthy, frightened, or happy.

Taken together, the studies we have discussed indicate that the problem of person perception is amenable to empirical analysis. They suggest also that we do respond immediately, or at least very quickly, to the "look" of things or of people and do so in terms of special categories. One might say that we are "cognitively tuned" in such a way that we can usually tell something about each other's feelings and emotional states without too much error. Furthermore, it may also be true that much effort and learning is required to "untune" ourselves from others. Children are so highly expressive that their personality moods are easily read by most adults. This often leads to difficulties with parents. A child who is told to stop doing something undesirable may display his defiance—often unintentionally—by little gestures and expressive movements that are very clear. However, for most parents these are hard to label verbally and, in any case, are not so bad in themselves. The parent may consequently find himself feeling quite angry without a clearly localizable target for his anger. This simple example perhaps typifies the subtlety and complexity of the problem of person perception.

One authority, Renato Tagiuri of Harvard University, says in reference to it:

> Do we not all "know" enough about this? Is not our relatively smooth interaction with others witness to this? To those who feel this way, we can give only a general reaction.... [It] is quite clear that insufficient attention has been given in theories—if we may call them such—of person perception to the broad and allegedly "well-known facts" of interpersonal behavior [Tagiuri, in Tagiuri & Petrullo, 1958].

There is no doubt that Tagiuri is right. The phenomenon of person perception may not, at first, seem to offer any problem, but closer analysis will reveal many. Let us look at one of these in particular.

There probably exists a good deal of variation between individuals in their manner of experiencing other people. Some persons are very sensitive to nuances of behavior and expression; others are quite insensitive. The simple hypothesis that individual differences exist in respect to person perception is certainly a sensible one that is capable of being explored experimentally. Once we think about how this can be done, a number of other problems immediately arise. How, in fact, do we measure the ability to perceive other people correctly? How can we know what is, in fact, a "correct" perception as opposed to an "incorrect" one? Is it one unitary ability, or is it multiple and complex, varying greatly with circumstances and stimulus persons? Is it something largely inborn, or is it mostly learned? If it is learned, how does this learning occur? What part does maturation play? Has person perception something to do with liking and disliking? For example, do people who are better at it form favorable or unfavorable opinions about acquaintances more readily than those who are poor at it? These are but a few of the many questions we can ask about the general problem, and the answers to them are not immediately obvious.

In order to illustrate the active line of research that has been going on in this area over the last fifteen or twenty years, we will examine two research foci. One of these is concerned with the constancy and the other with the variation in perception of persons. Assuming that all of us are basically able to interact with others, except perhaps those who are seriously mentally ill, can we say (1) that all social situations or stimuli are equally easily interpreted or (2) that with a constant situation there exists variation between perceivers in their ability to experience it correctly or veridically? Let us look at the first possibility.

Much of our communication with others is based on our perception of their actions or movements—what they do, how they look and speak, rather than the meanings they attempt to convey through words. As Heider (1944) points out, for example, the French philosopher Sartre has made much of the power of "the look." Someone else looking or staring at us will produce feelings of tension, constraint, or discomfort that were previously absent. "Staring down the other person" is a favorite game of childhood and certainly is a form of behavior by no means absent in the interactions of adults. Likewise, intonations of speech, use of certain grammatical forms, "significant pauses," and emotional expression all serve as a background against which we assess the meanings of verbal communication. The simple phrase "I love you" can be used to convey a dozen different ideas, depending on the surrounding context and the manner in which it is uttered. Consider simply the matter of emphasis. "*I* love you" means "I" as distinct from other people. "I love *you*" means "you" as against other people. "I *love* you" means "love" as against indifference or hate. Spoken in a crescendo, the phrase would signify desperation or climax; said in a diminuendo, it would carry a note of despair. Many other variations are possible in addition to these. It is fair to say, in fact, that the phrase is made *socially significant* only by reason of the emotional overtones it possesses. Stripped of these, it would convey very little.

It is, therefore, of some importance to find out, at as basic a level as possible, the accuracy with which people can respond to the behavior of others —particularly their emotional expressions. A good deal of work has been done on this topic; some examples follow.

Example 8–3 *Interpretation of emotional expressions (Feleky, 1924)*

A. M. Feleky obtained from 100 untrained observers their judgments of what emotion was being displayed in each of eighty-six photographic poses by a professional actress. The first impression given by the results was that judgments of emotion are highly inaccurate. However, examination of the names of the emotions being displayed revealed that many of them are no more than synonyms. For example, surprise, amazement, astonishment, wonder, and awe were all treated as separate categories, so that to judge "surprise" as "amazement" was counted as a mistake. This defect was remedied in a subsequent reanalysis of Feleky's data by Robert Woodworth of Columbia. His results are shown in Figure 8–4. The use of more inclusive categories reveals clearly that judgments of emotional expression are, on the whole, quite accurate. In fact, the correlation between pose and judgment turns out to be very high: $r = +.92$.

We must add a footnote to this conclusion. The manner in which emotions are expressed does vary a good deal with the culture, in respect to both intensity, or degree of expressivity, and form. For example, the Oriental commonly is regarded as being more "inscrutable" than the Westerner—a view that seems to have some basis in fact, according to the anthropologist Otto Klineberg (1940). This is not necessarily because of any anatomical differences in facial musculature—though there is some slight evidence for this—but more likely because of cultural dictates against free expression of feelings.

Again, we find quite wide differences in the form an emotion may take in different cultural groups. Both Italian and Jewish immigrants in New York City "talk with their hands" a great deal, but they do so quite differently, according to Efron and Foley (1947), two psychologists interested in ethnic differences. They found, for example, that the gestures of the Italians were more symmetrical and more expansive than those of the Jewish group. Again, it may well be true that the gestures of both groups can be reliably interpreted, different though they are, by any observer. Underneath the variations in form and intensity, there do appear constancies, and it is these that constitute the basic stuff of our experience of social reality. When they are in sorrow or in pain, human beings weep, and when they are happy, they smile and laugh; society regulates only the manner in which they do so.

The above experimental example, then, suggests that there do exist in our behavior certain dimensions to which other persons are *immediately* tuned in, in the sense that they do not have to make an inference or deduction but at once grasp the basic meaning of the behavior. The data also suggest, though they do not prove, that some individuals may be better at this than others. This pertains to the second problem area.

Example 8–4 *Sex differences in social perception (Sarbin, 1954)*

In Section II we discussed briefly the Freudian view that women had relatively underdeveloped superegos in contrast to men and could be considered, for this reason, to be less well socialized. As we pointed out in this chapter, "socialized" may mean several different things, two of which concern us here: it may mean institutionalized—and this is the meaning Freud uses—or it may mean socially perceptive. Evidence obtained by P. L. Sullivan and T. Sarbin at the University of California suggests that women may be superior to men in respect to this second definition.

In Sullivan's experiment, male and female subjects were asked simply to sort, or categorize, forty pictures of men into groups. The pictures varied according to a number of dimensions, for example, mood being expressed, type of clothing, features. Analysis of the groupings made showed that women tended to group predominantly in terms of traits or emotional expressions, for example, "moody," "quizzical," whereas men tended to use purely descriptive categories, for example, "well dressed," "executive type."

Sarbin's experiment supported this conclusion. He used a somewhat different technique. Instead of judging photographs, his subjects were asked to free-associate to persons who simply rose to their feet in a classroom and stood for 10 seconds. They wrote down the first three words that "came to mind" on viewing the stimulus persons. Responses were later grouped into two classes—those representing inferences about personality, for example, "shy," "cold," "aggressive," and those that were simply descriptive, such as "student," "tall girl," "gray suit." Again, it was found that women preferred, significantly more than men, to use the inferential words designating perceived personality traits.

Now these two experiments do not, of course, *prove* that women are actually better tuned in so-

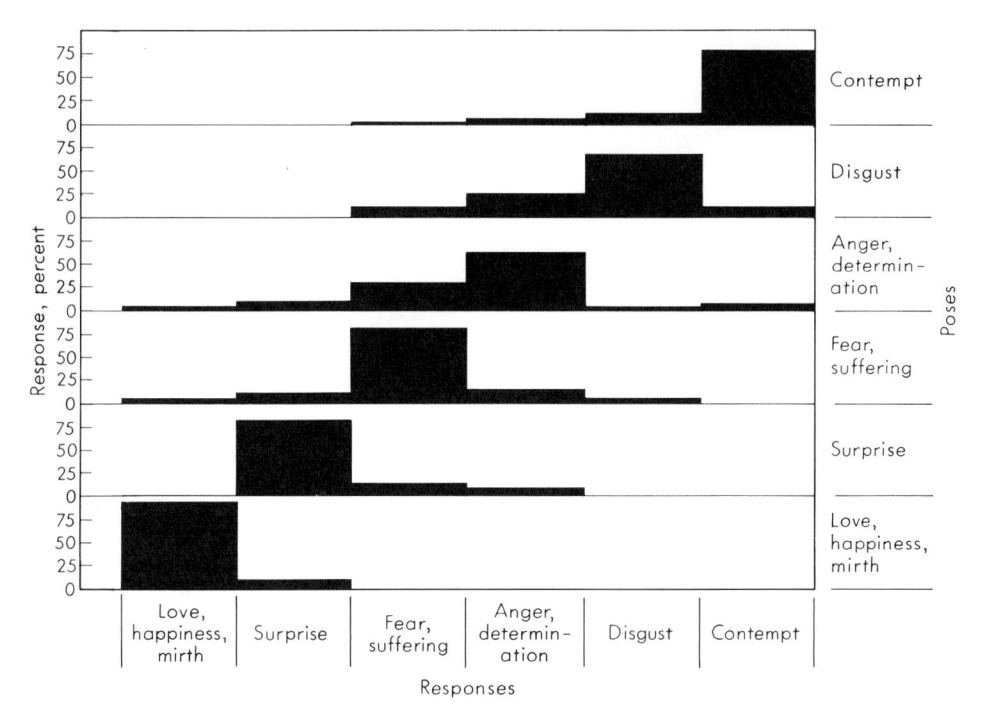

FIG. 8–4 Accuracy of judgment of facial emotional expressions. (*Woodworth, 1940*)

cially than men are, but they do suggest that women tend to be more prone to view the animate world in a manner conducive to social interaction in the sense in which we are using it here. Men, on the other hand, are apparently geared toward using simple indicators which society has designated to order social behavior and social roles. Clothing is such an indicator. We treat a doorman differently from a bellboy and a policeman differently from both of these.

The third study, presented in Example 8–5, involves an examination of both the questions raised above. If person perception tends to be fairly accurate on the average and if individuals differ in their ability in person perception, we can ask whether we are dealing with a general trait—that is, a skill which, in a particular person, maintains a stable level across different situations. Popular opinion would probably favor the view that it is a general trait. Administrators are especially inclined to think that they are able in general to assess character accurately. They implicitly regard this ability as one that is relatively independent of the specific person or type of person being judged and the sort of judgment being made. The following example describes a study that attempts to examine this problem.

Example 8–5 *Accuracy of interpersonal perception—a general trait? (Cline & Richard, 1960)*

Faced with contradictions in previous research on this problem, V. B. Cline and J. M. Richard, Jr., at the University of Utah attempted a fresh attack on it. They filmed interviews of persons recruited from various places in Salt Lake City—a supermarket, a theater lobby, and a university laboratory. The interviewer, a member of the university theater staff, attempted to probe the following areas: (1) personal values, (2) personality strengths and weaknesses, (3) reaction to the interview, (4) hobbies and activities, (5) self-concept. Of all the films made, ten were finally selected on the basis of various criteria. The ten persons involved were later given a battery of nine personality tests, and each person was also rated by five close associates on a fifty-item trait-rating scale.

115   SOCIAL EXPERIENCE: PERCEPTION AND ATTITUDE

Next, the films were shown to fifty men and women summer school students, who were asked to fill out five judging instruments. These included:

1. *Postdiction behavior.* For example, when Mr. M gets angry, he usually:
   a. Ends up cursing obscenely.
   b. Gets so upset he has to walk out or leave.
   c. Tends to keep it to himself and hides his feelings.
2. *Trait rating:* Twenty-five traits were involved, each on a 6-point scale.
3. *Opinion prediction:* Twenty items which the interviewees had already answered, for example, "I fall in love rather easily." The judge is asked to answer as he thinks the interviewee did.
4. *Sentence completion:* One hundred items such as "When I make a mistake, I:
   a. Am embarrassed.
   b. Laugh it off.
   c. Don't give a damn.
   Again judges try to guess the interviewees' answers.
5. *Adjective checklist:* The judge is asked to check which of a pair of adjectives (twenty pairs in all) an interviewee has marked as being descriptive of himself.

Results of the experiment were as follows:

First, it seems to be true that persons who are accurate in respect to one dimension of personality (i.e., judging instrument) tend to be accurate on the others also. Significant relations between the five measures were found. This fact indicates that *interpersonal sensitivity tends to be general across different aspects of personality.*

Second, the data showed that *accuracy was general across persons being judged.* Judges accurate at judging person A tended to be accurate at judging other persons also. The relation between accuracy of judgment for five of the films as against that shown for the other five was also high ($r = .71$).

Third, there appear to be two factors that make up interpersonal perceptiveness: One of these is what has been called *stereotype accuracy,* or sensitivity to the *generalized other.* It refers essentially to the ability of a judge to determine how deviant an individual is, in respect to his general personality, from the average man. Some people can apparently spot an "oddball" quite readily; others cannot. The other component is designated as *differential accuracy,* or *interpersonal sensitivity.* This refers to a judge's ability to assess actual personality differences between any two people without reference to an average person. Thus a person may perceive people not simply according to their degree of conformity to some general norm but as unique individuals, each different from the other.

The results obtained by Cline and Richard are most interesting and suggest a number of other studies that could be carried out. For example, it would be good to know something about the personality of people who use predominantly one judging component as against the other. The conclusions of Sullivan and Sarbin suggest that a sex difference might also appear, men favoring stereotype accuracy and women favoring differential accuracy. Again, if interpersonal sensitivity is a general trait, as they seem to show, how far can it be trained? Most programs in clinical psychology or clinical psychiatry hold to an implicit faith that it can. However, we have little solid evidence as to whether this is so or not. It would be useful to find out.

We have now analyzed the nature of social perception and have suggested how its properties serve to explain why and how man is sociable. The separation we make in an experience between animate and inanimate objects serves to define the difference between physical reality and social reality. The characteristics of social reality, in turn, require us to formulate special sets of rules in order to comprehend it properly. Some of these rules relate to ethical behavior and entail our perception of such behavioral categories as responsibility, blame, trustworthiness, and duty; others relate to behavior that has to do with what we call personality and involves our perception of traits, for example, impulsiveness, dominance, submissiveness, compliance.

By itself, any perception we have of objects or of people is free of possible associated values or beliefs. Thus we can look at a cow grazing in a field and see it simply as that and nothing more. However, this same percept may give rise, in certain people, to particular memories—for example, of early childhood days on a farm. That is to say, for them the cow has also some associated ideas and values. Likewise, we may perceive another person's behavior to be impulsive, and, on top of this, we may react negatively to it if we have the belief that impulsive behavior is inappropriate in a certain context, for example, a work situation. Again, we have added something to the bare percept. Such additions are very common indeed. In fact, in our everyday lives, it is more usual than not for us to have feelings and beliefs about the different parts of the world we perceive. Consequently, psychologists have found it necessary to define a category of experience more complex than that encompassed by the term "percept." This category has been called *attitude*.

ATTITUDES AND COGNITIVE ORGANIZATION

Nature of Attitudes

We have treated perception, or the direct experience we have of other human beings, as the basic process which allows people to be social and to communicate with each other according to a common set of primitive rules. Though it has been the position of Gestalt psychology that the way in which perception works is not acquired, we do not necessarily have to accept this view. It is possible that all human beings learn social perception by interacting with their environment in early life but that those aspects of environment that are relevant to such learning are so fundamental and universal that all individuals come to learn essentially the same modes of social experience. If such is the case, we would expect that only very drastic alterations in early experience would be capable of producing truly deviant social behavior. Harlow's monkeys raised with surrogate mothers appear to constitute a good example of this (see Chapter 7), as do also human infants who have been given inadequate amounts of mothering. However, these are unusual occurrences. The basic requirements are not great, and, provided these are present in the environment of the young organism, the ability to socialize with others will inevitably appear.

As we noted in the previous section, however, there is still some variation between individuals in their ability to make social judgments. Some of this has to do with direct social experience. That is, one person may be simply better attuned to social reality and be more sensitive to the fine nuances of behavior and action. Most of the variation, however, is probably to be found at the more complex level of attitude. This involves, as we indicated, factors such as values and ethical standards, affective states, and general cognitive structure. These are acquired by training and hence are relative to the culture in which the person is raised. We thus come to have dispositions to view the world in certain ways that go a long way beyond the basic percept.

Let us suppose we are watching a ten-year-old boy running down the street. Close behind him is a grown man also running. At its simplest level, depending on how certain physical relations between the two appear in our perception, the situation offers several possibilities of interpretation. First, the man may be *chasing* the boy—that is, following him with an intent to catch him. Second, the two may be *racing*, the man having previously given the boy a handicap. Third, the two may be *playing follow-the-leader* with the boy as leader. And, finally, *the two may not be interacting socially at all:* the boy may be running simply because he enjoys running, the man because he is afraid he will miss a bus at a stop down the street.

We make a decision from these alternatives on the basis of whether the two persons appear to be entrained to each other and on the basis of the outcome of the action. Thus if the boy slows down and the man then does the same, we may conclude we are seeing a game of follow-the-leader. A chase, on the other hand, should involve attempts to elude on the part of the pursued and attempts at capture on the part of the pursuer. A race may be indicated if the impression of effort is given without the impression of pursuit. Finally, coincidence is established if any kind of entrainment is seen to be at a minimum, for example, if the boy suddenly stops or turns, and the man continues running.

These simple components of the situation will usually be sufficient to evoke in us some feelings, such as wonder, amusement, concern, or excitement. In real life, however, our experience is more complex. Thus if the boy happens to be our son or brother and the man behind him is dressed in the uniform of a policeman, we will undoubtedly run a wider gamut of emotions and cognitions—surprise, worry, annoyance at the boy for what he must have done, indignation at the policeman for chasing a small boy, and nagging fears about possible lawsuits. These feelings will be compounded out of the immediate social interaction going on and the values we have earlier come to assign to "relatives," "policemen," the "law," and the "act of chasing." Sons are "good," but "crime" is bad. Likewise, policemen are "good," but men (including policemen) who chase our relatives are "bad." The result is a highly complex and conflicting situation arising out of the beliefs and values we impose on the components of our perception.

The above example suggests that attitudes are *dispositions to believe, feel, and act in certain ways toward objects in the world.* Any attitude thus has these three *components*—the *cognitive,* the *affective,* and the *behavioral.* Thus we *know* or *believe* that persons wearing a certain kind of uniform are employed by the state to uphold the law. Toward them we may *feel* fear, respect, devotion, or hate, or perhaps a mixture of all these, depending on our background. Finally, we may be disposed *to obey* policemen when they tell us to do something, or *to watch carefully* for them when we are speeding, or *to avoid* them if we have committed a felony.

We may infer from the above definition that these dispositions have a number of *properties.* First, they *have a valence sign;* that is, they may be positive or negative toward their object. Second, they *are relatively enduring,* so that the sight of a policeman elicits in us habitual reaction. We are not faced with the difficulty of trying to grasp the concept of "policeman" over and over again every time we see one. In this sense, attitudes are shortcuts that enable us to live more easily in a complex world. Like any shortcut, however, they can sometimes get us into trouble. Prejudices, for example, are shortcuts to understanding rather difficult social problems. The existence, in a country, of a minority group inevitably raises such problems, and it is an easy shortcut solution to deport symbolically all its members, attributing to them plainly undesirable traits. The task of changing such prejudiced attitudes is difficult in proportion to the amount of endurance such attitudes have.

A third property of attitudes—one perhaps implied by what we have already said—is *degree of intensity.* They can be held strongly or weakly, be highly resistant to alteration or readily changeable. Fourth, they may vary in respect to *salience.* A salient attitude is one that permeates the way we approach the world. For example, an authoritarian attitude may be so salient in a person as to color his whole life style. He is always obsequious to supervisors, harsh to inferiors, and quarrelsome with equals; he views society as a hierarchy in which those at the top must constantly guard against displacement by those immediately beneath them and these, in turn, must always be trying to push aside those higher up. Presumably, highly salient attitudes are always held strongly. However, nonsalient attitudes can be intense or weak; thus a person may have a deep dislike of Pekingese dogs, but this will probably not appreciably affect his way of life. On the other hand, some attitude about a little-known ethnic group, say, Eskimos, may be neither strong nor salient.

It should be noted that the word "attitude" is not a new one invented by psychologists. It is a very old one that occurs in many languages, perhaps precisely because it does refer to something very fundamental—namely, the orientation of a person to his physical and social world. Psychologists have recognized the usefulness and importance of the concept and then attempted to analyze carefully the meanings implicit in it.

We have introduced it as if it historically followed work on person perception. It must be emphasized that this sequence has a logical basis only and not a historical one. The concept of attitude was developed earlier and quite independently, and it was only later that the two currents of research came together. Whereas work on perception both of persons and of objects is rooted in German philosophy and psychology, interest in, and use of, attitude as a unit of analysis in social psychology arose mainly in the United States. Gordon Allport (1954, p. 43) says of it:

> This concept is probably the most distinctive and indispensable concept in contemporary American social psychology. No other term appears more frequently in experimental and theoretical literature. Its popularity is not difficult to explain. It has come into favor, first of all, because it is not the property of any one psychological school of thought, and therefore serves admirably the purpose of eclectic writers. Furthermore, it is a concept which escapes the controversy concerning the relative influence of heredity and environment. Since an attitude may combine both instinct and habit in any proportion, it avoids the extreme commitments of

both the instinct theory and environmentalism. The term likewise is elastic enough to apply either to the dispositions of single, isolated individuals or to broad patterns of culture (common attitudes). Psychologists and sociologists therefore find in it a meeting point for discussion and research. This useful, one might say peaceful, concept has been so widely adapted that it has virtually established itself as the keystone in the edifice of American social psychology.

The attributes of attitude we have listed above may be summarized as follows:

Components	Properties
Cognitive	Valence (positive or negative)
Affective	Endurance
Behavioral	Intensity
	Salience

Having set up such a definition, we may then proceed to translate it into concrete terms and subsequently to study it experimentally. A great deal of work has been done along these lines, and we can look at only a small sample. Making a concept concrete has to do first with *measuring* it.

Attitude Measurement

In the late 1920s a large amount of work was initiated, especially by L. L. Thurstone at the University of Chicago, on the problem of developing opinion and attitude scales. Such research has had many immediately useful applications. Particularly in times of national emergency, it may become imperative to assess the temper of different segments of the population in respect to many vital issues. Examples might be attitudes toward black platoons in white companies, attitudes toward conscientious objectors, attitudes toward rationing, or attitudes toward policies of leaders, such as use of nuclear devices, conscription, or social welfare. The vast increase in the use of communications has allowed information to be massively channeled from leaders to the people. Obviously, leaders themselves have an equal need to know something about the effects their messages have. Attitude and opinion scales are devices that readily supply this need for feedback.

The purpose of attitude scales, of which they are several types, is to allow statements to be made about how strongly an attitude is held by an individual or by whole groups as compared to another individual or whole group. With highly refined statistical methods, it becomes possible to say, for example, that Jones has a positive attitude to religion that is twice as strong as that of Smith. Usually, however, we must be content to speak in terms of rank order or percentages. Thus we might state only that Jones' attitude is more negative than 90 percent of the group which is being measured—a far less precise but still useful piece of information. To illustrate the general method by which attitudes are scaled, let us look at Example 8–6.

Example 8–6 *Attitude scaling (Thurstone, 1929)*

In 1929 and during the early 1930s, Thurstone and some collaborators at the University of Chicago undertook to develop formal attitude scales that could be applied to almost any group or concept—for example, Negroes, war, pacifism, capital punishment, evolution, and many others. The essential steps in their procedure were as follows: (1) the collection of a large number of *items*, or statements, about the object, ranging from very positive to very negative; (2) the judgment by a group of experts as to the relative positivity or negativity of each item on a scale from 1 to 11, called the *method of equal-appearing intervals;* (3) the rejection of items for which there was little agreement between judges and the selection of those for which there was good agreement in respect to scale position; (4) assignment of a scale value to each acceptable item, this being the *median of values assigned to it by all judges*. Items are also chosen so that they are distributed fairly evenly along the entire scale from one pole to the other.

The following items—a few from the scale developed by Thurstone and Chave (1929) to measure attitude toward the Church—represent the end result of the above procedures:

Item	Scale value
I believe the Church is the greatest institution in America today.	0.2
I enjoy my Church because there is a spirit of friendliness there.	3.3
I believe the Church is losing ground as education advances.	7.4
I think the Church is a parasite on society.	11.0

An individual taking the test is asked simply to check those propositions with which he agrees. His score is then computed as the *average* of the values of all items he checked. For example, if he checked the first and second of the four listed above, he would receive a score of 1.75. This would indicate a strongly positive attitude toward the Church.

On the whole, such scales seem to work very well and give highly reliable results. They do seem to probe the basic attitude they are set up to measure—that is to say, they are valid—and also they tend to give the same results when a group of individuals is given a retest—that is, they are reliable.

There are a number of other ways of measuring attitudes besides the Thurstone method of equal-appearing intervals. The Likert (1932) method, for example, requires the subject to express his degree of agreement or disagreement with each item on a 5-point scale, from strong agreement to strong disagreement. The propositions that make up the test are deliberately chosen so as to represent rather extreme positions, since a neutral item will probably not evoke either strong agreement or disagreement. Again, a scale can be made up for any attitude object.

A final method, one that antedates those of both Thurstone and Likert, is the Social Distance Scale devised by Bogardus (1925) to measure mainly ethnic attitudes. This uses the simple expedient of asking the subject how closely he would be willing to affiliate with the group under consideration. Five "distances" are used, ranging from "close kinship by marriage" to "citizenship in my country." At the time the scale was first constructed, Bogardus found suprisingly that out of a large population of native-born white Americans, only 54 percent were willing to admit Jewish people to citizenship and only 57 percent were willing to admit Negroes to citizenship. A more recent retest showed happily that such negative attitudes are not nearly so common as they used to be.

Before leaving the topic of attitude measurement, we should strike a cautionary note. The scales described above seem very simple, but this is deceptive. The greatest care goes into their construction. Often thousands of items are given to thousands of people representing as wide a sample of the total population as possible before the final scale is ready to be used. Many statistical analyses are carried out to give greater precision and sensitivity, instructions are made up and examined carefully for ambiguities, and sometimes several trial runs are made on large preliminary samples of subjects. Consequently, the attitude scales we often see in popular magazines should be viewed with skepticism. They usually have no known validity or reliability and are consequently largely meaningless.

Relations between Components in Measured Attitudes

We indicated above that attitudes have several components, these being the cognitive, the affective, or emotional, and the behavioral. The kinds of scales we have just described may assess the first two components, but they certainly do not evaluate the third. Thus, the fact that we may establish reliably that an individual dislikes pacifism intensely does not necessarily mean that his overt behavior will reflect this attitude. For example, he may never discredit pacifism to his friends and acquaintances. What we feel and think and what we actually do are often quite different. This fact is illustrated in Example 8–7.

Example 8–7 *Verbal attitudes and overt behavior (Kutner, Wilkins, & Yarrow, 1952)*

Kutner, Wilkins, and Yarrow set out to examine the extent to which verbally expressed attitudes toward Negroes would spill over into overt behavior. They did not use a conventional attitude scale, though this might also have been feasible. Instead, they obtained the simple assent or dissent of a group of restaurant managers to a discriminatory practice. Specifically, their procedure was as follows: three young women, two white and one black, entered eleven restaurants in a fashionable community and asked for a table. In none of these were they refused. Two weeks after each visit, they sent to the manager of each restaurant a letter requesting a reservation for a "social affair," explaining that the party would have both white and black guests. Seventeen days later a telephone call was made to each asking the same thing. Finally, one day later, a control call was made asking simply for a reservation for a group without mention of race.

The results were interesting. Letters tended uniformly to be ignored, except in a few cases when they were sent later as a result of the telephone call. The telephone calls themselves evoked rather ambiguous responses. Most of the managers said they had not received the letter and expressed a distinct reluctance to accept a reservation for a mixed party, in spite of the fact that they had previously done so. In almost all cases, they made a reservation immediately in response to the control call.

These results suggest that a discriminatory attitude is a highly complex structure and that its cognitive components may not necessarily be reflected in a behavioral component. In the case discussed, this is presumably because such behavior would conflict with other strongly held attitudes, for example, a negative attitude toward making a scene in one's business establishment and possibly hurting one's public image. The potential conflict this would cause was strong enough to force acceptance of the lesser conflict caused by behaving positively (acceptance of reservations) to objects of a negative attitude (Negroes).

Relation of Attitude Properties

Another set of relationships worth examining is that between attitude properties. Let us look at the relationship between how extreme an attitude is and the intensity with which it is held. We have already suggested that there must be a relationship between salience of attitude and its intensity. Now we are asking whether, for any attitude of given salience, assent given by a person to the more extreme propositions about the attitude object implies a greater intensity of commitment. For example, individual A might say yes to the statement "All Communists or Communist sympathizers should be run out of the country." Individual B might agree only to the neutral statement "Communists and Communist sympathizers represent merely another political group and should be treated accordingly." Can we predict that the assent given by individual A has more intensity than the assent given by individual B? It is difficult to supply any general answer to this question; in fact, a general answer may be impossible, in the sense that every case may be a little different. However, the following example illustrates how the problem can be attacked:

Example 8–8 *Extremeness of attitudes and their intensity (Suchman, 1950)*

The question we have posed above was examined empirically by the following procedure: Army personnel were asked first to respond to a number of statements concerning various issues, for example, the Women's Army Corps, satisfaction with their job in the Army, and a number of others. Following this, they were asked to state on a four-point scale, from very strong to not at all strong, the intensity, or strength, of each of the responses they had given. Results for one of the attitude objects are shown in Figure 8–5. The relation is obviously not a simple one. In Figure 8–5a, up to a point on the favorability scale, the less negative the attitude, the less intensely it is held. Note that this point is fairly high on the favorability scale. Here the intensity is at its lowest. With more favorable attitudes, the function inflects and becomes strongly intense again. This interesting result presumably means that servicemen, for the most part, found it difficult to feel neutral about the Women's Army Corps. In addition, it is a curious fact that those who felt *quite* positive were more intensely committed to this position than those who felt *strongly* positive, and these, in turn, were less committed than those who felt *extremely* positive. One might have expected the curve to inflect at the middle point of the favorability curve, but it does not.

Other curves drawn for other object attitudes gave different results. Attitudes to do with job satisfaction, for example, were strongly held only by those having highly negative or highly positive views (Figure 8–5b). All those in between tended not to feel strongly about their jobs.

The two examples above will serve to illustrate the manner in which we can study the relationships between the different components and properties of attitudes. They also indicate that these relationships are liable to be very complex and often highly particular to a single situation. Thus highly negative cognitive and affective components need not result in highly negative behavior. Nor is there always a uniform relation between extremeness of a position and intensity with which such a position is held. If there are general rules covering these relationships, they are as yet undiscovered.

Apropos of this last point, the examples we have given suggest a principle of some universality that may underlie the particular structure that an attitude may have in an individual. This is the principle of *balance* to which we have already referred several times. Attitudes can be considered to be systems made up of parts, or elements, each of

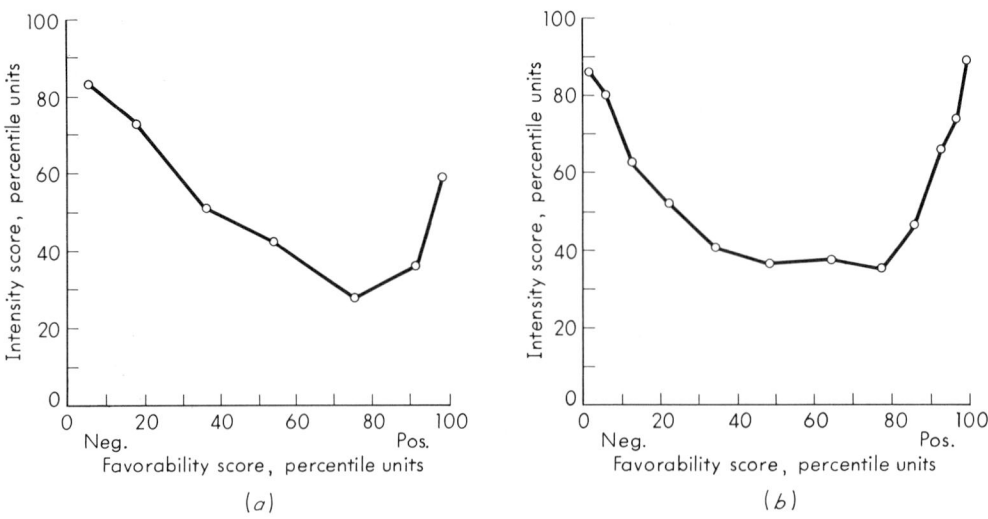

FIG. 8-5 Intensity of (a) attitude toward the Women's Army Corps as related to favorability; (b) attitude toward job. (*Suchman, 1950*)

which has a certain valence and intensity. It is obvious that circumstances may force situations in which conflicts or imbalances between different attitude structures arise. Such imbalances give rise to tension which in turn leads us to take steps to restore a balanced state. For example, our learning that an admired professor disliked a book we liked would cause in us a cognitive imbalance which we would have to try to resolve as best we could. We might revise our estimate of the professor, or we might revise our estimate of the book. Thus, we might conclude that perhaps the book was not so good after all or decide that the professor was not as bright as we thought he was before. The analysis of attitude structure, or more broadly "cognitive structure," and the modes by which balance in them is maintained has represented lively interest in social psychology. Let us look at it more closely.

ATTITUDES, COGNITIVE STRUCTURE, AND BALANCE

It is difficult to say exactly where the idea of imbalance had its origin. It would probably be fair to give some credit again to Freud and his thesis that the mind is made up of parts, each of which has a dynamic quality and which may conflict with each other. These are certainly general ideas that have influenced and still influence a great many psychologists in various fields. Gestalt psychology has made more explicit use of the same notions. It contrasts sharply in this respect with the structuralism of Wundt and others who were attempting simply to analyze the mind into its simplest dimensions—mental anatomy, as it were. Wertheimer, Koffka, and Köhler, on the other hand, regarded the mind as being governed by a dynamic principle which regulated the relationships between its parts. Each component in our experience of some sector of the world can be thought of as generating tension. Other things being equal, the mind acts so as to correct imbalances between these separate sources of tension, so that the total amount is distributed as evenly as possible.

The application of such ideas to social psychology was first made by Kurt Lewin, himself a junior associate of Wertheimer and the other founders of the Gestalt movement. Lewin's field theory considered the phenomenal world of the person, including objects and other persons and the relations between them. These parts of the field may have a valence, positive or negative, insofar as they are attractive or unattractive to the perceiver. To give a simple example, a hungry dog may see another larger dog eating a bone. Its phenomenal field thus contains an object with a high positive valence—the bone—

and an associated object with a high negative valence—the other dog. One attracts, the other repels, and the final result is the oscillating, approach-avoidance behavior we would expect to see in this situation. Note also that the oscillation tends to be an uneven one, in the sense that the approaches are usually slow and cautious, and the retreats are sudden and sharp (cf. Miller, 1951). This may suggest additional properties accruing to objects having negative as opposed to positive valences.

If we turn back to the contemporary scene in social psychology, we can assign the responsibility for putting the ideas of balance and conflict to work in the specific context of social psychology mainly to one man—Fritz Heider. It will be recalled that Heider specified as a basic dimension of social perception the "attribution of origin" to persons. Other persons are experienced as acting on us and on our shared environment, and we, in turn, are seen by them in the same way. Thus the simplest social situation will consist of two persons sharing a common environment, having certain dispositions toward this environment and toward each other, and each being aware of the other and the other's dispositions. Heider has represented such situations using the following terms: "P," a person or perceiver; "O," another person perceived by P; "X," an object; and "R," a positive or negative relation between O and X. The components O and X may be seen by P as being positive or negative also. This generates a number of different possibilities, some of which will produce imbalance, some of which will not. In the experience of P, the following eight possibilities exist, an odd number of minuses (i.e., 1 or 3) making for imbalance, an even number making for balance:

		O	R	X	
The experience of P	1	+	+	+	Balanced
	2	−	+	−	
	3	−	−	+	
	4	+	−	−	
	5	+	−	+	Unbalanced
	6	−	+	+	
	7	+	+	−	
	8	−	−	−	

By way of example, number 4 represents the case where someone we like dislikes something we dislike. Number 6, on the other hand, is a case of someone we dislike who likes something we also like. It is no strain for friends to dislike the same thing, but it is often very disturbing to us to find that an enemy has a pattern of values and wants similar to our own.

The other six cases given above can readily be translated into common social situations. We will leave this to the reader and go on to discuss some of the explications that have been made of this basic model. In this respect, it has been astonishingly fruitful with theorizing and research. At least eight separate models dealing with attitude and cognitive organizations have come out of Heider's original formulation. Let us look at a few examples.

Newcomb's Model of Communicative Acts

One of the earliest explications of the notion of imbalance was attempted by Theodore Newcomb (1953) at the University of Michigan. He starts with a unit he calls an A-B-X system, in which A and B stand for persons having some orientation or attitude toward each other and X stands for an object in the environment toward which each person also has an orientation. Orientations may be broadly positive or negative. The unit may be represented as follows:

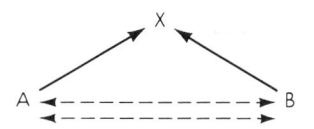

As in Heider's model, balance or imbalance of the system is given by the signs of the four relationships shown in the diagram. When there is imbalance and also some necessity or demand for coorientation, the persons of the system will take steps to bring about a more balanced situation. For example, if person A is positive about religion (X) and likes B while B, though he likes A, is negative about religion, then it is likely that one or both will initiate communication in an effort to restore symmetry. We have this situation:

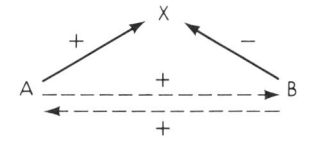

123   SOCIAL EXPERIENCE: PERCEPTION AND ATTITUDE

Presumably, whether A or B is the initiator of communicative acts will depend on the relative strengths of the demands for coorientations that are placed on each. A may not be at all disturbed by B's rejection of something he values, whereas B, for various reasons, may feel very upset by the asymmetry. If communication fails to alter the relevant signs in the system, other consequences may ensue. For example, A and B may decide they no longer like each other and break off relationships. Either may change his attitude toward X voluntarily without being persuaded to do so or else agree on a compromise, A by toning down his fondness for religion and B by permitting himself to see in it some virtues. Finally, there may occur, in either person, *cognitive dissociation,* that is, a refusal to admit that the other's orientation to X has any relevance to their relationships. Presumably such a solution is not a very satisfactory one and will work up to a point. There is a limit on the "allowances" we can make to preserve a positive relationship with another person, though this limit may vary rather widely with different individuals.

Newcomb's model is a rather general one and has been more valuable in suggesting an orientation for future work rather than in generating very specific testable hypotheses. We will now look at two other models which have been productive of a good deal of empirical study.

Festinger's Theory of Cognitive Dissonance

Basically, Festinger's theory of "cognitive dissonance" (Festinger, 1957) explores the *outcomes* of having components of experience that are in disagreement with each other. The components he calls "cognitive elements." These may be beliefs, attitudes, data of experience, opinions, values, or expectations. For example, one element could be "Smoking is pleasurable to me." Another, dissonant with this one, could be "Much evidence indicates that smoking causes cancer." Formally speaking, these two elements are dissonant *because the obverse of one element follows from the other.* Thus expanding, the above elements,

> Smoking is pleasurable.
> Pleasure is good.
> Smoking is good.
> But: Smoking causes cancer.
> Cancer is bad.
> Smoking is bad.

Dissonance between elements thus varies with the *relevance* of the elements to each other. This is implicit in the definition of dissonance given above. Obviously, one proposition can imply the obverse of another only if the two are relevant to each other. However, it is well to state this fact quite explicitly. Also, dissonance varies in magnitude with the *importance* of the elements involved. The fact that a friend likes oysters, which I dislike, may create only very mild dissonance. If he insults my wife, however, the dissonance is likely to be a good deal greater.

Having defined cognitive element and dissonance and suggested two factors determining the magnitude of dissonance, we may examine Festinger's hypotheses about the outcomes of a dissonant situation.

In common with Heider and the Gestalt theorists, Festinger postulates that dissonance, or imbalance, produces discomfort, which motivates the person experiencing it to seek its reduction. Three main ways of doing this are available: In the first place, there may occur a change in a *behavioral cognitive* element. Thus, in the example given above, the dissonance between smoking and health may be alleviated most directly simply by giving up smoking. Doing this presumably reflects a commitment to the cognitive element: "Smoking is *not* pleasurable." Though clearly very sensible, such a course of action may be a rather difficult one to follow.

A second means of dissonance reduction is by changing an *environmental cognitive element.* This is naturally only feasible when the person has sufficient control over his environment. For example, a person who drinks a good deal but is worried about the bad effects of alcohol may avoid the company of nondrinkers and associate only with heavy drinkers. Such selection of an environment friendly to his habit will lessen the likelihood of dissonance.

A third way to reduce dissonance is to add more information, that is, *new cognitive elements.* This has the effect of increasing either the negativity or positivity of the object, thus reducing the dissonance to the point where it is relatively slight. A person who buys a house more expensive than he can really afford experiences dissonance. He may reduce this by telling himself that an expensive house will impress his clients or his boss and this will lead to an eventual increase in his income level or that his family life will be much easier in more spacious quarters and this will, in turn, allow him to work more productively. It is important to note that the addition of such cognitive elements may itself lead to behavior that validates them. He may entertain more, be nicer to his wife, work during his evenings at home, and generally behave in ways that he would not have done had he not put himself into a dissonant situation.

Using his model, Festinger and his colleagues, as well as others, have tested many interesting predictions. Following is an illustrative study that examines some aspects of the point just discussed, namely, the behavioral and cognitive effects of making a decision. It is clear, first of all, that any decision, especially a so-called difficult one, will give rise to some dissonance. When we choose one of two attractive alternatives, we invariably feel some regret at losing the nonchosen one. The bachelor who finally commits himself to marriage will probably find that his new happiness may be tinged with a slight sadness over the loss of his other girl friends. As we have already stated, this dissonance is hypothesized in the model to have certain outcomes in behavior and attitudes, these all being essentially ways of increasing the value of the chosen alternative and decreasing the value of the one rejected. This hypothesis certainly does not strain common sense. Nevertheless, before it can be of any scientific value, it must be tested. The example following has attempted to do this:

Example 8–9 *Postdecisional change in attractiveness of chosen and rejected alternatives (Brehm, 1956)*

The hypothesis to be tested by the experiment was, as stated above, that the attractiveness of an object chosen over another would increase in the degree of attractiveness it had prior to the decision, whereas the rejected object would correspondingly decrease in its attractiveness.

The subjects were women college students taking a course in introductory psychology. They were told that their opinions about certain manufactured products were being sampled as part of a market-research survey being undertaken by the experimenter. Each subject was told she would be paid for her time by being given one of the products involved in the survey.

Procedure was as follows: The eight products were arranged in front of each subject. These were an automatic toaster, an electric coffee maker, a small portable radio, a desk lamp, a silk-screen print of a painting, a stopwatch, an art book, and a sandwich grill. Each could be inspected at leisure, after which all of them were given a rating by the subject on an 8-point scale ranging from "extremely desirable" to "definitely not at all desirable."

The next step was to offer a subject her choice of one of only two of the products and to explain that there was an insufficient number of them to go around. The two presented in any particular case were not, however, selected arbitrarily. Half the subjects, the high-dissonance group, were given a choice between two products which they had rated closely (a 1-point difference); the other half, the members of the low-dissonance group, were given their choice of two they had rated as being rather different (2½ points' difference). Thus, a subject in the first group might have had to choose between an electric toaster (rating of 5) and a radio (rating of 6); and a subject in the second group might have had to choose between a coffee maker (rating of 6) and a stopwatch (rating of 3). Another group of subjects was not allowed a decision but simply given a "gift" of one of the items wrapped in paper; these subjects served as controls for the effects of actually making a decision as the other girls did. After a subject had made her choice, she was asked to read a "research report" on each item. One purpose of this step was to allow some time to elapse before the final phase of the study.

The final part of the experiment consisted of obtaining a second rating, this being requested on the pretext of checking the first impressions on which the subjects had based their initial ratings. Another purpose was to see if reading reports specifically about the objects presented for choice had a different effect on postdecisional attitude than reading reports about nonchoice objects.

In summary, then, the procedure involved these steps: (1) estimation of initial attitude to a set of objects; (2) a forced choice of one of two objects having either similar or dissimilar ratings, i.e., a highly dissonant or mildly dissonant choice; (3) reestimation of attitude to the chosen and nonchosen alternatives.

Let us now look at the results. Dissonance theory predicts that postdecisional attractiveness of chosen objects should increase whereas that of nonchosen

Table 8-1 Postdecisional changes in attractiveness of chosen as against rejected alternatives*

Condition	Net change from first to second rating — Chosen object	Rejected object	Total dissonance reduction
Without research reports:			
Low dissonance	+.38†	+.24	+.62
High dissonance	+.26	+.66	+.92
With research reports:			
Low dissonance	+.11	.00	+.11
High dissonance	+.38	+.41	+.79
Gift	0		

* This table is Festinger's summary of Brehm's data (Festinger, 1957).
† A plus sign means change in direction of dissonance reductions, i.e., increase in attractiveness of chosen alternative, decrease in attractiveness of rejected alternative.

objects should decrease, and that this effect should operate more strongly in the case of more dissonant as against less dissonant decisions. The data are shown in Table 8-1. They need to be studied rather carefully.

Perhaps the first point to notice is that the members of the "gift" group, who did not have to make a decision, showed no change in attitude from the first to the second measurement. In contrast, all decision groups showed a change. This confirms the hypothesis that decision making per se produces a complex change in attitude. Second, the kinds of changes that occur are generally in the predicted directions. Chosen objects become more attractive; rejected objects become less attractive. Decisions tend thus to polarize phenomenal reality. "Good" things become better; "bad" things become worse. Third, this effect is greater when dissonance conditions are high—that is, when the alternatives are rather close in estimated value. The difference, though it occurs overall, applies mainly when research reports about the items were not read. This result is due to the very small amount of dissonance reduction shown by the low-dissonance group which had the reports (+.11). We can only make guesses as to why this should be so, since the description of contents of the reports is rather vague. It may be that they contained enough "factual" statements, both positive and negative, to make any change in attitude rather difficult. The subjects operating under such a condition would be forced to maintain their initial opinions about the objects they had chosen or rejected. One might then expect that their *satisfaction* with their choice would be less. Brehm gathered further data which appear to support this conclusion.

One final point is worth making. The change in attractiveness is greater for rejected objects in the high-dissonance groups, whereas in the low-dissonance groups the chosen object gains more than the rejected one loses. This seems sensible: if one is sure of one's positive choice, one need not bother very much if at all about the rejected alternative. But it is difficult to offer any formal explanation of such a result in terms of dissonance theory. One would presumably have to construct a postulate dealing with the magnitude of change as a function of initial scale position.

In general, Brehm concludes that his experimental results fit rather well with the dissonance model, which they indeed seem to do. They have, in fact, been supported by a good deal of later work.

The Osgood-Tannenbaum Congruity Model

This theory focuses directly on degree of *measured change* that occurs in attitudes toward some object about which incongruous beliefs are held. Suppose we read in a reputable newspaper that a highly respected political figure was seen dining with a known underworld leader. This would clearly be an incongruous situation which should produce, according to the theory, a shift in the attitudes we formerly held toward both these social objects. Osgood and Tannenbaum (1955) have concerned themselves with the prediction and measurement of such changes.

Festinger arrived at his model via earlier interest in, and work on, group dynamics and social behavior. Charles Osgood, trained originally at Yale, came out of a behavioristic rather than a Gestalt tradition. It was specifically his program on the analysis and measurement of connotative meaning (cf. Section Five) that led him to a concern with incongruity—that is, a conflict between the attributes a person assigns to a particular object. If for some reason, as in the example given above, the same object is judged to be both good and bad or powerful and weak at the same time, some resolution or redefinition of the meaning that object has for us becomes necessary. Thus Osgood, though he traveled by a rather different theoretical road, arrived at a consideration of the same problem that concerned Festinger. Note, however, that unlike Festinger's model, that of Osgood and Tannenbaum actually attempts to predict *amount* as well as direction of change.

The major components of the model are *attitudinal objects, scale positions of such objects,* and *associative or dissociative bonds between objects*. The first of these components needs no further explanation. The second refers to the value that an object has for a person, this being defined on a scale having both a positive and a negative pole. A heartily disliked object may thus have a scale position of -3.0, a highly attractive one a position of $+3.0$, and so on. The term "bond" is somewhat loosely defined. It generally means a junction or disjunction between two (or more) cognized attitude objects. If we see our best friend deep in amiable conversation with our worst enemy, we form an associative bond simply by observing their social interaction. The combination would, in fact, produce sharp incongruity. On the other hand, if the two were engaged in a sharp altercation, we would be perceiving a dissociative bond, and this would be *for us* quite congruous. We may represent the model graphically as shown in Figure 8–6.

Note that the scale positions occupied by the attitude objects as well as the designated relationship between them are as experienced by a subject. To generate any one of the four cases, we would have to ask him to rate each of the two objects on a 7-point scale and also to state what the relation between the two was—that is, whether it was associative or dissociative.

The figure illustrates two cases of relatively congruous and two cases of relatively incongruous relations. Case *a* might be exemplified by a person having a friend ($+2$) who dislikes sports, which he also dislikes (-2). Here we have *perfect balance, or equilibrium,* since the two objects dissociatively linked have equal values with opposite sign. Case *b* is also a congruous relation. Here, the friend likes turnips, which we also like. Note, however, that the equilibrium is not perfect as in the previous case. One object is not liked as well as the other. It is an assumption of the model that whenever there is associative linkage between objects of the same sign, a shift in attitude will occur if their scale values are different. This would mean that turnips at $+2$ should become even better liked by us since they are valued by a person we think very highly of ($+3$). On the other hand, by the same token, the value placed by our friend on an object we do not value that highly should cause him to sink slightly in our estimation. In the model, *the distance each one shifts is determined by the inverse of its degree of polarization*. This principle is based on the documented fact that intense attitudes are more difficult to change than less intense ones. Since the objects stand in a ratio of 2 to 3 in respect to their scale positions, then turnips at 2 should move $3/5$ ($5 = 2 + 3$) up in the next unit and the friend $2/5$ down. Both objects would thus end up with the same scale position of $2\,3/5$.

Case *c* represents incongruity. Here we have an associative linkage between something we like and something we do not like. For example, a racial segregationist who is also a Catholic may experience considerable discomfort if he hears his bishop promulgating integration between the races. Theoretically, the attitudes should both end up at the zero point given the equilibrium postulate and given their respective scale positions. Something else may also happen, of course, namely, a refusal on the part of the person to believe that the bishop's position really reflects that of the Catholic Church. This possibility is allowed for by an additional variable in the model, called by Osgood and Tannenbaum an "incredulity" factor.

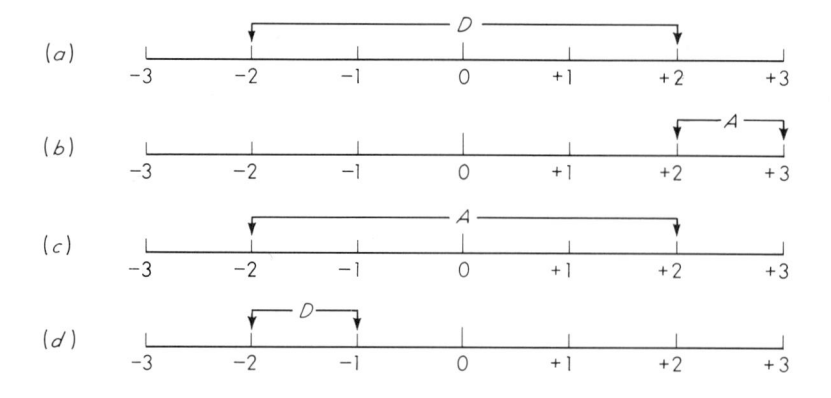

FIG. 8–6 Examples of congruous (*a* and *b*) and incongruous (*c* and *d*) attitude structures. *D* = dissociative linkage; *A* = associative linkage.

The final case in Figure 8–6, case *d*, also represents an incongruous situation: two negative objects linked dissociatively. For example, a political liberal, also a confirmed atheist, hears a spokesman for the Church (−1) speaking out *against* segregation (−2). This is quite a complex event. The shift toward equilibrium is as follows: The attitude to the Church will tend to move to the mirror image (+2) of the scale position occupied by segregation (−2). Likewise, segregation, because it is being criticized by a disliked institution, should move to +1. *But the more polarized the object, the less the shift.* The distance either object moves is 3 units (2 + 1). Of these, segregation will move less—1 unit (⅓ × 3)—ending up with a value of −1, and the Church should move 2, ending up at +1 (⅔ × 3). We then have equilibrium.

Notice that the result of this seemingly highly negative situation is that *both* objects gain in positivity for the subject. Had both objects started out as positive, both would have lost. When a husband and wife, for example, quarrel in front of friends, both suffer the consequences. However, one can imagine a circumstance in which only one of the two might shift to negative, leaving the other still positive according to the model. This could happen if one was much better liked than the other. Also, further interactions could produce further changes, depending on the associative or dissociative character of each. The model does not specifically deal with this kind of contingency, though it is easy to see that if such a case were sufficiently well defined, the model could generate predictions about it. Life is very complicated. Our liking of a friend may diminish not only because he likes one object we dislike but also because of a host of such linkages, both associative and dissociative, which contradict our own. Some of these linkages may become apparent to us only over time as we get to know the person in a wide variety of situations.

Two additional refinements of the Osgood-Tannenbaum model should be mentioned. The first, referred to already, is the *correction for incredulity*. A linkage between two attitude objects may be rejected as simply unbelievable. For example, even at a time when many people were prepared to think of United States government circles as being susceptible to alien influences, few were willing to take seriously the charge made by the John Bircher Robert Welch that Eisenhower was a Communist. Roughly, one would expect that the greater the attitude changes required to achieve equilibrium—that is, the greater the incongruity involved in the initial linkage—the greater will be the effect of incredulity in dampening change. Osgood and Tannenbaum have, in fact, worked out a fairly exact mathematical way of correcting for incredulity according to the above principle, though we need not go into this here.

The second additional refinement of the model is contained in what Osgood and Tannenbaum call the "assertion constant." This deals with deviations from expected change according to which the object is the source of the assertion. Thus the awarding by Queen Elizabeth of the O.B.E. to the Beatles caused a good deal of consternation among medal holders in Great Britain. According to the model, the esteem in which the Queen was held by these people must have dropped as a result of her action, though not very much. Assuming the Beatles had for them a negative value, this too would become less.

Suppose, however, the Beatles publicly acclaimed the Queen—certainly not an unlikely event—would the positions of each shift to the same extent? The answer given by Osgood and Tannenbaum is that an object is less affected when it is the source of the assertion. If A praises B, then B is more affected. If B praises A, A is more affected. This is in addition, of course, to changes predicted from magnitude and sign of scale position and type of linkage. Such a notion as this certainly fits with common sense and is, in fact, verified by an experimental test of the model made by Tannenbaum. Note, however, that it is an educated guess and does not follow from the theory in any particularly logical way. Furthermore, it applies only in cases where the linkage between the two concepts is directional in character. There is a difference between the news item "President Johnson praises Nelson Rockefeller" and the news item "President Johnson had lunch with Nelson Rockefeller." The assertion constant can be used only in the former case, where there exists a *causal relation* of the kind discussed by Heider. This distinction is not explicitly dealt with by Osgood and Tannenbaum.

Let us now look briefly at some experimental data gathered by Osgood and Tannenbaum.

Example 8–10 *Test of the Osgood-Tannenbaum model (Osgood & Tannenbaum, 1955)*

Osgood and Tannenbaum, in their attempt to test the model, found that, in general, its predictions were fairly well confirmed by observed results. For the six attitude objects involved in three source-concept pairs (e.g., labor leaders, legalized gambling) initial attitudes were assessed in a large group of subjects. Following this, linkages were established for some subjects by exposing them to a set of fake newspaper clippings, for example, "Labor leaders approve legalized gambling." Attitudes were then retested. The data were treated only in terms of general direction of changes. In this respect, the model fared well. All observed changes agreed with those predicted by the model as far as being positive, negative, or close to zero was concerned. Much still remains to be done in the way of testing the model, particularly in respect to the magnitudes of the changes it predicts.

The above discussion is perhaps sufficient to illustrate the kind of theorizing and experimentation that has been done on the problem of cognitive structure and attitude change. Other models have been formulated by Cartwright and Harary (1956), McGuire (1960), Rosenberg and Abelson (1960), Katz and Stotland (1959), Peak (1958), and Kelman (1961). All these have special features but share in common the principle that balance or consistency among cognitive elements is a basic need of human beings. Human beings seem to need a symmetry and order, and lack of them we find disturbing and hence motivating. There is, however, a qualification to this: as we will see in Chapter 22, there are still situations in which certain kinds of persons, especially creative ones, actually seek imbalance.

CHAPTER 9
SOCIAL INFLUENCE: COMMUNICATION IN SOCIAL SITUATIONS

So far we have discussed the nature of interpersonal experience and the structure of attitudes. These have been dealt with mainly from the standpoint of the experience of the individual. In the real world, however, individuals do not keep their perceptions and attitudes to themselves. In one way or another, they communicate them to other people and often attempt to influence these others. The nature of communication is thus an important topic for social psychology. The context in which it occurs is, of course, crucial. It may go on between a speaker and an audience, or between the members of a small group attempting to arrive at the solution of some specific problem, or in a very large group such as a society or a culture.

Accordingly, in this chapter we will consider first the process of communication itself and the major variables that affect it; second, we will look at social interactions and communications as they occur in small groups; and, finally, we will turn to the broadest sphere in which social behavior is carried on—namely, the society or culture.

THE NATURE OF COMMUNICATION

Dealing specifically with influences that one person can have on another or on a group is a body of research done on human communication. One of the important centers for studies of this kind has been Yale University. The Communication and Attitude Change Program was instituted there by Carl Hovland and came out of research done by himself and some colleagues on the effective use of training and indoctrinational films by the armed services during World War II. Initially, at least, the work at Yale and elsewhere was empirical and aimed simply at studying the effects of varying such factors as the order of presentation in respect to "pro" or "con" arguments, the length of the message, or the status characteristics of the communicator. As often happens in science, as the mass of empirical data grew, it became more and more evident that some theoretical formulations were needed to order it and to suggest which problems were likely to give the most basic and fruitful answers. The models of McGuire (1960) and of Rosenberg and Abelson (1960), which were mentioned above, are examples of the theorizing that came out of the Yale program.

The nature of social influence obviously represents a problem of major practical importance. A large proportion of the lives of human beings is occupied with the business of trying to influence others or else being influenced by them. For a sizable sector of behavior, society lays down rules which stipulate that certain communications from persons of a certain status or position be accepted. The Commandment "Honor thy father and thy mother" is such a rule. Legal obligations, traffic regulations, and the intricate niceties of etiquette are other examples. For these, conformity is demanded. There is usually no question of debate or doubt in many such matters. If we rob a bank and are caught, we go to jail. If we exceed a speed limit and are caught, we must pay a fine. These cases are fairly clear-cut. Consider, however, a teacher who wishes to convince his students of the value of learning philosophy or a political candidate who wishes to gain public acceptance of his party's platform. In these instances, no rules are laid down, assuming that the arenas of education and politics are reasonably free. Likewise, in wartime, it is imperative, for reasons of morale, to know what kinds of information are liable to be accepted both by military and civilian groups. It is these kinds of problems that we will discuss here.

Three main categories have occupied the attention of investigators. These are the communicator, the communique, and the recipient, that is to say, the characteristics of the person who delivers the message, both objectively and as understood by the recipient; the characteristics of the message itself; and the personality and "set" of the person to whom the message is directed. Let us look first at the effects of communicator characteristics.

The Communicator

Common sense would suggest that, other factors being equal, a communicator of greater prestige and status, and possessing some formal accreditation of expertise will be more readily believed. This indeed turns out to be the case. Hovland, Janis, and Kelley (1953) have fully documented this point and in so doing have identified *trustworthiness* and *expertness* as the two major parameters of persuasiveness. This sounds all very simple and obvious. Nonetheless, some problems are raised when it comes to defining just what trustworthiness is and why one person may be perceived as more trustworthy than another. To some degree, physical appearance, mannerisms, voice quality, and other such characteristics are important. But, in addition, the way the communicator is able to use what he has and gear his message to the level of the audience is equally so. That is to say, a good potential communicator counts for little without a good communiqué.

Interestingly enough, the influence of one communicator variable—his credibility—has an effect on attitude change that is large at first but that wears off over time, as demonstrated by the data in Example 9–1.

Example 9–1 *Attitude changes over time (Hovland, Janis, & Kelley, 1953)*

Two groups of subjects were given identical communications, but one communication issued from a source having high credibility, the other from a source having low credibility. Results are shown in Figure 9–1. Evidently, a highly impressive source produces a large amount of immediate

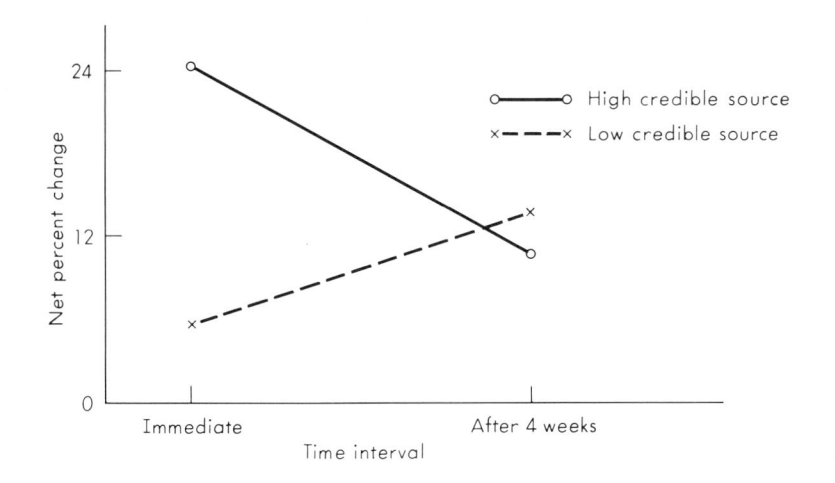

FIG. 9–1 The "sleeper effect" in attitude change. Changes in acceptance of message as a function of source credibility and time. (*Hovland, Janis, & Kelley, 1953*)

change in attitude compared with a communicator who is not considered believable or trustworthy. After a few weeks, however, the attitude changes in the two groups tend to equalize. This phenomenon has been called by Hovland and his colleagues the "sleeper effect." It is generally attributed to the fact that some of the negative or positive feelings about the source initially rub off on the message but that after a time interval this association is forgotten, thus attenuating the first exaggerated effect. Subsequent studies have supported this notion.

The Communication

Any communication has a great many characteristics potentially capable of influencing acceptance of it by a listener. Common sense does not help us to decide which of these are, in fact, the most crucial variables. Some will argue, for example, that it is always better to ignore the opposition and the available arguments against one's position; others will assert that both sides should always be presented. Supposing one takes the second view, there is room for further debate as to which to present first—the negative or the positive side. Certainly, it is somewhat anticlimactic to end a talk discussing the opposing position; on the other hand, it is likely that an audience will remember better whatever is said earlier. Again, should a speaker use "fear appeals" to emphasize his message, or should he avoid these at all costs, on the ground that a shocked audience may form a bad opinion of him and hence be reluctant to believe anything he tells them?

These are a few of the kinds of questions we can ask about the subject. Though a great deal of empirical work has in fact been done on such questions, the data so far yielded are far from supplying us with any simple general rules that a speaker can take and use.

An interesting example of research on the characteristics of the communication that can influence the audience is a study done by Janis and Feierabend (1957). One part of Hovland's program at Yale, it is published in the first of several volumes completed under his editorship. It deals specifically with the effects of order of presentation of "pro" and "con" arguments on persuading an audience.

Example 9–2 *Alternative ways of ordering pro and con arguments in persuasive communication (Janis & Feierabend, 1957)*

The writers started off by posing the problem as to how a speaker can keep the advantages given by a two-sided presentation while minimizing the risk of "boomerang effects," or the loss of persuasiveness that may occur as a result of a speaker's presenting the arguments against the position he is taking. Under some conditions, the audience may be less impressed by his fairness than by the force of the counterarguments.

Janis and Feierabend undertook the study with a view to specifying those conditions which minimize the risk of boomerang effects. Their theoretical positions relating order effects to acceptance or rejection of the communiqué is rather complex, and consequently we will present here only its essential outlines. Briefly they hypothesized that the tendency to accept a message is greater if the arguments in favor of it are presented prior to the arguments against it, *provided that the audience has no spontaneous awareness of the con arguments before the communicator presents them.* This hypothesis does seem to fit fairly well with common sense. Generally speaking, it is usually the first part of any material to be learned that is remembered the best. This is a rather well-documented fact (cf. Section Five). However, it seems likely that anyone who is aware of both sides of an issue can be made suspicious by too one-sided a presentation and, for this reason, discredit the speaker's views. By the same token, someone not previously aware of the con arguments should have no reason for not accepting the message and, furthermore, should be favorably impressed by the fairness of a speaker who takes the trouble to put forward the negative side.

To test their hypothesis, Janis and Feierabend used 182 high school students divided into three groups. These were asked to read a pamphlet urging students to join a local civil defense organization. The material consisted of fourteen paragraphs, seven of which stressed the positive advantages, seven the disadvantages of such a course of action. For example, a positive argument might involve a theme of patriotic duty; a negative paragraph might point out the tedium and inconvenience that aspects of this job would entail. A final paragraph simply asked for volunteers. In the pamphlet given to one of the groups, the seven positive paragraphs were put first, the seven negative ones last; for the second group, this order was reversed. Subsequently, both groups, plus a third control group not exposed to any pamphlet, all were given a questionnaire designed to measure attitudes with respect to volunteering for civil defense.

Results are shown in Table 9–1. This shows the percentage of subjects in each group displaying a positive attitude toward volunteering for civil defense. The group that read the pamphlet presenting the positive arguments first was more favorably disposed to the message than either of the other two groups. The differences are, in fact, statistically significant. Accordingly, we have good grounds for believing that the hypothesis made by Janis and Feierabend is a correct one.

We should note, however, that its correctness holds up only within rather narrow limits. This makes it difficult to apply in practice. However, if a speaker is an astute judge of his listeners and is able to assess quickly their attitudes about a position he wishes to take and gauge the information they are likely to have about the subject, he may profit by paying some attention to the order of presentation of his arguments.

Obviously, many other message variables determine the degree to which a communication is accepted. Order of presentation is merely one of the more important ones. The interested reader may consult the Hovland volumes or any recent textbook in social psychology for a discussion of others involved.

The Recipient

As we have already stated quite explicitly, the speaker who expects to be believed should know his audience. Every teacher is aware of this, though he may not be able to make it work for him. There are certainly many recipient variables that have been given attention. One is simply persuasibility. It is possible, in other words, that some people have personalities that are highly resistant to change, others personalities that are very easily influenced by a communication. This problem has been examined in some detail by a number of investigators, notably by Janis. It may be broken down into more specific questions, the first of which is whether persuasibility is a characteristic that is independent

Table 9–1 Overall index of positive attitude to volunteering

Groups	Percent
A. Pro arguments given first	87.3
B. Con arguments given first	73.0
C. Control group	69.6

of the type of communication—that is, as Janis and Field (1956) have put it, whether persuasibility is *topic-free*. Their study can be taken as illustrative of research in the area.

Example 9–3 *The trait of persuasibility (Janis & Field, 1956)*

This second volume in the Yale series on attitudes and communication was devoted to the problem of personality and persuasibility. The research presented in it was aimed at examining so-called unbound persuasibility factors—that is, dispositions in persons to be affected by social influence, independently of the content of the message, or of the characteristics of the communicator, or of general situational variables. In the twelve chapters of the book, a number of different approaches to the general problem were used. These centered mainly around (1) the definition of the hypothetical trait of persuasibility and its personality correlates and (2) the development in children of persuasibility. Some examples of the researches carried out follows.

In a study reprinted in the volume, Janis and Field developed a Persuasibility Test involving three components: (1) An Initial Questionnaire intended to assess opinions of subjects on a variety of controversial topics, for example, amount of defense spending of the United States, amount and money and time devoted to cancer research, radio and TV programming; (2) Booklet I, consisting of a set of "comments by prominent news reporters" on the controversial issues specified in the Initial Questionnaire, a definite position being taken on each of the five issues; (3) Booklet II, in which comments also were involved but in which conclusions opposite to those of Booklet I were reached. Subjects were asked for their opinions not only in the Initial Questionnaire but also following their reading of Booklet I and again following the presentation of Booklet II. The appeals in respect to the five issues were classified as fear-arousing threat statements, logical argument and specialized information, stereotyped characterizations (overidealized hero or exaggerated villain), social incentives (social approval), hedonic incentives (given choice will lead to pleasure or not).

The Persuasibility Test was administered to about 185 high school juniors in history classes. Booklets I and II were presented orally. In general, a score was calculated from the sum of the numbers of questions on which a subject had changed from his Initial Questionnaire position in the direction advocated by any given communication.

Reliability of scores turned out to be high, and, likewise, the test had high internal consistency. This means, essentially, that the tendency to be persuaded is largely independent of content and is general across different subject matters. In other words, persuasibility seems to be a general personality trait of some kind.

Next, Janis and Field attempted to find out some of the correlates of persuasibility. Table 9–2 shows an interesting sex difference, girls apparently being more susceptible than boys to persuasion. The difference is statistically significant. The following personality traits showed up as related to persuasibility:

1. Feelings of social inadequacy (in males only)
2. Richness of fantasy life—yielding more vivid anticipation of possible reward or punishment consequences depicted by a communicator

Relationships, it should be mentioned, though statistically significant, were of a very low order. Further studies also indicated such variables as these to be important:

1. Admitting to having unpleasant emotional reactions, such as episodes of intense anger, irritability, and worry.
2. Perceptual field dependency, that is, the tendency of perception to be affected by the surrounding field (e.g., perception of verticality as influenced by making the judgment in a tilted chair (cf. Section Four).
3. Disposition to take group conformity rather than inner values as the standard for behavior. This is called "other direction" after David Riesman (Riesman, Glaser, and Denney, 1956).

In general, we may conclude that persuasibility

Table 9–2 Sex differences in persuasibility

	Males	Females
Test score	10.7	12.2

does seem to be a general trait and that it is probably dependent on some personality factors. However, the latter were not very clearly identified by the research reported. As Janis and Field readily admit, there are still many large gaps in our knowledge in regard to this important aspect of the problem of communication.

The above study and several others done subsequently by different investigators do seem to point to the conclusion that persuasibility is to a large extent (though not completely) independent of topic. This means, in turn, that to this extent it is a character that must be tied closely to the enduring personality structure. The next question we must raise concerns other traits that might be expected to underlie persuasibility. Several possibilities have been examined, particularly intelligence, self-esteem, and aggressiveness. However, the general results that have been found are so ambiguous and subject to so many qualifications that they do not permit any general conclusions to be validly drawn. Persuasibility is probably a highly complex trait, so that a certain amount of it appearing in any particular individual may result from any one of a number of different combinations of values of the subunits comprising it.

The resumé given above of the process of communication is brief and is not intended to supply the reader with any techniques for successful persuasion. Nonetheless, it has, hopefully, pointed up some of the major variables that must be given attention by any worker in the area.

The kind of communication we have so far been discussing is of a one-way variety; that is to say, it deals with the effect that a message issued by a speaker or writer has on the attitudes and beliefs of the recipient. Equally common in the social matrix, and perhaps more important, is the two-way communication that goes on between people in some kind of face-to-face contact, for example, in a committee or a discussion group, or even in an informal "bull session." These have been called by

Cooley *primary groups*. To deal adequately with these means focusing on the actual process of reciprocal communication as it goes on over time rather than on the end result of a simple one-way message from a speaker to his audience. This different focus requires different methods and different conceptualizations. In a small group engaged in solving some problem, there is no unitary communiqué that remains constant over time. Instead, there is only a topic which different persons in the group will approach with different strategies and about which each person may have opinions that are fixed or fluid. Furthermore, we find that some groups seem to "work," in the sense that the results of their deliberations are productive and often creative, whereas other groups get "bogged down" and manifest only tension and acrimony.

There is, in social psychology, a large body of research that has been devoted specifically to an analysis of the process of small-group interaction and to a specification of the variables that operate. Most of this work, it is fair to say, has been empirical rather than highly theoretical and to this extent has been a little out of the mainstream of thought in social psychology as we have described it. At the same time, some of the concepts that have emerged out of work in this area will be recognized as being similar to some of those we have already encountered in our discussions of person perception, cognitive structure, and attitude change, notably, the concept of balance, as applied, however, to the relations between different individuals rather than to the relations between different cognitive elements in a single person. Likewise, the concept of role is as important to our understanding the functioning of small groups as it is to our understanding of the general relation of man and society—though this broader usage of the term still remains to be discussed. We now turn directly to the topic of small-group interaction.

COMMUNICATION IN SMALL GROUPS

As we have just indicated, much of the decision making that goes on in our modern world emerges from the activities of small groups, such as Senate committees, PTA groups, or subcommittees of management or labor. They consequently represent a most important unit for sociopsychological study. It will shortly become clear that a description of them involves two somewhat related major concepts, namely, *structure* and *role*. Any group involves a balance and distribution of power and modes of communication. These features define the structure of the group. In addition, groups usually designate special roles which define certain limits of behavior and action. Some of these are formal ones, such as "chairman" and "secretary," and others are less formalized, such as the group "wit," the "arbitrator," and the group "conscience." Before going into these basic concepts more fully, we will discuss two methods commonly used to study groups. These are interaction process analysis and sociometry.

Interaction process analysis refers to a method developed by R. F. Bales (1950) at the Massachusett Institute of Technology for all the interactions that occur in a small group over time. Two major dimensions are involved: (1) *who-to-whom dimension*, that is, the identification of the initiator and recipient of any interaction; (2) *type of interaction*, this being specified according to twelve observational categories as shown in Table 9–3.

Bales has developed a mechanical device for recording these categories as they occur over time. This is generally done by an observer seated behind a one-way window. With a good deal of practice and training, observers can achieve a high degree of reliability or consistency. It should be recognized, of course, that the categories are not absolute. But they do allow us to analyze groups in terms of the two major concepts mentioned above, namely, role and structure, and the manner in which these change over time. Thus, any role may be defined in terms of the kinds of things that are said by a person, to whom he says them, and the kinds of things that are said to him. Likewise, the structure of a group may be defined in terms of the patterns of communication that develop in the group—where information originates and how it is disseminated.

The second method for analyzing group interaction hits at a different dimension. In the sociometry of Moreno (1934), group structure is described in terms of "liking" choices and the number of these that are unilateral or reciprocated. Generally, a sociogram is represented in the manner shown in Figure 9–2. The figure indicates that individual A

Table 9-3 Categories used in observation of social interactions in small groups (Bales, 1950)

Problem areas	Observation categories*
Expressive-integrative social-emotional area: positive reactions	1. Shows solidarity, gives help, reward 2. Shows tension release, jokes, laughs, shows satisfaction 3. Agrees, shows passive acceptance, understands, concurs
Instrumental-adaptive task area: attempted answers	4. Gives suggestion, direction, implying autonomy for others 5. Gives opinion, evaluation, analysis, expresses feeling, wish 6. Gives orientation, information, repeats, clarifies, confers
Instrumental-adaptive task area: questions	7. Asks for orientation, information, repetition, confirmation 8. Asks for opinion, evaluation, analysis, expression of feeling 9. Asks for suggestion, direction, possible ways of action
Expressive-integrative social-emotional area: negative reactions	10. Disagrees, shows passive rejection, formality, withholds help 11. Shows tension, asks for help, withdraws from field 12. Shows antagonism, deflates others' status, defends or asserts self

* The twelve categories fall into pairs as follows:

Problems of orientation, 6 and 7
Problems of evaluation, 5 and 8
Problems of control, 4 and 9
Problems of decision, 3 and 10
Problems of tension management, 2 and 11
Problems of integration, 1 and 12

FIG. 9-2 A sociogram. It represents the positive relationships among individuals A, B, C, and D.

Using these two basic methods, or variations of them, investigators have now provided us with a good deal of information about the operation of groups and the variables that are important in determining group performance.

Essentially communication in small groups involves, as we have seen, two distinct though related aspects. The first of these is represented by the so-called who-to-whom matrix, which deals with the problem of specifying which people in the group do the communication, the absolute and relative amounts of communication between them, and the relation of these variables to such dimensions as group efficiency, satisfaction, and morale. The second aspect relates to the *type of communiqué or interaction,* that is, the characteristics of *what* is said. To illustrate, we may start first by asking a few simple empirical questions. Let us look first at the effects of controlling artificially extent of participation in problem-solving groups.

Example 9-4 *Communication networks and behavior (Leavitt, 1951)*

The purpose of the experiment was to explore the relation between behavior of small groups and certain fixed patterns of communications imposed on them. As will be obvious, the situations studied were highly artificial. Nonetheless, by highlighting some variable of importance, we may often get clues as to how it works in more natural or spontaneous circumstances. Twenty groups of five members each (M.I.T. undergraduates) were observed while engaged in problem solving. The problem given was as follows: each subject in a group was given

is best liked in the group but he, in turn, likes only C. C, on the other hand, is liked by no one except A and thus fills a kind of "henchman," or "court favorite," role—one of considerable interest, as we shall see later. B is liked by C and D but likes only A, who does not like B.

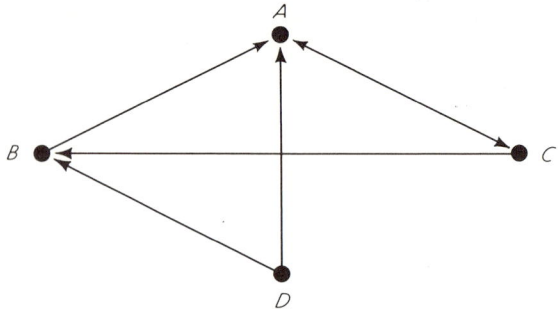

a card with five figures on it. Of these five, only one was common to all sets of cards. The task for the group was to find as quickly as possible the common figure by means of written communiqués, whose flow was specified beforehand by the experimenter. Four modes of communication flow, or "nets," were used. These may be depicted as follows:

```
  Circle         Chain             Y              Wheel
    C              C                               B     E
   o              o              P    B            o     o
  / \            / \              o    o            \   /
 B   D          B   D              \  /              C
 o   o          o   o               Y                o
 |   |          |   |               o C             / \
 A---E          A   E               |              o   o
 o   o          o   o               o D            A   D
                                    |
                                    o E
```

The circles represent individuals; the lines connecting them represent permitted channels of communication. Thus in the diagram labeled "Circle," individual B can send messages directly to C and to A but only indirectly to D and E. Such nets involve at least four dimensions of possible importance. These are:

1. *Sum of neighbors*, that is, the number of other individuals with whom one individual is in direct communication. Thus in the circle each individual can communicate with two others. The sum of neighbors is then $10 = (5 \times 2)$.

2. *Centrality*, a rather more complex index that involves the previous dimension. It is essentially intended to reflect the degree to which the information circulating in a group is funneled to one central figure. Leavitt has suggested a method of defining exactly a measure of centrality. Without going into details, we may state that roughly this involves a kind of average of the degree to which individuals in the group can communicate *directly* with the same individual. Such an average is high in case of the wheel, low in the circle, representing the fact that in the wheel all individuals communicate directly with C and with all others through him as the single intermediary. By the same token, the chain has more centrality than the circle, and the Y has more than the chain but less than the wheel.

3. *Pattern flexibility*, defined as the number of alternative links that persons in the group have available on the average for transmitting messages.

4. *Operational flexibility*, rather similar to pat-

Table 9-4 Efficiency and enjoyment in differing groups as a function of type of communication network

Type of net	Group characteristics		Group performance		
	Centrality	Sum of neighbors	Enjoyment	Efficiency	
				Mean no. of messages sent	Mean errors*
Circle	25	8	66	83	8
Chain	26.1	8	59	55	3
Y	26.2	8	58	46	0
Wheel	26.4	10	44	43	1

* Last 8 trials.

tern flexibility. It is the number of *ways* in which a pattern can be used by the whole group. For example, a net may have no *pattern* flexibility but may still be operated in different ways with different individuals serving as message centers.

The major results of the observations indicated that centrality was the most important dimension. High centrality in a group produced high efficiency but relatively low satisfaction. Conversely, nets with low centrality tended to produce a more enjoyable but less efficient situation. These data are shown in Table 9-4.

At an individual level, the findings were similar. Those persons who had a position with low centrality as compared with others in the group were the least satisfied and also the least active. Those with high centrality—C in the chain, in the Y, and in the wheel—enjoyed the task the most and were the most active.

The results of the above experiment may strike the reader as rather simple and commonsensible when set against the complexity of the theoretical structure used in setting up the study. This may be true. Nonetheless, it is rich in its implications. All human groups and institutions as they occur in society involve implicitly or explicitly some kind of communication structure which is capable of fairly precise definition. It is obviously of value for us who spend most of our lives within such structures to be fully aware of the kinds of effects that certain arrangements can have on our behavior and feelings.

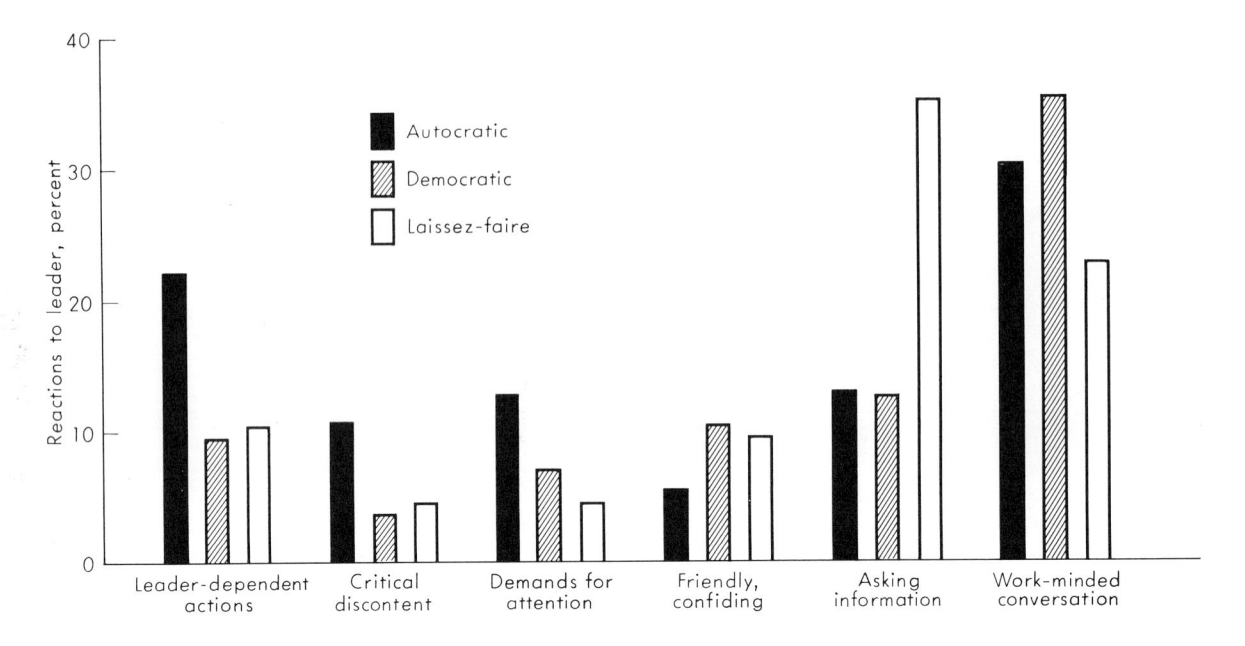

FIG. 9-3 Reactions of groups to different types of leaders. (*Lewin et al., 1939*)

A more practical application of the kinds of concepts and data discussed above is given by some early, classic observations of Lewin, Lippitt, and White (1939). These were done in what might be called "natural" groups.

Example 9-5 *Social climates in children's clubs (Lewin, Lippitt, & White, 1939)*

In this study, communication was structured in natural groups (children's clubs) engaged in craft and recreational activities by imposing on them different types of adult leadership. Three types were used: "authoritarian," "democratic," and "laissez faire." They were defined as follows:

Authoritarian: Virtually all policies regarding club activities were determined by the leader. Steps to be taken to a goal were communicated one at a time without presenting a view of the final goal. The leader remained aloof from participation in group activity except for demonstrating.

Democratic: Policies were a matter of group discussion and decision with active assistance by the leader. Final goals and steps to them were presented and discussed. The leader acted as a "resource" person by being available to suggest alternative modes of action. Choice of work partners was left up to individuals, as was assignment of various responsibilities. The leader showed active group participation.

Laissez faire: The leader played a passive role and gave the group complete freedom. He supplied help or information only when asked. He made no attempt to evaluate positively or negatively the performance of individuals or of the group and showed a minimum of group participation.

The effects of these three types of leadership on the feelings and behavior of the children in the clubs were then observed in detail. Only part of the obtained data is presented here.

1. *Patterns of group reaction to leaders.* Figure 9-3 shows how individuals in the three groups reacted to the leaders in terms of several dimensions. It is clear that some quite marked differences appeared. Autocratic leadership produced more dependency and also more critical aggression than did the other two types. The orientation to work appeared to be greatest under the democratic conditions.

138 MODELS OF SOCIAL BEHAVIOR

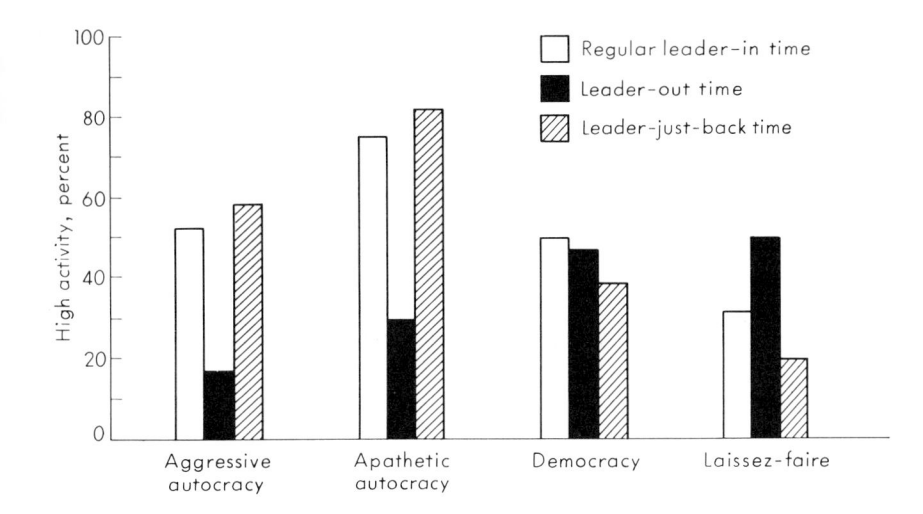

FIG. 9–4 Reactions to a leader's absence and return. (*Lewin et al., 1939*)

2. *Reactions to the leader's absence and return.* Data are presented in Figure 9–4. The graph indicates that, of the three groups, the democratic is most independent of the leader. Both the others show fluctuations, interestingly enough, in opposite directions, depending on the leader's absence or presence. The autocratic leader appears to potentiate activity. In his absence, activity declines sharply. The laissez faire leader, on the other hand, actually seems to interfere with the work production of the children. Supplementary data indicated that the activities of the members of the autocratic group turned sharply to outbursts of horseplay when the leader left.

In general, the results of the study suggest that the democratic leadership condition produces a social climate in which children are more work-oriented and more independent of authority than they are in either the autocratic or laissez faire conditions. It should be added that the main results obtained by Lewin and his colleagues have held up remarkably well in a number of repetitions and extensions that have been carried out since 1939. These have served only to qualify the way the major variables operate under different special conditions. Consequently, it seems that we are dealing with some rather basic kinds of principles.

It is evident that, in any kind of small group, interactions are not distributed evenly in amount. Usually, it seems that the strongest participant participates a great deal more than the others and between the others there are much smaller differences. Furthermore, this is much more true for acts directed to the group as a whole than for those directed to individuals. This is common experience. It is usually characteristic of a leader, in fact, that he attempts to deal with the group as a unit rather than focus on the separate individuals that comprise it, though he is sensitive to the individuals also.

This tendency of participation to focus has been called by Bales (1952) "centralization." It appears to happen more or less automatically. Aside from the possible consequences it may have, we may now ask under what conditions it applies. Experiments on this are numerous, and we will sample only a few of them.

Example 9–6 *Centralization in small groups*

In the first place, Bales (1952) has shown that the general form of the participation curve is J-shaped and that this applies to groups of about any size. This point is illustrated in Figure 9–5.

However, the degree of centralization is a function both of amount of leader activity (or passivity) and of total volume of group interaction (Stephan and Mishler, 1955). These relationships are shown in Figures 9–6 and 9–7. Thus we see that a group composed of individuals who are classified by past performance as low participators tends to be considerably more "unbalanced" than one composed of

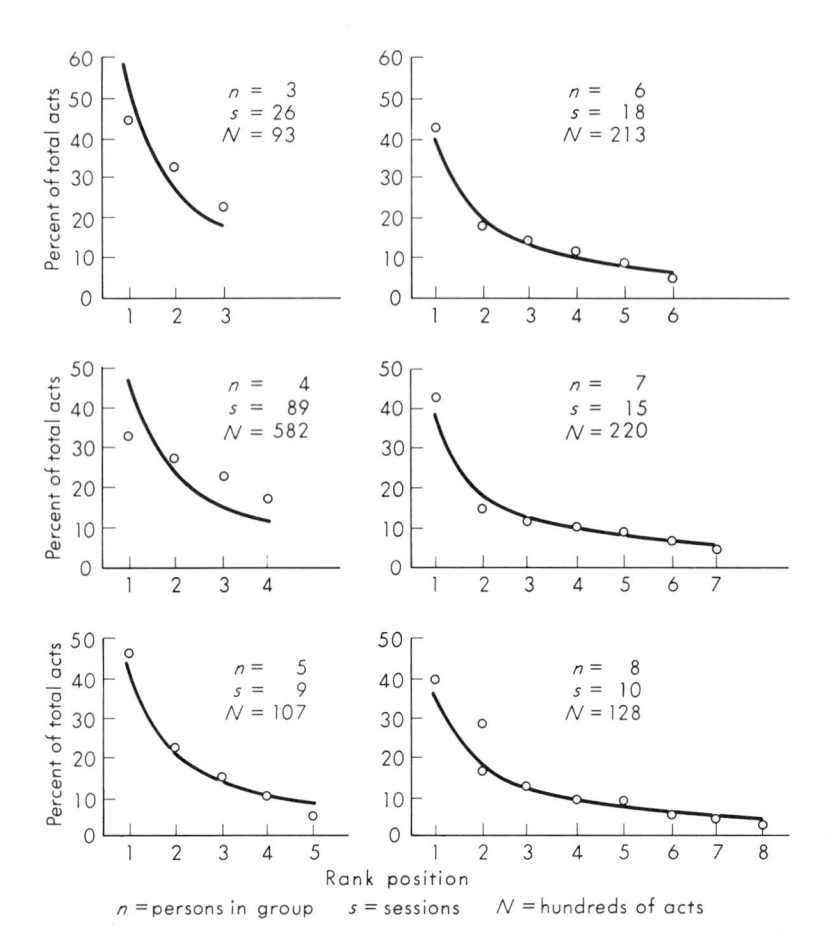

FIG. 9-5 Participation curves in small groups. (*Bales, 1952*)

n = persons in group *s* = sessions *N* = hundreds of acts

high-participation members. Active leadership similarly produces more imbalance than does passive leadership.

This notion of "imbalance" is an important one in developing a theoretical framework for analyzing group activity. Most workers in this field have looked to some kind of homeostatic, or equilibrating, mechanism as being basic to group activity, analogously to the principle that seems to govern cognitive structure. According to this view, the group tends to maintain a certain balance over time by automatically compensating for deviations from this balance which occur during the course of its lifetime. Obviously there can be many different kinds of imbalances and likewise many types of corrective mechanisms. A concrete example of the equilibratory process is given by the distribution of participation discussed above. It is clear that power is uneven in small groups. The question now before us is whether any homeostatic action is taken toward reducing the leader's power in some way.

Example 9-7 *Homeostatic mechanisms in small groups (Bales, 1955)*

Bales gathered evidence that bears on this theoretical question by studying data gathered from twelve meetings of five-man groups. They were given the task of analyzing and making recommendations about a "human relations" case. A case consisted of a summary of facts about a person in an administrative setting who is having problems with his subordinates and also receiving pressure from a superior to get an important job done. No leaders were appointed for any of the groups, which were

140 MODELS OF SOCIAL BEHAVIOR

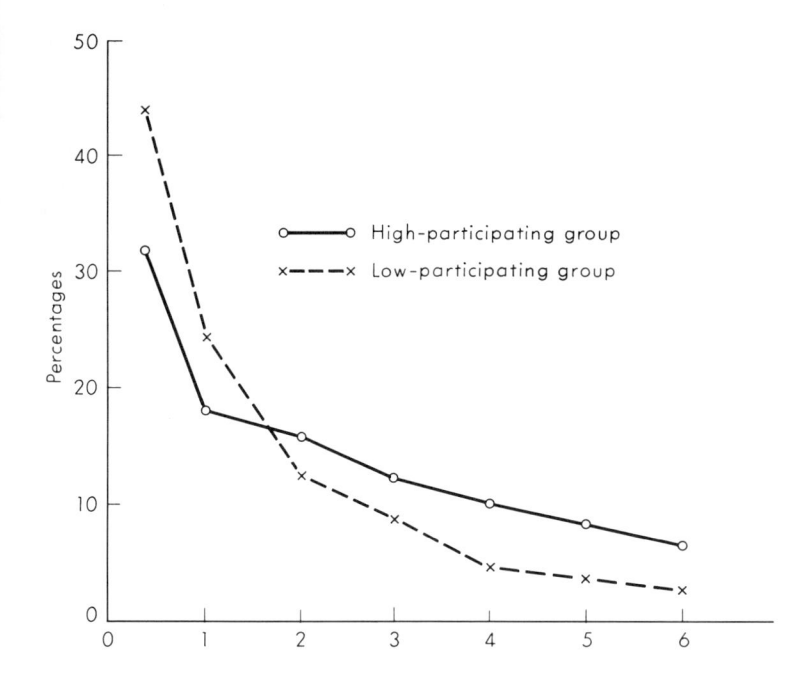

FIG. 9-6 Relative amount of participation in groups composed of high-participating or low-participating members. (*Stephan & Mishler, 1955*)

simply given forty minutes to come to some decision. Interactions during these discussions were recorded and analyzed by the Bales method.

The data from this program that have a bearing on the problem of homeostatic adjustments in small groups are summarized in Figure 9-8. The graphs show the interaction of individuals in many groups. Members are ranked on the horizontal axis according to the number of interactions each initiated. The most votes on "best ideas" and "guidance" are

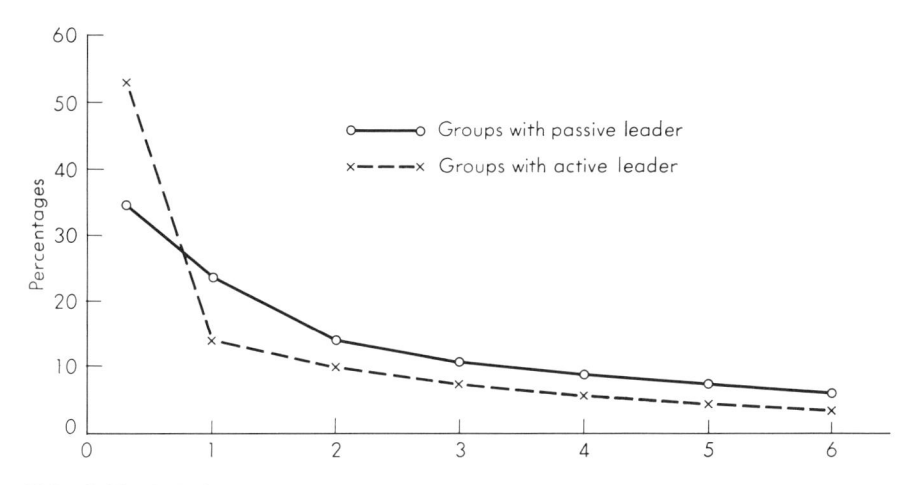

FIG. 9-7 Relative amount of participation in groups with active or passive leaders. (*Stephan & Mishler, 1955*)

141   SOCIAL INFLUENCE: COMMUNICATION IN SOCIAL SITUATIONS

received by the man ranked first, a fact which clearly fits with his role as leader. The second man, however, is rated rather lower than he should be on these same dimensions. On the curves of "likes" and "dislikes," we find that the top man is very little better off than number 5. Number 2, however, is the highest on "likes," and on "dislikes" he is lower than the leader.

These data suggest the following: The top man holds his position as director of the sphere of instrumental adaptive acts at a price which he has to pay in the socioemotional sphere by being the target for some hostility. Thus the imbalance produced by his ascendancy in one area of group activity is equilibrated by his lack of ascendancy in another area. Correspondingly, the tension produced by this compensatory response of the group is, as it were, "drained off" (to use Bales' term) by centering of positive affect (liking) on a secondary man. In this way the group adjusts homeostatically and preserves solidarity. As Bales says:

> The centering of positive affect on a secondary man is another mechanism by which the solidarity of the group—its integration as a collectivity of persons—can be reestablished. Such a man can be warm, receptive, responsive and rewarding, can "conciliate" and "bind up wounds," without diverting the movement of the system too far from the kind of movement in the instrumental-adaptive direction which is also felt to be necessary. He can do this because he does not assume responsibility for the movement of the system in these directions, but leaves this to the technical or executive specialist [p. 454].

This kind of coalition between the "brains" and the "heart" is an exceedingly powerful one. Bales suggests that it lies at the basis of most family systems. The father is generally the intellectual authority figure—the symbol of abstract justice, of reward and punishment. The mother, on the other hand, represents love and kindness, completely devoted and selfless, uncomplicated by rational considerations. Many other examples could be cited. The "kingmaker" role is an inverted example of such a coalition—an intellectual with political skills who sets up in nominal leadership a charismatic figure to be used as an instrument of power. Political history and literature are replete with such cases.

We do not suggest that the separation between "being liked" and "leading" is invariable. Certainly, they frequently occur together, and even in the data of Bales presented above there is at least some relationship between them. In the small group, in addition, as may be inferred from Figure 9–8, some of the tension also becomes directed to

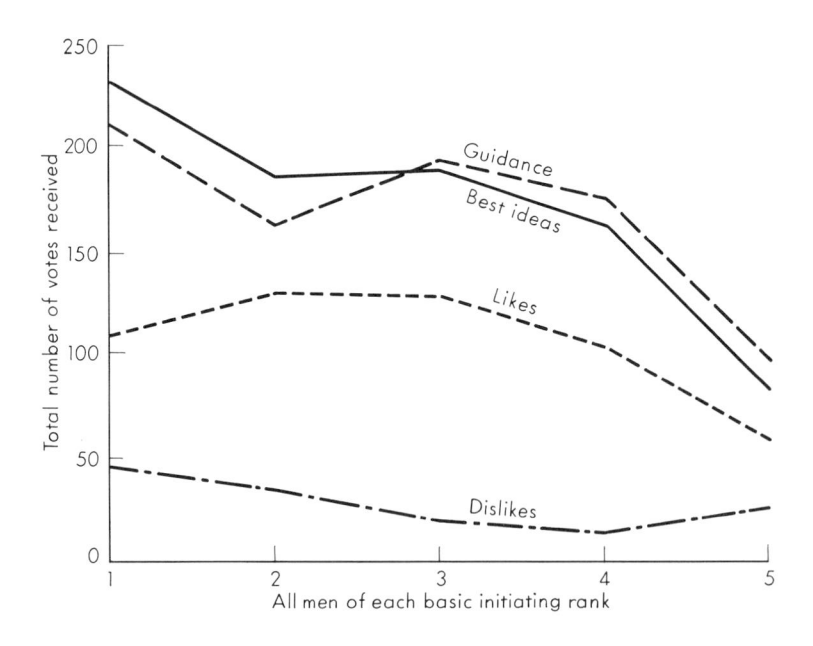

FIG. 9–8 Ratings on several dimensions of individuals ranked according to amount of participation. (*Bales, 1955*)

the "low man," who is estimated as contributing little to the problem and who is also disliked. Much of the hostility generated by the power of the leader is displaced to the scapegoat. This is another equilibrating mechanism.

So far we have been discussing only volume and direction of communication independent of its type. It is true, however, that not only the distribution of communication but also the *types* of communiqués initiated by particular individuals in a group have a bearing on the development of *roles*. As we have already indicated, the notion of role is crucial to a full understanding of groups and their relation to individual behavior.

It is clear first of all that the distribution of types of communication is different in different groups and in the same group at different times. These two points are illustrated by data gathered by Bales, as part of the project referred to in Example 9–8.

Example 9–8 *Roles and types of communication in small groups (Bales, 1955)*

The general situation and methodology were the same as in the previous example. One part of all the data gathered bears on the question of how types of interaction vary with time. These types are summarized in Figure 9–9. According to Bales, the curves describe the group's tendency to move qualitatively from a relative emphasis on problems of *orientation* ("What are we doing?") to a relative emphasis on *evaluation* ("How do we feel about it?"). There is an increasing emphasis on problems of *control* ("What shall we do about it?"). Affective reactions, both positive and negative, show a concomitant upswing as there arise tensions resulting from disagreements at the cognitive level.

The average balance between these areas of interaction tends to be different in different groups. Figure 9–10 compares a "satisfied" with a "dissatisfied" group. The data shown indicate that the chief differences lie in the sphere of affective reactions. The dissatisfied group shows a much greater proportion of negative responses than the satisfied group. It also shows more orientation and evaluative responses but fewer in the area of control. Presumably this means more tension and hence more negative affect.

The final problem concerning communication in small groups has to do with individual differences in types of social interaction. An examination of this problem will serve to introduce the concept of role. We have already demarcated at least implicitly three roles in a small group, namely, (1) "the leader," who communicates more than others and is communicated to more than are the others; (2) the "best liked," or specialist in the area of

Table 9–5 Roles and problem-solving patterns (Heyns, 1950)*

Role	Patterns
Problem-solving:	
Reality tester	Sets goals
	Prepare problems
	Clarifies
Expert	Gives information
Interrogator	Seeks information
	Seeks clarification
Idea man	Proposes solutions
Goal reminder	Sets goals
	Seeks summary
	Gives summary
Distractor	Behaves in non-problem-directed ways
Passive participant	Opposes
	Supports
Interpersonal patterns:	
Rejecter	Dismisses and ignores contributions
Supporter	Reacts in a positive way to contributions
Social oiler	Reduces frictions
	Aids cooperation
Isolate	Says nothing
	Is ignored
Dictator	Tries to dominate others

* From "Effects of variation in leadership on participant behavior in discussion groups." Unpublished doctoral dissertation, University of Michigan. Used by permission of T. M. Newcomb, *Social psychology*, New York: Dryden Press, 1950, p. 505.

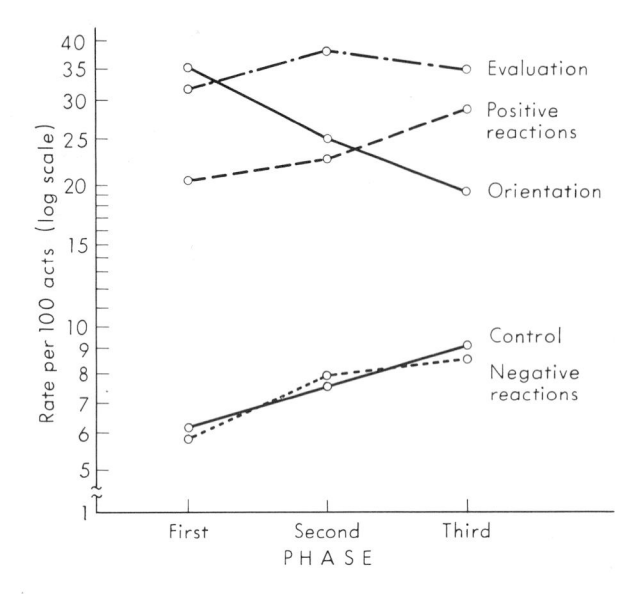

FIG. 9–9 Equilibration of types of interactions over time. (*Bales, 1955*)

socioemotional interactions; (3) "the scapegoat," who contributes least to the group and is a prime target for negative reactions from others in the group. A number of others may also be found in many groups. Heyns (1950) suggests that the roles and patterns in Table 9–5 can usually be fairly reliably identified. The reader can probably think of other roles in addition to the above that persons in a group situation frequently occupy. The "jester," the "kingmaker," the "arbitrator," the "wit," and the "goldbrick" are common examples. All these, like those in Table 9–5, can be specified fairly exactly in terms of Bales' interaction categories.

As it turns out, the concept of role has a much broader application in social psychology. We will examine it more closely and present a little of its historical development.

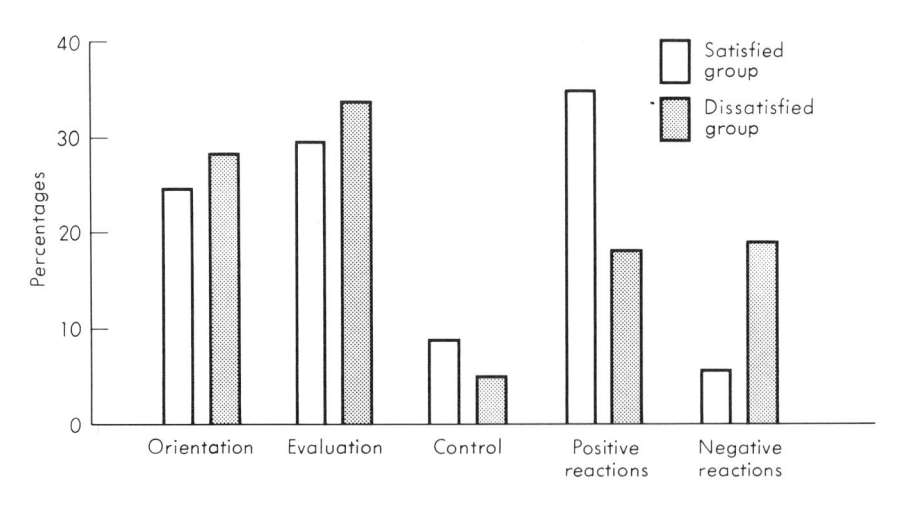

FIG. 9–10 Interactions of a "satisfied" and a "dissatisfied" group. (*Bales, 1955*)

144 MODELS OF SOCIAL BEHAVIOR

THE ROLE CONCEPT

The essential value of the notion of role is that it attempts to specify more closely those predictions made about an individual's behavior from knowledge of what he is like *as an individual* by adding statements about what he is like *as part of a social system*. Theoretically, explanations of a person can be made best from examining the dialectic between these two poles—the individual self and the social self.

Though most of us like to think of ourselves as unique personalities, all of us are nonetheless embedded firmly in society and occupy various social positions that determine much of our behavior. For example, being a university student means that much time will be given to reading, writing, and listening to lectures. Being a father implies all the kinds of behaviors associated with providing and caring for a wife and children. Many other examples could be given. The question to be asked now is whether, if all of a person's social self were taken away, there would be anything at all left.

This is a problem that we raised early in this section. It will be recalled that the philosopher Hegel tended to underplay the importance of the individual, emphasizing instead the whole social organism as the most compelling reality. One of the great founders of sociology, Emile Durkheim, dramatized this point of view in his statement "The individual does not exist." He did not mean this literally, of course. What he meant was that a true and full explanation of man's behavior was not to be found by looking at individual character traits; rather it would emerge only from a study of broad sociological variables.

In the United States, this emphasis was most influentially put forward by the social philosopher George Herbert Mead of the University of Chicago. The following quotation sums up much of his thinking:

> We are not, in social psychology, building up the behavior of the social group in terms of the behavior of the separate individuals composing it; rather, we are starting out with a given social whole of complex group activity, into which we analyze (as elements) the behavior of each of the separate individuals composing it. We attempt, that is, to explain the conduct of the individual in terms of the organized conduct of the group, rather than to account for the organized conduct of the social group in terms of the conduct of the separate individuals belonging to it. For social psychology, the whole (society) is prior to the part (the individual), not the part to the whole; and the part is explained in terms of the whole, not the whole in terms of the part or parts. The social act is not explained by building it up out of stimulus plus response; it must be taken as a dynamic whole—as something going on—no part of which can be considered or understood by itself—a complex organic process implied by each individual stimulus and response involved in it [Mead, 1934, p. 7].

The alert reader may pick up, in this passage, several phrases which have a familiar ring and which suggest some of the thinkers who influenced Mead's thought. Thus, the notion of analyzing something (society) into elements comes from Wundtian structuralism. The priority given to the whole rather than to the part is certainly similar to the point of view of Gestalt psychology. It is a fact that Mead did study in Berlin and was familiar both with Wundt's work and the writings of Köhler and the Gestalt group. Notice, finally, the use of the terms "behavior" and "stimulus" and "response." This again indicates the influence of John B. Watson and the early school of behaviorism. In fact, Mead called his system "social behaviorism."

In this system, there are several key concepts that have proved to be very useful to present-day social psychology. These are *self, other, generalized other*, and, most especially, *role*. Mead sees what he calls the self as a structure built up on top of the physiological organism through social interaction with others, especially in play and game situations. He is very explicit in stating that without social interaction no self is possible; in his own words, "... it is impossible to conceive of a self arising outside of social experience [1934, p. 40]."

The manner in which a self or personality develops, then, is through a process of learning to take the *role* of the *other*, that is, acquiring a facility in empathizing with the attitudes of other people with whom we interact. This is most readily seen in a game like baseball, in which, in order to perform properly, each player must be able to take on the attitudes of all others in the game. Only by virtue of its members' possessing this ability can a team act as a smoothly functioning unit. Thus the shortstop knows without looking, for example, that the second baseman will be in the correct position on a double play and throws the ball accordingly. And he knows this because he is able, implicitly, to take the role of second baseman in that situation. The organization of all social roles which the individual learns to take Mead calls "the generalized other." In the baseball example, the whole team constitutes such a generalized other. In a whole culture, it is the common experience shared by all members of it. It is this communality of shared experience that gives the group its cohesion and that allows the individuals that make it up to move in it comfortably and without too much conflict.

The notion of role, then, as defined by Mead, affords us a kind of bridge between our conceptualizations about the individual and our conceptualizations about society or culture taken as a whole. People become socialized, or acculturated, by taking roles, and consequently we should be able to understand much more fully just how this takes place by explicating more fully the meaning of the term "role."

Mead himself laid the groundwork for such an enterprise but did no empirical work on the subject. He was, after all, technically a philosopher and could hardly have been expected to venture too far away from his own field. It was left to psychologists to take up the concept and analyze it in a manner that permitted and suggested experimentation. Notable among those who attempted this successfully has been Theodore Sarbin of the University of California at Berkeley, starting in the 1940s. Chiefly from his thinking have emerged a number of aspects of role and a number of related concepts that need to be defined at this point.

In the first place, almost all societies—certainly all civlized ones—designate what are called "positions," for example, mothers, fathers, bosses, employees, policemen, teachers. People who occupy these positions are *expected* to behave in certain ways and not behave in other ways, the *expectations* being firmer for some sorts of behavior than for others. Likewise, a certain position carries with it certain expectations regarding the behavior of others toward the position. For example, consider a father and child. The father expects loving and respectful behavior from his child. Likewise, the child can expect protecting and loving behavior from his father.

A position category together with the expectations of behavior associated with it define the term "role," or "social role." These terms thus merely refine and further specify the meaning of a position. Note that the expectations of one person about a role may not agree with those of another. The role of boss may be thought of by one employee as embodying a notion of a kindly and charismatic leader; by another, as involving qualities of strength and authority. The person who is the boss may have a view quite different from either of these. Furthermore, his actual behavior in the position may agree or disagree with the expectations of others and also with his own. A professor who teaches poorly obviously behaves in a way that does not conform either to the ideas of most students or, probably, to his own definition of the position he is occupying. It is most likely that he simply cannot help being a poor teacher and suffers a good deal of discomfort on this account.

Several additional dimensions are suggested by the above discussion. One of these relates to the clarity with which any particular role is defined. Some are clearly demarcated by society, others not so clearly. This fact immediately suggests the possibility of conflict's occurring between the expectations of different persons about a given role and between the actual behavior of a person occupying a certain position and the expectations of others as to how he should be behaving. The general term used to designate the tension arising from such conflicts is "role strain." It is quite analogous, at the level of society, to the concepts of balance, symmetry, and congruity which we discussed earlier at the level of the individual and his cognitions about the world of things and people. Another source of role strain is any discrepancy arising between different roles occupied by the same person. For example, the role of employer can seriously interfere with the role of friend. Having power over another person is seldom conducive to maintaining a friendship with him. Such situations as this one are very commonly used in novels and dramas, for example, the military commander who has to mount a risky attack using a unit of which his own son is a member or the judge whose son gets involved in a hit-and-run accident. The reader will undoubtedly be able to think of many other such cases.

It may be well at this point to retrace our steps a

little. The reader may have, by now, the notion that personality, as treated in terms of role theory, is a kind of artificial entity made up of many different roles that are acted out—as if the world were really all a stage, to paraphrase Hamlet, and we were merely actors on it. Many people may feel that this implied lack of genuineness, or sincerity, about themselves is a rather repelling idea. Actually this is not the case. The concept of role as used technically is neutral in regard to this point. Roles that are adopted early in life are presumably a real and well-integrated part of the total personality. This may also apply to roles acquired later on. Nobody is born a minister, a professor, or a business executive, and the initial entry into these roles may cause discomfort to some people. But usually, the behaviors they involve soon come to be enacted without hesitation and without conscious effort.

Whether there is a center, or core, of personality that can be called the self on the basis of which roles are developed is a moot point. Mead, for example, evidently conceived of personality as being synonymous with social roles. Sarbin (1965), on the other hand, has separated the two concepts of self and role. He finds this necessary in order to account for the range of individual differences that can be found in respect to role enactment. People are different not only in the way in which they fit a role but also in how congruent they are with it—that is to say, some are more at home in it than others. An example of the work done on this general topic has aimed specifically at finding out what self-characteristics are congruent with the ability of a person to become engaged in, and attached to, the role of "hypnotic subject." The latter technique has a special usefulness for exploring the problem, since it is likely that ability to be hypnotized should maximally reflect aptitude for role taking, if such a general trait exists. Some data bearing on this question are shown in Example 9-9.

Example 9-9 *Aptitude for role taking (Sarbin, 1965)*

Two types of questionnaires were administered to a large sample of students. One type was designed to tap dispositions to do with the self. It was made up of such items as "I can study a subject rather well when I'm tired" or "I would hesitate to take drugs that produce mood changes out of the ordinary." These statements called for "true" or "false" responses.

The second type of questionnaire specifically measured hypnotizability. It was assumed that hypnotizability reflects the ease with which a subject can enact a role—in this case the role of hypnotic subject. The questionnaire was made up of rating scales for self-report of responsiveness to suggestion. The criterion tasks included such items as taste hallucination, hand lowering, and arm rigidity. The rationale of these can be explained by an example. Some persons, when it is suggested to them that a limb is becoming rigid, find that this is actually happening to a greater or lesser extent. It is their job, then, to report on a scale the magnitude of this reaction. Persons high and low on this second type of questionnaire were picked out and an examination made of their responses to the self-evaluation scales.

Results indicated that 23 of the pool of 117 items discriminated between persons high and low on role enactment. These items fall into five groups, with the high-response subject describing himself as:

1. Able to concentrate and become absorbed
2. Ready to accept mood changes
3. Enjoying new experiences and "as-if" behavior
4. Interested in hypnosis and cognate phenomena
5. Unconcerned about responsibilities and social reward and punishment

The general finding agrees partially with the results of another group of researchers.

The study thus starts to uncover the dimensions of self that are independent of any particular role but that may be necessary for all role enactments and, indeed, perhaps for the general ability to be sociable and socializable, assuming hypnotizability reflects the latter characteristics.

In any given situation, then, there occurs an interaction between self-dispositions and role demands. The congruity between the two will determine to a great extent how comfortable and how effective the person is in that situation and also how other people will react to him. We saw earlier that most small groups involve various roles, some more clearly specified than others. The activity of the group will be at least partly explicable by reference to the role concept, which usefully bridges, as we have pointed out, the gap between individual variables and group variables.

We have stressed the way roles can differentiate the social behavior of individuals in a group. By understanding the role each person occupies, we can start to predict not only his behavior but also the behavior of the group as a whole. We may then start to compare one group with another. It is obvious that by reason of their imposing common sets of roles they may share much in common. Thus all groups, large or small, will probably have a leader; most long-term ones, at least, will probably develop over time some kind of hierarchical structure—castes or classes, for example, to which special obligations, privileges, and attitudes may accrue. Large groups, such as societies, all tend to have persons delegated to formulate a set of rules or laws, others to enforce these, and others whose job it is to punish transgressors. In spite of such shared similarities in structure, groups differ enormously in the expectations they have as to how the roles they specify are to be enacted. The witch doctor in Central Africa is analogous to the general practitioner in the United States, inasmuch as both are concerned with healing and both hold respected positions, but the similarity does not go much farther than this.

These communalities of, and differences between, large groups are the direct concerns of sociology and anthropology. In the remainder of the chapter we will look at some examples of work done by investigators in these sciences and also examine the concepts of cultural relativity and conformity.

CULTURE AND SOCIETY

All of us, in our behavior, attitudes, and personality, are to some extent the product of the culture or society we live in. This idea quite explicitly emerges from role theory, which attempts to account not only for the dissimilarities but also for the similarities and uniformities between individual members of the group. Most groups will tolerate only a modicum of variation from behavior considered to be normal, right, or proper, and against persons falling outside certain limits they will employ various sanctions. Thus behavior is relative to culture. This idea has most forcibly been expressed by such anthropologists as Boas, Sumner, and Benedict. We began this section with a quotation from Ruth Benedict. Here is another from the same book, *Patterns of Culture* (1959):

> The life history of the individual is first and foremost an accommodation to the patterns and standards traditionally handed down in his community. From the moment of his birth the customs into which he is born shape his experience and behavior. By the time he can talk, he is the little creature of his culture, and by the time he is grown and able to take part in its activities, its habits are his habits, its beliefs his beliefs, its impossibilities his impossibilities. Every child that is born into his group will share them with him, and no child born into one on the opposite side of the globe can ever achieve the thousandth part. There is no social problem it is more incumbent upon us to understand than this role of custom. Until we are intelligent as to its laws and varieties, the main complicating facts of human life must remain unintelligible [Benedict, 1959, p. 2].

This emphasis placed on the differences between cultural groups and the great plasticity of human beings represented, at the time when it was first stated, a needed reaction against the idea that all men were basically alike—or at least should be—and that deviations from a Western ideal of behavior and morals were essentially peculiar or even bad. Kipling's classic phrase in reference to peoples in the outposts of the British Empire, "lesser breeds without the law," summed up this point of view nicely. Today, through the impact of anthropology and because of greatly increased communications between societies in all parts of the globe, the average educated person takes cultural relativism for granted. An American may feel a little uneasy about the outlook of Europeans, but he is not usually surprised or shocked to find it is different from his own. The following example, drawn from Benedict, may not startle the reader, either. Nonetheless, it is worth including, since it is a classic of its kind.

Example 9–10 *The Zuni, the Dobuans, and the Kwakiutl (Benedict, 1959)*

Ruth Benedict, a student of the great anthropologist Franz Boas of Columbia University, spent much of her time doing fieldwork on different cultures. One she studied intensively was the Zuni people, a Pueblo Indian tribe of the Southwestern United States. Two others on which she compiled information from secondary sources, notably Boas and Fortune, were respectively the Kwakiutl Indians of the Pacific Northwest and the Dobuans of an island near New Guinea. Here is a sketch of each:

The Zunis are a quiet and ceremonious people with a great love of detailed ceremonials and complex religious observances. The ideal life for them is a pleasant, peaceful one that passes without incidents. Likewise, the ideal man in this culture is polite, self-effacing, and never in the limelight. He takes responsibility and position only if these are thrust on him, and then with great show of reluctance. He avoids, at all cost, the appearance of leadership. In his capacity as a leader, he gets little real authority, in any case. Individual personality tends to be completely subordinate to the group.

The Dobuans, by contrast, are considered lawless and treacherous, which traits they apparently hold in high esteem. Between the large units of social organization—the so-called "locales"—there is a permanent and complete state of war. But even within locales there is strong aggression, expressed mostly in the form of magic and sorcery. Thus the most immediate problem for a Dobuan is not so much his enemy in a different locale but rather his neighbor who may at any time cast an evil spell and bring disaster upon him and upon what is his most precious commodity, namely, his crops. Benedict summarizes Dobuan life as follows:

> Life in Dobu fosters extreme forms of animosity and malignancy which most societies have minimized by their institutions. Dobu institutions, on the other hand, exalt them to the highest degree. The Dobuan lives out without repression man's worst nightmares of the ill-will of the universe, and according to his view of life, virtue consists in selecting a victim upon whom he can vent the malignancy he attributes alike to human society and to the powers of nature. All existence appears to him as a cutthroat struggle in which deadly antagonists are pitted against one another in a contest for each one of the goods of life. Suspicion and cruelty are his trusted weapons in the strife and he gives no mercy, as he asks none [Benedict, 1959, p. 159].

The Kwakiutl Indians of Vancouver Island are descendants of a much larger civilization who originally occupied a strip of Pacific seacoast between Alaska and Puget Sound. They are described as a vigorous and overbearing people whose culture was built upon an inexhaustible supply of goods and food that could be harvested from the ocean—fish of all kinds, seals, whales, and an abundance of shellfish. In spite of this, their culture is strongly competitive and entrepreneurial. Accumulation of wealth is their main purpose in life and a means to self-glorification. They fight with property, and paradoxically the most highly valued way of demonstrating one's success was either by giving away to a rival more than he could give back or else by deliberately destroying his own property in a dramatic display of conspicuous consumption. The reaction to such shaming, on the part of the rival, was often equally dramatic—suicide, usually preceded by a long and intense period of sulking, during which he retreated to his pallet and spoke to no one. This paranoid, megalomaniacal attitude toward life is one which we in civilized societies have branded as abnormal and undesirable, but we may also recognize that it is not so totally alien that we cannot recognize seeds of it in ourselves.

The above sketches of Zuni, Dobuan, and Kwakiutl personalities illustrate dramatically how culture casts the individual in a mold from which it is difficult for him to escape. National differences in the less primitive world are perhaps not as compelling but certainly seem to exist in a sense that is best defined in terms of *ideal or mythical types* rather than in terms of statistical averages. Every country, through its folktales and legends, through its history and its heroes, through its fine arts and its philosophy, seems to formulate a vision of a personality that it considers the most desirable. It is in these ideals, perhaps, that what we call national character is best explored. Thus it is likely that we can best understand Americans by finding out what most Americans would like to be like rather than by finding out what they actually are like. This makes sense when we consider that most critical decisions made by people during their lifetimes are on the basis of certain ideals they hold, rather than on the basis of simple circumstantial factors.

Unfortunately we cannot pursue this interesting problem further. A great deal of work has been done on national character, but it lies beyond the scope of our discussion. Of more relevance is the notion we started with, namely, cultural relativity. The emphasis of anthropology, at least until recently, has been on cultural differences. Allowing that these are very real and are of great interest, we must nevertheless be careful not to overstate their importance. People everywhere may also show certain similarities, and perhaps these, especially in the divided world we now live in, are very much worth examining.

One of the first people in psychology to question critically the concept of cultural relativity was the Gestalt psychologist Karl Duncker. His point of view was later taken up by Solomon Asch (1952). Their position is essentially this: underneath the differences in values and customs that exist between cultures lie basic communalities that are less obvious. According to Asch and Duncker, it usually happens that the diversity of practices we can observe do not necessarily imply a relativity of values but rather a differing comprehension of the situation involved, this being referable to differing amounts of information, differing intellectual capacities, and differing surrounding circumstances. The assumption, then, is that if these were held constant, the valuations made would also be constant across cultures.

Consider the treatment accorded to the aged by most civilized cultures as compared with that accorded by the Eskimos. Though not always realized in practice, the goals of our society with respect to old people are to provide them with sufficient care, comfort, and respect, so that they can live out their declining years in contentment. Eskimos, on the other hand, simply used to turn out the aged to die of exposure. Clearly, this does not necessarily mean that Eskimos were vicious and insensitive but rather that the harsh circumstances in which they lived forced them to adopt a custom that was in the best interests of the society. Their valuation of the situation is different because the meaning it has for them is different.

Thus the thesis of cultural relativism should not be overstated. People are shaped differently according to the culture they occupy, but nonetheless they may, in the end, share basic points of view and attitudes. And it is on these communalities that we must pin our hopes for mutual understanding between nations. As Asch says:

We do not know of societies in which bravery is despised and cowardice held up to honor, in which generosity is considered a vice and ingratitude a virtue.... We still have to hear of a society to which modesty, courage and hospitality are not known [Asch, 1952, p. 379].

CONCLUSION

This section has treated social psychology as a rather abstract discipline whose basic ideas may seem remote from the many pressing problems of society. We must emphasize now that this remoteness is only apparent. Just as an understanding of basic physics and chemistry is essential to the successful presentation of such practical goals as building houses and bridges, so also an understanding of the fundamental ideas in social psychology is a prerequisite to the tackling of the many pressing social problems that face us today. There can be no doubt that the greatest and most difficult issues concern the relations between individuals and how they can live together in harmony and good will. This is true whether we are considering the social interactions between two single individuals or between two great national powers.

We are very far from reaching any easy solutions. Yet it is perhaps not too optimistic to suppose that some may be forthcoming before very long. Social relationships are perhaps no longer being taken for granted as much as they used to be. People everywhere are starting to realize that social patterns are not fixed and absolute but are indeed vulnerable to manipulation and change along prescribed lines. This is probably especially true in the case of young children whose *social* education has so far been left largely to guesswork and chance. There is no reason why social ability should be treated in such a casual manner. Were the whole apparatus of theory and methods used by social psychologists brought to bear on the problem, we might see astonishing results.

Certainly, much is, in fact, being done along these lines with adult groups, particularly in business and managerial settings. So-called "sensitivity" training, or T groups, have, according to reports, yielded striking improvements in the social relationships and effectiveness of coworkers. There is every reason to believe that the implementation of such programs for children in schools might produce even greater effects.

This kind of possible application of social psychology is only one of many that can be made. Of all the areas in psychology perhaps this is the one that has potentially, at least, the greatest usefulness; and it does seem to be true, in the authors' experience, that those entering it characteristically have, besides their scientific commitment, a strong humanitarian orientation. In this, they are quite faithful to the spirit of those who founded and developed the field: Comte, Lewin, and many of the other thinkers we have discussed in the chapters of this section.

SECTION THREE: REFERENCES

ALLPORT, G. W. The historical background of modern social psychology. In G. Lindzey (Ed.), *Handbook of social psychology.* Vol. 1. Cambridge, Mass: Addison-Wesley, 1954.

AMBROSE, J. A. The development of the smiling response in early infancy. In B. Foss (Ed.), *Determinants of infant behaviour.* London: Methuen, 1961.

ASCH, S. E. *Social psychology.* Englewood Cliffs, N.J.: Prentice-Hall, 1952.

BALES, R. F. *Interaction process analysis: A method for the study of small groups.* Cambridge, Mass: Addison-Wesley, 1950.

BALES, R. F. Some uniformities of behavior in small social systems. In G. E. Swanson, T. M. Newcomb, & E. L. Hartley (Eds.), *Readings in social psychology.* (Rev. ed.) New York: Holt, 1952.

BALES, R. F. The equilibrium problem in small groups. In A. P. Hare, E. F. Borgatta, & R. F. Bales (Eds.), *Small groups: Studies in social interaction.* New York: Knopf, 1955.

BANDURA, A., & WALTERS, R. H. *Social learning and personality development.* New York: Holt, 1963.

BENEDICT, R. *Patterns of culture.* Boston: Houghton Mifflin, 2d ed., 1959.

BOGARDUS, E. S. Measuring social distance. *Journal of Applied Sociology,* 1925, **9**, 299–308.

BREHM, J. W. Post-decisional changes in the desirability of alternatives. *Journal of Abnormal and Social Psychology,* 1956, **52**, 384–389.

CARTWRIGHT, D., & HARARY, F. Structural balance: A generalization of Heider's theory. *Psychological Review,* 1956, **63**, 277–293.

CLINE, V. B., & RICHARD, J. M., Jr. Accuracy of interpersonal perception—a general trait? *Journal of Abnormal and Social Psychology,* 1960, **60**, 1–7.

EFRON, D., & FOLEY, J. P., Jr. Gestural behavior and social setting. In T. M. Newcomb and E. L. Hartley (Eds.), *Readings in social psychology.* New York: Holt, 1947.

FELEKY, A. M. *Feelings and emotions.* New York: Pioneer Publishing, 1924.

FESTINGER, L. *Theory of cognitive dissonance.* Evanston, Ill: Row, Peterson, 1957.

HARLOW, H. F. The heterosexual affectional system in monkeys. *American Psychologist,* 1962, **17**, 1–9.

HEIDER, F. Social perception and phenomenal causality. *Psychological Review,* 1944, **51**, 358–374.

HEIDER, F., & SIMMEL, E. A study of apparent behavior. *American Journal of Psychology,* 1944, **57**, 243–259.

HEYNS, R. W. Effects of variation in leadership on participant behavior in discussion groups. Unpublished doctoral dissertation, University of Michigan. Permission: T. M. Newcomb: *Social psychology.* New York: Dryden Press, 1950, p. 505.

HOVLAND, C. I., & JANIS, I. L. (Eds.) *Personality and persuasability.* New Haven: Yale University Press, 1959.

HOVLAND, C. I., JANIS, I. L., & KELLEY, H. H. *Communication and persuasion.* New Haven: Yale University Press, 1953.

HUME, D. An enquiry concerning human understanding. In E. A. Burtt (Ed.), *The English philosophers from Bacon to Mill.* New York: Modern Library, Random House, 1939.

JANIS, I. L., & FEIERABEND, R. L. Effects of alternative ways of ordering pro and con arguments in persuasive communications. In C. I. Hovland et al. (Eds.), *The order of presentation in persuasion.* New Haven: Yale University Press, 1957.

JANIS, I. L., & FIELD, P. B. Behavioral assessment of persuasibility: consistency of individual differences. *Sociometry,* 1956, **19**, 241–259.

KATZ, D., & STOTLAND, E. A preliminary statement to a theory of attitude structure and change. In S. Koch (Ed.), *Psychology: A study of a science.* Vol. III. New York: McGraw-Hill, 1959.

KELMAN, H. C. Processes of opinion change. *Public Opinion Quarterly,* 1961, **25**, 57–78.

KLINEBERG, O. *Social psychology.* New York: Holt, 1940.

KRECH, D., & CRUTCHFIELD, R. *Theory and problems of social psychology.* New York: McGraw-Hill, 1948.

KUTNER, B., WILKINS, C., & YARROW, P. Verbal attitudes and overt behavior involving racial prejudice. *Journal of Abnormal and Social Psychology*, 1952, **47**, 649–652.

LEAVITT, H. J. Some effects of certain communication patterns on group performance. *Journal of Abnormal and Social Psychology*, 1951, **46**, 38–50.

LEWIN, K., LIPPITT, R., & WHITE, R. K. Patterns of aggressive behavior in experimentally created social climates. *Journal of Social Psychology*, 1939, **10**, 271–299.

LIKERT, R. A technique for the measurement of attitudes. *Archives of Psychology*, 1932, No. 140.

McDOUGALL, W. *An introduction to social psychology.* London: Methuen, 1908.

McGUIRE, W. J. A syllogistic analysis of cognitive relationships. In C. I. Hovland & I. L. Janis (Eds.), *Attitude organization and change.* New Haven: Yale University Press, 1960.

MEAD, G. H. *Mind, self, and society.* Chicago: University of Chicago Press, 1934.

MEAD, M. *Growing up in New Guinea.* New York: Mentor Books, New American Library, 1953.

MICHOTTE, A. E. *The perception of causality.* London: Methuen, 1963.

MILL, J. S. *On liberty.* (People's ed.) London: Longmans, 1865.

MILLER, N. E. Learnable drives and rewards. In S. S. Stevens (Ed.), *Handbook of experimental psychology.* New York: 1951.

MILLER, N. E., & DOLLARD, J. *Social learning and imitation.* New Haven: Yale University Press, 1941.

MORENO, J. L. *Who shall survive?* Washington: Nervous and Mental Disease Monograph, No. 58, 1934.

NEWCOMB, T. An approach to the study of communicative acts. *Psychological Review*, 1953, **60**, 393–404.

OSGOOD, C. E., & TANNENBAUM, P. H. The principle of congruity in the prediction of attitude change. *Psychological Review*, 1955, **62**, 42–55.

PEAK, H. Psychological structure and psychological activity. *Psychological Review*, 1958, **65**, 325–347.

PIAGET, J. *The child's conception of causality.* London: Kegan Paul, 1930.

RIESMAN, D., GLAZER, N., & DENNEY, R. *The lonely crowd: A study of the changing American character.* Garden City, N.Y.: Doubleday, 1956.

ROSENBERG, M. J., & ABELSON, R. P. An analysis of cognitive balancing. In M. J. Rosenberg et al. (Eds.), *Attitude organization and change.* New Haven: Yale University Press, 1960.

SARBIN, T. R. Role theory. In G. Lindzey (Ed.), *Handbook of social psychology.* Cambridge, Mass: Addison-Wesley, 1954. Vol. I.

SARBIN, T. R. Role theoretical interpretation of psychological change. In P. Worchel and D. Byrne (Eds.), *Personality change.* New York: Wiley, Pp. 176–219, 1965.

SPITZ, R. A., & WOLF, K. M. The smiling response: A contribution to the ontogenesis of social relations. *Genetic Psychology Monographs*, 1946, **34**, 57–125.

STEPHAN, F. F., & MISHLER, E. G. The distribution of participation in small groups: An exponential approximation. In A. P. Hare, E. F. Borgatta, & R. F. Bales (Eds.), *Small groups: Studies in social interaction.* New York: Knopf, 1955.

SUCHMAN, E. A. The intensity component in attitude and opinion research. In S. A. Stouffer et al. (Eds.), *Measurement and prediction.* Princeton, N.J.: Princeton University Press, 1950.

TAGIURI, R. Introduction, in R. Tagiuri & L. Petrullo (Eds.), *Person perception and interpersonal behavior.* Stanford, Calif.: Stanford University Press, 1958.

THURSTONE, L. L. Theory of attitude measurement. *Psychological Review*, 1929, **36**, 222–241.

THURSTONE, L. L., & CHAVE, E. J. *The measurement of attitude.* Chicago: University of Chicago Press, 1929.

WOODWORTH, R. S. *Psychology.* (4th ed.) New York: Holt, 1940.

SECTION FOUR
APPROACHES TO THE PROBLEMS OF PERCEIVING AND KNOWING

SOCRATES: And were we not saying long ago that the soul when using the body as an instrument of perception, that is to say, when using the sense of sight or hearing or some other sense (for the meaning of perceiving through the body is perceiving through the senses)—were we not saying that the soul too is then dragged by the body into the region of the changeable, and wanders and is confused; the world spins round her, and she is like a drunkard, when she touches change?

CEBES: Very true.

SOCRATES: But when retiring into herself, she reflects, then she passes into the other world, the region of purity, and eternity, and immortality, and unchangeableness, which are her kindred, and with them she ever lives, when she is by herself and is not *let or hindered; then she ceases from her erring ways, and being in communion with the unchanging, is unchanging. And this state of the soul is called wisdom?*

(Plato, 1928, p. 139)

PROLOGUE

In this section, we will discuss some approaches made to one of the most basic of all problems in psychology and in philosophy—namely, how we know and establish contact with the world we live in. For the most part, we get around in the world with such ease and assurance that it is difficult for us to understand that any problems exist at all. But it is precisely the commonplace character and the universality of their occurrence that give to the processes of perceiving and knowing such fundamental significance.

Consider a championship tennis game. A good server can usually deliver a ball across the net to the receiver's service court at a speed of as much as 100 miles per hour, that is, about 150 feet per second. This means that the receiver will have probably not more than ¼ second in which to make a decision as to where the ball will bounce, how he will position himself, what kind of stroke he will use to try to return the serve, and, if possible, the direction of his return as well. That a human being is able to carry out all these tasks so efficiently is quite remarkable, though most of us probably take it for granted. Such feats are almost commonplace in a great variety of sports.

Again, many men, in their practical lives, must perform daily tasks of the same order of difficulty. A jet-fighter pilot, for example, may be required to land on the pitching and rolling deck of an aircraft carrier at a speed of as high as 200 miles per hour. In this case, a mistake in judgment, a slight error in perception, can cost him his life as well as endanger the lives of many others involved in his landing.

Yet these rather dramatic examples of perceptual skill are only extensions of those same mechanisms that allow us to walk across a room toward a friend we recognize, stop in front of him, and shake his hand; or to look across a valley and know that the house we see on the far side of it is not a tiny doll's house but a full-sized one; or to look at grass in bright sunlight and know that it is not yellow (as it actually appears) but green as grass should normally be. All these cases involve perception, and in all of them there is, at least in some sense, *a coincidence between the way things are and the way they appear to us.*

The psychologist Kurt Koffka, whose name we encountered in Section III, posed the central question in the study of perception as being, "Why do things look as they do?" A naïve person might answer, "Because they are what they are." Such an answer assumes that objects have certain definable existential properties—constituting "reality"—and that these are responsible for the manner in which we perceive them—that is, their "appearance." This seems a sensible postulate, but it is one that answers nothing, since the central problem is precisely to define these properties and to state how they produce a certain perception. Furthermore, it is not always true that there is such a coincidence between reality and appearance. Very often things appear different from the way they are, and these instances must also be explained; and we must consider seriously the possibility that the rules which explain *veridical* perception—that is, correct perception—may also explain the failures of perception, as, for example, in the case of so-called *illusions*.

It is an interesting fact that most of those who have thought about the problem have been more impressed by the failures of perception than by its successes. The quotation from one of Plato's dialogues with which we opened this chapter reflects this very clearly and commenced a tradition about the relation between the person and his reality that has lasted 2,000 years. Plato, speaking through his old teacher and friend Socrates, expresses clearly his view that appearances of things which come to us through our senses are so changeable and ephemeral that they are to be strongly distrusted. The sensory world is merely a pale and inadequate reflection of a set of eternal truths—and these we find only by looking inward into the soul or mind in which they lie hidden.

This notion, whatever merit it has, led to an important distinction between what reality is and what our mental impression of it is. There exist objects which emit physical energy—light waves, sounds, and smells. These energies excite our sensory receptors—our eyes, ears, and olfactory organs. Out of these sensations we somehow obtain information about objects in the form of percepts, which may or may not coincide with the actual objects. An important problem concerns the alchemy by which we are able to "transform" raw sense data—for example, an array of patches of color—into a meaningful perception of, say, a cathedral. And we must ask, having made such a transformation, "Are we still dealing with the real cathedral as it is out there in front of us?"

This last question is one that has been central to the whole history of art. Anyone who understands what many great artists were trying to do will realize that they were heavily involved in a quest to show what reality was like. The well-known art historian E. H. Gombrich, in his book *Art and Illusion*, suggests that "art itself becomes the innovator's instrument for probing reality." He goes on to say:

> The boldest of these experiments led to the conviction that the artist's vision is entirely subjective. With impressionism, the popular notion of the painter became that of the man who paints blue trees and red lawns and who answers every criticism with a proud "That is how I see it." This is one part of the story, but not, I believe, the whole. This assertion of subjectivity can also be overdone. There is such a thing as a real visual discovery, and there is a way of testing it despite the fact we may never know what the artist himself saw at a certain moment. Whatever the initial resistance to impressionist paintings, when the first shock had worn off, people learned to read them. And having learned this language, they went into the fields and woods, or looked out of their windows onto the Paris boulevards and found to their delight that the visible world *could* after all be seen in terms of these bright patches and dabs of paint. The transposition worked. The impressionists had taught them, not, indeed to see nature with an innocent eye but to explore an unexpected alternative that turned out to fit certain experiences better than did any earlier paintings. The artists convinced art lovers so thoroughly that the bon mot "Nature imitates art" became current. As Oscar Wilde said, there was no fog in London before Whistler painted it [Gombrich, 1961, p. 324].

A striking example of "impressionism" is Monet's painting of Rouen Cathedral. This shows a view of the western facade, its details and its outlines blurred and almost liquefied by the bright blue of the background sky and the dazzling sunshine striking directly against it.

The reader may object that this is not the view that a camera will give us and hence it has little connection with the cathedral as it really is. But it must be remembered that a camera, contrary to popular belief, is a highly particularized way of viewing reality—not the best way or the only way, but simply one way. A fast shutter and a small aperture will cut out the dazzle, and a good lens will yield fine detail. But these are very special conditions and do not replicate how all persons on all occasions must see the same scene. Indeed, using a slower speed and wide aperture, a photographer could undoubtedly produce a picture very much like Monet's painting. Thus there are many ways of viewing the world.

Let us look at one other example. The modern American painter Andrew Wyeth is noted for his so-called "magic," or "sharp-focus," realism. Here is representation so "real" that it goes beyond realism. By holding, as it were, a microscope to conventional scenes, Wyeth, as Samuel Green has put it, "gives to the ordinary world a sharpened intensity that sometimes makes it mysterious or even frightening [Green, 1966, p. 581]." One of Wyeth's most famous paintings, called "The Open Window," though it represents simply a curtain blowing in the breeze, has overtones of a definitely sinister quality. Looking at it we feel a sense of emptiness, foreboding, and sadness. How much we can see in the world, if through art we are "taught really to see it."

This short excursion into art history is not intended to supply the reader with answers. However, it should serve to give life and substance to the abstract problem raised initially, namely, the relation between reality and appearance. We turn back to psychology and show how this discipline can contribute to our understanding of how man grasps reality. Here, indeed, is an epic question but one, we hope, on which we can bring to bear some of the precision of science.

CHAPTER 10
THE PROBLEM OF PERCEPTION

The general discussion in the preceding Prologue does not specify directly how an attack can be made by empirical methods on the problem of perception. However, it does hint at those sectors of it on which we should initially focus. In this chapter we will attempt to make those sectors of the problem explicit.

THE PHENOMENOLOGICAL METHOD AND THE CATEGORIES OF EXPERIENCE

It will be recalled from Chapter 1 that psychology started out as the science of mind. The task that the nineteenth-century German experimental psychologists defined for themselves was the analysis of consciousness, and in this choice they followed the tradition of the British empiricist philosophers Hume, Mill, Bentham, Hobbes, and others. The main difference was that the psychologists rejected the method of philosophy by carrying out their observations in a laboratory setting under carefully controlled conditions. The experimental method of the German school consisted mainly of specifying different situations in which introspective reports were obtained. Thus, instead of asking the general question (as an empirical philosopher might) "What is 'feeling'?" these psychologists asked questions about the makeup, or contents, of feelings under such-and-such specific conditions, for example, feelings in response to the pleasant odor of lavender or feelings while awaiting a signal. This was a useful step forward in the development of a scientific psychology. The great problem that remained was the lack of control over the dependent variables—that is, the observations by the subject about his own mental state, usually reported verbally to the experimenter. Such observations were essentially private ones; that is to say, they were not about the stimulus or the outside world, but rather about the subject's own mind. Thus an experimenter, faced with two subjects who disagreed completely as to what their respective mental contents were under conditions X, was never able to decide which one was making a "true" report, if, indeed, either one was, or if both were.

The two major reactions to this ambiguity in the method of introspection were supplied, around 1912, by Gestalt psychology in Germany and behaviorism in America. Since we deal with behaviorism and its offshoots in another section, we will not discuss it here but will confine ourselves to Gestalt psychology and the phenomenological method. We have already seen something of it in our discussion of social perception in Section III. The key assumption in this method is that empirical truth may be obtained through an assessment of a subject's direct experience of the world. The word "phenomenological" itself means, simply, the study of the world *as known*. It is derived etymologically from a Greek word meaning "appearance," that is, the way things *seem* rather than the way they are. Gestalt psychology arose from a background of German and especially Kantian idealism. For Kant, a thing as it really was—the thing in itself, or *noumenon*—was unknowable. Truth was to be found only in the study of the phenomenal world. Such a point of view was one response to the English philosopher Bishop Berkeley, who had posed this question: If our only knowledge of the existence of the world is obtained through observation, how can we ever be sure that such a world exists independently of observers?

Kant's answer was that we can never be sure but can deal only with a world we ourselves construct out of sense data. This, of course, is not really an answer, though perhaps no real answer is possible. Certainly for most people no answer is even necessary. Be this as it may, Kant's axiom that the study of experience was in itself a valid enterprise clearly influenced the thinking of the founders of Gestalt psychology, Wertheimer, Köhler, and Koffka.

Thus, Köhler, in his book *Gestalt Psychology*, defines "objective (or direct) experience" as an interaction between the world (stimuli) and the observer (senses). Such objective experience contrasts with the so-called subjective experience of the introspectionist, this being essentially an interaction, not between the person and the world, but between the person and his own consciousness. Stimuli are accessible to an experimenter and can be manipulated, controlled, and refined with a good deal of precision. The situation is thus public and repeatable. This is not true in the case of subjective experience.

In our brief reference to art history, we indicated that the world "looks" different to different people and thus the view that Monet had of Rouen Cathedral was not merely the recondite and highly intellectualized construction of an avant-garde artist but rather a genuine and legitimate alternative to that immediately experienced by most people. Monet's painting represents the way this great church *looked* to him, perhaps at a very special and tiny moment in time but nonetheless in a direct and immediate experience. To this extent, his statement on canvas was, in Gestalt terms, objective rather than subjective.

From the standpoint of science, however, the study of such direct experience raises certain difficulties. A report made by a subject as to how a stimulus looks to him is not the same as behavior. In the first place, it is difficult to know whether the subject is making an accurate report of what he experiences. He may be very uncertain about it, he may not be able to articulate it accurately in words, and he may be unduly influenced by various attitudes he brings with him to the experiment. In the second place, it is never certain whether a certain experience would be reflected in behavior were the occasion to arise or, for that matter, if it were so reflected, whether this would detract from its validity. Consider the two sets of "parallel" lines in Figure 10–1. The top pair, to most observers, appear to curve out, the bottom pair to curve inward. The experience is a rather compelling one. Nevertheless we would probably not hesitate to use any of the lines as a straight edge if we had to. Behavior and experience are not necessarily coordinate domains of investigation, and it is silly to deny the legitimacy of either one because it does not entirely conform to the standards set up to handle the other.

At the same time, it is obvious that as many reasonable precautions as possible must be taken to reduce ambiguity in a report of direct experience. This can usually be done by narrowing the range of stimuli with which the subject is asked to deal and by reducing the complexity of the response involved in his report. In fact, if at all possible a simple digital response of the yes-or-no type is highly desirable. Repetition of the observation is also, of course, essential (cf. Allport, 1955).

The art of knowing the world involves a succession of steps from object to knower. The object, in the first place, emits energies of various kinds such as light rays, displacement of air molecules, and volatile chemicals. The impingement of these on the sensory receptor surfaces constitutes *sensation*, or *sensory stimulation*. At another level, especially in the case of vision, we have a percept, that is, the apprehension of an actual object in a spatial context. Finally, we have what may be called a *cognition*, taking this term to mean a percept to which the observer has given meaning or information beyond that which it immediately yields. A snake can constitute a percept, but in addition it may be cognized by some persons as something evil, a sexual symbol, something horrible and fright-

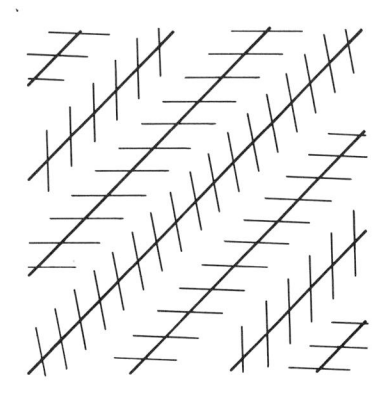

FIG. 10-1 An example of an illusion. Are the lines parallel? (*Morgan, 1956*)

ening, and so on. One of the central problems in the area we are considering is how we get from one level to another, whether, for example, percepts and cognitions are ultimately understandable in terms of sensory input or whether each requires its own level of explanation.

This problem has a long history, and to understand it better we must look at the way ideas about it have developed.

HISTORICAL BACKGROUND

John Locke, the seventeenth-century philosopher, in reaction to several thinkers before him, put forward the view that all ideas the mind has (perceptions and cognitions) are derived from information we get through the senses and our reflections about these. He says:

> But all that are born into the world being surrounded with bodies that perpetually and diversely affect them, variety of ideas, whether care be taken about it or not, are imprinted on the minds of children. Light and colors are busy at hand everywhere when the eye is but open; sounds and some tangible qualities fail not to solicit their proper senses, and force an entrance to the mind; but yet I think it will be granted easily, that if a child were kept in a place where he never saw any other but black and white till he were a man, he would have no more ideas of scarlet or green than he that from his childhood never tasted an oyster or a pineapple has of these particular relishes [Locke, 1939, p. 250].

For Locke, "simple ideas" constituted essentially the building blocks of complex knowledge about the world and of thinking in general. Interestingly enough, Locke saw little problem in how raw sensory data were transmuted into such ideas. For him, this was done by learning or "habitual custom." Thus a round globe of gold or alabaster, for example, that for the eye consists only of a flat plane with gradation of hue and color, nevertheless is perceived by us as a convex figure of uniform color. Such a percept is based upon a very rapid judgment made about sensory information with which we have had a good deal of experience.

Such a formulation will probably be acceptable to most readers and seem to them perhaps to be no more than plain common sense. Indeed, it was taken on faith by most nineteenth-century psychologists, one of whose major enterprises was to try to analyze, by careful introspection, complex mental functions down to the basic elements out of which they had been built. The great German physiologist H. von Helmholtz held such a view and in the third volume of his handbook *A Treatise on Physiological Optics* (1962) gave a formal name to the judgmental process that orders sensory data. He called it *unconscious inference*—"unconscious" because we are usually not aware we are doing it, "inference" because the process essentially involves the decoding of a set of sensory signals. It is as if information about the real world were transmitted to us by a code (sensory input) which we gradually learned through experience how to break. After practice, we are able to make an interpretation of any particular combination of signals without thinking—that is, unconsciously.

Such a theory as this appeals perhaps because it seems so obvious and so broad. In fact, it is still with us in the *transactionalist functionalism* of Ames, Kilpatrick, Ittleson, and others (cf. Kilpatrick, 1961). The rather formidable sounding title of the theory is merely a way of summing up the main assumption of this group of men that we come to have organized perceptions of the world through the useful (or functional) encounters (transactions) that we have with it. Playing with a ball teaches a child what round objects (as opposed to flat circular ones) are like—that is, look like. Thus the theory is not too far from that of Helmholtz and has the same attractiveness. The only trouble with such a point of view is that it is pitched at such a broad level that it explains too much too easily and, for the same reason, is almost incapable of being disproved; in other words, it is not capable of empirical check. Furthermore, it glides too smoothly over many important problems without really analyzing them. Thus we do not really know what is meant by a sensory element, if such a thing exists, nor do we know how the mind comes to make a judgment when confronted with an array of sensory elements. In fact, these questions constitute precisely the basic problem of perception. Restating it in other terms does not necessarily solve it.

Be this as it may, the distinction these theories have made between the *sensory level and the perceptual level* is an important one. It has been explored in several interesting ways by other workers in the area. We will look at two other major theoretical positions concerning it.

The first of these is represented by Gestalt psychology. As we pointed out earlier, this school of thought, originating in Berlin, is closely linked to the philosophical heritage left by the philosopher Immanuel Kant. Besides its stress on the phenomenological method, Kantian philosophy postulated, as we saw in Section Three, that we can experience the world of objects only by virtue of certain categories of the mind which we impose automatically on sense data. We do not proceed, as Locke had it, through a gradual transition from simple ideas to more and more complex ones; rather our experience is immediately ordered and organized by rules which are a basic part of the makeup of our minds. The mind is rather like a prism which, receiving the mixture of hues that together constitute white light, orders it into component parts. Kant says:

> When I speak of objects in time and in space, it is not of things in themselves, of which I know nothing, but of things in appearance, that is, of experience, as the particular way of knowing objects which is afforded to man. I must not say of what I think in time or space, that in itself, and independent of these my thoughts, it exists in space and in time, for in that case, I should contradict myself; because space and time together with the appearances in them, are nothing existing in themselves and outside of my representations, but are themselves only modes of representation, and it is probably contradictory to say that a mere mode of representation exists without our representation [Kant, 1783, pp. 108–109].

Gestalt psychologists, in exploring perception, have simply extended Kant's notion of "modes of representation" and attempted to specify them by empirical methods. Consider this statement from Wolfgang Köhler:

> Let us begin with objective experience. Under normal conditions, objective experience depends upon physical events which stimulate sense organs. But it also depends upon physiological events of the kind which we now wish to explore. The physicist is interested in the former fact: the dependence of objective experience upon physical events outside the organism enables him to infer from experience what those physical events are. We are interested in the latter fact: since experience depends upon physiological events in the brain, such experience ought to contain hints as to the nature of these processes. In other words, we argue that if objective experience allows us to draw a picture of the physical world, it must also allow us to draw a picture of the physiological world to which it is much more closely related [Köhler, W., 1947, p. 57].

Thus Köhler went a step beyond Kant in suggesting that it should be possible not only to find out more about these modes or categories of experience but also to specify their neural counterparts in the brain. The idea that there exists, in fact, such a correspondence between the physiological and the experiential is called the postulate of *isomorphism*. This word means literally "equal form" and as applied in the present context refers to the identity between ordering principles governing experience and those principles governing brain function.

As we shall show shortly, the basic goal in the Gestalt approach to perception has been the specification of these ordering principles, or principles of organization, through the study of direct experience.

Now it is clear that, for this school of thought, objective or direct experience is not explicable by reference to the sensory elements which may go into it. Analyzing percepts into sensations will not explain them. In this way, the Gestalt position differs from that of Locke and the structuralists such as Wundt who followed his tradition. At the same time, it is true that the raw material of perception is still considered to be sensation. On this point—that the senses do not tell us about the world of objects, but perception does—there is agreement between the different theories. This idea seems commonsensical. After all there is nothing in the rods and cones—the sensory receptors of the eye—that can yield to us anything except hue and lightness differences. The "innocent eye," to use Ruskin's phrase, sees only patches of color, not objects that have permanent sizes, shapes, and position. Likewise, touch will give us impressions of temperature and of hardness and softness but will not supply us information about object qualities.

It is because this idea has such intuitive appeal, perhaps, that it is only quite recently that someone has taken a second look at how much information the sensory receptors can give us. James J. Gibson, of Cornell University, has supplied a completely fresh outlook on the problem.

Gibson has been interested in demonstrating that, at least to some extent, we do "know" with our eyes or with our fingers, that is to say, that the senses do have rich informational content. For him, the main problem involved in building up a coherent picture of the world is not through some higher sorting or associative process that gives meaning to meaningless and chaotic sensory elements, but rather through learning to cope, in an economical way, with the vast amount of meaning at our fingertips and in the sensory receptors in our eyes.

In his book *The Perception of the Visual World* (1950a), as well as in a later summarizing article (1958) Gibson distinguishes between two kinds of visual experience we can have: one is of the *visual field*, the other is of the *visual world*. The first of these is the array of patches of color, of shifting sizes, and of fluid contours to which we have already referred. It is what the painter often tries to see—and it is difficult to do this—when he starts his composition. It is also what was commonly thought to be the one uniquely furnished by the sensory receptors working alone before being corrected by some kind of "conversion" process. The visual world, by contrast, is the orderly world we normally occupy, the world in which objects maintain their size, shape, lightness, and color despite our angle of regard and the distance we are from them. This is the world that many thought to be the one produced by correction of the visual field, either by associations built up or by categories imposed on it.

Gibson's position holds that these two types of experiences are merely alternatives. The visual world does not *depend* on the visual field, but rather either may appear depending on the stimulating conditions. This point of view breaks down the traditional distinction between sensation and perception by offering a new definition of sensation. To understand this, we will first look more closely at the old definition.

This derives from a model, well developed in the nineteenth century, that takes sensation to be the excitation by a quantum of the appropriate kind of energy (the adequate stimulus) of a discrete and isolated unit on the sensory surface—whether this be in the retina, in the organs of hearing in the inner ear, or in a free nerve ending in the skin. Such stimulations produce the so-called qualities of sensation—a red hue, a loud sound, or a feeling of pain. The establishing of such dimensions of sensation involves a highly specialized experimental situation, one in which a motionless observer focuses carefully on the specific modality involved. In such a setup, it is clear that the observer is not concerned at all with the real world of objects—only the excitations that some of them may produce in his experience. As we have pointed out already, it is on the basis of this model of sensation that most thinkers have felt that our perception of the real world of objects, by virtue of some transformation process, is constructed.

Gibson's work on some practical problems of perception in such highly mobile situations as that involved in landing aircraft led him to see the artificiality of the experimental paradigm described above and hence its inappropriateness for understanding the "useful dimensions of sensitivity [Gibson, 1963]." The fact of the matter is, that we make meaningful contact with the world *by moving around in it*. The whole organism is, with all its sensory modalities, constantly searching and exploring its environment. Even when we are sitting motionless looking at an object such as a piece of sculpture, our eyes are constantly in motion, not only with those fairly gross voluntary motions by which we visually explore an object, but also with the fine involuntary tremors that guarantee stimula-

161   THE PROBLEM OF PERCEPTION

tion of multiple units in the retinal mosaic. Under normal circumstances, the movements of an organism are much more pronounced. The result of this is that stimulation continually sweeps across the receptor surfaces; rarely is it focused on the component parts that make up these surfaces.

This being so, then what must be important for perception is not so much whether particular sensory units are excited or not excited but rather the range of them which is excited and the *order* in which members of a sensory array are discharged by stimulation. Thus, for Gibson, *ordinal stimulation* is the key to veridical perception, that is, perception of the visual world—not which units are triggered, but the order and pattern of their triggering. Though specific units may change, the pattern may remain invariant, and thus our percepts will be the same, much as a melody may remain constant no matter what key it is played in. Hence, sensation comes to have two meanings. In Gibson's words:

> The first meaning refers to the effects of stimulation in general. The second refers to conscious impressions induced by certain selected variables of stimulation. We can now assert that in the first meaning sensory *inputs* are prerequisite to perception, but that in the second meaning sensory *impressions* are *not* prerequisite to perception. In other words, the *senses* are necessary for perception, but *sensations* are not. In order to avoid confusion it might be better to call the senses by a new term such as *esthesic system*. We can then distinguish between sensory perception and sensory experience, between perception as a result of stimulation and sensation as a result of stimulation [Gibson, 1963, p. 8].

Whether Gibson is correct in his assertion that sensations, as he defines them, are not necessary for perception remains to be seen. As we shall show in the next section, there are many perceptual situations in which what he calls ordinal stimulation seems to be reduced to a minimum—as for example, in viewing a line cube drawn on paper. Consequently, it is possible that his position does not have universal applicability. But let us reserve judgment about this until we have had a chance to look at some data.

Whatever the case may be about sensation and perception, there is still a third level which we will explore more fully later on in this section. This is the level of cognition, as we have termed it. Besides the fact that we may be able to see a house as a unit—rather than just as patches of color—we may also have feelings and thoughts about it that are not contained in the bare perception of it. A highly ornamental Victorian dwelling, with its encrustation of nonfunctional turrets and windows, its conglomeration of straight and curved lines, may offend us. The simpler lines of a Saarinen or a Neutra may please us. We may associate a particular house, whatever its architecture, with death and sadness or with happiness and life. Most of the things we perceive have *meaning*. Furthermore, it is also true that our actual percepts may undergo deformation as a result of motives and wishes that are part of our makeup. And we have available on the subject a good deal of experimental material. Some of this we touched on in Section Three, but we will consider more of it in a later chapter. For the moment, we wish only to establish that besides sensation and perception (whether at one level or two) there is yet another level that must be taken into account when we analyze the process of knowing in human beings.

THE NATURE OF THE UNITS: WHOLES AND PARTS

In the previous sections, we saw that the units of analysis used to understand behavior were fairly gross ones. For example, Freud and many of those who followed him dealt with such large units as a dream, or thought, or an actual piece of behavior. No attempt was made by these men to reduce these macroscopic observations to their more molecular constituents. Certainly, it would be possible to take, say, a compulsion to drink and analyze it into specific muscular movements, but it is doubtful that it would any longer be capable of being handled by the psychoanalytic model. The same applies in the case of social acts. To break them up into their more molecular structure is to lose something of their essential nature.

In the field of perception, Gestalt psychologists have made a strong formal argument for this "antireductionist" position. It will be recalled that this school arose partly as a reaction to Wundtian structuralist psychology, whose main goal was precisely, in fact, the dissection of consciousness into its most elementary components or dimensions. This may be a legitimate idea, and certainly, modern biology has opted in recent years for a greater and greater stress on the molecular, an orientation that has had remarkable results; nonetheless, it may well be that such a bias is not the only one likely to produce interesting results in psychology.

The German word *Gestalt* means, in fact, "whole," or "totality." Thus the claim of this school was that we experience the world in terms of wholes which are immediately given rather than in terms of the summations of many parts. As Wertheimer says:

> I stand at the window and see a house, trees, sky. Now on theoretical grounds, I could try to count and say: "Here there are ... 327 brightnesses and hues." Do I have "327"? No, I see sky, house, trees; and no one can really have these "327" as such. Furthermore, if in this strange calculation the house should have, say, 120 and the trees 90 and the sky 117, I have in any event *this* combination, this segregation, and not, say, 127 and 100 and 100; or 150 and 177. I *see* it in this particular combination, this particular segregation; and the sort of combination or segregation in which I see it is not simply up to my choice: it is almost impossible for me to see it in any desired combination that I may happen to choose. When I succeed in seeing some unusual combination, what a strange process it is. What surprise results, when after looking at it a long time, after many attempts, I *discover*—under the influence of a very unrealistic set—that over there parts of the window frame make an N with a smooth branch [Wertheimer, 1923].

The decision to take naïve objective experience of such organized entities as houses and trees is crucial to Gestalt psychology. The search for rules and laws is then made at this level rather than at the more microscopic level of the specific brightness and color receptor mechanisms of vision. If it is accepted that the world is immediately experienced in this way, then certainly it would seem to make sense to follow such a course; and it can seriously be questioned whether such laws as apply at the microscopic level can fully explain laws that operate at the macroscopic level. This is the question raised by Gestalt psychologists and answered by them in the negative. Thus a house is made up of, let us say, bricks and mortar. But to know all about the properties of bricks and mortar hardly tells us everything about the house; for example, the reasons why the house is not blown down by a high wind or why its architect wins a prize must be found in the way in which the parts of the house—not only individual bricks but also particular arrangements of them such as arches—are all put together. In point of fact, the architect operates in practice at several levels. He must know something of the chemical composition of different building materials, something of structural engineering, and something of art. The notion that knowledge of the first of these, the most microscopic, will be sufficient, even potentially, is certainly doubtful.

A corollary of this stress on "wholes" by Gestalt psychology is the notion that the kind of approach we must take to their study must be a *dynamic* one rather than a *mechanical* one. What do these terms mean? It may help if we look at what Köhler had to say on the subject.

> In a physical system events are determined by two sorts of factors. In the first class belong the forces and other factors inherent in the processes of the system. These we call the *dynamic* determinants of its fate. In the second class we have characteristics of the system which subject its processes to restricting conditions. Such determinants we will call *topographical* factors [Köhler, 1947, p. 107].

As Köhler goes on to point out, most machines or mechanical systems are so arranged that the operation of dynamic factors is severely limited by imposing a maximum number of topographical conditions. For example, in a car, the forces generated by the combustion of gas fumes in the cylinders are harnessed to drive the car forward. This is done by the mechanical arrangements of a cylinder with rigid walls, a closely fitting piston inside the cylinder, connected in turn to a crankshaft which transmits the motion of the piston to the wheel axle. Thus the forces of the system are constrained and directed to a single end, namely, to move the car forward.

Such a mechanical system may be contrasted with a more dynamic system. A good example is the soap bubble. Essentially, this is a system in which a balance is struck between (1) the tendency of the soap particles to adhere together, (2) the pressure of the air inside, which tends to burst the bubble, and (3) the pressure of the air outside, which tends to hold the bubble together. The resultant system is a sphere which provides the maximum volume for the minimum surface. Thus the air pressure is distributed evenly and kept at a minimum while as many soap particles as possible are allowed to adhere together, since with a finite number of particles, more can be together when the surface is smaller. Note that in such a system there are no rigid mechanical constraints, only the balanced operation of dynamic forces.

It has been the Gestalt view that both the mind and the nervous system are dynamic rather than mechanical systems. Such a position is more axiomatic (i.e., based on faith) than logical. What we know about the nervous system, at least, does not compellingly indicate that it is a completely dynamic or a completely mechanical system. It is true that it is made up of discrete receptor organs and neuronal conducting units. But there are so many and they are so complexly interconnected that to think of them as constituting a kind of machine in the usual sense may be misleading.

It may be evident to the reader that Gibson by his redefinition of sensation has also opted for an approach to perception that involves a stress on *patterns*, or *totalities*, of stimulation. Though he differs from the Gestalt psychologists in some important ways, to this extent he holds a position similar to theirs. The perceptual world is not to be explained by reference to the specific excitations of isolated sensory units. Stimulation patterns of entire receptor surfaces will supply the answers.

THE TONIC SYSTEM: THE RESPONSE SIDE

If one grants that all sensory inputs that affect an organism during perception must be taken into account, then the position taken by Gibson and the Gestalt psychologists can be extended even further. In the active exploration that perception of the real world involves, muscles also play a part, and these constitute what may be called the *tonic* system. The tonus of a muscle is roughly the extent to which it is in a state of excitation. Thus as our eyes or hands move over an object, there is a continual feedback of stimulation from this system, and this must inevitably affect our perception.

Such a point of view has been put forward by Heinz Werner and Seymour Wapner of Clark University. They have labeled it the *sensory-tonic theory*. The key notion of the theory is that "organismic states are part and parcel of perception... perception may be affected equivalently by various kinds of stimulation and direct muscular changes [Werner & Wapner, 1952, pp. 325–326]." If their theory is correct, then any alterations in muscular tonus should affect the way we perceive the world. This indeed turns out to be the case as we shall see later on. At this point, we only wish to make the point that perception tends to be a dynamic process in the sense that its explanation must be couched in terms of the interactions of many factors. It is probably not a phenomenon which is understandable by searching for the smallest or most microscopic events that underlie it.

We have spent a good deal of time setting out the theoretical background of perception. This is perhaps more necessary in this field than in many others. The problems we have been considering may seem to the reader to be somewhat philosophical and rather removed from empirical test. To a certain extent this is quite true, but they are of the greatest importance insofar as the stance one takes toward them determines, in a broad sense, the research directions one chooses and the kinds of experiments one carries out. We hope that this will become clear in the following chapter, which describes some key studies that have been done on various perceptual phenomena.

Perhaps the major point to be emphasized before continuing concerns the general style of approach to psychology taken by those involved in the field of perception. All of them—the gestaltists, the transactional functionalists, Gibson, and the sensory-tonic theorists—have felt that a proper starting point to understanding human beings is the study of their experience—that is, how individuals process the information that continually impinges on their sensory receptors. Much behavior can be referred to facts at this level. Because we see a wall as solid, we do not walk into it. Because we see a cliff in front of us as a cliff, we do not walk off it. Work in this area of perception is aimed simply at finding out how we arrive at such conclusions concerning solidity and depth and what it is about the physical aspects of the stimuli that allow us to do this so quickly and easily.

CHAPTER 11
THE PHENOMENA OF PERCEPTION

THE BASIC ARTICULATION OF THE VISUAL FIELD

The Ganzfeld

Even the visual field, as we defined it earlier—that is, patches of brightnesses or colors—contains some information. It is experienced not just as a homogeneous "nothingness" but as a surface having, at least, parts that are differentiated one from the other and from a background. Furthermore certain of these parts may appear to "go together," and others do not appear to do so. In other words, the visual field is articulated. Note, however, that the character of the articulation is highly unstable. With every movement an observer makes, the pattern of these color patches and the size and shape of each will change. Thus a color patch occasioned by a red book lying on a table, for example, will become smaller and also more and more foreshortened as the observer steps back from it. Likewise, if the illumination is altered from dim to bright, the brightness of the red patch will also change. Still, it does throughout maintain its integrity as a unit against a general background.

Thus the experience of unity against a ground does appear to be a primitive or basic one that pertains both to the visual field and to the visual world. That this is so is indicated by the fact that people who were born blind of congenital cataract and then have their sight restored are able immediately to see *unities* in the field but not *identities;* the latter are unities which have stable characteristics that can be recognized again and differentiated from other unities (von Senden, 1960). We will examine these data in more detail shortly.

Now to see figures and backgrounds, we must first be able to see surfaces. What allows us to do this? According to Gestalt psychology, a necessary condition for this is *inhomogeneous* stimulation of the optical system. When stimulation is homogeneous, then, we should not be able to see surfaces. This follows from the position of this school that perceptual experience results from the operation of dynamic laws, that is, laws governing the interaction of parts. In other words, it is not simply the punctate firing of single receptors but rather the relative amount of firing of some of them as compared to that of others that counts. Such a relational approach implies that the simplest visual experiences will not occur when stimulation is distributed as evenly as possible over the whole visual field, that is, when stimulation is homogeneous. How do we produce such a condition? The follow-

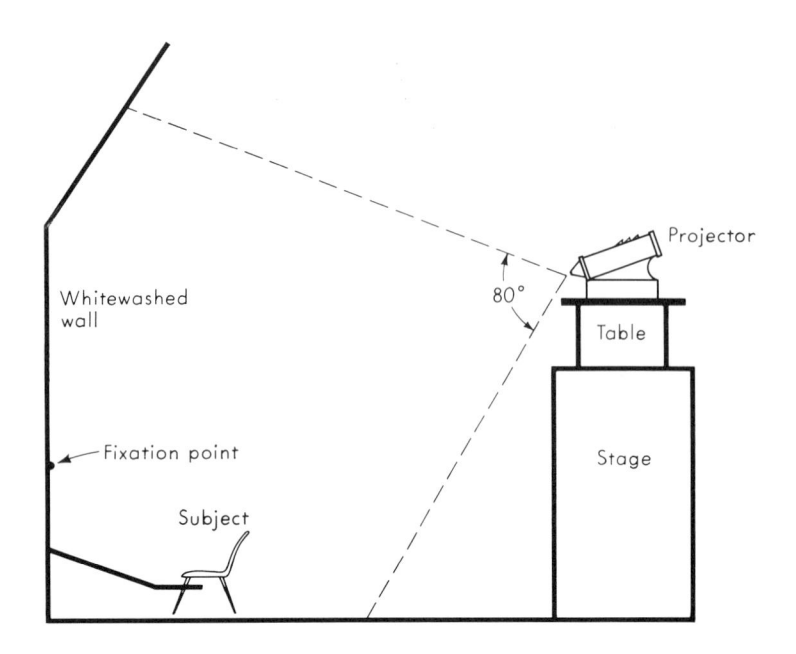

FIG. 11-1 Ganzfeld setup. (*Metzger, 1930; Engel, 1930*)

ing example gives us an answer to this question and also tells us what happens when we impose homogeneous stimulation.

Example 11-1 *The experience of homogeneous stimulation: the Ganzfeld experiments (Metzger, 1930; Cohen, 1957)*

In 1930, Metzger in Germany initiated research on this interesting problem. He had subjects sitting in front of (1.25 meters distant from) a carefully whitewashed wall 4 by 4 meters in area. On all four sides of the wall, wings were added, these being bent in somewhat toward the observer (cf. Figure 11-1).

Under low illumination, the subjects failed to see the surface of the wall but saw, instead, *a fog-filled space stretching an indefinite distance*. It could thus be concluded from these data that under conditions of homogeneous stimulation percepts tend toward the simplest possible condition. The one perceptual dimension that does remain is depth.

Some of the repetitions of Metzger's experiment have failed to give such definite results (e.g., Gibson & Waddell, 1952). One by Cohen (1957), however, appears to verify it completely. Cohen used as his apparatus two intersecting hollow spheres, 1 meter in diameter, as shown in Figure 11-2. The surfaces of these spheres had a minimum of texture and could be indirectly illuminated at various intensities. Sixteen observers gave relatively reliable reports of a foglike volume extending an indefinite distance in space. Consequently, there seems to be little doubt about the validity of the phenomenon.

In addition, both Metzger and Cohen found that an increase in the level of illumination led eventually to the appearance of surface. According to Koffka, this was due to the inhomogeneity of stimulation arising from the *microstructure*, or *texture*, of the wall (a sphere in Cohen's experiment). Thus whereas the experience of depth (though not accurate judgment of it) seems primitive, the experience of surface apparently is not.

Some of the available data thus seem to support Gestalt theory. This is not to say they do not support other theories as well, but they do at least suggest that even such a seemingly simple perceptual phenomenon as surface, one we take for granted, is a result of the operation of dynamic forces arising from inhomogeneities of stimulation.

There are many other interesting features of the Ganzfeld—for example, if it is colored as well with a homogeneous red or green light, this color also tends to disappear in a short time (Hochberg, Triebel, & Seaman, 1951). This is not due to adapta-

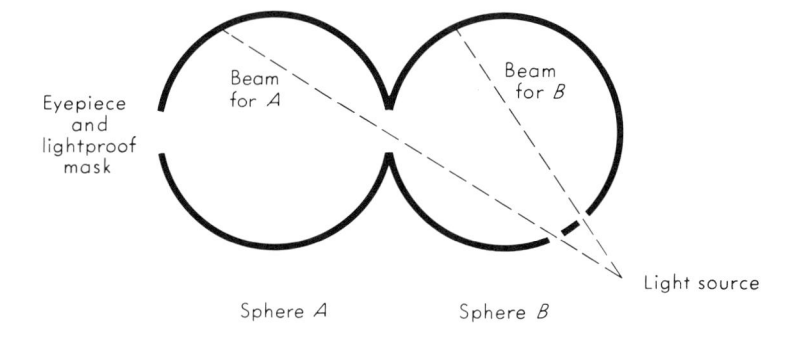

FIG. 11-2 Cohen's apparatus for studying the Ganzfeld effect. (*Cohen, 1957*)

tion—as, for example, when we adapt quickly to a smell or a taste—and must consequently be attributed to properties of the Ganzfeld.

Thus inhomogeneous stimulation is needed to articulate the visual field in experience—to see a surface ground and then to see unities standing out against this ground. Let us look at the figure-ground problem.

Figures and Ground

So-called figures, in the most primitive sense, might be regarded simply as rather large inhomogeneities in the visual field. However, they are usually more than this. Figures as we experience them in our *visual world* have a distinctness of size and shape and of other features that make them stand out from the surface ground. We will be discussing here flat surfaces rather than objects in three-dimensional space, though the properties of figures probably apply in both cases.

One worker of the Gestalt school, Edgar Rubin, examined in detail the laws governing "figure formation." These are set out in Example 11-2.

Example 11-2 *Figure and ground properties (Rubin, 1958)*

The characteristics of figure and ground are fundamental to much of our experience. Before we can talk about shape or size, we must be able to distinguish figures and attend to them. Rubin's studies of the experience of figure and ground have yielded a number of phenomenal facts as follows:

Figures tend to be seen as being in front of the ground which gives the appearance of having continuity behind the figure. This point is illustrated in the example in Figure 11-3. If the arcs with the radial lines are seen to constitute the figure, then

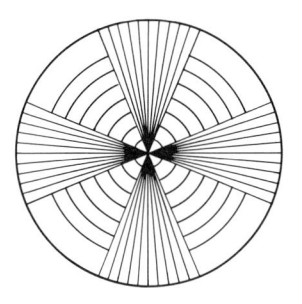

FIG. 11-3 Figures have the property of appearing to be in front of the ground. (*Rubin, 1958*)

the concentric lines usually appear to be continued *behind* the figure. The opposite applies equally. If we stare at the whole unit for any length of time, the figure will tend to reverse.

Other things being equal, the figure tends to be simpler and more symmetrical than the ground. This is illustrated in Figure 11-4. It is very easy to perceive the wavy white stripes as figures against a black ground, but the reverse is difficult.

The figure tends to be unified. To some extent figures are independent of the ground. This point is interestingly demonstrated by the so-called Wertheimer-Benussi effect shown in Figure 11-5. The gray ring, if inspected fairly naïvely, appears to be a uniform gray in spite of the fact that one half of it lies on a white, the other half on a black ground. However, if a pencil or some thin object is placed in the middle of the ring going from point A to B, this unity is quickly lost. Now one half appears darker, the other half lighter. This *contrast effect,* whereby one hue *induces* in another its own complementary, is a well-known phenomenon. Thus red will induce green and vice versa. The point of

167   THE PHENOMENA OF PERCEPTION

FIG. 11-4 Simpler and more symmetrical parts of the field are seen as figures. (*Krech & Crutchfield* [*modified*] *1953*)

interest here is that this effect is limited as long as the unity of the ring is preserved. Once it is broken by a contour, induction occurs.

We must emphasize, however, that the figure is never completely independent of the ground. Thus whether we see the central figure in Figure 11-6 as a square or a diamond depends a good deal on the orientation of the ground. Thus b is definitely seen as a diamond, d as a square. The figures in *a* and *c*, however, can be seen as either, though both more readily as squares. Consequently, it seems clear that the total effect we get from viewing a visual field is the resultant of a rather complex interaction between figure and ground. This last point illustrates a concept that goes slightly beyond that of ground, namely, *framework*. This notion implies a property of *directionality,* or *orientation*.

The figure is more definite and better articulated than the ground. According to Koffka (1935, p. 186) the same hue looks less deeply colored (i.e., less saturated) when it is ground, more when it is figure. In an ambiguous figure, such a transition in color occurs as reversal takes place.

The above are a few of the major features of figure and ground that have been described. There are others which need not concern us here. We will turn instead to the problems involved in the perception of several figures or objects in a field and the question of how we are able to organize these in our experience.

The Laws of Perceptual Grouping

According to Gestalt psychology, lines, points, or figures or other sharp inhomogeneities in the visual field tend to be organized perceptually according to the three principles illustrated in Figure 11-7:

Proximity. Stimuli tend to be perceived as belonging together if they are close to each other in space or time.

Similarity. Stimuli which are similar to each other in terms of some dimension are grouped together.

Continuation. Stimuli which tend to form some kind of simple ordered sequence tend to be grouped together.

All three laws follow a principle basic to Gestalt psychology. This is that we tend to organize the perceptual field in the easiest manner possible. Thus it is quite easy to group stimuli that are close to each other, or that are like each other, or that form some class. It is considerably harder to group otherwise. We could perceive in the first drawing in Figure 11-7 two groupings, one of black squares and one of white according to a similarity principle, but since it takes considerably more effort to do this, it tends to be avoided, unless we set out to do it deliberately. We will see more of this principle farther on.

The fact that groupings occur at all is significant and represents, of course, the central point in Gestalt theory that perception involves "wholes," or "configurations," which are organized according to some principles. The parts grouped, further-

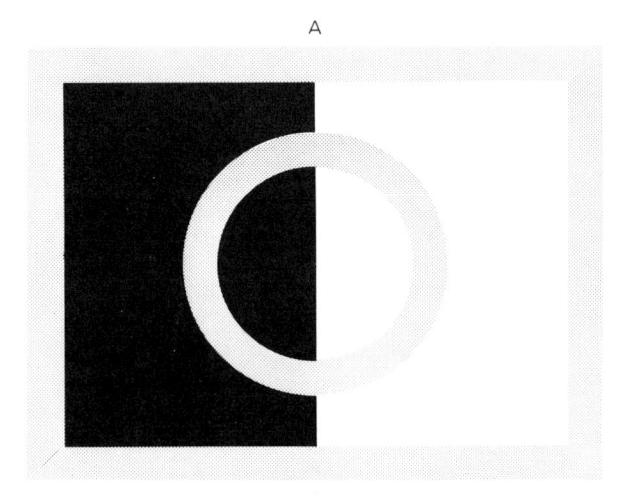

FIG. 11-5 Figures tend to be unified. (*Kendler, 1963*)

168   APPROACHES TO THE PROBLEMS OF PERCEIVING AND KNOWING

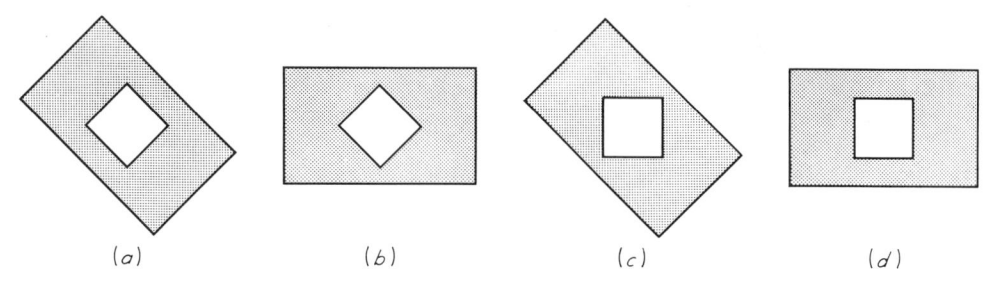

FIG. 11–6 Dependence of the figure percept on ground orientation.

more, actually are supposed to exert on each other a positive attraction, much as do two physical masses through gravitational forces. Perception is an active, dynamic affair, not a passive one (Koffka, 1935, p. 167). Now while the laws outlined above state those conditions under which grouping occurs, they do not specify either the psychological or physiological nature of the forces of attraction between two parts of the visual field. The term "grouping" itself also requires more precise definition than is usually given to it. Some experimental data presented below have at least indirect bearing on these questions.

Example 11–3 *Visual perception studied by the method of stabilized images (Pritchard, Heron, & Hebb, 1960)*

It is well known that our eyes are never still but are constantly making fine, rapid movements. Due to this constant tremor, an image falling on the retina is never really stable, although it may appear to be so in perception. Now curiously enough, it has been shown by a number of investigators that the stabilization of the image by eliminating fine eye movements produces intermittent disappearance and reappearance of any visual object. This is known, after its discoverers, as the Ditchburn-Riggs effect. The main point of interest for us here is that some figures or parts of figures show this kind of change more than others and that there are apparently some "rules" governing these differences. These rules have considerable bearing on the laws of grouping, as well as on some other aspects of Gestalt theory that were discussed above.

Let us first look at the method used by Pritchard, Heron, and Hebb. One eye of a subject is fitted with a contact lens which, because it fits tightly, follows small eye movements accurately. To one

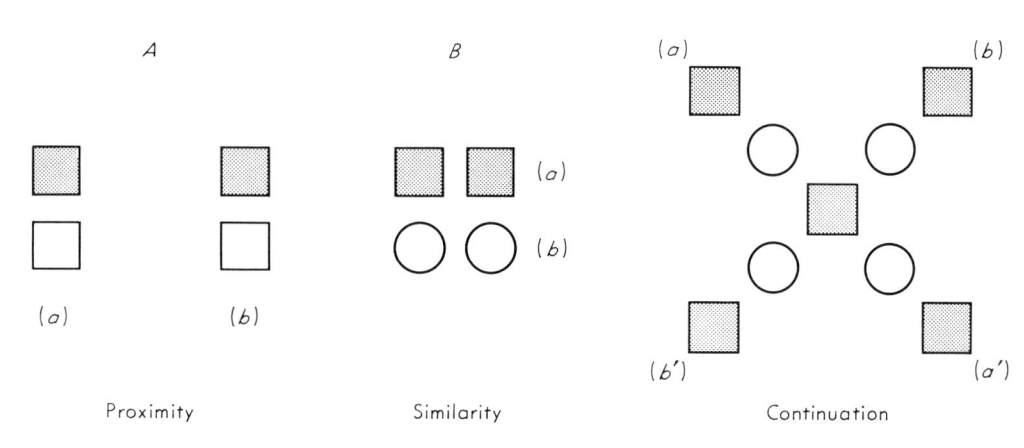

FIG. 11–7 Three laws of perceptual grouping: proximity, similarity, and continuation.

169 THE PHENOMENA OF PERCEPTION

side of the lens is attached a stalk to the end of which is fixed a small assembly consisting of a miniature high-power lens, target (a figure), and light source. The diagram in Figure 11-8 shows the main features of the apparatus. With such an arrangement, any movement of the eyeball produces in the target a movement corresponding in intensity and direction, thus maintaining a stabilized retinal image.

All viewing was done with one eye only, the other being covered. Observations were made by the subjects lying on a couch in a quiet room. Some fifty visual forms were used, of which eighteen are shown in Figure 11-9. The results of the experiment were quite startling—especially to the subjects involved. The following are of importance to us here:

Depth effects are striking. A hexagon (number 7), for example, is often seen as tridimensional. Even when it is not, it is seen in a plane different from that of its background, usually in one closer to the observer. The Necker cube (number 8), while sometimes losing its shape, always maintained compelling depth. Such findings lend considerable weight to the Gestalt notion that depth is a very basic and primitive feature of perception.

Meaningful figures (e.g., a profile in number 3) disappear less readily than meaningless ones. Likewise, some figures tend to disappear as wholes, others in terms of their parts. Thus single lines tend to act as units; for example, the three sides of a triangle tend to disappear and reappear independently. Rounded figures (as in numbers 3, 9, 10) are relatively "stable" and "quiet," while jagged figures (numbers 11, 12) are unstable and generate an effect of violent motion. These data suggest the reality of primitive organizations, though they may be of a very simple order.

Figures or parts of figures near each other or similar to each other tend to act as units. In the waffle pattern (number 4) rows acted as units. Likewise in number 5, a random arrangement of dots, a row running from A to B tended to become organized and to remain when the other dots disappeared. In number 17, the line and arc close to each other or continuous with each other acted as units. Likewise, the round parts of number 13 all tended to be stable, the angular parts unstable. These results give support to the three laws of grouping.

Closure. This is illustrated by an effect found with number 18. Sometimes the part above the dotted line would be lost. When this happened, the gap remaining would appear to subjects to be closed. This is a special case of the tendency to simplification in perception when the external situation is ambiguous.

A final comment: The observations presented above are taken from only four subjects who had had considerable experience with the conditions of the experiment. Consequently, we should be a little cautious about accepting the results without qualification.

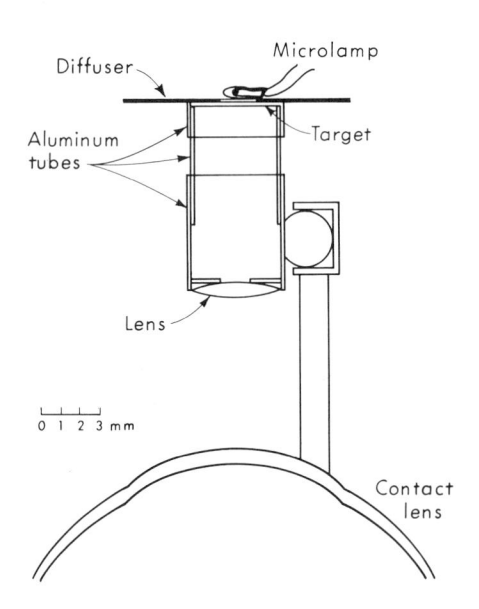

FIG. 11-8 Apparatus used to study perception under conditions of stabilized retinal images. (*Pritchard, Heron, & Hebb, 1960*)

The laws of grouping and the data we have presented describe the way in which the visual field is segregated and organized in perception. It is clear that different parts of it—its inhomogeneities—affect each other by virtue of their various characteristics. Thus we see surfaces, or grounds, and on these grounds we see groupings, or figures, that is, unified regions segregated from the rest of the field. Perception is not chaotic, but meaningful and

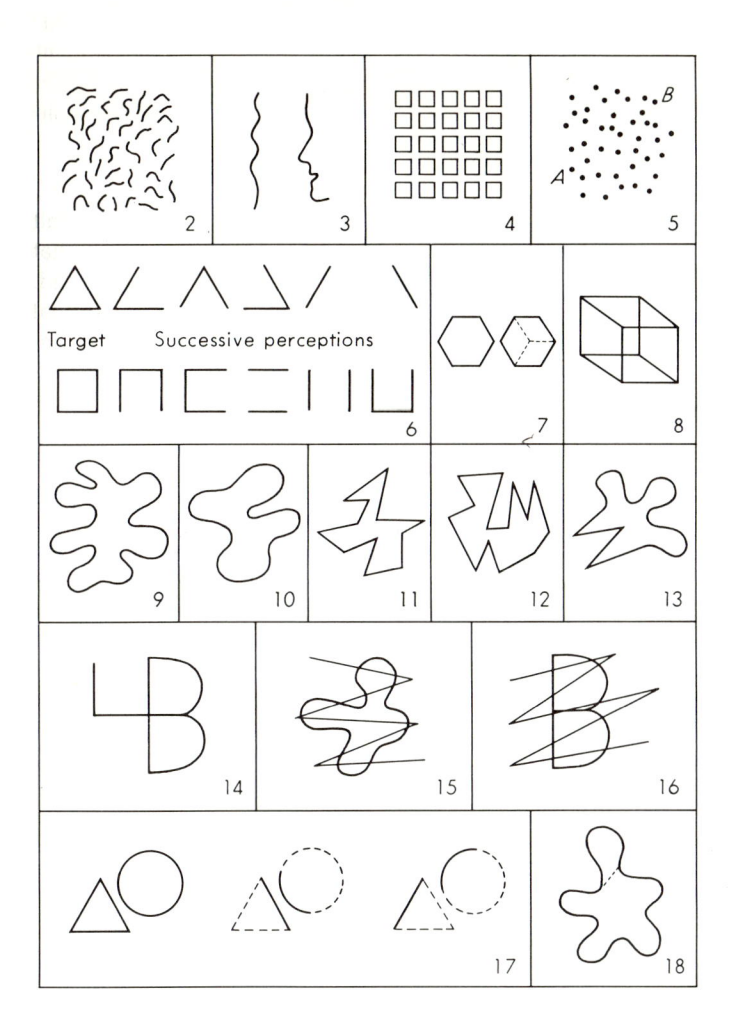

FIG. 11-9 Some of the visual forms used in the experiment on stabilized images. (*Pritchard, Heron, & Hebb, 1960*)

orderly. Let us turn now to a somewhat higher-order level of perceiving, namely, that involving figures.

Perception of Simple Line Figures

Let us start with simple figures like those known as Kopfermann cubes, shown in Figure 11–10. The first of these seems to produce depth inevitably. Notice that X and Y produce an experience of depth less readily and Z hardly at all. Thus it is difficult to see W as anything but a cube, but Y and especially Z can be seen as two-dimensional patterns. Such simple experiences raise a number of interesting questions.

In the first place, we can rightly ask just how much validity such data really have. Do we really "see" a three-dimensional figure, or do we merely *interpret* it in this way, especially in view of the fact that we know it is actually a two-dimensional drawing? Different answers would be given to this by different theorists. Unfortunately, there are few experimental data bearing directly on the point.

A second question relating to the first can also be asked: if, in fact, the experience of depth is real, is it due to innate factors (i.e., inborn properties of mind and brain), or is it something acquired through experience? Gestalt psychologists have, of course, insisted on its innateness. For them, the perception of depth is given by the simple fact that we have a three-dimensional brain and, if conditions allow, we

171   THE PHENOMENA OF PERCEPTION

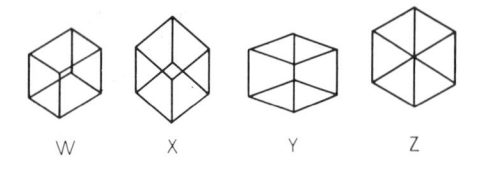

FIG. 11-10 Tridimensionality in simple line figures: the Kopfermann cubes. (*Kopfermann, 1930*)

automatically perceive objects in three dimensions. The phrase "if conditions allow" is an important one and will shortly be explained further. Other psychologists would feel that we occasionally see two-dimensional drawings as three-dimensional because we have had experience with real cubes and know the convention of representing them on a flat surface.

The third point is this: assuming that the experience of depth is real and also assuming for the moment that this is immediately or innately given in perception (and not inferred), how do we explain it? We will look first at the Gestalt explanation and then at a more recent extension of it.

Koffka and Köhler and others, we noted, consider the brain as subject to the same kinds of physical laws as are other physical bodies. One such law that pertains to the free distribution of energy in a system is the so-called *minimax principle*. It states simply that any given parameter of a system will take on, not just any value, but the *maximum* or *minimum* that the given conditions will allow at any moment. Thus in the example of the soap bubble mentioned earlier, the maximum number of soap particles become associated by reason of the bubble's assuming a shape which supplies the maximum volume for the minimum surface, this shape being, of course, a sphere. It is the Gestalt view that the same principle holds true for perceptual organizations and the underlying brain processes. One difficulty in such an application is knowing what maxima and minima, which are quantitative terms, can mean in terms of perceptual qualities. The solution of Koffka, Köhler, and Wertheimer is the equation of these with simplicity, symmetry, and regularity. Thus the minimax principle may be stated for perception as follows:

Psychological organization will always be as "good" as the prevailing conditions allow. In this definition, the term "good" is undefined. It embraces such properties as regularity, symmetry, simplicity . . . [Koffka, 1935, p. 110].

The phrase "as the prevailing conditions allow," as we noted, requires a little explanation. Gestalt psychology conceives of two kinds of forces that interact to produce a percept. On the one hand, there are *external forces,* which refer to the actual physical characteristics of the stimuli as they impinge on sensory receptors, for example, a particular light intensity or a particular retinal projection. On the other hand, there are *internal forces,* which refer to those processes of perception that operate on the sensory impression and tend to organize it in the simplest possible manner. The *weakening* of external forces by various experimental procedures allows us to see more clearly just how the internal forces, which are the main focus of interest, operate.

Weakening is usually accomplished by the following procedures: (1) short time exposures, (2) low light intensity, (3) small size, (4) afterimage. We can illustrate each of these by reference to Figure 11–11. Looked at under normal illumination, it is clearly seen to be a polygon. However, if the figure is inspected under low illumination, by half-closing the eyes or by simply taking it into a darkened room, it appears to be a circle. Likewise, if this book is opened and closed very quickly at this page, it will again look like a circle. Third, if we place the book open at this page several yards away, the same thing will happen. Finally, if we stare at the figure for about 30 seconds and then transfer our gaze to a wall or any plain surface, we will see a black circle on a white ground. All four procedures weaken external forces, thus allowing the freer operation of internal forces, which in this case *simplify* the polygon into a circle. For laboratory study, there are available various pieces of apparatus that allow us to use these same procedures in a well-standardized and precise manner. They are essentially extensions of the rather crude and simple techniques described above.

The minimax law, first formulated by Wertheimer as the "law of Prägnanz," or the "law of good figure," is basic to the Gestalt theory of perception

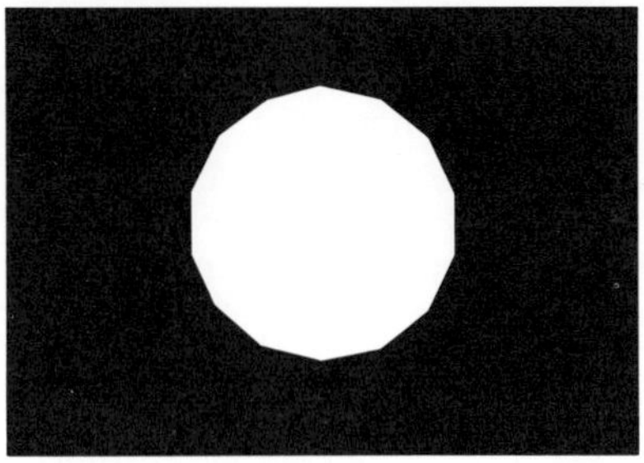

FIG. 11–11 External and internal forces in perception of text.

as will become evident shortly. Let us see how it applies in the case of the Kopfermann cubes shown in Figure 11–10.

The four figures may be seen either as cubes in three dimensions or as hexagons in two dimensions. In other words, *the prevailing conditions* allow two alternative perceptual responses in each case. Accordingly, we should expect, according to the law of Prägnanz, that the percept will dominate which represents the more regular, symmetrical, and simple figure. Figures W and X are rather more complex when seen as hexagons than when seen as cubes. This is less true for figure Y and not at all true for figure Z. Hence we should expect to get mainly three-dimensional cube perceptions for W and X and far fewer for Y and Z. Such perceptions as these are thus essentially compromises between what the object is actually like and what pattern of stimulation it produces on our sensory receptors and what our brain and nervous system impose because of their own properties. The former relates to what Koffka calls external forces, the latter to what he calls internal forces (Koffka, 1935). It is precisely by reducing the strength of the external forces or by making their operation ambiguous that we are able to see more clearly the nature of the internal forces and thus learn more about mind and brain.

This kind of experimental procedure, as the reader may recall, is in line with the general orientation of Gestalt psychology toward our knowledge of the world. What is important is not so much reality but rather appearance, or the phenomenon—that is, sensory data as transformed by mind into something orderly. Since all reality is ambiguous, we should be able to learn the most about the laws governing such transformation by studying our experience of ambiguous figures or illusions.

Since the law of good figure is so basic in the operation of internal forces, it is worth considering some recent efforts to define it more exactly and quantitatively. One interesting attempt made by Hochberg and McAlister (1953) is described below.

Example 11–4 *A quantitative approach to figural goodness (Hochberg & McAlister, 1953)*

Hochberg and McAlister took as their primary goal the translation of the qualities of so-called good figure into quantitative terms. Their definition of the term is implied in the statement of their hypothesis as follows:

Other things being equal, the probabilities of alternative perceptual responses to a given stimulus (i.e., their "goodness") are inversely proportional to the amount of information required to define such alternatives differentially, i.e., *the less the amount of information needed to define a given organization as compared to the other alternatives, the more likely that the figure will be so perceived* [p. 364].

To test this hypothesis, Hochberg and McAlister presented to 80 college-student subjects each of the four Kopfermann cubes, each one being shown for 100 seconds in balanced order. Subjects were asked during each presentation to indicate, by marking a test sheet whenever they heard a tone, whether they saw the figure as two- or three-dimensional. During each presentation, thirty-three tones were sounded at random intervals.

The results are shown in Table 11–1. Each cube is described in terms of its complexity, or "goodness," by reference to the characteristics indicated. Judgments of dimensionality are shown in the last column at the right. The investigators concluded that their initial hypothesis was not contradicted by these data. In other words, in the case of a stimulus situation which can yield two or more percepts, that percept is chosen which involves the *least amount of information*. In this experiment, a

Table 11-1 The relation between figure information and tridimensional perception

Stimulus	Stimulus characteristics Number of stimulus line segments	Number of angles	Points of intersection	Responses Bidimensional responses, %
W	16	25	10	1.3
X	16	25	10	0.7
Y	13	19	8	49.0
Z	12	17	7	60.0

figure was more readily seen in depth if seeing it in this way gave a greater gain in simplicity and symmetry. All angles in a cube are right angles, and all sides are equal. These two properties describe a cube completely. Seen as bidimensional, however, depending upon its orientation, a cube contains many inequalities of lines and angles, so that it cannot be explained or described simply.

A more general statement of this rule has been made by Hochberg and Brooks (1960). Using ten more sets of ambiguous figures (in addition to those dealt with above) they were able to make a plot between the amount of two-dimensional complexity (as defined above) and judged tridimensionality. The relation is shown in Figure 11-12. The more complex the description required with a two-dimensional experience, the more likely is the experience of depth. The phrase "least amount of information" implies that we attempt to order our world in the simplest manner that circumstances allow. This is, of course, just a restatement of the minimax principle, or law of Prägnanz. This is extremely important to Gestalt theory and runs through almost all their explanations of specific perceptual phenomena.

Before leaving the subject of simple figures, we must mention one interesting and important characteristic associated with such percepts. This is the phenomenon of *figure reversal*.

Figure Reversal and Satiation

In such a figure as shown in Figure 11-13, there exists an indeterminacy in respect to which corner ab is seen as nearest and which as farthest away from the observer. Fixation on the cube for a short period of time will produce a reversal, first $abcd$ in front and then $a'b'c'd'$ in front. There are many other examples of this phenomenon. It may be made particularly compelling if it is observed during the movement of an ambiguous figure as in the simple demonstration described in Example 11-5.

Example 11-5 *Reversal in moving frames*

An outline figure constructed of wire in the shape shown in Figure 11-13 is rotated slowly in front of an observer. With continued fixation (particularly monocular) rotation will be seen to reverse its direction. Thus if the rotation is actually clockwise, it will *appear* to be counterclockwise. When this occurs, the ends of the figure, which are square and are usually seen as such, no matter what their orientation, now start to change to trapezoid with rotation. The total effect is thus a curious one: not only does a rigid figure appear to be rotating in the wrong direction, but also it appears to change shape as it does so.

Some indication of reversal can be obtained by looking at Figure 1-13 and allowing first square $abcd$ and then square $a'b'c'd'$ to be perceived as the leading or nearest part of the figure. If $abcd$ is seen as closer with ab as the leading edge, then it and also $a'b'c'd'$ appear square, just as a book does even when we look at it from an angle. However, if $a'b'c'd'$ is seen as closer, with $c'd'$ as the leading edge, then the situation is quite different. Of two objects of equal size, the nearest one usually appears larger. But $c'd'$, though it is nearer in the perspective defined, is also much shorter than $a'b'$. This must mean, perceptually, that $a'b'c'd'$ is a trapezoid with side $a'b'$ much longer than side $c'd'$. When seen rotating in this perspective, the rigidity of the frame is lost, and the trapezoidal sides actually change shape, the ratio of the long to the short sides becoming first greater and then smaller as the frame turns. Such a distortion does not occur when the frame is seen in its real perspective.

These kinds of effects are due to depth reversal, as we have noted already. The important point to emphasize is that when depth cues are so ambiguous that reversal can occur, simplicity, symmetry, and stability of shape can be sacrificed, in the sense that a real square can come to be seen as a trapezoid, and, seen as such, shows alteration of shape with movement through space.

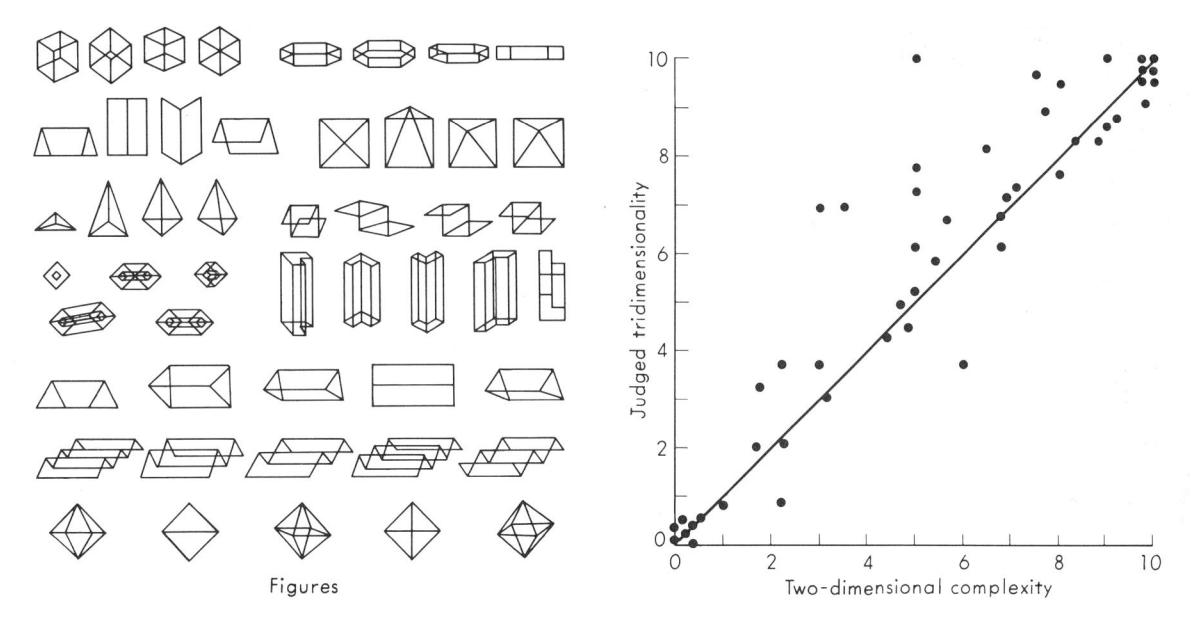

FIG. 11–12 Relation between figural information and experience of depth in a variety of figures. (*Hochberg & Brooks, 1960*)

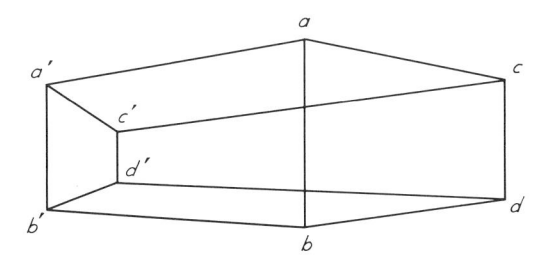

FIG. 11–13 Moving frame used in the experiment on figure reversal.

This raises two questions: First, is this a real exception to the minimax principle, and, if so, why does it occur? Second, if the experience of shapes can be so unstable under the conditions of the demonstration, just what is it that keeps it stable under "normal" circumstances? The answer to the second question is rather complex and must wait until we have presented some basic information about the perception of surface, size, and distance. Let us look at the first question.

The Hochberg-McAlister experiment showed that bidimensionality gives way to tridimensionality in the service of figural (i.e., shape) "goodness." Now it will be clear, if we look at Figure 11–13, that it is rather easier to see it with *abcd* in front rather than *a'b'c'd'*. This contrasts with the Necker cube, which can be seen about equally well in either perspective. If this is true, then it represents a perceptual preference that conforms to the minimax principle. That is, we prefer the perspective yielding the simpler figure. It is only the *reversal of the figure that occurs with continued fixation over time* that represents a deviation from the principle. Consequently, we must envisage some process, strongly dependent on time, that is capable of producing a change from the simpler percept initially preferred to the more complex, less-preferred alternative. The name that has been given to this process by Köhler is *satiation*. Although we know only a little about the physiological mechanisms underlying it, we do know that it occurs reliably, and we know something about the conditions that favor its occurrence.

We have already cited two examples of figure reversal. Both of these had to do with depth. Other examples shown below have to do with figure and ground. Thus Figure 11–14 is usually perceived

175 THE PHENOMENA OF PERCEPTION

FIG. 11-14 Figure reversal. (*Kendler, 1963*)

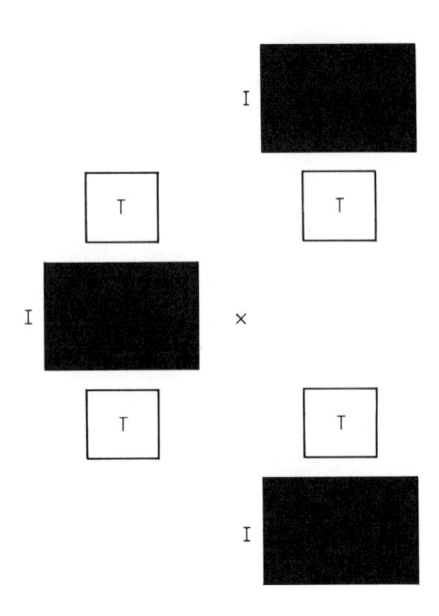

FIG. 11-15 Inspection and test figures used to study satiation effects. I = inspection figure; T = test figure. (*Köhler & Wallach, 1944*)

alternately either as a vase or as two profiles. We cannot usually exert voluntary control over this oscillation. It occurs quite spontaneously. Somewhat the same applies in the case of Figure 11-3, in which we may see either a cross whose four arms have arcs on them or a cross whose four arms are crosshatched. It is not quite the same, however, for the arced cross is usually seen more often and for longer. The reason for this, according to Koffka (1935, p. 183), is that the arced cross constitutes a "better figure," since the arms, although separated, are given some continuity with each other by virtue of the arcs. Such continuity is not supplied by the crosshatch in the case of the alternative figure. Consequently, it is less "strongly organized" (i.e., more complex) and therefore less preferred. However, this difference in "goodness" is small enough that some oscillation will occur. Furthermore, we can readily induce a preference for either one by previously satiating with the other. Then if we were to fixate on the arced cross by itself for a short period and then look at the circle, we would probably see the other cross as the figure and the satiating cross as the ground.

The notion that perceptual preference for a figure can be reduced by continued exposure to that figure suggests that satiation must somehow alter the perceived characteristics of a figure. Some clues as to the nature of the alterations are afforded by a famous experiment done by Köhler and Wallach (1944).

Example 11-6 *Satiation and figural aftereffects (Köhler & Wallach, 1944)*

The purpose of the experimental series (of which this demonstration was one example) was to explore the effects of satiation and to compare percepts in satiated sensory areas with those in nonsatiated sensory areas. The subject was asked to fixate the cross in the inspection figure in Figure 11-15 for approximately one minute, with only the black inspection squares present. Following a minute or so, the inspection figures were replaced by the white test squares, with the subject still fixating on the cross. He was asked then to report his experience.

What many subjects found (and the reader can check this himself) was that the two open squares on the left looked clearer and also farther apart. Those on the right looked less clear and closer together. Köhler and Wallach interpreted this to mean that there is a tendency for figures projected (on the retina and brain) near a satiating area to be displaced away from it. Thus the left-hand squares are displaced outward, the right-hand squares are displaced inward. Whether this is correct is not really known. Köhler and Wallach have built up an elaborate theory of brain activity to correspond to their psychological interpretation. It is based essentially on the notion that cells in certain visual areas which have been firing for some time because of stimulation are likely to fire less rapidly and that, consequently, cells near them fire more vigorously instead. The effect of this is that a stimulus having a certain locus in the visual field will give rise to neural firing in a part of the brain that is normally associated with a different locus in the visual field; hence, the perceptual displacement. We should add that the Köhler-Wallach theory is only one of several put forward to explain satiation phenomena (cf., for example, Osgood & Heyer, 1952; Ganz, 1966).

Such effects as those reported above may not have much in common with figure reversal. We should note that in the Necker cube, for example, the shift in perspective can hardly be due to differential satiation of different parts of the visual field. All the lines comprising the cube are actually equidistant from the eye and must be producing equal amounts of satiation. The reversal in perspective must therefore be due to a very phenomenal kind of satiation. We may get "tired" of seeing one corner as the front end and therefore switch it to the back, but if so the term "tired" must mean something a little different from what it means in the Köhler-Wallach experiment, in which amount of stimulation in different parts of the visual field is deliberately varied. Consequently, figural reversal and figural aftereffects may well be separate phenomena requiring different explanations.

To return now to the major point: We have seen that the minimax principle is supported nicely by the data on figure reversal and satiation. According to Köhler's theory, the maintenance of a particular perceptual organization for some length of time itself requires the expenditure of energy. Such expenditure will reach a point at which an alternative organization, even though it is more complex, will involve less effort. Reversal then occurs. Empirical verification of this point is, of course, needed. Presumably, this would involve comparison of the relative rates of satiation or reversal of organizations whose "goodness" is already defined in terms of criteria such as those of Hochberg and McAlister (1953) or of Attneave (1954).

Let us now look at another application of the minimax principle. This takes us back to the perception of surface. Obviously most surfaces are not regular. The outside of any solid is usually slightly irregular and may also be quite unstable at the molecular level. Consequently, not only will the distribution and density of light-dark gradients be arranged rather randomly, but also they may change over time. With fine-grain textures we do not tend to notice these differences, even though we are sensorially capable of doing so. Though an artist, by virtue of his training, can be very sensitive to these nuances, most of us ignore them and perceive surfaces as uniform. That we do so is in accord with the minimax principle. Some data illustrating this point are presented in Example 11–7.

Example 11–7 *Operation of the minimax principle in the perception of surfaces (Krech & Crutchfield, 1958, p. 86)*

The subject sits with his head inside a hollow hemisphere which is evenly lighted at low illumination to keep external forces weak. This produces the experience of a surfaceless fog-filled space. When illumination is increased slightly, the texture of the sphere reaches the threshold of usual acuity, and therefore surface appears. Next, the illumination is so arranged that a brightness gradient is generated across the surface. Under these conditions the subject still perceives the surface as *uniformly lighted*. Finally, a thin vertical shadow line is projected down the middle of the field. Immediately this is done the subject perceives the two halves as being very different in brightness, though within each half he perceives brightness as being uniform. The three steps of the experiment are shown in Figure 11–16.

The perceptual experience resulting from the last step constitutes a clear case of the minimax principle. In the previous step, the quite large differences existing between the left and right side of the field are ignored, presumably because the transition in light intensity is very gradual and nothing separates the right from the left halves. This homogenization of the field is sometimes called *assimila-*

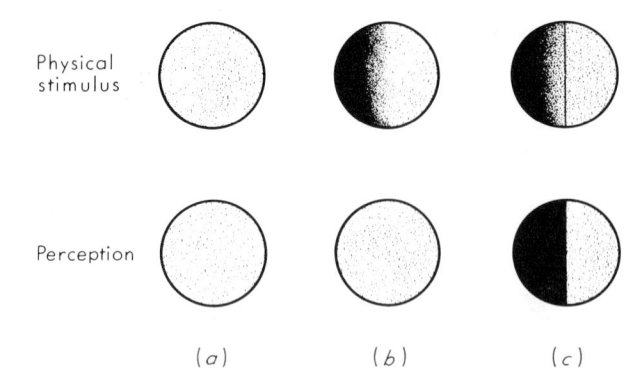

FIG. 11-16 Minimization or maximization in the perception of surface differences. (*Krech & Crutchfield, 1953*)

tion. In the final step, however, the insertion of a contour appears to split the field into two discrete parts such that a unified perception is no longer possible. The difference between the two halves now becomes maximized, the value of each being a resultant of all brightness values within it. This kind of differentiation is sometimes known as *contrast*. Thus in the service of generating as simple a perception as possible, some differences between the halves are maximized, others within the halves are minimized.

It is clear from the above that the introduction of a contour into a field has rather a large effect and forces a segregation of the field into parts. This presumably happens because a contour represents a very abrupt kind of inhomogeneity in the surface texture. Thus if the inhomogeneities are arranged merely randomly and are about equal in degree, we tend to see a surface in a frontal plane (i.e., directly in front of us); but if a few inhomogeneities are very large, we may see units, or figures, or shapes lying on a surface or ground. Surface and figures are thus dependent on the same basic principle of inhomogeneous stimulation.

The minimax principle is perhaps one of the most important and fruitful legacies of Gestalt psychology. It does seem to be true that the mental processes of human beings are somewhat lazy, in the sense that they favor percepts that are as simple as possible. It is perhaps this fact that accounts for the success of caricatures in art. The essential ability of the great caricaturists like Töpffer, Daumier, and Hogarth was that of simplifying experience in a satisfying manner—so satisfying, in fact, that the caricature often seemed more real than the "reality." As Gombrich says, "For there is a secret of good caricature—it offers a visual interpretation of a physiognomy which we can never forget and which the victim will always seem to carry around with him like a man bewitched [Gombrich, 1961, p. 344]."

Gestalt theorists, notably Wulf (1922), have tried to apply the minimax principle to memory as well as perception. Thus they have argued that complex and asymmetrical figures which are memorized and then later reproduced tend to become simplified and symmetrical because of internal forces working upon them. The evidence that has been gathered concerning this notion is extensive but by no means conclusive either for or against the Gestalt position (cf. Riley, 1962).

Besides visual forms, memory for stories is also considered by some to be subject to normalizing or simplifying internal forces. Thus in recalling a narrative of some kind, we tend to omit details, to sharpen the salient features, and to assimilate the plot to various expectations we may have. Allport and Postman (1947) have used these facts to formulate a theory of rumors. They suggest that the kinds of alterations shown in the transmission of a story by word of mouth essentially follows Gestalt principles. This accounts for the curious distortions we find in rumors.

In all these cases, it has always been uncertain whether the evident distortion that occurs between initial exposure to some material and the reproduction of it later on are due to perceptual processes, memory processes, or response processes. Changes in any of these or all of them might be responsible. A discussion of this point is beyond the scope of this section, however, since our major concern here is with perception.

The kinds of perceptual situations we have been considering so far are rather artificial, in the sense they do not involve the solid objects in the real world, although they constitute perhaps the most important part of our experience. We will now examine a more complex level of experience.

THE THREE-DIMENSIONAL WORLD

The study of simple figures, especially illusions, as carried out by Gestalt psychology, indicates fairly clearly that the mind may impose on sensory data certain organizations of its own. The Gestaltists, following their Kantian leanings, have tended to take the position that such situations constitute the rule for all perception, which is then always a kind of compromise between the bare sensory input and the transformation that mind works on this. If we suppose that the mind does make such transformations and that these are part of our essential makeup as living organisms, then we may well concede that the best way to study them—and thus find out about mind—is by using ambiguous perceptual situations such as illusions in which the mind is allowed more freedom and scope.

However, one may also argue that, in the first place, illusions are not typical of an ordinary everyday experience. Usually, we are not puzzled about the real world and do not find it ambiguous, but rather move about in it with ease and freedom. In the second place, it may well be that the way in which we make experiential decisions about ambiguous cases is not by virtue of innate properties of mind and brain but rather by virtue of the long practice we have already had with the world of objects which we have experienced through all sensory modes since birth. From this point of view, it would seem more sensible to give a good deal of study to our *successes* in perception rather than to the indecisions that illusions force on us.

As we noted earlier, it is precisely this real world of solid objects in which the observer is constantly moving about—whether walking or landing an airplane—that J. J. Gibson takes as a starting point for the study of perception. We will give special attention here to his analysis of three-dimensional perception.

It will be recalled that according to the Gestaltists we see surfaces by reason of inhomogeneities of stimulation. Solid objects have surfaces, and hence the perception of them might be expected to involve similar principles. Solids exist in three dimensions: an up-and-down dimension, a near-far, or depth, dimension, and a right-left dimension. It is exactly the differences in these dimensions that yield us the impression of an object in space. Thus, in this section, we will be concerned essentially with those aspects of stimulation that convey information about relative depth of different parts of an object: *slant, sidedness, angularity,* and other features of the three-dimensional world.

With simple line figures, we may see depth rather than bidimensionality when such a percept yields the simpler figure. However, real solids provide a perceptual situation that is much more complex; they involve stimulus variables that may demand tridimensional percepts even when a bidimensional view might be simpler. A sphere represents a good example. Obviously, in some ways, it can be seen more simply as a flat circle. The fact that it is not a flat circle implies that additional kinds of factors are working. The description and analysis of these factors has concerned thinkers since Euclid, in 300 B.C. As we shall see, Gestalt psychologists like Koffka have felt that the perception of both depth and solidity is governed ultimately by the minimax principle. Other workers have taken rather different positions. Let us start with the classical position, represented, for example, by Helmholtz.

According to Helmholtz, much of perception, including depth, is given by means of *cues*. Note that the term "cue" implies some kind of signaling stimulus in the object that allows us to make some guess, judgment, or inference about its positional characteristics. Thus it is by no means a neutral word but carries with it an important theoretical position, the basic postulate of which involves the traditional distinction between sensation and perception.

Generally, two classes of clues are recognized, depending on whether the sensory input is monocular or binocular.

Monocular Cues

SIZE The size of an object tells us something about its distance. Hence one part of a figure that is smaller than another will be seen as also farther away, other things being equal. Of course, other things are not always "equal," so that an edge which is seen as smaller than another edge may really be smaller and not any more distant from the observer. In addition, our knowledge of an object may influence our judgment of its size. Look at the

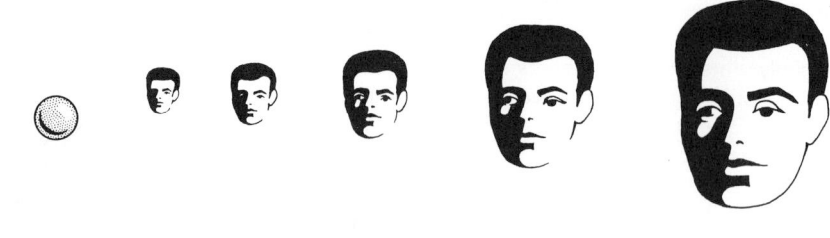

FIG. 11–17 Perceived size dependent on knowledge of object character. (*Life magazine, 1950*)

picture in Figure 11–17. Whether we see the ball as being in the same plane as the man's head depends on whether we see the ball as a ping-pong ball, a baseball, or a basketball. Such a notion, we may recall, is rather antithetical to Gestalt psychology, which has always tried to explain a percept in terms of the dynamics of forces operating at the moment rather than in terms of learning and experience. We shall return to this theoretical problem later on. For the moment, we can state merely that, at least in some size-distance judgments, experience does seem to play a role.

LINEAR PERSPECTIVE This is illustrated in Figure 11–18. Parallel lines appear to converge as they become more distant from an observer. It will be obvious that this set of cues is really only a special case of the size-distance effect discussed already, whereby farther objects appear smaller than near ones. Thus the railroad ties that are actually nearer simply project a larger image on the retina, the distant ones a smaller image. Linear perspective is commonly used by painters to convey depth, though surprisingly enough they did not start to use perspective in this way very much until about the fifteenth century.

INTERPOSITION One object that partially blocks another is usually judged to be in front. This is probably a case of figure-ground relations, the features of which we have already outlined. Its usage may yield some rather interesting effects as in a demonstration by Ames (1946), shown in Figure 11–19. The card in (*c*) that appears to be behind is actually closer to the observer. This is due to an interposition effect produced by cutting corners of the middle and right-hand cards and placing them in an appropriate position in relation to the observer. The result is to give the illusion that the two playing cards are very different in size even though they are objectively equal.

SHADOW Shading is another factor contributing to depth, as illustrated in Figure 11–20. The craters on the surface of the moon appear as hollows when the pictures are viewed right side up. When they are turned upside down, we see bumps rather than hollows. The reason for this is not entirely clear. Some writers have suggested that we are used to a world in which light comes from above, so that a surface whose upper half is shaded can be only concave, while one whose lower half is shaded can be only convex. Gestalt psychologists would discount such a notion because of its assumption of the priority of learning over perception.

MOTION PARALLAX The final cue to distance and depth involves the relative speed of perceived movement of near and far objects. Near ones appear to move faster than far ones when they are actually traveling at the same rate. This is, again, a case of the size-distance effect. The distance between two far points must be much greater for it to be perceived as equal to the distance between two near points. Thus an object moving at a constant speed must necessarily seem to move much more slowly when it is farther away. A jet airplane flying at 30,000 feet appears to an observer on the ground to drift rather slowly. Viewed from only 300 feet it would be seen as going very fast indeed.

Binocular Cues

CONVERGENCE In order to fixate on a near object, the eyes must converge, or turn inward. At least within a fairly short distance range, there will be a relation between degree of convergence and nearness of the object. The sensory feedback arising from the movements of the eyeballs could thus

FIG. 11–18 Example of convergence, or linear perspective, as a distance cue. (*Morgan, 1956*)

supply us with a cue as to distance and depth. It is obvious, of course, that fixation must occur first; that is, each eye must move to such an angle as to yield a single rather than a double image. If we hold a pencil about a foot from our eyes and fixate on a point on a wall behind it, we will see two pencils, that is, a double image. Similarly, if we fixate on the pencil, objects in the background are actually seen as double, though we tend not to notice this effect. This disparity between retinal images in the two eyes furnishes the basis for binocular disparity, the binocular depth cue to be discussed next.

BINOCULAR DISPARITY, OR PARALLAX The receiving part of the eye, that is, the retina, is made up of very small individual units called rods and cones, each of which can send an impulse to a specific area in the cortex. Thus we have a so-called *topographical correspondence* between retina and visual cortex. For each unit in one eye that sends an impulse to a point X in the cortex, there is a corresponding unit in the other eye that also sends impulses to X. These retinal units are designated as *corresponding points*. Now any three-dimensional object of moderate size fixated at a moderate distance (e.g., a matchbox 6 feet away) will probably stimulate corresponding areas in the two retinas and will thus be perceived as a single unified obejct. However, any one part of the object outside the fixation point will stimulate noncorresponding points within corresponding areas. Thus a moderate degree of disparity will exist, not enough to produce double vision, but enough so that fusion

FIG. 11–19 Interposition effect. (*Ames, 1946*)

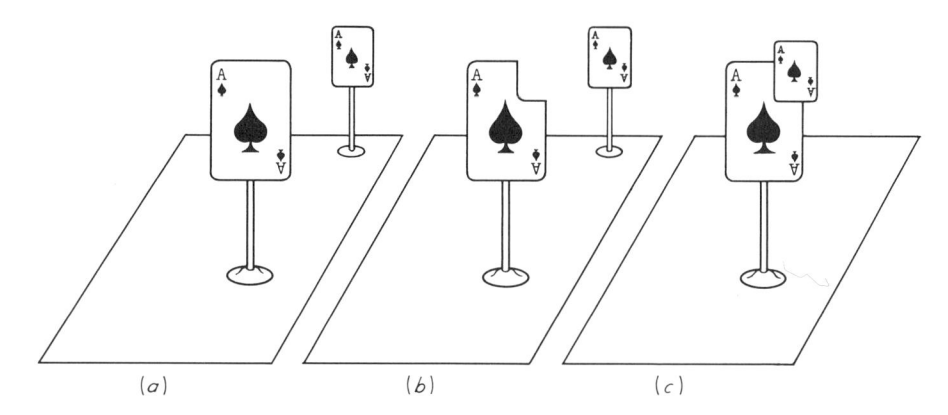

(a)   (b)   (c)

181   THE PHENOMENA OF PERCEPTION

FIG. 11–20 Shadow as a cue to depth. A shot of the lunar surface shows a crater when viewed right side up. Inverted, the photograph shows a bump rather than a crater. (*National Aeronautics and Space Administration, 1967*)

can occur only in three rather than two dimensions. The farther away from the fixation point a part of the object is, for example, a rear edge of a cube, the greater will be the disparity for that part, and hence the greater the difficulty of producing fusion in respect to it.

Such gradients of disparity will continually shift as the point of fixation changes, which it is bound to do involuntarily, thus giving the object depth and solidity (Gibson, 1950a). An example of the manner in which an object is seen by the two eyes is shown in Figure 11–21. Discrimination of the pyramid as a "thing" separate from the rest of the visual world will probably be achieved by virtue of the sudden jumps in disparity that occur at its boundaries.

If binocular disparity can serve as a cue for depth, then it should be possible to simulate depth in flat

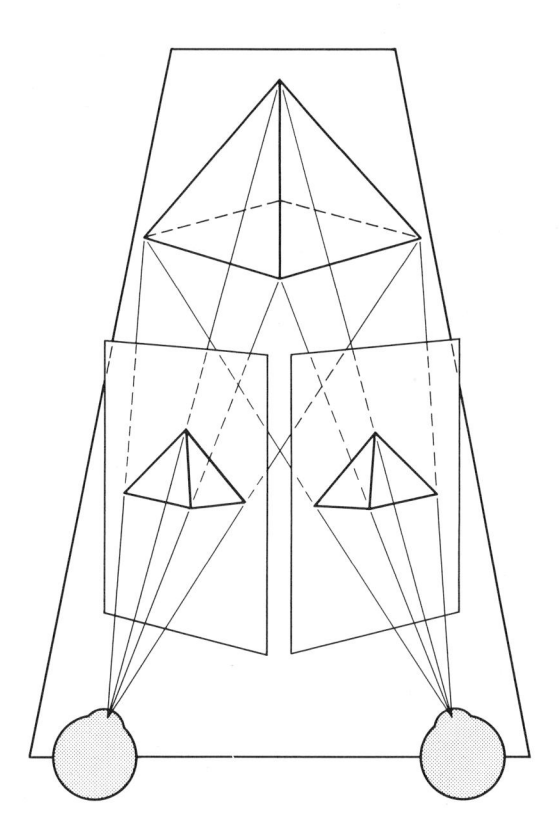

FIG. 11–21 Binocular disparity. (*Gibson, 1950a, p. 106*)

pictures by presenting each eye with a slightly different view of the same picture. This can indeed be done, as was shown by Wheatstone, inventor of the stereoscope. The same scene is photographed from two angles and the resulting pictures inserted in the stereoscope, which allows one eye to see only one picture, the other eye only the other. The result is a rather compelling experience of depth. Essentially the same principle was used in the 3-D movies of the 1950s. In these, different pictures were superimposed on each other by means of two projectors, each using a different color filter. The use of spectacles with a red filter for one eye and a green one for the other allowed the viewer to have disparate views. The result again was a striking impression of depth.

Now it is obvious that binocular disparity cannot be the only important cue for perception of depth

and solidity. Many one-eyed people have apparently good depth perception, as do also (so it is thought) many species of animals whose eyes are set so far apart that the field of each eye overlaps very little with that of the other. Aside from this, we must mention a theoretical issue that has been raised by Koffka (1935) in connection with binocular disparity. He points out, first of all, that although disparity is certainly known to be a cue for depth, the reason why it is still remains a problem. In line with major Gestalt theories, Koffka suggests that some dynamic processes, central in locus (i.e., in the brain), must be responsible. Now it must be true that whenever we view some object, corresponding points all over the two retinas will be stimulated even though by different parts of the figure. When we speak of disparity, then, we must be speaking not simply in respect to stimulation but rather in respect to *the kind, or pattern, of stimulation that emanates from a certain part of the figure,* for example, a particular side or a particular corner.

Thus if we are fixating the front corner of a pyramid, as shown in Figure 11–21, then fusion of the rear corners will occur with the addition of depth. That is, the other corners will be seen as single fused units; the rear left seen by the left eye will fuse with the rear left as seen by the right eye. This happens not only because these retinally stimulating points are closer but also, presumably, because they are more alike. Which components of a figure can be fused is governed by the laws of proximity and similarity that we discussed earlier. That fusion occurs at all is probably governed by the minimax principle—that is to say, the percept of the object is kept as simple as possible, and a single unified image, rather than a highly complex one, is given by virtue of tridimensionality. Thus Koffka has suggested that the production of depth in actual three-dimensional figures is perhaps not too different, in principle, from the production of depth in actual two-dimensional line figures.

Gradients of Stimulation

As we indicated, the notion that cues are necessary to yield an experience of depth represents the theoretical position that sensation and perception are different and that through learning we come to associate certain kinds of stimuli (i.e., cues) with objects' being farther from us or nearer to us. This implies that primitive sensation, as in an infant, is two-dimensional. However, through his behavior and its consequences, the child gradually comes to discriminate between those stimulus conditions which signify a *near*—for example, reachable—object and those stimulus conditions which signify a *far*—or nonreachable—object. Thus he may initially try to reach for the moon but soon finds that he cannot reach it. A ball in his crib, however, does turn out to be within his grasp. Furthermore, he will find that as he brings the ball closer to his eyes, the pattern of sensory stimulation it yields will change. Thus a certain kind of muscular, or kinesthetic, sensation (flexing the arm) in reaching becomes associated with a systematic change in visual sensation. In other words, perception is the result of compounding simple sensory impressions, themselves initially meaningless, and this is achieved through learning.

The Gestalt position allows the distinction between sensation and perception but does not give any place to learning, preferring instead the notion that the brain, because of its basic makeup, immediately organizes sensory input in such a way as to yield the experience of depth.

Perhaps the most cogent analysis of three-dimensional perception, however, has been made by Gibson. As the reader will recall, this writer abandons the traditional distinction between sensation and perception by giving a new meaning to the former. By defining sensory stimulation in a more holistic way, he has been able to specify, unlike those holding the traditional views, variables at the receptor level capable of immediately yielding depth. Let us now look at Gibson's ideas.

Grades of texture produce, in the retina and in the brain, a differential pattern of excitation, or as Gibson (1950a, p. 64) has called it, *ordinal stimulation*. Thus in any of the textures in the figure, stimulation occurs in the order light-dark-light-dark, etc. The retina itself is made up of a mosaic of neuronal elements, the rods and cones, as shown in Figure 11–22. The density of cells is extraordinary, being as high as 140,000 to 160,000 per sq mm at or near the center (the fovea), though somewhat less in the periphery. The width of each element is about two-millionths of a meter—very small indeed (Bartley, 1958). Thus, in terms of ordinal stimulation, we should be able to see as surface any texture in which shifts in the light gradient (i.e., light to dark to light) occur as often as 500,000 times or more in 1 meter, or 5,000 times per centimeter. Texture much finer than this, however, should be seen as a Ganzfeld, that is, as nonsurface.

As Gibson points out (1950a, p. 65), many artists used to paint with a magnifying glass in order to reproduce surfaces with the particular density and distribution of light-dark gradients that are found in various kinds of material such as velvet, silk, or the human skin. The key notion is that of stimulation gradient. Most surfaces are not homogeneous but have textures which give such discontinuities of stimulation. A wall made of bricks affords a good example. The closer a part of the wall is to an observer, the fewer the bricks that will make up a certain angular area of the visual field. The farther away a part of the wall is, the more closely packed and dense its texture will be. Thus, depending on the gradualness or abruptness of the change in density, we will see slant of a greater or lesser sharpness.

Figure 11–23 shows differences in surface textures. Some data on the influence of texture on depth perception are given by Gibson (1950b). Let us look at his experiment.

Example 11–8 *Texture and judgment of depth (Gibson, 1950b)*

Gibson studied the effects of different texture gradients on the perception of surface slant. Other depth cues, such as binocular parallax and linear perspective, were carefully controlled. The subjects looked through an aperture at photographs of texture gradients varying in sharpness. All photos were actually kept vertical. Judgments of perceived slant were then made by subjects. Results indicated that the perceived slants agreed very closely with the actual slants of the surfaces which had been photographed. This agreement indicated clearly that texture gradients make an important contribution to our perception of slant and depth, in the absence of any of the traditional cues.

An extension of the idea of textured gradients and their retinal effects can also explain most of the so-called cues of depth. Size, interposition, linear perspective, shadow, and parallax, for example, all

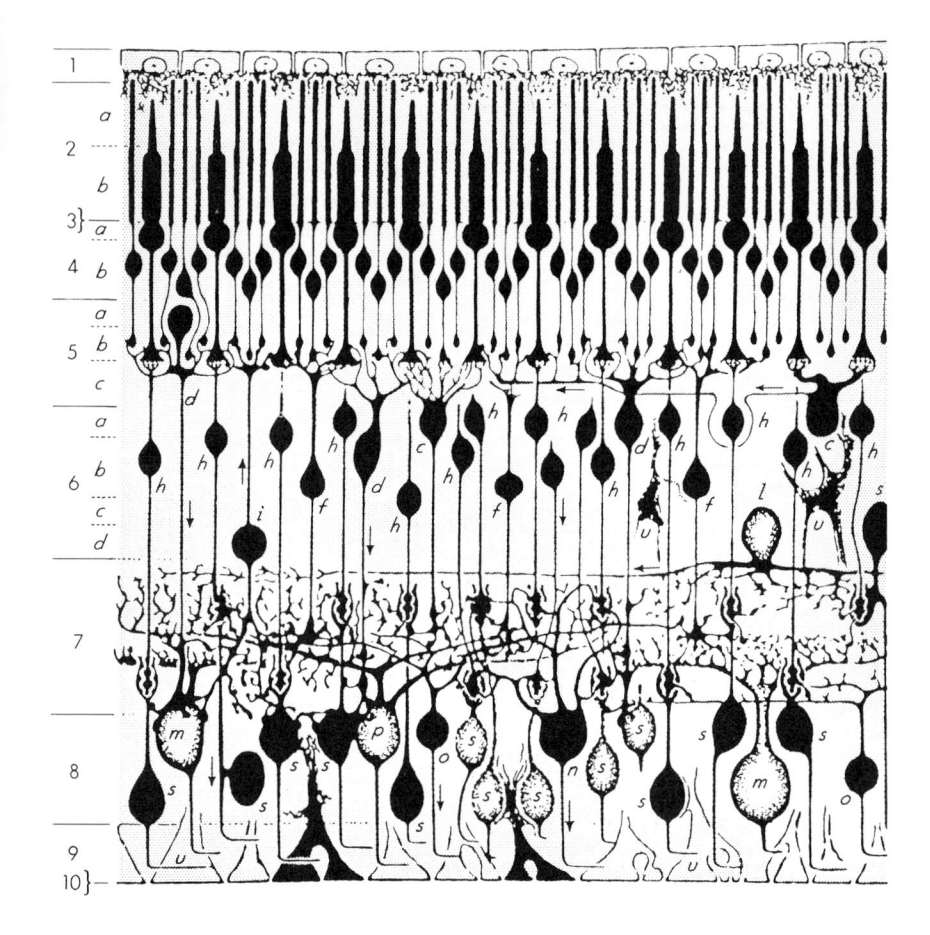

FIG. 11-22 Structure of the retina. (*Gibson, 1950a*)

involve gradients of stimulation or a sudden discontinuity in gradients, such as occurs at corners or edges.

Perceptual constancy

As we move around our visual world, we see the same objects at many different distances, from many different orientations, and under many different conditions of illumination. This means that the *proximal*, or retinal, impressions produced by these objects are continually shifting and changing. In spite of this, the world—though not the visual field—remains a stable and constant place. Thus a white cylindrical wastebasket, for example, remains perceptually the same shape, the same size, and the same brightness whether we stand directly over it or sit on the floor 10 feet away from it. Were we to draw pictures of it from these two views, we would have to make them very different indeed. This phenomenon describing the fact that different retinal images can give rise to the same perceptual experience is known as *perceptual constancy*.

Since the real world does in fact remain stable, it is fortunate for us that we do possess such mechanisms as are responsible for constancy. It would certainly be difficult to get around in a world in which objects changed their appearance every time we changed our own position.

The theoretical explanation of these general facts

FIG. 11-23 Textural gradients can be a basis for experience of depth. (*Gibson, 1950a*)

is less obvious. The one that will immediately occur to most laymen is that the perceptual constancies are dependent on experience, that is, on learning and memory. Originally, according to this view, which was put forward by Helmholtz (1962) and Tichener (1909), we are not born with constancies, so that a table would change in size and shape for every orientation in which we viewed it. Gradually, we would come to learn that when the image changes, the real table does not, and we make suitable "corrections."

As the reader will guess, Gestalt theorists and others, including Gibson, have rejected this view and find explanations of constancy in the dynamics of the immediate situation. Evidence bearing on one aspect of this point will be considered later when we discuss the innateness of perceptual characteristics. For the moment, we can say that the constancies certainly can be affected by experience but probably are not directly dependent on it. Given a *normal environment* in which to develop, an organism will undoubtedly show perceptual constancy, though a very abnormal environment may produce defects. Taking this as our basic assumption, we may now inquire directly into the dynamics of the constancies, looking at shape, size, and brightness constancy in turn.

Shape Constancy

If a rectangular piece of cardboard is held up in front of an observer at a distance of, say, 10 feet and then gradually turned on its horizontal axis, it will become trapezoid, that is, it will become compressed or foreshortened in its vertical dimensions. An example of this, from Gibson (1950a), is shown in Figure 11–24. The use of a checkerboard texture gives a compelling perception of slant, so that we see, not a trapezoidal shape in the frontal-parallel plane (i.e., perpendicular and directly in front of us), but rather a rectangle with the top tilted away from us. This highlights an important fact, emphasized both by Koffka and by Gibson, that we do not perceive disembodied shapes but rather "shapes-in-a-given-orientation [Gibson, 1950a, p. 171]." Koffka (1935, p. 228) suggests that any given shape has what he calls a "normal" position, this being a position in the frontal-parallel plane. In this orientation, a figure is "well balanced" within itself, that is to say, as simple as it can possibly be.

Thus a square figure or a circular figure is *simpler*, in the sense in which we have previously used the word, than the same figure slanted along its vertical or horizontal axis. If we then invoke the minimax principle that a percept tends to be as simple as circumstances will permit, we can understand that some extra forces will be necessary for us to perceive the figure in a nonnormal position. These forces, supplied by depth cues, or texture gradients, tell us that the figure is slanted and that one part is closer to us than another. The final percept will then be some kind of compromise between the shape of the retinal image and the actual shape of the slanted figure. Depending on how these various stresses are balanced, this resultant may be closer either to the real object or to the retinal image. If depth cues are minimal, for example, a trapezoidal figure may be seen about as easily as a tilted rectangle, or as a real trapezoid in a frontal-parallel planes. Adding some depth cues will produce a percept that favors the rectangle. Thus constancy will be complete to the extent that we can see tilt.

In Gibson's terms, gradients of stimulation will be yielded by the orientation of the figure; these will relate to the surface texture and also to the contours of the figure. Both will indicate something about the angle of tilt. Thus if the vertical edges of the figure are seen as sharply tilted but the texture gradient is seen as rather gradual, then the final percept will be of a trapezoidal rather than a square shape, with its longer side on the bottom. Clearly, a great many different combinations are possible.

The explanations given by Koffka and Gibson are probably not contradictory. Perhaps the main difference lies in the fact that Koffka looks to hypo-

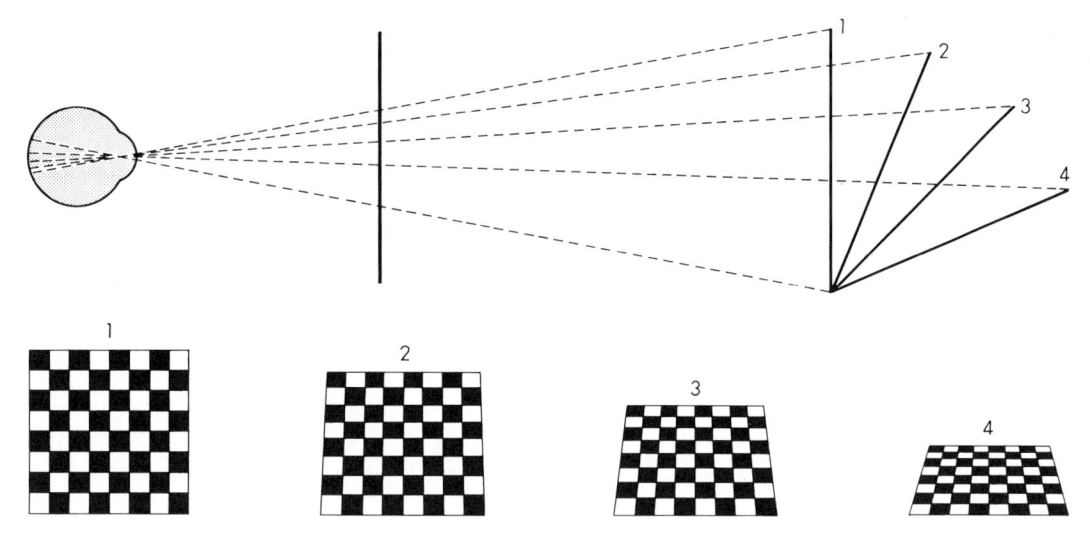

FIG. 11-24 Textural gradient can be a factor in shape constancy. (*Gibson, 1950a*)

thetical central processes to account for constancy whereas Gibson uses the more economical notion of invariants in stimulation gradients.

Size Constancy

As Koffka has pointed out (1935, p. 236), the size of an object is rather different from its shape, inasmuch as a "normal" size cannot be uniquely specified as can "normal" shape. The latter has been defined as the shape of the object as it is in a frontal-parallel plane. Such an orientation is uniquely defined and serves as a base line against which the size of a certain deviation can be judged. For size, however, there is no standard "normal" comparable to a "normal" orientation. Nevertheless, within a certain range of distances our perception of object size does remain remarkably constant in spite of variations in size of retinal image. Another person walking toward us from 20 yards away does not gradually get bigger as he approaches but remains the same size, one that we can judge quite accurately. As with shape, size constancy depends greatly on distance perception. If two objects project the same retinal size, the one farther away will be perceived as being larger.

A compelling illustration has been arranged by Ames (1946) as shown in Figure 11-25. This is called the Honi phenomenon, after the nickname of

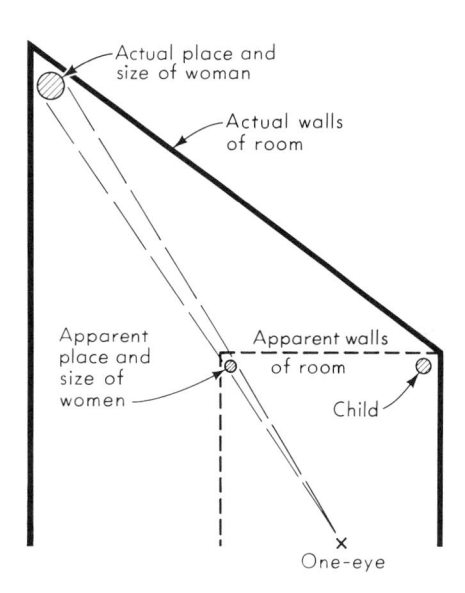

FIG. 11-25 Honi phenomenon and the distorted room.

the woman who first reported it. We see, on looking into the room through a peephole, what appears to be an adult midget and a giant child standing in the far corners of a square room. The illusion is due entirely to the architecture of the room, which is so distorted as to destroy distance cues.

187 THE PHENOMENA OF PERCEPTION

Actual dimensions of the room, as compared with its apparent ones, are shown in Figure 11-25. One side is three times as long as the other, so that the retinal image projected by the adult is smaller than that projected by the child. Were distance cues available, each would be seen as a normal size, but due to the elimination of binocular vision, they are severely reduced. In accord with the experience most of us have with square or rectangular rooms, however, the asymmetry is not perceived. This has the effect of pulling the far corner of the room and the adult occupying it to a distance equal to that of the other wall as shown by the dotted lines in the drawing. The result of this is that we see a child who is actually a normal size but is perceived as very large, and an adult who is very tiny. It is important to note that a lifetime of close experience with adults and children does not reduce the distortion. On the other hand, continued experience with the room, as, for example, bouncing a ball against the back wall, eventually produces a perception of its true shape.

Note that an interpretation of this curious phenomenon can be made from at least two points of view. Ittleson and Kilpatrick (1952), who studied it extensively, have argued that the distortion occurs because we have had such long experience with traversing and having transactions with symmetrical rooms that we make an automatic correction even at the expense of a distortion in the perceived sizes of a child and an adult. However, it could equally well be counterargued that, according to the minimax principle, we see the shape of the room in the simplest manner that prevailing conditions allow—that is, as symmetrical. The minimax principle cannot apply, however, to size, since it has no norm, or standard. There is no "best" or "simplest" size. Consequently this dimension suffers a distortion.

The close relation between apparent distance and perceived size has been analyzed experimentally by Holway and Boring (1941). This is described below.

Example 11-9 *Size constancy and distance (Holway & Boring, 1941)*

The purpose of the investigation was to examine the dependency of size constancy on depth cues. The subjects were required to adjust the size of a comparison disk so as to equal a set of standard circular images projected on a screen placed at eleven different distances (10 to 120 feet) away. Four conditions of viewing were used: (1) both eyes open, allowing the full operation of depth cues; (2) only one eye open, eliminating all binocular cues; (3) viewing with one eye only and through a peephole, eliminating depth cues arising from head movements; (4) the same as condition 3 with the addition of a long reduction tunnel made of black cloth between the observer and the stimulus, to eliminate the visual frame of reference provided by the walls, floor, and ceiling of the corridor. The size of the stimulus was so varied that at each distance it would project an image on the retina of a constant size (1 degree visual angle). In other words, it was made larger as it became more distant from the subject. Figure 11-26 depicts the two extreme possibilities by the broken lines, the upper being the case of complete constancy, in which perceived size increases with size of object, and the lower one the case of complete lack of constancy, in which size judgments follow retinal image size. The composite judgments for five subjects are shown in between. The dependence of size constancy on depth cues can clearly be seen. As more cues are removed, so size judgments tend to approach the law of the visual angle. Under optimal condition 1, it should be mentioned, *overconstancy* was actually found; that is, the plot was higher than it should be for perfect size constancy. Holway and Boring took this to be due to error and corrected it downward as shown in the figure, but recent studies have shown it to be a genuine phenomenon (cf. Wohlwill, 1963).

Brightness and Color Constancy

It is clear that the color and brightness of some opaque surfaces depend on the color and brightness reflected by the object. This reflectance must, in turn, depend on the color and brightness of the surrounding illumination. Thus, as Hering once pointed out (cf. Helson, 1958, p. 243), a piece of chalk on a dark day is actually measurably darker than a piece of coal on a sunny day, but in spite of this, we continue to perceive the chalk as white and the coal as black. The same applies to colored objects placed in illuminations of varying hue. This phenomenon is color and brightness constancy.

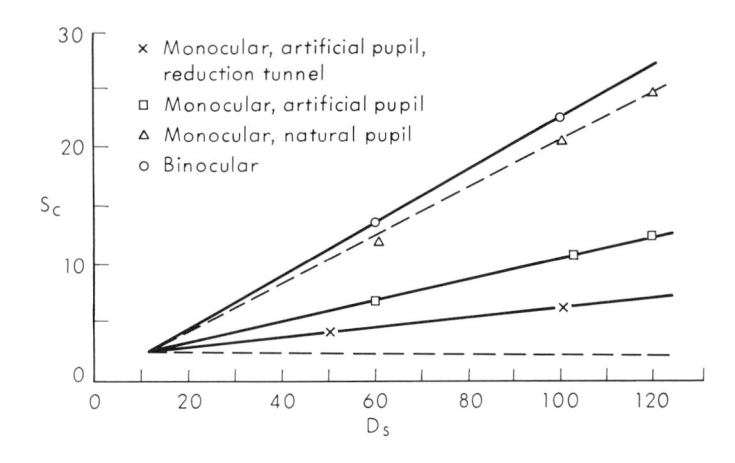

FIG. 11–26 Relation of size constancy to depth cues. (*Holway & Boring, 1941*)

The basic experimental setup used for studying color constancy was developed by David Katz (1935), one of the pioneers in this field. It is illustrated in Figure 11–27. As shown, the observer sits in front of two color mixers separated by a screen so that one is in direct illumination and the other is in a relatively shaded area. His task is to match a certain hue or brightness of one of these by adjusting the other. For example, one may be set to yield a gray made up of a combination of white to black in a 4 to 1 ratio. If we suppose this is the one in the lighted area, the problem then is to find out what white-black ratio is necessary in the other mixer to produce a match. In such a case, it would be found that much more white is needed on the dark side. If, however, the observer then views his matched brightnesses through a peephole, so that the illumination surrounding each is not seen, he will be struck by the actual inequality of the two. The same applies to color, or hue, matches.

The principle involved is well known. It is simply that perceived surface brightness and surface hue here depend on the ratio of the reflected light to the incident light. This ratio is known as *albedo*. Generally speaking, we maintain constancy because of albedo. Thus chalk in shadow and chalk in daylight are very different, but the albedos are approximately equal. We therefore perceive the whiteness of the two as also being approximately the same.

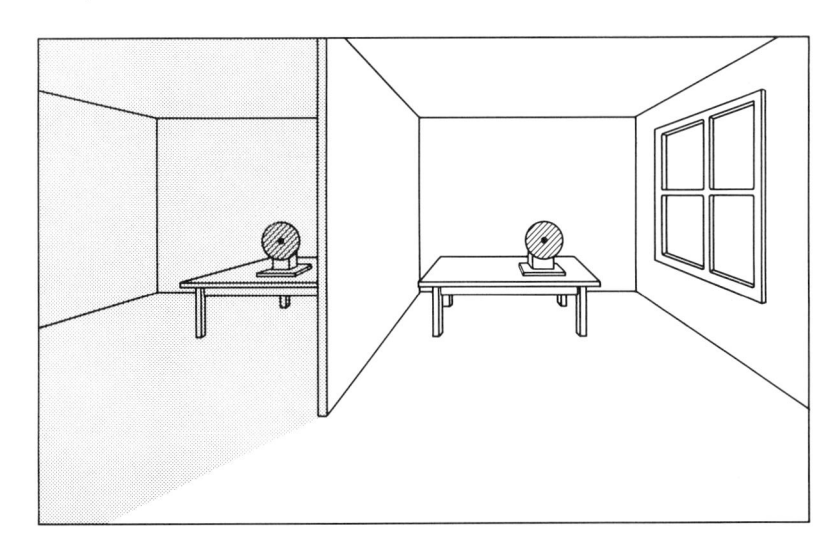

FIG. 11–27 Experimental setup for studying color and brightness constancy. (*Katz, 1935*)

189 THE PHENOMENA OF PERCEPTION

As with shape and size, color and brightness constancy varies a good deal, depending on many complex variables, which are not always the same for color as for brightness. Such problems are, however, beyond the scope of this book.

Movement Constancy

Besides those discussed already, one more type of perceptual constancy may be mentioned, namely, movement constancy. In this, three factors appear to be at work: size of moving object, distance from observer, and actual velocity of the object. If we hold size constant, we find a good degree of speed constancy over a range of distances. That is to say, we tend to judge as moving equally fast objects that really are moving at the same velocity but at different distances from us. This is somewhat of an achievement, since the displacements of the retinal image of a moving stimulus will obviously vary as a direct function of distance. On the other hand, if constancy is not disturbed by distance, it is seriously disturbed by size when distance is held constant.

It will be clear by now that whatever particular explanation of the constancies may be given, it must be one that depends on Gestalt, interactional, or higher-order variables. The isolated and punctate stimulation produced by the object in isolation is not sufficient. Only by considering it in relation to its position in space or to the total surround can we begin to understand how we can experience such a remarkably stable and orderly world rather than a fluid and shifting visual field. At just what point in our receptor systems—the peripheral sense organs or the central brain areas—we can most profitably search is still a problem. However, Gibson is probably correct in suggesting that the receptors themselves can yield much more information than has been generally supposed and that, consequently, it may make a good deal of sense to start at this level by elaborating a psychophysics of perception involving higher-order variables.

CHAPTER 12
EXTENDING THE STUDY OF PERCEPTION

The study of perception as considered so far may give the reader the impression that perception is a rather specialized subject somewhat divorced from the rest of psychology, a technology of interest to painters, factory managers, airplane pilots, and others concerned with the problem of how people contact the world and how errors arise in such contacts but not an area supplying a theoretical framework broad enough to take in the more general questions about personality and behavior.

Some workers in the field have perhaps shared this feeling and have therefore attempted to extend in various directions the scope and breadth of their research. One extension was initiated by Heinz Werner and Seymour Wapner (1952) of Clark University, another mainly by Bruner and Postman (1950), then of Harvard. The first of these two pairs of workers have put forward a formal organismic theory of perception that takes special account of the contribution made to our perception by the tonic, or motor, system.

SENSORY-TONIC THEORY

Perception is not just a passive affair. Organisms behave and move, and these movements have *sensory* consequences which feed back into, and therefore might be expected to affect, the operation of the more conventional sensory systems. Gibson, of course, took account of this fact by considering, for example, the sweep of stimulation across the optical array as a person moves in his environment. However, he did not explicitly consider, as Werner and Wapner do, the sensory feedback from the contracting and flexing musculature. This is definitely a source of stimulation and is called, formally, the *kinesthetic system*. Thus there are sensory nerve endings embedded in our muscles, and as these are used, sensory impulses are set off.

Consideration of this rather specific problem is only one part of the general and holistic theory put forward by Werner and Wapner. They also see other systems, such as drives, motives, and attitudes as affecting even the most simple of our perceptions of the world. At the same time, it is also true that their starting point is with sensory-tonic events. They state:

> The perceptual properties of an object are a function of the way in which the stimuli coming from an object will affect the existing sensory-tonic state of the organism. Instead of talking, as traditional psychology does, about a visual object stimulating the retina and other visual areas, we talk about a stimulus object always arousing sensory-tonic events, i.e., events which involve the whole organism [Werner & Wapner, 1952, p. 325].

Werner and Wapner have shown a special ingenuity in specifying this rather broad theory at an experimental level. They put forward, as a basic construct designed to deal with the resultant of several interacting sources of stimulation, the concept of *equilibrium*. According to this, the organism automatically tends to establish a steady state, so that equilibrium disturbance is at a minimum. Such an idea is not very different from the Gestalt minimax principle. Thus if a person sits in a chair that is tilted to one side, stimulation is greater on that side due to the greater effects of gravity. As a result, counterforces come into operation on the other side to restore a state of equilibrium. This has the effect of producing a body axis (normally perpendicular to the earth's surface) that is biased in the direction of the counteractive forces. A simple example will illustrate this. As many readers who have flown in an airplane may have observed, when the descent is rather sharp, the horizon outside the window appears to swing downward in the direction of flight from the horizontal. In terms of Werner's and Wapner's theory, the gravitational pull on the front half of the body of a passenger is countered by a force on the back half. This results in a vertical axis biased posteriorly. The result is an alteration in our perception of what is horizontal. *Phenomenal* horizontal is now tilted upward to maintain a 90-degree angle with the new vertical. As a result, the *real* horizontal (the horizon) now appears to be tilted down. The opposite will hold true in the case of a steep ascent.

Werner and Wapner and their colleagues have examined this phenomenon under more controlled conditions in the laboratory. The following experiments are representative of some of the work done in their research program.

Example 12-1 *Body tilt and perception of verticality (Werner, Wapner, & Chandler, 1951a, 1951b; Werner, Wapner, & Morant, 1951)*

Werner and Wapner and two colleagues published in 1951 three preliminary studies aimed at testing their sensory-tonic theory. All three involved analysis of perceptual effects produced by applying to subjects some kind of disequilibrating stimulation. In the first experiment, the investigators used electrical and auditory stimulation administered to one side of the body. Forty subjects were asked to move a rod to what they considered to be a vertical position under conditions of such stimulation or of no stimulation. Results are shown in Table 12-1.

Table 12-1 Phenomenal vertical as a function of left or right stimulation

Condition	Degrees of counter-clockwise (left) tilt
No stimulation	1.4
Auditory stimulation left	1.0
Auditory stimulation right	2.1
Electrical stimulation left	1.0
Auditory stimulation right	2.1

In the first place, even under controlled conditions observers tended to judge a rod as vertical when it was in fact slightly tilted counterclockwise, or to the "left." In the second place, stimulation on the left produced a clockwise deviation, i.e., to the "right" of phenomenal vertical, whereas stimulation to the right produces a counterclockwise deviation—to the "left" of phenomenal vertical. The differences, although small, are statistically significant. In the third place, the *type* of stimulation does not make any difference. Electrical and auditory stimulation are, in other words, *functionally equivalent*, an essential contruct in sensory-tonic field theory.

In the second study, Werner, Wapner, and Chandler examined the effects of supported versus unsupported body tilt on the perception of verticality (the E phenomenon). They argued that the greater muscular involvement in the second condition should produce that much more effect on phenomenal vertical.

Forty subjects were used with two angles of tilt—15 degrees clockwise (right) or counterclockwise (left) and 30 degrees clockwise or counterclockwise (right or left), either in a supported or in an unsupported condition. Tilting was done by means of a special chair whose tilt could be accurately calibrated either by the experimenter or by the subject himself when in the unsupported condition. Results are shown in Table 12-2.

Two conclusions can be educed from the table: First, the greater the angle of tilt, the greater the displacement of phenomenal vertical from real vertical. Second, unsupported tilt produces a larger deviation than supported tilt. Both effects were

Table 12-2 Phenomenal vertical under different experimental conditions

	Body tilt, degrees			
	Clockwise (right)		Counterclockwise (left)	
	15	30	15	30
Supported	2.5 L*	7.6 L	1.3 R*	3.4 R
Unsupported	4.1 L	10.0 L	4.6 R	6.9 R

* L and R stand for judgment to left (counterclockwise) or right (clockwise) of objective vertical, respectively.

statistically significant. Thus *amount of muscular involvement*, and not simply position of the body, is a crucial factor in perception. This fact again fits with sensory-tonic field theory.

In their final experiment, Wapner, Werner, and Morant examined the effect of body rotation on perception of verticality. The extraneous stimulation in this case involved, in sensory terms, activation of receptors in the inner ear. When excessive or extensive, such stimulation will usually produce the symptoms of vertigo and nausea. Twenty-eight subjects were tested. Five conditions were set up: control or nonstimulation; acceleration clockwise; deceleration clockwise; acceleration counterclockwise; deceleration counterclockwise. Subjects were rotated in a specially designed chair up to or down from a maximum speed of 25 rpm. A luminous rod rotated in front of them. Its verticality could be varied by the experimenter.

Results indicated that clockwise (to the right) acceleration produces a phenomenal counterclockwise tilt (to the left), whereas counterclockwise acceleration (to the left) produces a clockwise tilt (to the right). Decelerations had just the opposite effects. Thus clockwise deceleration produces, like counterclockwise acceleration, clockwise displacement of the phenomenal vertical (to the right).

Wapner et al. again conclude that the data are in agreement with sensory-tonic theory.

The notion of *symmetrization* is extended by Werner and Wapner to other problems. One of these involves what they call *visual dynamics* and the so-called *physiognomic*, or *demand*, qualities of objects and persons. The asymmetry of a face in profile, for example, sets up vectorial forces that suggest to us directionality on one side, not because we are familiar with faces (i.e., have *learned* about them), but because of an imbalance of stimulation producing in us an automatic response or feeling tone. The reader may recall that a rather similar idea guided some of the thinking and research of Heider and Simmel and of Asch in social psychology.

ATTITUDES, MOTIVES, AND DRIVES: THEIR EFFECT ON PERCEPTION

An extension of the work in perception, less formalized than that of Werner and Wapner, was initiated at about the same time by Bruner and his colleagues. This movement has usually been labeled the "new look" in perception. Its major postulate—reasonable enough—is that the work on perception such as that done by gestaltists has failed to take into account the influence of the whole personality and all that this implies. A useful distinction made by Bruner and Postman has been between *autochthonous* and *behavioral* variables. The former category refers to those factors that determine how the average organism, "purified" of values, needs, and personal biases, perceives the world; all the variables we have so far been considering belong to this category. The latter category refers to all dimensions of personality that can influence the manner in which those in the first category have an effect. Needs, values, attitudes, and motives can thus produce deviation from those rules describing the operation of variables of the first category.

A great deal of research has been done on this problem. The general conclusion to which all studies point is that the way a person perceives the world can indeed be affected by his personality, defined both in terms of immediate manipulations introduced by an experimenter—for example, by reward and punishment—or in terms of long-range variables commonly identified with the enduring structure of personality—for example, values and needs.

Example 12-2 *Value and need and estimation of size (Bruner & Goodman, 1947)*

A classic experiment in this field was done by Bruner and Goodman in 1947. Although its methods and conclusions were less tightly controlled

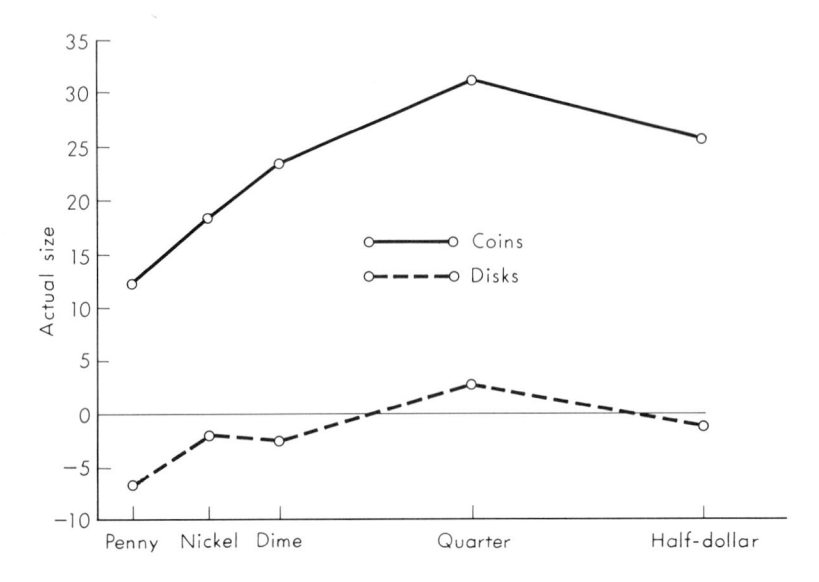

FIG. 12-1 Estimate sizes of coins versus disks. (*Bruner & Goodman, 1947*)

than they might have been, it can still be regarded as a seminal study. They start off with a specification of the distinction to which we have already alluded, that between autochthonous and behavioral determinants of perception, and follow this with a review of the "fruitful if slim body of literature on behavioral factors in perception [p. 35]." They specified three empirical hypotheses as follows:

1. The greater the social value of an object, the more it will be susceptible to organization by behavioral determinants.
2. The greater the individual need for a socially valued object, the more marked will be the operation of behavioral determinants.
3. Perceptual equivocality will facilitate the operation of behavioral determinants only in so far as equivocality reduces the autochthonous determinants without reducing the effectiveness of behavioral determinants [Bruner & Goodman, 1947, pp. 36–37].

The manner in which they translated these hypotheses into experimentally testable terms is ingenious. They used 30 ten-year-old children of normal intelligence and divided these into three groups—two experimental and one control. Subjects were asked to manipulate a knob controlling the size of a circle of light on a screen, until they felt it matched the size of certain objects. For the experimental groups, these objects were coins: a penny, nickel, dime, quarter, and half-dollar. Controls were given cardboard disks of the same respective sizes as the coins. Judgments, expressed in deviation from actual sizes, are shown in Figure 12–1. It is very clear that there is a difference—and it is highly significant statistically—between the judgments of experimentals and controls. Coins are judged much larger than they really are, though this is not true for the cardboard disks. The first hypothesis was thus confirmed.

The second hypothesis was examined simply by comparing the judgments made by "rich" children as against "poor" children. Again the difference, shown in Figure 12–2, is statistically significant, thus confirming the notion that distortion is greater the greater the need for an object (in this case, money).

The final hypothesis, which need not concern us so much here, since it is less explicit than the first two, was only partially confirmed, by data based on judgments of remembered size as against judgments based on perceived size.

The Bruner and Goodman study was by no means the first done in this area, but it did more than perhaps any other to generate interest and excitement in this area of research. Many points about it can be questioned. One important one, for example, is the question of value or need versus usage. Poor children may value money more, but even if they

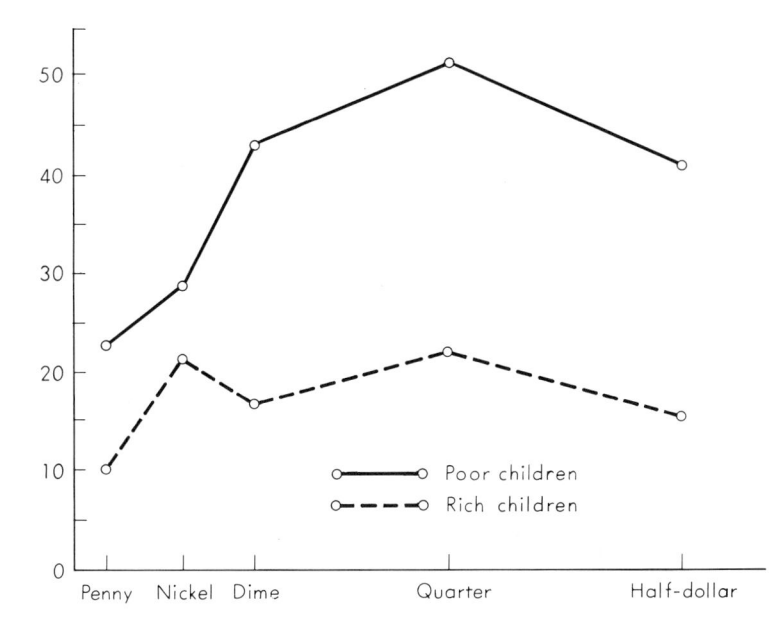

FIG. 12-2 Size judgments of coins by "rich" as compared with those made by "poor" children. (*Bruner & Goodman, 1947*)

do, they also probably handle it less frequently than rich children. It may have been this factor of *amount of contact* that produced the greater distortion of perceptual judgment in the poor group. On the other hand, it is equally true that if this were the only factor operating, the judgments of size should not deviate only in the direction of overestimation but might as well also go in the direction of underestimation. Consequently, it does seem as if something else besides familiarity or lack of it is operating. Let us now look at another experiment that relates to the distinction we have been making between value and usage.

Example 12-3 *Familiarity and the Honi phenomenon (Wittreich, 1952)*

We have already referred to the Honi phenomenon, occasioned by a distorted room: a face in the foreshortened corner looks a great deal larger than a face in the corner on the lengthened side. However, Wittreich had previously observed one instance in which a woman observing her husband saw his face as normal size. A stranger in the same place, however, she saw as distorted in the expected manner. The present study was simply an attempt to replicate and extend this isolated instance.

In his first experiment, the experimenter used ten married couples, six of whom had been married less than 1 year. The other four couples had been married 2, 3½, 5, and 10 years, respectively. Two distorted rooms were used, one large and one small. Both were viewed with one eye only. Among other features of the room, they were asked to view two pairs of heads through the rear windows: (1) two strangers and (2) a stranger and the marital partner.

An analysis of the protocols showed that spouses were always distorted less than strangers. This applied both to the small room and to the large distorted room. Here is an example of a protocol:

Female married 4 months to Bob: Good night! Well, now the difference is tremendous because Bruce [stranger] is so small. You see, I can't be objective about it. I know Bob is tall, therefore the difference between his and Bruce's height seems tremendous, more so than the other two. (Experimenter: Does Bob look taller than usual?) Yes, I think. Uh, that's hard to say; he doesn't look taller than usual. Not especially. It's just that Bruce looks so small. He's just minute. That's just about it [Wittreich, 1952, p. 708].

This kind of difference was also found in the second experiment, whose purpose was to present it in more quantitative terms. Table 12-3 summarizes the findings: with strangers, particularly of the op-

Table 12-3 Differences in mean position scores for groups observed: marital partners, strangers of sex opposite to that of observer, and strangers of same sex as observer

Groups compared	Difference between respective mean position scores, visual angle	Statistically significant
Strangers of opposite sex and marital partners	1.45	Yes
Strangers of same sex and marital partners	1.17	No
Strangers of opposite sex and strangers of same sex	0.28	No

posite sex, the distortion is greater, measured in degrees of visual angle, than with marital partners.

Thus familiarity operates here to increase the veridicality of perception. Wittreich considered the result to be compatible with the so-called transactionalist point of view—that is to say, the position taken by Ames and Ittleson that we learn to perceive things and to "make sense" out of sensory data through the transactions we have with the world.

The notions of value and need as against familiarity or amount of contact have figured in another series of experiments, two of which will be presented here. The first deals with the problem of whether objects on which we place a negative value, apart from whether they are distorted, tend to be *perceived less readily* than objects on which we place a positive value.

Example 12-4 *Personal values as selective factors in perception (Postman, Bruner, & McGinnies, 1948)*

This experiment was intended to study the effect of values on perceptual selectivity. The writers specified two types of selectivity: *spatial selectivity*, which involves picking some relevant item out of a complex field, and *temporal selectivity* which involves the speed with which a certain relevant item can be recognized. Only the second of these was studied here.

Twenty-five subjects, students from Harvard and Radcliffe, were given the Allport-Vernon Study of Values Test. This categorizes subjects according to six value orientations: theoretical, economic, aesthetic, social, political, and religious. Thus any single individual obtains a profile according to the kinds of values he considers more important or less important. The perceptual part of the study was carried out as follows: each of the twenty-five subjects was shown thirty-six words, one at a time in a tachistoscope, a device by which the length of time a word is exposed can be accurately controlled. The initial duration was very short—1/100 second. If, after three presentations at this speed, the subject failed to recognize a word correctly, duration was increased, first to 2/100 second, then 3/100 second, and so on, in 1/100-second steps, until recognition occurred. All prerecognition responses, that is to say, wrong responses guessed at by a subject, were also recorded.

The results averaged over all subjects are shown in Figure 12-3. It is clear that there is a definite and positive relation between value and recognition time. The higher the value for a subject represented by a word, the more quickly it is recognized. On the basis of these results and also of those obtained from the prerecognition-response data, Postman, Bruner, and McGinnies postulated three mechanisms by which value orientation can affect perception. These are *selective sensitization*, according to which the organism's perceptual threshold is lowered for objects it values; *perceptual defense*, by which the organism erects barriers against perceiving objects it regards as unpleasant or threatening; and *value resonance*, by which a subject tends to make prerecognition responses which relate to his dominant value orientation.

This study led to a fascinating line of research that is still going on. The main problem to which it has been directed has concerned the nature of sensitization and more especially of perceptual defense. As critics point out (Eriksen, 1960, Dember, 1960), it is a little difficult to know how the human organism can initially grasp enough information about a presented object to know that it is repellent or dangerous and then defend against it by not seeing it. The only way this might be possible would be through a highly sensitive and alert un-

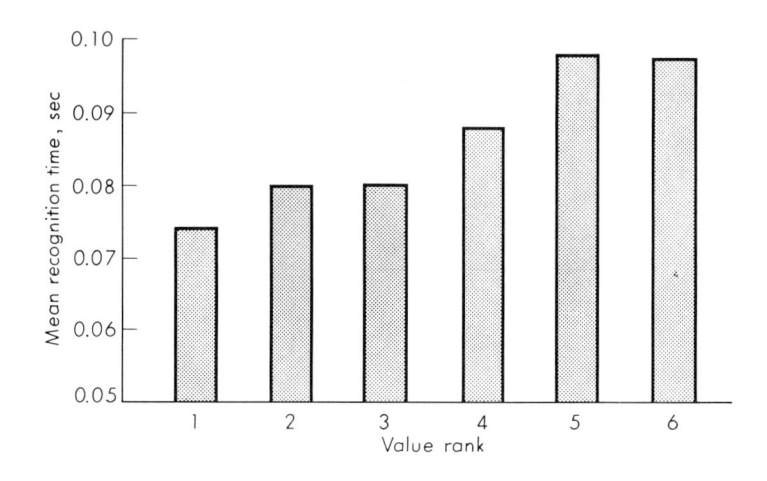

FIG. 12–3 Relation between value of word and durations of exposure at which it is correctly recognized. (*Postman, Bruner & McGinnies, 1948*)

conscious that screens selected perceptions before they can enter consciousness. Such a position would be quite in line with Freudian psychology, but most experimentalists have become a little wary of it, since it is not a notion that lends itself very well to experimental test. One expert, for example, writes:

> It appears that the organism is extracting information continuously from the stimulating situation, and likewise, there is no need to introduce the notion of unconscious. What we call unconscious is merely the condition wherein the subject is extracting very little information from the stimulus [Forgus, 1966, p. 266].

Whatever we may consider the mechanisms to be, we can hardly doubt that values and needs do affect perception in some manner. Which aspects of them are the most important in this respect is another problem. Two other workers, Solomon and Howes (1951), have suggested that our values reflect the amount of contact we have had with certain classes of subjects including words. Their study testing this hypothesis is presented in Example 12–5.

Example 12–5 *Word frequencies and recognition thresholds (Solomon & Howes, 1951)*

These researchers essentially repeated the Postman, Bruner, and McGinnies experiment with one important addition: the word lists they used to cover the six Allport-Vernon value categories were divided into two types: high-frequency, or common, words and low-frequency, or uncommon, words. Thus under the category "aesthetic," for example, they had listed:

Relatively frequent:
- poetry
- picture
- painter
- orchestra

Relatively infrequent:
- vignette
- etcher
- ensemble
- metaphor

Nineteen subjects were exposed to these words for various durations until recognition thresholds were established. They were also given the Allport-Vernon test. Results are shown in Figure 12–4. It is fairly clear from the graph that the relation between a word value and its recognition threshold is slight in the case of high-frequency words but is slightly positive for low-frequency words. Even this trend, however, is attributed by Solomon and Howes to frequency differences within the low-frequency category. Consequently, they suggested that a linguistic formulation was certainly at least as adequate as, and more economical than, any explanation drawn from a rather complex personality theory.

Postman and Schneider (1951) repeated the Solomon and Howes experiment and obtained essentially the same results. However, they concluded that, at least in the case of the infrequent words, values were the major factors determining recognition threshold. In view of more recent work, it seems very likely that this conclusion was a correct

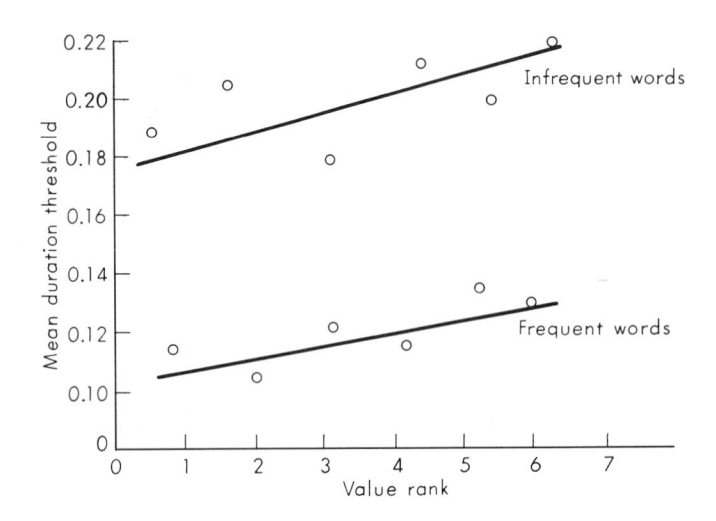

FIG. 12-4 Relation between value rank and recognition thresholds for frequently and infrequently used words. (*Solomon & Howes, 1951*)

one. Certainly word frequency is important, but as a number of investigators have pointed out, it is difficult to assess. Furthermore, it may be highly idiosyncratic and directly dependent on an individual's value system. Thus a word that is very uncommon for the average person may be quite common for one particular individual simply because of his unique patterns of interests and activities. Obviously, then, the term "word frequency" has meaning only in terms of the life history of the individual and the history of the culture in which he lives. Different cultural values will be reflected in different language structures and hence different word frequencies. Thus it is likely that values, needs, and attitudes may be the ultimate causative agents affecting perceptual thresholds, though word usage may well be the more immediate one. The situation can be represented as follows:

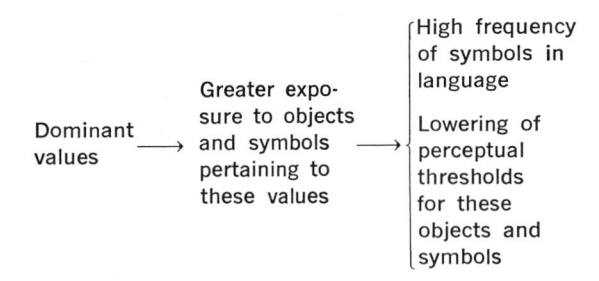

Dominant values → Greater exposure to objects and symbols pertaining to these values → {High frequency of symbols in language; Lowering of perceptual thresholds for these objects and symbols}

The "new look" in perception at first was a theoretically rather informal position. However, during the past number of years it has grown to be part of a stronger and more coherent movement in psychology commonly labeled "cognitive psychology."

DEVELOPMENT OF PERCEPTION

One of the problems with which psychologists have been concerned for a very long time has been what is often called the "nature-nurture" issue. Are there any determinants of our behavior—and, particularly in the present context, of our perception—that are innate? Or is everything due to learning, or nurture? As we saw earlier, the British empiricist philosophers, for example, Locke, Berkeley, Hume, and Mill, tended to hold the view that the way in which we see the world is acquired through experience. The raw sensory elements, which are all we have at birth, yield nothing in terms of perceptual dimensions such as depth, distance, size, shape, and meaning. Only through *contact* with the world do we gradually learn to see it in a way that is veridical.

The notion made quite explicit by these philosophers is that the sensory system that is the ultimate indication of reality is touch, used in the rather broad sense above of making contact with an object. By his direct contacts with limited aspects of its environment—for example, a room and the objects it contains—a child gradually learns to extrapolate from the contactual to the visual and auditory modes. Thus notions of space and depth are built up. As we pointed out before, this is probably the most commonsense point of view (at least in present-day Western culture) about perceptual development. It is a position nicely stated by Helmholtz as quoted by Hochberg (1962, p. 282):

> This relation between distance and size ... can only be acquired by long experience, and so it is not surprising that children are ... apt to make big mistakes. I can recall when I was a boy going past the ... Chapel ... where some people were standing in the belfry. I mistook them for dolls and asked my mother to reach up and get them for me, which I thought she could do.

The chief virtue of this empiricist position was that there was no real evidence against it. It is to the credit of those in the empiricist tradition that they did try to suggest how evidence that perception developed with learning might be obtained, but their suggestions did not very easily translate into definitive experimental research.

Perhaps because of this difficulty, the opposite point of view, that of nativism, did gain adherents and still has many today. According to this theory, organisms are born with at least the potential for perceiving the world veridically. A normal maturation guarantees immediate grasp of all the aspects of depth, shape, size, and color. The translation of this notion into some experimental procedures is equally difficult. However, as an idea it is certainly as sensible as that put forward by empiricism. Ewald Hering was an important nineteenth-century sensory physiologist like Helmholtz but stood in opposition to the latter's empiricism.

According to Hering (1861), the experiences of light, color, height, breadth, and depth are innately furnished by every retinal point. Separately and together they immediately give us all relevant information about the visual world. No learning is necessary. A similar position was put forward by Lotze (1881) based on this notion of "local signs." The doctrines of Hering and Lotze supplied a mechanism at the sensory level that was innately capable of handling all spatial dimensions. Again, however, experimental evidence definitely proving this is difficult if not impossible to obtain.

A strong nativist position was also taken by the Gestalt psychologists Wertheimer, Koffka, and Köhler, as we pointed out earlier in this section. They differed mainly from Hering in postulating that the innate processes that organize sensory input pertain, not to the peripheral receptors, but to the brain or central nervous system. These processes constituted the so-called "laws of organization" whose operation we have already discussed in connection with two- and three-dimensional space perception and the constancies.

Finally, we may mention two contemporary points of view on the nativism-empiricism issue. Gibson is a quasi nativist to the extent that he sees in the so-called optical array certain invariants that immediately produce an organized perception of the visual world. If any learning is involved, it is, for Gibson, not an associative kind, whereby basic elements gradually become connected together into compounds, but a *differentiation learning*, whereby, through exposure to the world, we gradually come to make finer and finer discrimination between various sensory inputs, for example, between a more pronounced versus a less pronounced gradient of stimulation. Thus we achieve closer and closer contact with a world potentially rich in meaning.

The other contemporary theorist, Donald O. Hebb of McGill University, takes a somewhat similar position, though his emphasis is more directly physiological. Hebb (1949) makes a useful distinction between perception of *unities* and perception of *identities*. The first of these is essentially what Gestaltists would call *object perception*, that is, the ability to perceive a thing as distinct from its background. This does not involve, however, the ability to recognize the same object—same, that is, in respect to such discriminated qualities as form, shape, or brightness—when it is presented a second time.

Perception of identity, on the other hand, is defined as the ability precisely to perform such an act of recognition—that is, to be able to tell one object from another through an awareness of its identity. According to Hebb, there is some evidence to indicate that perception of unity is built into the organism. Perception of identity, however, is not; it is learned early in life through the process of scanning with the eyes the outline of an object. With much practice we soon come to be able to identify an object with one quick glance. This is done by even relatively young organisms with such ease and rapidity as to mask its dependence on learning and to suggest an innate ability.

On the physiological side, Hebb has suggested a "dual trace" mechanism that corresponds to the two kinds of perception. Initially, the receptor systems have sufficient organization to yield differentiation between figures and ground—that is, perception of unities. With the searching and scanning activities of the organism, certain particular sequences of neuronal firing come to be consolidated. These correspond to particular perceptual configurations. Once such an assemblage has been formed in the brain, it can be triggered off by the stimulation of any small part of it. Although this takes time, it happens fast enough to give us the impression of instantaneous recognition at the perceptual level.

It would be foolish to say that any one of the above points of view contains the whole truth. Certainly the evidence on hand does not suggest this, and at this stage of research it would be best to regard each as no more than a general strategy, pointing research in a certain direction. It will probably be some time before we can say definitely which direction is the most fruitful.

In the meantime, then, let us look at such evidence as is available on the nature-nurture issue. The experiments to be discussed represent, of course, only a small sample of a very large number done on this topic.

Example 12–6 *Perception following recovery from congenital cataract (von Senden, 1960)*

It is interesting that the experimental data reported by von Senden take their start directly from a hypothetical experiment suggested by Mr. Molineux in the eighteenth century and described by both Locke and Berkeley. This "ingenious and studious promotor of real knowledge" wrote in a letter to Locke:

> Suppose a man born blind, and now adult, and taught by his touch to distinguish between a cube and a sphere of the same metal, and highly of the same bigness, so as to tell, when he felt one and the other, which is the cube, which the sphere. Suppose then the cube and the sphere placed on a table, and the blind man to be made to see: quaere, whether by his sight, before he touched them, could he now distinguish and tell which is the globe, which the cube? . . . Not. For though he has obtained the experience of how a globe, how a cube, affects his touch; yet he has not yet obtained, that what affects his touch so or so, must affect his sight so or so; or that a protuberant angle in the cube, that pressed his hand unequally, shall appear to his eye as it does in the cube.

Locke agreed strongly with this conclusion of the "observing" Mr. Molineux.

It was not true, of course, that the gentleman in question was an "observing" one, and it is an interesting commentary on the empiricist philosophers that they were nonetheless willing to put so much faith in an experiment which had not (to their knowledge) been performed then and was not performed systematically until much later. Happily, Mr. Molineux's guess turned out to be quite accurate.

What von Senden did was simply to collect as many accounts as he could find of the first visual experiences of patients successfully operated upon at maturity for blindness due to congenital cataract. Not all of them would be considered totally blind, but even those who had some sight could perceive the world as no more than a vague gray mass yielding only intensity differences.

The critical conclusion educed from reports of the first visual impression of these patients when sight was restored was that they had the ability to discriminate objects—or *unities*, to use Hebb's terms—on the basis of color. There was also some impression of depth or distance, though judgment of its *extent* was poor. Appreciation of *form* and the ability to perceive *identity* was not present at first. Considerable practice was required before even a circle or a triangle would be recognized and distinguished. Furthermore, generalization was deficient, in the sense that after, say, a triangle came to be recognized, a slight change in it caused the patient to see a completely new figure.

One case is described as follows:

> He gradually became more correct in his perception, but it was only after several days that he could or would tell by the eyes alone, which was the sphere and which the cube; when asked, he always, before answering, wished to take both into his hands; even when this was allowed, when immediately afterwards the objects were placed before the eyes, he was not certain of the figure [von Senden, 1960, p. 183].

This is more or less typical of the kind of slow progress and reorganization of spatial understanding that has to be undertaken by such patients. It is of some interest that not only is the effort required to do this very great but that it also often produces great emotional upset. Von Senden quotes Beer on this point as follows:

> Among the most remarkable psychological phenomena presented to my observation in all the patients so far operated upon, is the rapid and complete loss of that striking and wonderful serenity which is characteristic only of those who have never yet seen; for hardly are the first lively sallies of their curiosity satisfied after the operation, than already they evince this striking transformation of their attitude. Gloomy and reserved, they now shun for a time the society of others, which was so indispensable to them while they were blind that they lamented every moment they were obliged to spend without it [von Senden, 1960, p. 161].

Thus, we must learn to see. All the subtle dimensions of visual perception which we use so quickly and easily every day of our lives apparently are not built into us from the beginning but must be acquired through early experience. In the main, then, Mr. Molineux's educated guess proved to be fairly accurate.

Von Senden's data seem very convincing. At the same time, it should be noted, as one critic, Michael Wertheimer, has pointed out (1951), that the study is very anecdotal in character and is based on cases widely scattered in time and place. Of the 74 used, the first dates from around A.D. 1020, and 57 are from the nineteenth century. Consequently, we must be a little cautious about accepting them as completely valid scientifically. However, a single case study reported by Gregory and Wallace (1963) on the visual experience of a patient recovered from early blindness is in substantial agreement with the findings of von Senden. In addition, two sets of data now to be discussed also support and extend the conclusions of his work.

Example 12–7 *Monkeys reared in conditions of light deprivation (Riesen, 1950)*

Austin H. Riesen started off his research with a view to correcting some of the difficulties inherent in the studies of cataract patients. These he considered to arise from the intrusion of too many uncontrolled variables such as (1) the degree of the patient's previous blindness (2) the limit that is imposed on potentiality for improvement when the eye operated on lacks a lens; (3) the fact that, in all these cases, there remains another visual handicap, namely, spontaneous nystagmus, that is, jerky and uncontrollable movements of the eyeballs. To achieve more control than is possible with human cases as they occur in nature, Riesen undertook to set up a careful experiment using another higher primate, the chimpanzee.

The first study of a long series continued at several centers was done by Riesen at the Orange Park Primate Center in Florida. Seven chimps were involved. These were subjected to a variety of amounts and durations of light deprivation early in life. For example, Debi, a female, was raised in complete darkness for seven months, and another female, Kora, was allowed, during the same period, a "ration" of an average of 1½ hours daily of diffuse, unpatterned light as transmitted through a white Plexiglas mask.

The general results may be summarized as follows: (1) Newborn animals and those somewhat older (e.g., seven months) that have been kept in darkness for some time show usual visual reflexes when first subjected to light. Some semivoluntary acts, such as rapid eyeblink at an approaching object, become automatic only after considerable practice. (2) Spontaneous nystagmus tends to be pronounced. (3) Visual pursuit of moving objects, coordination of the two eyes, convergent fixation, and ready identification of objects tends to take many hours or even weeks of experience. Depth perception is poor. (4) Severe light deprivation (and hence the most severe perceptual deficits) is associated with marked pallor of the optic disk and retina. In such cases the physiology of the visual system can no longer be regarded as normal.

Riesen's further studies done over the following fifteen years on rats, cats, and rhesus monkeys have verified these basic conclusions, as well as refining them and extending them in various directions (cf. Riesen, 1961). We will not consider this work here, however. Let us turn instead to another basic set of observations.

Example 12–8 *The visual cliff (Walk & Gibson, 1960)*

The series of studies summarized in this article

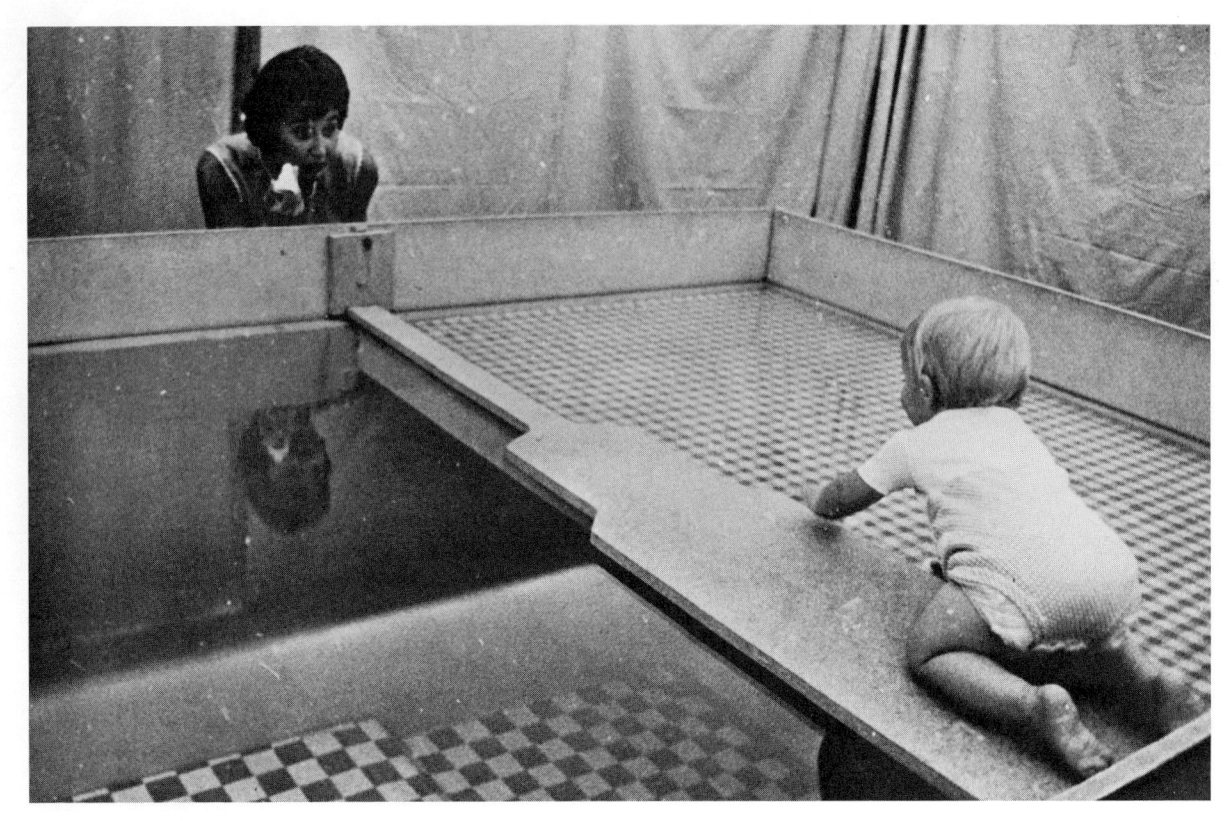

FIG. 12–5 Visual-cliff apparatus used to study depth perception. (*Gibson and Walk, 1960; William Vandivert,* Scientific American)

used an ingenious experimental situation called by the investigators the "visual cliff." It is shown in Figure 12–5. As indicated, a piece of heavy glass covers two sides, one a shallow side, the other deep. Between the two is a central starting platform raised several inches above the glass. To highlight the difference between the two sides in terms of other optical-array qualities, a checkerboard material was used on the middle and on both sides. The general technique, employed with human babies (six to fourteen months) and with a variety of species of lower animals, was to place them initially on the center and observe any preference as to deep or shallow side, particularly when there was an incentive favoring traversal of the deep side.

Of 36 human infants tested, 27 moved off the center board when the mother called. But of the 27 only 3 went over the deep side to her. Thus most human infants can apparently discriminate depth as soon as they can crawl. Under a variety of testing conditions, young goats, lambs, chicks, and kittens behaved in the same way. Rats showed little preference provided they could feel the glass with their vibrissae, or whiskers. However, if the two sides were lowered so that the glass floor was beyond the reach of their whiskers and they therefore had to choose on the basis of visual cues, 95 to 100 percent of rats would descend to the shallow side. Turtles, which may have mixed up the glass with the surface of a pool of water, showed no particular preference. Walk and Gibson in an ensuing set of experiments found that both optical density and motion parallax were responsible for the shallow-side preferences. If these were controlled by manipulating the size and spacing of the checkerboard squares on the deep side and its distance below the glass, then avoidance of this side diminished sharply.

Finally, it was found that rats reared in the dark during the first part of their lives (ninety days) showed depth discrimination as soon as they were tested. They must have relied, in this case, on motion parallax rather than on pattern density differences. Likewise, kittens reared in the dark, though showing no immediate preference when first tested at twenty-seven days, did so within a week after transition to a visually normal environment.

Walk and Gibson conclude from these interesting data that a seeing animal will be able to respond to depth as soon as it has adequate locomotion (though not necessarily to judge it accurately), this being from birth, in the case of precocial animals like sheep, goats, guinea pigs, and chicks.

The results of this last example are clearly in line with the observations of von Senden. Apparently depth perception is a very basic property of organisms, in the sense that it is resistant to manipulation of early visual experience and, in the course of normal development, appears very early in life. Walk and Gibson further suggest that the basic feature of the visual field that permits this is motion parallax—that is, the differential rate of stimulation of different parts of the receptor system as the eyes sweep across surfaces of different density gradients. Why it is that an animal will automatically avoid the gradient that sweeps across the eye more slowly (the more distant pattern) is not known.

A similar kind of attack on the problem of perceptual development has been made by a former student of Riesen's, Robert Fantz. Walk and Gibson drew conclusions about perceptual development inferred from the extent to which animals approach or avoid visual configurations representing, respectively, a near distance and a far distance. One of Fantz' studies was based on essentially the same principle but involved observations of *eye fixations* rather than whole-body movements. Since this has now become quite a popular technique for studying perception in neonates, we present it here.

Example 12–9 *Form preferences in human neonates (Fantz, 1967)*

The purpose of the study was to find out the extent to which newborn human beings can discriminate different visual forms. Infants between the ages of one and fifteen weeks were tested in a "looking chamber." This was a uniformly lighted enclosure on the ceiling of which could be placed various kinds of patterns. The infant subjects were simply placed on their backs, and the experimenter observed which pattern they fixated for the longer duration of time. This was accomplished by a peephole in the top of the chamber through which the experimenter could see which of the patterns was reflected in the infants eye. Duration of visual fixation was taken as an index of interest. Widely disparate durations between fixations would indicate that the infant (by showing a preference) was discriminating between the patterns involved. Note, however, that lack of such a difference would not necessarily indicate lack of discrimination.

Results were as follows: Infants seemed to prefer more complex patterns over simpler patterns. For example, a checkerboard was fixated longer than a uniformly colored rectangle. A bull's-eye was preferred over horizontal stripes. Secondly, a picture of a human face was strongly preferred—again, presumably because of its complexity. Color and brightness were not important determinants of fixation time.

Fantz' data are very interesting. However, it is not certain that differential visual exploration really indicates discrimination in the sense of "identity" perception. Most likely it simply represents the transitional process by which such an ability comes to be built up. As such it is of fundamental importance as a subject of scientific inquiry.

As a debate, the nature-nurture question is pointless. Both heredity and environment, both maturation and learning contribute in some measure to every aspect of perceptual and cognitive development. As a *problem for analysis*, however, it is very relevant indeed. Through the kinds of experimentation we have described above, we will make gradual progress toward anwering some of the fundamental theoretical stances taken toward the problem of perceptual development by the various schools of thought we examined earlier. So far, we cannot say which of these is the most valid. Perhaps each one of them is, in some sense, valid. The fruitfulness of each will be judged finally only in terms of the amount of useful experimentation it has generated. In any case, let it be emphasized, in contradiction to the suggestion of some writers, that the nature-nurture issue is by no means dead; as a research area it is very much alive.

THE OUTER LIMITS OF PERCEPTION

There are two problem areas in perception that because of their bizarre character usually arouse a good deal of interest in most people. These are the phenomena of *extrasensory perception* and *dermo-optical perception*. We will discuss each of these here, not necessarily because we admit their genuineness, but rather because we wish to convey to the reader the need for great caution in assessing their validity as well as the need for keeping an open mind. Strictly speaking, neither belongs to any of the theoretical traditions which we have examined in this chapter. Both stand off by themselves as empirical phenomena whose main interest lies immediately in whether they are real or fictitious.

Extrasensory Perception

The general field of so-called parapsychology, or psychical research, can be divided as follows:

1. *Extrasensory perception proper, or ESP:* Reading off correctly cards laid face down before the subject
2. *Clairvoyance:* Same as ESP, except performed with the cards at some distance from the subject
3. *Telepathy:* Transferance of thoughts or ideas between two persons
4. *Psychokinesis:* Ability to influence behavior of physical objects, e.g., dice, merely by thought
5. *Precognition:* Ability to predict events prior to their occurrence

All categories involve in some manner the notion that information can be transmitted to the brain by some channel other than those represented by the conventional sensory pathways; hence the label "extrasensory" perception.

What is the evidence for such an ability? There is a great deal that is of so uncontrolled and anecdotal a nature that it is most difficult to evaluate. One writer, J. S. Dunne, in *An Experiment with Time* (1939), for example, presented a number of cases of persons who had foreseen and predicted future happenings. Beyond this, he also constructed an elaborate theory postulating that consciousness not only extended over the past and present but also over the future. Thus with an almost unused portion of our mind, we could actually be aware of future events as if they were occurring in the present. Now it is certainly true that we can often predict the future, provided we have a grasp of present circumstances and can estimate their possible outcome. But this is different from saying that consciousness has a direct awareness of future events. Most people would be willing to predict the sun will rise tomorrow, but few would say it is certain in the same sense as perceiving the sun above them at a moment in the present.

Apart from this, such case histories as Dunne presents can be treated only with skepticism. Anecdotal evidence cannot be taken as sufficient to validate a hypothesis, particularly one as unconventional as that being considered.

Perhaps the person most responsible for an experimental approach to ESP has been J. B. Rhine of Duke University. In 1930, he commenced an intensive program of research in this area. Let us now look at some examples of his work.

Example 12–10 *Data on ESP (Rhine, 1964)*

We will consider here some early data summarized by Rhine in a 1964 book. To a reader accustomed to the typically formalized description of an experimental series, the account by Rhine (and also others of his persuasion) may seem curiously inexact. Nevertheless the results he reports are fairly compelling.

The usual procedure in these experiments, which started around 1930, involved mostly the use of special packs of cards with five designs. Subjects were asked simply to guess which card was which, either as each was removed from the pack by an experimenter or as they had been ordered by random shuffling without being further touched. Quite elaborate procedures were taken to avoid any possibility of cheating or collusion. These are obviously mandatory in such studies, whose potential payoff is so great. Results up to 1933 summarized by Rhine (1964, p. 217) involve probability values which, by any usual statistical standards, are astronomically high. His data also show—and this appears to be a crucial point in ESP—that certain subjects seem to be extraordinarily better than others. Hubert Pearce, for example, was one of Rhine's star subjects. On one occasion, he was able to name correctly 25 ESP cards in a row, a feat having chance odds of 298,023,876,953,125 to 1! Such figures as these must give us pause.

Similarly good results have been obtained in respect to psychokinesis. We will now look at some data reported by Dale (1946) (cf. Murphy, 1961).

Example 12–11 *The psychokinetic effect (Dale, 1946)*

As we have already stated, psychokinesis is the supposed ability of a subject to influence directly physical events, in this case, the fall of dice. The subjects were fifty-four students from colleges in New York City. The dice used were four standard commercial dice, 5/8 inch on a side. These were thrown by each subject down a so-called "randomizing shoot"—a device consisting of fifty-five waffles on a shoot leading down onto an enclosure. Dice were simply shaken up in a dicebox and then deposited in the top of the shoot. Different groups of subjects "tried for" as many of a certain number as possible, for example, all ones, all twos, and so on. Results are summarized in Table 12–4. The possibility of chance's operating is only 5 in 1,000.

Note also that such departure from chance cannot be explained by a hypothesis of loaded dice, since different groups were trying for different dice faces. Another point of interest is that the effect was greatest in the initial runs and gradually declined *in an orderly way* up to the fourth run. This is again a statistically signficant effect and is one that is quite often found in work on ESP.

How do we interpret results like these? There is no easy answer to this question. Taken by themselves, such studies seem to yield evidence that is unassailable. Unless we have very good reasons for not doing so, we can usually rule out fraud, incompetence, and use of subliminal sensory cues as explanations (Rhine, 1964). There seems little reason to suppose that ESP workers such as Rhine are willing to pursue a career of calculated dishonesty in a general sector of life which demands, over everything else, honesty. Some critics, however, have indeed suggested this. Martin Gardner (1966), *Scientific American* mathematics editor, for example, writing in *The New York Review of Books*, has suggested that one of Rhine's series, the famous Pratt-Pearce distance tests, could readily

Table 12-4 Results of psychokinesis experiment in terms of deviation from chance

Number of trials	31,104
Hits obtained	5,355
Hits expected by chance	5,184
Deviation	+171
Mean score per run	4.132
Standard deviation	65.727
Critical ratio	2.60
p value	.005

be explained by cheating. These clairvoyance studies, done with each subject located in a different building on the Duke campus, were remarkably successful. But Gardner suggests that one of the two, Pearce, could easily have left his cubicle in the library, sneaked back to Pratt's office, and read the cards through the transom as Pratt was recording their order. It is difficult to credit a hypothesis of such skulduggery, yet there have been documented cases in which such did occur. This is one of the reasons why many professional psychologists remain very dubious about ESP.

There are also other reasons. Probably thousands of studies of ESP have been done by investigators all over the world. They are not difficult to perform. Yet only a fraction of these turn out to yield positive conclusions, such as the two studies described above (cf., for example, Sprinthall & Lubetkin, 1965). Furthermore, the most positive of these usually have depended on the unusual skill of particular persons who seem to "have ESP." If true, this would suggest that such subjects possess to a high degree a special ability not possessed by others. By itself, this is not implausible. Any trait follows such a pattern in a large population.

Yet we also find that the high-ability subjects do not always maintain a high level of performance. Such failures are usually explained as being due to extraneous circumstances—feeling ill, being worried or nervous, being fatigued, and so on—but they might also be explained as due to the operation of chance. If we were to give a thousand subjects some ESP tests, it is almost certain that of these a few would perform extremely well, just by chance. If we then were to concentrate on further studies of these few subjects only, we might well expect that if their earlier results have been due only to chance, they might now show fluctuations, if not a drift to a chance level. However, if we were to accept the hypothesis that they have ESP, we could quite easily find reasons that would explain any declines in performance they might show. The critical question would then be whether good performers tend, on the whole, to maintain a consistently high level. Obviously, most of those committed to a belief in ESP feel that they do (e.g., Rhine, 1964; Bateman & Soal, 1950; Murphy, 1961). Most psychologists remain skeptical.

The final problem concerns the explanation of ESP, assuming that it is a genuine phenomenon. At present, it can be stated categorically that no explanation exists. For one thing, if it involves some kind of physical energy transmission, it should follow the usual inverse-square law governing energy exchanges over distance. *It does not.* Clairvoyance and telepathy are no better at 2 feet than at 200 miles (cf. Rhine, 1964). This has led Rhine to conclude that it is a purely psychical rather than a physical phenomenon. Well and good; but what exactly does this mean? We have no answers.

In conclusion, we can only recommend to the reader that he adopt toward ESP phenomena an attitude of great caution. While many individual studies appear to demonstrate telepathy, clairvoyance, and psychokinesis at very high levels of statistical significance, there are also many others that have found nothing. Furthermore, the alleged properties of ESP appear to fall outside the theoretical explanation of phenomena we know anything about.

Dermooptical Perception

Dermooptical perception refers to the ability to sense color or optical stimulation through touch. One of the first accounts of this phenomenon was given by the well-known French novelist Jules Romains in his book *Eyeless Vision* (1924). More recently it was "rediscovered" in Russia by Isaac Goldberg, who claimed to have observed this ability in a twenty-two-year-old girl named Rosa Kuleshova. According to the report, she was able to read newspapers when blindfolded simply by moving her fingers across the printed page. A number of other such cases quickly followed this one in Russia. In the United States, after several rounds in the popular press, dermooptical perception was taken up seriously by Richard Youtz of Barnard College in New York. He dealt with the case of a Mrs. Patricia Stanley, who allegedly had the ability to discriminate colors with her fingers, though she was not able to read print in that way. Youtz (1966) did not claim "vision" but hypothesized that different colors generate very slight thermal differences that can be detected by touch, particularly with practice.

Again we are faced with a perceptual phenomenon which, if valid, is almost as extraordinary as ESP. What a boon to the blind such an ability would be, especially if it were improvable through proper instruction. Can we really sense words or colors through our skin?

Again, we must urge skepticism. It is certainly true that we have thermal receptors in our skin, but their sensitivity is not that great. It is extremely doubtful if such differences as might exist between black letters and the white paper on which they are printed or between different colors having the same surface characteristics could possibly be large enough to be perceptible. Purely apart from this, in the reported cases there appears to be a distinct possibility of cheating—which, if true, tells us more about properties of the subject's personalities than about properties of their perceptual ability. The strongest case for such a possibility has been made by Martin Gardner, to whom we referred in connection with ESP. According to him, all the blindfold procedures used in the positive instances reported were such as to allow the subject, by sniffing or moving his facial musculature, to form a large enough aperture between the blindfold and one side of his nose to permit him to see any object in front of him. Such "nose peeking" is a standard procedure of magicians and stage clairvoyants. Gardner's suggestion to Youtz that he employ a box over the head to eliminate such a practice was apparently not taken up by this investigator. Youtz has continued to affirm his findings, and he claims that anyone who doubts them can readily prove them to himself. We would concur in this advice and pass it on to the reader.

BEYOND PERCEPTION

There remain still many questions into which the study of perception leads fairly logically. Perhaps the most important of these is the research to do with cognitive processes and thinking, and, of course, the formal problem of learning. Perception, learning, and thinking may all be regarded as related, as Forgus (1966, p. 1) has pointed out, in the sense that all involve *information extraction*. At the same time, the core of the work and theorizing done in these three areas flows from somewhat different traditions. Certainly, many of those workers whose major interest has been perception—for example, the gestaltists—have concerned themselves with learning and thinking. The researches of Duncker (1945), Katona (1940), and Wertheimer (1945) on thought processes are good cases in point. However, the most central contemporary work on thinking seems to emerge more directly from behaviorism and functionalism.

These we will examine in detail in the next chapter. Thus, just as one of the central themes of Section Three—social perception—led into this chapter, so here our analysis of perception leads us to a consideration of the processes of learning and thinking.

CONCLUSION

Most of this section has dealt with visual perception. For human beings and many of the lower animals this certainly seems to be the sensory channel most capable of yielding rich information content about the world. Yet, as the reader will recall, the British philosophers felt that touch is even more basic and ultimately supplies a standard against which visual experience is judged. There seems to be a good deal of truth in this notion. Haptic space given by active touch—that is, touch together with the sensory feedback occasioned by moving tactile receptors systems over surfaces—is a rich one indeed and used to its limit can almost compete with sight.

To realize this, we have only to consider the case of that extraordinary woman Helen Keller. Born a normal child, she contracted in early years a malady that produced blindness and deafness. Until adolescence she lived totally at the mercy of these handicaps, more an animal than a human being, given to violent outbursts of temper, uncontrollable, and uncommunicative. The miracle—about which a biographical play was written—was brought about through the dedicated efforts of an Irish nurse, Anne Sullivan, who taught her the basic meaning of symbols and of communication—the notion that a certain sound she could emit and feel, though not herself hear, went with a certain tactually experienced object. So for Helen the feel of water from a pump running coldly over her fingers came to be definable by a word.

From this time on, the progress made by Helen with Anne's help was remarkable to say the least. She attended one of the best girl's colleges in New England, wrote a book before she was graduated *summa cum laude,* learned several languages, wrote more books, and conversed and corresponded with some of the best minds of our time—all this without the benefit of two of our most important sensory channels.

The story of Helen Keller is perhaps an unparalleled one. Few of us could face and conquer such a grave handicap. But unusual as her case is, it does serve to point out to us the extraordinary potentiality that our sensory receptors have for extracting information about the world. On this are built up all our abilities, our capacity to learn, to solve problems, and to think, and, in the end, to transcend all these in creativity.

SECTION FOUR: REFERENCES

ALLPORT, F. H. *Theories of perception and the concept of structure.* New York: Wiley, 1955.

ALLPORT, G., & POSTMAN, L. *The psychology of rumor.* New York: Holt, 1947.

AMES, A. *Some demonstrations concerned with the origin and nature of our sensations: A laboratory manual.* Hanover, N.H.: Dartmouth Eye Institute, 1946.

ATTNEAVE, F. Some informational aspects of visual perception. *Psychological Review,* 1954, **61,** 183–198.

BARTLEY, S. H. *Principles of perception.* New York: Harper, 1958.

BATEMAN, F., & SOAL, S. G. Long-distance experiments in telepathy. *Journal of the Society for Psychical Research,* 1950, **35,** 257–272.

BRUNER, J. S., & GOODMAN, C. C. Value and need as organizing factors in perception. *Journal of Abnormal and Social Psychology,* 1947, **42,** 33–44.

BRUNER, J. S., & POSTMAN, L. Perception, cognition and behavior. In Bruner & D. Krech (Eds.), *Perception and personality: A symposium.* Durham, N.C.: Duke University Press, 1950.

COHEN, W. Spatial and textural characteristics of the Ganzfeld. *American Journal of Psychology,* 1957, **70**, 403–410.

DALE, L. A. The psychokinetic effect: The first A.S.P.R. experiment. *Journal of the American Society for Psychical Research,* 1946, **40**, 123–151.

DEMBER, W. N. *Psychology of perception.* New York: Holt, 1960.

DUNCKER, K. On problem solving. *Psychological Monographs,* 1945, **58** (5), 270.

DUNNE, J. W. *An experiment with time.* London: Faber, 1939.

ENGEL, W. Optische Untersuchungen am Ganzfeld. I. Mitteilung: Die Ganzfeldanordnung. *Psychologische Forschung,* 1930, **13**, 1–5.

ERIKSEN, C. W. Discrimination and learning without awareness: A methodological survey and evaluation. *Psychological Review,* 1960, **67**, 279–300.

FANTZ, R. L. Visual perception in infancy. In E. E. Hess & H. L. Rheingold (Eds.), *Early behavior.* New York, Wiley, 1967.

FORGUS, R. H. *Perception: The basic process in cognitive development.* New York: McGraw-Hill, 1966.

GANZ, L. Mechanism of the figural after-effect, *Psychological Review,* 1966, **73**, 128–150.

GARDNER, M. ESP: A scientific evaluation by C. E. M. Hansel. *The New York Review of Books,* 1966, **6** (9), 27–29.

GIBSON, E. J., & WALK, R. D. The "Visual Cliff." *Scientific American,* 1960, **202**, 64–71.

GIBSON, J. J. *The perception of the visual world.* Cambridge, Mass.: Riverside Press, 1950. (a)

GIBSON, J. J. The perception of visual surfaces. *American Journal of Psychology,* 1950, **63**, 367–384. (b)

GIBSON, J. J. Perception as a function of stimulation. In S. Koch (Ed.), *Psychology: A study of a science.* Vol. I. New York: McGraw-Hill, 1958.

GIBSON, J. J. The useful dimensions of sensitivity. *American Psychologist,* 1963, **18**, 1–15.

GIBSON, J. J., & WADDELL, D. Homogeneous retinal stimulation and visual perception. *American Journal of Psychology,* 1952, **65**, 263–270.

GOMBRICH, E. H. *Art and illusion: A study in the psychology of pictorial representation.* (2d ed.) New York: Bollingen Foundation, 1961.

GREEN, S. *American art: A historical survey.* New York: Ronald Press, 1966.

GREGORY, R. L., & WALLACE, J. G. Recovery from early blindness. *Experimental Psychology Society Monographs,* 1963, No. 2.

HEBB, D. O. *Organization of behavior.* New York: Wiley, 1949.

HELMHOLTZ, H. VON. *A treatise on physiological optics.* New York: Dover, 1962.

HELSON, H. Some factors and implications of color constancy. In D. C. Beardslee & Michael Wertheimer (Eds.), *Readings in perception.* New York: Van Nostrand, 1958.

HERING, E. *Beitrage zur Physiologie,* Part 1. Leipzig: Engelmann, 1861.

HOCHBERG, J. E. Nativism and empiricism in perception. In L. Postman (Ed.), *Psychology in the making: Histories of selected research problems.* New York: Knopf, 1962.

HOCHBERG, J. E., & BROOKS, V. The psychophysics of form: Reversible-perspective drawings of spatial objects. *American Journal of Psychology,* 1960, **73**, 337–354.

HOCHBERG, J. E., & McALISTER, E. A. A quantitative approach to figural "goodness." *Journal of experimental Psychology,* 1953, **46**, 361–364.

HOCHBERG, J. E., TRIEBEL, W., & SEAMAN, G. Color adaptation under conditions of homogeneous visual stimulation (Ganzfeld). *Journal of experimental Psychology,* 1951, **41**, 153–159.

HOLWAY, A. H., & BORING, E. G. Determinants of apparent visual size with distance variant. *American Journal of Psychology,* 1941, **54**, 21–37.

ITTLESON, W. H., & KILPATRICK, F. P. Experiments in perception. *Scientific American,* 1951, **185** (2), 50–55.

KANT, I. *Prolegomena to any future metaphysics.* Chicago: Open Court, 1949.

KATONA, G. *Organizing and memorizing: Studies in the psychology of learning and teaching.* New York: Columbia University Press, 1940.

KATZ, D. *The world of colour.* London: Kegan Paul, Trench, Trubner, 1935.

KENDLER, H. H. *Basic psychology.* New York: Appleton-Century-Crofts, 1963.

KILPATRICK, F. P. *Explorations in transactional psychology.* New York: New York University Press, 1961.

KOFFKA, K. *Principles of Gestalt psychology.* New York: Harcourt, Brace, 1935.

KÖHLER, W. *Gestalt psychology.* New York: Liveright Publishing Corporation, 1947.

KÖHLER, W., & WALLACH, H. Figural after-effects. *Proceedings of the American Philosophical Society,* 1944, **88**, 269–357.

KOPFERMANN, H. Psychologische untersuchungen über die Wirkung Zweidimensionaler Darstellung körperbcher geblde. *Psychologische Forschung,* 1930, **13**, 293–364.

KRECH, D., & CRUTCHFIELD, R. S. *Elements of psychology.* New York: Knopf, 1958.

LOCKE, J. An essay concerning human understanding. In E. A. Burtt (Ed.), *English philosophers from Bacon to Mill.* New York: Modern Library, Random House, 1939.

LOTZE, R. H. *Grundziige der Psychologie: Diktat ans den Vorlesungen von Hermann Lotze.* Leipzig: Huzel, 1881.

METZGER, W. Untersuchungen am Ganzfeld: II. Zur Phänomenologie des homogenen Ganzfelds. *Psychologische Forschung,* 1930, **13**, 6–29.

MURPHY, G. *Challenge of psychical research: A primer of parapsychology.* New York: Harper, 1961.

OSGOOD, C. E., & HEYER, A. W., JR. A new interpretation of figural after-effects. *Psychological Review,* 1952, **59**, 98–118.

PLATO, *Phaedo.* In I. Edman (Ed.), *The works of Plato.* New York: Modern Library, Random House, 1928.

POSTMAN, L., BRUNER, J. S., & McGINNIES, E. M. Personal values as selective factors in perception. *Journal of Abnormal and Social Psychology,* 1948, **43**, 142–154.

POSTMAN, L., & SCHNEIDER, B. H. Personal values, visual recognition, and recall. *Psychological Review,* 1951, **58**, 271–284.

PRITCHARD, R. M., HERON, W., & HEBB, D. O. Visual perception approached by the method of stabilized images. *Canadian Journal of Psychology,* 1960, **14**, 67–77.

RHINE, J. B. *Extra-sensory perception.* Boston; B. Humphries, 1964.

RIESEN, A. H. Arrested vision. *Scientific American,* 1950, **183**, 16–19.

RIESEN, A. H. Stimulation as a requirement for growth and function in behavioral development. In D. W. Fiske & S. R. Maddi (Eds.), *Functions of varied experience.* Homewood, Ill.: Dorsey, 1961.

RILEY, D. A. Memory for form. In L. Postman (Ed.), *Psychology in the making: Histories of selected research problems.* New York: Knopf, 1962.

ROMAINS, J. *Eyeless vision.* New York: Putnam, 1924.

RUBIN, E. Figure and ground. In D. C. Beardslee & Michael Wertheimer (Eds.), *Readings in perception.* New York: Van Nostrand, 1958.

SOLOMON, R. L., & HOWES, D. H. Word frequency, personal values and visual duration thresholds. *Psychological Review,* 1951, **58**, 256–270.

SPRINTHALL, R. C., & LUBETKIN, B. S. ESP: Motivation as a factor in ability. *Journal of Psychology,* 1965, **60**, 313–318.

TITCHENER, E. B. *Lectures on the experimental psychology of the thought process.* New York: Macmillan, 1909.

VON SENDEN, M. *Space and sight.* London: Methuen, 1960.

WALK, R. D., & GIBSON, E. J. A comparative and analytical study of visual depth perception. *Psychological Monographs,* 1961, **75** (Whole No. 519).

WAPNER, S., WERNER, H., & CHANDLER, K. A. Experiments on sensory-tonic field theory of perception: I. Effect of extraneous stimulation on the visual perception of verticality. *Journal of Experimental Psychology,* 1951, **42**, 341–345. (a)

WERNER, H., WAPNER, S., & CHANDLER, K. A. Experiments on sensory-tonic field theory of perception: II. Effect of supported and unsupported tilt of the body on visual perception of verticality. *Journal of Experimental Psychology,* 1951, **42**, 346–350. (b)

WAPNER, S., WERNER, H., & MORANT, R. B. Experiments on sensory-tonic field theory of perception: III. Effect of body rotation on the visual perception of verticality. *Journal of Experimental Psychology,* 1951, **42**, 351–357.

WERNER, H., & WAPNER, S. Toward a general theory of perception. *Psychological Review,* 1952, **59**, 324–338.

WERTHEIMER, MAX. *Productive thinking.* New York: Harper, 1945.

WERTHEIMER, MAX. Principles of perceptual organization. In D. C. Beardslee & Michael Wertheimer (Eds.), *Readings in perception.* New York: Van Nostrand, 1958.

WERTHEIMER, Michael. Hebb and Senden on the role of learning in perception. *American Journal of Psychology,* 1951, **64**, 133–137.

WITTREICH, W. J. The Honi phenomenon: A case of selective perceptual distortion. *Journal of Abnormal and Social Psychology,* 1952, **47**, 705–712.

WOHLWILL, J. F. The development of "over-constancy" in space perception. In L. P. Lipsitt & C. C. Spiker (Eds.), *Advances in child development and behavior.* Vol. I. New York: Academic, 1963.

WULF, F. Über die Veranderung von Vorstellungen (Gedächtnis und Gestalt). *Psychologische Forschung,* 1922, **1,** 333–373.

YOUTZ, R. P. Dermo-optical perception. *Science,* 1966, **152** (3725), 1108.

SECTION FIVE
BEHAVIORISTIC MODELS IN PSYCHOLOGY

"Habit is thus the enormous fly-wheel of society, its most precious conservative agent. It alone is what keeps us all within the bounds of ordinance, and saves the children of fortune from the envious uprisings of the poor. It alone prevents the hardest and most repulsive walks of life from being deserted by those brought up to tread therein. It keeps the fisherman and deck-hand at sea through the winter; it holds the miner in his darkness, and nails the countryman to his log-cabin and his lonely farm through all the months of snow; it protects us from invasion by the natives of the desert and the frozen zone. It dooms us all to fight out the battle of life upon the lines of our nature or our early choice, and to make the best of a pursuit that disagrees, because there is no other for which we are fitted, and it is too late to begin again. It keeps different social strata from mixing. Already at the age of twenty-five you see the professional mannerism settling down on the young commercial traveler, on the young doctor, on the young minister, on the young counselor-at-law. You see the little lines of cleavage running through the character, the tricks of thought, the prejudices, the ways of the "shop," in a word, from which the man

can by-and-by no more escape than his coat sleeve can suddenly fall into a new set of folds. On the whole, it is best he should not escape. It is best for the world that in most of us, by the age of thirty, the character has set like plaster, and will never soften again."
(William James, 1890)

"Man is, of course, a system—roughly speaking, a machine—like every other system in nature subject to the unescapable and uniform laws of all nature, **but** *the human system, in the horizons of our contemporary scientific view, is unique in being most highly self-regulatory. Among the products of man's hands, we are already familiar with machines which regulate themselves in various ways. From this standpoint, the method of investigating the system of man is precisely the same as that of any other system: decomposition into parts, study of the significance of each part, study of the connections of the parts, study of the relations with the environment, and finally the interpretation on this basis of its general workings and administration, if this be within the capacity of man...."*
(Ivan P. Pavlov, 1941)

PROLOGUE

In the last section, we looked at the problem of how human beings perceive the world in which they live. The emphasis was on extraction of information from the sensory input that impinges on us every day of our lives. Here we will consider mainly the problem of *output*—that is to say, the actions or responses organisms perform in order to adapt to the environment they occupy and how these actions change and crystallize with time.

The two quotations given above, one from the American psychologist William James, the other from the Russian psychologist Ivan P. Pavlov, both reflect concern for this problem of action—habit, as James calls it, or "general workings . . . of the system of man," as Pavlov calls it.

Both writers are quite positive in their view of habits. For Pavlov, habits are highly changeable and can lead to a host of noble realizations of man's potential. For James, habits are the very stuff of which a society is built. Both these men were major contributors to the development of modern behavioristic models.

The passage by William James is a graphic description of habitual behavior. Yet, in his very influential textbook, *The Principles of Psychology*, written at the close of the last century, James began by defining psychology as the science of *mental life*. His definition of psychology in terms of mind seems to be at odds with his emphasis on habit, which is, of course, behavior. This apparent contradiction leads us to our first important idea in behavioristic psychology: the problem of the proper subject matter of psychology. The problem was not, however, new with James; it has persisted in philosophy and psychology from the Greeks to the present day.

Idea of Objectivism

The problem can be broken into two parts, in the sense that there have been two allied controversies in the history of psychology as a science. The first has been concerned with the proper methodology for gathering information in any science. The second part is the question of what evidence is admissible in the science of psychology. Discussion of objectivism has passed through several stages, each forming a hurdle of resistance to the achievement of agreement among theorists of the mind. Perhaps the first step was the development of naturalistic explanations of the nature of mind. The particular way in which this problem is expressed for a science of psychology has concerned the difficulty of observing the content of the minds of others. William James appears to have been concerned about this problem, for he placed the chapter on habit at the beginning of his book and emphasized the automatic quality of such behavior. Yet, the problem remains: what sort of evidence can a psychologist accept when dealing with the subject matter of mental life? It is quite clear that we cannot look directly into other minds and thereby know what is happening in them. The mind of another person is not open to our direct observation. Of the various strategies which psychologists have adopted to deal with this problem, we will consider in this section those methods which rely on the *objective observation of behavior* as the basis for the study of mental life. Therefore, we have called the section Behavioristic Models in Psychology.

Aristotle emphasized naturalistic explanation of psychic phenomena by his stress on observational methods for classifying the events in the mind. In his writings, he discussed the laws of associative memory and appealed to direct evidence, a tendency toward classification of observed cases which foreshadowed modern methodology.

In his speculations, Aristotle anticipated both Francis Bacon, who championed empirical science, and the later development of theories of psychology which were based on actual observation of objects of a material sort. A little later, we will examine further historical development of objectivism; now let us turn to a second major theme of this chapter, that of the mind as process.

The Idea of Process in Psychology:
The Stream of Consciousness

Physics and other sciences deal with situations which can be reproduced again and again for purposes of validation. But psychology has no such easy task in its search for the truth about behavior. It is a truism to say that life involves change. In the study of psychology nothing stands still and waits to be observed again. Growth and maturation, the interference of later activity, decay and old age all bring profound changes of a sort which we all observe about us. Further, as we shall see, there are even more subtle processes going on in the organism which prevent exact reobservation of a static kind such as in the case of other sciences. Certainly the Greeks were aware of this too. Heraclitus' dictum is something of a cliché: "You can never step into the same river twice." Again, we can savor the thought of William James about process as a psychological reality:

> Thought is in constant change.—I do not mean necessarily that no one state of mind has any duration—even if true, that would be hard to establish.... [The result on] which I wish to lay stress ... is this, that *no state once gone can recur*

and be identical with what it was before [James, 1890].

The idea which dominates James' passage is that *time* is a relevant dimension in psychological science and that therefore process is a central theme in the study of behavior. We shall return again to this idea when we begin our study of the *process* of learning. Now we turn to the third idea which will structure our discussion in this chapter, the idea of *function*.

The Idea of Function in Psychology: The Utility Dimension in Behavior

If any event in recent Western thought can be described as an intellectual explosion, it was the publication in 1859 by Charles Darwin of his theory of evolution (Darwin, 1859). Its appearance shattered many then current preconceptions. Although evolutionary theory is commonplace in our thinking today, in Darwin's time it aroused a storm of criticism and controversy. In its simplest terms, the theory held that species have arisen by natural selection of particular attributes, behavioral as well as morphological, *which favor survival,* and that those attributes which serve some function persist because they lead to survival.

Darwin's ideas were paralleled by the ideas of a school of psychologists called *pragmatists* in the development of functionalism. The pragmatic theorists suggested that the validation of any knowledge must be in terms of its consequences, values, or utility. The prime target which the movement opposed was the structuralist tradition which had grown up in Europe. In this passage from James Rowland Angell, later president of Yale University, the juxtaposition of the two schools is sharply made:

> ...functional psychology [is concerned] with the effort to discern and portray the typical *operations* of consciousness under actual life conditions, as over against the attempt [by structuralism] to analyze and describe its elementary and complex *contents* [Angell, 1907].

However, it was Angell's senior at the University of Chicago, John Dewey, who was the pioneer in the functionalist tradition. His position was strongly against the psychology approach of his time which insisted on breaking behavior down into elements and studying it in a fractionated way. One of Dewey's most famous and truly prophetic papers was entitled "The Reflex-Arc Concept in Psychology." It appeared in 1896, and the ideas expressed in it might have been said much later by critics of behaviorism, which had not arisen at that time. We include the following passage from that paper to present the flavor of Dewey's concerns. While the passage introduces many concepts for which the reader is not yet prepared, the dominant theme should be emphasized at this point in our discussion:

> The fact is that stimulus and response are not distinctions of existence, but...distinctions of function, or part played, with reference to reaching or maintaining an end.... There is no question of consciousness of stimulus *as* stimulus, of response *as* response. There is simply a continuously ordered sequence of acts, all adapted in themselves and in the order of their sequence, to reach a certain objective end, the reproduction of the species, the preservation of life, locomotion to a certain place. The end has got thoroughly organized into the means [Dewey, 1896].

The Study of Animals

A fourth tradition aided the development of behaviorism, namely *the study of animal behavior,* which arose after Darwin. With Darwin's pronouncement that species are continuous from man down to the lowest forms of animal life, a controversy arose over the nature of animal minds. The adherents of evolutionary theory held that animals did have intelligent mental life and were capable of cognitive activity which had previously been thought to occur only in human beings.

A succession of books on the animal mind appeared. Among the earliest of these were those of George Romanes. His method of gathering evidence was to collect anecdotes about the behavior and cognitive processes of animals. His books were filled with stories of problem solving in animals.

Romanes was followed by C. Lloyd Morgan, also a Darwinian and one of the founders of comparative psychology as we know it. Morgan differed from Romanes, however, in one very important aspect: he advanced a canon of parsimony which placed a strong burden on psychologists to strive after simple explanations when they observed the behavior of animals. Combined with his dictum of parsimony, contained in the following passage, is a plea for methodological sophistication, which would be timely in any era:

> For in the study of animal psychology as a branch of scientific inquiry, it is necessary that accurate observation, and a sound knowledge of the biological relationships of animals, should go hand in hand with a thorough appreciation of the methods and results of modern psychology....
>
> There is one basic principle.... *In no case may we interpret an action as the outcome of the exercise of a higher psychical faculty, if it can be interpreted as the outcome of the exercise of one which stands lower in the psychological scale* [Morgan, 1894].

Morgan himself wrote a book on animal psychology which was, like that of Romanes, largely based on anecdotes and descriptions of problem solving by pets. Perhaps for our discussion here the most interesting instance of influence which Morgan exerted was on Edward Thorndike, whom we will discuss more fully later. Thorndike studied Morgan's writing while a student at Wesleyan University. Thorndike's copy of Morgan's book, which is in the Wesleyan library, has marginal notes and marked passages which seem to document this influence. When he began laboratory studies of behavior, Thorndike's experiments bore a remarkable likeness to the anecdotes which he marked in Morgan's book. So, from chance influences, a science has developed.

In summary, then, four traditions in Western thought have led to the behavioristic dominance of American psychology. The first influenced the methods to be used: observation of objects in the world. This methodological stance is called *empiricism*. As it developed this heritage, psychology became the study of observed behavior. The second stressed the notion of studying process—that is, acts over time. In a third, evolutionary theory emphasized adaptive function, and psychologists became interested in seeking to understand the way in which man adapts himself to his environment. Finally, the study of animal behavior led to theory building based on the behavior of lower animals. As we emphasized early in this book, the use of animals in theory building is not intended to answer comparative problems but rather to permit the examination of behavior as it occurs in simple forms.

Having skimmed rapidly through the antecedents of behavioristic models, we can now limit our discussion to that single problem which has dominated the thinking of the functionalists and the behaviorists: the process of learning. This section, then, will emphasize the study of learning, its historical development, and finally, an examination of a few current models of the learning process. Our presentation will be selective and will focus rather sharply on ideas and selected experimental illustrations of problems which arose during the development of learning theories.

CHAPTER 13

THE DEVELOPMENT OF THEORIES OF THE LEARNING PROCESS

At the turn of the present century the dominant cultural concern was with things practical and with maximizing efficiency. True to this cultural environment, psychology turned to the problem of understanding the learning process. As populations increased in size and democratic principles became entrenched in the West, nations turned their interest to solving the problems of providing every child with a good education. To do this meant that the conditions under which learning best proceeded should be explored and understood. Of course, as we have pointed out, theories of learning did not simply spring into being *de novo*. They had long traditions behind them which shaped the forms which they took. This tradition arose in philosophy beginning with the Greeks and continuing in the philosophical speculation of the British empiricists. One of the main empirical problems with which this tradition attempted to deal was the nature of the association of ideas.

Among the first statements about the associative nature of events in the human mind was Aristotle's writing on memory and recollection. He stated that the process of recollecting involved the association of ideas, because the two usually occurred together.

Aristotle's notions of order in the train of thought persisted through a thousand years in the teaching of the scholastics. The first man to rediscover Aristotle's principle of contiguity was Thomas Hobbes in 1651, who added to it the principle that the stream of thought reflected personal experience.

A second English philosopher, John Locke, advanced the associationistic view of the connection of ideas because of prior experience. He separates, in the following passage, ideas which have a natural connection and those which are the result of experience.

> ... Some of our *Ideas* have a natural correspondence and connection one with another: It is the office and excellency of our reason to trace these, and hold them together in that union and correspondence which is founded in their peculiar beings. Besides this, there is another connection of ideas wholly owing to chance or custom: Ideas that in themselves are not at all of kin, come to be so united in some men's minds, that it is very hard to separate them; they always keep in company, and the one no sooner at any time comes into the understanding, but its associate appears with it; and if they are more than two, which are thus united, the whole gang, always inseparable, show themselves together [Locke, 1700].

Following Locke, George Berkeley made an explicit statement that the mind operated according to the principles of association. Although Aristotle, Hobbes, Locke, and Berkeley all wrote of the association of ideas, David Hume, who evidently did not know of their work, refined the notions. He impelled philosophical explanations of the manner in which associations occur toward the problems which modern psychologists still debate: the laws of contiguity, similarity, and effect, which govern the formation of associations.

We may skip ahead from Hume to a much later writer, Herbert Spencer. In his *Principles of Psychology,* which appeared in 1855, he focused on two sources of habits in a given person: The first source is the direct experience of that individual. The second source of habit is the inherited experience from the person's ancestors. Darwin's *Origin of Species* was yet to appear, in 1859, and therefore Spencer was already concerned with mechanisms of inheritance before he became aware of Darwin.

> The multitudinous facts commonly cited to illustrate the doctrine of association of ideas, supports it. It is in harmony with the general truth, that from the ignorance of the infant the ascent is by *slow steps* to the knowledge of the adult. All theories and all methods of education take it for granted—are alike based on the belief that the more frequently states of consciousness are made to follow one another in a certain order, the stronger becomes their tendency to suggest one another in that order.... The only orders of psychical sequence which do not obviously come within this general law, are those which we class as reflex and instinctive—those which are as well performed on the first occasion as ever afterwards—those which are apparently established antecedent to experience [Spencer, 1855].

This passage calls attention to the fact that some behavior is reflexive and not learned. Further, it suggests that instinctive behavior is vital to the individual.

Again, having followed a slightly different path through history, we have arrived at the turn of the present century. Next we will examine the theories and experimental work of four men of that time whose early approaches to the study of learning have profoundly influenced the field as it is today.

EARLY APPROACHES TO THE STUDY OF THE LEARNING PROCESS

Russian Reflexology: I. P. Pavlov

A major source of influence on modern learning theory came out of the physiological tradition in Russia. The important names are Sechenov and Pavlov. These men, even before the Russian Revolution, had shown an anti-mentalistic inclination in their study of psychology. Sechenov's *Reflexes of the Brain,* which appeared in 1863, advanced a theory which stated that mental functions are fundamentally physiological. He held that a knowledge of the brain would provide us with an understanding of psychical life.

Ivan Pavlov was very impressed by Sechenov's edict of objectivism, and he went on to apply himself diligently for all of his long life to experimental work in the laboratory. Pavlov has been described as the great model of the dedicated scientist. While the Russian revolt raged around his laboratory, he admonished his students to stick to their workbenches. But, again, the ideas of these men can be better understood if we explore the history of the concepts which they inherited and so skillfully reworked into a theme which still dominates in psychology. The basic concept is the reflex.

As is true in many scientific discoveries, Pavlov's great contributions to psychology arose from observations of an accidental nature. To say that his original discoveries were accidental, however, in no way detracts from his brilliance involved in making the correct interpretation of the observations. Pavlov received the Nobel prize for his work on the digestion of animals, mostly dogs. In the course of his work, he wished to look into the stomach of a living, and, if possible, eating animal, and observe the digestive juices which were secreted during eating. To accomplish this, he developed an ingenious operation which opened up the animal's stomach to observation.

Using great surgical skill, Pavlov made an artificial channel from the stomach out through the side of the animal. The stomach thus had a fistula, as it was called, through which Pavlov was able to observe secretions. As in many such preparations, the presence of food was a source of contamination which made it difficult to measure the secretory substances in a pure way. To combat this difficulty, Pavlov used a simple operation in which food fed to an animal did not reach the stomach but was taken out at the level of the esophagus through a tube fitted into the animal's throat. Pavlov observed that stomach secretions occurred even though no food actually reached the stomach. Consequently, he deduced that learning had occurred. That is to say, the sight and taste of the food had come to elicit secretions originally brought on by food in contact with the stomach. In further experiments, Pavlov observed that a variety of stimuli could apparently come to connote to the animal the arrival of food and that the animal would then make so-called preparatory responses, for example, salivation or orientation of the head toward the place where the food was usually presented.

To those who have worked with animals in domestic situations, this situation may scarcely seem surprising. Certainly, any dairy farmer is well aware that the rattling of his pails as he comes into the barn acts as a signal to the cows to release their flow of milk. In a similar way, our pet dog will respond to the sound of our tapping his dish with a spoon by rushing into the kitchen and salivating copiously. However, we should not underestimate the importance of Pavlov's observations. Hindsight may blind us to the brilliance of his work. He himself called attention to the commonplace nature of conditioning, as the following quotation from his paper before the International Congress of Medicine held in Madrid in 1903 shows:

> I have stated easily and exactly reproducible facts. It is evident that many striking instances of animal training belong to the same category as some of our phenomena, and they have bourne witness for a long time to a constant lawfulness in some of the psychical manifestations in animals. It is to be regretted that science has so long overlooked these facts [Pavlov, 1928].

With the development of the classical conditioning situation, as it came to be called, Pavlov brought the learning process into the laboratory and was able to demonstrate carefully, under controlled conditions, a basic fact of learning. He showed clearly that a stimulus which prior to conditioning did not result in a particular response was later capable of eliciting that response. In his particular case, the sound of a tone which was not followed by definite salivation before the experiment would, after it was paired with food, cause the animal to salivate. Let us consider, in some detail, one of Pavlov's experiments. After we have done so, we can reexamine the situation to understand the importance of each part of the experimental procedures:

Example 13–1 *An experiment in classical conditioning: A psychical process observed under controlled conditions (Pavlov, 1928)*

As a result of his work with gastric secretions, Pavlov conceived of experiments in which salivation would be brought under the control of stimuli which were formerly neutral to the animal. He developed an operation in which a small tube was implanted in the duct of one of the glands which normally secretes saliva into the mouth. This arrangement permitted an actual count of the drops of saliva secreted by the animals under a variety of experimental conditions. In order to induce salivation in the first place, he made his animals hungry before the experiments and then presented them with a stimulus which would elicit salivation automatically without prior learning, for example, dry meat powder or weak acid squirted into the mouth. These stimuli Pavlov called the *unconditioned stimuli* (UCS) because they elicited the response without conditioning. Pavlov was able to condition his dogs to make the salivary response to a previously neutral stimulus, such as a metronome, by pairing the neutral stimulus with the unconditioned stimulus. The neutral stimulus was given the name *conditioned stimulus* (CS) because it *acquired* its capacity to elicit the response.

Pavlov's experimental situation is shown in Figure 13–1. The setup was designed to minimize distraction to the animal and to allow the dog to be quite comfortable and under minimal restraint. After some training, the animals would stand quietly in the apparatus during an experiment without showing signs of distress. The stimulus used in this particular experiment was a tuning fork. All events during the experiment were controlled by automatic devices to allow a careful control and accurate recording of the results of the experiment.

The experimenter began the experiment by sounding the tone, and 7 or 8 seconds after this stimulus began, he moved a plate containing a small quantity of dry meat powder into reach of the dog's mouth. No salivation occurred when the tone sounded, but when the dog began to eat the meat, a large flow of saliva was observed. The combinations of food and tone were presented three times a day, with varying amounts of time between each presentation, or trial. In order to assess the strength of learning, the tone was presented alone for 30 seconds, and the amount of saliva which the animal secreted was measured. After ten presentations of the paired stimuli, there was only a slight

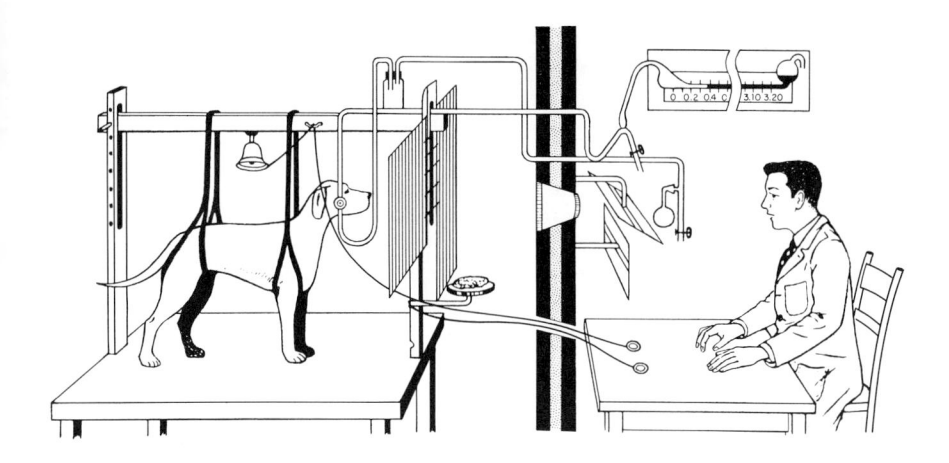

FIG. 13-1 Arrangement of Pavlov's apparatus with dog and observer. (*Pavlov, 1928*)

conditioned salivation response. However, after thirty trials, the tone elicited a response of thirty drops of saliva.

A second measure, the time required for the conditioned response to appear, was taken. After only a few trials, the conditioned salivation did not appear until 18 seconds after the tone was sounded. Later, after the response was well established, the conditioned reaction appeared within 1 or 2 seconds following the onset of the tone. Learning of the salivation response involved both the amount of the response and the speed with which it appeared.

Now let us examine the basic concepts in classical conditioning more closely. They can be divided into two groups: those which are a part of the situation *during* learning and those which are part of the situation *after* learning has taken place.

VARIABLES IN CLASSICAL CONDITIONING DURING LEARNING As we have said above, prior to learning the subject must be capable of a definite response, called the unlearned, or *unconditioned, response* (UCR), which is made to a known stimulus, the UCS. Pavlov believed that the connection between the UCS and the UCR was innate.

In a given experiment, a UCS may give rise to more events than the response selected for measurement, a fact that has been of increasing interest to students of learning as they have refined their studies of the effects of stimulation. For instance, a brief electric shock is likely to produce vocalization, a change in skin conductance, and a variety of internal responses. All these may occur in addition to such responses as running or jumping, which may be of major interest in an experiment on learning to cross a hurdle. Recently, these side effects have become increasingly prominent as possible *mediators* of responses, and more attention has been paid to measuring them. However, the response to shock or other normally pain-inducing stimuli is not of a fixed automatic sort. Even quite noxious events such as electric shock can be brought, by conditioning, to elicit positive reactions while their usual negative effects disappear.

The classical conditioning situation is defined by the following paradigm, which is diagrammed in Figure 13-2. A CS is paired with the UCS. The CS can be virtually any stimulus or change in level of stimulation to which the subject is sensitive. Consequently, we find that the UCR comes to be evoked by the CS when originally it was not so evoked.

How does the newly established CR relate to the UCR? On close examination in some cases, it is only a part of the UCR. In other cases there are important differences between the CR and the UCR. It is possible to speak of a connection, in the sense in which the word was used by the classical philosophers, as having been established between the CS and the UCR only to the extent that the CR is equiv-

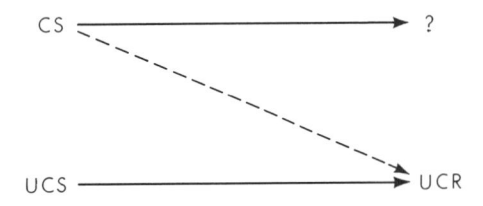

FIG. 13–2 CS, CR, UCS, and UCR relationships.

alent to the original UCR. Pavlov, who of course was examining salivation, was aware that the speed of the CR changed but, nevertheless, believed that it was in fact the same as the UCR, so that learning, for him, was a matter of *stimulus substitution*. The definition of learning as stimulus substitution has been adopted by a number of learning theorists interested in the analysis of classical conditioning. According to this notion, the classical conditioning situation involves a response which is already in the subject's repertoire. When this form of learning occurs, the subjects simply learn new occasions on which to make the same response. A crucial question, however, is whether, in fact, the CR is really identical with the UCR. This question has not been fully answered, and there has been a good deal of controversy among psychologists, because the CR often appears to differ somewhat from the UCR. Let us look at the problem more closely.

The CR may differ qualitatively from the UCR, as appears to happen in the case of eyelid conditioning discussed in Example 13–2.

Example 13–2 *Classical conditioning of the eye blink (Hilgard & Marquis, 1938)*

A good deal of research on classical conditioning has been done with human subjects using the eyelid response. In brief, the situation involves a UCS of blowing a brief puff of air at the eye. The situation regularly elicits a blink as the UCR, as shown in the top section of Figure 13–3. Also shown in that section is the slight reaction of the subject to the light which was used as a CS. Figure 13–3 is based on photographic tracings of the movement of the eyelid on a moving paper. The record starts at the left and moves right. At the extreme left the low position of the eyelid line denotes that the eyelid is open. The top line in each section records the onset of the CS, and the bottom line is a record of the puff of air used as a UCS. The top section of the figure shows the sequence of events before learning begins. The UCR is a rapid closing of the eye, that is, a quick blink. The next three sections, from the second one down, show the progressive change which comes about in the response as learning progresses. In the second record, there is a slight response between the light and the puff. Later the closure becomes anticipatory, and, finally, the subject avoids the puff with a smooth, relatively slow closure of the eye. Clearly, there has been a

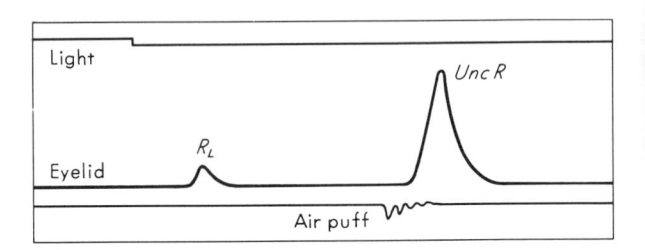

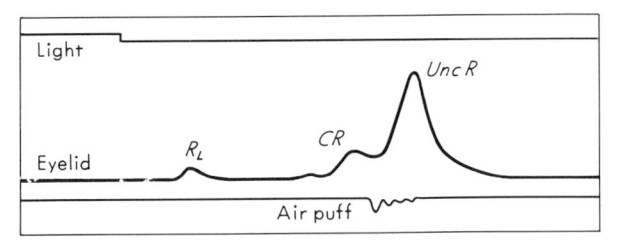

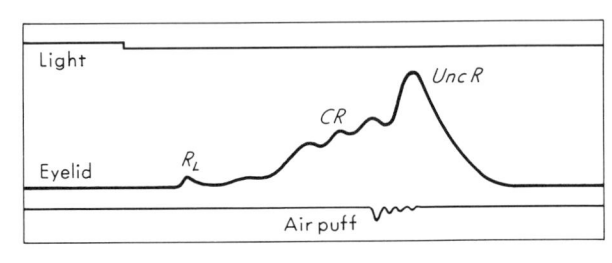

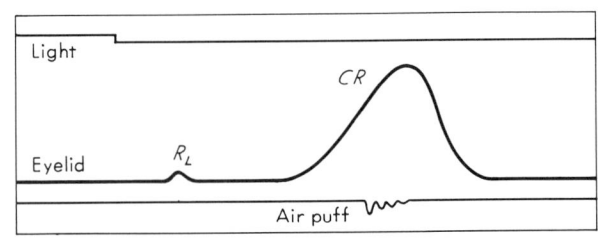

FIG. 13–3 Eyeblink responses and stimuli. (*Hilgard & Marquis, 1938*)

220 BEHAVIORISTIC MODELS IN PSYCHOLOGY

dramatic change in the way in which the eye is closed. The CR differs greatly from the UCR.

In addition to qualitative changes, there are often quantitative changes in the CR; for example, the magnitude of the CR may be less than that of the UCR. This is especially true in cases involving a noxious stimulus as the UCR. When the animal learns to respond to the CS, the force of the response may lessen a good deal. Third, it is sometimes found that the CR represents a single component of the UCR in the sense that it is more specific than the UCR. For example, the UCR to electric shock tends to be diffuse and general, and the subject shows alimentary disruption and displays a lack of direction in his motor responses. But after he has learned to respond to a CS, thereby avoiding the shock, a subject may show a CR that is highly specific. One foot may be raised to remove it from a shock grid or one finger withdrawn from the electrodes. There may be a few or none of the concomitant reactions shown to the shock prior to conditioning.

In contrast to the differences we have been discussing, there may also be a kind of equivalence between the UCR and the CR which is "cognitive" in character. This term is used here to refer to the fact that subjects may freely substitute for the appropriate CR another which they apparently deem to be equivalent or they may, if they find themselves in a new situation, perform a response which now accomplishes the same result as did the former CR. A situation which has demonstrated such equivalence was developed by D. D. Wickens. His study is presented in Example 13–3.

Example 13–3 *Classical conditioning of finger withdrawal: Different responses may accomplish the some outcome (Wickens, 1938)*

Wickens, in this experiment, had subjects learn to avoid a mild but annoying electric shock by lifting a finger from an electrified grid when a CS occurred. The situation is a classical-avoidance-conditioning paradigm. After each subject showed reliable avoidance, his hand was turned over and repositioned with the same finger on the grid but with the back of the finger on the grid. On the next trial, when the CS sounded, almost all subjects removed their fingers from the grids by flexing, in the finger, the muscles antagonistic to those which had figured in the original learning.

Now, since the subjects made an "equivalent" response which was not the CR and used muscles which were not conditioned, an explanation of classical conditioning in terms of the learning of new stimuli for old muscular movements is inappropriate. It appears that the stimulation which the person receives from the position in which his hand is strapped is important in determining the response he will make in this situation. We appear to learn more than muscle twitches. Our behavior has a goal toward which it is directed. In the sense that one response may be substituted for another when it will accomplish the same result, learning may be said to involve "cognitive" components; that is, it may involve relationships such as equivalence of responses, which requires that we consider the nature of higher mental processes to be more than simple reflex action.

From our examination of these several problems, it appears that we can accept only a qualified interpretation of the stimulus substitution concept. It must be taken to imply that the shift of a response to a new stimulus which occurs during classical conditioning may also entail a modification in the character of the response. The new response often is not quite the same as the original one.

VARIABLES IN CLASSICAL CONDITIONING AFTER LEARNING Beyond the experimental situation itself, there are several factors which affect the way in which the classically conditioned response will be performed. The first of these is the presence or absence of the UCS on each trial. During learning in Pavlov's situation, the food powder, which is his UCS, is said to *reinforce* the animal on each presentation, because it rewards the anticipatory salivation to the CS with food. If, however, a CR has been established in an animal and then the CS is repeatedly presented without the food powder or other UCS, the subject will show *experimental extinction*. That is, it will show a progressive response decrement and finally will stop salivating.

In order to explain this loss of CR, Pavlov developed a theory of *inhibition*. In his formulation, each time the animal makes a conditioned response, inhibition builds up, and this acts to compete with the excitatory process of the CS. When the UCS fails to occur, response inhibition brings the animal's responding to a halt. The response has been extinguished. We will have a good deal more to say about the mechanisms of extinction later, but here we will only suggest that the concept of inhibition used by Pavlov suggests an active mechanism such as fatigue which builds up and stops the animal from responding. It would appear that if extinction is due to a buildup of a fatigue of some sort, then a long rest between extinction trials should slow down the rate at which the response disappears in terms of the number of trials required to make the response stop. This deduction has been tried by a number of experimenters, and the results have not been in agreement with each other. Sometimes massing of extinction trials speeds up extinction. Sometimes it does not. In one particular case, however, that of the eye blink which we studied earlier, massed extinction trials do seem to speed up the process.

One surprising phenomenon seems to support the notion that extinction is indeed the result of an active process of inhibition. If an animal's response is extinguished and then after a period of rest is again presented with the CS, the CR reappears. Pavlov called this *spontaneous recovery*. He explained the reappearance of the CR by postulating a dissipation of response inhibition over time. Unfortunately for this otherwise neat idea, spontaneous recovery is only partial. The extinguished response does not come back with the strength it had before. A simple dissipation of inhibition is not an adequate model of spontaneous recovery, and later theorists, such as Hull, have introduced more complex models to account for these data.

A second factor which may vary during learned performance is the degree to which the stimulus conditions at that time are similar to those present during conditioning. It is easy to demonstrate that a learned response will be given to other stimuli than the one to which it was learned. Everyone knows that we may learn to avoid certain items because they are painful, say, sitting on a dark-colored chair which has been in the hot sun. If we leap up in pain on several occasions, we tend not to sit down on such chairs in such places again. We may also choose to be wary of other objects than chairs, such as benches, boards on the ground, stones, decks, and even sidewalks. We have generalized our response to the chair to a variety of objects which are similar to it. The fact of this partial equivalence of different stimuli in eliciting responses is called *stimulus generalization*. The concept was developed when Pavlov found that a dog which salivated to a stimulus of one value would tend also to salivate to other stimulus values along some dimension of the stimulus, for example, pitch in the case of a tone used as a CS. An example of a laboratory study of stimulus generalization is presented in Example 13–4, which describes a famous study by Carl Hovland (1937a, 1937b) used by Clark Hull (1943) in the development of his learning theory.

Example 13–4 *Stimulus generalization: A conditioned response will occur to a range of stimuli (Hovland, 1937a, 1937b)*

In order to study stimulus generalization, Hovland used a measure of response called the *galvanic skin reaction* (GSR). In this situation, sensitive measuring devices are placed on the skin of a person, usually on the palm of the hand or foot. These areas are particularly sensitive to the emotional state of the person: when the person is aroused the palms tend to sweat, changing the resistance of the skin to electric current. Sometimes the measure is called the *palmar conductance*. In his experiment, Hovland used a pure tone as the CS and a shock as the UCS. He used twenty subjects. First, they were conditioned, and then their GSR response was measured to the CS alone and to three other pitches separated from each other by an equal number of discrimination thresholds. A discrimination threshold refers to the amount a pitch, for example, must be changed before a subject can tell that it has, in fact, deviated. This is also called a *just noticeable difference*, or j.n.d. Hovland used pitches that were 25 j.n.d.s apart. Figure 13–4 is a plot by Clark Hull (1943) of the average GSR the twenty subjects gave at each pitch. Hovland used frequencies of 153, 468, 1,000, and 1,967 cps. Half of his subjects were conditioned to 153 cps and half to 1,967 cps, and they were tested on all four frequencies. Thus, each point of the graph represents the data for ten subjects, except the midpoint, which is based on an average response by all the subjects. Notice that the am-

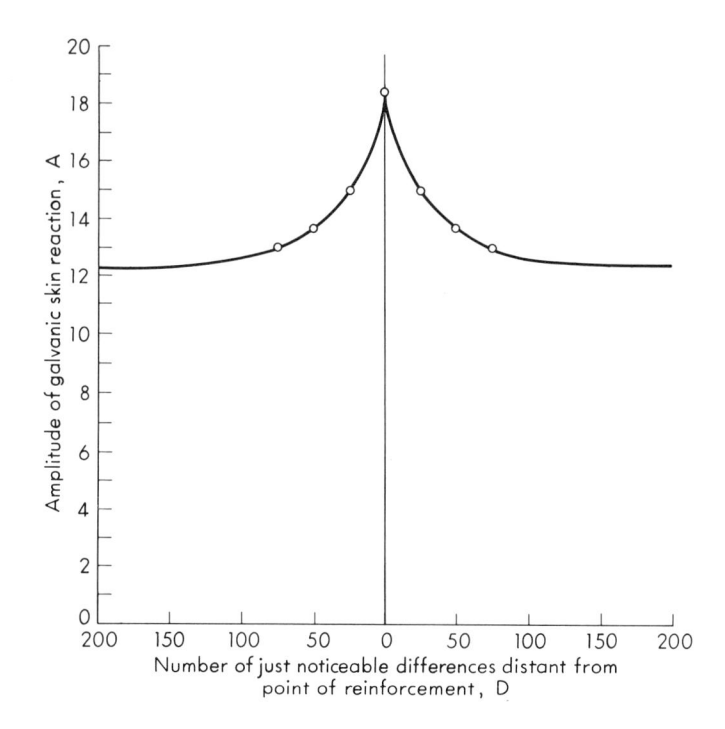

FIG. 13–4 Galvanic skin reaction. (*Hovland, 1937a & b*)

plitude of the response drops off as the distance from the CS increases. This reduction in strength has been called the *generalization gradient*. It should be noted, however, that a plot of the results of individual subjects did not always yield such orderly gradients.

In his extensive exploration of generalization, Pavlov used such stimulus dimensions as pitch, loudness, hue, and even location on the skin of the stimulus. Researchers since Pavlov have explored generalizations in most of the sense modalities, and in general the conclusion is that the farther the test stimulus is from the CS, the less will be the response.

Closely related to the concept of generalization is a second phenomenon of classical conditioning, *discrimination*, which involves teaching a subject to respond to one stimulus and not to another. Pavlov related generalization and discrimination by suggesting that generalization was a failure to discriminate between two stimuli. In his laboratory, a three-step procedure was used to establish a discrimination: First, a dog was conditioned to a specific stimulus value. Then a test was made for the generalization of the conditioned response to a second stimulus somewhat removed in value from the CS. Finally, differentiation training would be used to steepen the gradient of generalization. In this training period, various stimulus values would be presented, one at a time, in a random order. Every time a stimulus other than the CS was presented, no reinforcement was given; in other words, an extinction trial occurred. Pavlov called this technique the *method of contrasts*. There is one caution to be observed in undertaking this technique. If it is to be successful, negative stimuli which are used at first must be well removed from the CS. But as the animal begins to make his discrimination, values can be used which are quite close to the CS. As a matter of fact, the CS and the negative stimuli may be made to become closer and closer in value until the subject is no longer able to tell the stimuli apart.

Pavlov used precisely this procedure to develop *conditioned neuroses* in dogs. When the differentiation became too difficult for the animals, they showed severe behavioral disturbances. In addition to obvious physical activity such as snapping, vocalization, urinating, and struggling in the harness, the animals sometimes showed psychological effects in that they behaved in a withdrawn manner, rebuffing their handlers in the home environment.

Pavlov's work has been very influential, both in Russia and in the West. Of course, he did not formulate an explicit theory of learning. But his classical conditioning paradigm provided a structure and a mass of data which was later used by others to develop theories of learning. Such men as Hull and Guthrie built upon his work.

Since World War II, Pavlov's work has been extremely influential in the Soviet Union. It is rare to find an article in a Soviet journal of psychology which does not begin by paying homage to him. The reason for this popularity appears to be the nature of Pavlov's findings. Since he demonstrated that individual animals could be made to behave quite differently as a result of experience and he attributed such effects of training to the plasticity of the nervous system, his work fitted nicely into Marxist doctrine. Dialectical materialism holds that it is the role one plays, that is, his experiences during his nurture, which determine what he will become in later life. Pavlov's research could be interpreted to support the Marxist doctrine that the environment, as opposed to heredity, determines the adult's nature. Since the leaders of the Soviet Union wished to repudiate the value of inherited predispositions as determinants of behavior, they found his work very appealing. But we should not let political factors influence our appreciation of Pavlov. The results of his labors are easily reproduced in the main. Therefore, there can be no doubt of the great value of his scientific legacy. During his long and fruitful life he built upon careful observation and counseled his students to do the same, as shown beautifully in the following quote from a letter written shortly before his death in 1936, at the age of eighty-one:

> First of all, be systematic. I repeat—be systematic. Train yourself to be strictly systematic in the acquisition of knowledge. First, study the rudiments of science before attempting to reach its heights... Do not become a mere collector of facts, but try to penetrate into the mystery of their origin. Search persistently for the laws which govern them.
> The second important requisite is modesty.
> Never at any time imagine that you know everything....
> The third thing that is necessary is passion. Remember that science demands of a man his whole life. And even if you could have two lives, they would not be sufficient [Pavlov, quoted in Babkin, 1949].

Behaviorism: J. B. Watson

A second pioneer in the development of modern theories of the learning process was John B. Watson. His contribution stemmed from his ability to seize upon a major idea—radical objectivism—and make it widely influential through his enthusiasm and his skill as a popular lecturer and writer. Watson occupies a singular place in the history of psychology. Although, as we have shown, there was a tradition of empiricism and even objectivism before him, he became the champion of a radical metaphysics which he called *behaviorism,* and he excluded states of consciousness as a proper study for a science of psychology. Consider the following quotation which appeared in 1913. Certainly, Watson was vigorous and positive in his presentation of his views:

> Psychology as the behaviorist views it is a purely objective experimental branch of natural science. Its theoretical goal is the prediction and control of behavior. Introspection forms no essential part of its methods, nor is the scientific value of its data dependent upon the readiness with which they lend themselves to interpretation in terms of consciousness. The behaviorist, in his efforts to get a unitary scheme of animal response, recognizes no dividing line between man and brute [Watson, 1913]

One tenet underlies all of Watson's teaching. He held that psychology must use the methods of natural science and that the proper study for psychology was the study of behavior, which could be observed and measured. For him, behavior was composed of response elements, these being glandular secretions and muscle movements. Behavior thus becomes reducible to definable physiochemical processes. Watsonian behaviorism was strictly deterministic, in that it maintained that a response must have an effective stimulus which could be demonstrated to have elicited the response. Conversely, every effective stimulus was held always to elicit an immediate response.

We have emphasized that Watson was a popularizer. But he was also an experimenter in the tradition of the empiricists, and, further, he placed emphasis on the application of the findings of psychology to real life.

One of Watson's most famous experiments was a study, outlined in Example 13–5, of a learned fear in a human baby. It was a pioneer study that explored an area which had been brought to the attention of many people by Freud's writings on phobias.

Example 13–5 *Conditioned emotional reaction: Fear as a conditioned reflex (Watson & Rayner, 1920)*

In this study, Watson and his student Rosalie Rayner used one subject, a nine-month-old boy named Albert, who was reared from birth in a hospital environment. The child was reported to be "on the whole" stolid and unemotional. Prior to any conditioning, the experimenters ran the child through a series of tests of emotional activity which involved suddenly presenting the boy with a white rat, then a rabbit, a dog, a monkey, masks with and without hair, cotton wool, burning newspapers, and other objects which are not described in the experimental report. At no time during the testing prior to conditioning did the child ever show fear of any of the objects.

Following these tests, the child was exposed to a loud sound made by striking a hammer on a steel bar. The results of this test are reported by Watson:

> One of the two experimenters caused the child to turn its head and fixate his moving hand; the other, stationed back of the child, struck the steel bar a sharp blow. The child started violently, his breathing was checked and the arms were raised in a characteristic manner. On the second stimulation the same thing occurred, and in addition the lips began to pucker and tremble. On the third stimulation the child broke into a sudden crying fit. This is the first time an emotional situation in the laboratory has produced any fear or even crying in Albert [Watson & Rayner, 1920].

Building on this observation, the experimenters began procedures designed to condition fear to a visual stimulation. They presented Albert with a white rat and then struck the bar. After two trials at this, the boy began to cry. After a week's rest, the boy was given a series of pairings of the rat and the noise. By the eighth trial, when presented with the rat alone, the child appeared to be conditioned. He cried, fell over on his side, and crawled away from the situation vigorously.

After five days, Albert was tested to see if the fear response would transfer to other objects. No fear was shown to a set of toy blocks. But when the rat was presented to him, the boy whimpered. A rabbit produced an even more violent reaction, indicating that objects which resembled the original stimulus, the rat, would also produce fear. When the boy was tested after a year and twenty-one days, he showed signs of residual fear to the rat and the rabbit. In addition, he showed some apprehension to a fur coat and a dog. The conditioned emotional response appears to be very long lived. Of course, Watson's experiment lacks controls for evaluating the effects of maturation and the sudden presentation of these objects at the particular time in Albert's life when he was tested again, but this study is an important first step in the experimental study of learned emotional reactions. Watson himself was convinced of the generality of his findings:

> These experiments would seem to show conclusively that directly conditioned emotional responses as well as those conditioned by transfer persist, although with certain loss in the intensity of the reaction, for a longer period than one month. Our view is that they persist and modify personality throughout life [Watson & Rayner, 1920].

Watson served to focus an intellectual trend. His influence has endured, and his intellectual descendants, however modified their versions of Watson's behaviorism may be, owe him a great debt.

Stimulus-Response Connectionism: E. L. Thorndike

The work of the third pioneer, Edward L. Thorndike, actually antedated that of both Watson and Pavlov. Thorndike put forward one of the first stimulus-response theories and probably the most influential one. His influence was later attested by a leading modern psychologist, Edward Tolman:

> The psychology of animal learning—not to mention that of child learning—has been and still is primarily a matter of agreeing or disagreeing with Thorndike, or trying in minor ways to improve upon him [Tolman, 1938].

A student of William James, Thorndike was responsible for initiating the systematic study of animal psychology and learning, as well as the analysis of instrumental behavior. The expression "instrumental behavior" is defined in terms of the learning situation itself. A particular response of the subject is chosen by the experimenter as the one to be learned. However, the reward is not given until the subject makes the response himself. In the sense that the response is instrumental in bringing about the reinforcement, it is said to be instrumental conditioning. Noting that the subject must initiate the sequence, some theorists have used the term "voluntary" as a description of the instrumental situation. An example of an instrumental conditioning situation, taken from Thorndike's original work, appears in Figure 13–5.

In 1898, Thorndike published his doctoral thesis in a monograph called *Animal Intelligence*. In the work, he accepted evolutionary principles which emphasized the psychological continuity between man and other animals. He argued that learning, as it occurs in animals, depends on trial and error with accidental success. When a successful response is rewarded, a bond is formed between the stimuli and that response. Learning consists of a stamping in of such stimulus-response connections. Because of this terminology, Thorndike's theory came to be called *S-R connectionism*.

In order to understand Thorndike's theory of learning, it is necessary to examine his experimental situation carefully. As shown in Figure 13–5, Thorndike's first scientific apparatus was crude by today's standards. Nevertheless, Thorndike's puzzle box proved to be an instrument that had a remarkable influence on theoretical development in the study of learning. In his early experiments, Thorndike used cats, dogs, and chickens. Here we will consider only the results of his cat experiments. The general method he used is illustrated in Example 13–6.

Example 13–6 *Cats in a puzzle box: Learning by trial and error (Thorndike, 1898)*

In his experiments with the puzzle box, Thorndike's chief concern was not to develop a theory of learning but rather to answer those who held that animals were capable of reasoning. In designing his apparatus, he tried to present the animals with a situation which was well within their capacity as he saw it.

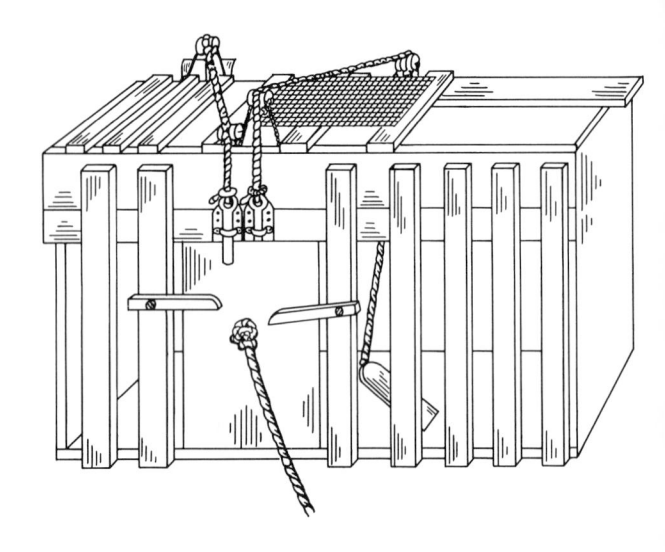

FIG. 13–5 Primitive puzzle box. (*Thorndike, 1898*)

The animals were first made hungry and then shut up in an enclosure 20 by 15 by 12 inches from which they could escape by performing some simple act such as pulling a wire loop or stepping on a pedal. In each case, the act operated an escape door by means of a simple mechanism. A piece of fish was placed outside the box in plain sight of the animals just beyond their reach.

If cats could reason, Thorndike argued, his situation was ideally designed to demonstrate that ability. Thus, if a cat was placed in the box, it might try to reach the fish; then when that failed, it might manipulate other objects in the box until it hit upon the device which opened the door. When it had eaten the fish, the experimenter would return the animal to the apparatus, close the door, and rebait the dish. If reason prevailed, the cat would then do immediately what it had just done successfully. But Thorndike found that his cats certainly did not show any such signs of reasoning.

As a criterion of performance, Thorndike measured the time it took the animals to escape from the box on each trial. When the animal was first put in the box, it showed signs of discomfort and attempted to escape from the box by squeezing through the openings between the bars. Eventually, the struggle led to an escape when the animal accidentally operated the escape mechanism. On the first trial the animal took 60 seconds to escape.

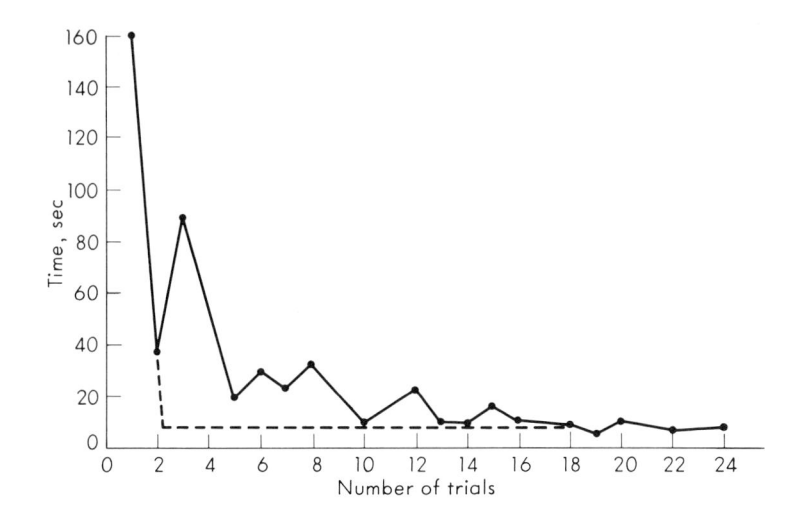

FIG. 13-6 A learning curve. (*Thorndike, 1898*)

On the second trial, 80 seconds. On the next four trials, 50, 60, 50, 40. A curve of such a performance is shown in Figure 13–6. Notice that the animals show a gradual decrease in the reduction of time it takes to escape from the box.

In Thorndike's view, there was no evidence for reasoning in these results. He argued that any animal which could reason would, as soon as it had operated the latch a few times, escape quickly, with a sudden drop in the curve such as is shown by the dotted line. Thorndike concluded that learning of situations such as the puzzle box could be attributed only to accidental success and the gradual stamping in of habits over a series of trials.

One important result of Thorndike's experimental observations was his formulation of the basic laws of learning—laws which have been most influential in psychology. The first of these was the *law of effect*, which was the precursor of the principle of reinforcement found in present-day learning theory. The law of effect places emphasis on the consequences of the performance of a habitual response. As formulated by Thorndike, the law stated that whenever a response was made which led to satisfaction, the bond, or connection, between the stimuli and that response would be strengthened. Indeed, he said that satisfaction stamped in the bond. If the connection was made and annoyance followed, then the bond was weakened. It is important to understand that the satisfier or annoyer was not the response itself but rather that the satisfaction or annoyance followed the performance of the response. In cases of both annoyance and satisfaction, the S-R bond was measured in terms of the probability that a response would occur in a given situation. Thorndike made no formal distinction between learning and performance.

An important problem for the law of effect was presented by the definition of a satisfying or an annoying state of affairs. Barring obvious cases such as fish to a hungry cat, it is not always easy to decide beforehand what will prove to be rewarding in any given situation. Thorndike dodged this problem by simply defining a satisfying agent as anything which animals would approach or work to maintain and an annoying agent as anything that the animal would work to avoid or escape and do nothing to maintain.

In his later career, Thorndike traced problems of learning in the educational situation. He wrote an extremely influential book on the psychology of education which was used widely in schools of education and influenced the methods used in the classrooms of the world. He worked extremely hard and in a direct way. When he asked himself what a child was taught, the answer he gave was "Words." Then he proceeded to count the frequency of occurrence of the words in the language used in a variety of media such as newspapers, novels, and magazines. He wrote a dictionary. He developed intelligence tests. He laid down principles for vocational guidance and the teaching of arithmetic and spelling, and he developed a scale for evaluation of handwriting. If a single word typified his effort, it was "practical." Thorndike strongly believed in direct attack on the problem of complex learning, and he did the work necessary to complete his aims.

The Study of Rote Learning: H. Ebbinghaus

The final trailblazer—and the term is particularly appropriate here—was Herman Ebbinghaus, whose particular contribution to psychology lay in his direct approach to the analysis of psychic processes, particularly memory (Ebbinghaus, 1885). Ebbinghaus developed an interest in problems of learning and recall, and thought it possible to study them in the laboratory. As a philosopher, he had studied the thinkers of associationistic tradition and had been influenced by their theories. In addition, he knew, from a study of the field of perception, how Fechner and others had developed the psychophysical methods to study thresholds of response in human beings. When Ebbinghaus applied psychophysical methods to the study of memory, he broke with the established doctrine of that time, which held that the higher mental processes of man were too complex for study in the laboratory.

The logic by which Ebbinghaus proceeded to study the higher mental processes can be outlined as follows: In psychophysics, the basic concept is the threshold. A threshold is that value of a stimulus which can just be perceived by the observer, or it is a change in the stimulus which is just capable of being perceived as a difference. In order to measure thresholds, psychologists had found that, first, they needed a criterion of discrimination; that is, they had to establish a method of measuring the ability of the observer to detect the presence or absence of a stimulus. Secondly, in order to measure thresholds, stimuli must be presented in such a way that marked changes in behavior would occur at the critical values. For example, to measure the intensity at which a light can just be seen requires that a number of intensities be used as stimuli, and the person's response to each must be observed. The threshold is that value at which the person suddenly says that he can see the light.

Ebbinghaus considered it possible to apply the idea of a threshold to the problem of measuring the memory. The criterion of performance which he chose was the threshold of mastery. For this purpose, Ebbinghaus used one perfect recitation of a memorization task as his threshold. He felt that the proper study of memory was the exploration of those stimulus conditions under which the criterion of performance would be reached. His materials were lists of syllables; his subject was himself.

While his conceptions may seem simple today, in his time, he accomplished an intellectual break away from tradition. Unique and first in this area of study, his work has stood the test of time in a singular way. Because it has shown such a robustness in the face of massive experimental attacks, we will summarize Ebbinghaus' findings and illustrate the major problems in verbal learning by his work.

The unit which Ebbinghaus used to study memory was the *nonsense syllable,* known as a trigram, or three-letter item which does not have dictionary meaning. His particular trigrams were in the form of a consonant, a vowel, and a consonant. These are usually referred to as CVCs. He chose these materials because he wanted memory items of comparable difficulty. That is, he wished to avoid errors in his study which were due to differences in the ease with which materials could be learned. For example, it is certainly true that two prose passages may differ greatly in the ease with which they can be learned as a function of the length of the words in the passages and the familiarity of the items to the learner. Surely, two passages of equal length, one from a first-grade primer and the other from a scientific report, would not offer equal ease of mastery for all subjects.

Beyond the problem of difficulty of the materials, Ebbinghaus also wished to study the "raw" learning process. In order to do this, he wished to avoid material which had meanings which might play a role in the task under study. Clearly, this is not truly possible. He later decided that nonsense syllables did have a potential for evoking associations. As we shall see, others have explored this problem by evaluating the association values of different nonsense syllables. To anticipate, we can say that there is quite a wide range of "meaningfulness," in that sense, among CVCs. Nonsense syllables have continued to be used by psychologists in an attempt to control the association value of the stimulus materials in experiments on learning.

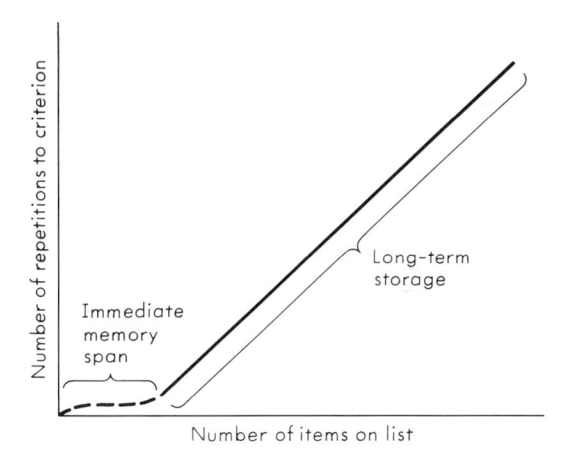

FIG. 13–7 Memory span and storage utilizing lists.

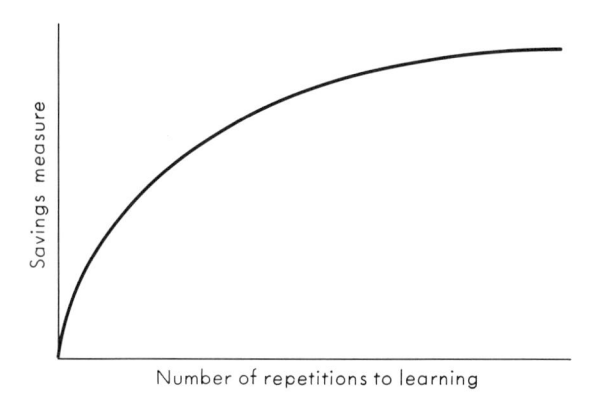

FIG. 13–8 Number of repetitions in learning.

However, direct approaches to the role of meaningfulness in verbal learning have led to the use of actual words in learning tasks, and the nonsense syllable has become less important as an experimental tool.

In the course of his work, Ebbinghaus devoted himself to four main problems: the length-difficulty relationship, practice effects in learning, forgetting, and remote association. We will consider each of these problems in turn. To a remarkable extent, as we shall see later, Ebbinghaus' work set the stage for modern theories of verbal learning. But he never advanced a formal theory of memory. He was a strict empiricist, and with true German thoroughness he observed and observed.

Ebbinghaus' first problem was that of the *length-difficulty relationship in rote learning*. In the study of this relationship, the experimental situation involves series of nonsense syllables. Ebbinghaus read this list at a controlled rate of one per second and then tested himself for retention. He read the list again and tested again, continuing in this way until he reached a criterion of one perfect reproduction of the list. In working at these tasks, Ebbinghaus discovered a discontinuity in the difficulty of the task with increased length. This relationship is illustrated in Figure 13–7. As the reader can see, there is a span of list lengths for which all the items could be retained in one or a few trials. Increasing the length of the list up through that span did not increase the difficulty of the task. However, as soon as the length of list went beyond this "immediate memory span," the time per item required for mastery increased with increased length of list.

It is clear to anyone who has attempted to master a difficult task that *repetition* plays an important role in learning and memory. Ebbinghaus devoted a great deal of effort to exploring the exact relationship between the number of repetitions of a learning task and the degree of learning or memory. He found a direct relationship between repetitions of a task and the amount learned, as shown in Figure 13–8. While the truth of this finding has a ring of obviousness, it had a profound influence upon theoretical psychology, because it gave rise to the notion that the strength of habits increased in an incremental fashion. That is, when it was clearly demonstrated that there was a change in the strength of habits which occurred on each trial of practice, some psychologists deduced that the final strength of a habit was built up from small gains on each trial.

In his exploration of the strength of retention, Ebbinghaus used the *method of savings*. In measuring the effect of practice on a learning task, he would first learn a list of syllables and then, after a period of time, relearn the same list. The savings score was computed by subtracting the number of trials required to relearn the list from the number of trials required on the original task. The result was always a number in the range from 0 to 1. Ebbinghaus believed this number to provide a meas-

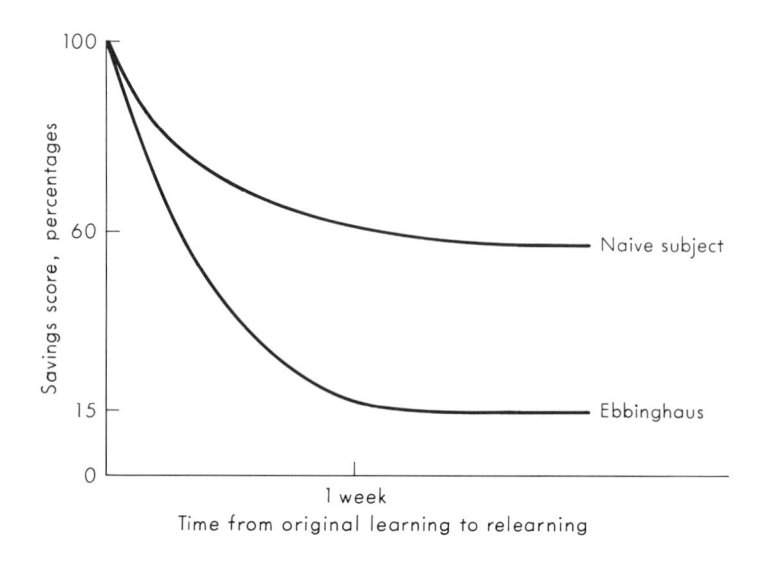

FIG. 13–9 Savings score versus time from original learning to relearning.

ure of the strength of association. To illustrate the method of savings:

If a list requires 30 trials on first learning and 10 trials to relearn, the savings score may be expressed as

$$\text{Savings} = \frac{30 - 10}{30} = .667$$

which in this idealized case means that on the second attempt the subject, by his memory, saved two-thirds, or 66.67 percent, of the effort required at first.

It was a part of Ebbinghaus' genius that he brought the study of the common human problem of forgetting into the laboratory. He was specifically searching for a quantitative law which would mathematically describe the course of forgetting over time. To quantify forgetting, Ebbinghaus first learned material to measure up to a criterion, and then at a later period of time, using the method of savings, he measured the amount retained. He made an effort to use a number of comparable lists to get a list-independent measure of the amount of retention after each period of time. What he found is what has come to be called the *classical curve of forgetting*. The curve is illustrated in Figure 13–9. Since Ebbinghaus' publication, psychologists have studied a wide variety of situations in many different animals and found the curve of forgetting to have great generality.

There are two important characteristics of the curve of forgetting: First, it involves a deep initial drop and then a period of negative acceleration. Second, the curve is not capable of being clearly extrapolated to the zero point. This gives rise to an interesting speculation: is forgetting ever complete? There have been a number of experimental studies of the problem of whether forgetting is final and complete. Suffice it to say, here, that evidence indicates that people retain materials after a very long time, and sometimes material thought to have been completely forgotten will reappear in the memory of a person.

With replications of his work, using naïve learners, it has become clear that Ebbinghaus' curves of forgetting are too low. This finding seems due to the fact that he learned a great number of similar materials and, therefore, his ability to remember suffered from a lot of interference. Of course, the experience of a subject influences his ability to learn. As a result of much study of the effects of experience, it appears that experienced subjects are fast learners and fast forgetters. They know how to do the job, but they also suffer a good deal of interference in remembering what they learn. Adults will agree that they tend to show failures of memory which are due to interference from the many things they have learned in the past. In contrast, their children show remarkable retention, possibly due to their lack of experience and, therefore, lack of interfering events in their memory store. "Kids remember everything" is a saying which reflects this state of affairs.

The final problem of Ebbinghaus which we will consider is that of *remote associations*. The question concerns whether we learn more than direct associations when we master verbal materials. Consider the case where a person learns a series of items such that A is followed by B; B is followed by C; C is followed by D; and so on. Clearly the associations between A and B, B and C, C and D are learned and correct. But it is also possible that there are remote and incorrect associations between items which are removed from each other in the list. Thus we might ask, is there an association formed between A and C? Further, is there a backward association between C and A? This problem of remote associations called the classical principle of contiguity into question. Since the time of the ancient Greeks, as we have seen, temporal contiguity was a law of association. Now, the possibility that associations could be formed between items remote from each other in time was bringing the ancient principle under closer scrutiny.

There are four possible associations by contiguity: The first is called *forward-adjacent,* and it is the correct response in the ordinary serial learning task. The remaining three, all of which are incorrect associations, are *forward-remote, backward-adjacent,* and *backward-remote*. Ebbinghaus recognized that if these incorrect associations were built up, along with the correct ones, then a simple analysis of the learning process would not suffice. The strength of the correct associations must be greater, or learning would not occur but the incorrect ones might also build up their strength. Possibly, he reasoned, forgetting is due to some gain over time on the part of the remote or incorrect tendencies. This bit of reasoning is the beginning of an *interference theory of forgetting*. It has proved quite difficult to demonstrate remote associations clearly. Ebbinghaus used the method of derived lists as transfer tests of remote associations. A derived list is defined as follows: If practice lists consist of items 1, 2, 3, 4, 5, 6, 7, 8, then a transfer list derived as a space of one item will consist of 1, 3, 5, 7, 2, 4, 6, 8. Remote associations would be indicated if there were savings in learning the derived list.

From this research, Ebbinghaus concluded that there were, in fact, remote associations built up during practice. He suggested that the length-difficulty relationship which we have discussed may be due to the rapid buildup of possible remote associations, which are, of course, errors, as the length of the list increases. This series of experiments on remote associations has had great importance because of two methodological points which they raised: First, they called attention to the importance of measuring and analyzing errors as well as measuring correct responses. Further, the use of a transfer test has proved to be a valuable tool in working with the study of learning. A measure of learning a second task can be a sensitive test of what was learned on the first task.

In summary, Ebbinghaus had great influence because he channeled the study of human learning into the investigation of rote processes. That is, he led psychology into a study of the linkage of discrete units. In addition, he passed on to his followers the conception of learning as being primarily the association of these discrete units. As a result of this conception, there came to be an interaction between classical conditioning theory, which had also been influenced by associationistic philosophy and rote learning theory.

THE DEFINITION OF LEARNING

As we have examined the antecedents of modern behavioristic models, we have focused on the process of learning without concerning ourselves overly much with a precise definition of just what it is we mean by learning. Everyone uses the term, and, in most situations, we do not have difficulty in understanding what is meant. But when the process of learning began to be subjected to careful study in the laboratory, a more precise definition was required. As is sometimes the case with concepts used in ordinary language, the task of definition has proved to be a difficult problem. In the first place, it seems fairly clear that, by the term "learning," we do not refer to an object which we can directly observe. There are no "learnings" running around in the world. Rather, learning is a change, or process. This is not an easy point to grasp, and particular attention should be paid to the difficulty of defining learning. Let us spell out the problem more carefully.

In order to infer that learning has occurred, we must observe the behavior of the person at least twice and take note of differences in the way he performs on the successive occasions. At first glance, this seems simple enough. To give an example, we may present a person with a passage which he is to memorize. After some patient practice, we observe that he is able to recite the passage, and we say that he has learned. However, we may be wrong in our inference if we are not certain that our student did not already know the passage. A test of performance prior to practice is important. Even at the outset of our attempt at definition, we find that there are two kinds of conditions which we must observe if we are to be right when we infer that learning has taken place: antecedent conditions, which are present prior to learning, and consequent conditions, which are present after the actual learning has taken place.

Within the antecedent conditions, by far the most important factor is practice. No one is going to be surprised by that statement. "Practice makes perfect." Provided the task is difficult enough to require more than one trial, everyone knows that the learner must be exposed repeatedly to a situation in order to learn. But the general acceptance of this rule leads to confusion in defining learning in terms of practice alone. Practice may produce other effects, such as fatigue. To give an example, if we observe a friend trying to master the skill of throwing a baseball accurately, we may find that he gets worse after a time. But we cannot be sure that his loss of accuracy is a failure of learning. He may be simply showing fatigue, and although he is actually learning to throw the ball well, the fatigue is interfering with his performance of the task.

By consequent conditions, we mean relatively permanent changes in the behavior of the learner which reliably occur whenever he is placed in a particular situation and which are the result of other variables than practice, such as maturation, changes in physiological conditions within the learner, changes in motivation, the effects of drugs. From this analysis, it should be apparent that a prediction of behavior depends on knowing the condition of the organism *during* learning and *after* learning, which brings us to an important distinction in behavior theory.

We have all learned a myriad of skills, but we do not always exhibit our abilities to their full extent.

Even when we are in situations which call generally for us to perform what we have learned, sometimes we are not able to do so. Because our learning fails to appear, psychologists have found it *necessary to distinguish between learning and performance.* An example may be helpful. Consider the case of a skilled athlete such as a golfer who is capable of performing the highly complex learned response of driving the ball straight down the fairway. If he is handicapped by an "off day" or by adverse physiological conditions such as a bout of rheumatism, he may not be able to hit the ball well at all. Certainly, his well-learned habit will appear only if the man is well motivated and is not suffering from ill health. Further, the large context in which he plays will determine his performance. Some golfers, for example, are readily thrown off their game by crowd noises; others are not. Every person learns a great number of skills which he can perform well only under appropriate conditions. A failure to make a response or failure to perform a known skill does not necessarily mean that the skill could not be performed well under other conditions.

From these considerations of the distinction between learning and performance, we may conclude that learning is a change in behavior potential. That is, what is learned is a potential to perform a particular response under appropriate conditions. During the early states of the psychological study of learning, many investigators failed to make the learning-performance distinction.

Keeping in mind the problems discussed above, we may now attempt a definition of learning, as follows: *Learning is a relatively permanent change in behavior potential which occurs as a result of practice.* Learning is conceptualized as setting an upper limit to the level of performance under appropriate conditions.

FACTORS WHICH ARE IMPORTANT IN LEARNING ABILITY

Although the different models of the learning process which we will discuss emphasize each of the following factors to a different degree, there is partial concensus that these variables always effect learners.

The first variable is *heredity*. It is necessary to consider the genetic endowment of the subject, since individuals may have inherited different degrees of ability to learn. No modern learning theorist, with the possible exception of Tolman, has included heredity as an explicit factor in determining performance of habits. Most theorists have chosen to avoid the problem of variation in learning due to hereditary factors by using carefully selected subjects, such as rats which are all from the same bloodline or people who are identical twins. But increasing attention is being paid to the genetics of behavior, as we will see in Chapter 16.

Maturation, a second factor, has come to occupy more of the interest of theorists of learning. In recent years, a good deal of experimental work has emphasized the process of development and the manner in which the ability to learn emerges at each stage of this development. Although few formal theories have accorded much importance to this problem so far, the situation is now changing, since educators are all directly concerned with developmental stages in children.

We alluded in our definition of the learning process to *practice*. But, practice can be done under a variety of conditions, and the conditions of practice are important in learning. For instance, practice may be massed or spaced, involve the complete task or only part of it at a time. Much experimentation has been done on the conditions of practice because of the great interest which these matters have for classroom teachers.

A prominent concern in the study of learning has been the role of *motivation*. It appears obvious that the motivational condition of the learner determines the degree to which he will learn. Indeed, one of the clichés of education has it that failure to learn may be simply due to poor motivation on the part of the student. But a lot of educational dust has thus been swept under the rug. As we shall see, there has been little agreement among psychologists on the role of motivation in learning.

Of course, learning by adults can never be studied in a pure situation, in the sense that every adult subject studied has learned before. For this reason, most studies of adult learning are really studies of the *transfer* of learning. By transfer, we refer to the fact that past learning can affect learning of a new task. If past learning causes poorer performance on a second task, we call the effect negative transfer. If, on the other hand, prior learning facilitates a new task, we refer to it as positive transfer.

We have treated the early period of development of theories of learning somewhat lightly, because the pioneers were working new ground and, therefore, many of their conceptualizations have undergone great change as experimental evidence has been gathered. But with our knowledge of how the study of learning began from behavioristic and associationistic foundations, we can study the further development of theories of learning with a better understanding of the basic issues.

CHAPTER 14

IMPORTANT ISSUES IN THE STUDY OF THE LEARNING PROCESS

For psychologists in the 1930–1940 period interested in the learning process, certain problems stood out from the theorizing which had preceded them. Leading workers took up the difficult issues and attempted solutions. While it is true that they did not always agree, they cleared the air by settling down to work in the laboratory. Their controversies have furthered our grasp of the learning process.

In this section, we will change our approach from a consideration of individual theorists and their theories as a whole to an emphasis on problems and the positions advanced by the theorists who dealt with them. Two major problems will concern us: how formal a theory does psychology need, and what is the major "law" of learning? We shall deal with each problem in turn.

THE FORMALIZATION OF LEARNING THEORY

Quite obviously, theories of behavior differ greatly in their degree of formalization. Some writers, among whom Clark Hull (1943) is a good example, felt that a high degree of formality would allow more precise predictions of behavior. For such thinkers, physics is the best model for theory building, and the mathematicodeductive method is the one to use. In contrast, other theorists have gone so far as to reject the necessity for any formal theory at all. B. F. Skinner (1950) is prominent among such thinkers. For him, an empirical law of reinforcement can successfully explain most of behavior. Of course, there is a great middle ground, and we will examine one theory, that of Edward Tolman (1932), which has a quasiformal structure.

The Hypotheticodeductive Method in Behavior Theory

Beginning in the late nineteen twenties, Clark Hull, at Yale University, attempted to synthesize the methods and theories of Thorndike and Pavlov. He evolved a formal postulate system, based on the mathematicodeductive model, which had had success in the physical sciences. The following quotation illustrates Hull's thinking about behavior theory.

> The major task of science is the isolation of principles which shall be of as general validity as possible. In the methodology whereby scientists have successfully sought this end, two procedures may be distinguished—the empirical and the theoretical. The empirical procedure consists primarily of observation, usually facilitated by experiment. The theoretical procedure, on the other hand, is essen-

tially logical in nature; through its mediation, in conjunction with the employment of the empirical procedure, the range of validity of principles may be explored to an extent quite impossible by the empirical procedure alone. . . .

Scientific theory, in its ideal form, consists of a hierarchy of logically deduced propositions which parallel all the observed empirical relationships comprising a science. This logical structure is derived from a relatively small number of self-consistent primary principles called postulates, when taken in conjunction with relevant antecedent conditions. The behavior sciences have been slower than the physical sciences to attain this systematic status, in part because of their inherent complexity, . . . but also in part because of the greater persistence of anthropomorphism [Hull, 1943].

Hull was a dedicated worker, capable of intensive effort and creative innovation. When he came to the study of learning, the field was dominated by vague constructs and imprecise methods of studying behavior. Hull introduced precision, both in the prediction of behavior and in its measurement. Like Thorndike, Hull was oriented toward the *empirical*. His postulates were based on laboratory findings. We will not present his system in detail. Those who have an interest in formal behavior theory can consult Hull's book *Principles of Behavior*, which is a fascinating example of theory building and the search for precision in the prediction of behavior. However, several of Hull's postulates have had a profound influence on the development of the field, and we will briefly consider those.

Hull's model of the learning process is an example of a stimulus-response-effect (S-R-effect) theory. In the tradition of Thorndike's law of effect, Hull held that learning depended on the *outcome* of a behavior. But Hull added an important modification to the traditional associationistic view. He developed the postulate of *primary reinforcement*, which states that a stimulus-response connection, or habit, will be increased in strength if the response is followed by a rapid decrease in drive. The notion that learning depends on such an event has been called the *drive-reduction hypothesis*. Later we will consider in detail Hull's principle of reinforcement, which was his most important "law" of learning, but at this point, to give the flavor of Hull's complexity and the manner in which he relied on empirical constructs, we will scan his system. Figure 14–1 presents a summary by Hilgard of Hull's constructs. Hull's variables can also be presented in equation form:

$$_sE_R = (_sH_R \times D \times V \times K) - (I_R + _sI_R)$$

In this formula, the symbols presented in Figure 14–1 are shown to relate to the production of behavior. Each symbol is defined as follows: $_sE_R$ is the *reaction potential*, or the tendency to perform a previously learned habit. By introducing a separation between habits and reaction potential, Hull makes quite explicit the distinction between learning and performance discussed in Chapter 13. Notice, in Figure 14–1, that the measures of reaction potential are the speed or latency of a response, the amplitude of a response, and the resistance to extinction of a response. $_sH_R$ stands for *habit strength*. Hull used the symbol to show that H (for habit) is a bond between stimuli in the environment and the response of the organism. The strength of $_sH_R$ depends on the number of times the response has been made and reinforced in a given situation. As the formula above shows, $_sH_R$ places an upper limit on performance but does not ensure that a response will be performed. Hull used example 14–1 to develop his definition of $_sH_R$.

Example 14–1 *Reaction latency and the number of reinforcements (Simley, 1933)*

In a nice example of the use of response latency, Simley used college students to measure the relationship between the number of reinforcements and the strength of a habit.

The apparatus consisted of an automatic exposure device which presented nonsense drawings of characters, one at a time for five seconds, before the subject. When the device was turned on, a very accurate stop clock was started. After about three seconds the characters appeared, and a particular nonsense syllable, that is, a string of letters, was spoken by the experimenter. The subjects were told to speak each syllable as quickly as possible when the appropriate symbol appeared. A microphone picked up a subject's voice and shut off the clock, through automatic devices. The time which elapsed between the onset of the symbol and the speaking of the syllable by the subject gave a measure of his response latency.

The data from one subject were used. That person spoke the associated syllable before being prompted at the second presentation of about 125

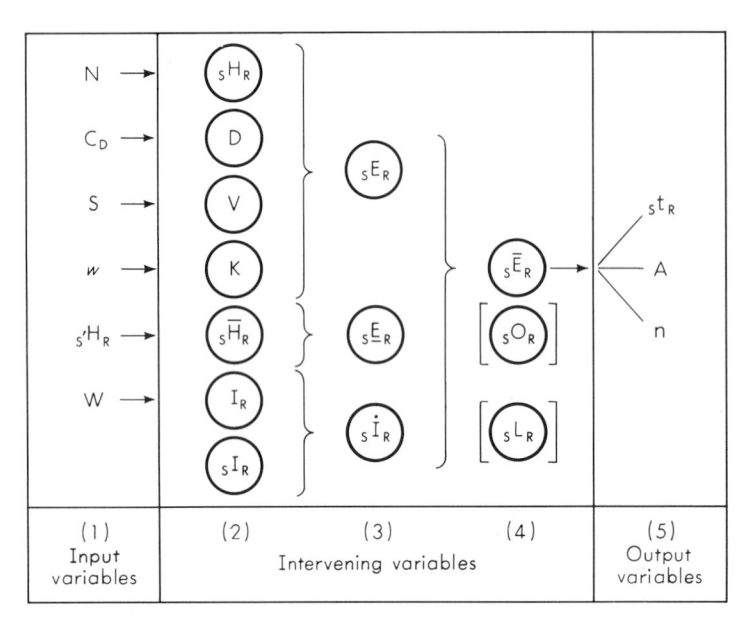

FIG. 14–1 Summary of Hull's final system. (*Hilgard, 1956*)

COLUMN 1
- N, number of prior reinforcements
- C_D, drive condition
- S, stimulus intensity
- w, amount (weight) of reward
- $_S'H_R$, strength of a habit based on same response conditioned to another stimulus
- W, work required in responding

COLUMN 2
- $_SH_R$, habit strength
- D, drive
- V, stimulus-intensity dynamism
- K, incentive-reinforcement
- $_S\overline{H}_R$, generalized habit strength from related habit
- I_R, reactive inhibition
- $_SI_R$, conditioned inhibition

COLUMN 3
- $_SE_R$, reaction potential
- $_S\underline{E}_R$, generalized reaction potential
- $_S\dot{I}_R$, aggregate inhibitory potential

COLUMN 4
- $_S\overline{E}_R$, net reaction potential
- $_SO_R$, oscillation of reaction potential
- $_SL_R$, reaction threshold

COLUMN 5
- $_St_R$, reaction latency
- A, reaction amplitude
- n, number of non-reinforced responses to extinction

characters. Figure 14–2 is a plot of the average latency of response on fifteen successive presentations of those 125 symbols. Thus, each point is the mean of 125 latencies.

It appears that reaction latency is inversely related to the number of reinforcements. That is, the greater the number of reinforcements, the faster the person makes the response. The curve which is fitted to the points is the reciprocal of a positive growth function, which indicates that habit grows most rapidly at first and then by smaller and smaller amounts. Hull asserted that the growth of habit strength was related to the amount which remained between its strength at the beginning of a trial and the maximum strength which it could empirically reach. He expressed this relationship in the following formula, which illustrates Hull's attempt at exact quantification of his constructs:

$$_SH_R = 1 - 10^{-aN}$$

where a is determined empirically as a constant and N is the number of trials.

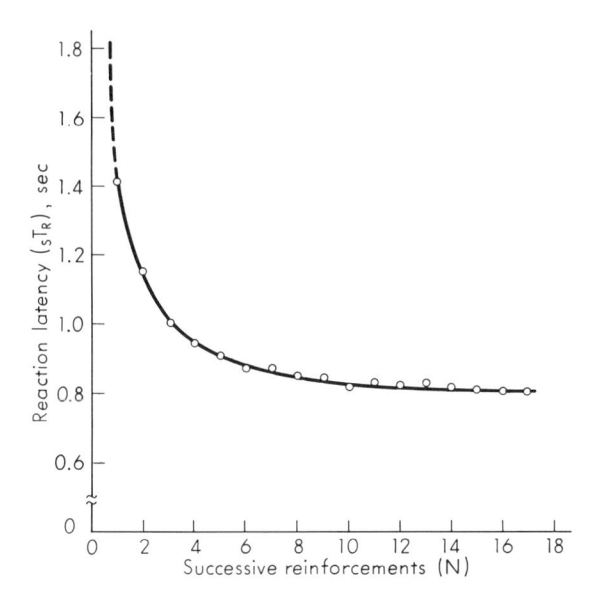

FIG. 14–2 Empirical learning curve (reaction latency versus reinforcement). (*Hull, 1941*)

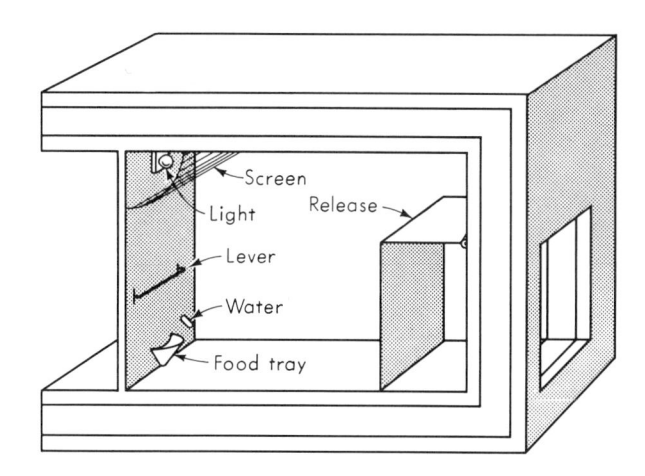

FIG. 14–3 Typical experimental box. (*Skinner, 1938*)

In the system used by Hull, the symbol D was used to refer to the motivational state of the organism, that is, its level of drives. The relationship of D to $_sH_R$ is multiplicative; that is, the strength of motivation will determine the amount of performance of a habit. In Example 14–2, we present the experiments which Hull used in deriving their relationship.

Example 14–2 *Strength of drive performance: Poor motivation results in low performance (Williams, 1938; Perin, 1942)*

Using a refinement of the Thorndike instrumental learning situation, two experimenters, Perin (1942) and Williams (1938) trained albino rats to obtain food by pressing a lever. A diagram of such an apparatus is shown in Figure 14–3. Each time the animals press the lever, a tiny pellet of food falls into the box, and the animals can eat. Under such conditions, hungry rats soon learn to press at very high rates. The apparatus is called the Skinner box after the psychologist B. F. Skinner, who made much use of it (Skinner, 1938).

Perin and Williams gave separate groups of their animals different numbers of reinforcements, which varied from five to ninety. During learning, all animals were food-deprived for 23 hours. Later the groups were subdivided in half. Each group was put back in the box at different levels of food deprivation: either 3 hours or 23 hours. Now, the lever was disconnected and lever pressing yielded no food. In other words, the animals' responses were subjected to experimental extinction.

The number of responses which the rats made until extinction was produced is plotted in Figure 14–4. It is clear from the figure that both the number of reinforcements and the state of deprivation of the animals were potent factors in determining performance of a habit. The curve for a group in which the habit was extinguished under a high degree of hunger reveals that they were willing to work long after the lever no longer yielded food. While we would all agree that this result is one to be expected from common sense, the careful work of these experimenters has given us a quantitative demonstration of the relation between drive and performance.

Hull used the symbol V to stand for a factor that he called *stimulus intensity dynamism*. It refers to the ability of strong stimuli to activate organisms. Hull observed that habits are activated by strong stimuli even when the motivational level of animals is not changed. He added V to account for this dynamic quality of increased stimulation.

The symbol K was used by Hull to refer to *incentive motivation*. K was developed to account for

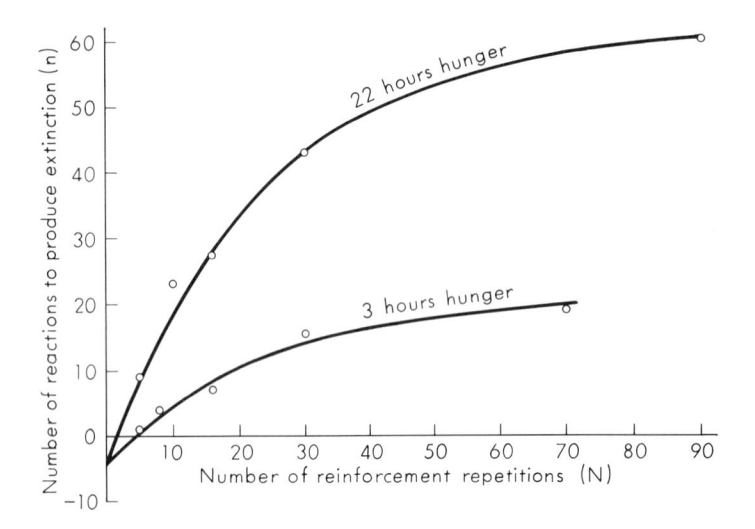

FIG. 14-4 Number of reactions to produce extinction versus reinforcement. (*Hull, 1941*)

the ability of certain goal objects to activate behavior according to their size, or amount, or other dimension, e.g., sweetness, for which psychological preference is shown. Thus, we all know that people will work harder for a larger amount of money than they will for a small amount. It is also true that a larger amount of food is a greater incentive for rats even though their level of drive (D) has not been changed.

There are also subtractive factors which decrease the level of performance of a habit. I_R, the first of these, we have already referred to in our discussion of Pavlov's work. Hull called it *reactive inhibition*. The construct describes the fact that making a response decreases the probability that it will be made again soon thereafter. Although I_R is often referred to as a conventional physiological fatigue factor, it is incorrect to equate I_R with fatigue. There is clearly a psychological component to fatigue. For example, a response which has been extinguished will often reappear if a strong distraction is introduced into the situation. This is called *disinhibition* and indicates that fatigue alone does not cause the diminution of responding or extinction.

$_sI_R$ is of special interest in the system, because it refers to a habit which competes with the main habit in the situation. $_sI_R$ is a habit of not responding. Hull observed that spontaneous recovery, which we discussed earlier under the work of Pavlov, was never complete, and he introduced $_sI_R$ to account for that fact. The concept is logical enough, because not responding is reinforced when I_R, which has motivational properties, is reduced. Fatigue is a drive to stop responding. When we stop, fatigue dissipates, which is drive-reducing and reinforcing. The response which led to the reinforcement is therefore increased in likelihood; that is, a habit of not responding is built up in strength.

The presentation given here is much simplified and does not do justice to the work involved in the development of Hull's system. Suffice it to say that the system was built to be precise and therefore it was a relatively easy matter to test Hull's predictions. Such a theory is also one which can be proved wrong. To say that subsequent research showed some of Hullian theory to be wrong is a compliment to his precision in defining his constructs. We will return to his work in a later section. We can close with Hull's own testimony to his commitment to the mathematicodeductive theory:

In scientific theory logic is employed in conjunction with observation as a means of inquiry. Indeed, theoretical procedures are indispensable in the establishment of natural laws. The range of validity of a given supposed law can be determined only by trying it out empirically under a wide range of conditions where it will operate in simultaneous conjunction with the greater variety and combination of other natural laws. But the only way the scientist can tell from the outcome of such empirical procedure whether a given hypothetical law has acted in the postulated manner is first to deduce by a logical process what the outcome of the investigation *should* be if the hypothesis really holds. This deductive process is the essence of scientific theory [Hull, 1943].

Operant Conditioning: Observation without Theory

Not every psychologist has been enamored of theory building as the path to understanding behavior. At least one vigorous and highly influential school of psychology has actively rejected theorizing in favor of a programmatic empiricism and objectivism. The school consists of the followers of B. F. Skinner, who are therefore referred to as Skinnerians. Their viewpoint stands in sharp contrast to that of Hull: it consists of no theory at all. Few psychologists who are still active on the psychological scene today have had the impact and the audience beyond the range of their own discipline that Skinner has had. He is the symbol of behaviorism to the intellectual world of our time.

The latter-day Skinner is the result of an evolutionary attitude in scientific method. In his early period, he began as a somewhat orthodox behaviorist who wrote at length on the reflexes, following Pavlov and Sherrington. At least during the period following his doctoral dissertation, he was still readily classified as an S-R psychologist whose work flowed from that of Thorndike. Indeed, Thorndike's influence is clear, since most of Skinner's later experimentation has made use of a greatly refined Thorndikean puzzle-box, the one which has come to be called the Skinner box. Skinner broke with the S-R tradition later when he subdivided responses into two classes: *respondent behavior* and *operant behavior*. Traditional associationistic S-R formulations had placed emphasis on the stimulus which elicits a response, and it was always assumed that every response had a stimulus. But Skinner, unwilling to make any assumptions, simply called responses which occurred without a known stimulus *operants*. Operants were contrasted to respondents, for which the stimuli were known. Thus Pavlov's salivation situation involved respondents, but the Thorndikean situation was an operant-conditioning situation.

Most of the work done by Skinner and his students has involved the exploration of the conditions which control operants, the first and most important of which is reinforcement. For Skinner, reinforcement, in its simplest terms, the empirical law of effect, is the major determinant of behavior. When an operant is reinforced, its rate of emission is increased. That is all that Skinner is willing to say. The stark simplicity of his system gives it a classic beauty. The role of the psychologist becomes one of reinforcing operants so as to control behavior. Since most human adult behavior is operant in nature, the respondent can be easily relegated to a minor position of concern.

Two measures are regularly used in the study of operants: resistance to extinction and the rate at which the response is emitted. The first measure, resistance to extinction, refers to the number of times a subject will continue to emit an operant, say, press a bar, after reinforcement has ceased. To illustrate this measure, let us consider Figure 14–5. The graph is what Skinner calls a cumulative record. It works in this way: Every time the subject, in this case a rat, presses the bar, a pen is moved upward a slight amount. The pen is marking a paper which is moving from right to left. In this way, whenever the animal does nothing, the pen marks the paper with a horizontal line. Upward movement, that is, areas where the curve shows a sharp rise denotes times when the animal was pressing at a fast rate. The angle, or slope, of the curve indicates the rate at which the operant is being emitted. Because the responses each add to the height of the curve, they are said to cumulate.

Note in Figure 14–5 that two curves are shown, representing the behavior of two different rats which had had different numbers of reinforcements before the food-delivery apparatus was turned off, subjecting their responses to extinction. Quite obviously, there are more responses emitted following a larger number of reinforcements, but the single reinforcement still leads to well over fifty responses.

The second measure, steady rate of response emission, was developed by Skinner as the result of a problem which he faced during his early laboratory experience. As he was using rats and reinforcing them with small pellets of food fed by an automatic device, he required great numbers of these pellets of food. Since he rolled his own pills, using an old apothecary pill press, the task of keeping up with the rats was a tremendously time-consuming one. To save time, he decided to let his animals press freely, but he gave them a pellet only after a fixed amount of time passed. Thus, he was able

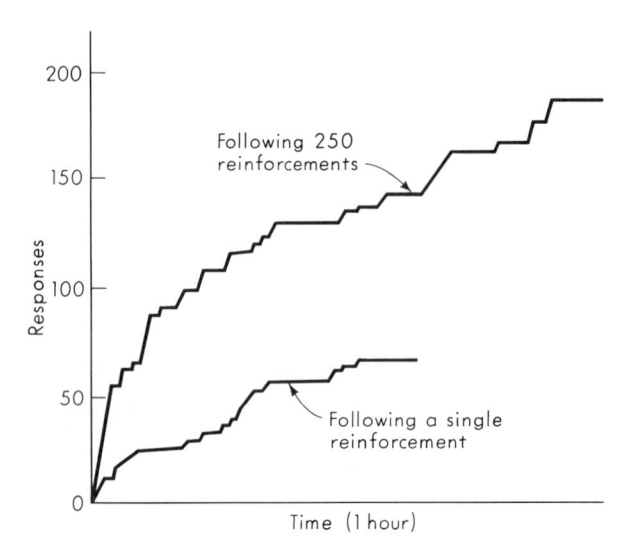

FIG. 14–5 Extinction of lever press by rats. (*Skinner, 1938*)

to test his rats for long sessions with only a few pellets. If he simply gave a pellet every three minutes, for instance, he would have his animals on what has come to be known as a schedule of reinforcement of fixed intervals of three minutes.

Rather remarkably, Skinner found that his rats pressed away happily on the fixed-interval schedule, settling down to a steady rate of pressing for hour-long experimental periods in the apparatus. The curves which he obtained suggested a steady state of behavior, which he felt to be highly desirable for the study of operants. Other sciences, such as physics, had made much use of steady-state conditions, and here was a possible analogy in behavior. If animals could be kept in a steady state of responding by scheduling their reinforcements, then it might be possible to study the parameters of operant behavior, such as the effects of different schedulings of reinforcement on the behavior of the animal. To accomplish this end, he placed animals under different fixed-interval schedules and found, indeed, that the rate of emission of operants was much changed under different periodic reinforcements. The left side of Figure 14–6 is a plot of the responses of four different rats during a one-hour session on different fixed intervals. The right side of Figure 14–6 is a plot of the responses of the same animals over twenty-five daily one-hour sessions.

The steady-state hypothesis is supported in both records. Animals seem to settle down to a rate which is related to the temporal frequency of the reinforcement. The more often they are reinforced, the higher the rate at which they press. Although the curves in Figure 14–6 appear quite smooth, actually there is a stepwise character to them. This consists of a slowing down just after reinforcement and a speeding up as the time for the next reinforcement approaches. It appears that the animals learn to tell time and to regulate responding accordingly. This phenomenon of scalloping can be corrected by varying the intervals at which the reinforcements occur in what is called a variable-interval schedule. Under such conditions, extremely uniform and stable rates of responding occur, and resistance to extinction can be remarkably great. In one reported case, at least, a pigeon emitted 10,000 responses during extinction following variable-interval training.

It is a mistake to conclude from the effects of fixed-interval scheduling that all partial reinforcement affects behavior in the same way. We saw that, under interval schedules, rates of responses increase with more frequent reinforcement. That is, the more reinforcement an animal receives in, say, an hour, the more responses he will make. But something quite different happens when an animal is placed on a different type of schedule in which he is reinforced after a constant number of responses. Such a schedule is called a fixed ratio. Rather paradoxically, the animals show higher rates of responding the *less frequent*—that is, the higher—the ratio of reinforcements. This finding is illustrated in Figure 14–7, which shows three cumulative records of animals under different fixed-ratio schedules. The animals who were being reinforced for only every 192 responses show much faster rates of responding.

In addition, the scalloping effect seems pronounced when fixed ratio is used. This effect is much like human behavior, in which high bursts of activity at times slow down when a part of the ultimate goal is reached. Perhaps the "sophomore slump" shown by so many college students is an example of the effect of reaching the reinforcement of the end of the freshman year with a burst of ac-

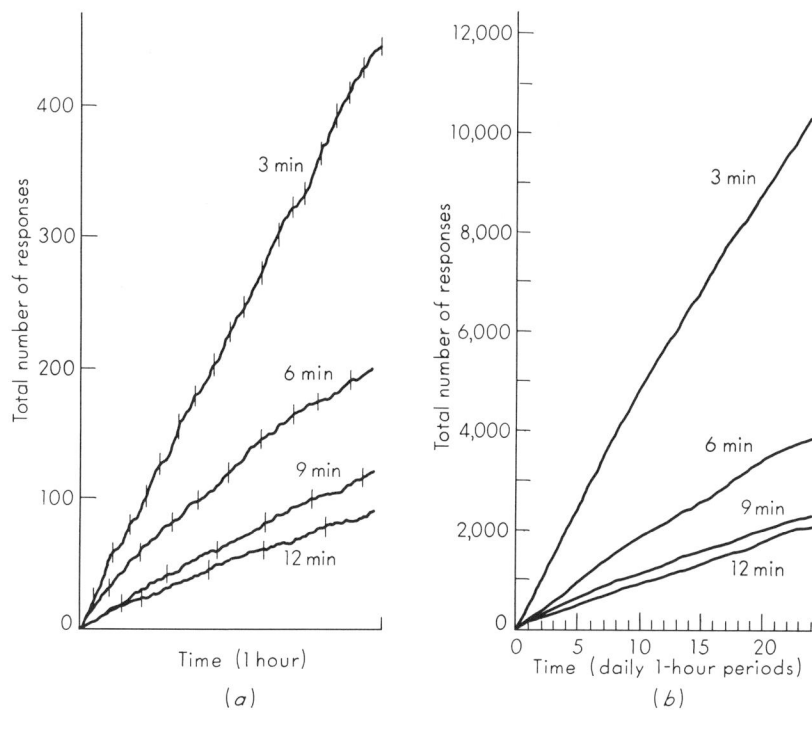

FIG. 14-6 Responses within one session of fixed-interval reinforcement. (*Hilgard & Marquis, 1940*)

tivity. Then, the student finds it difficult to pick up the high level again, and he slumps for a time. The scalloping can be smoothed out by placing the subjects under a variable ratio in which reinforcement is given after different numbers of responses are averaged out to a given number. For example, more or less at random, an animal might be reinforced after 10, 2, 6, 8, 4 responses. The variable ratio is then said to be 6.

Although Skinner has rejected elaborate theory construction, he has not been at all averse to the application, in practical, real-life situations, of principles derived from the laboratory study of behavior. In his textbook *Science and Human Behavior* (1953), he extends the principles of operant conditioning to many of the problems faced by society and the individuals in it. In addition, he has written a utopian novel in which he presents an ideal social order built on his experimental analysis of behavior. Although the book is really more a polemic for his own view of the techniques for control of behavior than a work of literary art, it has been accorded wide attention. There has been a good deal of protest over his strong emphasis on control of behavior. That his critics are somewhat unfair to Skinner, whose social concerns appear to be as humanistic as theirs, is testified to by the following quotation, which appears at the end of an article in which Skinner describes the use of his principles to develop programed machines for classroom teaching:

> Not only education but Western Culture as a whole is moving away from aversive practices. We cannot prepare young people for one kind of life in institutions organized on quite different principles. The discipline of the birch rod may facilitate learning, but we must remember that it also breeds followers of dictators and revolutionists.
>
> In the light of our present knowledge, a school system must be called a failure if it cannot induce students to learn except by threatening them for not learning. That this has always been the standard pattern simply emphasizes the importance of modern techniques. John Dewey was speaking for his culture and his time when he attacked aversive educational practices and appealed to teachers to turn to positive and humane methods. What he threw out should have been thrown out. Unfortunately, he had too little to put in its place.

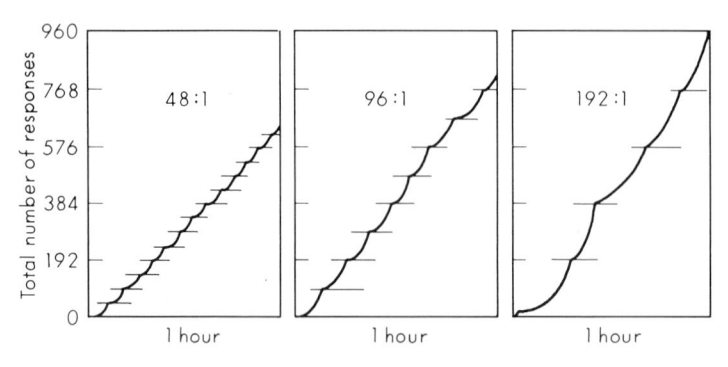

FIG. 14–7 Responses within ratio reinforcements. (*Hilgard & Marquis, 1940*)

Progressive education has been a temporizing measure which can now be effectively supplemented. Aversive practices cannot only be replaced, they can be replaced with far more powerful techniques. The possibilities should be thoroughly explored if we are to build an educational system which will meet the present demand without sacrificing democratic principles [Skinner, 1958].

In a very real sense, Skinner followed in the footsteps of Pavlov, Thorndike, and Ebbinghaus, all of whom made strong attempts to solve practical problems using the methods derived from their work in the laboratory. However, Skinner differs from them in that he has disavowed theory in the laboratory and yet has freely theorized about society.

Having considered the two extreme positions on the question of how complex a theory of learning should be—Hull opting for a high degree of formalization and Skinner for relatively little—we can turn our attention to some other important psychologists of the period who have held less extreme views. We will consider two men, Edwin Guthrie, whose position has been more like that of Skinner, and Edward Tolman, who has developed quite a complex theory of behavior, almost as intricate as that of Hull, but who has chosen not to make use of constructs which could be measured and quantified as Hull's were.

Contiguous Conditioning: A One-principle Theory of Learning

Edwin Guthrie's theory of behavior is a relatively simple one. It flows directly from the behavioristic model of John Watson and the reflexology of Ivan Pavlov. Like Watson, Guthrie adhered directly to the notion that we must analyze behavior and eschew introspective data about states of consciousness. He viewed Pavlov's classical conditioning as the basic paradigm for studying learning.

Central to Guthrie's theory (Guthrie, 1952) is the very narrow definition he gives to the basic units to be used in the analysis of learning. In his stimulus-response system, a response is taken to be a highly specific motor reaction, these being evoked by stimuli in the environment. Guthrie interprets this S-R relationship as only a small part of a total effector movement. His point is that we should not analyze behavior in terms of gross acts but rather study subunits of behavior. When we consider the manner in which these subunits are learned and assembled into functional units, we will have a better understanding of behavior as a whole.

Likewise, a stimulus is defined by Guthrie as a highly specific sensory excitation which is a very small part of all stimulus elements present in the environment at any one instant. Thus, in a large room, the stimulus elements would be all the objects within the room. We do not respond to a whole room during the course of learning, but rather to some smaller parts of the room. As we shall see, it is only when we have undergone a repeated learning experience in an environment, such as a room, that we learn to perform the response well. This is because it must relate to all stimuli present before it will predictably occur. Otherwise, if one object has not been learned as the stimulus for the response, it may, later on, inhibit the response.

Guthrie also stressed those stimuli which are produced internally within the organism by its movements. These *movement-produced cues*, or feedback stimuli, were introduced by him to explain the way in which the organism maintains its reactions when external stimulation is not adequate to explain the pattern of behavior which is exhibited. As an example, a person may learn to dance on the basis of these movement-produced cues, or he may learn the complex coordination of a skilled sport on the basis of a combination of internal and external cues. A good example of this is the ice-hockey player who falls off balance, slides across the ice, regains his feet, and races off after the puck without ever losing his stick or using his hands to raise himself. The action takes place in one quick flow of motion, and the player is obviously using external cues to guide himself in the direction of his recovery; internal cues appear to direct the balancing which restores him to his skating posture. There is no break in the movements. There appears to be no time for thinking about recovery. Yet, the action is dominated by direction and sensitive response to change.

Guthrie made an important distinction between a response and an act. A response he defined as a highly specific motor reaction at the muscular level. In contrast, an act is defined in terms of the consequences it produces. The distinction is between molecular motor movements and action systems which accomplish certain ends. For Guthrie an act is composed of a number of responses which are chained together to produce a desired consequence. Movements are the units of learning in his theory. He strongly emphasized that the specific result of learning was the connection of a stimulus and a response element of movement, which must be carefully defined for any learning situation. Within this system, it was important to examine the individual movements which were made in a given learning situation so as to be able to predict on later occasions what movements would occur.

There was only one principle in Guthrie's theory: the law of contiguity. Actually, as he stated the principle of contiguity, it had implicit in it another principle—the principle of postremity. This states that the last response made will be what will most probably occur in a subsequent occasion. This was so, according to Guthrie, because a bond was formed between the stimulus and the response by contiguous occurrence. Note that *every* situation is a learning situation in such a theory. It follows that the contiguous occurrences of a stimulus and a response are the necessary and sufficient conditions for learning. The reader may also realize that Guthrie has written an explanation of forgetting into into his theory by simply stating that it is the last response that is learned. Presumably, previous responses will no longer be bonded to the stimuli, since new ones have taken their place.

It should be emphasized that theorists who have advanced an "effect" interpretation of learning, such as Thorndike and Hull would not agree that contiguity is sufficient for learning.

Perhaps the most important logical implication of the principle of contiguity developed by Guthrie is the assertion that all learning can take place in a single trial. The question of whether one-trial learning is the model for all learning has stirred up a great deal of controversy among learning theorists. Guthrie's hypothesis may be stated more rigorously as follows: when an organism is in the presence of a stimulus, it will always do what it did the last time it was in the presence of that stimulus, provided the stimulus is, in fact, identical. The last condition is crucial. The stimulus situations must be identical in order to allow the prediction of behavior. This point follows from the way he analyzes stimulus situations into their component elements, as we have said above.

There is, however, a caution to be observed in applying the identity notion to predictions of behavior. According to Guthrie, the law of one-trial learning applies only to the basic units of analysis, that is to say, to movements or responses. An act, that is, behavior, which is considered as an action system, such as escaping from a puzzlebox, includes several different movements, and these movements all have the property of changing the patterns of stimulation present, both because of the internal stimulation they produce and because of the reorientation of the sense receptors which results from movement. Therefore, one-trial learning does not occur with acts, since each component segment of an act is conditioned. To accomplish this integration of the subunit movements into a learned act requires a number of learning trials. To repeat, movements are learned in one trial, but integrated acts which consist of several movements require a number of trials to be learned. When a complex act is to be learned, Guthrie's theory, in common with the theories of Hull or Thorndike, predicts that there will be a gradual, *seemingly* incremental change in proficiency.

As an outgrowth of his thinking, Guthrie placed a good deal of emphasis on the stereotyped nature of movements in any particular stimulus situation. It follows from a combination of the principle of contiguity and the principle of one-trial learning that behavior should not change when stimulus conditions do not change. Guthrie pointed out that in most experimental situations used by psychologists, such as mazes, there is too much variation in effective stimulation from trial to trial to permit a demonstration of this stereotypy of behavior. To prove his point, Guthrie devised a puzzle box for cats, something like that of Thorndike but designed to allow careful control of environmental stimuli from trial to trial and to demonstrate stereotypy of movements by which the animal escaped. Example 14–3 presents the experiment in outline.

Example 14–3 *The stereotypy of behavior (Guthrie & Horton, 1946)*

Some behavior is successful only if it is highly stereotyped. Consider, for example, the basketball player throwing from the foul line. If he is an expert, he will go through a sequence of movements which is very, very carefully reduced to an exact pattern. He holds the ball so, he bends his knees, rises with exact care, and flips the ball with a spin designed to drop it through the hoop. Again and again, any one player will do exactly the same thing, and the good player will score with great frequency. Guthrie and Horton set out to demonstrate in the laboratory that behavior has such repetitiveness. They built a puzzle box for cats which had a glass front permitting the use of photographic techniques to record the behavior of animals at the exact point in time when they escaped from the box. A pole placed in the center of the floor was hooked to the release so that any movement of the pole dropped the door and allowed the animal to escape. When the release was tripped, a trigger photographed the scene.

Guthrie's work was not designed to test the intelligence of the cats. It would have been easy for him to devise a situation which would have required far less stereotypy on the part of the animal. The point which he wished to make was that the animal would tend to do whatever it last did in any situation, and the puzzle box was a good setup in which to demonstrate this phenomenon.

In Figure 14–8 are presented four tracings made from photographs of a single cat taken at the time of escape. Clearly the cat exhibits an unusual method of getting out of the box. He hits the pole with his tail. These pictures were taken on trials 9 through 12 consecutively. From these pictures, Guthrie asserts that associative connection of stimuli and movements is the model of learning.

Because he did not recognize the law of effect, Guthrie had to account for the obvious fact that reinforcement increased the probability of repetition of a response. Certainly, he, in common with all theorists of learning, had to accept the empirical law of effect, but the burden was placed on him to account for this generality of the efficacy of reinforcement within his simple contiguity theory. To accomplish an explanation of the effects of reinforcement, he argued that the occurrence of the reward makes a drastic change in the stimulus situation. This change "protects" the last response made before reinforcement from being unlearned. This follows because the new stimulus changes the situation and the bond between the stimuli present before the reinforcement is protected. However, there are difficulties with this interpretation. In some laboratory learning situations, such as the Skinner box, it does not seem resonable to say that the small amount of food used as a reinforcement can much change the situation. A second problem arises because punishment also readily changes the stimulus situation. Yet, punishment does not protect associative bonds and increase the probability of response.

Aside from these criticisms, Guthrie's theory of learning, like that of Skinner, has an attractive simplicity which has perhaps been responsible for its being used as a basis for the development of some mathematical theories of learning. William Estes, in particular, has built upon Guthrie's model. Finally, we should mention that Guthrie was first of all a teacher and stressed that fact in his writing. He spelled out in detail practical methods to be used in teaching. These were based on his view of the way in which the process of learning proceeds. He admonished parents to put their children through the exact behavior which they wished to have them learn, because it was stereotypy which was necessary. Further, he emphasized changing behavior by having it recur in the proper form. In an amusing, yet highly instructive way, he insists that parents

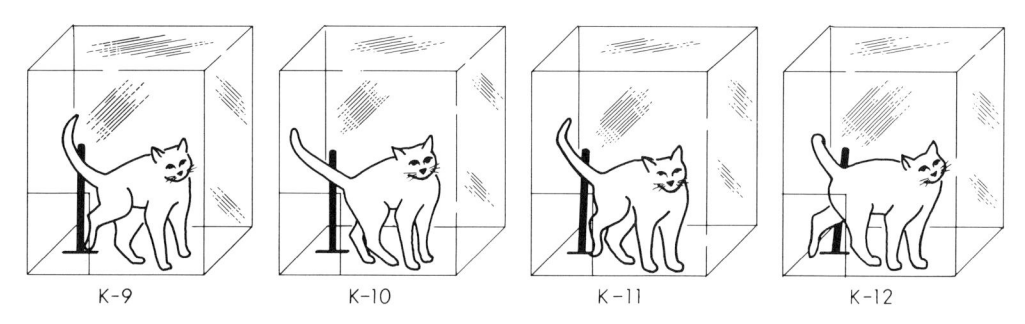

FIG. 14–8 Four trials in the escape of a cat from a puzzle box.

not punish their children; rather, children should be led through the correct behavior and then rewarded.

From Guthrie we will turn to Edward Tolman, a theorist who developed a system which was much more complex than that of Skinner or Guthrie yet which was not designed to be quantifiable in the way in which Hull's theory was. An examination of the structure of Tolman's system will provide us with our fourth approach to theory building in behavioristic psychology.

Purposive Behaviorism: A Complex Cognitive Theory

As early as 1917, Edward Tolman espoused the behavioristic viewpoint in psychology (Tolman, 1917). As his system evolved, however, it differed in important ways from the other behavioristic models of both that and later periods. It was these differences, which we will spell out shortly, which led to a lengthy debate between Hull and Tolman as to the nature of the learning process. But in spite of certain fundamental divergencies from orthodox behaviorism, Tolman's system was a true behaviorism (Tolman, 1932). Tolman acknowledged that he owed a debt to Watson. He also placed emphasis on his indebtedness to Gestalt psychology, which directed the attention of psychology to the goal-directed nature of behavior and its essential unity, or "wholeness." Although well aware of the differences of his theory from other behavioristic theories, Tolman firmly maintained that his system was a genuine behaviorism which rejected introspection as the methodology of psychology. We will consider three aspects of the theory which characterized Tolman's work from its beginning until his later formulations.

As we have said, Tolman strongly rejected the method of introspection, particularly as it was used by the American structuralists, who were at their strongest during Tolman's student days. In this, he was a rebel who insisted that Watson's formulations were useful. However, in his writings Tolman refers often to "cognitive states," seemingly contrary to Watsonian doctrine. The contradiction, however, is not real. Tolman was very careful to spell out the fact that such constructs as expectancies and beliefs were really carefully defined in terms of observable behaviors. His *intervening variables*, as he called these constructs, were introduced as interpretations of the behaviors observed. They were not to be used alone, but only insofar as they were firmly anchored to the behavior of the organism being studied. Thus, when Tolman observed an animal in a maze making head movements from side to side, he called such behavior "vicarious trial and error" (VTE). The phrase may seem to imply that the animal is thinking or reasoning out a choice, but Tolman defined VTE in terms of the movements of the head of the animal. Thus, although his terminology suggested that the animal was thinking, he presented evidence only in terms of the behavior of the animal, that is, in terms of movements which oriented its eyes and ears when it had to choose between two paths to a goal.

On the other hand, Tolman quite firmly rejected the reduction of behavior to physiology or to molecular fractions of an act. Included in this repudiation of reductionism was any explanation of behavior by consideration of those muscular, glandular, or neural processes which might underlie it. Tolman insisted that behavior must be studied on its own level, because it had distinctive attributes all its own. He argued that the study of muscle

245   IMPORTANT ISSUES IN THE STUDY OF THE LEARNING PROCESS action is not the study of behavior as it occurs in the living and behaving organism. The reader may remember the quotation in the Prologue to this section from John Dewey on the use of the reflex arc in psychology to explain behavior. Tolman's position is in the tradition of Dewey's argument that behavior must be considered as a whole and not reduced to its parts.

Finally, Tolman's system can be described as a *purposivism*, because of the emphasis placed on the degree to which behavior is regulated by a recognizable goal toward which it is directed. Thus, purposive behavior is goal-directed behavior. The organism must be understood in terms of the objects which are effective in regulating its behavior. At this point, there is a possibility of misunderstanding which Tolman carefully avoided. To say that an organism is goal-directed does not imply, in his system, that the organism had a self-conscious mind which was actively seeking a goal. Rather, the system placed an emphasis on the inclusion of the effect of the goal on behavior. There are many other determinants of behavior besides goals, such as the stimuli in the environment and past experience with them. Tolman did not intend to make the effects of the goal the overriding concern in his system; however, he placed emphasis on goal seeking as an attribute of behavior.

Particularly important within Tolman's analysis of behavior was the emphasis placed on environmental supports or determinants of behavior. The world of the organism is a world of tools and paths by which to arrive at goals. There are also obstacles and detours with which the organism must interact on the path to his goal. The cognitive nature of Tolman's system stems from his development of constructs which referred to hypothetical and unobserved states within the organism. These hypothetical states were used by the organism in making paths and tools serve its purposes.

Tolman emphasized the *principle of least effort*. In his version, the principle stated that there is a selective preference on the part of the organism for easy rather than more difficult ways to achieve particular goals. As a companion principle, he underscored the *docility* of behavior. That is, behavior is plastic, or changeable. Thus, when one is considering the process of learning, the most important attribute of behavior is the manner in which it is readily varied so as to bring about success in goal seeking.

Among his many insightful contributions to psychology was Tolman's development of the concept of the *intervening variable*. He hypothesized that a complete act of behavior was the result of cognitive processes which assumed control of behavior which had been initiated by environmental stimuli and physiological states such as needs. While this language seems formidable, what is being said is that the organism begins its behavior because of some internal state of bodily need or environmental stimulation. For instance, the animal may be hungry and then begin to seek food, or it may be lying near a place where a loud sound suddenly occurs, and it may be frightened and run. However, once cognitive processes are directing behavior, they intervene between immediate states of affairs and the final act which occurs. Thus an animal seeking food when hungry would not just run because it felt need. Rather it would act in terms of goals which it had previously experienced and about which it had expectancies. It should be clear, however, that Tolman was careful to define the data of psychology as being rooted in the external world. He was thus able to maintain his position as a behaviorist.

In his presidential address, before the American Psychological Association in 1937 (Tolman, 1938), he listed those variables which he considered to enter into the determination of behavior. Table 14–1 is the list of variables taken from Tolman's paper. The list can be divided in two ways: One division separates environmental variables from variables which reflect individual differences. The second division correlates intervening variables and environmental variables, so that one can easily understand the manner in which Tolman defined his intervening variables.

As we indicated at the beginning of our discussion, Tolman's theory differs in one important way from that of Hull and other behaviorists: it does not aim at quantitatively precise predictions about behavior. In his description of behavior, Tolman's use of molar constructs led to a concern with what it was the animal was trying to achieve rather than with the measurement of the movements or rates of responding which it made en route to the goal. In

Table 14-1 Environmental and intervening variables

I. Environmental variables
    M—Maintenance schedule
    G—Appropriateness of goal object
    S—Types and modes of stimuli provided
    R—Types of motor response required
    $\Sigma(OBO)$—Cumulative nature and number of trials*
    P—Pattern of preceding and succeeding maze units

II. Individual difference variables
    H—Heredity
    A—Age
    T—Previous training
    E—Special endocrine, drug or vitamin conditions

Intervening variable	Correlated environmental variable
Demand	Maintenance schedule
Appetite	Appropriateness of goal object
Differentiation	Types and modes of stimuli provided
Motor skill	Types of motor response required
Hypotheses	Cumulative nature and number of trials
Biases	Pattern of preceding and succeeding maze units

* $\Sigma(OBO)$ is a shorthand formula which means some consequence or summation of previous experiences in which one occasion (O) has led through behavior (B) to another occasion (O). The occasions are such features as a choice point, a goal at the left, and so on.

spite of this difference in emphasis and technique in analysis, Tolman maintained the necessity for operational definitions of the terms which he used within his system. In one of his last papers, he listed those variables which he thought must be operationally defined. Table 14-2 presents the list taken from his paper.

Later, we will return to Tolman's theory, particularly in respect to its treatment of "ideas." Here, however, we will conclude our discussion of the complexity of the different theories by presenting an example which illustrates a controversy which arose between Hull and Tolman. The issue at stake was the question of "what is learned—(during the solution of complex behavior)—a sequence of responses, or a behavior route or cognitive map which contains information about what leads to what?"

Table 14-2 Variables to be operationally defined

Need systems:
1. List of needs
2. Magnitude of a given need at a given moment

Belief-value matrices:
1. Magnitude of the gratification and deprivation "values" of the given matrix at a given time
2. Shape of the cathexis belief attaching the various types of goal object (arrayed along a given generalized dimension) to the gratification end of a given matrix
3. Shape of the means-end belief attaching types of means object (arrayed along a given generalization dimension) to a given type of goal object or subgoal object

Behavior spaces:
1. Perceived qualities, distances, and directions in the behavior space
2. Strength of a need push
3. Strength of a positive or negative valence
4. Strength and direction of a field force
5. Identification of a locomotion.

Example 14-4 *What is learned? Place learning versus response learning (Tolman, Ritchie, & Kalish, 1946)*

In most S-R theories, the learner is described as learning to make a series of responses which are evoked by the cues present in the situation. Thus if an animal is placed at the starting point (S_1) in a maze, such as the one shown in Figure 14-9, he is said by S-R theorists to learn to find food at the goal (F_1) by learning to respond by turning right at the choice point (C). The important idea is that the stimuli, or cues, present at C evoke the behavior of turning right when the animal has learned the maze. But in Tolman's theory, the animals are said to learn the maze according to signs which they understand to be significant for finding the goal. They have a cognitive map which contains behavior routes. Thus in the view of the S-R theorists learning consisted of acquiring movements, while in Tolman's view it consisted of developing an understanding of what leads to what.

To test this defined difference between the the-

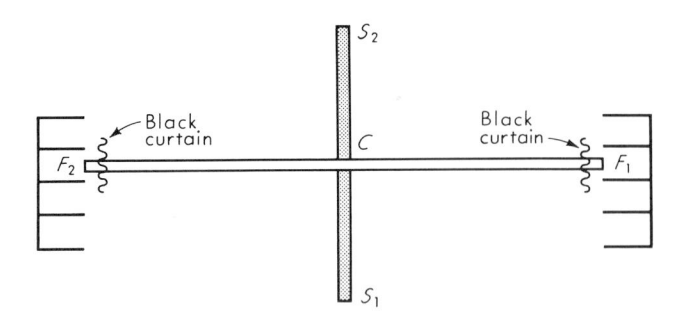

FIG. 14–9 Maze used to test the relative ease of learning. (*Tolman, Ritchie, & Kalish, 1946*)

ories, Tolman, Ritchie, and Kalish made use of the cross maze shown in Figure 14–9. They designed their experiment so as to pit a movement habit against a space-learning habit and measure which is more easily learned. And, of course, the logic of this type of experiment depends on the notion that the type of habit which is more easily learned is the one which the animal must be better equipped to use, or the one which is ordinarily used by the animals.

The apparatus was an elevated maze in the form of a cross. There were two groups of rats. The first group, called the response-learning group, was started at random alternation of trial from either S_1 or S_2 and could always find food by turning to the right. On any one trial there was food only in one goal box. Thus, if the animal was started from S_1, food was in F_1. When it was started from S_2, food was in F_2. On the other hand, the place-learning group always found food at the same place, regardless of where they were started.

The place-learning group was far superior to the response-learning group: all 8 place-learning rats learned in 8 trials. None of the response-learning group of 8 rats learned that fast, and 5 did not learn the task in 72 trials.

In special conditions posed by the learning of an elevated cross maze, which has very many extra-maze cues, place learning is easier than response learning. However, later experimental work indicated that the animals might have been using extra-maze cues to solve the problem. When salient extra-maze cues were reduced, the animals appeared to learn responses more easily than places.

The example dealing with place learning versus response learning, with its overtones of cognitive processes, leads us to the second major problem faced by theorists of learning during that period, the question of the major law of learning. As we will see, the controversies became more difficult to resolve, since it proved difficult to design experiments which could be agreed upon as true tests of the theories involved.

WHAT IS THE MAJOR LAW OF LEARNING?

During the middle period of the development of theories of behavior there was one major question about which much controversy raged: what is the major law of learning? Without an understanding of the issues involved in this controversy, it is difficult for a student to comprehend the experimental and theoretical debates of the period. Indeed, in retrospect, the period is marked by its concentration on problems generated by theoretical differences. To say that there were many debates which had only limited interest for those outside the discipline is not to say that the outcomes were not important.

In our discussion of Hull and Skinner, we were very much concerned with the principle of reinforcement. As we have seen in Thorndike's system, the law of effect seemed to hold up under experimental test, and, therefore, the attention of learning theorists was focused on the question of just how the law of effect worked. The theorists whom we will consider are those we have discussed before: Hull, Tolman, and Skinner. In addition, outgrowths of the controversy, such as the extension of the concept of motivation, will be of interest to us here.

A Theory of Reinforcement: Drive Reduction as the Most Important Law of Learning

During our survey of Hull's (1943) system earlier in this chapter, we alluded to Hull's emphasis on the principle of reinforcement as the most important law of learning. Now, we will examine the relevant parts of Hull's system in greater detail, because it is fair to say that it was Hull's formulation of the role of motivation in learning which touched off the debates that marked the psychology of the period.

The central construct in Hull's system is habit strength. In the study of learning, Hull suggests that the growth of habit strength is the crucial matter. Now Hull made several separate formulations about the way in which habits were developed. The first of these postulates related habit to reinforcement. Primary reinforcement was defined as a strengthening of a stimulus-response connection which occurs if there is contiguity of the stimulus and the response and the response is followed by a rapid decrease in drive level. As we said earlier, the statement that a reduction in motivation is a condition for learning is called the drive-reduction hypothesis.

But there are a number of difficulties inherent in theories of the relationship between motivation and learning. It is a fact that a small amount of food given to a food-deprived subject cannot have much effect in decreasing its biological drive state, in the sense of putting nutrient substances into its cells. Whatever decrease in drive occurs must be a very slow process. It takes a good deal of time for food which reaches the stomach to be absorbed and reach the cells of the body that have a deficit caused by deprivation. Because of these problems, Hull suggested that deprivation had two consequences for the organism: First, he stated that there is a general state of drive or motivational level, which, as noted earlier, he symbolized by the letter D. This is a nonspecific drive state which is the summation of all of the motivational factors present in the organism. The basic notion is that every possible source of motivation is capable of summation with the others to give a single "excited" state.

In addition, Hull stated that there is associated with any particular deprivation a specific drive which he called the s_D, a notation which clearly indicates the emphasis on the stimulus properties of the specific drive. In fact, these drive stimuli are quite parallel in their function to the cue-producing responses which we discussed earlier. Both sources of stimulation play a role in the evocation of responses. That is, they can act as the stimuli for responses just as stimuli in the external environment can. To put it in another way, s_D is very important in Hull's system because specific responses were assumed by Hull to become associated with a particular set of internal stimuli which included these stimulus effects of deprivation.

In addition to its role as a stimulus, Hull was also able to use the concept of specific drive stimuli to deal with the problem of need reduction. He argued that the component of reinforcement critical to its influence on learning is not a decrease in a biological need state but a decrease in the intensity of the s_D which is specific to the deprivation. Since Hull considered that the arrival of food, for instance, might decrease the intensity of the drive stimuli associated with food deprivation, he concluded that reinforcement is not dependent on the lengthy time periods involved in need reduction at the biological level. Therefore, the concept of drive reduction was still relevant in the learning situation.

A second motivational concept used by Hull was that of *secondary reinforcement*. A secondary reinforcer is a stimulus which becomes a source of reinforcement by virtue of learning. Thus a previously neutral stimulus might acquire the power to act as a reinforcement for the formation of habits as a result of its contiguous occurrences with a primary reinforcer, such as food. Pavlov, in his classical-conditioning situation, was able to demonstrate quite easily learning based on secondary reinforcement. In a standard experimental situation, he would pair a bell with food powder. When the animal was regularly and reliably salivating to the bell, Pavlov would then present the bell paired with a metronome, but no food powder. The bell would elicit salivation, and the metronome would occur at a time when the animal was salivating. After several trials, the bell would be omitted, and the metronome would then be found to have acquired the power to elicit salivation, even though it had never itself been associated with food powder. Though Pavlov called this phenomenon "higher-order conditioning," this term is synonymous with "secondary reinforcement."

In spite of the frequent use made of the concept of secondary reinforcement and the obvious need for such a construct in theories which attempt to describe behavior, the actual mechanism by which it is developed is not well established. Colloquially, we all speak of money and status as the rewards for learning. Since they are not biologically needed in reinforcement, they must have some secondary effect. It was because of these commonsense problems for theories of reinforcement that the notion of secondary reinforcement was postulated. However, in spite of some vagueness in definition, there are, in the literature on secondary reinforcement, several illustrative studies which Hull used in his development of the concept. Example 14-5 describes one of the better known of these.

Example 14-5 *Secondary reinforcement in chimpanzees (Cowles, 1937)*

For human beings, the most obvious secondary reinforcer is money. People do a great deal of work for money which does not directly reduce any biological need. Therefore, money has reinforcing value of a complex kind. Clearly, money may stand for a variety of things—food, drink, status, power, or whatever. We all see this situation about us every day, yet it is not easy to demonstrate secondary reinforcement in the laboratory. An experiment by Cowles made a direct attack on the problem by using chimpanzees and token rewards.

The apparatus for this experiment consisted of a machine called a "chimp-o-mat" which, like many such devices used by man, dispensed desirable rewards. In this case, raisins became available whenever a chimp placed a poker chip into the machine. The animals were first trained to use the machine with poker chips given them without the requirement of work. Then the animals were placed in difficult discrimination situations in which they had to solve problems in order to receive the chips. If the chips were now secondary reinforcers, the animals would presumably work for them.

The animals did work to obtain the chips. However, there was a limit to the rewarding value of the poker chips. The animals would cease to work if they were not allowed to cash in their chips for raisins at fairly frequent intervals.

Although this experiment provides a parallel to easily observed behavioral facts about man, it does not supply an answer to the question of how a secondary reinforcer acquires its capacity to reward behavior.

If we examine the concept of motivation as it is presented within Hull's system, we find a very complex picture indeed. As we have seen, there are three different sources of motivation: drive (D), an intensity factor (V), and a value which has to do with incentives and goals (K). Drive itself has three distinct functions: (1) Drive plays a primary role in reinforcement. The rapid reduction in drive is defined as the necessary condition of learning. (2) Since drive is the basic activator of habits, there will be no response if there is no drive. Animals without drive simply do not perform habits. (3) Finally, the distinctive stimuli (s_D) which arise from the drive state act to determine what habits will be performed. In this sense, drives control the nature of responses which are made.

The concept of motivation was central to Hull's system, and it played a very versatile role. Not only was it an activator, in the sense of referring to a generalized drive state, but it was a selector of behavior and was the mechanism by which habits were acquired in the first place. However, at least one prominent theorist, Edward Tolman, did not agree with Hull on the role of motivation in learning. Tolman rejected the notion of reinforcement as a condition for learning, and his disagreement touched off a long experimental controversy.

Cognitive Structures: Latent Learning and Curiosity

From our former discussion, we know that Tolman made free use of mentalistic constructs such as *expectancy* and *hypotheses*. But he firmly rejected the law of effect as it had been propounded by Thorndike and later by Hull. Tolman used the concept of motivation in a somewhat different way than it had been used by Hull. First of all, like Hull, he emphasized the role of motivation in the performance of behavior. In addition, he held that motivation is important in learning, though not in an automatic stamping-in process like that suggested by Thorndike, but rather in the acquisition of cognitive structures. Rather than take the reduction of motivation as the exact mechanism of reinforcement, Tolman held that the presence of a goal object and its consumption might better be considered as giving *emphasis* to certain components of the environment. If reinforcement was not necessary to the acquisition of cognitive structures, Tolman felt that experiments could be performed in which animals would learn in the absence of reward. In Example 14-6 we examine one of a series of experiments on the phenomenon of *latent learning* which attempted to demonstrate the ability of animals to learn or gain knowledge that might not show up in performance until the animal has a reason to demonstrate its knowledge. This awareness of the dimensions of a problem which is not used until needed is called latent learning.

Example 14–6 *Latent learning: Does learning occur without reward? (Tolman & Honzik, 1930)*

The approach to the problem of latent learning first used by Blodgett (1929) was followed up by Tolman and Honzik (1930). Animals were given a chance to explore a maze for several days and then to find food at the end of the maze. If they then showed that they knew the maze, this meant that they had learned something on the days when they were not rewarded.

The apparatus was a multiple-unit T-maze arranged with doors which prevented the animals from retracing. Three groups of rats were used. The first group consisted of animals which were placed in the maze each day and found food at the end of the maze in a goal box. This group was called the "reward" group. The second group was run each day but never found food in the maze. Their group was called the "no reward" group. The third group, which was really the crucial group, found no food in the maze until the eleventh day, when they did find food. Thereafter, they were always reinforced in the maze. The number of times animals entered the blind alleys was counted, and this score was averaged for each group on each day. It should be noted that the animals in all groups tended to progress through the maze and reach the goal, at which point they were removed from the maze.

The error scores for the groups, over days, are shown in Figure 14–10. The two control groups showed the kind of performance which would have been predicted by reinforcement theorists. Those rewarded eliminated errors, those not rewarded tended to make a significant number of errors, although there was some suggestion that the number of errors was decreasing over days. The experimental group, however, presented quite a different picture. Again, on the first eleven days, before they found food in the goal box, they showed a slight tendency to eliminate errors, but they were roughly equal in performance to the control-group animals which did not find food. On the next day, after having found food in the maze only one time, they immediately reduced their errors to about the same level as the animals of the group which were being rewarded on every trial.

The interpretation made of these data by Tolman and Honzik is that the experimental animals which were not fed did indeed learn something in the first ten days. However, their learning was "latent" and did not show until the presence of food in the maze made a difference in the incentive to go to the goal box as quickly as possible.

When reinforcement theorists were faced with the results of the latent learning studies, they began to expand the notion of drives in order to encompass the findings of the experiments within the S-R effect position. Since they were committed to a notion that required that all behavior must be motivated and that learning depends on the reduction of some drive, they suggested that other motives were responsible for the learning occurring in the absence of ordinary drive reduction. Curiosity was the new drive which was suggested to account for the willingness to work without immediate rewards such as food or water. In Example 14–7 we will consider the work of Robert A. Butler, whose experiments with monkeys were designed to illustrate the concept of curiosity as a drive.

Example 14–7 *Curiosity as a drive (Butler, 1953)*

Common sense suggests that curiosity is a major determinant of human behavior. Parents and teachers make great use of common curiosity in order to teach children. Often, a child will perform some task in order to satisfy curiosity.

Until recently, there has been little attention paid to curiosity by psychological theories, particularly those advanced by behaviorists. However, researchers working with monkeys have found that the everyday behavior of the animals seems to be strongly motivated by curiosity. This fact is particularly evident in the great amount of manipulation of objects in which monkeys engage. Anything which is placed within their reach is given a thorough going-over. It is picked at, fondled, scratched, and generally handled with what seems to be an attempt to explore the nature of the thing. But it is not so simple to demonstrate that there is in fact

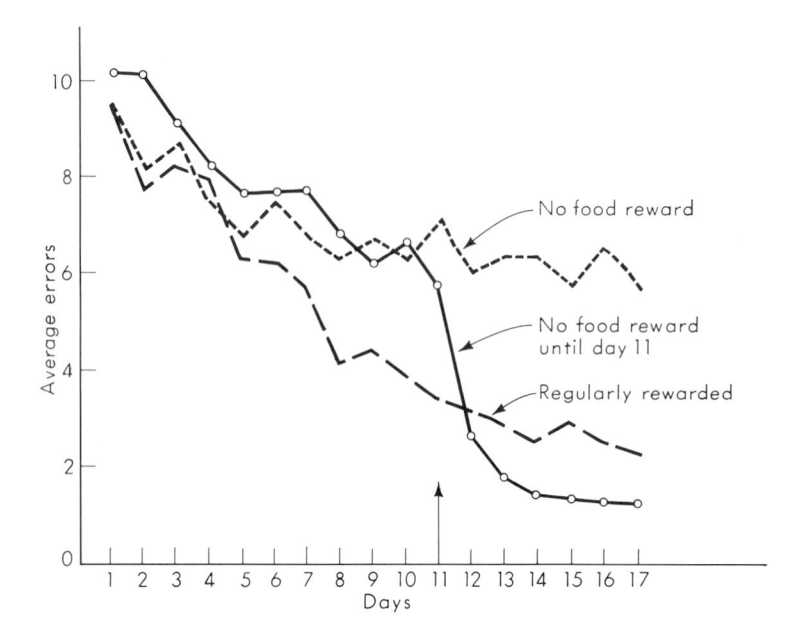

FIG. 14–10 Latent learning in the maze. (*Tolman & Honzik, 1930b*)

a curiosity drive in the sense in which the term is used to describe a drive for food or water or pain avoidance. Before we can be certain that there is a curiosity drive, we have to demonstrate three points: (1) that the subjects will work for a long time with nothing but the satisfaction of curiosity as a reward for their efforts, (2) that curiosity drive will produce learning, and (3) that no other drives are implicated.

Robert Butler, working in the Wisconsin Primate Laboratory noticed an interesting behavioral trait in monkeys which led him to set up an experiment to demonstrate curiosity as a drive (Butler, 1953). In a series of earlier experiments, he had used an apparatus in which the experimenter and the monkey were on separate sides of a screen. Because the experimenter could not see what the monkey was doing between trials, there was a strong temptation to look around the edge of the screen. When Butler did this, the monkey was distracted and the experiment was spoiled. When Butler drilled a small hole in the screen so that he could peek through at the monkey, he found that the monkey would spend its time with its eye glued to the peephole, watching him. This suggested a series of studies on curiosity in the monkey.

The apparatus was an enclosed animal cage equipped with a built-in discrimination problem for the monkey to solve. In one of the enclosures there were two 5- by 5-inch doors. The doors could be fitted with colored panels between which the monkey was required to choose in order to open one of the doors. Since the monkeys were in a very dull, uninteresting environment, it was thought that the opportunity to open one of the doors and look out into the busy outside laboratory would be rewarding to them. At the beginning of the experiment, the monkeys were allowed to look through the doorways, and then they were closed. Soon the animals learned to open the doors by pushing against them. Then, one door was locked. Two different-colored cards were placed behind the doors, and the monkey was allowed to push one and only one. If he chose the correct one, he was allowed thirty seconds of looking through the open door. Then, a screen was raised in front of him, and another trial began. Twenty trials a day were given for twenty days. Both the number of correct choices and the speed at which the monkey responded were recorded.

The outcome of the experiment was very clear. The monkeys worked throughout twenty days of testing without slowing down or showing any sign of loss of interest. They pushed at the doors rapidly and learned the problems only in order to look into the laboratory and for no other reward. Other monkeys were tested with running electric toys or companion monkeys as the objects which they had to work to see. It turned out that the objects could be graded for desirability, or as satisfiers of curiosity. Another monkey was the best object, the train next, and the bowl of fruit was last in terms of the length of time the subjects would work in order to look at them.

Fear as a Drive

Another motivational state is fear. Certainly, it is commonplace to say that much behavior is the result of anxiety or fear of punishment. But it is one thing to make commonsense assertions about the role of fear in determining behavior and quite another matter to bring the study of fear into the laboratory, where it might be possible to uncover the mechanisms by which fear develops. Among those who have explored the role of fear in behavior has been Neal E. Miller, who developed a two-part theory of the role of fear in behavior. He held that fear is, first of all, a drive which can be learned, and, secondly, he postulated that the reduction of fear can act as a reinforcement for the learning of new responses.

Perhaps the most important contribution made by Miller has been his demonstration of learned, or acquired, fear. Indeed, the study of learned motives, or drives, has engaged the interest of many workers, including Woodworth (1918), Tolman (1932), Allport (1937), and Miller (1951). As mentioned earlier, Watson was able to demonstrate that a child will become afraid of furry animals after being frightened in their presence. Since the child was not afraid before the experience, the fear was clearly learned, and, therefore, we may conclude that fear is an acquirable response. But it is necessary to demonstrate that fear can function in the same way as do other drives such as hunger and thirst before we may conclude that fear has drive characteristics.

Example 14–8 *Learnable drives: Fear as an acquired motive (Miller, 1948)*

Miller performed the following study in order to explore the possibility that fear could motivate behavior and also serve as a reinforcement to produce learning of a new response.

The apparatus which was used in the experiment is shown in Figure 14–11. The left compartment was white and had an electric-grid floor. The right compartment was painted black and had a smooth floor. When the experimental animal was dropped into the left side of the box, its weight started a timer which was stopped when the animal either rotated the wheel or pressed the bar. This caused the door to drop, permitting the animal to escape the right side of the box.

In the experiment there were five steps: (1) The animals were pretested with the door open and the grid turned off to see if they had a preference for either side of the box. (2) For ten shock trials, the animal was dropped in, the grid was electrified, and the animal was allowed to escape through the open door to the safe compartment. (3) For five nonshock trials, the grid was turned off and the animal allowed to escape through the open door. (4) Then, the animals were given sixteen nonshock trials with the door closed but connected so that turning the wheel dropped the door; thus, the animal could escape the cues of the white compartment by turning the wheel a small fraction of a turn. (5) Finally, the animals were given ten nonshock trials in which the wheel was no longer operative but the bar would cause the door to drop if it was pressed.

In the pretest, before-shock trials, the animals showed no preference between sides. During the trials with the primary drive of electric shock, all animals learned to escape the shock quickly by running to the black compartment. On the next five trials, without shock, the animals ran quickly to the black compartment, which behavior was, of course, quite different from that on the pretest. Now they appeared quite afraid of the white side of the box or they may be said to have had a clear preference for the black side.

When the door was closed for the next series of trials, the animals exhibited a variety of behaviors which appeared to indicate that they were afraid. They became highly agitated, and some moved the wheel, causing the door to drop. Of these, some then ran through the door to the black compartment. Thirteen of the original animals eventually learned to move the wheel and drop the door. The others tended to show either long-term exploration or startle responses when the door dropped. Since a response must occur before it can be reinforced,

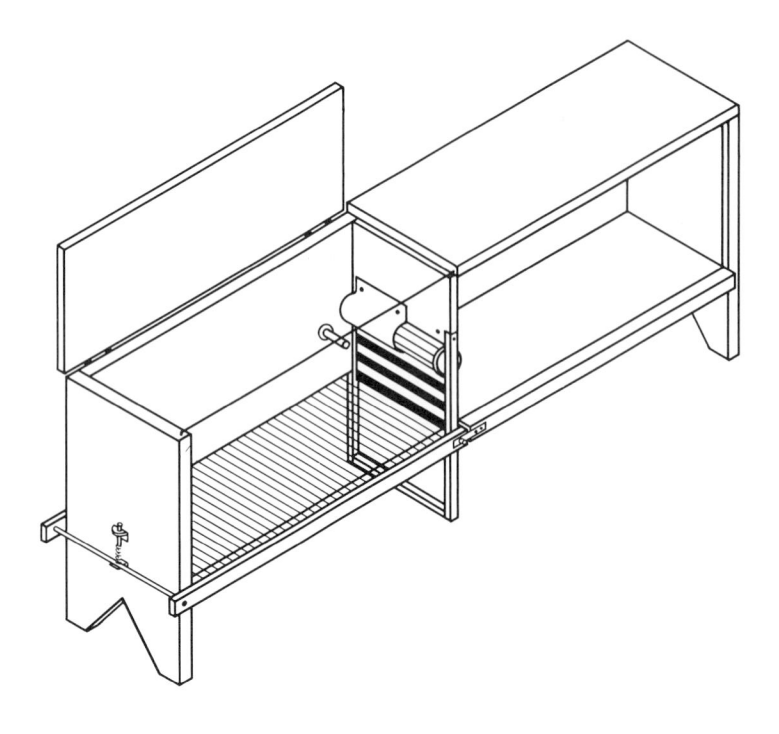

FIG. 14-11 Learned-drive apparatus. (*Miller, 1948*)

Miller analyzed the latency of wheel-turning response in the thirteen animals which made the wheel response.

When the apparatus was changed so that the wheel no longer worked but the bar did, the animals gave up turning the wheel and learned the new habit of pressing the bar.

Miller concluded from his study that fear is an acquirable drive which can motivate the learning of new habits. His animals not only showed the ability to learn to move a wheel in order to escape the cues of the box in which they had been shocked, but they also learned to give up the wheel-turning response and adopt a new habit of pressing the bar when this led to escape. Figure 14-12 shows a graph of the performance of the subjects.

The logic of Miller's situation does seem to be quite straightforward. The drive of fear was learned to the cues of the white box as a result of the association of the cues with an electric shock. Later, the drive of fear motivated the learning to escape.

In addition to extension of theorizing about drives and motivators, there were other reformulations of learning theories during the latter part of the 1940s.

One particularly interesting attack on classical reinforcement theories of learning was made by Harry Harlow. We will conclude our discussion with a brief view of some of his contributions.

Learning Sets: Elimination of Errors

Out of a quarter century of experimental work at the Wisconsin Primate Laboratories, Harry Harlow published, beginning in the 1940s, a series of papers critical of classical reinforcement theory. Two major concepts were introduced by Harlow: *learning sets* and *error factors* (cf. Harlow, 1959). We will attempt to define each of these important concepts and then to present Harlow's conclusions about the nature of the learning process.

The apparatus used by Harlow in the development of his theories—the Wisconsin General Test Apparatus—is shown in Figure 14-13. It was especially designed for the presentation of discrimination problems, which involve a choice between two or more stimulus objects. The problems cannot be solved by making the spatial orientation of the objects the method of solution. To be concrete, in Figure 14-13 there are two objects on the tray in front of the monkey. Under each object is a food

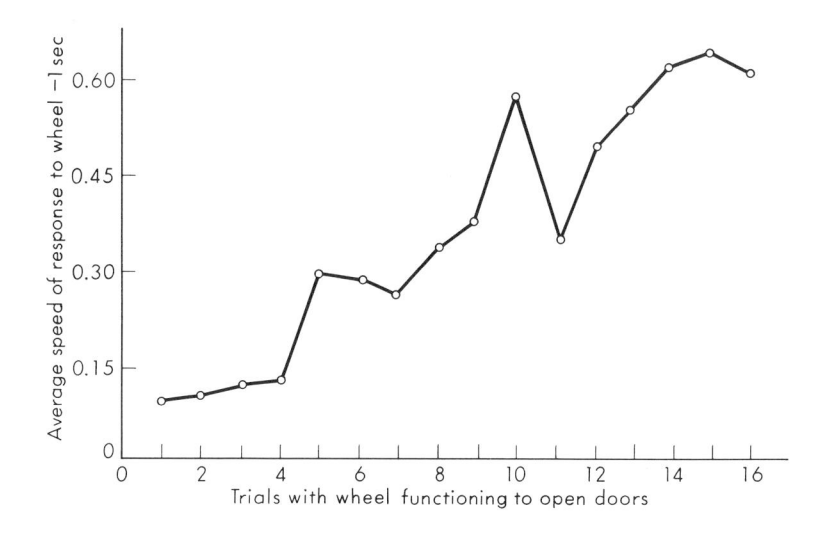

FIG. 14–12 Average speed versus trials with a wheel. (*Miller, 1948*)

cup, but only one cup has a raisin or other reward in it. The monkey is allowed one and only one choice on each trial. When he chooses, a screen promptly drops down in front of him and prevents him from correcting his behavior in the case where he has made an incorrect choice. On each trial, the objects are placed in different positions at random, and, therefore, the monkey cannot solve the problem simply by choosing either right or left or even by alternating his choices. Thus the problems involve the necessity of focusing on the attributes of the stimulus objects themselves rather than on their spatial arrangement.

Using the Wisconsin General Test Apparatus (WGTA), Harlow presented monkeys with a large number of problems of the same kind. Each problem involved learning a discrimination. As a result of a number of such experiments, Harlow discovered that the monkeys developed a facility for solving successive problems. They transferred what they learned on early problems to the solution of later problems. In other words, they appeared to "learn to learn." This phenomenon of acquiring a disposition to learn Harlow called a "learning set." Out of this formulation he developed an interesting distinction: learning sets refer to "interproblem learning"; that is, they refer to something which the animal learns about solving problems in general. "Intraproblem learning" refers to the course of learning which goes on during the animal's solution of any single discrimination problem. It will be obvious that all the individual problems must be of comparable difficulty if measurements of interproblem learning are to be valid.

The formation of a learning set can be illustrated by the presentation of a large number of discriminations each of which is only presented for a few trials. Thus, the animals do not overlearn the problems, and the situation is one in which the gradual development of transfer can be illustrated. In Example 14–9, the data from one of Harlow's early experiments are presented.

Example 14–9 *Learning sets (Harlow, 1959)*

Harlow was very critical of learning theories which placed too much emphasis on internal drives and which understressed the role of external stimuli in the determination of behavior. To illustrate the importance of external stimuli, he developed a method of problem presentation which forced attention to the stimulus dimensions of objects. As we have said, he presented the animals with a large number of problems, in this case 312. His monkeys were given only six trials on each problem but were run through 14 problems a day for several months until they had been run through the entire set of 312 problems. For any given problem, two objects were placed over the food cups, and the animal had to learn which object was the correct cue for food. On each trial, the placement of the objects was changed according to a random sequence, as we have explained. Regardless of how

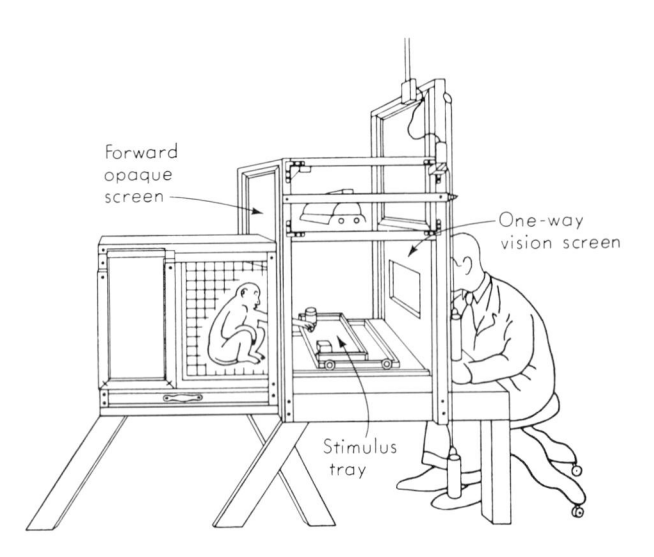

FIG. 14–13 Wisconsin General Test Apparatus. (*Harlow, 1959*)

well the animal was doing, after each six trials new objects were used; that is, a new problem was presented.

The results indicate that the ability of the animals to solve a problem is greatly improved after a number of problems have been attempted. Figure 14–14 is a family of learning-set curves. When the curves are examined carefully, it becomes clear that the nature of the learning exhibited changes over problems. At first, when the animal had not yet learned to learn, the learning took place slowly, and the curve looks more like one of those which describe "trial-and-error" learning. There appeared to be no advantage gained from one problem to the other during these first few problems. The monkey seemed to solve each problem by itself with no gain from his experience with the previous problem. But as experience with problems increased, the subjects began to improve, until by the time 100 problems had been presented there was a sharp difference between the performance of the first trial on any problem and the ensuing trials. From the hundredth problem on, the curves look very much like curves descriptive of "insight" learning. At this stage, the monkeys performed at a very high level after only one trial on a problem. Quite obviously they had learned to learn.

As a result of his studies, Harlow suggested that learning can be managed efficiently according to a plan which maximizes the gain from problem to problem as learning to learn proceeds. He concluded that the amount transferred from any one problem to the next is an increasing function of the amount learned on the first problem. What this suggests is that the best way to proceed in any situation involving the development of learning skills is to run trials on a problem only until large gains have been made. Beyond that point, the return is not worth the effort and time involved. Clearly this formulation runs contrary to many theories of education which assume that overlearning and intensive practice on early tasks will maximize the effectiveness of the learner throughout the course of learning. Harlow has concluded that the best procedure is to allow only small amounts of practice on any one problem but to have many different problems for the learner. In this way, the learner will learn to learn.

From his studies of learning sets, Harlow came to consider those factors which lead the monkey in the WGTA to make mistakes. He calls these mistake-producing dispositions *error factors* (EFs). Presumably, the factors which produce errors differ from one particular learning situation to other learning situations, but in the case of WGTA, Harlow has identified four error factors. He calls them *stimulus-perseveration*, *differential-cue*, *response-shift*, and *position-habit* error factors.

The actual analysis of which of these factors leads an animal to make an error in any one trial is a difficult problem. We will simply consider the defi-

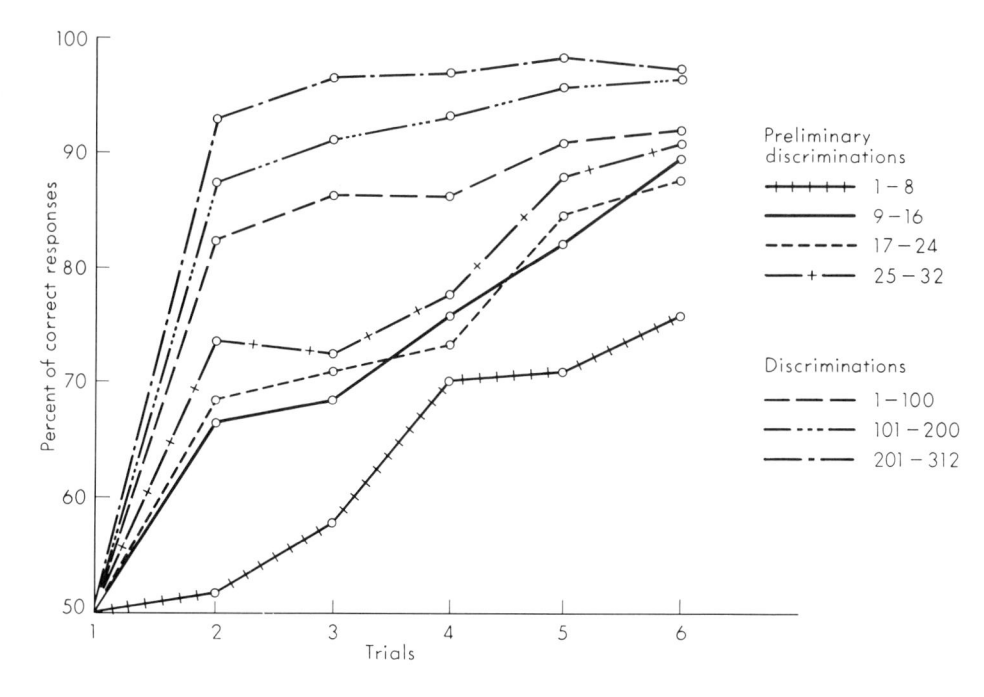

FIG. 14-14 Percent of correct responses versus trials in a learning curve. *(Harlow, 1959)*

nition of each error factor. The first error factor, stimulus perseveration, describes errors involving repeated choice of the incorrect stimulus object. Thus, when an animal chooses the wrong object on trial after trial, we conclude that he is showing stimulus perseveration. One interesting fact about stimulus-perseveration errors is that they are more prevalent in younger monkeys than they are in older animals which have had the same amount of experience in laboratory work.

The differential-cue error factor operates in discrimination situations because on any one trial the monkey not only is rewarded for choosing the correct stimulus but he is also rewarded for choosing that spatial position which the stimulus object happens to occupy on that trial. But, in order to solve the nonspatial discrimination problem, the animals must be responding in terms of the object and not in terms of the place where it happened to be. Differential cue is a more persistent error factor than stimulus perseveration.

In line with the fact that monkeys are prone to manipulate all objects within their grasp, animals in the WGTA tend to respond to both objects when they are in the object-discrimination learning situation. This tendency leads to an error factor called by Harlow "response shift." Harlow discovered response shift when he noticed that animals tended to make more errors on the fourth trial of a series if they had been rewarded on all of the first three trials than they would if they made an initial error and then had two correct trials. To put it in anthropomorphic terms, the animals seemed to be curious about what was under the other object, and they could not restrain themselves from satisfying this curiosity beyond the fourth trial.

The final error factor is position habit. This is perhaps the simplest of the error factors in that it is defined by a consistent response to either the right or the left food well regardless of the objects which are over them. This is a relatively unimportant source of error for monkeys, although it has been reported by Lashley and Krech that position habits are important in rats.

A rather novel theory of learning, cast in terms of error factors, has been advanced by Harlow. He suggests that learning may be conceptualized as the suppression of all the factors in the situation which lead to errors. Thus, a monkey or for that matter any other organism may be considered to have learned perfectly when it is no longer responding in terms of the error-producing stimulus factors in a problem situation. Obviously, such a formulation is not unreasonable but is quite contrary to the usual formulations of S-R theories, which place an emphasis on the acquisition of connections as the bases for formation of habits. In Harlow's subtractive process, the tendencies to make correct responses are there at the outset of learning. It is required only that the animal give up tendencies to make errors in order to exhibit mastery of the task. Learning is thus a process of eliminating error tendencies.

SUMMARY

So much for our selective sampling of learning theories which grew out of behaviorism. As we have seen, they have been marked by a concern for principles and laws. Many of the experiments were designed to decide "crucial" issues. As a result, the field lost some of its crispness when seen in retrospect. However, even if the modern theorist or research worker does not emphasize problems such as "what is learned" and avoids the question of the most important laws of learning, he is free to pursue his concerns only because earlier workers have already developed and defined the study of learning. Now, we will turn to a consideration of problems which engage the interest of today's psychologists. As before, we will be selective in our approach and omit far more than we include. However, we will attempt to reflect the change in emphasis from a behaviorism which concentrated on the acquisition of habits to the neobehaviorisms which are oriented to specific problems, particularly to the learning of language and verbal behavior.

CHAPTER 15
VERBAL BEHAVIOR AND LANGUAGE

The behavioristic analysis of behavior has been extended beyond simple learning situations into the realm of problem solving, verbal behavior, and language. As these efforts have developed, there has been a firm attempt to make a consistent application of associationistic language and to retain the rigor of the associationistic tradition. However, one modification in emphasis has occurred. In place of theoretical reliance on the direct elicitation of responses by the stimuli in the environment, greater weight has been placed on mediational responses which lead to internal cues previously conditioned to observable responses. In this new class of theory, the *mediational chain* is the object of analysis. The general program of research is usually designed to explore implications for educational programs of the way in which language acts as a mediator of behavior. In most approaches, the design of the research explores the effect of increasing the number of associations that an individual has learned to the stimulus elements of a situation. Further, complex behavior is thought to proceed by changing a person's hierarchy of habitual responses in a situation.

ASSOCIATIVE NETWORKS

In our discussion of S-R psychology and the manner in which complex mental processes depend on the connection of responses in the behavioral repertoire of the learner, we have referred to *association* as the mechanism by which such learning proceeds. But theory alone is not convincing. Actual data about the nature of such associations are required. Several research workers have been concerned with providing such data, and we next discuss their explorations of the nature of the network of associations between words.

Simple Associations

Most experimentation on verbal association has involved the presentation of words to a group of persons who are instructed to say or write down the first word which is suggested to them by a particular stimulus word. The method was pioneered by Carl Jung, the famous psychoanalyst whose work is discussed in Chapter 4. Of course, not all persons report the same word. But when the frequencies of occurrence of the associations are tabulated, there are found to be large commonalities within the list of words reported. Such lists are called *association norms*. In Table 15–1 an example of the associative norms for twenty-five words is presented. The reader may wish to check the representativeness of these norms by doing a simple study involving one of his friends. This can be done simply by asking the person to say the first word which

Table 15-1 Words and associations with their frequency in 1,000 responses

1. Table—chair 840, food 41, desk 21, top 15, leg 11
2. Dark—light 829, night 55, room 33, black 31, white 9
3. Music—song 183, note 168, sound 124, piano 51, sing 28
4. Sickness—health 376, ill 159, death 153, bed 64, well 58
5. Man—woman 767, boy 65, girl 31, dog 18, lady 17
6. Deep—shallow 318, dark 131, water 101, sea 76, high 52
7. Soft—hard 445, light 87, pillow 81, bed 42, smooth 28
8. Eating—food 390, drinking 138, sleeping 122, hungry 45, full 22
9. Mountain—hill 266, high 127, snow 65, valley 64, climb 46
10. House—home 247, door 93, garage 47, barn 40, roof 33
11. Black—white 751, dark 54, cat 26, light 22, night 20
12. Mutton—lamb 365, sheep 295, meat 96, chops 56, beef 32
13. Comfort—chair 117, bed 99, ease 76, home 71, soft 69
14. Hand—foot 255, finger 237, arm 131, glove 53, shake 38
15. Short—tall 397, long 336, fat 76, small 21, man 18
16. Fruit—apple 378, vegetable 114, orange 94, fly 62, berry 46
17. Butterfly—moth 144, insect 117, wing 104, bird 84, fly 78
18. Smooth—rough 328, soft 206, hard 135, silk 40, hands 29
19. Command—order 196, army 102, obey 78, officer 65, performance 33
20. Chair—table 493, sit 205, leg 45, seat 38, soft 26
21. Sweet—sour 434, candy 162, sugar 80, bitter 76, music 33
22. Whistle—stop 131, train 89, noise 73, sing 62, blow 56
23. Woman—man 646, girl 88, child 75, mother 16, lady 15
24. Cold—hot 348, snow 218, warm 168, winter 66, ice 29
25. Slow—fast 752, cars 23, stop 22, down 17, snail 12

comes into his mind, as each word is read, and then checking his responses against the list. It is quite probable that the results will show many of the words which appear in the norms.

It is perhaps surprising to realize that so many other people have the same linguistic habits as our own, built in by their experiences. However, this seems to be the case. It is, of course, just this similarity in our linguistic frames of reference which enables us to communicate with each other in the way we do. Often, two people who have known each other for many years, such as a husband and wife, will find themselves each anticipating what the other is going to say when something happens to both of them. They have strong commonalities in their linguistic associative networks.

Working from an associative viewpoint, Charles Cofer and his coworkers have examined the way in which the common word-associative responses help or hinder the solution of problems. In such research, the assumption is usually made that the process of association is an automatic one, in much the same way that Thorndike's theory of the connection of stimuli and responses was conceived to be an automatic process.

Directional Associations

So far we have been discussing simple associations, that is, associations which are made when the subject is told only to report the first word which comes into his mind. But there is another type of association which has been studied extensively and which has been of theoretical importance: directed associations of a particular kind. For example, the person may be asked to give a synonym or an antonym of a word, or he may even be asked for such responses as superordinate concepts. In the case of being presented with the word "chair," a superordinate reply might be "furniture" or "four-legged." When instructions which involve directions are used, the process of association is greatly changed, and the person making the association takes more and more time. In addition, he will report a process of searching for the correct response in the class of responses to which he has been directed.

In Example 15-1 an interesting experiment from Cofer's laboratory is outlined. It combines the notions of direction in problem solving with the theory of associative responses to words. The effect of such associations on the solutions subjects make to problems is explored.

Example 15-1 *Reasoning as a directional associative process (Judson & Cofer, 1956)*

Cofer and one of his students, A. J. Judson, performed a series of experiments in which they explored the hypothesis that the directedness of reasoning processes arises through the activation of verbal habits of an associative nature. They examined two hypotheses in their study: First, they suggested that the way in which a person solves a problem is a function of the way in which it is presented to him, because the first material presented will evoke associative "sets" which will influence the attempted solution. Secondly, they predicted that solutions will depend on the habit systems already built into the subject. That is, the verbal associations which the person brings to the problem-solving situation will greatly influence his method of solving problems which involve words.

The experimental task for the subject consisted of solving a series of four-word problems. In each problem, four words were presented which could be grouped into sets of three words in two different ways. The subject was asked to eliminate the word which did not belong to the set. Each problem had two possible answers. For example consider the words "powerless," "blessed," "meek," and "poor." They may be grouped in two ways: "powerless," "meek," and "poor" may be placed together, or "blessed," "meek," and "poor" may be. In this set, two of the words, "meek" and "poor," are unambiguous, since they belong to either group. The other two words are ambiguous.

In order to test their first hypothesis, Cofer and Judson presented 129 college students with forty-five sets of four words. Sixty-five of the students were given the crucial words in one order in the set of four words. The other sixty-four students had the unambiguous words reversed. Thus, the hypothesis that order of presentation would influence the set chosen was tested.

A second study added another variable, which was based on the habit patterns of the subjects. Several items were used which had a religious or a nonreligious solution. The solutions which were used by each student related to his religious affiliation and his frequency of attending church. In this second study 311 students were used.

The results were striking in their confirmation of the first hypothesis. For items which were changed in the test, the order in which the items were presented to the subjects appeared greatly to influence the specific solution which was made. The results of the religious variable, however, were not so clearcut: only four of the twelve items which had both a religious and a nonreligious solution showed a relationship to church affiliation and attendance. But those four items did show a pattern of solution which was related to the religious orientation of the subjects.

Cofer also demonstrated that order of presentation determines, to a degree, which of two possible solutions will be applied to a verbal problem. He interpreted his results in terms of the patterns of associations which each word elicited as it was presented. Thus, if the first word elicited an associate which had some bridging connection to a later word, it would tend to be chosen as a part of the set of words. This is, of course, an associationistic interpretation of the results.

The data on the sets which had a possible religious interpretation were not as striking. Cofer suggested that the results might have been weakened, not because the religious effect was not there, but rather because even those subjects who reported that they did not regularly attend church may have made the religious grouping. In other words, the religious interpretation of the ambiguous words might well have held even for nonreligious students.

SYNTACTIC STRUCTURES: THE ANALYSIS OF LANGUAGE AND COGNITION

The linguistic theory of Noam Chomsky (1957) attempts to describe the way in which decisions are made during the utterance of speech. Quite clearly, an understanding of the process of speaking, that is, the process by which one decides what unit of language will be said at any given time, is crucial to an understanding of the way in which the mind works during problem solving and thinking.

Although it is clear that when we speak our language, we utter words one at a time, whether we actually have to make a decision after each word as to which word we will then use is not so clear. Somehow we have, before we begin to utter our sentence, a foreknowledge of what it is we are going to say. Chomsky calls this intended message a "deep structure." At times, this foreknowledge is quite clear, and we may actually know verbatim just what words we are going to say. At other times, however, just which words or which phrases we are going to use is not clear in our minds. A very famous quotation from William James (1890) aptly describes this process of making decisions about words we use to express ourselves:

> And has the reader never asked himself what kind of a mental fact is his *intention of saying a thing* before he has said it? It is an entirely definite intention, distinct from all other intentions, an absolutely distinct state of consciousness, therefore: and yet how much of it consists of definite sensorial images, either of words or of things? Hardly anything! Linger, and the words and things come into mind; the anticipatory intention, the divination is there no more. But as the words that replace it arrive, it welcomes them successively and calls them right if they agree with it, it rejects them and calls them wrong if they do not. It has therefore a nature of its own of the most positive sort, and yet what can we say about it without using words that belong to the later mental facts that replace it? The intention *to say so and so* is the only name it can receive [James, 1890].

This quotation rather sharply calls our attention to the fact that we seem to know something about what we are going to say before we say it and while we are saying it we are able to check the things we say against some plan of action which we had. However, this is not the only sort of evidence which seems to rule out the possibility that we choose our words one by one.

Chomsky has suggested that perhaps the best way to introduce the second kind of evidence is to make a more complete analysis of the kind of process which would in fact be correct if we *did* make our choice of words one at a time. Such a process is called a "Markov process." Put somewhat simply, it is a situation in which an event is determined only by the state of affairs which obtains just before it occurs. For example, if language was in fact a Markov process, then the speaker would choose each word only on the basis of that word which immediately preceded it during his utterance. When such a model of language behavior is discussed, it is usually referred to as a *left-to-right model of the sentence planner*.

It is not difficult to show that a child could not learn a language using a Markov model for sentence development. To illustrate such difficulties, we can consider the case of a child required to learn how to generate and recognize all those sentences which are grammatically correct in a language of a fixed length, say, twenty words. Miller, Gallanter, and Pribram (1960) have suggested that there are about 2^{100} different strings twenty words long which would have to be dealt with if one were to master the English language. Since each of these different sequences would produce different effects upon the person who was learning, the person would have to hear each string at least one time. Thus, in this system, the left-to-right generator of grammar, there is only one grammatical rule, which is:

> ... [At] any one point you may examine the words you have produced and then choose your continuation from the set of all English sentences which have the required number of remaining words and which continue to be well-formed. That is, which are grammatically correct [Miller et al., 1960].

Since this is the only rule, there appears to be no alternative, in teaching the child, to having him hear all 2^{100} sentences which exist. Now 2^{100} sentences are, in fact, about 10^{30} sentences. Miller, Gallanter, and Pribram have called attention to the ridiculous nature of such a plan by pointing to the fact that there are only about 3.15 by 10^9 seconds in a century. Because of this a child would have to listen to about thirty sentences per second in order to be exposed to all the information that he would have to have in order to produce a sentence according to the Markov model. Finally, it becomes apparent that a childhood greater than 100 years long without interruptions for sleeping, eating, and so forth, with perfect retention for everything presented would be required in order to have a child learn to speak the language. Since every parent knows that his child begins to produce well-formed sentences—that is, grammatically correct ones—long before such an exorbitant amount of time has passed, we will not consider this argument further.

Chomsky (1957) has presented a simple and yet very elegant proof that a left-to-right system cannot form certain grammatically correct sentences. What he has done is to show that sentences which are themselves grammatically correct can be imbedded inside other sentences. Consider the following example: "The woman who said X has left." One can substitute for X the sentence "Either Y, or I leave." Again one can substitute for Y the sentence "He finishes Z." This process can continue indefinitely. Note that in each example there is a grammatical dependency which extends across the sentence which is inserted. English grammar enables us to develop such nested sentences within a sentence of an infinite length. It should be clear that a Markov sentence generator, which has a purely historical left-to-right type of message source, cannot generate such sentences. From our previous example, it becomes apparent that in order to produce an infinitely long nest of sentences such as this, the sentence generator would have to have an infinitely long memory. But there is no biological system, let alone the sentence-generator capacity of a child, which is capable of such a prodigious feat. So we must assume that the left-to-right system is incapable of producing certain perfectly acceptable sentences. For this reason, it is clear that chains of words will not suffice as a model for the production of English grammar.

Having thus eliminated the possibility that a Markov process can account for the generation of English sentences, let us present a simple model, taken from Chomsky's theory of language (1957). In order to develop this model, we must assume that the producer of a message can know something about what he is going to say as well as about those things which he has said. In addition, we may then imagine a system for the production of sentences in which a whole sentence is manipulated as a unit and is gradually developed from the inside out. We can symbolize the whole sentence by the letter S. Our first rule is that S consists usually of a noun phrase (NP) and a verb phrase (VP). This rule we shall write as

(1) S ⟶ NP + VP

In this form of expression the arrow symbolizes the fact that S can be rewritten as NP + VP in order to derive the eventual sentence which is uttered. In certain English sentences the noun phrase may consist of an article (T) and a noun; thus we might rewrite

(2) NP ⟶ T + noun

and we might wish to expand the verb phrase into a verb and a noun phrase:

(3) VP ⟶ verb + NP

(We will limit ourselves to this simple grammar. The reader will be aware that a complete grammar would contain a number of alternative ways of expanding NP and VP.)

Finally, we will add a few new rules about vocabulary:

(4) T ⟶ a, the
(5) noun ⟶ man, car, woman
(6) verb ⟶ struck

Miller, Galanter, and Pribram have postulated an imaginary machine, which operates to produce grammars according to the six rules which we have developed. If we ask their machine to produce a sentence, the only thing it can do with S is to apply rule 1 to it. Figure 15–1a shows the outcome. S is rewritten NP + VP. Then the machine would expand either NP or VP, and either the structure in Figure 15–1b or the one in Figure 15–1c would accordingly be produced. The machine would continue until finally it produced the structure shown in Figure 15–1d. Then it could use the vocabulary rules and convert T + noun + verb + T + noun into any one of a small set of different sentences:

A man struck the woman.
The woman struck the man.
The car struck a car.

and so on. The machine would be extremely simple in its ability to communicate, but then it is, as Miller, Galanter, and Pribram intended, only an illustrative construct.

Now let us ask whether the machine can be criticized using the two arguments with which we attacked Markov's processes. At least one argument against Markovian sources is dealt with successfully by the model. It is possible to show that the sentence generators such as the ones we have out-

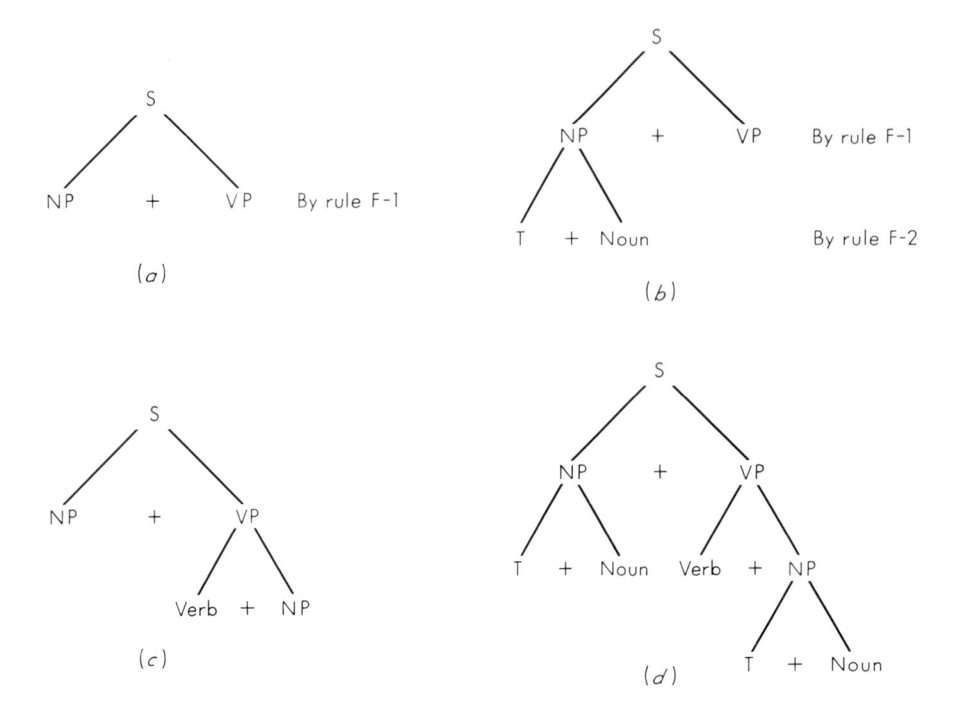

FIG. 15-1 Miller, Galanter, and Pribram's language machine.

lined do not have difficulty in dealing with the nested dependencies which we showed to be embarrassing to the left-to-right planner. All that is needed are rules of the forms $S \longrightarrow a X^1 a$ and $X^1 \longrightarrow b X^2 b$ and $X^2 \longrightarrow c X^3 c, \ldots$, etc. Miller, Galanter, and Pribram have argued that such rules can generate both future and past elements simultaneously and leave the growing part of the sentence in the middle of the developing utterance, rather than at the right end. Thus, Chomsky's argument against Markovian processes has been answered successfully by the development of the machine.

However, it is not as clear that the scheme which Miller, Galanter, and Pribram have developed is as successful in reducing the number of rules required to be learned in a finite childhood. We have made use of only a few rules to generate the simple sentences shown above. However, when one begins to develop a serious attempt at constructing an English grammar, it becomes clear that a very large number of rules may become unnecessary. Without going into too great detail, we can state that it is possible to reduce greatly the number of rules which must be learned by using what are called *transformations*. A transformation is any rule which enables a well-formed sentence to be transformed into any other well-formed sentence in a simple manner. We will give only two illustrations of such transformations: The first is the passive transformation. If one is capable of producing the well-formed sentence "The girl hit her friend," we may make use of a passive transformation rule to develop the sentence "The girl was hit by her friend." Thus, we have by a single rule almost doubled our repertoire of available sentences.

A second transformation which has a great deal of power to increase the repertoire is the negation transformation. Thus, if we have a sentence of the form "The boy ran the mile," we can apply the negation transformation to attain the sentence "The boy did not run the mile."

In this theory of grammar, the basic sentence forms are of a very simple kind and are called "kernel strings." When one has the set of kernel strings, a system of transformations operates upon them to combine or permute them into a large variety of grammatically well-formed sentences. Miller, Galanter, and Pribram have estimated that 100 rules will generate the kernel strings for a fairly complete English grammar. It would require an additional 100 transformational rules to operate upon them, and finally it would require additional rules for vocabulary and pronunciation in order to produce a child who can speak the language. When one compares this number with the immense number of rules required by a finite-state Markov process, it is immediately apparent that a very great reduction in the number of rules has been accomplished. Miller, Galanter, and Pribram have suggested that "even a child should be able to master that much after ten or fifteen years of constant practice."

Thus far our discussion of the Chomsky model has taken place only at the theoretical level, but it will be more convincing if an empirical demonstration and some evidence are presented. To do this, Chomsky has called attention to the ambiguous nature of many English sentences. Consider for example, the sentence "Running horses can be exhilarating." Most speakers of English recognize that this is an ambiguous sentence. Using the rules which we have elaborated above, it is not possible to distinguish between the interpretation "Horses which run are exhilarating" and the alternative interpretation "The act of running horses is exhilarating." Many of us speak our language quite well without being aware that many of the sentences which we use are ambiguous in this way. When one becomes aware of such ambiguity, it is the occasion for humor as in the pun. Since it is clear that there must be two rules for the development of exactly the same well-formed sentence, we must go beyond the grammatical process in order to resolve the ambiguity which can be found. The resolution of this problem seems to depend upon understanding by the listener of the underlying "deep" structure of the sentence. In other words, the listener must have some knowledge of the intention of the sentence generator, that is, the speaker.

We will leave this question without attempting a solution for the problem of ambiguity, except to point out that the fact that Chomsky's transformational grammar is capable of reproducing this kind of ambiguity is strong evidence that his grammatical formulation is close to an adequate description of the process by which sentences are generated. Beyond that, certainly it is true that much of the process of communication which goes on during the speaking of a language is dependent on variables outside the actual strings of words which are being uttered and received. Subtle nuances of behavior, gestures, contacts, a knowledge of the other person, and many other factors are involved. It is not clear just how far a grammatical theory must be extended into these realms before it is considered to be an adequate model for the communication and decision process.

THE ROLE OF MEANINGFULNESS IN VERBAL LEARNING

The Acquisition Process in Rote Learning

One of the most important lines of research which has developed in the study of verbal learning has been the study of the acquisition process in rote learning tasks. Many individual researchers have contributed to the study of this problem.

There are a number of basic requirements for successful performance of a rote-learning task. One has to do with the division of the process of acquisition into two stages, the stage of *response learning* and the stage of *associative hookup*. In the response learning stage, the subject must learn what responses are required of him. This task involves different problems depending on the material which is to be learned. If the responses are not already part of the subject's repertoire, he must first integrate them. For example, the integration of the "syllable" QRB as a response can be conceived of as the learning of a three-unit serial list. Once the subject has integrated this response, he can learn to restrict his responses to the population of required ones. If the units are already a part of the subject's knowledge, he still must learn to restrict his responding to the items required for the task.

This process is not well understood. It is clear, however, that there is a highly developed and easily used ability on the part of the learner to achieve response restrictions. This can be readily demonstrated when we consider our behavior in entering a room containing a group of people whom we do not know. As we attempt to learn their names, we are usually familiar with all the first names which we will hear. If we leave that group and later reenter it, we may have the problem of remembering which name goes with a particular person. We usually are able to restrict the problem of remembering which name is which to the group of names which we have heard. We have in a sense restricted our responses, or names, to the actual group without a great deal of difficulty.

Beyond the question of how response restriction is accomplished, psychologists have become aware that response restriction can occur while response integration is going on. Further, during the course of learning the responses, the errors which are made rarely include items which are imported from outside the learning task. From this observation, it has been suggested that a subject has a selector mechanism which enables him quite early in learning to restrict himself to a given population of recognition and recall items. The learner can recognize the wrong, or extra-list, items before he can recall the correct ones. An example of this occurs when we attempt to recall a person's name. Frequently, we can say with certainty many of the names which are not correct long before we are able to say which name it was we tried to remember.

The associative, or hookup, stage involves the actual linking together of the items of material to be learned. Logically, it is clear that we cannot have an associative stage before the responses are available. But this does not mean that the entire population of responses must be learned prior to the beginning of association. The stages of learning occur together; that is, they overlap in time. The associative stage appears mainly to involve a process of discrimination between the stimuli.

Psychologists have developed techniques for making relative estimates of the durations of these two stages. The fact that the stages overlap must be recognized in interpreting these estimates. In order to measure the duration of the response-learning, or response-integration, stage, it is necessary to find the trial on which an item is given that is in fact on the response list and ignore whether this response was given to the correct stimulus. There is a difficulty in this procedure in that many learners tend to hold back giving responses until they know the stimulus to which it is the correct response. Because of this reticence on the part of the learners, the response-integration stage may appear to be too long. A measure of duration of the associative stage can be obtained by observing the first time an item is given in the correct place and subtracting from that value the time it took to give it first.

Measuring Meaningfulness

There are a number of ways of using these measures of stages in learning. One of these is to compare stimuli of high and low similarity with the same responses. When this is done, it is found that there is no difference in the response-learning stage but there is a difference in the duration of the associative stage. An enduring problem in the study of the associative process has been the effect of *meaningfulness* on these stages of learning. It has proved very difficult to define meaningfulness. One way of doing this is by examining the techniques which are used to measure meaningfulness. These various techniques present methods of classifying materials in terms of preexperimental learning. When an experimenter seeks to evaluate the effect of meaningfulness, he is asking about the amount of prior experience with the particular items which his subjects will have had. This previous experience can be classified in terms of the numbers and types of associations which a verbal item will elicit from subjects. In Example 15–2, several methods of measuring meaningfulness are discussed.

Example 15–2 *The measurement of meaningfulness*

Historically, there have been several ways of measuring meaningfulness. First, association value has sometimes been measured in terms of the number of subjects who have an association to a given verbal item. This method was first developed for use with nonsense syllables. In 1928 Glaze scaled the meaningfulness of nonsense syllables of the CVC form by showing each of them items to fifteen subjects. He asked each subject to signify directly, within five seconds, whether or not it produced in him a meaningful association. He measured the percentage of subjects who signified an association to the item. Although this method seems somewhat imprecise, there have been replications of the technique done with greater numbers of subjects which have correlated well with Glaze's results. It should be clear that this method simply asks how many subjects can associate to an item and ignores the number of different associations which they may have.

A later replication by Archer (1960) used 200 subjects and found association values which correlated well with Glaze's results except for some trigrams such as DUZ that had become commonly heard in the language.

A second method for measuring association value is in terms of the number of different associations which a subject has to an item. Noble (1952), who has used this technique, has suggested that what we mean by the term "meaningfulness" is the number of different associations to the particular item. He used stimulus materials ranging from two syllable nonword items through quite common English words of two syllables. Noble insisted that in studies of verbal learning the distinction between word and nonword is irrelevant to the process of learning. Rather, he suggests, learning is based on the associability of the items. He used a procedure in which subjects were asked to give as many different associations per unit of time as they possibly could. The instructions emphasized that each association should be independent of the others. An average of the number of associations to the stimulus over subjects yielded a meaningfulness value which was considered by Noble a better measure of the meaningfulness of the item than the Glaze-type technique.

A third method for scaling association value is that of free association. In the free-association method a stimulus item is presented, and the subject is instructed to respond with the first item that comes to mind. This yields a distribution of associative strengths, and a function is developed which is usually referred to as the rank-frequency function.

It is possible, when a large number of people have made a single response, to locate that association given with the highest frequency by subjects. This is called the primary response, and a rank of 1 is assigned to it.

Using such data one can draw a rank-frequency (R/F) function for each word showing the percentage of associations versus the rank. The function usually drops sharply. For example, the R/F function for "table" is very steep, indicating that there is a high agreement in the population about the association of "chair" to "table." If we plot the function for the word "butterfly" on the same set of axes, the function is much flatter. The R/F function can thus be regarded as reflecting the relative strength of different associations, if we assume that the item given by a large number of people is also the strongest for each individual. However, this assumption does not always work when it is subjected to experimental test.

The relationship between the frequency of response in a population and the strength of the response in an individual member of the population has been described by Marbe's law. Marbe's law was originally formed in reference to the latency of response. It predicted that a response common to the population would have a shorter latency. Recently, however, there have been attempts to validate the law by using speed of learning. As Marbe's law is usually stated today, it relates the frequency of response in a population to the strength of the response in the individual, and in the interpretation given by many psychologists, this is considered to be due to cultural factors.

Cross validation of the free-association method with Noble's measure of meaningfulness is not very satisfactory. Words appearing in Noble's situation overlap only 50 percent in their measured meaningfulness with words in the free-association situation. It has been suggested by some writers that this definite discrepancy between the two methods of measuring meaningfulness is due to a kind of association chaining in Noble's situation. By associative chaining we mean a situation in which a person first makes an association to a word and then associates again not only to the word but to the association which he has just made. In this way, a long chain of associative responses can be made which is not made up of associates to the original word. The procedure used by Noble is quite likely to lead to erroneous measures of association value due to associative chaining.

Much learning takes the form of paired associates. That is, we learn to give a particular response to a particular stimulus. A good example of paired-associates learning is in the learning of foreign vocabulary words. We see the English word and learn to pair a foreign word with it. For many psychologists who have studied the learning process, the paired-associates situation has been used as the model of the process of acquisition. Our consideration of the role of meaningfulness in verbal learning can be divided into two parts: meaningfulness, or association values, may have a different effect on the stimulus side of the paired-associates situation than it has on the response side. A number of experiments have been performed to explore the role of meaningfulness in this situation.

The first type of experiment, which we shall discuss in Example 15–3, is the familiarization experiment. The general procedure which has been followed in such work has been to allow the prospective learner prior access to the stimulus items and/or the response items which he will be required to learn and to see if the familiarization has an effect on learning. Certainly, for the response side this prior exposure should aid the integration of responses.

Example 15–3 *The effect of familiarity of material upon learning (Underwood & Schulz, 1960)*

In an experiment designed to test the hypothesis that familiar verbal items would be learned more easily, Underwood and Schulz (1960) used a method of familiarization in which the subject was allowed to read the items over and over again. Having been familiarized with either the stimulus items or the response items the subject then learned material which contained both familiar items and items to which the subject had not been exposed. When the results were examined, it was found that there was a difference between the effect of familiarization on stimulus items and on response items. This is illustrated in Figure 15–2.

When we consider the effect of familiarization on response items, we find a large and progressive effect on increaing familiarization with the response items on the rate of learning of paired-associates tasks. However, for stimulus items effects are uniformly negligible. In fact, there may be a very slight negative effect.

A second technique used to explore the role of meaningfulness in verbal learning has been to measure learning as a function of scaled meaningfulness of either the stimulus items or the response items, or both. The selections of the items which are used is not made on the basis of experimental experience as in the familiarization experiment, but rather it is based on scaled values obtained prior to the experiment. In this work, it is necessary to make a distinction between experiments which use only non-

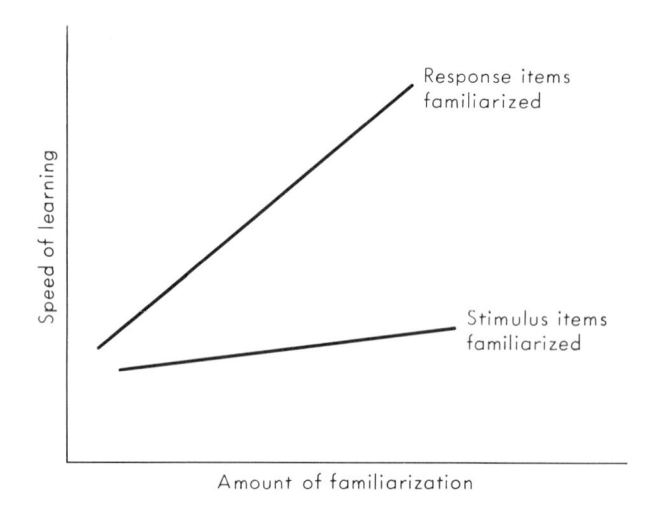

FIG. 15–2 Speed of learning versus amount of familiarization.

sense items and those using entirely meaningful words, since the results of these two turn out to be quite different.

In a series of studies, Noble developed a continuum of nonsense syllables and words. He defined meaningfulness as the average number of different associations per item per unit of time, as we mentioned above. The continuum of meaningfulness goes from nonsense syllables to real but unusual words and then on to common words. When these materials are used in paired-associates learning situations, response meaningfulness has large and significant effects. Increased response meaningfulness increases the speed of learning. This result is the same as that obtained in the familiarity studies. On the other hand, in these experiments, stimulus meaningfulness also has small but positive effects. This result is different from that obtained in familiarization studies. However, response-meaningfulness effects appear to override stimulus-meaningfulness effects. In this type of experiment, the usual design included four conditions in respect to stimuli and responses: high meaningfulness–high meaningfulness (HH); high meaningfulness–low meaningfulness (HL); low meaningfulness–high meaningfulness (LH); low meaningfulness–low meaningfulness (LL).

An exhaustive attack on this problem was made

by Underwood and Schulz, who attempted to develop a continuum of nonsense syllables and three-letter words. They used all the permutations of consonants and vowels such as CCV, CVC, CCC, and so on. In addition, they scaled both frequent and generated trigrams. In their frequency counts, they made especially elaborate tabulations of the occurrences of three-letter sequences in the language. In addition to counts which they made themselves, Underwood and Schulz used the counts of cryptographers. The work on generated trigrams involved a procedure by which subjects responded to a pair of letters with a third letter. The experimenters simply provided the subject with all possible choices of two letters and asked them to supply the third letter. This yielded a distribution of third letters for each trigram over the normative group. The data showed that the generated trigrams correlated fairly well with sheer frequency of occurrence in the language of the same materials but that the correlation was not perfect, since other habits of human beings entered in, such as emission preferences, alphabetic sequence preferences, and preferences of CVC forms.

When these scaled syllables were used as stimuli or responses, the results showed a difference between the results obtained for learning tasks which involved homogeneous lists. A homogeneous list is one in which all the items have the same scale value of meaningfulness. For homogeneous lists there was found to be a large difference on the response side and a small difference on the stimulus side. On the other hand, when mixed lists were used which contained some highly meaningful items and some of medium and low meaningfulness, the results changed. What was measured was the correlation between the number of correct responses on any one item and its scaled meaningfulness.

For the response side of the task, meaningfulness sometimes yielded the predicted results and sometimes it did not. An examination of the actual results showed that there was a difficulty hidden in the experimental procedure and that this had to do with pronounceableness. In general, high meaningfulness correlates with pronounceableness, but this is not always so. There are words which have a high frequency in the language and therefore a high meaningfulness but which are not easily pronounced. Because of this discrepancy between meaningfulness and pronounceableness, it was necessary to use a larger number of learning tasks, since any one list of verbal items may have peculiarities in the pronounceableness of those items of which it is constructed. The results showed, in general, that in those lists in which high-frequency items were also easy to pronounce, the relationship between response meaningfulness and learning was that which had been found by previous workers. In lists where high-frequency items were not also easy to pronounce, the relationship broke down. To explore the relationship between pronounceableness and frequency, experiments were performed in which pronounceableness was varied while frequency was held constant. The results showed that response pronounceableness predicts learning very well. Frequency also predicts learning well but only because of its association with pronounceableness. If a special situation is set up in which frequency and pronounceableness are made to work against each other and pronounceableness is held constant, the remaining effect of frequency is close to zero.

From these results, Underwood and Schulz concluded that effects on the response side of paired-associates tasks were due to pronounceableness, which reflects the item as an integrated unit. However, such a conclusion is not fully justified in Underwood's work, because he obtained his frequency counts by counting across syllabic boundaries. If the frequency of occurrence of an item is counted within syllabic boundaries, then one obtains the usual frequency effect on the response side of the paired associates.

On the stimulus side, the Underwood and Schulz data yield results like those of Noble. There is a small but quite consistent effect of the meaningfulness of the stimulus on learning. Pronounceableness was again found to be the best predictor of stimulus effect on learning. Frequency, as measured by the Underwood technique, did not add much to the effect of pronounceableness.

From these results a rationale for Marbe's law can be worked out. All individuals in a culture are basically alike in respect to exposure to verbal materials. But there is not equal exposure to all items, and, therefore, one builds up a response hierarchy in which different responses have different probabilities of being made by an individual in a particular stimulus situation. Those responses which are quite common in a population should have very short latencies in the free-association situation. Any one individual is quite able to give a primary association characteristic of the population in which he lives if he is specifically asked for it and will often do so even if he is not specifically asked to give it. It is because of this commonality of associative networks that the effects of meaningfulness on learning appear.

From the experiments which we have discussed, it is clear that scaled meaningfulness has different effects on the response side as against the stimulus side. Underwood and Schulz suggested that the speed of learning on the response side depends on the speed with which any of the responses can be emitted by the subject. The readiness to emit the response items is important in paired-associates learning. Further, it can be argued that the more frequently an item is used, the higher its scale of meaningfulness will be. During the first stage of learning the availability of responses is an important factor. Stimulus availability is not so important, since the learner does not have to pronounce or give the stimulus. He needs only attend to as much as will allow him to discriminate it from the other stimuli in the task. From this analysis, Underwood and his coworkers have suggested that the response side of paired-associates learning can be accounted for in terms of the pronounceableness and, therefore, the ability of a subject to make the responses rapidly.

There have been several approaches to the analysis of effects of the stimulus side of the paired-associates task. One of the most prominent theories has suggested that any stimulus has a very certain probability of eliciting associations which can be used in learning by establishing a link or a series of links to the response. Familiarization with the stimulus items has very little effect, since just familiarization does not increase the number of associations and, therefore, the number of potential mediating links which the stimulus evokes. In fact, the results show that as long as we remain in the nonsense-syllable meaningfulness range, we can expect little variation in the number of associations among nonsense syllables. But when we use words of different levels of meaningfulness, a U-shaped effect occurs. One possible explanation is that as a word becomes more meaningful, the number of associations with it increases the number of associations available as links to correct responses. But with further increases in meaningfulness, the number of associations available as links to the wrong responses also increases. One of these two contradictory trends may increase more slowly than the other. If this is true, the U-shaped function would be explained.

SHORT-TERM MEMORY

Thus far in our discussion of the psychology of learning we have been primarily concerned with evidence for long-term learning. However, we cannot limit our consideration of learning to retention after a long period of time, because it is quite apparent that at any time in the process of learning there is a good deal of variation which is due to short-term memory. When the learner attempts to master material which is so difficult as to require more than one trial, there must be a carry-over from trial to trial. If there were no carry-over, then the person could not learn the task. The amount of material which can be recalled after one presentation is usually referred to as the memory span.

Memory Span

The study of the memory span is by no means new to psychology. The classical memory span (CMS) was and still is used as a measure for IQ. We will consider some of the classical work on this topic.

The classical memory span is usually defined as the number of discrete units which can be reproduced in correct serial order after one exposure to the material if measurement occurs as soon as possible. Thus, the four defining characteristics are (1) the number of discrete units, (2) correct serial order, (3) measurement after one exposure, and (4) measurement as soon as possible. Stated another way, the classical memory span is a measurement of how much a person can retain at one time with an emphasis on correct serial order.

The measurement of the classical memory span is closely related to the measurement of thesholds in perception. It was found that the classical memory span varied from moment to moment much as threshold does in a sensory discrimination task. Therefore, the classical memory span is usually taken as an average of the subject's capacity for reproducing discrete units. The moment-to-moment variation which is usually observed may be due to the use of test materials which are not truly equivalent on each measurement trial. Further, there may be changes which are within the subject, causing him to vary in his ability to reproduce the items. The standard psychophysical practices were adapted to the measurement of the classical memory span.

In the *method of limits*, the person is presented with a stimulus list of a length much longer or shorter than that which he can easily reproduce. Then, the length of the list is changed in single-unit steps until the threshold is reached. In an ascending series, one might start with a three-item list and then a four-, five-, and six-, and so on, until the person failed to reproduce the list in one trial. The ascending series is the type of measurement most frequently used. On the other hand, a descending series starts with a much longer stimulus list than any subject can be expected to learn. For digits this might be a fifteen-item list, and the lists are shortened until the subject is correct. For certain types of tests, a subject is presented with first an ascending and then a descending list and his memory span taken as the average length of the two lists at the transition point. It is easy to see that this is not an economical method for measuring the memory span. Many trials are required which do not yield information about the subject's memory span. Only the point of transition is of use to the measurer.

A second method often used to measure the memory span is the *method of constant stimuli*, in which the person is presented with each of a series of stimulus items, the series being selected to cover a range from low to high probability of retention. Each length of list is presented randomly many times, and a plot is made of the psychometric function of percentage correct reproduction versus list length. The classical memory span is usually statistically defined as the length of list which results in 50 percent correct reproductions. This percentage may sometimes vary, but it is usually taken as the percentage correct over a number of trials in one subject or over a number of subjects.

Units in Memory

One interesting finding about the classical memory span is that it is not invariant with respect to the type of unit which is used in its determination. A large number of experiments have been done which use different units. Digits, letters, words, dot patterns have all been used. In general, there is some variation in classical memory span with different types of units, but the variation is not very large. For example, the classical memory span for digits is about seven or eight, but for letters it is about five or six in the general population. Further, with consistent training the classical memory span can be increased somewhat.

Example 15-4 *An informational analysis of the classical memory span (Miller, 1956)*

In an article which has stimulated a great deal of research on the measurement of immediate memory, George Miller has suggested that the unit of what is remembered has not been correctly defined in immediate-memory methods. Historically, units have been nominal and have not necessarily been equivalent to psychological functional units. Miller has pointed out that in reference to immediate memory span, a human being might be envisaged as a communication system having a certain number of channels each of which will allow only limited amounts of information to be transmitted. On the basis of this analysis, a hypothesis can be stated as follows: regardless of units, the organism can transmit only a constant amount of information. According to this hypothesis, variation in the classical memory span occurs because of different amounts of information carried in different kinds of units. That is, there is a different amount of uncertainty as to what the message will be in different sequences of units.

If we are to use this type of informational analysis, we must define the term "information." In this case, the amount of information is determined by how much an item reduces the uncertainty as to what a message will be. For example, if the population of possible stimuli contains only one member, giving the subject this stimulus does not reduce his uncertainty, since he is completely certain. Thus, it carries no information. On the other hand, if the population contains two stimuli, presentation of one of them reduces uncertainty by 50 percent. It is possible to state for any population how much uncertainty is reduced after the presentation of one of the members of the population. It can be seen that an increased number of possible alternatives increases the amount of information that can be carried in any given message. The amount of information in such statements is measured in terms of the extent to which the number of possible outcomes is reduced.

If we consider the amount of information carried by different units, which are ordinarily used in measuring the classical memory span, we see that a string of words carries more information than a string of digits. Thus, if the span for decimal digits is seven, then the classical memory span for words should be only two. But the classical memory span is actually five or six for words. When one examines the data from a number of experiments on the classical memory span, the facts are much more in agreement with the hypothesis stating that a constant number of units will be remembered than they are consistent with a constant-information hypothesis. In actuality, a person can remember a very wide amount of information depending on the unit. According to Miller, persons can remember 7 plus or minus 2 units.

From this analysis, a second hypothesis is suggested. Perhaps we are looking at the wrong units in determining information. We know that most subjects have certain grouping habits. From our knowledge of these grouping habits we can introduce a new functional unit which we will call a "chunk." The chunk is defined as a functional unit already integrated by a subject that he will use as a unit. Our hypothesis then states that the number of chunks of information contained in the classical memory span is constant. The size of a chunk may vary from one kind of material to another. Miller advanced this hypothesis to account for the fact that there is no apparent correlation between span and amount of information per unit.

In one experiment, Miller produced evidence for chunking by teaching persons to increase the size of their functional units through training and, therefore, to increase the amount of information in a chunk. Therefore, such persons increased the amount of information in their memory span by using binary digits. The method went as follows: the binary-digit span of a naïve subject is equal to about eight. But when the subject is taught different recording methods, his ability to remember series containing more information is increased. For instance, if a 2-to-1 code is used, there are four possible labels: series 00 has the label 0; series 01 has the label 1; series 10 has the label 2; series 11 has the label 3. If a subject masters this code and is then capable of correctly recalling eight items, he will actually be able to write sixteen binary digits. Miller found that it takes a long time to train a subject in the use of such a recoding method. The subject obviously must learn some strong symmetrical associations. However, one subject was able to learn as high as 5-to-1 recoding. With this technique, it was possible to raise the binary digit span from eight to forty. From this work it is possible to draw several conclusions: A subject can carry in his memory seven plus or minus two chunks, but each chunk can carry a range of amounts of information. There seems to be something like an invariant span in the classical memory situation. This invariant number refers to the number of chunks that the subject can process. The size of each chunk will vary from situation to situation and from subject to subject. The size of the classical memory span, therefore, depends on how successful the subject is at coding information into a smaller number of units.

There have been a number of further developments of the idea of the memory span. Various psychologists have drawn attention to the fact that messages rarely reach an individual in the form of a discrete series of approximately the same length as the memory span. Most of us, in dealing with such situations in our daily lives, simply retain that which has most recently been presented to us. Because of these considerations, the memory span has been redefined as the length of a subseries within a longer series which can be correctly recalled in the proper serial order after a single presentation. This is a more general and powerful definition of memory span than the classical one. Clearly, this definition requires that points of reference in the measurement procedure be defined for determining what is available in immediate memory. We will not consider all the experimental data relating to immediate-memory span, but we will list some of the methods which have recently come into prominence.

The first of the immediate-memory methods is the initial-memory span, whose point of reference is the beginning of a series. The initial-memory span is that span which is obtained when the beginning of the list is used as a point of reference, whether or not the series exceeds the memory span. In this situation, the subject is presented with an instruction which tells him to retain those items at the beginning of the list. He is then presented with a list and asked to present the initial items.

The second memory-span method is the terminal-memory span, which has as its point of reference the end of the series. In this situation the experimenter finds out how far back the subject can go without errors to the end of the list. A long list of items is read to a subject, and he is asked to report as correctly as he can the last items. One may, from these considerations, redefine the classical memory span as a special case in which the initial- and terminal-memory spans overlap and the subject is required to give his response in certain order.

Of course, other positions within a list could be designated as points of reference. A special case of the terminal-memory span is the running memory span, which involves a situation in which the subject is uncertain as to the length of a list. This type of memory span is important in any situation in which a continuously changing input must be monitored and the action that the monitor has to take depends on the most recent input. When faced with a running-memory-span task, a subject is required to drop out old events from his memory store and retain new ones.

There is one important fact about the immediate-memory span which has emerged from recent experimentation. This is that all measures of immediate-memory span systematically underestimate what is available in immediate memory. This seems to be due to the fact that when a person recalls, he must do it in some sequential order which takes time and results in intervening activity. As a person's recall progresses, the interval between presentation of the series and point of recall increases. There also occurs interpolated recall activity which causes errors, and, therefore, the amount of material which could actually have been correctly recalled, were it possible to give all of the responses at once, is underestimated.

A second approach to the problem of determining the storage capacity of memory is that of studying so-called storage load. Storage capacity is defined as the average amount of information that has to be retained in order to recall when one is required to do so. The storage load for any particular task is defined as what the subject is required, on the average, to carry in his memory on any one trial.

The storage capacity is the limit of a person in successfully carrying any particular storage load. The storage capacity is estimated from that level of storage load at which performance deteriorates.

Example 15–5 *Storage load and the immediate-memory span (Lloyd, Reid, & Feallock, 1960)*

Lloyd, Reid, and Feallock performed a series of experiments on storage load. We will consider only one of these. In this study, the experimenters used overlearned words as the members of common classes. For instance, the class "tree" might have as its members "oak," "maple," "birch," and so on. Before the experiment began, the subject was told what the classes were and was familiarized with all members of the classes which would be used. Then, the words were presented to the subject, and every so often the presentation was interrupted by giving the subject a class name and asking him to recall the last member of that class. When a subject is faced with this task, he must drop out old items and respond in terms of the newest ones. In this experiment, an auditory presentation technique was used. For different lists, the average storage load was varied. In general, two members of any class were never given without intervening recall for one item. Therefore, the task involved remembering those items which had been given since the last request for a recall for that class. The results showed that, as the average storage load increased, there was an increase in the number of errors which were made. Varying the number of classes used had no effect, and varying the number of items within the classes also had no effect. This series of studies is very important, because it has led to a great increase in interest in the contextual factors involved in learning and recall.

Continuous-memory methods alternate input and output in a haphazard fashion, and, in general, recall is used as an index of what is retained. However, recognition methods can also be used in continuous-memory tasks, and we will report one experiment which has tested recognition memory in a continuous test.

Example 15–6 *The recognition method in measuring memory (Shepard & Teghtsoonian, 1961)*

Shepard's experiment used long series of three-digit numbers written one to a card. These cards formed a deck which was so arranged that each number occurred twice but the sequence of second occurrences, that is, old numbers, and first occurrences, that is, new numbers, was random. In this task, the subject had to look at each number and say whether it was old or new. It was possible to vary the number of intervening items between the first and second occurrence of a number and generate a curve which showed retention as a function of the number of intervening items (Figure 15–3).

The results of Shepard's experiment showed that the occurrence of correct recognitions decreased with the number of intervening items between the first and second occurrences of the number. There were still a significant number of recognitions after large numbers of intervening items. An information analysis of this situation indicates that the subject can carry an average of thirty-two bits rather than the twenty-three bits found in the recall situation after one exposure. This indicates that the recognition method is more sensitive.

Memory of Single Items

In the history of the study of memory there have been many theories which apply only to a single item, whereas most experiments which have been done have used lists of items. One such theory is the decaying-memory-trace theory of short-term retention which can best be applied to the trace of a single item and says little about the possible effects of interactions between items in a list of items. A good deal of experimentation has been done on memory for single items. Some classic work by Peterson and Peterson (1959), which tests retention for a single verbal unit, will be discussed here.

Example 15–7 *Short-term recall of single items (Peterson & Peterson, 1959)*

The researchers used low-meaningfulness list trigrams, that is, three-letter items, and they tested retention after intervals of three to eighteen seconds. Each subject was tested eight times at each interval. Now it should be clear that during the intervals between presentation of an item and the test for retention, something must be done to prevent rehearsal. If no intervening activity is used and the subject is allowed to rehearse, the trace will be strengthened by rehearsal in the direction of correct items and weakened by rehearsal of errors.

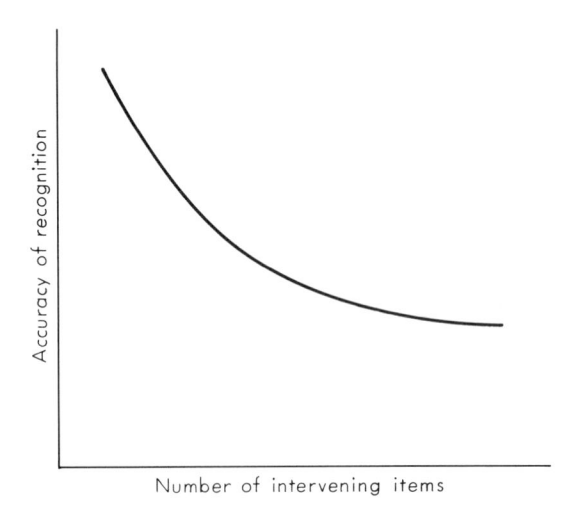

FIG. 15–3 Accuracy of recognition versus number of intervening items.

The traditional problem is that during the process of controlling rehearsal it is necessary to avoid introductory interference effects from other verbal material. Therefore, Peterson and Peterson had their subjects count backward during the interval time. They found that the percentage of recall divided by the opportunities for recall decreased with increased lengths of intervals.

With the learning-recall interval filled by the backward-counting task, which prevents rehearsal and has low interference, a rapid forgetting curve is obtained for a single item. The result could be considered as evidence for rapid decay of trace without rehearsal, or it may be due to extremely powerful interference even from unrelated tasks. In general, however, the follow-up studies of the Peterson work have indicated that there is strong evidence that the rapid decay over time is due to the rapid falling off of the amount recalled with very short increases in time if the subject is prevented from rehearsing.

CONCLUSION

In looking back over the history of the functionalistic and behavioristic movements, one must be profoundly impressed by the degree to which they have dominated the academic scene. Many, if not most, departments of psychology at major American universities have had a functionalistic and a behavioristic bent during the last thirty or so years. However, now the emphasis seems to be subtly shifting toward a reconsideration of higher mental processes and the use of theoretical orientations that are more cognitive than those which were in favor earlier. However, one must not underestimate the major contribution made to psychology by the behaviorists and functionalists. Beginning with the period in which departments of psychology were established in American universities, they have continuously sought to provide theories and bodies of data which would help solve the problems current in psychology as they viewed it. Their emphasis on learning and, therefore, on the methods to be used in teaching have generated some dramatic ideas. Every child who is being taught fundamentals by the use of programed books or apparatus is under the influence of functionalism and behaviorism. The principles which have been used to set up these programed learning techniques are directly derived from such theories.

The future of functionalistic and behavioristic models seems to lie in the direction of a rapprochement with the cognitive movement. In the place of prohibitive dicta against the study of states of consciousness as data to be used in psychology, there has been an increasing tolerance of verbal reports as providing potentially useful data. A new kind of functionalist and behaviorist is appearing on the scene, and we can look forward to a widening of interest, on the part of psychologists of these theoretical persuasions, from considerations of simple learning to the analysis of complex cognitive processes.

SECTION FIVE: REFERENCES

ALLPORT, G. W. The functional autonomy of motives. *American Journal of Psychology*, 1937, **50**, 141–156.

ANGELL, J. R. The province of functional psychology. *Psychological Review*, 1907, **14**, 61–81.

ARCHER, E. J. Re-evaluation of the meaningfulness of all possible CVC trigrams. *Psychology Monographs*, 1960, **74** (Whole 497).

BABKIN, B. P. *Pavlov: A biography.* Chicago: University of Chicago Press, 1949.

BLODGETT, H. C. The effect of the introduction of reward upon the maze preformance of rats. *University of California Publications in Psychology*, 1929, **4**, 113–134.

BUTLER, R. A. Discriminated learning by rhesus monkeys to visual exploration motivation. *Journal of Comparative Physiological Psychology*, 1953, **46**, 95–98.

CHOMSKY, N. *Syntactic structures.* The Hague: Mouton Press, 1957.

COWLES, J. T. Food-tokens as incentives for learning by chimpanzees. *Comparative Psychology Monographs*, 1937, **14** (5).

DARWIN, C. *The origin of species by means of natural selection.* Garden City, N.Y.: Doubleday, 1859.

DEWEY, J. The reflex-arc concept in psychology. *Psychological Review*, 1896, **3**, 357–370.

EBBINGHAUS, H. *Memory.* New York: Teachers College, 1885.

GLAZE, J. The association value of non-sense syllables. *Journal of Genetic Psychology*, 1928, **35**, 255–269.

GUTHRIE, E. *The psychology of learning.* (Rev. ed.) New York: Harper, 1952.

GUTHRIE, E. R., & HORTON, G. P. *Cats in a puzzle box.* New York: Holt, 1946.

HARLOW, H. F. Learning set and error factor theory. In S. Koch (Ed.), *Psychology: A study of a science.* Vol. III. New York: McGraw-Hill, 1959.

HILGARD, E., & MARQUIS, D. *Conditioning and learning.* New York: Appleton-Century-Crofts, 1938.

HOVLAND, C. I. The generalization of conditioned responses: I. The sensory generalization of conditioned responses with varying frequencies of tone. *Journal of Genetic Psychology*, 1937, **17**, 125–148. (a)

HOVLAND, C. I. The generalization of conditioned responses: II. The sensory generalization of conditioned responses with varying intensities of time. *Journal of Genetic Psychology*, 1937, **51**, 279–291, (b)

HULL, C. L. *Principles of behavior.* New York: Appleton-Century-Crofts, 1943.

HUMPHREYS, L. G. Acquisition and extinction of verbal expectations in a situation analogous to conditioning. *Journal of Experimental Psychology*, 1939, **25**, 294–301.

JAMES, W. *The principles of psychology.* Vols. I, II. New York: Holt, 1890.

JUDSON, A. J., & COFER, C. N. Reasoning as an associative process: I. "Direction" in a simple verbal problem. *Psychological Reports*, 1956, **2**, 469–476.

LLOYD, K. E., REED, L. S., & FEALLOCK, J. B. Short-term retention as a function of the average number of items presented. *Journal of Experimental Psychology*, 1960, **60**, 201–207.

LOCKE, J. *An essay concerning human understanding.* Vol. I. (4th ed.), New York: Samuel Marks, 1700.

MILLER, G. A. The magical number seven, plus or minus two: Some limits on our capacity for processing information. *Psychological Review*, 1956, **63**, 81–97.

MILLER, G. A., GALLANTER, E., & PRIBRAM, K. H. *Plans and the structure of behavior.* New York: Holt, 1960.

MILLER, N. E. Studies of fear as an acquirable drive: I. Fear as motivation and fear reduction as reinforcement in the learning of new responses. *Journal of Experimental Psychology*, 1948, **38**, 89–101.

MILLER, N. E. Learnable drives and rewards. In S. S. Stevens (Ed.), *Handbook of experimental psychology.* New York: Wiley, 1951.

MORGAN, C. *An introduction to comparative psychology.* New York: Scribner's, 1894.

NOBLE, C. E. An analysis of meaning. *Psychological Review*, 1952, **59**, 421–430.

PAVLOV, I. P. *Lectures on conditioned reflexes.* New York: International Publishers, 1928.

PAVLOV, I. P. *Conditioned reflexes and psychiatry.* New York: International Publishers, **1941**.

PERIN, C. T. Behavior potentiality as a joint function of the amount of training and the degree of hunger at the time of extinction. *Journal of Experimental Psychology*, 1942, **30**, 93–113.

PETERSON, L. R., & PETERSON, M. J. Short-term retention of individual verbal items. *Journal of Experimental Psychology*, 1959, **58**, 193–198.

SECHENOV, I. M. *Reflexes of the brain.* Cambridge, Mass.: M.I.T., 1863.

SHEPARD, R. N., & TEGHTSOONIAN, M. Retention of information under conditions approaching a steady state. *Journal of Experimental Psychology*, 1961, **62**, 202–222.

SIMLEY, O. A. The relation of subliminal to supraliminal learning. *Archives of Psychology*, No. 146, 1933.

SKINNER, B. F. *The behavior of organisms.* New York: Appleton-Century-Crofts, 1938.

SKINNER, B. F. Are theories of learning necessary? *Psychological Review*, 1950, **57**, 193–216.

SKINNER, B. F. *Science and human behavior.* New York: Macmillan, 1953.

SKINNER, B. F. Teaching Machines. *Science*, 1958, 128.

SPENCER, H. *Principles of psychology.* London: Longmans Press, 1855.

THORNDIKE, E. L. Animal intelligence: An experimented study of the associative processes in animals. *Psychological Review*, 1898, **2** (Monogr. Suppl. 8).

TOLMAN, E. C. Retroactive inhibition as affected by conditions of learning. *Psychological Monographs*, 1917, **25** (Whole No. 107).

TOLMAN, E. C. *Purposive behavior in animals and men.* New York: Appleton-Century-Crofts, 1932.

TOLMAN, E. The determiners of behavior at a choice point. *Psychological Review*, 1938, **45**, 1–41.

TOLMAN, E. C., & HONZIK, C. H. Introduction and removal of reward, and maze performance in rats. *University of California Publications in Psychology*, 1930, **4**, 257–275.

TOLMAN, E. C., RITCHIE, B. F., & KALISH, D. Studies in spatial learning. II. Place learning versus response learning. *Journal of Experimental Psychology*, 1946, **36**, 221–229.

UNDERWOOD, B. J., & SCHULZ, R. W. *Meaningfulness and verbal learning.* Philadelphia: Lippincott, 1960.

WATSON, J. B. Psychology as the behaviorist views it. *Psychological Review*, 1913, **20**, 158–177.

WATSON, J. B., & RAYNER, R. Conditioned emotional reactions. *Journal of Experimental Psychology*, 1920, **3**, 1–14.

WICKENS, D. D. The transference of conditioned excitation and conditioned inhibition from one muscle group to the antagonistic muscle group. *Journal of Experimental Psychology*, 1938, **22**, 101–123.

WILLIAMS, S. B. Resistance to extinction as a function of the number of reinforcements. *Journal of Experimental Psychology*, 1938, **23**, 506–521.

WOODWORTH, R. S. *Dynamic psychology.* New York: New York University Press, 1918.

SECTION SIX
BIOLOGICAL MODELS

"As long as mind is thought of as a special kind of being... so long will its relation to the brain be incapable of investigation. Mind is a complex organization, held together by interaction of processes and by the time scales of memory, centered about the body image. It has no distinguishing features other than its organization."
(K. S. Lashley, 1958, p. 17)

"The effect of physiology was to put mind back into nature. The neurologist traces first the effect of the stimuli along the bodily nerves, then integration at nerve centers, and finally the rise of projective references beyond the body with a resulting motor efficacy in renewed nervous excitement. In biochemistry, the delicate adjustment of the whole organism composition of the parts to the preservation of the whole organism is detected. Thus the mental cognition is seen as the reflective experience of a totality, reporting for itself what it is in itself as one unit of occurrence. This unit is the integration of the sum of its partial happenings, but it is not their numerical aggregate. It has its own unity as an event. This total unity, considered as an entity for its own sake, is the prehension into unity of the patterned aspects of the universe of events."
(Alfred N. Whitehead, 1925, pp. 134–135)

PROLOGUE

Zoological and Physiological Orientations toward an Understanding of Behavior

While we have titled this section Biological Models, for contrast with the other sections of this book, it is well, at the outset, to make an important distinction. Biological models of behavior can be divided into two general types. The first type of theory has a zoological orientation. That is, the units of behavioral analysis are based on classic concerns of biologists, such as the genotype or the taxonomic category of the animal which is under study. Thus, *behavior genetics* is concerned with the role of genotype in the determination of behavior. Likewise, *comparative psychology* and *ethology* deal with species as these show specific behavior patterns. The zoological orientation, therefore, involves the study of the whole animal in its emerging nature.

Somewhat in contrast with the zoological approach are the *physiological models of behavior*. Here the emphasis is on the underlying structures of the organism and their relationship to behavior. The chief concern has been with the nervous system, particularly the brain, the traditional subject matter of psychophysiology. But in addition, there has been a good deal of work on two other dimensions derived from a physiological orientation: *psychochemistry,* which is concerned with the relations between body chemistry and behavior, and *psychopharmacology,* which studies the role of exogenous chemical compounds on behavior. Research has been done with such agents as the tranquilizers, sedatives, and hallucinogens. In our discussion, we will first consider the history and something of the present status of the zoological tradition in the study of behavior and then turn to the other fields delineated above.

Origins of the Biological Approach to Behavior

Man's interest in his biological makeup is very old indeed. Perhaps stemming from the struggles for survival which must have marked his own evolutionary emergence, he has given animals a prominent role in his mythology, in his religious rites, and in his more formalized study of nature. From the earliest periods about which we have evidence, man has made highly anthropomorphic judgments about the nature of animal behavior. A good example of this tendency is contained in Aesop's fables, in which animals are portrayed as wise and witty, foolish and scheming, much like men. In a parallel way, many of man's religions have involved the worship of animals, which were given symbolic roles or thought to have the souls of human beings embodied in them.

The first extensive record of the formal study of animals which has survived is contained in Aristotle's writings. His work is a combination of collected animal lore and some of his own original observations. In the light of our present-day scientific insistence upon observable facts, Aristotle's work is somewhat weak, in that much of the evidence is based on *anecdotal method,* which is often uncritical and extreme in its interpretation of the causes of animal behavior. But Aristotle firmly believed in direct observation, and his writings contrast greatly with the fables and legends which constituted discussions of animal behavior up to his time. In addition, he made wide-ranging observations of many forms of life and, thus logically provided the beginnings of a truly comparative psychology. During the middle ages, the growth of biological thought was less evident, but with the Renaissance interest in experimentation was revived, and the study of anatomy and physiology quickened.

Perhaps the most exciting of the events in the history of this period, from the viewpoint of biological psychology, came with the publication in 1735 by Carolus Linnaeus of his *Systema Naturae*. In this work, he described over four thousand species of animals and plants. The tradition of taxonomy was begun, and not only was the great diversity of living forms demonstrated, but the apparent functional similarity in the forms of life laid the cornerstone for the idea that some organisms had developed from others. During this period, J. B. Lamarck (1809) advanced his now famous doctrine of the inheritance of acquired characteristics. This doctrine states that the deliberate efforts of an animal could modify the parts of the body involved and that the offspring of the animals would inherit these acquired features. Although Lamarck's doctrine proved incorrect, at least at the level of gross behavior, it was important because of its emphasis on the evolution of biological forms. In effect, Lamarck and his contemporary theorists provided the springboard for the most momentous event of modern biological science: Charles Darwin's theory of evolution.

The Evolution of Behavior: Survival of Behaviors by Which the Organism Profits

In Chapter 14 we discussed the influence of Darwin's theory on the development of functionalistic and ultimately behavioristic psychology. By introducing the notion that there was a natural selection for those behaviors which had functional relevance for the survival of those animals, which were therefore "fittest," he brought the notion of behavioral function into prominence. In addition, we examined Darwin's contribution to the study of animal behavior. Because he placed man on a continuum with the lower animals, we concluded that he gave impetus to the study of the "animal mind" and thus to the study of animal behavior. Here, in the context of our present discussion of biological models of behavior, we will examine a third facet of Darwin's influence, that having to do with the problem of inheritance of behavior.

In Darwin's theory, the key concepts which are relevant to the present discussion are *natural selection* and *heritable variability of behavior*. Natural selection refers to his notion of the "struggle for life" and the influence of a hostile environment on the behavior of those animals which occupy it.

Owing to this struggle, variations, however slight and from whatever cause proceeding, if they be in any degree profitable to the individuals of a species, in their infinitely complex relations to other organic beings and to their physical conditions of life, will tend to the preservation of such individuals, and will generally be inherited by the offspring. The offspring, also, will thus have a better chance of surviving, for, of the many individuals of any species which are periodically born, but a small number can survive [Darwin, 1859].

Notice that behavior, as such, is not mentioned in this selection, but it is clear from his later writings that Darwin regarded instinctive behaviors as being a very important part of his theory of evolution.

The second important concept for biological psychology is the notion of variability in the behavior of the offspring. The explanatory power of the theory of evolution depends on there being heritable variations in each generation. Without such variation, the process of evolution would stop. After a good deal of speculation, Darwin was not able to develop a satisfactory theory of how variations in behavior or other characteristics were passed on. This problem remained until the work of an Austrian monk, Gregor Mendel, was rediscovered. Although working with morphological characteristics of plants, Mendel developed a theory of inheritance which formed the basis for all of modern genetics.

CHAPTER 16
BEHAVIOR GENETICS

Darwin presented his theory of evolution at a time of intellectual ferment. The work was greatly controversial, and a storm of reaction arose. A half cousin of Darwin's, Francis Galton, responded to the controversy by initiating a careful study of the inheritance of mental traits, particularly the trait of genius. Obviously this was a highly interesting subject, even to those most opposed to the theory of evolution. Everyone is strongly concerned about the effect of his own intelligence on the intellectual capacity of his children.

Example 16–1 *The inheritance of intelligence (Galton, 1869)*

Galton gathered biographical data on 100 eminent men. "Eminent" men were defined as those whose achievements ranked them as one of only 250 persons in each million men. Thus, 1 man in 4,000 could achieve such a rank. In fact, most of Galton's cases fell into his category of "illustrious," which comprised those individuals whose talents ranked them as one in a million. In his description of such persons, Galton labeled them as being leaders of opinion, originators of ideas, and acknowledged determiners of the affairs of the world. His sample included men who were judges, statesmen, ministers of state, military leaders, scientists, poets, writers, musicians, painters, religious leaders, and their families. Famous athletes were also included. Using the most illustrious person in a family as a reference point, the other members of the family were tabulated according to the closeness of kinship with him. Table 16–1, which is a compilation in terms of percentage of cases, gives Galton's results. It is clear from the table there is a decrease in the tendency to attain high status as the distance from the most illustrious member of the family increases.

Galton's data were interesting and informative, but though they did indicate that individuals in families tended to be similar, they indicated next to nothing about inheritance in a genetic sense. Kinship groups often share as much in common culturally and environmentally as they do biologically or genetically. The two sources of variance are thus confounded (i.e., confused) in the pedigree method and give us no more exact scientific information than does common sense. Galton was aware of this problem. In his writings he remarks that both heredity and environment together determine differences between individuals. The following is a modern equational statement of this notion:

$$\sigma^2_{pop} = \sigma_G^2 + \sigma_E^2 + 2\,\text{cov}_{GE}$$

where σ^2_{pop} = total observed variance between individuals for trait in question

σ_G^2 = that part of observed variation due to only genetic differences

σ_E^2 = that part of observed variation due to only environmental causes

cov_{GE} = that part of observed variation due to interaction effects between genetic and environmental causes

The last term perhaps requires some additional explanation. An environmental agent may have an

Table 16-1 Percentages of occurrence of eminence in relatives of eminent men (Galton, 1869)

	Judges	States-men	Com-manders	Writers	Scien-tists	Poets	Artists	Divines	All classes
Father	26	33	47	48	26	20	32	28	31
Brother	35	39	50	42	47	40	50	36	41
Son	36	49	31	51	60	45	89	40	48
Grandfather	15	28	16	24	14	5	7	20	17
Uncle	18	18	8	24	16	5	14	40	18
Nephew	19	18	35	24	23	50	18	4	22
Grandson	19	10	12	9	14	5	18	16	14
Great-grandfather	2	8	8	3	0	0	0	4	3
Great-uncle	4	5	8	6	5	5	7	4	5
First-cousin	11	21	20	18	16	0	1	8	13
Great-nephew	17	5	8	6	16	10	0	0	10
Great-grandson	6	0	0	3	7	0	0	0	3
All more remote	14	37	44	15	23	5	18	16	31

effect whose size and direction relates to the genotype, or the genetic makeup, of the individual on which it acts. Thus so-called "rich" environments (e.g., nursery school, interesting toys) may be associated strongly with children who are genetically bright. In other words, the effects of genes and environment on intelligence are not always independent, but they may covary. The covariance term allows for this possibility.

There has been a great expansion of interest in behavioral genetics in recent years. We will first consider the effects on human behavior of specific chromosomal anomalies. We will then deal with problems of the inheritance of intelligence, aptitudes, personality, and mental illness. A consideration of these problems must be based on naturally occurring populations, since it is out of the question for scientists to control breeding patterns in human beings. However, in the second area of research which we will consider—that of animal behavioral genetics—it is quite usual to develop specially bred strains of animals in order to study the mechanisms of inheritance of behavior characteristics such as level of activity, emotionality, social behavior, and learning ability.

BASIC MECHANISMS OF HEREDITY

Physical Basis of Heredity

In order to discuss some of the facts which are known about the inheritance of human traits, we will first need to define some terms which are regularly used in discussions of genetic mechanisms.

Clearly, if offspring are like their parents, then "information" of a highly specific kind which determines such characteristics as growth, form, and, as we shall see, behavior must somehow be passed to the offspring through the sexual cells, the sperm and the egg. Such information is carried in the *chromosomes*, which are contained in every cell of the body. In the human being, there are forty-six chromosomes, which are divided into twenty-two pairs of *autosomes* and one pair of *sex chromosomes*, as shown in Figure 16–1. Other species have different numbers and patterns of chromosomes. In each case, however, one of each pair of chromosomes comes from the father and one from the mother.

In the cell division of ordinary body cells, such as happens during the process of growth, each chromosome duplicates itself so that each of the two cells which result has the same number of cells as the parent cell. This process of division, known as *mitosis*, results in a proliferation of cells which have the same chromosomal characteristics as the original cell. It is the process by which the embryonic creature becomes the fully formed adult and by which the adult repairs any damage to its cellular structures. Figure 16–2 is a schematic representation of the process of mitosis.

In the case of the sex cells, however, there is a different pattern of cell division, called *meiosis*. The germ cells, that is, the sperm and ova, do not contain a full set of chromosomes but have only half of the complement of chromosomes found in so-

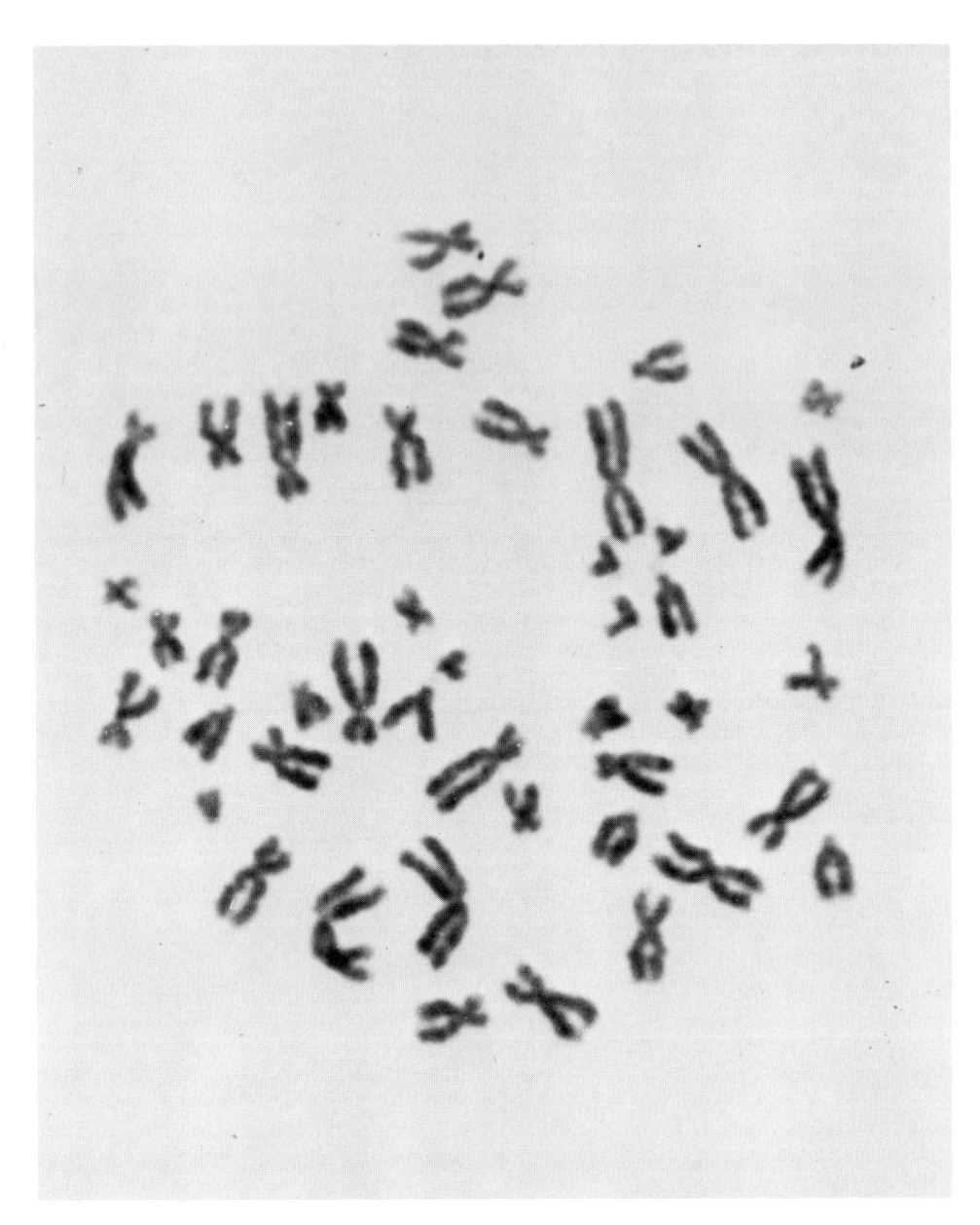

FIG. 16–1 The human chromosomes. A cell, in the act of dividing, was pressed between glass plates and photographed. The figure on page 283 was made by cutting a copy of the photo on page 282 and matching the pairs. Notice the X and Y chromosomes, which are the sex pair. The other pairs are the autosomal, or nonsex, pairs. (*Dr. C. C. Li, personal communication*)

A 1-3   B 4-5

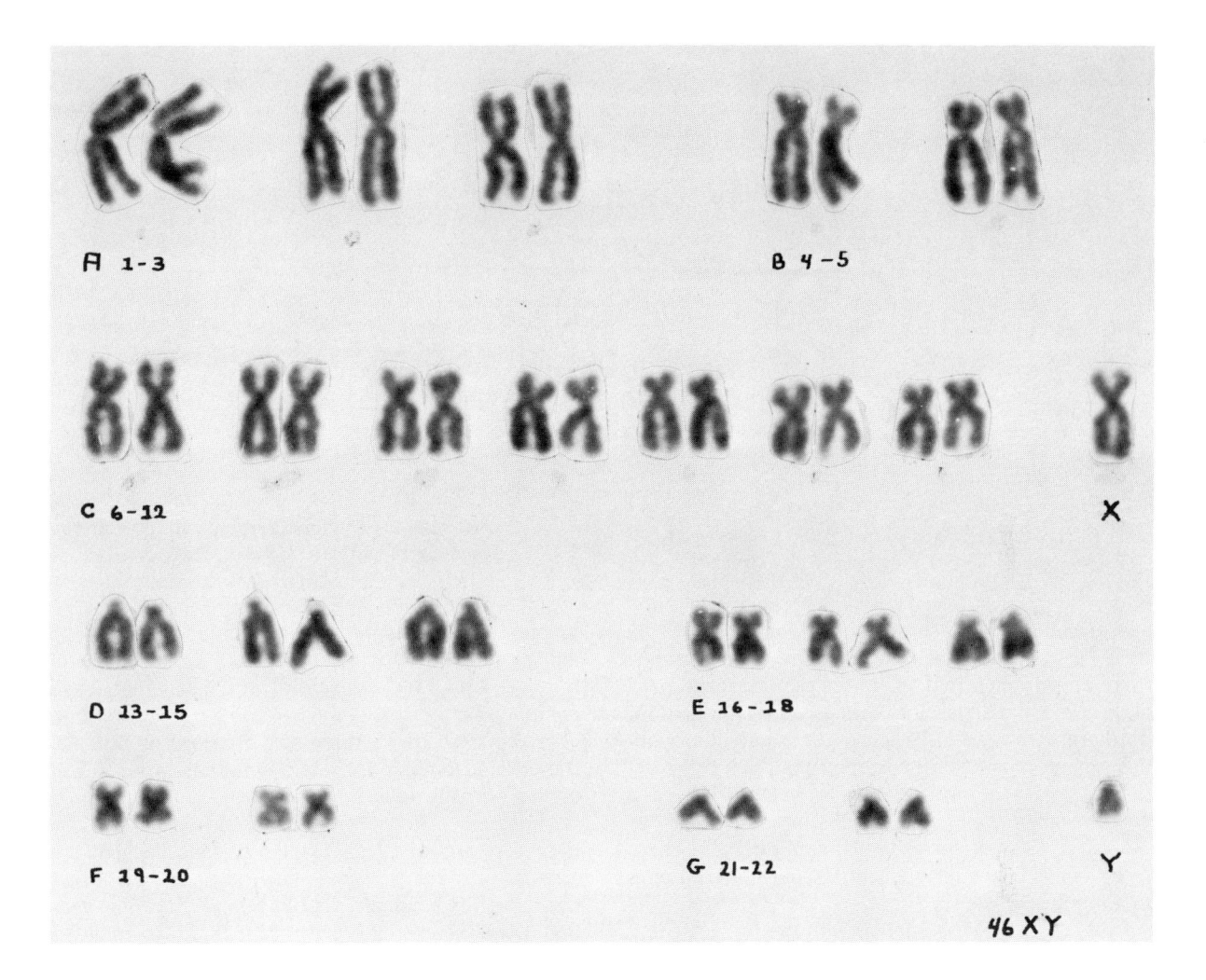

C 6-12   X

D 13-15   E 16-18

F 19-20   G 21-22   Y

46 XY

matic cells. Put simply, meiosis consists of a reshuffling of the chromosomes and produces germ cells which have different combinations of the parental chromosomes. These different types of germ cells are called *gametes*. The process of meiosis is represented in Figure 16–3. Since the number of distinctive gametes can be computed as 2^n, there can theoretically be 8,388,608 different human gametes from each parent. From this, it is clear that the probability of any particular combination of human chromosomes in an individual human being is $8,388,608^2$.

As we mentioned in the preceding paragraph, one pair of chromosomes is concerned with determining sex of the offspring. In the case of females, there are two similar chromosomes called X chromosomes. Males, on the other hand, have one X chromosome and a Y chromosome. Since in meiosis the pairs of chromosomes separate, the sex of a particular offspring is determined by the gamete which the child receives from his father. This results from the fact that the mother is capable of donating only X chromosomes. The father, however, produces both X chromosomes and Y chromosomes. Thus if a sperm cell, that is, a male's gamete, which has an X chromosome unites with a particular ovum, the offspring will be a girl, since its sex chromosome pair will be XX. But if the

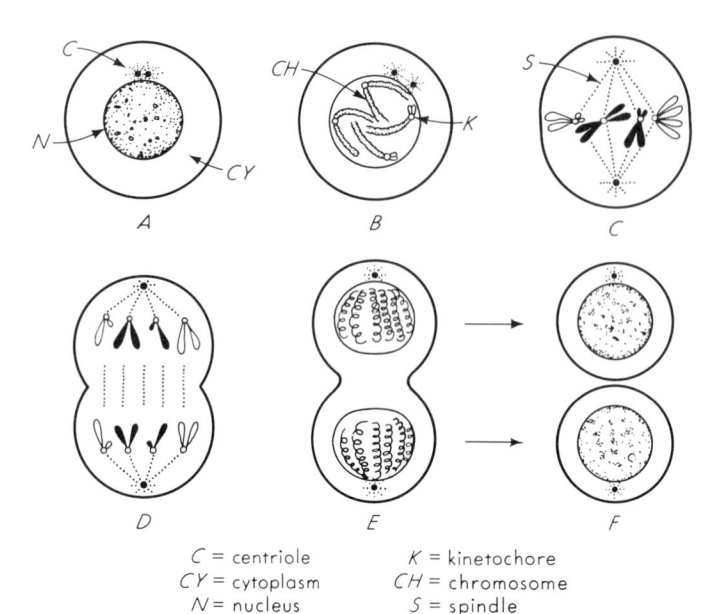

FIG. 16–2 Schematic representation of the process of mitosis. (*Stern, 1949*)

C = centriole
CY = cytoplasm
N = nucleus
K = kinetochore
CH = chromosome
S = spindle

sperm cell has a Y chromosome, the child will be male, with an XY sex chromosome. Very rarely, there appear abnormalities in the chromosomal pairing. We will discuss this matter more fully below, but here we should point out that certain abnormalities, or anomalies, of chromosomal pairings produce sexual aberrations. Thus the pairing of a sperm and an ovum may result in more than two sex chromosomes, for example, XYY or XXY. There is evidence that such individuals may be defective in a number of ways.

Every reader will be familiar with the term "gene." Unfortunately, there is a good deal of confusion about just what a gene is. In our discussion, we will define the gene as *the chemical code that exists at a particular place on a chromosome which determines a specific trait in a species*. In a number of genera, such as the fruit fly, *Drosophila*, it is possible to map on each chromosome the location at which certain traits are encoded. In addition, recent work by biochemists has shed light on the mechanisms by which the genes act.

The chromosomes are made up of very large macromolecules called deoxyribonucleic acids, or DNA. DNA consists of two extremely long strands of material which are curled together in a helical form. The chemical bonds, which are base compounds, are thymine, guanine, adenine, and cytosine. It is thought that the sequence of bases along the DNA helix may differ both as to order and relative amounts of each of the particular base compounds.

In the case of ordinary cell division, or mitosis, the chromosomes duplicate themselves, prior to cell division, in the following manner: The DNA strands begin to separate. As the separation occurs, a duplicate strand of DNA is built up along each of the original strands. These new strands are exact copies of the originals, and in this way the information contained in the base sequences is retained during mitosis. The new cells thus have the same genetic information in them which was carried in the chromosomes of their parent.

The genes are thought to work in the process of the buildup of the protein structures of the body. Thus, protein synthesis is controlled by bases connecting the strands. Since the production of protein takes place outside the nucleus in which the DNA is contained, a messenger substance is required to carry the information from the DNA to the sites of protein buildup. This messenger substance is called ribonucleic acid, or RNA. It is very similar to DNA in chemical structure. RNA is built up using the DNA as a template, and then the RNA migrates to the sites at which protein is constructed. Thus, the information contained in the

284   BIOLOGICAL MODELS

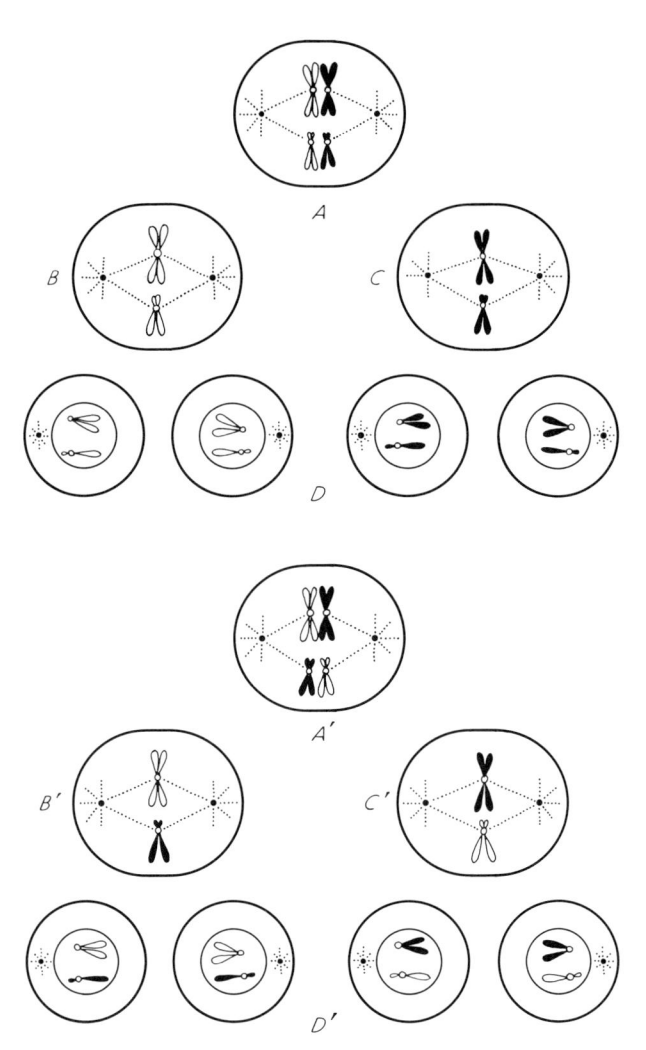

A, A': The two alternative arrangements of the chromosome pairs on the first meiotic spindle. *B–D*, and *B'–D'*: The second meiotic divisions and the different types of reduced chromosome constitutions of the gametes.

FIG. 16–3 Schematic representation of the process of meiosis. (*Stern, 1949*)

DNA ultimately determines the form of the protein which is built up in a particular locus of the body.

Transmission of Characteristics

In the Prologue to this section, we mentioned the name of Gregor Mendel and attributed the foundations of modern genetics to his discoveries. Now we turn to a consideration of some of Mendel's work and the nature of Mendelian theory.

Mendel worked with hybrid peas in the garden of an Austrian monastery. He observed that the peas differed in form; that is, they had different morphological features which appeared with different frequencies. Having noticed the difference in frequency of occurrence of the different forms of the peas, Mendel discovered that by a careful program of cross pollination between the parents of the peas he was able to predict the percentages of the different forms of peas which would occur in the offspring.

285 BEHAVIOR GENETICS

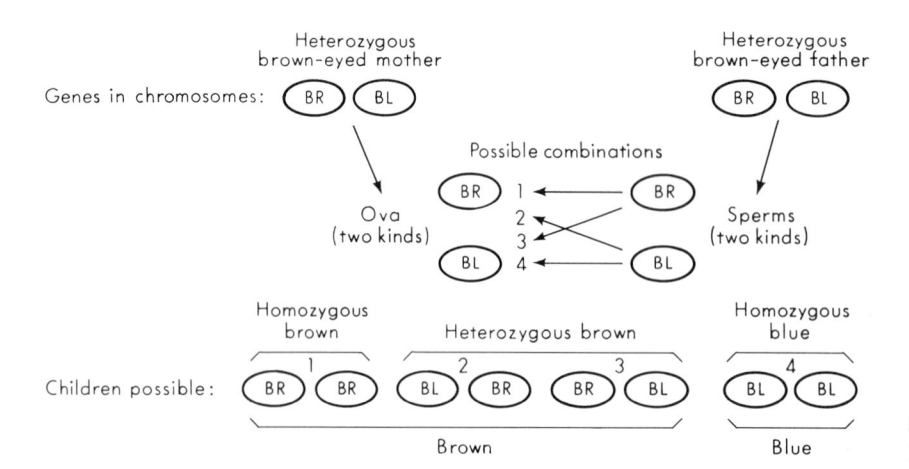

FIG. 16–4 Gene combinations for eye color.

We may illustrate the rules that Mendel discovered by an example based on a trait in human beings which is of some interest: eye color.

Example 16–2 *Eye color in human beings: Gene dominance and recessivity*

A key concept in Mendelian theory is gene dominance. A gene is dominant if, whenever it is present in the chromosomes of an individual, the characteristic which it determines appears. It is usual practice to indicate dominant genes by capital letters. Thus, if we symbolize a simple trait by letters which represent the contribution of each parent to the chromosomal compliment of the offspring, we have four possible combinations of contribution, when the parents have either of two possible alternative forms: AA, Aa, aA, aa. Consider the case of eye color illustrated in Figure 16–4. Every individual is seen to have a pair of genes determining eye color. Thus, the gene pair may consist of genes both of which act to produce brown eyes. When both genes produce the same character, we refer to the individual as *homozygous*. If, on the other hand, the individual has a mixed pair of genes, he is classified as *heterozygous*. In our example, an individual who is heterozygous will always have brown eyes, because the gene for brown eyes is dominant in the human being.

Several deductions follow from these simple assumptions: If both parents are homozygous for blue eyes, all their children will have blue eyes. If both parents are homozygous for brown eyes, all the offspring will have brown eyes. The interesting case, however, comes when both parents are heterozygous for eye color. Figure 16–4 illustrates this case. As can be seen, there are four possibilities for kinds of gene combination: BB, Bb, bB, bb. Three of these combinations of genes will result in individuals whose eyes are brown, but one-fourth of the offspring can be expected to have blue eyes, even though their parents both had brown eyes. This principle sets aside the folklore that blue-eyed children of brown-eyed parents are difficult to explain.

The schema which we have presented represents traits determined by genes at single loci. Yet, with many traits, both morphological and behavioral, we notice that there appears to be a continuous variation in respect to the amount and quality of the characteristic. In the case of such traits, it is necessary to postulate that they are determined by the action of many gene pairs. Such a situation is referred to as *polygenic determination of traits*. In such a case, the number of different forms which a trait may have in a given individual becomes very great, as can be seen by the example given in Figure 16–5.

CHROMOSOMAL EVENTS AND BEHAVIOR

Although our presentation of the mechanisms of inheritance is highly simplified, it is sufficient to enable us to consider several human traits which are known to be due to chromosomal anomalies. We will consider two kinds of anomalies, those due to errors in autosomal, or nonsex, chromosomes

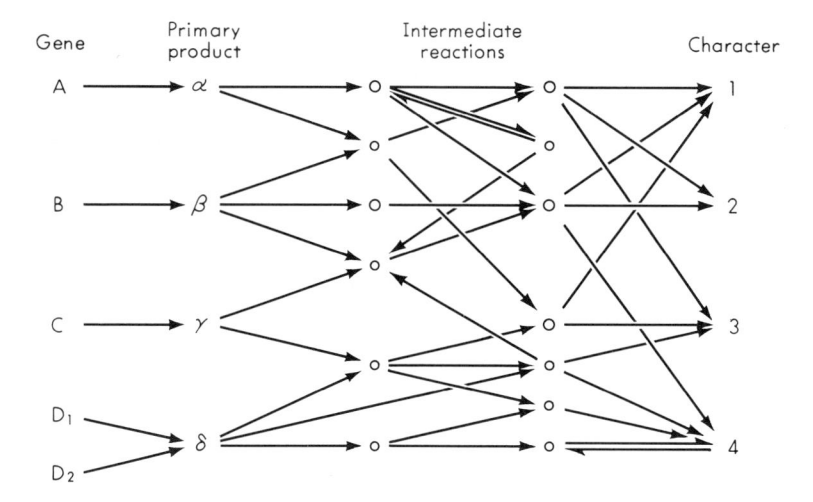

FIG. 16–5 Polygenetic determination of traits.

and those due to aberrations in the sex chromosomes.

Autosomal Trisomies

The most common feature of autosomal abnormality is mental retardation. The first of these syndromes of mental retardation which was found to be due to chromosomal abnormality was *mongolism*, or Down's syndrome, as it has come to be called. It has been discovered that mongoloid individuals have forty-seven, instead of forty-six chromosomes. The extra chromosome is a third member of a particular chromosome number, number 21, which results in a triplicate where there should only be a pair. This condition is called *trisomy*.

Most cases of mongolism are due to an accident which occurs during the process of meiosis in which the gametes are produced. For reasons which are not known, both chromosomes of a pair go to the same pole, resulting in a gamete which has an extra chromosome. The other gamete is a monosome, a condition which is thought to be lethal in man, since no cases of monosomic development have yet been reported. When a trisomic condition develops on chromosome 21, mongolism results. It is estimated that the frequency of occurrence of this defect may be as high as 1 in 600 births.

The causes of errors in chromosome segregation, such as result in mongolism, are not well known. From the days of the ancient Greeks, it has been known that the risk of mongolism increases as the age of the mother increases. This may be due to some environmental condition whose effect on the mother increases the likelihood of aberrations in gametogenesis. There has been some evidence that the incidence of mongolism varies a good deal from year to year in a particular locality and that there is a good deal of clustering of cases in such localities. This has been interpreted as being due to an infectious agent. Such an interpretation is supported by the observation that mongolism is more prevalent in urban areas than in rural areas.

Sex Chromosome Anomalies

We have already referred to sexual anomalies which result from errors in the sex chromosomes. Not only do many of these abnormalities affect sexual development, but frequently they are accompanied by mental defect.

One condition, known as Klinefelter's syndrome, results in a phenotypic male, that is, an individual who has the appearance of a male but in whom there is incomplete sexual development. The testes are usually underdeveloped, and there may be development of the breasts, accompanied frequently by mental defect. In this case, there is an extra chromosome, which is an X sex chromosome. Thus, the individual has a sex chromosome complement of XXY. There have also been reported cases of XYY sex chromosome complements in males. Such a condition has been suggested to be associated with high aggressiveness and criminal tendencies (Forsmann & Hambert, 1967).

The study of biochemical and embryological

mechanisms which lead to chromosomal errors is proceeding at a very rapid rate. We have only touched on the field and refer the interested reader to an excellent review by McClearn and Meredith (1966) for more detailed discussion of the area.

Metabolic Errors and Mental Defects

There are a number of genetically determined "errors of metabolism" which result in behavioral effects. Here we will consider only one of these: defective amino acid metabolism. The syndrome called *phenylketonuria* (PKU) has been studied quite thoroughly from the genetic point of view. The defect is dependent mainly on a single recessive gene.

In PKU, the critical biochemical defect is an inability to metabolize phenylalanine, an amino acid. As a result of the defect, the products of metabolism accumulate in the body, and one or more of these is thought to be the agent responsible for the mental defect. Children who have this condition become mental retardates if they are not diagnosed and treated in early infancy. Treatment consists of feeding the infant commercially prepared diets which are extremely low in the amount of phenylalanine which they contain. When such a diet is fed, the biochemical situation often becomes partly normal, and severe mental retardation is less likely to occur. However, at this writing, the commercially prepared diets have not been available for a sufficiently long time to permit the evaluation of their remedial effect on intellectual performance by affected children.

In untreated cases of PKU, a rapid decline in intelligence is detectable at four to six months of age. If treatment is delayed beyond six months of age, the outcome is increasingly worse. However, there is some favorable effect gained by treatment of older patients, since therapy appears to lessen their irritability and motor defects and make them more manageable.

A number of other metabolic diseases have been approached in the same manner as PKU, with some hope that successful treatments may also be developed.

We can turn at this point from the study of chromosomal defects in behavior to methods which involve the study of the human being in natural population.

HUMAN BIOMETRICAL GENETICS
Population Studies

Up to now, our discussion has emphasized the Mendelian concept of the gene. We have discussed the role of the gene in the determination of human traits in cases where the traits were largely determined by single gene pairs. But much interest for behavior genetics lies in the study of the occurrence of traits in larger populations of individuals. Thus, methods have been developed which allow quantitative prediction of the occurrence of traits in populations. Such questions are asked as (1) What are the proportions of different genotypes in a population? (2) How are these proportions related from generation to generation?

A simple example of the theoretical systems which have been used in the development of population genetics is given in Example 16–3.

Example 16–3 *Panmixis and the Hardy-Weinberg law: random mating*

We can illustrate the random-mating situation by the following analogy: If it were possible to do so, we could throw all the sperm and ova of a species into a lake and thoroughly mix them together and allow them to combine to form zygotes. At any particular chromosomal position, therefore, there might be a gene from a parent either of type A or of type A', but not both. If we make the assumptions that the proportion of A is p, the proportion of A' is q, and the proportions are the same in both ova and sperm, and that $p + q = 1$, then the probabilities of the various combinations which are possible are as given in Table 16–2.

Since the two heterozygotes are genetically equivalent, the proportions of the three genotypes may be expressed as $p^2(AA) + 2pq(AA') + q^2(A'A')$. As the mathematically sophisticated will already have realized, this is the binomial expansion of $(p + q)^2$. Now, the proportions may vary a great deal, and we can show how such variation affects the proportion of types of individuals by giving two cases: When $p = q = 0.5$, as in the case of certain generations of two pure-breeding lines, the resultant proportions are $0.25(AA) + 0.50(AA') + 0.25(AA\,A')$. This means that the result of a random mix of pure breeding lines is a population of offspring in which one-fourth are homozygous for one trait, one-fourth are homozy-

Table 16-2 Frequency of zygote types in panmixis

Sperm type	Frequency	Ovum type	Frequency	Zygote type	Frequency
A	p	A	p	AA	p^2
A	p	A'	q	AA'	pq
A'	q	A	p	A'A	pq
A'	q	A'	q	A'A'	q^2

gous for the other trait, and one-half of the population consists of heterozygous individuals. If, however, $p = 0.9$, and $q = 0.1$, a very unequal mix, then the proportions are .81(AA) + .18(AA') + .01(A'A'). Thus, the frequency of occurrence of homozygotic individuals for the gene which has the lower proportion is greatly reduced in each generation.

Quite important to an understanding of population genetics is the fact that the attainment of these frequencies of individuals bears no relationship to the exact nature of the individuals who were the source of the genes, provided that the genes were mixed thoroughly before combining into zygotes. The gametes might have come from two pure stocks, consisting of only AA and A'A' individuals, or they might have come from a single population already in panmictic equilibrium. All that is necessary is that there be present genes of the two types in the proportion indicated. The amount of previous assortment is of no consequence, so long as completely random mating occurs. Two scientists, working independently, discovered this law, which is called after them the Hardy-Weinberg law.

In working with human populations, it is often quite difficult to analyze genetic mechanisms, since human beings usually choose their mates selectively and not randomly. Whenever such a mating bias occurs, the postulate of random mating does not hold, and appropriate corrections must be made. However, there is one very interesting case in which the postulate of random mating probably does hold: taste blindness. This is discussed in Example 16–4.

Example 16–4 *Taste blindness: Panmixis in human beings (Snyder, 1932)*

There exists a rather unusual taste deficiency in about 30 percent of the human population. People with this defect are unable to taste a chemical substance called phenylthiocarbamide (PTC). In normal persons, low concentrations of PTC are tasted as very bitter. About 70 percent of the population have this reaction to the substance. In individuals who have the taste blindness, PTC tastes insipid or does not produce a reaction at all. Thus, although there are some differences in type of reaction, the population can be divided into two categories: tasters and nontasters.

Now, ordinarily, people do not choose their mates on the basis of ability to taste special substances. We say "ordinarily" since it is possible that special interests might dictate special cases, such as in the case of a wine connoisseur who might insist on appreciation of such aesthetic taste sensitivity in his mate. Yet, in the ordinary population, the sense of taste does not enter into mating, and therefore the genetic determiners for PTC tasting may be safely considered to be randomly distributed through the population. We may conclude that in a randomly drawn sample from an intermarrying population the proportion of tasters to nontasters would approximately reach the 70/30 figure.

One study of population genetics based on PTC taste blindness made use of the Hardy-Weinberg rule (Snyder, 1932). He assumed that the ability to taste PTC is a simple dominant trait determined by a single gene pair and that taste blindness is recessive. Several deductions follow from this assumption: If all PTC taste blindness is recessive, all offspring of nontasters should be taste-blind for PTC. If both parents are heterozygous, then the Mendelian ratio of 3 to 1 should appear in the children. Finally, whenever one parent is homozygous for the ability to taste, all the children should be tasters. Given an estimate of the frequency g of the nontasting t, and given the fact that tasters may be homozygotes or heterozygotes, certain expectations can be calculated regarding frequency of nontaster and taster offspring in different types of marriage. As the data in Table 16–3 show, observed proportions agree very well with those predicted, thus giving confirmation to the genetic model.

From the Hardy-Weinberg law, various applications have been made to many forms of behavior, including schizophrenia, enuresis, and various forms of mental defects.

Table 16-3 Inheritance of taste deficiency to phenyl-thiocarbamide (Snyder, 1932)

Matings of parents	Children with taste deficiency	
	Predicted, %	Observed, %
Taster × taster (N = 425)*	12.4	12.3
Taster × nontaster (N = 289)	35.4	36.6
Nontaster × nontaster (N = 86)	100.00	97.9

*N = number of families tested.

Family Studies

Since the geneticist has no control over the breeding plans of human society, he must make his inferences on the basis of data which, from a scientific standpoint, are not always as orderly as he would like them to be.

As indicated earlier, the basic method involved in assaying genetic and environmental influences in the determination of a trait is by comparing its occurrence among individuals known to be genetically more alike with its occurrence among individuals known to be genetically less alike. The most obvious way of doing this is by comparing individuals within a family unit and finding out whether these are more alike than are individuals chosen without respect to immediate ancestry (i.e., from different families). Thus, if a trait is heritable, siblings would be more alike in respect to it than would unrelated persons; similarly with parents and offspring, cousins, uncles and nephews, and so on. Depending on whether the trait is discrete or continuous, we will use frequency counts or some form of variance or covariance analysis.

INHERITANCE OF HUMAN INTELLIGENCE This general technique of studying family resemblances has been widely used to study the heritability of a great variety of traits, for example, intelligence, school achievement, personal "tempo," persistence, neuroticism, handwriting, and attitudes (cf. Fuller & Thompson, 1960). In the great majority of cases, there is no doubt at all that related individuals are more alike than unrelated, but very few of these studies allow us to infer that the likeness is due to genotypic rather than environmental causation.

Much the same is true of the *twin method*, essentially an extension of the family-resemblance approach. Comparisons are made here between similarity of the members of identical, or monozygotic, twin pairs and similarity of the members of fraternal, or dizygotic, pairs. The former, originating from the same *zygote*, or fertilized egg, have identical genotypes. The latter, coming from two different zygotes, are no more alike genetically than siblings, though they are likely to be more similar due to their age identity and to their sharing similar prenatal and postnatal environments. Even here, however, it can be argued that identical twins grow up in environments even more similar than do fraternal twins and hence are more likely to be alike anyway, quite apart from the fact of genetic identity. Although intuitively we may not regard such a notion as very compelling, it is nevertheless one that cannot be dismissed (or accepted) without scientific proof.

A classic experiment can serve as an example.

Example 16-5 *A comparison of identical and fraternal twins (Newman, Freeman, & Holzinger, 1937)*

Newman, Freeman, and Holzinger managed over a number of years to locate nineteen pairs of identical twins that had been separated early in life and reared in different home environments. As the reader will probably realize, this was no easy task. Comparisons were then made between the similarity within identical pairs reared together and with fraternal twins reared together. Similarity was assessed by means of correlations computed between members of one pair from two standard IQ tests as well as from an achievement test. Results are shown in Table 16-4.

It is clear from the table that the genetic identity of members of monozygotic pairs produced greater similarity in IQ even when they were reared in quite different home environments. This did not apply in the case of the achievement test, which is understandable enough, since this test is not intended to tap innate potentiality directly.

Two additional points should be noted. First, there was a fairly strong relationship between the discrepancy of home environments in which separated twins were reared and the discrepancy between them in IQ. If the homes were very different,

Table 16-4 Twin resemblances in intelligence with environmental influences controlled

Test	Monozygotic Reared together	Monozygotic Reared apart	Dizygotic reared together
Binet	.91	.67	.64
Otis	.92	.73	.62
Stanford achievement	.95	.51	.88

then so were the test scores. However, discrepancy was little more than chance level in homes rated as moderately unequal and relatively similar. This indicated that the similarity generated by heredity apparently resists environmental pressures to dissimilarity, though only up to a point.

Secondly, it is worth mentioning that a comparison between identical and fraternal twins necessarily underestimates the importance of heredity, for the simple reason that fraternal twins (or siblings) are themselves quite similar genetically. A fairer comparison might be between identical twins and two foster children of as different genetic backgrounds as possible but adopted by the same family. Of course, as we have already pointed out, heritability estimates are relative to the population studied. There is nothing absolute about them.

The study of Newman and his colleagues gives us some reason to suppose that heredity is very important in determining IQ level, though a drastic shift in environment can produce fairly sharp deviations from expected level.

A number of other studies have been done on the intellectual resemblance of twins. Erlenmeyer-Kimling and Jarvik (1963) have collected the results of fifty-two of these. In general, the findings support the conclusion that there is a reliable difference in correlation between the intelligence of identical twins and fraternal twins *whether reared together or apart*. Thus, fourteen studies of intellectual resemblance of identical twins yield an average correlation of .87, while the same correlation for fraternal twins was, on the average, .53. The conclusion is clear: identical twins are more alike in intelligence than fraternal twins. A substantial difference is maintained even when identical twins are reared in different environments.

INHERITANCE OF PERSONALITY   Less of the kind of evidence obtained above for intellectual factors is available for factors of personality and temperament or for mental disorders. One study exceptional to this has been done by Cattell, Stice, and Kristy (1957).

Example 16-6 *Analysis of heredity versus environment in personality (Cattell, Stice, & Kristy, 1957)*

In this study, Cattell and his coworkers used a method Cattell had previously developed called *multiple abstract variance analysis* (MAVA). It is essentially an application of variance-components analysis adapted to natural human populations. As such, it relies on the collection of genetically related subjects—including twins, sibs, and half sibs—some raised in different homes and others together. The observed variation among such groups can then be expressed in terms of abstract or hypothetical components. For example, the variation between identical twins reared apart must be totally environmental and be made up of two parts, one arising from the differences between the families and the environments they supply, the other arising from differences that arise within each family in the manner in which it treats a particular child compared to others in the same family unit. Algebraically we may express this as follows:

$$\sigma^2_{ITA} = \sigma_w^2 + \sigma_b^2$$

where σ^2_{ITA} = observed variance between identical twins reared apart

σ_w^2 = environmental variance component within families

σ_b^2 = environmental variance component between families

It is not difficult to see how for any particular set of observations, for example, sibs reared together, sibs reared apart, or unrelated children reared together, a similar equation can be constructed expressing the observed variance in terms of a number of unknown abstract genetic and environmental variance components plus the covariations between these. Solution for the unknown is obtained by the method of simultaneous equations.

Using this analysis, Cattell and his associates examined the relative contribution of hereditary and environmental factors to scores on the Objective-Analytic Personality Test Battery, a test measuring general intelligence as well as a number of "basic" personality factors. Some of the results of the study are shown in Table 16–5. The obtained figures shown in the table should not be considered absolute. There is every reason to believe that they will vary according to the population studied. If they have generality, this is yet to be established. Keeping this qualification in mind, we may draw attention to a few points of interest.

With only one exception, variation within family units is due more to environmental than genetic factors. This is true even of general intelligence. Apparently, siblings are intellectually different more because of the different upbringing each has. On the other hand, variation in intelligence between children in different families is far more dependent on genetic than on environmental causes. Apparently, families in our society treat the average child in very much the same way. But each also tends to encourage diversity among its members. Cattell et al. therefore suggest that if we are interested in environmental influences on intelligence, we should focus on patterns of rearing the different children within a family, rather than on general differences in rearing patterns between different families.

The same is not true, however, of a trait like gregariousness. Differences in this characteristic are due more to genotype both between and within families. Neuroticism, on the other hand, if the data are valid, apparently arises from a kind of general "climate" that is typical of particular family units and not others. This result, incidentally, is not in agreement with another investigation, one done by Eysenck and Prell (1951) in England. These workers, using standard monozygotic-dizygotic comparisons in twins, found evidence for strong hereditary determination of neuroticism.

In general, the MAVA method appears to have some merits and does start to separate environmental from genetic influences. This represents a major step forward in the study of behavior inheritance.

The next example illustrates a similar approach to the genetic study of personality. It involves an improved version of the classic twin method and standard tests of personality.

Table 16–5 Genetic and environmental components of variance for some basic personality traits

	Within family		Between families	
	σ_G^2	σ_E^2	σ_G^2	σ_E^2
General intelligence	122.5	179.1	83.3	6.7
Inhibition (cautiousness, timidity)	1.8	2.6	0	3.2
Comention (gregariousness, acceptance of social and ethical values)	24.0	16.7	21.1	4.6
Exuberance (fluency, fast judgment)	3.1	5.2	2.4	0.4
Corticalertia (speed in basic reactions)	1.2	5.8	0.9	2.3
Neuroticism	1.6	2.2	1.0	5.8

Example 16–7 *Heritability of personality (Gottesman, 1963)*

Gottesman gathered further evidence that personality and perhaps psychopathology in man may indeed have a genetic component. By means of the Minnesota Multiple Personality Inventory (MMPI) and the High School Personality Questionnaire (HSPQ), he assessed the degree of relationship in the personality traits of both identical and fraternal twins. He then computed the amount of each trait which could be attributed to inheritance.

The subjects were volunteer pairs of twins from public high schools. Thirty-four pairs each of identical (MZ) and fraternal (DZ) same-sex twins were used in the study. Each was administered the MMPI and the HSPQ. In addition, their zygosity was diagnosed by means of blood samples. Through the use of the blood tests, a highly accurate determination of whether the twins were identical or fraternal could be made, a necessary condition for accurate work.

The heritability index which Gottesman used is similar to one we will discuss later in the section on animal-behavior genetics. The formula for heritability is

$$H = \frac{V_{DZ} - V_{MZ}}{V_{DZ}}$$

where V_{MZ} = within MZ pairs estimate of variance of a trait

V_{DZ} = within DZ pairs estimate of variance of a trait

An examination of the formula shows, the index may vary from 1 to +1, depending on the difference between the two sets of twins in the amount of intragroup variability of a trait. Gottesman used a somewhat more statistically refined version of this basic formula.

In his results, he found that two of the scales on the HSPQ appeared to have significant gene determined components: sober versus happy-go-lucky and group-dependent versus self-sufficient. Five of the MMPI scales of personality traits appeared to have significant gene determination: depression, psychopathic deviation, psychaesthenia, schizophrenia, and social introversion. The reader should be aware that the results indicate only that identical twins are more alike on these scales. They say nothing about any possible directional differences in scores which might be attributed to twin type.

In a second analysis, Gottesman had expert clinical psychologists judge the similarity of the MMPI results for the two types of twins. These clinical judgments supported the results of the personality tests. The judges found that the greater the gene similarity, the greater the similarity of MMPI profiles.

THE INHERITANCE OF MENTAL DISORDERS In view of the prevalence of mental disorders, the question of this inheritance represents a pressing social as well as scientific problem. Like much of the work done on normal behavior traits, studies on the genetics of mental disorders have also tended to take it for granted that environmental influence is relatively unimportant. Let us now look at some typical data.

Example 16-8 *Inheritance of mental illness (Kallman, 1953)*

One of the leading investigators in the field in the United States has been Franz Kallman. The method he and many others have typically used to study the inheritance of mental illness has been the so-called *proband*, or propositus, method. This is based essentially on the same principles outlined above for the family unit studies. A number of index cases (probands, or propositi) manifesting the trait (e.g., schizophrenia) are selected randomly from a population. The relatives of these cases are then located and examined. Incidence of the trait among relatives of probands is established, and this is compared with its incidence in the general population. Comparisons can also be made between incidence among relatives of varying degree of kinship to the proband, for example, second cousins, first cousins, half sibs, full sibs, identical cotwin.

Applied to mental illness, the propositus method involves certain difficulties, not the least of which are *diagnosis* of the illness and the fact that it may have a certain typical *age of onset* (for example, adolescence). Keeping these reservations in mind, we may turn to the actual data obtained by Kallman, first on *schizophrenia*, secondly on *manic-depression*, these being the two major forms of psychiatric illness.

The data in Table 16-6 clearly indicate that if a person has a psychotic relative, the chances that he himself or his parents or siblings or children also have had, have, or will contract the disease are enormously increased. Such a fact has been taken by many as strong evidence for hereditary factors at work. Even if true, of course, what would be in-

Table 16-6 Kallman's propositus data on mental illness

Relationship to proband	Expectancy, %
Schizophrenia:	
Unrelated (general population frequency)	0.5–1.0
Stepsibs	1.8
Halfsibs	7.0–7.6
Full sibs or fraternal cotwins	11.5–14.3
Identical cotwins	86.2
Children	
One parent affected	16.4
Both parents affected	68.1
Parents	9.3–10.3
Grandparents	3.9
Grandchildren	4.3
Nephews and nieces	3.9
Manic-depression:	
Unrelated (general population frequency)	0.4
Sibs or fraternal cotwins	23.0
Identical cotwins	92.6
Children*	2.8–38.7
Parents	23.4

*Data of other investigators.

herited would be only a *disposition to manifest the illness,* not the illness itself. There would still be a strong dependence on environmental factors. Due to the rather poor control of environment in the studies done on the subject, the real problem is simply the relative importance of genetic and environmental influences. If this can be worked out more exactly, then it should be easier to make decisions about long-term strategies of research aimed at finding a cure for psychotic illness.

We can further illustrate the concern of those working on the problem of the inheritance of mental disease by considering, in Example 16–9, a carefully presented review of the theory and data on the inheritance of schizophrenia published by Gregory (1960).

Example 16–9 *The nature-nurture dilemma in studies of schizophrenia (Gregory, 1960)*

Gregory begins his analysis by accepting the fact that intelligence and high-grade mental deficiency are largely determined by polygenetic inheritance. In a similar fashion certain low-grade forms of mental deficiency, such as those we have discussed above, and other deficiencies of the nervous system are due to Mendelian inheritance. He then reviews the literature on the frequency of schizophrenia in relatives and suggests that the frequency of occurrence in relatives of different degrees of removal does not appear to support a simple Mendelian process based on recessive or dominant traits.

Because the monogenic hypothesis does not appear to account for the observed frequency of occurrence of schizophrenia, Gregory suggests three alternative hypotheses for the cause of the disease: (1) the disease may be predominantly caused by environmental factors; (2) the genetic component of the syndrome may be heterogeneous, and therefore there may be two or more types of genes which play a role in determining the onset of the disease; (3) the genetic component of the disease may be polygenic, in that expression of the trait may depend on many genes. He notes that there is a negative relationship between intelligence and schizophrenia and a positive relationship between oligophrenia and schizophrenia. Statistical analysis of these relationships and other somatic characteristics of schizophrenics support the polygenic hypothesis, i.e., that many genes are responsible for the disease.

It will be obvious that the task of analyzing how such traits as intelligence, personality, and mental illness are inherited is a very difficult one when one is working with natural populations. Although methods are available for doing this and these have occasionally been tried, particularly with the major psychoses, they have so far not yielded results on which different investigators agree. And it seems doubtful that any possibility of firm conclusion will be reached until a number of basic problems are solved, in particular, the problem of diagnosis or measurement and the problem of environmental control.

It seems clear from the data and discussion in the section above that genetic factors do influence behavior. It is likely that they work in two important ways: (1) they provide the organism with a modal, or most probable, form or level of behavior, for example, an IQ of 115; (2) they set fairly broad limits within which environment, depending on how "drastic" it is, can produce deviation from this modal value. Thus a very restricted or impoverished rearing condition might conceivably pull down an expected IQ of 115 by as much as 20 or 30 points; correspondingly, a very rich environment could perhaps shift it upward by the same amount. It is also possible that such environmental effects are not always symmetrical. That is to say, for certain traits, it may be easier for environment to pull them down than to push them up. Little information is available on this point.

Since most behavioral traits involve some genetic component, they must therefore be amenable to selection. Their response to any selection pressure will be a function of their heritability. This means that behavior can evolve in directions determined by its adaptiveness for various environmental circumstances.

THE GENETICS OF ANIMAL BEHAVIOR: ARTIFICIAL POPULATIONS

By artificial populations, we mean populations of individuals whose hereditary origin and environmental upbringing can be manipulated by the experimenter. Much of the work done in this way has come from agricultural geneticists. Their aim has been primarily practical—namely, to find what kind of manipulations, genetic or environmental, will maximize economic gains. If a character like egg yield, for example, is highly heritable, by the same token, it is minimally susceptible to environmental influences. In such a case, the poultry farmer will be better advised to spend his capital on breeding hens which lay many eggs than on providing special diets or highly controlled temperature and light conditions to a genetically random flock. Thus it is useful in economic terms to be able to partition the sources of variance of a trait. The same information can also contribute to our basic knowledge of heredity. Similarly, our understanding of the etiology of behavior traits will be greatly aided by the same kinds of data. For example, if it were definitely established that severe mental illness was strongly dependent on genotype, then it would seem more sensible to focus our attention on biochemical causes than on, let us say, early parental patterns of rearing and to think of therapeutic measures more in terms of pharmacology and eugenics than in terms of psychoanalysis. We will now turn directly to some methods available for separating out the hereditary and environmental components of trait variance in experimental populations.

Strain, Breed, and Litter Comparisons

In animal populations, due both to natural and artificial selection, we have available groups which are of the same species but between which breeding does not occur. Thus, though accidents do happen, the world population of dogs is divided into large numbers of breeds which are reproductively isolated (mostly by dog breeders) from each other. The same is true, to a lesser degree, of cats, sheep, swine, horses, cattle, and many other domestic species. This isolation of groups means that the individuals in one group constitute a single breed, since each breed has its own ancestry common to all its members. With animals, at least, we can largely control the major aspects of environment, so that any differences between breeds can be attributed mainly to genetic factors or heredity. Thus a rough estimate of heritability may be obtained from this ratio of the variation between breeds to the total variation between individuals in both breeds—that is, the ratio of genetic to total variation. We may express this as follows:

$$h^2 = \frac{\sigma_G^2}{\sigma_G^2 + \sigma_E^2}$$

where
h^2 = heritability
σ_G^2 = genetic (between-breed) variation
$\sigma_G^2 + \sigma_E^2$ = total variance, or σ_{pop}

The actual calculation of these values is somewhat complicated by the fact that the individuals in each breed are unlike not only because of environment but also for genetic reasons, unless they have been deliberately inbred. Generally speaking, we may say that, on the average, about half of the genetic differences between any two individuals is due to the between-breeds component and about half due to the differences that normally arise between any two members of a family group. Without going into its derivation, the calculational formula for heritability may be stated as follows:

$$h^2 = \frac{\sigma_G^2}{\sigma_G^2 + \sigma_E^2} = \frac{\sigma_b^2}{\sigma_b^2 + \sigma_w^2}$$

where σ_b^2 = the variation between breeds
σ_w^2 = the variation within breeds

Note that in such a design no estimate for the genotype-environment interaction can be obtained. We can obtain only one if we deliberately introduce into our design different environments to which the different breeds are exposed. An example is shown in Figure 16-6 (Fuller, 1953). The data represent heart-rate changes in four dogs of different breeds under two environmental conditions, one involving a mild, the other a sharp change in stimulating conditions. It is clear that there is a strong genotype-environment interaction in this case. The breed which is most "aroused" in the mild state (Basenji) is least aroused in the more stressful condition, and the breed which is next-to-least aroused (in fact somewhat "calmed" in the mild situation—the Shetland sheepdog) is by far the most aroused in the "bell" situation. Obviously, a simple comparison of the four breeds in only one environment would not do justice to the kinds of genetic differences that exist between them. Such a variability or fluidity of genotype in changing environments is a crucial feature from the standpoint of behavior

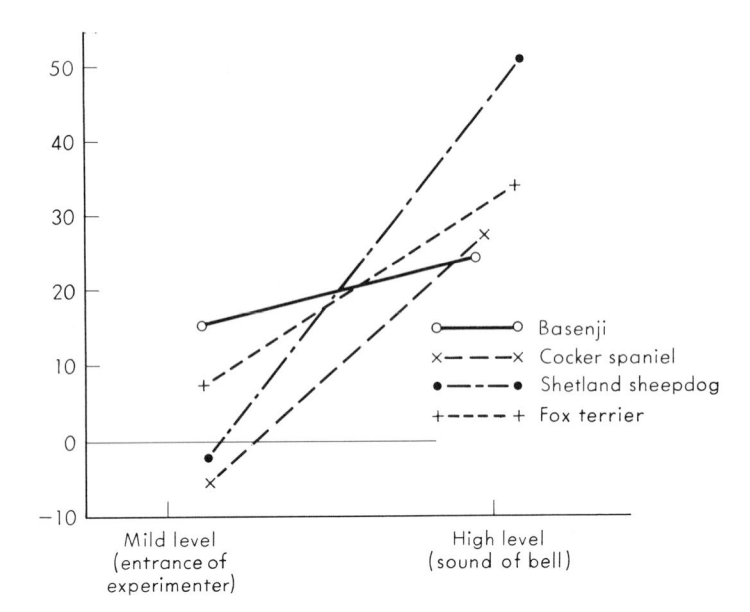

FIG. 16–6 Compared heartbeat of four different breeds of dogs. (*Fuller, 1953*)

traits, precisely because of their great plasticity relative to morphological characters.

We noted above that the basic calculation of heritability involved in a comparison of breeds or strains is not completely accurate due to the genetic heterogeneity that already exists in such groups. We can partly correct for this heterogeneity, and hence for the associated inaccuracy, by several procedures, which we will now discuss.

Inbred Stocks

In the first place, it is possible to select strains that are very similar genetically. The genetic homogeneity of the resulting groups at the end of selection will depend on the selection procedure we have used. Obviously, mating only brothers and sisters in each successive generation will produce genetic likeness. The less the consanguinity, or degree of kinship, between breeding pairs, the longer it will take to achieve likeness. In fact, the relationship between genetic homogeneity in the population and extent of inbreeding has been rather carefully worked out, as shown in Figure 16–7. The curves shown indicate that, theoretically, self-fertilization will produce virtually complete genetic homogeneity in about 10 generations. About 26 or more generations will be required using brother-and-sister pairs. Many such inbred mouse lines are available (80 or more). These so-called *isogenic strains* are the product of as many as 100 generations of brother-sister matings. Hence, any difference in some trait found between them may be fairly safely attributed to genetic causes, while differences between individuals within a strain may be regarded as being mostly dependent on environmental causation. There are likely to occur from time to time in any population some "spontaneous" genetic changes known as *mutations,* but these are relatively rare events. Consequently, we may effectively ignore them in any inferences we draw about strain differences.

Selection of Behavior

Inbreeding produces lines that have complete genotypic homogeneity. By selection, we may achieve a homogeneity that is limited to that part of the genotype underlying a particular trait or character. The basic procedure involves simply mating together, in a population, only those individuals which are both high in the trait or both low in it. Over a number of generations, such selection gradually results in two populations that are uniformly high and low respectively for the trait, provided, of course, the trait is heritable in the first place. The speed with which selection can be achieved is, in fact, a good index of heritability.

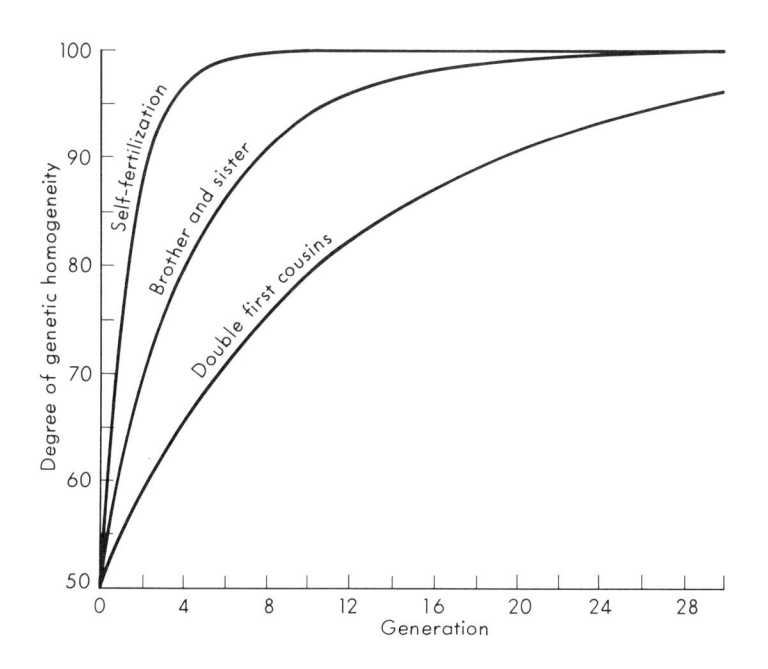

FIG. 16–7 Genetic homogeneity and inbreeding relationship of a population. (*Russell, 1941*)

This last point can be illustrated in Figure 16–8. This shows the relation of the two major variables on which an estimate of heritability will depend: R, the *response* to selection, or the difference between the mean phenotypic value of the offspring and the mean of the original base population, and S, the *selection differential*, or the difference between the mean of the base population. Without going into the derivation of the formula, heritability can be expressed as a function of R and S as follows (Falconer, 1960):

$$h^2 = R/S$$

where h^2 = heritability
R = response to selection
S = selection differential

It should be noted that this situation asumes that nongenetic causes do not contribute to the similarity between parents and offspring. Some other assumptions are also involved, but they are too complex to discuss here.

In agricultural genetics, as we have already indicated, selection is used widely to maximize the economic value of different products, ranging from cattle to crops. In behavior genetics, we can also find many examples of selection of behavior traits. This has been done partly as a demonstration that the trait is in fact inherited and partly as a means of establishing populations in which the physiological basis of the trait can conveniently be studied.

By such selection procedures, we can thus demonstrate that heredity determines some or most of the variance of a trait. Such selection procedures have been applied in the case of a wide variety of traits. These include maze-learning ability, emotionality, reactivity, activity-level, disposition to ulceration under stress, phototaxis and geotaxis, and disposition to drink alcohol (cf. Fuller & Thompson, 1960; Hirsch, 1967). In addition, we can use homogeneous material to examine the relation of a trait to other traits, particularly physiological and biochemical ones. Artificial selection mirrors natural selection. In the one case, an experimenter selects populations according to certain criteria, scientific or practical, that he has set up. In the second case, nurture, or environmental influence, exerts a pressure on a population that results in some genotypes having more survival value than others.

The complex manner in which both genotype and environment may contribute to phenotypic appearance of individuals is shown in Figure 16–9. Two populations of four each are shown, one having small variance. (Thus, the two groups differ in the

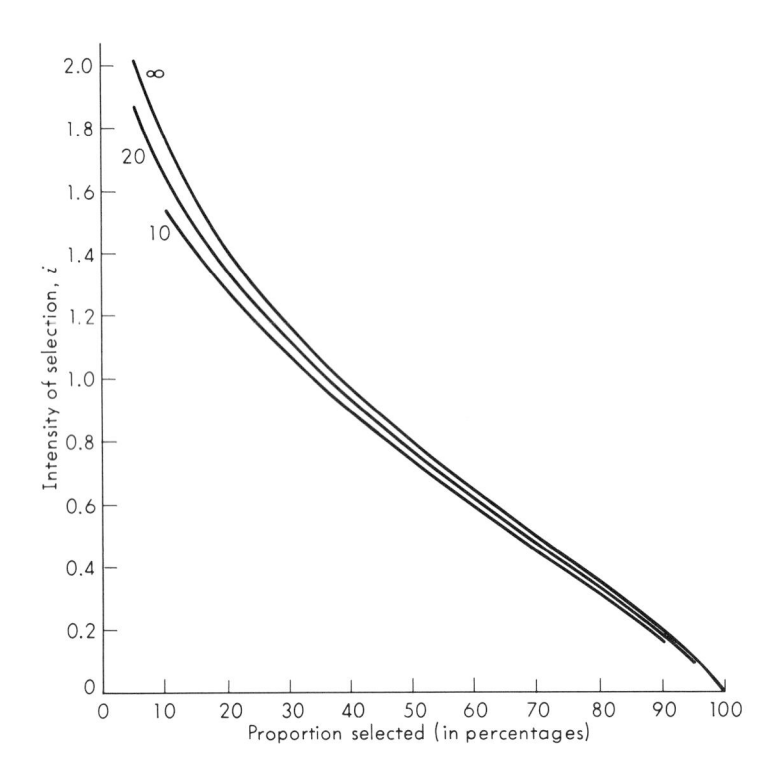

FIG. 16–8 Relationship of the two major variables on which an estimate of heritability will depend. (*Falconer, 1960* [*modified*])

range of scores they show on some tested traits.) But notice that the same range can be generated in a number of different ways, three of which are illustrated. In the figure, the columns represent the two populations which have the same range, and the rows are the three different methods of computing the range of scores of individuals. In the case of line *a*, the genotype is well "buffered," in that it is resistant to environmental influence. This fact appears in the form of small variance in the subgroups regardless of changes in environment. In *b*, where genotypes are poorly buffered, environment causes a directional shift in phenotype in both populations. In *c*, again a poorly buffered population, the environment causes a phenotypic shift in one direction for one group and in the other direction for the second group. In the cases shown, the directions given are in terms of movement toward or away from the mean of the subgroup.

Behavior genetics has become a well recognized and highly active research field in psychological laboratories. Although recognition of the importance of inheritance has been a part of discussions of behavior for a very long time, it is only recently that sophisticated modern programs of research have been mounted in order to parcel out the complex roles of inherited predispositions to behavior. The nature-nurture controversy is no longer an "either-or" issue. Every thoughtful worker in psychology will recognize that any comprehensive treatment of behavior must explore the built-in determinancies of organisms which potentiate or attenuate the effects of environment.

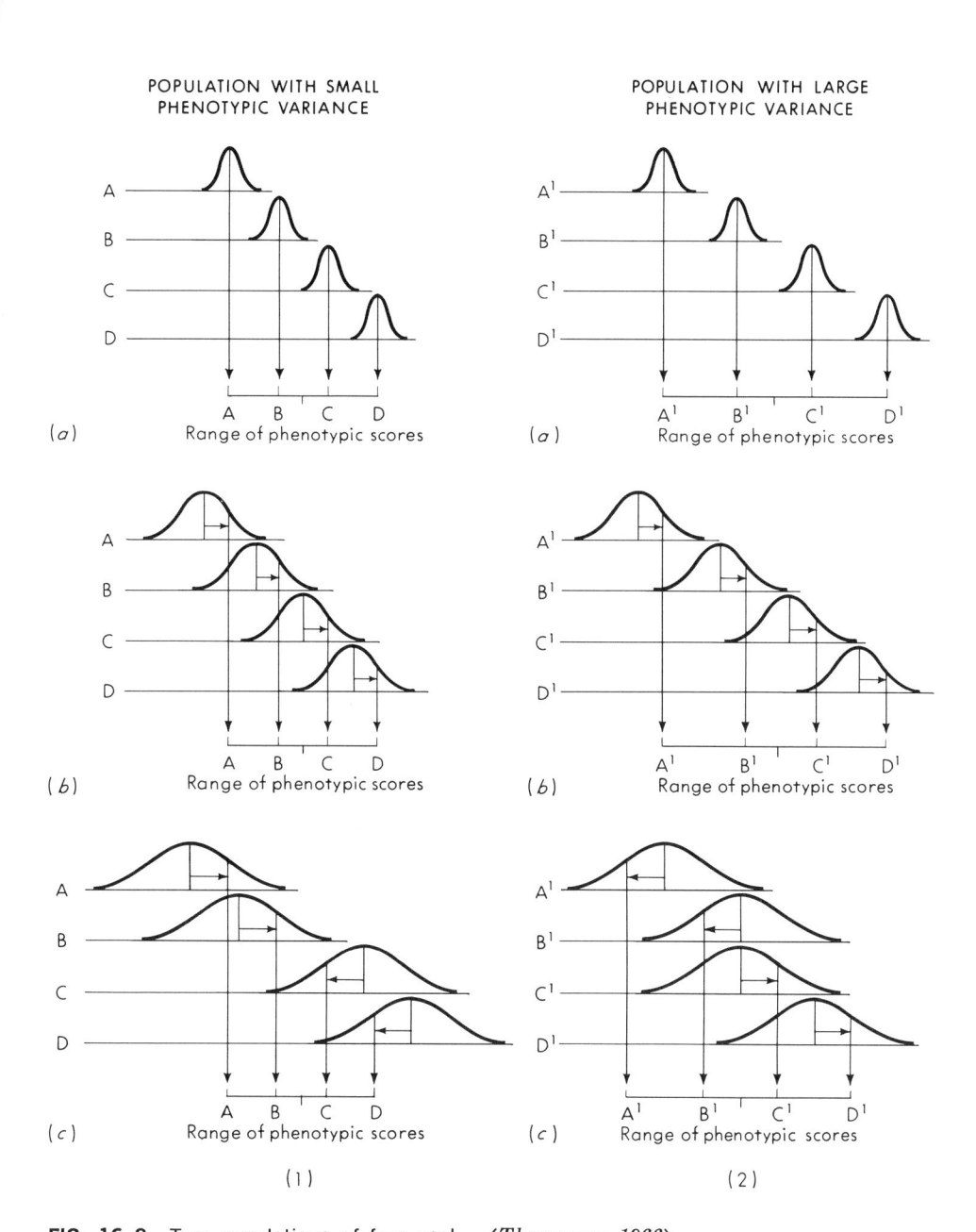

FIG. 16–9 Two populations of four each. (*Thompson, 1966*)

CHAPTER 17
ANIMAL BEHAVIOR

THE CONCEPT OF ADAPTATION: ECOLOGICAL BEHAVIORISM

The study of animal behavior is not clearly distinct from the study of behavior genetics which we surveyed in the last chapter. Modern discussions of the mechanisms of animal behavior involve concern for the mechanisms of inheritance. There is also a tradition within biology, called ecology, which has involved the study of behavior. In this chapter, we will commence our discussion of comparative psychology by a brief look at ecology. Our central concern will be the modes of adaptation of organisms to their ecological surroundings or habitats.

The term "adaptation" refers simply to the process by which an *individual or a population adjusts to, or fits into, a particular environment*. Environment, in this definition, includes the totality of factors, physical, chemical, biological, and psychological, that can affect the survival and hence the reproductive fitness of the individual. Those animals for whom an environment is suitable will produce progeny and hence multiply genotypes which are like themselves and can therefore also adapt; those for whom an environment is for some reason not suitable either will die out or will move to a new environment in which they can survive. This process of *natural selection* has two effects: (1) it produces changes in the distribution of animal forms over the earth, or parts of it at any particular point in time; (2) it produces changes in the kinds and numbers of animals that exist on the earth at a particular time, that is, evolutionary change. It is only the first of these types of change that we can actually observe happening. The second is simply a hypothesis about past events which are, of course, not directly observable. However, they can be reconstructed up to a point through the use of fossil structures. The results of such reconstructions are bound to be ambiguous. It seems more profitable to focus our attention on the first type of change brought about by natural selection.

Modes of Adaptation

If we consider adaptation at the level of the population, we can see that there are several ways in which a congruence can be established between certain individuals and a certain environment or habitat:

1. The individuals which cannot adapt to it for some reason, for example, because it is too cold or too hot, too wet or too dry, may simply die. This allows those individuals which do survive to reproduce offspring. These offspring, since they have genotypes similar to their parents, should, in turn, also be able to adapt.

2. The individuals which cannot adapt may simply move away to a new habitat in which conditions are more suitable to them. What may happen over

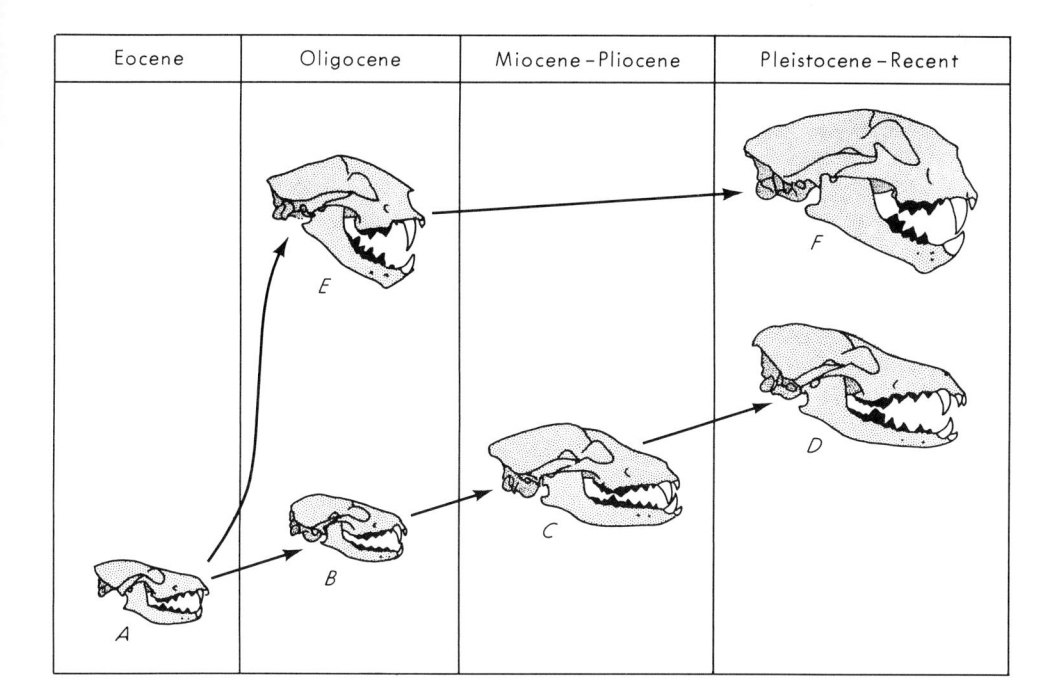

FIG. 17-1 Contrasting evolutionary development of the canids and felids.

time is that the two groups, originally related to each other, become isolated *reproductively* from each other, not merely in the sense geographical with less opportunity to interbreed, but also in the sense that they may no longer be capable of fertile mating or of mating at all.

3. Individuals whose genotypes are not directly adapted to the habitat may nonetheless adapt indirectly by altering their behavior in such a way as to make the environment more suitable to them. Such *learned* adaptations are not transmitted genetically, but the capacity that underlies them is heritable. Thus the genotypes possessing such a capacity will survive as well over successive generations as those genotypes whose mode of adaptation is more direct. We will consider modes of adaptation in respect to two types of behavior: food getting and homing.

FOOD GETTING Since food getting is a trait of such basic adaptive importance, it is not surprising that it figures importantly in classification. Thus among mammals we find such groups as carnivores (meat eaters), insectivores (insect eaters), and herbivores (green-plant eaters). The use of such categories arises, of course, from obvious morphological (i.e., pertaining to physical appearance) differences connected with food getting. Good examples of such differences in form and their relation to general behavior patterns are afforded by the dog and the cat. A comparison of these two forms has been made by Colbert (1958).

Example 17-1 *The predation adaptation of dogs and cats (Colbert, 1958)*

In considering the general relation of morphology to behavior, Colbert contrasts popular domestic pets, the dog and the cat. It is obvious that the two are very different. Dogs are very friendly and sociable and clearly like human company. They perform a great variety of tasks effectively for man, for example, guarding, hunting, and herding, and do these with an apparent enjoyment. Cats, by contrast, are friendly only in a limited way. They are highly independent and are not easily trained. As Colbert remarks "... one gets the impression that, whereas the dog is a truly domesticated animal, a cat is essentially a wild animal that tolerates man as a useful host."

This difference, Colbert thinks, is traceable to the evolutionary histories of the two groups. Figure 17–1 summarizes some of the fossil evidence available on carnivore origins. As indicated, both groups are thought to descend, together with all other modern carnivores, from a common Eocene ancestor known as the Miacidae. These were small predators about the size of a house cat, with large eyes and efficient teeth adapted to nipping (the front teeth), stabbing and killing (the canines) and cutting (molars and carnassials).

During the next epoch, the Oligocene, canids and felids underwent a marked divergence, with the cat family showing a rapid specialization which it has maintained since. This specialization in food getting, or predation, has involved an emphasis on the solitary hunt, ambush, or stalk and a sudden, short, extremely fast charge. A lion, for example, can maintain a speed of 50 miles per hour over a short distance, a cheetah 65 miles per hour. The jaw and tooth structure are geared also to killing and tearing their prey rather than masticating it. Canids, on the other hand, have emphasized pursuit of prey, tracking and hunting it and finally catching it on the move. Often, this is done in packs rather than singly. Their long legs, lean bodies, and compact feet, together with their jaw formation and dentition, form the physical bases of these behavioral adaptations. They also provide for considerably more versatility, or plasticity, in food-getting behavior than we find in the cat family. Their teeth are such that they can eat more foods satisfactorily, and their ability to cooperate in locating food allows more complex forms of behavior.

Thus Colbert concludes:

> If these two groups of carnivores are viewed in this way the difference in behavior between modern dogs and cats can be readily understood. Dogs are plastic in their behavior because they are relatively unspecialized physically, while at the same time they are highly intelligent and have a heritage of being very social animals. Cats are fixed in their behavior because they have been highly specialized carnivores, indeed the most highly specialized of land-living predators, for some forty million years. They are intelligent, but they have a long history of nonsocial behavior, of living by themselves and for themselves. Dogs have been growing up in an evolutionary sense to their present state for a long time, but during this long time cats have always been cats. These are facts reflected just as surely in their different behavior patterns as in their very different morphological specialization.

Such differences as we see between the dog and cat are found even more strikingly between other groups, for example, bird species. Here we find a large variety of bills adapted to different purposes. The hawk, for example, has a sharp curved beak and claws for grasping and tearing. The spoonbill, heron, and others have long beaks useful for dipping into marshes or shallow streams. The case of the pelican is well known and has been immortalized in a limerick.

Besides the physical structures which permit a certain range of eating activities, methods of locating food or prey also vary widely and are of considerable interest. In many carnivorous species, smell obviously plays a very large part. In other forms, techniques may be more complicated. Let us consider the case of the bat and the moth as described by Roeder and Treat (1961).

Example 17–2 *Echolocation in bats and moths (Roeder & Treat, 1961)*

It has been known for some time that bats and certain species of birds and possibly some mammals can locate objects in space by echo (cf. Griffin, 1958). This phenomenon is known as *echolocation*. It is essentially similar to sonar and involves the following sequence of events: A bat, while flying at a high speed, emits a series of high-frequency sounds. These are around 50,000 cps (the upper limit of human hearing is about 20,000 cps) and emitted at the rate of about thirty to fifty cries per second. These sounds bounce off solid objects ahead of the bat and return to his ears as echoes. The bat reacts appropriately to the echo by turning aside from the object. The bat, by using echolocation, can successfully navigate a room divided in the middle by a row of wires hanging vertically from the ceiling 1 foot apart (each 3/16 inch in diameter) without any collisions. Blocking the bat's ears or mouth, however, reduces its successes to a chance level.

It was later found that the bat also uses echolocation to catch and eat moths. The principle is exactly the same, except rather more complex since the object is now a moving one whose trajectory, or flight direction, must be anticipated for successful interception. This added difficulty apparently does not present a problem for the bat. However, moths have evolved defensive measures to cope with bat attack. Roeder and Treat (1961) found that moths have extremely good ears and can therefore hear a bat approaching. When the intensity of the bat's signals reaches a certain level, indicating he is too close for comfort, the moth simply folds its wing and does a nose dive into the grass, thus effectively putting himself out of harm's way. Furthermore, the moth emits sounds of its own. Their function is not at present really known, but it is possible they may act as a device for "jamming" the bat's sonar system.

The remarkable story of the bat and moth is typical of the complexity of prey-predator relations in nature. Sometimes the systems of location or the defenses are chemical; sometimes they are visual, sometimes auditory. For example, when the young wren first leaves its nest and is exposed to predators, it emits an alarm call which is very hard to localize because of its high, narrow frequency band and short duration. While it can convey to the mother that help is needed, it probably cannot convey to a passing hawk exactly where a potential prey is to be found. The young of the great tit, on the other hand, have vocalizations much easier to locate because of their relatively wide frequency range. However, this factor, which increases their vulnerability to predators, is compensated for by the fact that they do not emerge from the protective nest until they are more mature, compared to the young wren, and hence better able to look after themselves (Marler, 1959).

The kinds of communications that occur between prey and predator show how a balance—a kind of dynamic equilibrium—is achieved in nature between different species. In addition, they illustrate diverse ways in which animals respond to other animals, that is, the general problem of social communication and behavior.

A second type of adaptation studied by naturalists involves the mechanisms by which animals can return to their original territories, that is to say, so-called homing instincts.

HOMING BEHAVIOR Newspapers frequently report anecdotal data describing especially the ability of cats to return to their homes after having been taken to places many miles away. Many of these stories are, of course, exaggerated or untrue. Nonetheless, it is a fact that some species do really show homing ability to a remarkable degree. A case in point is the Pacific salmon. This species is first hatched in a stream quite far inland and then gradually makes its way down to the ocean. Here it lives for several years before it is ready to spawn. When this happens, it somehow locates the mouth of the river from which it came and swims steadily upstream. At all forks, it chooses the correct turn, proceeding in this way until it has arrived at the stream where it was hatched. Here spawning again takes place, and the whole cycle is repeated once more. Many studies have documented this homing ability in salmon, the usual method being by marking the young with tags and then attempting to recover them as adults later on. While the facts are clear enough, the actual mechanisms by which the fish accomplish such a feat are relatively little known. One study which helps to cast some light on the subject was done by Hasler and Larsen (1955).

Example 17–3 *Homing in salmon (Hasler & Larsen, 1955)*

The investigators hypothesized, on the basis of what is known about the sensory equipment of fish, that homing was accomplished primarily by smell, or olfaction. Their experiments involved several steps:

1. Fish (minnows or salmon) were blinded and then tested in a specially built tank for their ability to discriminate different odors. When one odor was released into the tank, the fish were rewarded by food for moving toward the jet which released the substance in one corner of the tank; when the other odor was released, the fish received a shock if they moved toward it. It was found that the fish quickly learned the differential responding that indicated discrimination. In all, they were able to tell apart dilute rinses from fourteen different aquatic plants, as well as other substances at very low chemical concentrations.

2. Having established that fish have a good sense of smell, Hasler and Larsen next established

chemically that different streams do, in fact, have different odors and further that salmon homing in particular streams failed to home "correctly" if their sense of smell was blocked. This was done simply by removing the fish from a stream during spawning migration, plugging the noses of half of them, then returning all of them to the river downstream from the point of initial removal and observing which ones followed their original path. Fish with unplugged noses swam back the same way, but those with plugged noses swam back in random directions.

3. The third step involved testing the notion that fish memory for odors is very good, especially when established young. This was confirmed in the laboratory by the procedure described in the first step. In addition, a field study gave additional support. This involved transferring salmon eggs spawned in one stream to a hatchery in another, then releasing the fingerlings back in the original stream to migrate down to the ocean. Some years later, thirteen of these fish were recovered in the *stream in which they had been hatched, rather than in the one from which they had migrated to the ocean.*

The data of Hasler and Larsen indicate that homing in salmon is governed by early olfactory conditioning. On the practical side, this finding suggests the possibility of controlling homing, directing it to the most suitable streams and spawning grounds, by conditioning the fish early to certain odors. This would be extremely valuable from the standpoint of fish conservation. On the theoretical side, the data indicate that at least some young systems are extremely plastic, so that memories can be established quickly and permanently if this is done early in development.

The phenomenon of homing in salmon is representative of the manner in which many animals are able to locate places and objects at a distance, as well as the compelling attraction that can be exerted by an early habitat. Numerous other examples could be given: eels which breed in the Sargasso Sea off the Eastern United States and cross the Atlantic to spawn in European streams; a species of bird which is able to navigate successfully over several thousand miles of ocean; the male mosquito which is able to locate a female at a distance of as great as 5,000 meters. These are just a few.

Although these examples from biological studies are concerned with adaptive behavior, they are not truly representative of the field of comparative psychology, which has more of an orientation to the behavioral concerns of traditional psychology, such as the processes of learning and motivation. We will consider this tradition in the next section of this chapter.

Comparative psychology and a closely related discipline, ethology, provide examples of two schools of thought, both of which are concerned with the study of animal behavior yet each of which has a quite different orientation and method. Such a situation is not unknown in the history of scholarly work. Consider the example of quantum mechanics versus electromagnetic field theory. Each is concerned with the nature of light, yet the concepts and the methods are quite different. So it is with the study of animal behavior. The basic datum is the same: the behavior of a variety of animals. Yet, as we shall see, the members of the two schools have differed a good deal on the methods to be used. Further, they have tended to place a different emphasis on variables deriving from genetics, learning, or formal cross-species analysis of behavior. We will first examine the tradition of comparative psychology as it has been developed primarily in the United States, and then we will turn to the ethological schools which began in Western Europe, primarily in the work of naturalists and biologists.

THE SEARCH FOR GENERAL LAWS OF BEHAVIOR: COMPARATIVE BEHAVIORISM

The principle concern of American psychologists who have been interested in animal behavior has been the development of theories of behavior which are applicable to many species and the major emphasis of which has to do with the analysis of *learning*. Such an orientation is highly desirable, since it tends to offset the tendency of behavioristic models to focus on only a few animal forms such as the laboratory rat. As both Beach (1959) and Bitterman (1960) have persuasively argued, theories of behavior based only on the behavior of the rat have a very low likelihood of being general throughout the animal kingdom. Consider the following:

Like any other responsible scientist the Comparative

Psychologist is concerned with the understanding of his own species and with its welfare; but his primary aim is the exposition of general laws of behavior regardless of their immediate applicability to the problems of human existence. Now this means that he will not be content with discovering the similarities and differences between two or three species. Comparisons between rats and men, for example, do not in and of themselves constitute a comparative psychology although they may well represent an important contribution toward the establishment of such a field. A much broader sort of approach is necessary [Beach, 1959].

The key concern, then, of comparative psychology is generally with laws of behavior. But a procedure for establishing generality or the lack of it is not so simple to design. Although the exact nature of study procedures may differ in various ways, we may indicate several steps often followed in the study of animal behavior. First, behavior of animals is identified and classified. The great innovator in this area was Carolus Linnaeus, who used a binomial system of classification. His major taxonomic categories were *genus* and *species* (e.g., Homo sapiens). Divisions were made in this system on the basis of morphological characteristics. Linnaeus believed that species were fixed and immutable—that is, collections of individuals reflecting, perhaps in slightly varying degrees, eternal and unchanging ideals.

The second step in this approach to the study of animal behavior has been the method of specifying those animals and situations which are appropriate for the analysis of particular problems. As we have noted, comparative psychologists have emphasized the process of learning. However, such behaviors as herd formation, schooling, social behavior, and reproductive behavior have also come in for attention. But the basic orientation has been the selection of a behavior in one species and then a more or less systematic attempt to extend the laws governing that behavior to other species. The third step involves the development of formal theories which relate aspects of behavior, such as learning and motivation, and subsequently seeking general laws which cover the range of species which have been studied. To exemplify this process, we will examine the work of three prominent American comparative psychologists: M. E. Bitterman, a theorist of learning; Frank A. Beach, a student of sexual behavior; and T. C. Schneirla, who has explored the patterns of socialization in animals.

The Comparative Psychology of Learning

After a distinguished career as a theorist of learning who worked almost entirely with the laboratory rat, M. E. Bitterman (1960) has turned toward the search for generality of laws of learning across species. His motivation for doing this is nicely expressed in the following passage:

> For many years, the field of animal learning has been dominated by a controversial, deductive spirit. Most of us have acted as though we knew all about the learning process, and as though the only purpose of our experiments was to demonstrate the validity of our convictions. The controversy was fun, of course, and to some extent even productive—we managed certainly to accumulate a considerable amount of data on learning in the rat—but in my recent dealings with fish, and fly, and crab, and worm, I have come again to a kind of research that is at once more satisfying and more productive. Its function is inquiry, not proof. Broadening the phylogenetic base of our work will facilitate the broadening of our outlook, and perhaps one day we shall be able to approach even the higher forms in the same spirit of discovery [Bitterman, 1960].

As is clear from the quotation, Bitterman was definitely dissatisfied with the way in which psychological study of the learning process had become a polemical pursuit for proof of extant ideas and theories. He has been asking for a new approach to the understanding of the behavior of animals. The experiments described in Example 17–4 illustrate how he has attempted to test laws of behavior in other species. It should be noted that his general methods are similar in the two experiments: he brings a species into his laboratory and performs on it experiments which elicit from it behaviors not normally a part of its mode of adaptation to the environment. This methodology is in sharp contrast to the techniques of the ethologists who have insisted on observation of animals in their usual habitats.

Example 17–4 concerns Bitterman's exploration of the partial reinforcement effect (PRE) in fish (cf. Chapter 14 for a definition of partial reinforcement effect).

Example 17–4 *Partial reinforcement in the fish: Are the laws of learning for fish the same as those for the rat? (Bitterman, 1960)*

Bitterman, as we have said, became dissatisfied with the great emphasis placed on the laboratory rat in the formulation of general laws of learning. When he decided to extend the study of the learning process beyond the realm of the mammal, he hit upon the fish as a desirable subject for experimentation, because it represented a form far enough removed from the rat so that possible differences in behavioral processes might emerge. After all, the behavior of an aquatic form is clearly a far cry from that of a terrestrial one. Further interest in the fish stems, of course, from its importance to man as a source of both food and sport.

In order to study learning in fish, Bitterman developed an experimental procedure which involved an operant behavior, namely, pushing a target suspended in the fish's tank. His apparatus is illustrated in Figure 17–2. The fish is first familiarized with the special tank and then gradually taught to press the target by reinforcing its behavior with food pellets or tubifex worms. Since the fish were quite hungry at the start of the experiment and the pellets or worms were a highly desirable food for them, they soon learned to push the pedal and then to rush back to catch and eat the food. This first phase of the experiment established that fish can be trained by an operant procedure, much in the same way that rats and human beings and many other species can. But Wodinsky and Bitterman (1960) performed a second phase of the experiment which seemed to cast doubt upon the notion that the process of learning is the same in fish as in mammals.

The subjects were African mouthbreeders (*Tilapia macrocephala*). The apparatus used was a single target version of the apparatus. Two groups of fish were trained: The first group was always reinforced during learning. The second group was given partial reinforcement; that is, they received a reinforcement on only some of the trials. This procedure produces an increased resistance to extinction in the human being and the rat; that is, as we said in Chapter 14, it appears that there is a tendency to make more unreinforced responses after training in which some responses are not reinforced. As discussed earlier, this finding cast serious doubt on the validity of classical reinforcement theory, which holds that each reinforcement adds strength to a habit. At least in human beings, rats, and other mammals, the opposite is true: partial reinforcement leads to increased resistance to extinction.

The effect of partial reinforcement on fish came as a surprise. After partial reinforcement the animals showed *less* resistance to extinction than they did after continuous reinforcement. This is in exact contrast to the results in mammals.

Without doubt, Bitterman's results raise questions about the generality of the partial reinforcement effect, at least as it has been explained in some theories of learning. His data support his contention that we should seek information about a variety of forms before we make wide generalizations about the nature of an abstract learning process. However, not all psychologists have been convinced that the observation of less persistence to extinction in fish after partial reinforcement in Bitterman's situation reflects some basic difference in the learning process. It is quite possible that the results are due in part to differences between the reactions of fish and rats to the nonreinforcement, if this is considered to be a frustrating event. Thus, the explanation of Bitterman's data might be found to be in terms of performance variables rather than learning ones. That is, the animals may learn in the same way, but they may differ in the extent to which they perform after frustration.

The Comparative Study of Sexual Behavior

Learning is not by any means the only phenomenon which has been studied by American comparative psychologists. Working over a long period, Frank A. Beach has extensively explored the patterns of sexual behavior of a variety of species. First of all we should point out that Beach agrees strongly with Bitterman that the study of behavior in animals should extend beyond the rat. However, in the experiments described in Example 17–5, Beach makes use of the rat in his studies of sexual patterns, primarily because of the great body of previous information which exists about its behavior. Again, we should note that Beach makes use of the same general methodology as that of Bitterman.

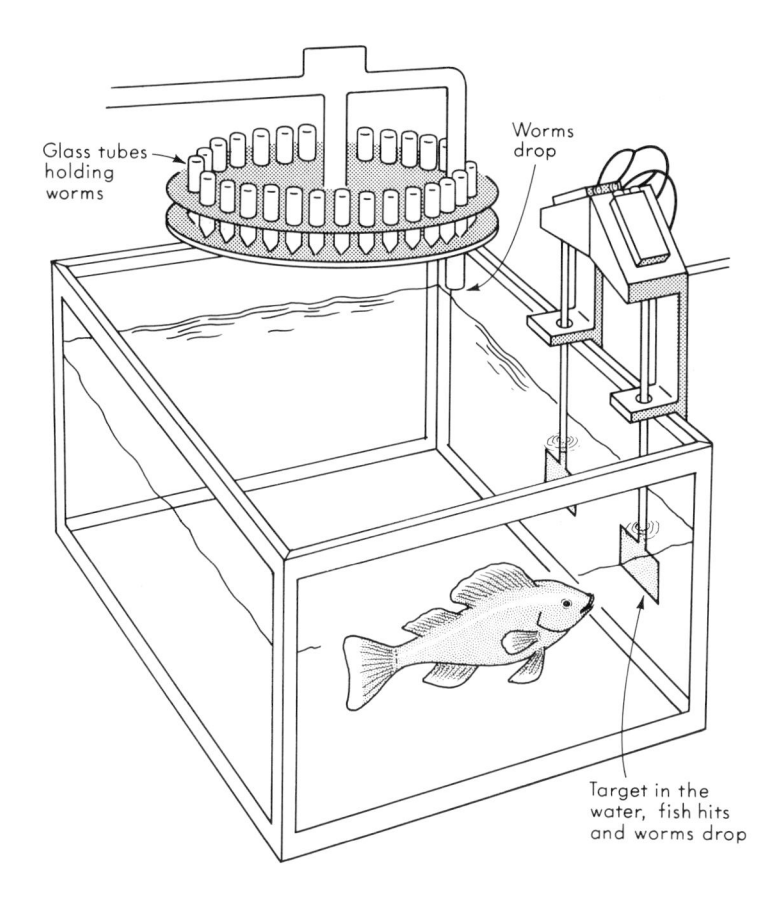

FIG. 17-2 Bitterman's experimental apparatus for operant behavior in fish studies.

He does experiments in the laboratory which are designed to change the conditions under which the animal is required to perform a response.

Example 17-5 *Sexual behavior after isolation during early life: Evidence for species difference in behavior (Beach, 1958)*

Beach is an interesting example of an animal behaviorist who almost bridges the gap between ethology and comparative psychology. In this experiment, he made use of the isolation-experiment technique, which, as we shall see later, is a method much used by ethologists. The method was used to explore the degree to which adult sexual behavior is dependent upon the amount of experience which the animals have with other individuals during the period of early development. Before Beach performed this particular experiment, Valenstein, Riss, and Young (1955) had carried out an experiment on guinea pigs in which they isolated the males at 10 days of age and at 25 days. They reported that animals isolated at the earlier age showed impairment of their ability to perform the sexual act. Beach had also previously reported (1942) that rats raised in isolation did not show impairment. In the 1958 study, he set out to validate this conclusion, using careful laboratory procedures.

The subjects were twenty-five male rats. Thirteen of the animals were placed in individual cages at 14 days of age. Since at that age rats are just beginning to open their eyes, Beach argued that they were unlikely to be able to mount other animals and thus have early experience in presexual behavior. Twelve littermates of the isolates served as controls. They were raised in group cages until they were 76 days old. Then they were placed in individual cages. Sex tests were begun two weeks later.

The sex tests consisted of placing the male rat in

an arena with a receptive female. Ten minutes were allowed for him to mount the female. If copulation was attempted, the male was allowed to continue until ejaculation occurred. As soon as an ejaculation occurred, the male was eliminated from the experiment. Testing continued until recalcitrant males had been tested on the sexual response five times.

Four experimental and four control males ejaculated in their first test. By the end of the fifth test, nine of the control and eight of the experimental animals had ejaculated. Thus, it was apparent that there was no difference in the efficiency of sexual performance which could be attributed to the isolation of the experimental group during rearing.

From these results, Beach concluded that there is a species-specific difference in the effects of isolation upon sexual performance. Since it had previously been shown that early isolation was detrimental to the sexual behavior of guinea pigs, these results with rats point to a difference between the two forms. He suggested that the difference may be due to the need for practice in mounting other animals during the early development which is specific to guinea pigs. Since the guinea pig is a precocial species and much more developed during the first days of its life, it may have a biological requirement for sexual maturity which is as yet unknown.

The Comparative Study of Social Behavior

We will conclude our discussion of comparative psychology with an examination of the work of T. C. Schneirla. Schneirla has made contributions to our understanding of animal behavior over a long period of time. Much like Beach, he has worked with a variety of species and seems to come close to bridging the gap between the comparative point of view and the ethological one. As we shall see from the work described in Example 17–6, he has done studies of animals in their natural habitats and also in the laboratory. In particular, he has been interested in the manner in which behavioral organization develops and has studied especially the emergence of social bonds. Certainly, as social beings ourselves, we are greatly attracted to the study of social processes, and, with the information that social bonds can be studied in the laboratory, much interest is generated. An example of this wide appeal is found in the reception accorded the appearance of Harry Harlow's work on the affectional system of monkey infants toward their mothers, discussed in another section of this book. But we will find that Schneirla dampens our enthusiasm for wide generalizations of the results of studies of the development of social bonds. He points out that the findings indicate that each species must be treated as a particular case and that wide generalizations are dangerous. In Example 17–6 we will examine the results of observations of the army ant. These are primarily naturalistic studies, yet some experimental manipulations are performed.

Example 17–6 *The functional system of the army ant: The mosaic process of species-typical behavior (Schneirla & Rosenblatt, 1961)*

The army ant provided Schneirla and Rosenblatt with a nice "preparation" for dissecting out those factors which are important in determining the way in which instinctive behaviors develop. As a result of his extensive observations of army-ant behavior, Schneirla has conceptualized the manner in which individual members of the colonies are incorporated into the group and maintained in their interindividual and group relations. An effective way of understanding this social system of ants is in terms of *reciprocal-stimulative processes*. The particular species which he studied, *Eciton hamatum*, is a tropical ant whose behavior is characterized by frequent predatory raids and by a wandering nomadic life. The animals engage in daily raids which are quite well organized. In fact, Schneirla suggests that the level of social organization of these raids by ants involves the highest degree of interpersonal behavior carried out away from the home by any animal other than man. In addition, the periodic migrations are also well organized in a social sense. Close observation has shown that these activities show regular fluctuations in their occurrence and intensity. On the basis of a careful study of these activities, Schneirla has developed an understanding of the functional pattern of the species. His schema is shown in Figure 17–3.

The functional pattern of the army ant involves a cyclic alternation between a *nomadic* phase, during which raiding is very heavy, and a *statary* phase, during which time there is little or no raiding. The phases of the functional cycle are related directly to the developmental stage of the brood, or

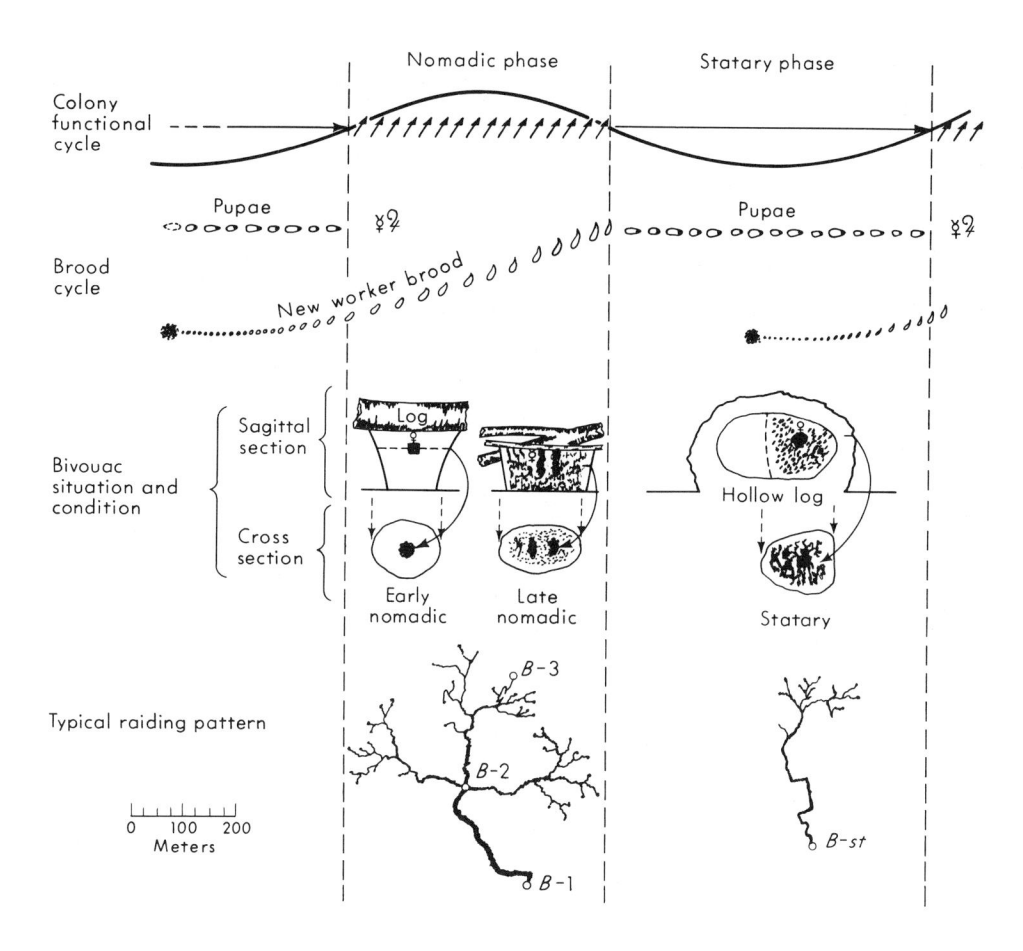

FIG. 17–3 Schema for the functional cycle of the army ant species. (*Schneirla, 1957*)

developing young. This correspondence shows that the adult ants are responsive to tactual and chemical stimulation by the young. Every thirty-six days an all-worker brood appears (as many as 200,000 individuals), which stimulates the adult to raid and migrate, probably because of the great voracious appetites of the newborn. This conception has been called by Schneirla the *brood-excitation theory*. In a comparable way, when a colony loses its queen, it maintains its cyclic activity only as long as the broods which she produced are developing. When all have been born, the colony enters a statary phase in which it perishes unless fused with another colony.

Two further observations extend the notion of chemical stimulation as the reciprocal methods of determining ant behavior. The first observation has to do with patterns of olfactory stimulation during raids. The animals lay down a chemical trail during their raids which is followed by other animals. Different species attack each other, and the following evidence suggests that the basis for combat is indeed olfactory. Ordinarily, different species attack each other upon first contact, but if they are kept in a chamber in which they are close together and separated only by a cheesecloth through which air can circulate, they appear to take on each other's odors. If they are then placed in a common container, they do not attack each other. Rather, they tend to form a circle of alternating members of each species in which the strong individual response to a common tactile-chemical stimulation is apparent. However, after a time the effects break down and combat begins.

A second phenomenon which appears to depend heavily on colony odor is the different location of the bivouac during the nomadic and static phases. The location appears to depend on the circulation of air at the chosen site. If ants are brought into the laboratory and allowed to cluster and then are exposed to a stream of air, they differ in the amount of circulation they will tolerate as a function of the phase they are in. Ants in the late nomadic phase, when they would normally be in the forest in enclosed bivouac sites, are the first to break their formation and recluster out of the stream of air. This phenomenon appears related to the state of excitation of the worker ants during the cycle. Finally, the presence of the queen odor alone is sufficient to induce army ants to cluster. When deprived of its queen, the colony gradually loses its capacity to form a cluster and soon becomes a diffuse spread of animals. Thus, it is assumed that the queen and her odor are central to colony cohesion.

Schneirla and Rosenblatt conclude that the species-typical development of any behavior is a complex process which involves many individual components of stimulation.

> The recurrence of each change in the cycle thus is a product of reciprocal relationships between brood, worker and queen functions, and not of a special timing mechanism or "biological clock" endogenous to the queen. The cyclic pattern of Army ants therefore is based upon numerous structural, behavioral and environmental factors capable of interacting under the conditions normal to the forest environment. The organization of this pattern is not determined through the heredity of any one type of individual—queen, workers or brood—nor is it additive from factors of maturation alone [Schneirla & Rosenblatt, 1961].

THE ANALYSIS OF INSTINCTIVE BEHAVIOR: ETHOLOGY

The third orientation toward the study of behavior—ethology—differs from both of the two approaches which we have so far discussed, animal behavior considered from an ecological point of view and comparative psychology. The major difference lies in the methodology used by ethologists and also in their strong emphasis on the innateness of behavior patterns.

Although ethology has only recently become prominent in American psychology, it is by no means a new science, nor does it owe its development to any one nation or locale. The biological study of behavior, from the point of view of inherited predispositions, has a long history. We can only skim the high points of that history here. As early as 1707, Baron von Pernau, a German zoologist, described in exhaustive detail the behavior of several species of birds which he maintained in aviaries. His work included an examination of feeding behavior, migration, nesting, social behavior, territoriality, voice, and care of the young. As a part of his analysis, he observed the fact that some birds must learn their song patterns and others show a species-specific song without prior experience of the song from another member of the species. In addition, Pernau investigated the inheritance of behavior from parents to offspring, long before either Gregor Mendel or Charles Darwin were born.

Of course, Darwin is an important forerunner of ethology. In his writings, he gave many examples of behaviors which appeared without dependence on learning. Since we have discussed Darwin at some length earlier, we will mention only the fact that he emphasized a phylogenetic approach to the study of behavior and the homology, or commonness, of behaviors across species. For example, he pointed out the attribute of hair-raising as common to many mammals and considered it an adaptive mechanism which made the beast appear larger and more formidable to its enemies. In addition, of course, the raising of the hair forms a protective function, since it thickens the coat and provides a more difficult purchase for the jaws of the enemy.

In the 1880s, Jacques Loeb advanced his theory of tropisms, this being a mechanistic analysis of "automatic" responding on the part of animals (see Loeb, 1900). In Loeb's view, all behavior could be explained in terms of physiochemical reactions to external stimulation. He made a number of observations of such behaviors. His theories have had a strong impact, and a residue of them persists in the language of psychology. A good example of a tropism is the behavior of the moth when it is attracted to a flame. Figure 17–4 is a simplified

FIG. 17-4 Sensory and motor pathways of a moth toward a flame.

illustration of the sensory and motor pathways which tropistic theory might advance to explain the manner in which a moth is drawn to fly into the flame. Note that the motion of the wings is seen as being under the control of the eyes in a contralateral way. Thus, when an eye sees the flame, the opposite wing beats more strongly. Then, the animal is turned toward the flame and drawn to its death.

Loeb's views were challenged by Jennings (1906), an American zoologist who made a strong argument for the "wholeness" and purposiveness of behavior in a way which is quite reminiscent of the arguments of John Dewey, to which we referred earlier. Since Jennings was writing in the early part of the twentieth century, he was expressing the spirit of the times quite well. A reaction to elementalism was underway, and it has thoroughly infused the thinking of the ethologists. Among the concepts stressed by Jennings was the idea that behavior in higher and lower animals is on a continuum. He suggested that a homology, or commonness, existed in the essential features of behavior of all animals.

Perhaps the earliest writer whose views have the flavor of today's ethology was Jakob von Uexküll (1909). He, like Jennings, insisted upon an exhaustive study of all features of the behavior of a species before theories of behavior were developed. In the language of modern ethology, such a complete catalog of behavior is called an *ethogram*. Two concepts advanced by von Uexküll have been highly influential in ethology. First, he held that of all the stimuli which impinge upon an organism, only certain select ones have the power to act as perceptual signs which *release* certain behaviors. The meaning of these perceptual signs may be innate, or they may be learned. Secondly, he postulated a *functional circle* of interaction between an organism and the stimuli in its environment. He pointed out that as an animal responds to a stimulus, the fact of responding changes the stimulus surround and leads to a new response, because the animal has completed a circle within itself consisting of the perception of the stimulus, an internal change in the receptive field, an analysis of the change, and the final motor act which changed the external stimulus situation. By their insistence on the study of the whole pattern of behavior, as against the reflex, and the use of neurophysiological models, Jennings and von Uexküll were the direct forerunners of modern ethology.

Two other zoologists, C. O. Whitman (1899), an American, and Oskar Heinroth (1938), a German, came to similar conclusions about the nature of inherited behavior patterns. Whitman studied behavior patterns which seemed to come from within, the so-called instincts, but he argued that they were behaviors which had similar patterns through the phylogenetic scale. Heinroth was truly a taxonomist of behavior who emphasized the species-specific nature of certain patterns, and the need for describing these exactly.

A student of Whitman's, Wallace Craig (1918), was one of the first to develop a theory of instinctive behaviors using an ethological model. He rejected the notion that survival value was the goal of appetitive behavior and substituted the notion that it is the consummatory response and the discharge of the energy involved toward which behavior is directed. Craig's theory was taken up and developed by Konrad Lorenz (1950), a student of Heinroth, in his theory of *action-specific energy*. Further, he argued that a lack of activity led to a pent-up reserve of energy. Another important figure in modern ethology was Niko Tinbergen (1951), who further advanced the Craig-Lorenz theory of action-specific energy and initiated many studies on the releasing stimuli for various innate behavior patterns. We will turn now to several concepts which have been of central importance to ethological theory and present examples of experimentation relating to them. The first concept which we will consider is the *fixed action pattern*, which was first described by Heinroth and Whitman.

Fixed Action Patterns (FAPs)

We may begin our discussion of the FAP with a definition by Hess (1962):

> The fixed action pattern is defined as a sequence of coordinated motor actions that appears without the animal having to learn it by the usual learning process. The animals can perform it without previous exercise and without having seen another species member do it. The fixed action pattern is constant in form, which means that the sequence of motor elements never varies.

As an example of the type of invariant behavior, we may consider the "fanning" of its eggs by a small fish, the three-spined stickleback.

Example 17–7 *Fixed action patterns in fish: Egg fanning in the stickleback (Tinbergen, 1951)*

Niko Tinbergen has reported the results of observation and experiment on a small freshwater fish, the three-spined stickleback (*Gasterosteus aculeatus*). These studies have become classics in the literature and we report them here both for their historical interest and because they nicely illustrate the notion of FAPs.

Ordinarily, the stickleback mates in early spring in shallow water. According to Tinbergen, the mating cycle follows an unvarying ritual which can be observed easily, since the fish will perform the sequence in aquaria. When kept in tanks, the fish form a group which swims more or less as a unit. When the mating cycle begins, the males leave the school and stake out a territory in a shallow place where each will build its nest. From then on, an intruder, male or female, is attacked if it enters the territory. Then the male builds a nest by scooping out the sand and putting in a roof of dead weeds and trash over the top, forming a hollow, covered depression in the sand. The tunnel which is formed is slightly shorter than the length of an adult fish.

When the male finishes the nest, it suddenly changes its color from a flat gray to a bright red on the chin and a bluish white on the back. Then the male seeks a suitable female. Since the females have also entered the reproductive cycle, by developing fifty to one hundred eggs, which cause the females to swell, the male is able to recognize them. As a female approaches, the male swims toward her in a zigzag pattern. When he has gained the female's attention, the male goes to his nest and puts his nose into it. This act induces the female to enter the nest, with her tail out one end and her head out the other. The male then prods her tail with a rhythmic set of thrusts, and she lays her eggs. The entire ritual takes about a minute. When the female leaves the nest, the male enters and fertilizers the eggs. He then goes looking for another female.

After the male has courted and consummated the

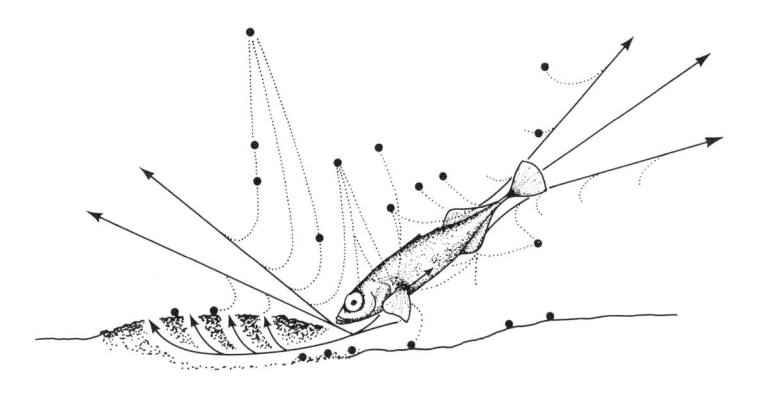

FIG. 17-5 Male three-spined stickleback giving ventilation to eggs. Dots indicate the position of KMnO$_4$ crystals; dotted and solid lines indicate observed currents. (*Tinbergen, 1942*)

pattern with several females, his mating impulse appears to subside, and his normal color returns. Then the male begins to fan or ventilate the eggs as shown in Figure 17-5.

The male positions himself near the nest and fans water over the eggs with his pectoral fins, presumably to enrich with oxygen the supply of eggs. Each day, as the eggs mature, they require more fanning, and the male spends greater time fanning them until the eggs hatch. When that happens, the male guards the nest, keeping the young together until they mature enough to leave the nest and join the school.

That this fanning behavior is controlled by internal as well as external factors was demonstrated by Tinbergen in the following way. Ordinarily, fanning increases in duration each day until the eggs hatch. But if the eggs are removed on the sixth day and replaced with a fresh batch of eggs from a fresh nest, the pattern of fanning changes markedly. The fish now spends a lower percentage of time fanning, and the duration of the fanning period in terms of days spent fanning is increased. Clearly, the fish is performing an FAP which depends on both internal and external sources of stimulation.

At this point, it is well to list four empirical properties of the FAP which have been presented by Moltz (1965). He suggests that FAPs are *stereotyped*, in that they are expressed in a highly invariant manner within a species. Further, they show *independence from immediate external control*. Also, FAPs show *spontaneity*, a term used to designate the apparent changes in the responses which are independent of changes in external conditions. One of the most striking phenomena in this category is the relationship of the strength of a FAP as a function of the time since it has last been performed. Thus, if a male stickleback is prevented from fanning its nest of eggs, when it is returned to the nest, it will show a large increase in the intensity of fanning. This is not due to changes in the chemical constituents of the eggs or water, since the experimenter (van Iersel, 1953) found the same results if the nest was completely enclosed during the experiment.

A second phenomenon which illustrates the concept of spontaneity is the appearance of FAPs *in vacuo*. The FAP will appear in an inappropriate situation if the animal has been kept from performing the response for a long time by elimination of those cues which ordinarily release the behavior. Thus, van Iersel (1953), reported that the fanning behavior of the stickleback is sometimes exhibited when there is no nest present. In their discussions of vacuum behavior, ethologists often contrast FAPs with reflex behavior, pointing out that FAPs must be considered to be different from real reflexes because they show this vacuum behavior. That is, there is something building up within the nervous system which tends to lead to FAP behavior, and the FAP will appear spontaneously without the usual releasing stimulus. The reflex, on the other hand, occurs only when the proper stimulus elicits it.

Finally, FAPS must be *independent of individual learning*. In order to investigate this attribute of FAPs, the ethologists have made use of a particular technique, the *isolation experiment*. The simplest example of the method consists of removing young from the nest at birth and rearing them apart from contact with adults. They are then tested at maturity to see if they exhibit species-specific behaviors. For instance, Tinbergen (1942) has reported that male sticklebacks reared in isolation perform the species-typical zigzag courting dance even though they have never seen another stickleback. Even more strikingly, they would perform the dance if they were presented with a cardboard model of a swollen female.

The FAP plays a central role in ethological theory as well as in empirical research. We have referred already to two attributes of theoretical concern. First, FAPs are held to be genetically determined, and in that sense, they are instinctive. In the second place, an FAP has a specific source of energy, referred to as action-specific energy. A nice illustration of the thinking of the ethologists on this aspect of FAPs is given by Bullock (1961):

> It seems at present highly likely that for many complex behavioral actions the nervous system contains not only genetically determined circuits but also genetically determined physiological properties of their components so that the complete act is represented in coded form and awaits only an adequate trigger, either internal or external.

Bullock's notion of an "adequate trigger" relates to another concept which has been of major importance to the ethologists, namely, a *releasing stimulus*, or *releaser*. Tinbergen and Lorenz have argued that certain innate reactions show a dependence on a certain set of sign stimuli, which leads to the conclusion that there must be a special neurological sensory mechanism which releases the patterned reaction and is responsible for its highly selective nature. They call this mechanism the *innate releasing mechanism*. This concept has led the ethologists into a consideration of the neurological bases of innate behavior. We will first discuss the nature of releasers and then conclude our discussion with an example of a neurological model derived from ethology.

Releasers and Innate Releasing Mechanism: (IRMs)

Thus far, we have dealt with FAPs without detailed discussion of the particular stimuli which release them. Much exploration of the nature of releasers has been done by the ethologists. We will examine two illustrations of their work which make fundamental points about the nature of releasers: animals react *automatically* to sign stimuli, with little insight, and the nature of the sign stimulus is both *qualitative* and *relational*.

Example 17–8 *Chick rescue reaction (Bruckner, 1933)*

The conservation and survival of many species depends on the care given the young during their early days. This is one of the truisms which we take for granted without question, yet we seldom ask just what events lead to the exhibition of care responses in the various species. Thus, the human mother responds to the cry of her child, but she also becomes concerned if the child shows struggling movements. Thus care is elicited by both visual and auditory cues. However, in lower animals such as the chicken, such is not the case. Bruckner performed an experiment on chickens which illustrates the dependence of the hen on auditory cues.

Ordinarily, if a chick finds itself in trouble and is away from the nest, it cries and beats its wings. The hen then rushes to it and performs a retrieval in which she guides the chick back to the nest. If, however, a chick is taken from the nest and placed in plain sight of the hen, *but under a glass bell jar*, the hen will simply ignore the chick, even if the chick engages in wild flapping and running about. Since the hen cannot hear the chick, evidently the FAP of rescue is not released. Proof of this comes when an opaque barrier is placed between a chick and the hen. Since she can hear the cries of the chick, even though she cannot see it, she rushes over the barrier and to the rescue. The situation is shown in Figure 17–6. We can therefore conclude that rescue behavior is indeed an FAP of a highly specific sort which is released by the auditory stimulus of the chick's cry.

Our second example is a classic in the literature, and we include it because it illustrates so well the relational nature of the sign stimulus. Since we have already discussed the behavior of the stickleback, in part, we will present the example without further explanation.

Example 17–9 *The relational nature of the releaser stimuli: Fighting behavior in the stickleback (Tinbergen, 1951)*

In Example 17–7, we discussed the pattern of reproductive behavior in the stickleback. It will be recalled that the male changes color when it has

FIG. 17-6 Experiments on reaction of domestic fowl to distress call of chick. (*Tinbergen, 1942*)

built a nest and then engages in fighting behavior toward any other male which happens to enter its territory. Tinbergen has also explored the nature of the stimulus which elicits this fighting behavior, by the use of models which more or less resemble the male stickleback in his nuptial markings.

Two series of models were used. The basic design put the red color, which appears on the belly of the male at this time, into direct competition with all other morphological characteristics of the fish. One series of models were very accurate models of the fish except that they lacked the red coloring of the nuptial male. The other series only approximately represented a fish at all but had two types of red figure markings. In one set, marking was placed in the correct position on the model, that is, on the underside of the model. To check on the importance of the position, the second set of approximately identical models had equal amounts of red markings, but they were located in inappropriate locations such as on the upper side.

The results indicated that sticklebacks attacked only those models which had red on them and then only if the markings were in the proper location, on the belly of the model.

Tinbergen's experiment illustrates the important point that FAPs are not solely under the control of qualitative differences in the stimuli. Since the two sets of approximate models had equal amounts of red color, it is clear that color alone was not the controlling factor in the behavior of the fish. Rather, there is a relational factor, namely, the position of the red coloring, which determines whether the fish will enter into an attack pattern against the model. Fixed action patterns are obviously complexly related to environment.

A final ethological concept which we will consider is the notion that innate behavior consists of an organized sequence of subacts arranged in a hierarchical way. This *hierarchical organization* can be found in an examination of instinctive behaviors. Tinbergen has applied a hierarchical analysis to the reproductive instinct of the stickleback and presents a diagram, shown in Figure 17–7, which illustrates the principles involved. Notice that the complex organization of reproductive behavior involves several distinct and quite independent lines of activity which coexist as propensities within the animal yet which involve different FAPs. Thus, the onset of the reproductive stage leads to dispositions for fighting, nest building, mating, and care of the offspring. Each of these can be classified as an appetitive behavior which shows two attributes: (1) the pattern of behavior has a purpose, that is, it leads to consummatory activity, and (2) it has variability and plasticity in that the exact form of the behavior which occurs is dependent on the external

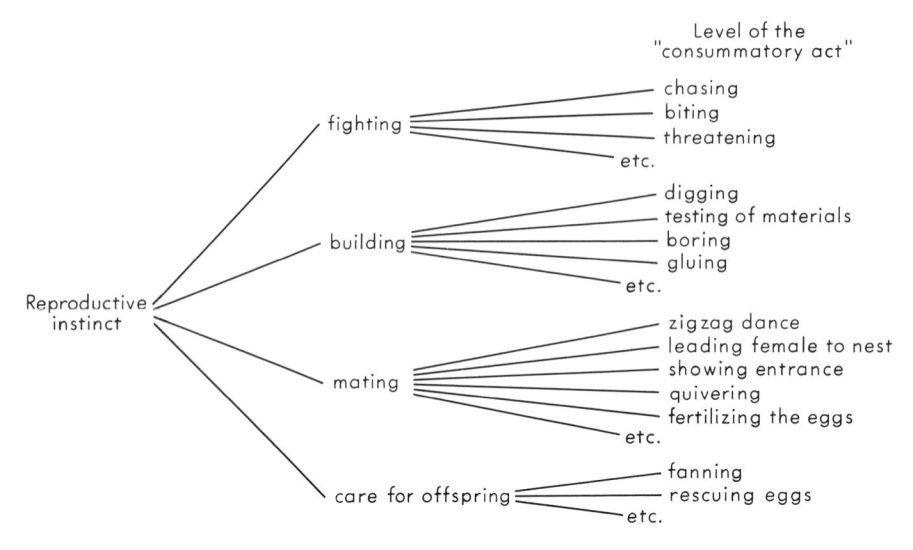

FIG. 17–7 Principle of hierarchial organization in the three-spined stickleback. (*Tinbergen, 1942*)

stimulation. Thus a stickleback will fight another male, but the nature of the fight will depend on the location of the other fish and its behavior. At the second level of the sequence, the consummatory act is characterized by simple stereotyped actions which depend closely on the stimulus surround. The hierarchy of behavior involves a complex sequence which results in a stereotyped consummatory act.

It may clarify our understanding of the ethological tradition to examine a phenomenon which illustrates many of the points which we have been making. This mechanism, called *imprinting*, establishes in certain young birds a tendency to follow or remain close to the mother or some mother substitute. A number of salient facts about it are described in the experimental data presented below.

Example 17–10 *Imprinting in chicks (Hess, 1959)*

The phenomenon is a well-known one familiar to anyone who has watched a mother hen with her brood foraging in a barnyard, or a mother duck swimming in a pond followed by a line of ducklings. It was not very clear until recently, however, how this tendency occurred, at what age it could be established, to what range of objects besides the mother and what evolutionary significance it might have.

One of the pioneers in the work on these problems has been Eckhart Hess (1959) at the University of Chicago. Hess has made use of the experimental situation shown in Figure 17–8. Chicks are hatched in incubators in the laboratory and then exposed to the surrogate mother in the apparatus at different ages. A record is made of the time during which the chick follows or is close to (e.g., within 1 foot of) the surrogate. Among other conclusions, the following emerge as some of the more important:

1. There appears to be a *critical period* during which imprinting occurs most readily as measured by later strength of following. The exact time of this critical stage will vary with the species and also with the manner of calculating age. Time of hatching from the egg is rather variable and does not take place in all individuals at the same degree of developmental age (Klopfer & Gottlieb, 1962). Nonetheless, the existence of a critical period for imprinting does seem well established.

2. Duration of exposure to the surrogate does not seem to be very important. The conditions of presentation, however, do appear crucial. Thus, imprinting occurs more readily to a moving as against a stationary object. The presence of barriers that have to be "hurdled" by the chick to keep

FIG. 17–8 Apparatus used in Hess' study of imprinting. (*Hess, 1959a*)

up with the moving surrogate also seem to produce a stronger attachment.

3. In chickens and ducks and probably a good many other species, the young will imprint to a wide variety of objects of varying shape, size, and color. Some of these are more effective than others. Examples are shown in Figure 17–9. It is important to note that, if opportunity for imprinting to some object is not permitted, following does not occur by itself later on. That is to say, genotype does not in this case rigidly determine the behavior—but only in conjunction with an environmental experience. There are exceptions to this, however. The European cuckoo and American cowbird are parasitic, in the sense that they lay their eggs in the nests of other species. In spite of not being exposed to their own species for quite a long time, these birds will later still flock and mate with members of their own kind. In this case, the genotype is strongly buffered against environmental contingency.

There are many more facts known about imprinting than we have the space to list here. There are also many more yet to be found out. It is an adaptive mechanism of great importance in helping to ensure, first, that young animals survive the early period of life during which they are relatively helpless, and, second, that later in life they associate and mate with members of their own species.

Physiological Basis for FAPs

As the ethologists have gathered more and more observational data, they have begun to consider the underlying physiological mechanisms of behavior. Specifically, they have come to be concerned with the manner in which the drives to behave in certain ways are related to the brain. By making use of a technique involving electrical stimulation of the brain, von Holst explored this problem with some success. In the following example, we will consider some of his findings on the effects of opposing two drives which are elicited by electrical stimulation to the brain.

Example 17–11 *The brain and action specific energies: The effects of conflicting drives (von Holst & von Saint Paul, 1963)*

These researchers adopted the methods pioneered by Walter Hess on electrical stimulation of the brain in order to relate FAPs to the central nervous system. The technique involves the placing of electrodes into certain parts of the brain. We will discuss the techniques in Chapter 18, in which emotional behavior is discussed. Here it is sufficient to mention that when a current is passed through the electrodes, it is possible to elicit chains of behaviors which are recognizable as the appetitive sequences to which we referred above. The experimenters were interested in the results of simultaneously eliciting two of these patterns of appetitive behaviors. Multiple electrodes were implanted in chickens and were positioned in those parts of the brain from which appetitive behavior chains could be elicited by electrical stimulation. Two sites were simultaneously stimulated in order

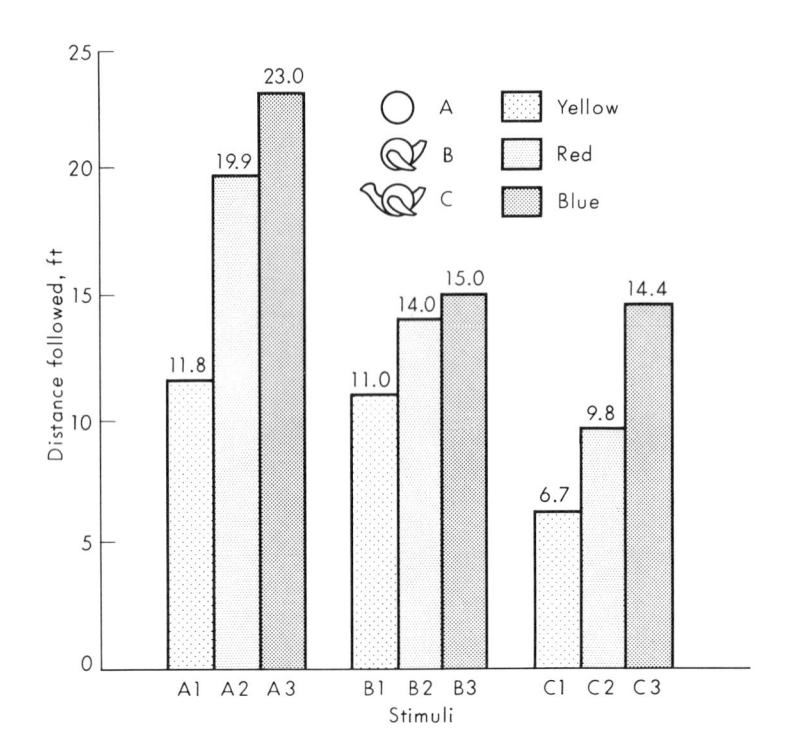

FIG. 17–9 Effectiveness of models in eliciting the following reaction, expressed as a function of stimulus complexity and color. (*Hess, 1959*)

to explore the functional relationship between the two appetitive systems.

Several effects were obtained. In the simplest case, the animals simply combined the behaviors of the two chains. Thus an animal might sit down and preen or turn its head while cackling, and so on. This type of reaction occurred when the behaviors were not antagonistic.

In a second class of responses, the animal would make a compromise between the two response systems. Thus, it might combine searching behavior involving raising the head and peering with the sweeping motion of the head shown in food seeking. In the combined form, the head was raised and moved only slightly. In a final class of combined behaviors, the animal showed an alternation between the elements of the two sequences, giving one behavior, then an element of the other.

Frequently, however, only one of the two classes appeared, the stronger behavioral force suppressing the weaker. However, a result appeared which is reminiscent of the behavior *in vacuo* phenomenon which we discussed above. When the stimulation is turned off, the behavior which was suppressed occurs.

Von Holst and von Saint Paul observed that there exist various processes within the organism which have a time course buildup. These processes, when released by an appropriate stimulus, lead to the behavior. If two or more of these processes interact, the stronger suppresses the weaker, and then the weaker will appear at a later time. As a result of his observations, von Holst and von Saint Paul postulated a cyclic nature of the processes of the brain. As a result of such processes, the drive to perform certain behaviors waxes and wanes over time.

The ethologists, then, have advanced theories which attempt to explain instinctive behavior in terms of functional models of the brain. The development of such models and the exploration of the relationship of brain and other body structures and behavior has traditionally been the province of physiological psychology, and we now turn to a consideration of this field.

CHAPTER 18
PHYSIOLOGICAL PSYCHOLOGY I: THE CENTRAL NERVOUS SYSTEM AND BEHAVIOR

THE CENTRAL HYPOTHESIS AND METHODS OF PHYSIOLOGICAL PSYCHOLOGY

Workers in physiological psychology have been guided by the principle that behavior can be explained in terms of the physiochemical reactions within the organism. This idea has a long history. As we have seen in Chapter 13, Descartes, in the seventeenth century, considered animals to be automatons; thus he used a mechanical model to explain their functioning. His ideas influenced many later French philosophers who formed a school of philosophical thought called *materialism*, which held that the brain is a physical organ which secretes thought. Materialism entered the biological sciences when four students of Johannes Muller, a very prominent physiologist, formed a pact to promote materialism in physiological theory; these were Ludwig, DuBois-Reymond, Helmholtz, and Brucke. All became highly eminent scientists, and it was through the influence of three of them that much of physiology developed in the way it did.

The father of Russian physiology and psychology, I. M. Sechenov, was a student of Reymond, Ludwig, and Helmholtz, and in his writings he adopted the framework of mechanistic thought. From his studies of the inhibitory action of the nervous system Sechenov concluded that all voluntary motions were due to reflexes within the nervous system. He published these views in his book *Reflexes of the Brain*. Sechenov's influence on his student Ivan Pavlov resulted in a profound materialistic bent in Russian psychology.

Among the most enduring problems for physiological psychologists has been the question of the loci within the brain responsible for learning and memory. The problem is a critical one, not only because of its theoretical interest to professional psychologists, but also because of its relevance to the causes of feeblemindedness, senility, and all forms of mental defect. Some of the most important studies of learning and the brain have involved the use of a particular technique: surgical removal of cortical tissue by *ablation*. We will summarize a few of these studies.

One cannot begin a discussion of studies of brain function based on ablation without mentioning the father of that method, Pierre Flourens, who lived in the nineteenth century. A very skilled surgeon at a time when the art was not yet refined to a high degree, Flourens performed a long series of studies on brain function in the period 1820–1867. He was profoundly influential in his arguments against the then current view that the brain functioned in an atomistic way. He argued for a unity of function and advanced a long set of postulates—in general, remarkably correct—which assigned to the various parts of the brain a specific function, yet argued that the brain acts as a whole. He stated that it was the principle of unity which dominates all brain function.

Following Flourens, perhaps the most famous researcher was Broca, who discovered a specific area in the brain responsible for speech. His work apparently indicated a return to a localization of function as the best model for the brain.

Broca's work seemed to support the viewpoints of the phrenologists Gall and Spurzheim, who had advanced the idea that there were particular areas of the brain responsible for specific functions. Although many of the tenets of the phrenological doctrine proved to be untenable—such as the idea that the shape of the skull reflects developmental differences between functional areas of the brain—the phrenologists were tremendously popular and "in vogue." In addition, they greatly influenced the course of history by directing attention to the problem of the role of the brain in determining the nature of mental life. Because the phrenologists put forward such an atomistic view of brain functioning, Flourens and later workers seemed less radical than they might have. Further work performed in the latter part of the nineteenth century was principally designed to explore the effects of brain lesions on perception and on motor control. But it was only with the work of Shepard Franz (1902) that a direct attack on the locus in the brain responsible for learning was begun.

Example 18–1 *Localization of function in the brain: Learning ability (Franz, 1902)*

Franz made use of the puzzle box developed by Thorndike, which we discussed in Chapter 13. He trained cats to escape from the box and then surgically removed their frontal lobes. The subjects showed a loss of retention after the operations. But his results did not fit the exact localization model of the phrenologists who had preceded him. In fact, he found that those cerebral areas whose ablation produced a loss of habit were not sharply defined, and even their approximate locations were subject to variability. Further, he discovered that destruction of an area might lead to loss of the memory of a learned function but would not cause total loss of the function. Lost habits might even be reestablished. Such findings seemed to swing the weight of evidence to a support of Flourens' view of unity of function in the brain. But research into the mind-body problem did not move into its modern high rate of productivity until some time later.

THE GEOGRAPHY OF THE BRAIN

We will now present an overview of the field with an examination of some of the major ideas which have dominated it. Perhaps the most important of these orienting attitudes has related to the relation between the anatomical structure of an organism—in particular its brain—and psychological function. In the short history just presented, we have alluded to one facet of this controversy: the search for the locus of ability to learn. The issue has been whether there was an exact localization of function in the brain or whether psychological functions are served by the whole brain in a general way.

At this point, it may be helpful to consider the views of a contemporary theorist in the area—Pribram of Stanford University, a surgeon and neurophysiologist, who has conducted many experiments designed to relate brain structure to behavioral function. From his own work and that of others, he has developed a model of brain function.

Pribram (1960) has stressed the manner in which the vertebrate brain has become more complex during its evolutionary history. Examination of the brains of successively more complex animals indicates some general patterns of developments. We find in very primitive forms, such as fish, reptiles, and to some extent birds and mammals, a spinal cord which follows the path of the vertebrate spine, ending in an enlarged complex of neural tissue, the brain. Such brains can be divided into three parts, the forebrain, midbrain, and hindbrain. This division applies through the phylogenetic series up to man. Of course, as the organisms themselves become more complex, their brains become more com-

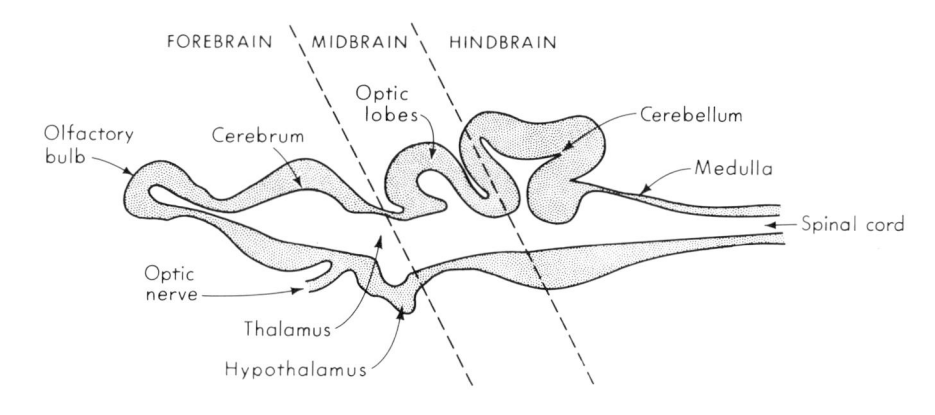

FIG. 18–1 A hypothetical primitive vertebrate brain. (*After Hilgard, 1962*)

plex, and it is this process of evolution of the brain which has interested Pribram.

It will help our discussion to be acquainted with the structures common to the brains of vertebrates. In Figure 18–1 a simple brain is sketched and labeled. In this primitive form of the brain, the chief parts of the forebrain are the olfactory lobe, the cerebrum, the thalamus. The latter consists of a clump of nerve cells and has several functions. Mainly, it directs messages coming into and going out of the brain. The next structure, considered in a "vertical" direction, is the midbrain, which consists of the optic lobes, which in this primitive brain control the eyes. The hindbrain consists of the cerebellum, which plays a role in coordination of movement, and the medulla, which acts in the maintenance of such basic functions as respiration and circulation of the blood.

Pribram suggests that the course of evolution of the brain has not been entirely vertical; that is, the brain has not simply grown more complex structures at the top as the higher forms have emerged. Rather, he suggests, the brain can best be divided into three concentric sets of structures each of which has a vertical organization, from the stem up the cerebrum as shown in Figure 18–2. The primitive core is, as the name suggests, the brain stem, consisting of the spinal cord and the structures just above it, the medulla and reticular formation, and the hypothalamus. These structures underlie those very basic processes necessary to the maintenance of life, such as breathing, circulation, regulation of the salt content of the blood, maintenance of body temperature, and control of heart rate.

Situated around the core are the structures of the old brain, which appear to have evolved from the core at a very early stage. They have been called the *visceral brain* by MacLean (1950), because part of their function seems to relate to such processes as digestion and emotion. Pribram has suggested that this part of the brain is in control of these behaviors, which have a "programmed" aspect in that they have a time course through which they run. Thus instinctive behaviors and other long-term patterned behaviors appear to depend on the old brain. Pribram has called this system the *internal system* of the brain and related it to basic adaptive functions.

On the other hand, the *external system* of the brain includes those portions of the brain which are quite specific in function, in that they are concerned with sensory and motor control. Principally, this involves the cortex. In using Pribram's analysis we will first consider the external systems, with their high degree of specificity of function, and then turn to the internal, more diffuse systems.

INPUT AND OUTPUT SYSTEMS OF THE BRAIN

For purposes of analysis of the external system, it is useful to consider the central nervous system as a means of transmission and storage of informa-

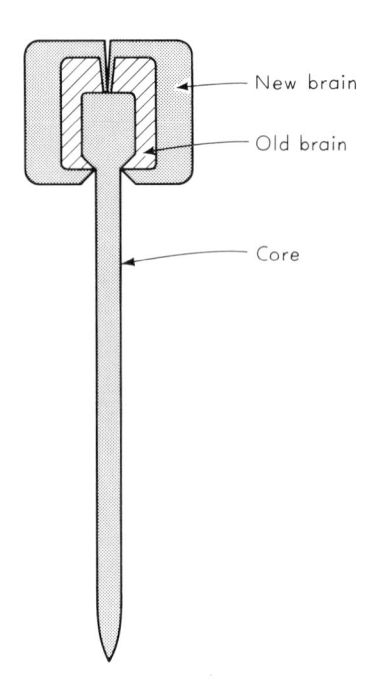

FIG. 18-2 Sketch of Pribram's model of a brain.

tion within the organism. Using an information-theory approach we can develop two notions about bodily processes: information is carried and stored in structures, and each structure has a particular informational function. Thus, the concepts of structure and function will guide us in our analysis.

The first system which we will consider is the sensory system, which delivers information about the world to the brain. Our discussion of perception stressed the phenomenological approach. Here, we shall consider sensory processes from the viewpoint of physiological psychology, which asks, essentially, what structures mediate the functions of sensation and how they do it. Historically, several questions about the nature of sensation have been of interest to biologically oriented psychologists. It has been apparent that not all physical events in the environment are encoded into neural events. One may ask which events in the world are encoded and which are not and, further, what the mechanisms are by which such a selection is accomplished. We will examine these problems by considering some generalizations about sensation without regard to any particular modality. Then we will consider two specific sensory systems, audition and vision.

The General Processes of Stimulus Reception

The receptor organs with which we are equipped have a selective nature in that they are set for a physical energy of a certain sort, usually referred to as the *adequate stimulus*, which is defined as that particular form of energy which best excites a receptor. In addition, receptors are selective as to what they report about the environment. Even in its own field, a receptor does not report all stimuli present. For example, there is an *absolute threshold* for the adequate stimulus. That is, there is a value of stimulus intensity which must be reached before the receptor will be activated. In general, our absolute thresholds are very low, indicating that our receptors are extremely sensitive. Further, in general, the more the energy by which a receptor is stimulated, the greater is its response. It is true that our perceptions change along a dimension of magnitude. However, changes in the intensity of our experience of stimuli are not the same as the changes in intensity of the external stimuli themselves. For different sensory modalities, there are different rates of change in the psychological experience, as shown in Figure 18–3.

As the figure shows, the increase in phenomenal awareness of a particular kind of event in the physical world is different for different modalities. By considering the figure, we can intuitively recognize the benefit to the organism of each of these functions. Notice that small increments in electric shock will give rise to large increments in felt shock, while large increments in luminescence are required to give rise to small increments in brightness. Clearly it is highly necessary that an organism respond to shock with small changes in the amount of stimulation present, while it would impair the behavior of an organism if small increments of luminescence gave rise to large changes in brightness.

A second type of threshold which is important is the study of sensory processes in the *differential threshold*, defined as that difference in stimulation which is necessary in order to detect the fact that a change has occurred. In many cases, the detectable differences are a function of the strength of the original stimulus. This relationship has been

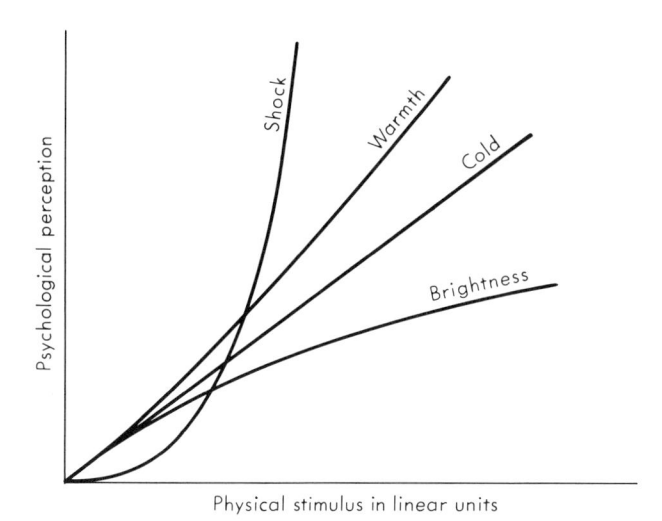

FIG. 18–3 Psychological perception versus physical stimulation.

expressed as *Weber's law*, which states that $\Delta I/I$ is approximately constant over the middle range of stimulus values for the modality being examined. In this expression, I is the intensity of the original stimulus and ΔI is the change in stimulation necessary for a difference to be perceived.

It may be stated as a generalization that changes in *intensity* involve the activation of more and more receptor units. Thus, as a stimulus is perceived as growing more intense, so there is the involvement of more and more receptor units within the organ responsible for that stimulus. On the other hand, discrimination of *qualitative* differences, within the same sensory modality, appears to require units attuned to slightly different stimuli. For example, the psychological dimensions of pitch and loudness are functions of different physical dimensions. Pitch is a function of the frequency of sound waves. Loudness is a function of the amplitude of sound waves. However, the two main dimensions are not completely independent, since they are mediated by the same receptor system. Thus, if one increases the pitch of high sounds, the loudness is decreased until the terminal threshold for pitch is reached. Thus, sounds which are increased in pitch require an increase in intensity in order still to be heard.

To understand the way in which sense organs convert the physical energy of the external environment into information within the nervous system, we may consider a *single neuron to be a model of a typical sense organ*. When the process of information transmission begins, a local potential is set up at the point of stimulation, on the neuron. If this local potential is large enough, it can stimulate an action potential which travels down the neuron. Thus, information is transmitted. In a specific sensory receptor, such as the touch receptor, the stimulus sets up a *generator potential*, also called a *local excitatory potential*.

Much work on the process by which receptors convert physical energy into nervous system events has been done on the Pacinian corpuscle, which is illustrated in Figure 18–4. The corpuscle is amazingly well designed to be sensitive to small deformations of shape. The corpuscles are located in the skin, the muscles, and in the connective tissues in the body cavity. They are quite large in size, for receptor organs, being 1 mm in length and 0.6 mm in width. Extremely small changes will set up a potential in the corpuscle. If a stimulus which causes a $\frac{1}{2}\text{-}\mu$ deformation occurs in the capsule which is 600 μ in width, a potential will occur. When the corpuscle is equipped with electrodes, it can be shown that the generator potential develops along the bare nerve fiber, which is in the center of the corpuscle. However, although the corpuscle is sensitive, the stimulus which is brought to bear on the corpuscle does not provide the energy for the generator potential to start. The corpuscle supplies

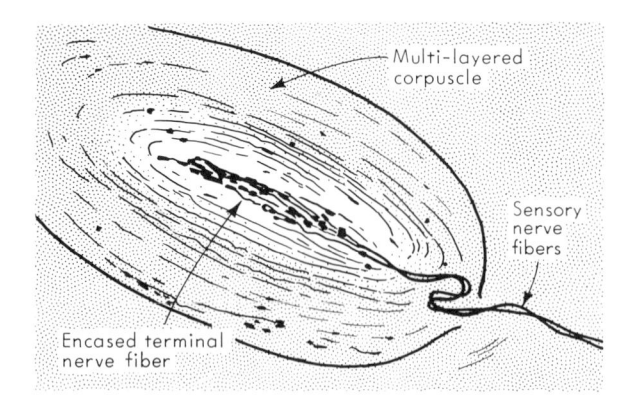

FIG. 18–4 Pacinian corpuscle.

the energy itself. The stimulus is just an initiator of events, in much the same way that the trigger pull does not provide the energy for the propulsion of the bullet from a firearm. The trigger pull merely initiates a sequence of events. The force for propulsion is provided by the chemical events within the cartridge. In the same way the metabolism within the neuron provides the energy for the generator potential.

Auditory Reception

In order to illustrate the importance of audition, we may compare it to vision. The visual receptor, that is, the eye, takes in more information per unit of time than does the ear. It is common to say that the human being is highly visual. But speech and hearing are very important, especially in social and intellectual development. For instance, totally blind students are able to attend regular colleges, but rarely can a totally deaf student do so.

Our sense of hearing is extremely sensitive. We noted above that the Pacinian corpuscle can respond to a pressure which deforms it by only 0.5 μ. The skin on the fingertips can respond to a vibration of 0.5 μ at 100 cps, its most sensitive frequency. On the other hand, the eardrum only has to move $0.5\ \mu \times 10^{-6}$ in order to respond. The eardrum is most sensitive to vibrations of about 3,000 cps, and at 3,000 cps the movement of the eardrum is only 10^{-9} centimeters. Thus, the auditory system is sensitive to extremely small movements of the eardrum. In addition, the ear can respond to different frequencies at the same time and to patterns of different frequencies such as occur in speech sounds. It is possible to study the visual patterns of different speech sounds by projecting the sounds on a visual display. In fact, deaf persons can be taught to read such sound spectra. The essential information in speech sounds seems to be contained in a frequency-intensity-time pattern.

In human beings, sound *localization* is a well-developed faculty. When many persons are talking, it is easier to listen to any one voice if it is possible to localize the source. In addition, we are able to ignore sound reflections of short intervals. Finally, the ear is quite sensitive to change in intensity. If the ear were a little more sensitive, we would be able to hear the movements of the molecules in the air or the noises made by our own muscle tremors.

The remarkable sensitivity of the auditory sense is achieved by the mechanical structure of the ear. This is illustrated in Figure 18–5. The eardrum surface is twenty times as large as the footplate of the stirrup, a bone in the transmission system of the middle ear. Therefore, the force on the oval window is increased by a factor of twenty as compared to the force on the eardrum. In addition, there is some mechanical advantage in the lever system of the bones of the middle ear. A cross section of the cochlea is shown in Figure 18–6. The cochlea is quite small compared to the eardrum. It sits close to the auditory centers of the midbrain; therefore, the auditory nerve is short. The cochlea is located within the bone of the skull under the outer part of the eye. The human cochlea has 2½ turns. The process which is involved in converting the stimulation to the eardrum by sound waves into nervous impulses proceeds as follows: The movement of the eardrum leads to movement of the bones of the middle ear which push on the cochlear fluid through the window. This motion causes the basilar and tectorial membranes to rock and pivot about the two points shown in the diagram. Small up-and-down motions of the two structures are converted into a shearing motion pulling the hair cells sideways, achieving a mechanical effect on the hair cells. The points of mechanical advantage are the difference in size between the eardrum and the oval window, the lever action of the bones of the middle ear, and the shearing action of

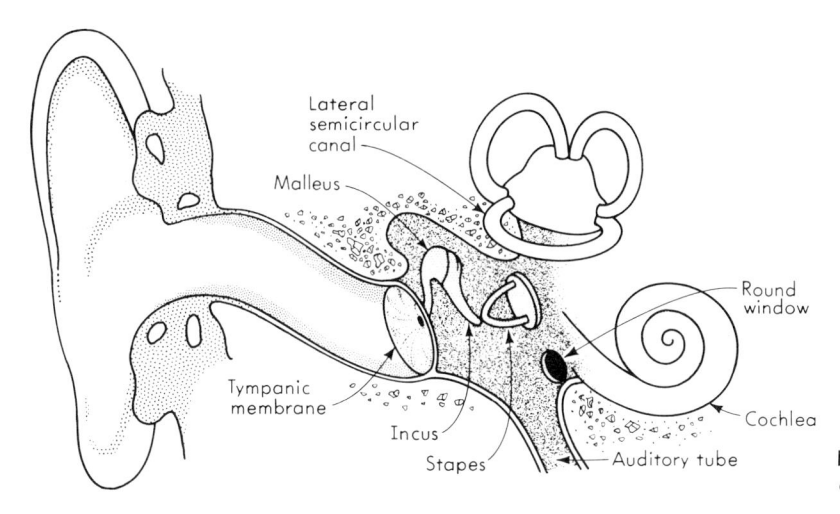

FIG. 18–5 Semischematic drawing of the ear.

the membranes. When the hair cells are bent, the auditory potential occurs. As this sequence indicates, remarkably enough, we hear by touch in the process of auditory transduction.

Visual Reception

It is difficult to overestimate the importance of vision in our daily responding to the environment. Many of our reflex reactions are in fact visually stimulated. However, even though we all use vision frequently, we are not usually aware that we have two visual systems. Table 18–1 illustrates this duality of vision.

The duality of vision, that is, the fact that there are two sets of receptors, the rods and the cones, is illustrated by a phenomenon called the *Purkinje effect*. As light becomes less yellow and red, and more blue, the rods participate more and the cones less. That means that as evening comes on we experience a brightness shift. That is, the rods, which are sensitive to lower intensities of light, become the effective organ of sight. Since the rods are "tuned" to bluish light, we see things as bluish in dim light.

With this brief examination of the way in which information enters the organism, we can turn back to our discussion of the relation of structure to function as exemplified by the search for the locus of memory.

INFORMATION STORAGE: SEARCH FOR THE ENGRAM

Lashley: Mass Action and Equipotentiality

Perhaps the greatest of modern psychobiologists was Karl Lashley (1929), who, while a student at

Table 18–1 A comparison between the rods and cones of the retina of the eye

	Rods	Cones
Specialization	Specialized response to low intensity light. Used in night vision.	Specialized for color vision and high acuity.
Connections	Many rods are connected to one retinal ganglion cell. The number of rods/ganglion cell increases toward the periphery of the eye. Such an arrangement is good for summation effects.	In the fovea, each ganglion cell receives information from only one cone. This is an arrangement which is good for acuity.
Pigments	Rhodopsin.	Probably more than one.

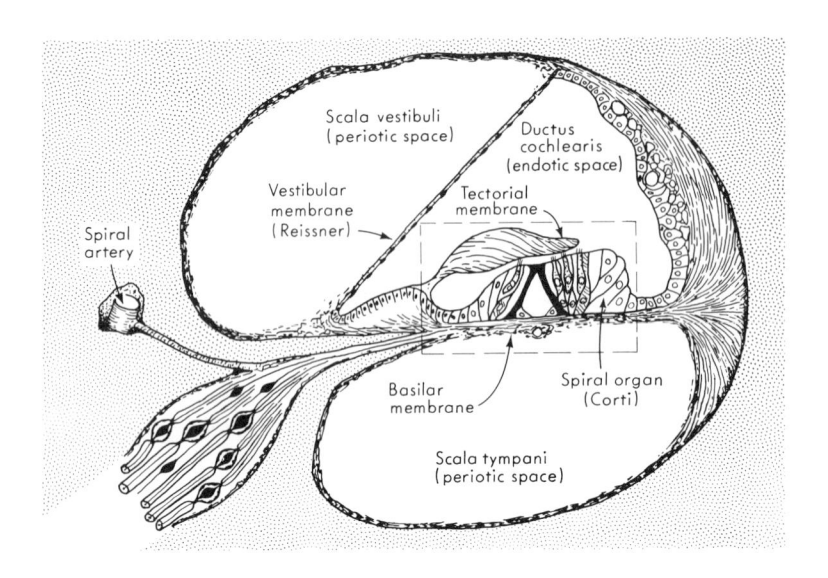

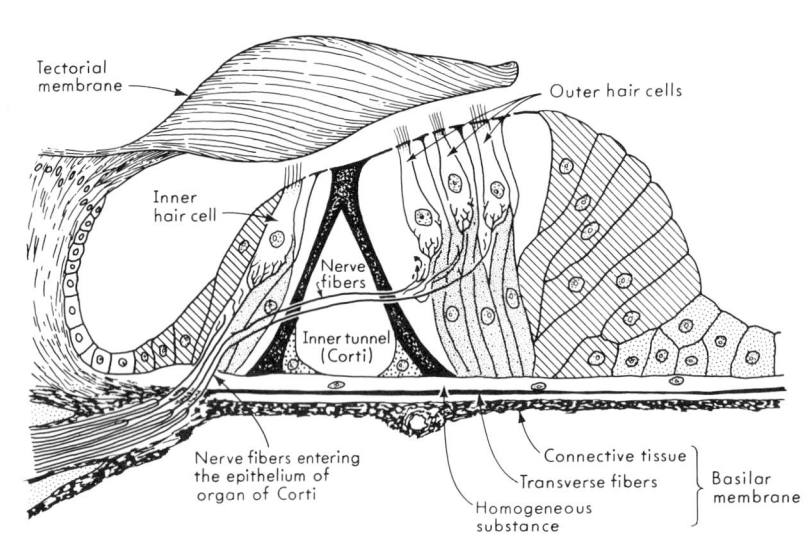

FIG. 18–6 Vertical section of the human cochlea. (*Rasmussen, 1943*)

Johns Hopkins University, worked with Franz at Walter Reed Hospital. It happened at this time that a second behavioral technique had been developed, by Stone: the so-called *spatial maze*, once a familiar part of every psychological laboratory which dealt with learning in animals. The development of the maze was one of the factors which enabled Franz and Lashley to explore further the effects of *brain lesions on behavior in rats*. Lashley continued his explorations during the period from 1917 through 1940. He varied the sites and sizes of the lesions in the cortex. The effects of these lesions on maze learning and retention of learning convinced him that the location of the lesion had little effect on behavior. However, he found that the size of the lesion was highly correlated with the number of errors which an animal made in the mazes he used.

On the basis of this observation Lashley educed a principle which he called the *principle of mass action*. He concluded that the cortex acted as a

326 BIOLOGICAL MODELS

whole in the sense that when a maze habit was formed through training, the trace of it was not localized in any one part of the cortex. Rather, after the removal of part of the cortex, the performance of the animal would depend on the quantity of the tissue which remained. This notion of mass action is a refinement of Franz' position and in direct contradiction to the extreme atomism of the phrenologists. Thus, the theories of Flourens were revitalized by Lashley.

However, an explanation of brain function requires some additions and qualifications of the principle of mass action. There are, as Broca and others have shown, areas of the cortex which are functionally important for some kinds of behavior. For instance, the occipital, or visual, cortex, the area to which the retina of the eye projects, is necessary if the animal is to make visual discriminations. Lashley did a good deal of work on visual discrimination and developed an apparatus for teaching rats to make visual discriminations: the Lashley jumping stand, which is shown in Figure 5–4. He found that when some part of the visual cortex is destroyed, the remaining parts are equal in their ability to carry out at least the simplest function of the area, for example, brightness discrimination. He formulated the principle of *equipotentiality* to describe this observation. The amount of the functional area which remains after the operation, not the exact locus which has been destroyed, is the significant variable.

Lashley's viewpoint that central integration in the brain is participated in by the entire cortex although some large subareas may be more or less devoted to specific functions did not go unchallenged. In particular, Walter Hunter (1935), who had been working with lesions and their effects on memory, took issue with Lashley. Hunter questioned Lashley's interpretation of the results from maze experiments. In Hunter's view, the most important function of the cortex is sensory integration. Since the maze situation involves many specific sensory cues, each with its own projection area, effects observed may be a function of the number of such areas which are damaged by the lesion. If the size of the lesion is increased, more and more projection areas are destroyed, and the number of sensory cues left to the animal is reduced. Hunter argued that Lashley's work was ambiguous because his findings may have been the result of either the loss of a large amount of equally potent tissue, as Lashley said, or the results may have been due to the loss of multiple functions which are a part of a highly differentiated brain.

Example 18–2 *What sensory input is required in order to learn a motor task? (Honzik, 1933)*

An experimental test of Hunter's hypothesis of the nature of the cues in a maze was made by Honzik (1933), using a complex maze which depended for its solution on cues from several modalities. Using at least forty-two rats in each group, he taught several groups of rats to run the maze. The treatment consisted of removing one or more sense modalities from each group of rats. Thus one group was made blind, one group was made deaf, one group was rendered anosmic, that is, unable to smell. Other groups had two or three of the modalities removed. The design of the experiment and the results were:

Group	Mean errors on 12th trial	On 24th trial
Normal rats	.1	.1
Deaf rats	.2	.1
Anosmic rats	.2	.1
Blind rats	1.5	1.1
Blind-deaf rats	4.2	3.9
Blind-anosmic rats	5.8	5.4
Blind-deaf-anosmic rats	6.2	6.4

Honzik reported that the initial score on running this maze was about 6.5, which indicated that the blind-deaf-anosmic rats made no improvement over twenty-four trials. These results can be interpreted as support for Hunter's notion that the solution of a maze depends on a number of sense modalities. When animals are trained in mazes which involve multiple possibilities for cue by which to solve the maze, different animals make use of different cues.

In an experimental reply to Hunter, Lashley attempted to show that sensory input was not the only important factor in learning. He compared the maze performance of animals which were blinded by removing their eyes, that is, peripherally blinded animals, with that of animals which were blinded centrally by ablation of visual cortex. He found that central blinding had a worse effect on maze performance than peripheral blinding. Lashley then argued that the visual cortex not only is important as a sensory projection area which receives input from the receptors. Rather, he argued, it also participates in central integration of behavior.

Lashley's work represented a major step in developing a theory of brain function. However, it is clear that he did not fully solve the problem of localization of the engram, or memory trace. In a sense, it appeared to be true that the brain as a whole unit was involved in many behaviors, but it was equally apparent that there must be some degree of localization.

A rapprochement was accomplished by D. O. Hebb, and he did this by switching to neurons as the major units of analysis, instead of the broad anatomical areas with which Lashley had been mainly concerned.

Hebb: Cell Assemblies

In 1949, Hebb directed attention to the manner in which the central nervous system comes to build up functional connections between neuronal units. He first noted that stimulation of the organism sets up activity in the nervous system which follows certain paths through the synaptic connections between them. A crucial postulate in Hebb's scheme states that whenever there is a transmission of excitation from one neuron to another, the ability of the first neuron to fire the second is increased. As a first approximation, Hebb suggested that this might be accomplished by a reduction in size of the synaptic gap between the two cells.

Hebb's second important suggestion was that the result of the development of functional relations between neurons is a new unit, which he called the *cell assembly*, a system having a particular functional significance and, in addition, involving a reverberating, or closed, loop as a part of its structure. Being a closed loop, the cell assembly can maintain activity over time and therefore has an importance in allowing the effects of external stimulation to perseverate. Psychological processes, such as learning or perception, occurring over time and based on the firing off of temporally ordered cell assemblies, Hebb called *phase sequences*. Thus, if a person looks at a particular form, say, a triangle, he may direct his glance at each corner in turn. When he has followed the path through the corners, he will have completed a phase sequence which forms the neural basis of the percept of the class *triangle*.

Although Hebb has said much more about the processes of learning and memory, we will consider only three deductions which can be made from his theories: First of all, by focusing so sharply on the development of the nervous system through experience, Hebb stressed the early period of life. Both in his lab and elsewhere, many studies were performed on the effects of early experience on later behavior. We will consider several of these. In addition, Hebb's theory of phase sequences led to a two-stage analysis of the learning process—the reverberatory stage and the consolidation stage. We will consider examples of research designed to explore these aspects of his ideas. Finally, Hebb's emphasis on the synapse as the locus of the effects of experience directed attention there, and in the next chapter we will consider one line of research on the chemical effects in the synapses which result from experience.

EARLY EXPERIENCE AND ADULT BEHAVIOR As we have seen, the work of Lashley emphasized the role of the brain in the behavior of mature animals but did not deal very much with the role of events in early life. But, with the advent of Hebb's ideas, a refocusing of effort occurred with a new emphasis on the role of the early environment. We will consider two studies on such efforts in the following example.

Example 18–3 *The importance of early environment for the development of problem-solving ability (Lansdell, 1953)*

In the usual laboratory situation, rats are raised in small cages which restrict their environments. They may have enough to eat and drink, but they probably lack the complex sensory and motor experiences such as those which are experienced by an animal in the wild. Building on the ideas of Hebb, Lansdell (1953) performed an experiment which made use of a special group of rats that had been raised in a relatively free environment which allowed them a good deal of enriched environmental experience. This condition can be abbreviated EC, for environmental complexity. The animals were operated upon to produce lesions in the anterior cortex or the posterior cortex or large lesions on only one side of the brain. The animals were then trained on a maze which required a high degree of flexibility in behavior from day to day (Hebb-Williams maze).

Lansdell's findings showed that destruction in the posterior cortex was much worse in terms of producing errors in the maze than were lesions in the anterior cortex or much larger lesions on only one side of the brain. The evidence seemed to be against Lashley's hypothesis of mass action and equipotentiality, because the area destroyed seemed important and the size of the area seemed not to be the crucial factor in causing errors. However, more recently, Smith (1959) has suggested that raising animals under complex environmental conditions may allow differential development of different areas of the brain. In a single experiment, he replicated both the Lansdell experiment and the Lashley experiment. He had rats which were raised under both complex and enriched environmental conditions and rats raised in the restriction of cages. The animals were all trained to criterion on the Hebb-Williams maze which had been used by Lansdell. Then, posterior, anterior, and control lesions were made in the cortex. The results of subsequent testing were quite interesting, in that they seemed to show that both Lashley and Hebb were correct. For the animals raised in cages, the rats with posterior cortical lesions were not different in behavior from the controls. But larger lesions in the anterior cortex produced more errors than either the posterior lesions or the controls. This finding supported Lashley, in that the concept of mass action seemed supported: the larger the lesion, the more the behavioral deficit.

But the animals raised in a complex environment showed different results. The rats with the smaller posterior lesions were much worse than either the controls or the animals with the larger anterior lesions. Thus, although the anterior lesions were twice as large as the posterior lesions, the animals with anterior lesions showed less behavioral loss. This finding goes against Lashley's principle of mass action.

The results appear to be interpretable in exactly the way in which Hebb predicted. Since the EC animals performed better on the whole, it appears that raising the animals in a free environment improved performance on problems such as the Hebb-Williams maze. Further, there appears to be a different effect of locus and size of brain lesion depending on the early environment in which the animal was raised. At this point, it would appear that Lashley's concept of mass action can be upheld only if one uses a maze which depends on many sensory modalities and on animal's having been raised in a restricted environment. The mind-body problem is an elusive one indeed. Yet, common sense, after the fact, can find itself in agreement with the results of this series of experimental explorations.

The Nature of the Memory Trace

In the chapter on behavioristic models we placed stress on the problem of memory. The question of how we manage to remember the myriad of events which have affected our experience is a question which has long fascinated man in his attempts to understand himself. The amount we remember is remarkable, and even more remarkable is the way in which we can search, purposefully, through our memory store and find some item of information which has been laid down in that store waiting, changed perhaps over time, for us to seek it out and use it. How easily we can make use of the idea of a memory store. It seems quite natural to speak that way, and yet it is the very notion of storehouse in which the memories are on file which has proved so difficult for biological psychologists to refer to actual functional units within the body. It is useful to divide the problem into three subproblems. First, we must somehow put information into the nervous system. But, the information seems, as we have said, to be much changed by the receptor systems and by the means of communication between the senses and the store. This poses a problem of just what sort of informational input we have to record after all. Secondly, there is the problem of where in the nervous system the memory trace *is* laid down. Finally, we must ask how it is that we are able to recall items from the memory banks of our storage, a challenging question which has seen very little research. We can ask questions about events which pop into our minds, uninvited as it were, and we can wonder why it is that some items resist our efforts to recall them and they reappear in our memories just when we have turned our minds away to something else.

These fascinating problems involve the question of what changes occur in the brain during learning or recording of experience, and then, what changes occur during recall. There are a number of possibilities: First, there is the question of whether the change in the organism is a dynamic one, that is, an ongoing part of a process, or whether the change is a static one. Put another way, we may ask whether the record of experience is simply an alteration of some activity in the nervous system such that the rate or rhythm or circuitry is changed or whether it is a structural change of a stable sort such that some part of the system undergoes a physical change by growing larger, or by developing new connections, or perhaps even by atrophying and being destroyed. One theorist, Ralph Gerard (1953), has espoused a static view of memory. He has likened the process to that of the calf muscles of the ballerina. When the dancer practices hard and long, these muscles reflect that experience by having grown larger and more powerful. So may the record of experience of a psychological sort be stored by structural changes in the nervous system.

On the other hand, as we have said, Hebb has argued that the fundamental mechanism of memory is the development of new functional pathways for ongoing activity. Activity is continuous in the nervous system, and when interconnections are changed, the records of experience are laid down. Actually, of course, the two theories have a similarity, in that the building up of connections must involve some structural change which is like that postulated by the static-change theorists such as Gerard. There is some evidence that it is unlikely that memory is held by continuous activity. An experimental situation and approach to the problem of the dynamics of memory is presented in Example 18–4.

Example 18–4 *The record of experience: Dynamic and flowing or static and fixed (Duncan, 1949)*

One experiment on the dynamic nature of memory used strong electric shock to disrupt the electrical activity of the brain. Carl Duncan (1949) trained eight groups of albino rats (a total of 120 rats) to avoid shock by running, on signal, from a grid box to a safe box. The groups were given strong electric shocks at different intervals after they completed each trial of training. The intervals were 20 seconds, 40 seconds, 60 seconds, 4 minutes, 15 minutes, 1 hour, 4 hours and 14 hours. The animals were given the shock to the head through electrodes attached at the ears. In a control group, the animals were shocked through the feet. The head shock resulted in convulsions on the part of the animals. Below 1 hour, the shorter the interval between training and shock, the poorer the performance of the animals which received the head shocks (see Figure 18–7). Duncan interpreted his results to indicate that newly learned material undergoes a period of consolidation and that up to 1 hour after a learning trial electroconvulsive shock can disrupt this process and thereby produce amnesia. This finding has been replicated by Gerard and others, but recent work has cast some doubt on the interpretation. For instance, Hunt and his coworkers have shown that electroshock given long periods after learning trials on bar pressing to avoid shock seems to cause a loss in ability to remember that the signal means that a shock is about to come but it does not impair performance on pressing the bar. The process of memory storage is a complex one indeed.

In a second example of the research on the nature of the memory trace Roger Sperry of the California Institute of Technology developed an interesting operative technique by which the brain of animals is divided into two separate parts. The method is usually referred to as the "split-brain preparation." We will consider one of Sperry's early experiments and the implications which it has for understanding nervous system function.

Example 18–5 *The split-brain preparation: The memory trace is stored in the cortex (Myers, 1961)*

Sperry and Myers (Myers, 1961) were interested in the question of whether memories were located in the cortex or in the lower parts of the brain. To that end, they used cats trained on visual discrimination problems as subjects. The animals were their own behavioral controls.

It is not difficult to train cats to learn a visual discrimination. Vision is an interesting modality to use, since the nervous pathways between the eyes and the brain are well known. As Figure 18–8 shows, each eye has a part of its retina which sends messages to each half of the brain. In the first experiment, Sperry and Myers cut the place where

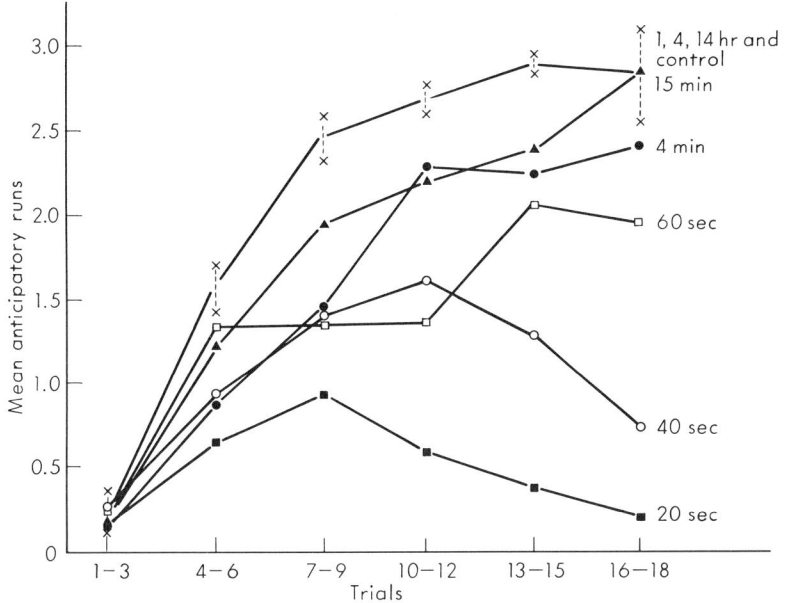

FIG. 18-7 Shocks and intervals. (*Duncan, 1949*)

the nerves from the eyes cross over, the *optic chiasma*, which makes each half of the brain a monocular system, in the sense that it receives information from only one eye.

Following the surgery, the experimenters covered one eye of their cats and trained them on a discrimination task. Then they changed the blindfold to the other eye and found that the animals were quite easily able to perform the learned response. Clearly the information necessary to perform was capable of moving from one hemisphere of the brain to the other. This suggested a second experiment, in which they not only cut the chiasma but also made a cut through the large tract of nerve fibers which runs between the two halves of the cortex—the corpus callosum. Now they repeated their procedures. Trained with one eye open and tested with the other eye, the second batch of cats *could not perform the learned response.* They were truly split-brained cats in a functional sense.

Sperry and Myers concluded that the locus of the memory trace for visual discrimination is in the cortex. Since the corpus callosum is a tract which carries fibers from the cortex of one hemisphere to the cortex of the other, cutting it interferes with communication between them but not with communication between the cortex and the lower brain. Thus, memory traces must be stored in the cortex.

The results, of course, do not decide the issue of whether the trace is a dynamic or a static one. Either type of system might be stored in the cortex.

The above discussion has briefly outlined the development of research on the external systems of the brain and the pathways by which information reaches them. Now we will turn to a consideration of research on the role of internal systems of the brain in behavior. As indicated above, Pribram suggested that the internal systems have to do with the regulatory functions of the brain in the maintenance of basic bodily conditions necessary for life, such as breathing and regulation of body temperature. In addition, these structures appear to play a role in control of activities which have a long time course, such as the emotional responses and the instinctive behaviors.

THE PHYSIOLOGY OF MOTIVATION

The theory of motivation advanced by Elliot Stellar (1954) has placed emphasis on the hypothalamus of the brain as the chief regulatory system in such behavior. In this respect, Stellar is a "locus theorist," in that he emphasizes the role of a particular

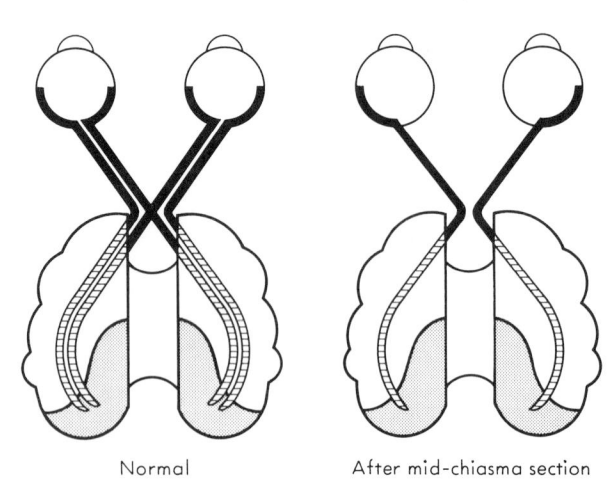

FIG. 18–8 The split-brain experiment. (*Myers, 1961*)

Normal | After mid-chiasma section

structure in the regulation of behavior. Stellar has underlined the fact that motivation involves more than sensory determinants and has suggested that some internal sources of programming of motives appear to be operating. Further, he has put forward the view that the amount of motivated behavior shown by an organism is a direct function of the amount of activity of neurons of certain excitatory and inhibitory centers of the *hypothalamus*.

In ascribing to such loci control over motivational activities Stellar makes the point that the state of excitement of these centers is the result of a combination of several sources of influence; that is, that they are integrating centers rather than initiators of function. The sources of influence which Stellar suggests are (1) sensory stimuli, which arise in the sense organs and send afferent impulses up to the brain, which ultimately reach the hypothalamus; (2) the internal environment, which influences the hypothalamus through blood supply to the hypothalamus, and the cerebrospinal fluid which also flows near the hypothalamus; (3) certain centers in the cerebral cortex and the thalamus of the midbrain which send excitatory and inhibitory influences to the hypothalamus; (4) centers in the hypothalamus itself which have an inhibitory function. Thus, the hypothalamus involves both inhibitory and excitatory centers which are influenced by outside agents including higher brain centers, the sense organs, and blood and other body fluids.

Figure 18–9 shows a simplified diagram of these relationships, modified so as to include all of the brain and to localize the regions within the central nervous system. We will not be able to consider all the evidence for the theory, but as we begin our discussion of motivated, cyclic, and emotional behaviors, we see that Stellar's scheme appears to describe the data quite well.

Emotional Behavior

A great deal of work has been done by psychologists on the emotions, beginning with the early descriptions by William James and others. However, we will limit our discussion in this section to a discussion of the role of brain centers in the control of emotional behavior.

THE EFFECT OF BRAIN DAMAGE ON EMOTIONAL BEHAVIOR It has been shown that emotional behavior is integrated at a number of different levels of the nervous system. The decerebrate preparation has been used to study this effect. If the central nervous system is transected above the midbrain, some emotional integration remains. There are both anger and rage behaviors. Transitory signs of rage are shown in handling, but they stop as soon as the stimulation stops. This kind of emotion has been called *pseudoaffective*. In general, when the animal is not being handled, it is asleep.

In the bulbar preparation the brain stem is transected below the midbrain. When this is done, there are no signs of emotional behavior, which indicates that the midbrain is capable of some emotional integration. The contribution of the dien-

FIG. 18–9 Schematic diagram of hypothalamus. (*Stellar, 1954*)

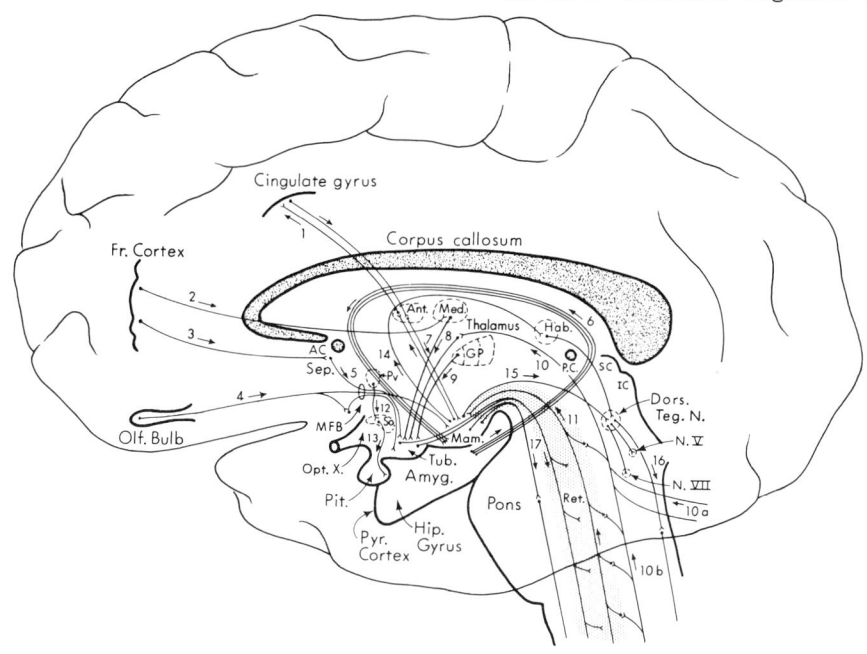

ABBREVIATIONS AND DESCRIPTION OF PATHWAYS

A.C.	= anterior commissure	MFB	= medial forebrain bundle
Amyg.	= amygdala	N. V	= motor nucleus, Vth nerve
Ant.	= anterior thalamic nuclei	N. VII	= motor nucleus, VIIth nerve
Cingulate Gyrus	= cortex of cingulate gyrus	Olf. Bulb	= olfactory bulb
		Opt. X	= optic chiasm
Dors. Teg. N.	= dorsal tegmental nucleus	P.C.	= posterior commissure
Fr. Cortex	= cortex of frontal lobe	Pit.	= pituitary gland
GP	= globus pallidus	Pv.	= paraventricular nucleus
Hab.	= habenular nucleus of thalamus	Pyr. Cortex	= pyriform cortex
		Ret.	= reticular formation
Hip. Gyrus	= hippocampal gyrus	SC	= superior colliculus
IC	= inferior colliculus	Sep.	= septal nuclei
Mam.	= mammillary nuclei	So.	= supraoptic nucleus
Med.	= dorsal medial thalamic nucleus	Tub.	= tuber cinereum

AFFERENTS TO HYPOTHALAMUS

1. Corticothalamic fibers
2. Frontothalamic fibers
3. Frontoseptal fibers
4. Olfacto-hypothalamic tract
5. Septo-hypothalamic fibers
6. Fornix
7. Mammillothalamic tract
8. Thalamo-hypothalamic fibers
9. Pallido-hypothalamic fibers
10. Sensory systems ascending to thalamus
    10a. cranial afferents
    10b. somatic and visceral afferents
11. Sensory collaterals to hypothalamus
12. Paraventriculo-supraoptic fibers

EFFERENTS TO HYPOTHALAMUS

13. Supraoptic hypophyseal tract
14. Mammillohabenular tract
15. Mammillotegmental tract
16. Dorsal longitudinal fasciculus
17. Descending efferents relaying in brain stem and medulla

cephalon has been studied by removing the cortex of the entire brain, leaving intact only the hypothalamus and thalamus. Under these conditions, there is a response known as sham rage. This is more than the pseudoaffective response found in the decerebrate animal. The response exhibits more direction and a lower threshold of response, and tends to outlast eliciting stimuli.

Walter B. Cannon (1929), a famous physiologist, stressed the role of the hypothalamus in the integration of emotional behavior. Later work with lesions of the central nervous system, electrical stimulation, and recording showed more integration in emotional behavior in animals with the hypothalamus intact than in animals with only the midbrain remaining. Various parts of the hypothalamus are important in rage behavior. A particularly important area in the hypothalamus—the ventromedial nucleus—is important in restraining rage as well as in restraining eating behavior. A lesion in the ventromedial area produces rage reactions. However, such reactions have direction only if the cortex of the brain is intact.

Example 18–6 *Role of the cerebral cortex in emotion (Jacobsen, 1939)*

The role of the cerebral cortex in emotional behavior has been explored in a series of experiments which date as far back as the last century, but only beginning in the 1930s has extensive behavioral work been done. Jacobsen (1939) used problem-solving situations to explore the effects on emotional responses of ablation of the frontal parts of the brains of monkeys. Since monkeys usually show a high degree of emotionality when they fail to solve problems, the choice of such a task was an appropriate one.

After the frontal operations, the animals seemed to care less about the outcomes of their actions. They rarely displayed anger at "frustrating" situations. Such anger as they did display was not prolonged. As a matter of fact, however, their actual performance on the problems was not much impaired.

In early work on human beings, a Portuguese psychologist, Moniz, treated emotionally disturbed patients by performing operations on their brains which interrupted connections between the lower brain and the frontal association areas of the cortex. When partial isolation is achieved by cutting connecting fibers, the operation is called a *lobotomy*. If the lobes are removed, we speak of a *lobectomy*. The results of these procedures appeared to produce improvement on the part of a number of patients who had previously exhibited psychotic behaviors. There followed a period in which extensive use was made of the technique. Now, however, the development of tranquilizing drugs has greatly lessened the use of lobotomy. Work on animals, however, has continued.

Several generalizations may be made about the effects of ablation of the cortex of animals. If only the neocortex, which is that part of the brain which has evolved most recently, is removed, the animals become placid and show little emotional response. On the other hand, if the phylogenetically old cortex is ablated, animals show rage reactions which have a very low threshold of elicitation. If one observes the patterns of emotions of animals at different levels of the phylogenetic scale, the patterns seem quite similar. This strongly suggests that emotions are served by a part of the nervous system which is relatively similar throughout the phylogenetic group. One such common set of structures is the *limbic system*, which is a part of the internal brain in Pribram's terms. It changes little throughout the scale of mammalian development. Figure 18–10 shows the structures which make up the limbic system.

In an early theory of emotions, Papez (1937) suggested that the hypothalamus and limbic system integrate emotional behavior. He examined evidence such as the fact that the disease rabies leads to lesions in the hippocampus of animals. This suggests that the emotional symptoms of the disease are based on the lesions and implicates the hippocampus in emotional behavior. Also, there is a difference between the sexes in the development of the cingulate gyrus. This difference may be the basis for sexual differences in emotionality. When there are tumors in this region, the patient shows marked changes in his emotional behaviors. Further, it has been shown that removal of the base of the temporal lobe of the cortex leads to decreased rage behavior and increased sexuality. If, on the other hand, lesions are made in the hippocampus, or ventromedial nucleus of the hypothalamus, in-

FIG. 18–10 A schematic view of the limbic system. (*MacLean, 1950*)

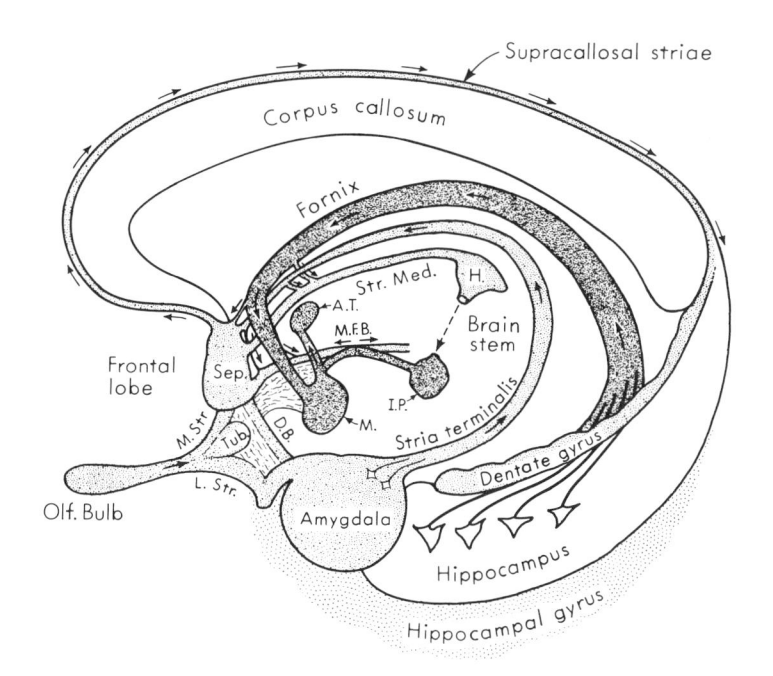

ABBREVIATIONS

A.T. = anterior nucleus of thalamus
D.B. = diagonal band of Broca
H. = habenula (a part of the epithalamus)
I.P. = interpeduncular nucleus
L. Str. = lateral olfactory stria
M. = mammillary body (a part of the posterior hypothalamus)
M.F.B. = medial forebrain bundle
M. Str. = medial olfactory stria
Olf. Bulb = olfactory bulb
Sep. = region of the septal nuclei
Str. Med. = stria medullaris
Tub. = olfactory tubercle (head of the caudate immediately underneath)

creased rage behavior is observed. All this evidence points, quite convincingly, to some control of emotional behavior by the limbic system.

Brain Stimulation and Motivation

In the early 1950s a set of studies by James Olds seemed to add even more weight to the idea that the limbic system was the mediator of emotions and, further, that it was involved in the process by which behavior is reinforced.

Example 18–7 *Brain stimulation as reinforcement (Olds & Milner, 1954)*

While working at McGill University, James Olds and Peter Milner (1954) made an interesting discovery about the brain. They were interested in the mechanisms of arousal and attention and had put fine electrodes into the brains of rats. One electrode was located in the septal area of the limbic system, and in the case of that animal they noticed that it seemed to enjoy the electrical stimulation. In a fine example of serendipity, they acted upon their hunch and soon discovered that they could use a shock to the brain as a reinforcement to shape the animal's behavior. Thus, if they placed the animal in an open field and administered brain shocks only when the animal was in one corner of the field, they soon had the rat spending all his time in that part of the apparatus. Figure 18–11 shows an x-ray picture of an electrode in place in a rat.

When the spot was located where the tip of the electrode had been placed, it was found to be in the limbic system. Olds followed up his first observations by placing many electrodes in many rats, each in a different location. He thus was able to map the brain for "pleasure" areas. Some of the structures which were "positive" were areas of the hypothalamus which are known to control digestive, sexual, and excretory processes. In addition, stimulating the limbic system also produced rewarding effects.

But the question remained: Is intracranial stimulation (ICS) really reinforcing? To answer this, Olds made use of the Skinner box. In the special situation he constructed, the animal was placed in an enclosure which contained a bar which when pressed delivered a small shock to the brain. The beauty of this experiment was that it forced the animal to do work to obtain the shock and presumably the

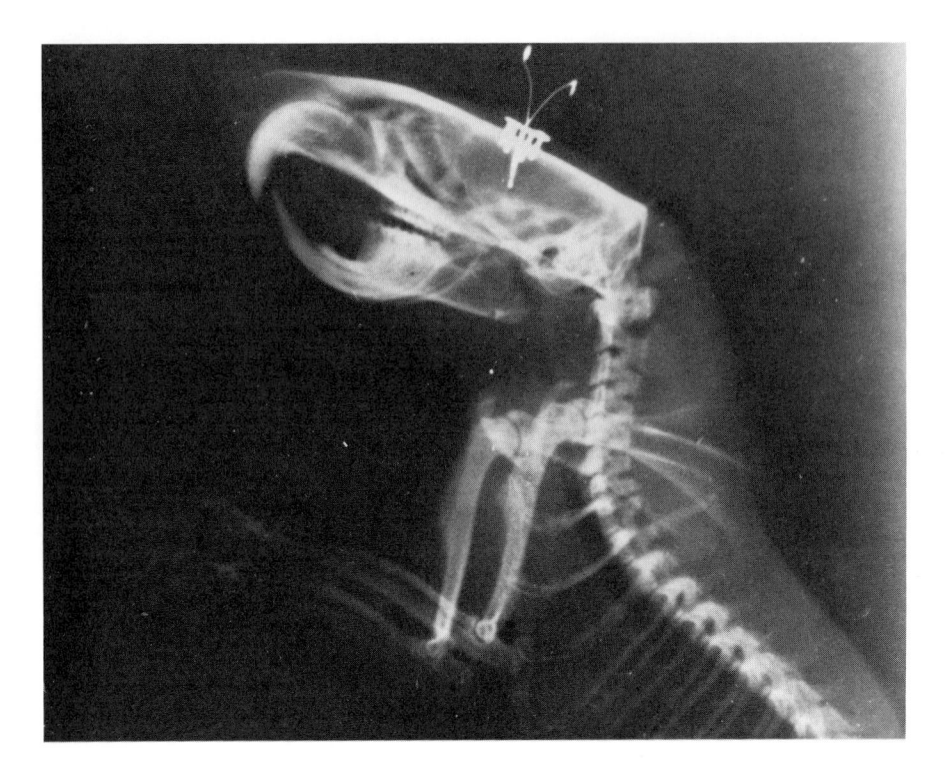

FIG. 18–11 X-ray of implanted electrode in intact rat. (*Olds, personal communication*)

pleasure of the reinforcement. If the animals would in fact press at rapid rates, they could be assumed to be reinforcing themselves with the shock.

The results were striking. Depending on the spot in the brain where the electrodes were placed, the animals would press at rates well above the rates of unoperated rats, with no other reinforcement than ICS. In fact, some rats, observed by Olds, pressed at the rate of 2,000 times an hour for twenty-four hours, a remarkable rate of responding indeed. ICS can only be assumed to be reinforcing, but it was not clear to Olds just how ICS compared with normal reinforcers. To explore this question, he compared the speed at which animals would run in order to receive ICS as against a food reward. More than twice as many of his animals ran faster to get to ICS than to food when they were run in a straight alley. When animals were run in a complex maze, both ICS and food resulted in faster running. However, at this point there appeared the first of many paradoxical effects of the ICS situation. It turned out that animals reinforced with ICS would regress considerably overnight on the maze problem. That is, they seemed to show a good deal of forgetting of the fact that there was a reinforcement at the end of the maze. Animals run for food did not show this loss.

There also appears to be an interaction of sexual behavior and ICS. The method used to study the relationship involved removing the sexual organs of rats and supplying sex hormones, androgens, by injection. When electrodes are placed in the caudate nucleus and used to administer ICS, there appears to be an interaction between the levels of the sex hormones in the animal and the willingness of the animal to work to obtain ICS. At first, after castration, the animal decreases the rate of responding for shocks in the caudate nucleus. However, when the sex hormones are replaced by in-

336 BIOLOGICAL MODELS

jection, the rate of responding for ICS goes up. Thus it appears that the ability of brain stimulation to act as a reinforcer in certain areas depends on the level of sexual hormones in the animal. Further, there appears to be a negative correlation between the effects of hunger and sex-hormonal level on the rate of responding for ICS. It appears that the sex drive and hunger drive interact within the brain in a negative way.

With further experimental work, the explanation of the Olds effect has become even more difficult. There are a number of paradoxical effects of ICS in addition to the regression of performance in the maze which we mentioned above. Miller and his coworkers at Yale (Delgado, Roberts, & Miller, 1954) were able to show that some areas of the brain could be used to establish avoidance responses to ICS. Their technique involved the implantation of multiple electrodes in cats, so that with one electrode implant it was possible to stimulate the animals at a number of different levels. When their animals were stimulated in the midbrain, the animals proved to be reluctant to return to the experimental apparatus. Now that fact in itself is not enough to prove that ICS is a negative motivator. It might be that the stimulation of the diencephalon simply resulted in emotional responses and that all that was happening was that the animal was going through the motions of being emotionally aroused; actually it was not "involved" emotionally. However, Miller's animals showed learning, which indicated that the effect was more than the simple elicitation of motor movement.

Miller and several of his students have gone on to the exploration of further fearlike reactions which are elicited by ICS. There are several areas of the midbrain where such reactions can be elicited. The reactions appear to have "drive properties." Using ICS in these areas, it is possible to teach animals to escape and to avoid ICS. Thus the animals could be trained to make instrumental responses which led to the cessation of the brain shock, or they could be taught to respond to avoid the onset of ICS. But Roberts (1958) was able to show that in different areas of the brain there were different reaction patterns of escape and avoidance. In some areas, ICS could be used to train animals both to escape and to avoid. In other locations, the animals could be taught only to escape, not avoid. It appeared possible that there was a double reaction to stimulation in some of the areas negative to ICS. Perhaps the onset of the ICS produced a positive effect, and the continuance of the stimulation produced a negative effect. The duration of ICS seemed to be important.

Clearly, the mechanisms of reinforcement by stimulation of the brain are not yet fully understood, but the discovery and exploration of the ICS effect has done a good deal to support the notion that the brain has specific areas which are responsible for specific functions. Further, the close relationship between the loci in which the ICS effect is found and the areas responsible for motivational behavior seems to provide a new source of evidence for the role of motivation in the learning of behavior.

Cyclic Changes in Behavior: Sleep and Wakefulness

Although many of us never consider it in quite that light, much of our behavior *is* cyclic, in that there are periods in which we engage in the behavior and other periods in which we do not. Of the cyclic behaviors, some are quite regular in their cycles, and others have an irregular pattern. For example, most of us sleep and are awake with a remarkable degree of constancy. It would be surprising to find a person who did not have a kind of biological clock which determined when he slept and when he was awake. Since sleep occupies about one-third of our lifetime, many psychologists and biologists have devoted a good deal of research to the problem of how and why we sleep.

From the viewpoint of physiological psychology, research on sleep has taken two paths: one line has concerned itself with the mechanisms in the central nervous system which are the control centers for sleep and wakefulness; other research has been directed to the content of dreams and their relation to physiological manifestations such as the way in which the electrical activity of the brain changes during such periods.

One of the signal contributions to an understanding of the role of the brain in sleep and wakefulness was made by Moruzzi and Magoun (1949), who explored the mechanisms of arousal by placing electrodes into the midbrain and the cortex of animals. The electrodes were mounted so that they could be used both when the animals were asleep and when they were awake. In addition, the electrodes were

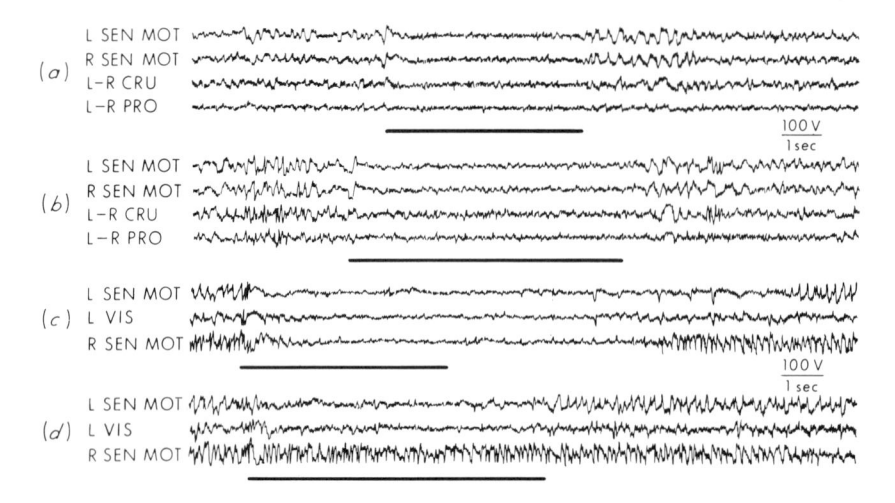

FIG. 18-12 EEG showing the effect of stimulation. (*Moruzzi and Magnum, 1949*)

designed to be used both to stimulate the brain by passing a very small electrical current through the brain and also to record electrical activity which arises in the brain spontaneously. They found that stimulation of the midbrain of a drowsy cat resulted in arousal of the animal, and, in addition, the brain waves of the animal were changed to a pattern which is usually seen in aroused animals. If an awake animal was stimulated, the animal showed an alerting reaction and an activation pattern in its brain waves, or *electroencephalogram* (EEG), as it is called. Figure 18-12 shows an EEG. If an animal is aroused by an external source of stimulation, such as a sound, the activation pattern first appears in the midbrain, which is a very complex region of nerve cells. Moruzzi and Magoun called this region of arousal the *reticular activating system.*

In addition to the activity of the brain which is recorded on the EEG, as will be recalled from Section II, there is another behavioral attribute of sleep which has been much studied recently; the ocular motor activity of the sleeping person. A sleeping person can be equipped with electrodes which will record his eye movements. When this is done, it is found that during the sleep periods in which there is a mixture of low-voltage, irregular, relatively fast waves on the EEG—the first stage of sleeping—there is an associated occurrence of rapid eye movements (REMs). These REMs are quite similar to the purposive eye movements which are associated with visual perception when the person is awake. Both eyes are involved in synchronous movements which are much like the movements made during changes in fixation when the person is awake.

Up to this point, our discussion has centered on the nervous system as the mediator of behavior. But, in addition to studies of the bioelectric message and the neuron and brain in physiological research of behavior, there has been a good deal of work on a second type of message within the body: the biochemical. As we shall see in the next chapter, there has developed an understanding that the neural and hormonal systems are not independent factors in behavior, but form a cooperative system.

CHAPTER 19

PHYSIOLOGICAL PSYCHOLOGY II: CHEMICAL SYSTEMS AND BEHAVIOR

Although we devoted the last chapter to a survey of the role of the nervous system in behavior, it is an error to think that only the nervous system plays a role in the regulation of behavior. There is a second major group of systems which play a role in behavior: the biochemical systems. The study of these systems is assuming a new prominence in psychology and biology, at least in part because of the very great advances which have recently been made in our understanding of biochemistry and also because of the recent emphasis on chemical forms of therapy, which has changed the very nature of care of the mentally ill.

In our study of biochemical systems and their role in behavior, we will first continue our analysis of the transmission of information within the body, this time considering chemical mediators of behavior: the hormones, the neural transmitter chemicals, and the chemical codes for information storage in the nervous system. Then we will turn to a consideration of the effect on behavior of chemicals which are introduced into the body. Our survey will include such factors as stimulants, tranquilizers, and the new hallucinogenic compounds.

INTERNAL BIOCHEMICAL SYSTEMS

Hormonal Systems

The most important of the mediators of biochemical messages in the body are substances called *hormones* which are secreted into the bloodstream by the endocrine glands. Considered from an evolutionary viewpoint, the endocrines are the result of the process of organism growth and increased complexity. In small unspecialized organisms, such as the amoeba, chemical communication is mediated by simple diffusion of materials. However, as animals become larger and more specialized, greater distances and more specific effects are involved. These facts pose problems, since the use of the bloodstream as a means of communication involves a good deal of inefficiency, and the organ which is to be affected may receive only a small portion of a secreted chemical.

To understand how the body solves this problem, we may compare two rather loose analogies: If we consider the nervous system as a kind of complex telephone hookup, involving direct lines between different places, we may consider the hormonal system to be more like a speech made to a crowd.

Even though the message of the speaker reaches everyone, specificity may still be obtained if the speaker and a selected hearer both know a special code. In a rough way, this is how the hormonal system works. Each hormone has target organs which are especially sensitive to it. For example, a gland connected to the brain releases follicle-stimulating hormone (FSH) into the blood. The hormone is spread throughout the body and reaches the ovaries, which are its target. Under the influence of the hormone, an egg matures and the female ovulates. Whatever other organs are reached by FSH are not affected. Because of this diffuse spread and wastage, the hormones must be very powerful in their action, and the target organ must be very sensitive. In general, the effects of the hormones are regulatory in function. They regulate the rates of certain processes, but they do not furnish material for the energy required for the process.

During the nineteenth century, medical observations led to this discovery of hormones. It was noticed that certain disease conditions were related to pathological conditions of glands. For instance, goiter is related to a pathological condition of the thyroid gland in the neck. Removal of diseased thyroids results in thyroid deficiency which had to be treated by feeding thyroid tissue from another animal. These facts suggest that something secreted by the thyroid is important in normal health. Further, a type of mental retardation called cretinism can be helped if thyroid tissue is fed early enough in life, which suggests that the thyroid has something to do with the growth process. In a similar way, when the pancreas is removed, the symptoms of diabetes mellitus occur. This fact was discovered incidentally with work which was done on the role of the pancreas in digestion and implies that the pancreas has functions other than the one of replacing digestive juices.

Work with the gonads furthered concepts about the chemical transfer of information. Early workers used chickens and discovered that castrated chickens, or capons, will keep their combs if testicular tissue is transplanted elsewhere into their body. Work with the transplantation of gonadal tissue indicated that some organs secrete into the blood some substances which are necessary to normal health. Ivan Pavlov, whose work on learning we discussed in Chapter 13, thought that pancreatic secretion of enzymes was neurally controlled. But he discovered that, even with transection of nervous innervation, the pancreas would still secrete if food was in the intestines. In addition, injection of an extract from the small intestines which had been recently stimulated with food into a host animal resulted in pancreatic secretion. The substance obtained from the small intestine was called *secretin*. In 1902, Starling proposed the word *hormone* for such a stimulating substance.

There is a great deal of similarity in the basic hormonal systems from fish through the higher mammals to men. For instance, insulin, which is involved in the control of sugar metabolism, can be derived from animals and used for human medical purposes.

Our general discussion of hormonal systems can serve as a background for a consideration of a specific process of chemical control within the body, namely, that involved in hunger and thirst. As we shall see, there has been a good deal of research on just how the body accomplishes control of these phenomena. The answer will turn out to be a complex one.

Mechanisms of Hunger and Thirst

As with many of the processes of the body which we have examined, there have been a series of hypotheses about the mechanisms of hunger and thirst. The major question, in this area, concerns the manner in which the nervous system learns about an internal deficit and sets about correcting it. We will examine several of these theories.

The first hypothesis we will consider is called the *local* theory of hunger and thirst. This theory assumes quite simply and directly that a message from the stomach goes to the brain stem and that information is ultimately transmitted to the cortex. For example, in the case of thirst, dryness of the mouth results in a message to the brain. The second theory is called the *general* theory of the origin of hunger and thirst. It holds that most of the tissues of the body are affected by hunger and thirst. This peripheral deficit is monitored and a message conveyed to the central nervous system about the condition of body tissues. The third hypothesis, called the *central* hypothesis, states that some specific part of the nervous system continually "samples" for the presence of food and water in the circulatory system. There has been a historical progress in the development of these three theories. First the local theory was advanced, then the general theory, and finally the central theory. Quite possibly there may be more than one mechanism at work.

One might suggest that there is a feedback control of hunger and thirst. That is, in eating and drinking, there is some control system which prevents large fluctuations in the condition of the organism much like the control systems we have already discussed. Of course, these feedback systems do not always work perfectly. Sometimes people become overweight or underweight. Various conditions sometimes lead to destruction of the feedback system. Further, some animals may not select the right diets and thus become vulnerable to pathology.

Although it is clear that many sources of external stimulation play a role in the eating and drinking behavior of organisms, many internal factors also play a role. Exploration of such changes has been accomplished under the rubric of specific hungers.

SPECIFIC HUNGERS There has been a good deal of interest in physiological psychology in this area, which has a certain taint of the bizarre because of its association with the often idiosyncratic eating habits of pregnant women. Many of us have had some experience with specific hungers. People will report that they can "almost taste" something they desire. With the wisdom of the marketplace, advertising men present billboards and display ads designed to induce such hungers and even to portray occasions in which they occur. How often we see in a newspaper a smiling face, redolent with satisfaction, with a dream, shown above the face, depicting something it finds marvelously desirable. The ad men clearly think such scenes are believable and that they will influence the reader.

Psychologists interested in the biology of motivation recognize that specific hungers are very central to the general problem of control of food intake. Often, this is discussed in terms of general caloric balance. The idea is that the amount we eat is somehow controlled by the amount of energy we burn up. The notion of caloric balance suggested the idea that there was one essential nutrient, much like a fuel which we required, the particular source being immaterial. In order to provide the energy for life, anything which contained energy could be eaten in any combination, and the requirements would be well met. But, by the end of the last century, it became apparent that there were many specific requirements for an adequate diet. By now, with massive educational efforts to disseminate this information, we are all aware that we must take in vitamins, minerals, and certain amino acids each day, or we will lack these essentials, to our detriment.

Out of this physiological research area emerged a fascinating psychological problem: Are there mechanisms which specifically monitor the balance of certain substances within the body, and does the information obtained influence the behavior of the organism? Early research on specific hungers led to observations on the behavioral effects of removal of the glands on the body. For instance, it was observed that removal of the parathyroid gland, in cases of tumors or hypertrophy, led to an avidity for foods which contain calcium. On the other hand, such persons avoid foods containing phosphorus. Along that line, an early textbook on animal husbandry shows a very starved-looking cow eating an enormous bone. The caption under the picture attributed the behavior to a need for calcium in the animal. Certainly, the general condition of the beast appeared so poor that the animal probably needed everything. But the writer of the book clearly was aware of specific hungers and dietary requirements. In another early study a second instance of specific hungers was observed, when the adrenal cortex of animals was removed. Such animals may compensate for the fact that they now excrete sodium very rapidly by increasing their sodium intake. The behavioral problem has been more systematically explored in a series of experiments which we will consider as a single example of research in this area.

Example 19-1 *Salt balance in adrenalectomized animals (Richter & Eckert, 1938)*

In order to explore one specific hunger, that for salt, Richter and Eckert removed the adrenal glands from rats and placed them in cages where they had access to both water and a saline solution. They observed, as others had before them, that adrenalectomy resulted in an increase in the apparent preference of the animals for the concentrations of salt; that is, they drank more saline solution. Richter and Eckert attributed the increased intake of salty water to an increase in the sensitivity of the receptors of the animal which monitored sodium level. They based their theory on the fact that the operated animals would choose successfully between a concentration of salt and water when the difference was so small that a normal animal was not able to make a discrimination between the two concentrations. Further, they found that when the nerves to the tongue of adrenalectomized animals were cut, the animals could no longer discriminate between the saline solution and water. But there are problems in Richter and Eckert's theory. If the adrenalectomized animals were more sensitive to salt, they should have been satisfied more easily when drinking saline solutions. It would appear that they were receiving a good deal more stimulation from the salty water than from the plain water, and this fact should have slowed down their intake in much the same way that richer foods seem to be more filling when we eat. On the other hand, if the animals were more sensitive to salt, strong solutions of salt should have repelled them in the way that strong concentrations of other substances do.

Pfaffman and Bare, using electrode recording techniques (1950), undertook a direct test of the Richter and Eckert hypothesis that the tongue of the adrenalectomized animal is more sensitive to sodium than that of the normal animal. They placed recording electrodes on the sensory nerves which come from the tongue and attempted to determine directly the thresholds for saline solutions. That is, they asked whether there was any difference in the messages to the brain from the tongue when saline solutions of different concentrations were placed on the tongue. Unfortunately, their results were negative, in the sense that the thresholds for both adrenalectomized and normal animals were the same. There was a threshold response at a salt concentration of .01%. This concentration turns out to be about that value at which Richter's adrenalectomized rats were first able to show a preference for saline solution over water. Pfaffman and Bare concluded that peripheral or sense organ sensitivity for salt does not seem to be altered by adrenalectomy. Thus the Richter and Eckert hypothesis does not appear to be tenable. The effect of adrenalectomy is to cause rapid excretion of sodium, but the loss of sodium evidently does not lead to greater sensitivity of sense organs.

As a result of the experiment in Example 19–1, the decrease-in-receptor-sensitivity hypothesis for specific hungers does not seem tenable. However, several other interesting questions may be asked about the way in which specific hungers operate. Continuing with the case of the adrenalectomized animal, we may ask whether these animals make discriminations between salt and water because of the beneficial effect of sodium, which they require in order to live, and whether the sodium is therefore somehow rewarding to them or whether they drink salt solutions as a result of the effects on the central nervous system. Perhaps these changes can occur in intake without the animal's having to learn. It would be as if the animal underwent an adjustment in the part of central nervous system responsible for diet selection and simply acted on the new schedule of preferences. We ordinarily prefer a sweet to a bitter taste; it may be that the effect of adrenalectomy is to change this "liking" pattern for salt concentrations.

Investigation of preferences in animals has usually, as we have noted, been done with the so-called two-bottle situation. But there are several strong criticisms to be made of that behavior test. Usually, the animal samples from both bottles. Since the effect of salt solutions takes some time and any reward due to the beneficial effects of sodium will reinforce drinking from both bottles, it is difficult to see how the animal could be associating the "good feeling" of drinking sodium-containing solutions with the correct bottle. Therefore, the two-bottle situation does not allow one to explain the increased intake of sodium as being due to learning. A rather creative and ingenious approach to the problem using modern technology was developed by Elliot Stellar, and his experiment is presented in Example 19–2.

Example 19–2 *Internal sampling for sodium: The ion-exchange experiment (Stellar et al., 1954)*

In this experiment, Stellar and his coworkers made use of ion-exchange resins that had been developed for use in water purification and other industrial applications in which it is desirable to remove sodium ions. The experimenters reasoned that these resins would affect animals to which they had been fed by binding free sodium and releasing calcium and other ions. Therefore, when animals were fed the resins, the amount of sodium in their systems would be radically reduced. About half of the salt which an animal takes in its diet cannot be used if the animal has been fed these resins.

The researchers asked the question, will feeding animals ion-exchange resins change their intake of salt? That is, they asked whether there is some way in which internal deficits were monitored either at the cellular level or at the level of the blood and whether such information could be used to influence the consummatory behavior of the animals. Both adrenalectomized and normal rats were used.

The results were quite clear. Normal animals did not alter their sodium intake after they were fed the resins. In sharp contrast, the adrenalectomized animals increased the amount of saline they drank from 11 to 18 cc of 3% saline solution after being fed resin. After the resin was removed from the diet, the adrenalectomized animals did not, however, return to the level of salt consumption which they had shown before the resin was placed in their diet. This finding may be interpreted as evidence for learning, or it may reflect some temporal effect of adrenalectomy.

The ion-exchange experiment is a nice illustration of how a long-standing problem can be solved through the development of technical methods and their application by creative researchers. The reader may have many questions about interpretation of the findings, but there is no doubt that somehow the resins led the adrenalectomized animals to drink more saline solution. Whether we can finally decide that the effect indicates central control of sodium level or whether in some yet undiscovered way the resin has a selective effect on the adrenalectomized animals which makes sodium consumption reinforcing, the fact remains that the experiment clarifies the issue of specific hungers as motivators by referring the behavior to some internal state which is monitored, as Stellar's theory requires, and which can be used to direct behavior.

From this brief consideration of feeding and drinking behavior, we will turn to a second complex consummatory behavior, sexual behavior, which involves both internal cues and external cues for its initiation.

Sexual Behavior

A variety of research data indicates that an excitatory center in the *hypothalamus of the brain* is implicated in sexual behavior. If we destroy a certain region of the hypothalamus, there is a cessation of mating, and replacement therapy with hormones does not lead to a resumption of sexual activity. There are two ways in which this may occur: lesions that directly affect sexual activity through effects on nervous tissue alone and secondary effects in which lesions affect the output of glands responsible for the release of the sexual hormones. There is also evidence of an inhibitory center whose locus is not yet clearly established.

In addition to these central nervous system effects, there are internal environment effects upon mating behavior. There is a strong indication that gonadal hormones are important in activating patterns which are already organized in the nervous systems of animals. If one injects sex hormones into young animals, the sexual pattern will appear. If an injection into the female sex organs is given during a period when a female is not in heat, she will come into heat. If sex hormones are injected in seasonally mating males such as rams during their quiescent period, they will become sexually active. And finally, if hormones are injected into gonadectomized animals, they will become sexually active. There is some evidence that within a species there are large individual differences in the sex drive. Experiments have shown that these individual differences are not due only to hormonal levels. It is possible to breed animals selectively for high or low sexual activity. Further, in the primates and in dogs and cats, castration of an experienced male animal may not result in cessation of sexual activity.

Beyond the factors we have mentioned there are sensory factors which are important in the control of sexual behavior. In many species the reactions of the male depend on the external environment. If the environment is unfamiliar, there may be a decreased amount of mating. The presence of a receptive female will frequently lead to initiation of sexual activity. Further, negative conditioning can occur which will disrupt sexual activity. But stimuli which have been associated with mating in the past will elicit mating reactions anew. Finally, the amount of learning involved in sexual behaviors differs across species. In rats the mating animal can function normally without previous experience, but in monkeys there is a period of trial-and-error learning.

Emotional Behavior

Few areas of psychology have engendered as much disagreement and controversy as the study of the emotions. We all use the term "emotional," yet few of us are able to define the emotions in a way which clearly delineates precisely what emotional states are. Because of this problem of definition, the area has been marked by a good deal of polemics. Hazy definition has not, however, kept researchers from the study of the relationship of the emotions to body chemistry, and it is to this subarea of the study of the emotions that we will limit ourselves in this section. It is usually known as *psychosomatics*.

We all know that our emotional state of mind is correlated with certain chemical states of our body. Just before an important event, such as an examination, an interview, or a speech, we all experience some bodily reaction to the stress. The effect may be slight, as a mild sweating of our palms, or it may take the form of queasy stomach or even violent nausea. While anyone will admit to these short-term changes, he may be less convinced that psychological processes have effects on the body that are long-term or permanent. Such effects are the province of psychosomatic medicine. Although work in this field has been going on for some time, it is only in the present century that experimental evidence has been presented which convincingly demonstrates this interrelationship of mind and body.

In Example 19–3, the work of one of the most famous pioneers of modern physiology is outlined—Walter Cannon's work on the interrelationship between the emotions and the body, which led to modern conceptions of psychosomatics.

Example 19–3 *The bodily reactions of animals to threat (Cannon, 1929)*

As a result of a long series of experiments, Walter Cannon concluded that an animal which was faced with a situation that evoked pain, rage, or fear responded not only with overt behavioral actions but also with a complex set of internal physiological adjustments. These adjustments prepared the animal to meet the threatening situation with "fight" or "flight." As Cannon recognized, these reactions were mobilized by the secretions into the blood of the hormone epinephrine, which was then carried to various loci in the body where it activated certain behaviors. Cannon held that the sight of a threatening stimulus caused the brain of the animal to send a message down to the adrenal glands, which then secreted the hormone.

The pattern of the reaction is as follows: respiration deepens; the heart beats faster; the pressure of the blood rises; the blood is shifted away from the stomach and intestines to the central nervous system, and muscles; digestive processes cease; the liver releases its reserve of sugar into the blood; the spleen discharges blood corpuscles into the vascular system; and the adrenal glands secrete epinephrine into the blood.

Cannon argued that this complex pattern of reactions could be understood by relating the transformation to the actions which an animal takes when it is faced with threat: escaping the stimulus by running away, or attacking in order to dominate the threat. Further, he argued that this pattern of physiological change is clearly preparatory for either flight or fight. The addition of stored sugar provides the energy needed for the muscular effort required in the struggle. Also, the effect is to increase the coagulation rate of the blood, which is of obvious value if the animal is wounded. An increase in rate of circulation coupled with a higher red blood cell count increases the amount of oxygen which is contained in the blood, thereby providing the brain and other parts of the body with the basis for increased activity.

Not all these complex physiological effects are due to the action of epinephrine alone. A second hormone is also secreted from the same source, the adrenal medulla: this is called norepinephrine. In contrast to epinephrine, which has diffuse effects, norephinephrine appears to have a very specific effect: it causes the contraction of the fine blood vessels, or capillaries, in the skin and in other organs, and thereby increases the resistance to the flow of blood through the vascular system. Of course, this results in higher arterial blood pressure, but it also lessens the danger from damage to the skin, since bleeding is decreased and the size of the vessels which must clot is reduced. Again, the action is preparatory to the struggle that the animal must face.

Combining these physiological considerations with some conceptions from dynamic psychology, particularly those of Sigmund Freud on the role of unconscious processes in behavior, Daniel Funkenstein et al. (1954) have attempted to relate physiological processes to the expression of fear and anger in man. We will consider an example of his theory and work in Example 19–4 and then turn to a second approach to the effects of emotion-producing stimuli on the body and on behavior.

Example 19–4 *Bodily concommitants of fear and anger in man (Funkenstein, King, & Drolette, 1954)*

Working at the Harvard Medical School, Funkenstein and his coworkers observed that patients who were classed as psychotic or deeply disturbed and who had high blood pressure could be separated into two distinct groups on the basis of the way in which they reacted when injected with a drug which stimulates the nervous system in a way which is opposite to the effect of epinephrine. One group of patients showed a long-lasting and marked drop in blood pressure; the others showed only a slight effect. Further, the two groups showed two other differences: they responded to treatment differently, and they showed a different pattern of responses on psychological tests such as the Rorschach inkblot projective test.

To Funkenstein these observations suggested that the patients might have different underlying emotional states. On the basis of independent analyses by psychiatrists, the patients could indeed be sorted into two groups: those who felt strong anger directed at other people, that is, outwardly directed anger, and those who were usually depressed or frightened, or whose emotional maladjustments were directed inward. In general, there was a high degree of correlation between the type of emotion exhibited by the patient and the reaction he showed to the drug. Patients who showed outward anger did not show much effect of the drug on blood pressure. However, patients who were depressed showed sharp lowering of blood pressure. It could be concluded that the physiological reactions of the two groups of patients were related to the emotional content of their psychoses.

Further work with normal people, medical students and college undergraduates supported these findings. In general, when a person shows anger directed outward, his reactions are like those produced by an injection of norepinephrine. When a person shows fear, his pattern of physiological responses is like those which result from an injection of epinephrine. This outcome is the same if different groups are studied which exhibit different emotions or if one person is observed at different times when he is exhibiting the two different states. It appears that the physiological state is specific for the emotion and perhaps that the mode of adaptation of an individual is related to the dominant physiological mechanism by which he responds to stress.

In our discussion, we have introduced the concept of a stressful situation without further exploring the nature of the pattern of reactions which individuals show when they are stressed. However, one group of research workers, under the leadership of Hans Selye (1950), working at the University of Montreal, has been studying the complex way in which the human being and certain animals respond to prolonged periods of stress. Perhaps the best way to illustrate the manner in which Selye's conceptions have evolved from those of Walter Cannon is to present Selye's system as an example and then to follow that presentation with a particularly interesting experimental finding which concerns the effects of prolonged physical stress on endocrine activity.

Example 19–5 *The alarm reaction: The responses of the organism to stress (Selye, 1950)*

In their study of the effects of stress on the physiology of animals, Selye's group has been concerned with a consideration of the organism as a system which responds as a whole. They have recognized that the living organism consists of separate subsystems, such as those which control salt balance, hormonal level, and energy reserves; but also they have pointed out that an animal which undergoes an unusual threat from outside itself responds as a whole, not in terms of these separate systems.

From studies which explored the effects of severe injury or prolonged noxious stimulation upon the physiology of animals, Selye has discovered that animals respond to such situations with patterns of change which are similar even when the types of damage, danger, or stressful stimulation vary a good deal. There are three major facets of the syndrome: the adrenal glands greatly increase in size and change in color from yellow to brown, the thymus gland atrophies, and the stomach lining shows bleeding ulcers. Selye called this pattern the "alarm reaction" (AR).

Working with several stress-producing situations, Selye discovered that it is the outer part of the adrenal gland which secretes several hormones mediating the AR. The outside part of the adrenal gland, called its cortex, secretes hormones which control the composition of body cells by retaining salts, especially sodium, in the solutions outside the cells. Perhaps the most important of these hormones is deoxycorticosterone, usually abbreviated DCA. In addition, adrenocorticohormone acts to convert protein into sugar, which is needed for energy.

But the adrenal cortex is under the control of another gland: the master gland, or pituitary. By secreting a hormone which stimulates the adrenal cortex into activity, the pituitary ultimately controls the AR. This has been proved by surgically removing the pituitary. When this is done, the adrenal cortex atrophies and becomes inactive. No AR occurs. It was concluded by Selye that acute stress acts on the pituitary gland, which sends a hormone to stimulate the adrenal cortex, which then discharges hormones that set up the AR.

In order to observe the effects of prolonged stress upon the AR and the organism, Selye subjected rats to sublethal daily stress for several weeks. He observed a rather startling sequence of events. At first, the animals showed a full blown AR. Their chemical and organic functions were typical: their sex and growth functions ceased, and the indications of tissue breakdown were present. With the continued presence of the daily stress, however, the animals which survived the AR showed a period of recovery. A stage of resistance, lasting from a few weeks to over a month, followed, and the animals showed a restoration of their physiological structures and mechanisms. However, this resistance was highly specific to the kind of stress imposed. If a new and novel stressor was introduced at this point, the animals immediately showed an AR and died. The resistance to the specific stress was increased, but resistance to other sources of stress were markedly decreased.

Finally, as the daily stress was continued, the animals lost their resistance, became weaker, and died. There was a very similar pattern of change to that which originally occurs in the AR: the adrenals became enlarged, the thymus shrank, and sugar and chloride levels fell. Selye referred to this final level as the "stage of exhaustion." The struggle to survive prolonged stress can therefore be seen as the expenditure of a limited amount of adaptation energy. He referred to the sequence of responses made by the organism as the "general adaptation syndrome" (GAS). A final finding uncovered by Selye's group was that a side effect of the GAS was damage to the kidneys.

As a speculative conclusion to a discussion of Selye's work, we may suggest that these findings, although they come from research on animals, can be applied to an understanding of human diseases. If the human being is placed under prolonged stress, it is possible that he undergoes the phases of the GAS, resulting in the AR, the period of resistance, and finally the exhaustion phase in which the individual succumbs. Perhaps an understanding of these effects in human beings will lead us to discover remedial measures, even though we may not be able to eliminate the stimulus conditions which bring on the GAS and ultimately death.

Since the publication of Selye's ideas and research results, much work has been done on the relationship of stress to the activity of the adrenal glands. A report by Hoagland (1958) illustrates these studies.

Example 19–6 *Endocrine stress response of athletes. (Hoagland, 1958)*

In a report which was supportive of the conclusions made by Funkenstein et al., Hoagland (1958) outlined an experiment in which determinations were made of the amount of epinephrine and norepinephrine contained in the urine of hockey players before, during, and after a game. He argued that hockey is a fast aggressive game in which the players un-

Table 19-1 Excretion of norepinephrine and epinephrine in members of a professional hockey team—defensemen and forwards versus nonparticipating players*

Urine collection	No. of hockey players sampled	Norepi-nephrine	Epinephrine
Active hockey players (defensemen and forwards):			
Pregame	20	2.7 ± 0.43	0.36 ± 0.07
Postgame	20	15.3 ± 2.20	0.95 ± 0.21
		$t = 5.66$	$t = 2.68$
		$p = <0.001$	$p = <0.05 > 0.01$
Two players who did not participate in game:			
Pregame	1 (No. 18)	2.2	0.23
Postgame		3.3	0.75
Pregame	1 (No. 10)	5.6	0.78
Postgame		5.3	1.42
Player involved in fistfight:			
Pregame	1 (No. 16)	3.5	0.18
Postgame		29.3	3.30

* From Elmadjian et al., *Journal of Clinical Endocrinology,* 17:608, 1957.

dergo a prolonged period of stress. The data are shown in Table 19–1. Clearly, the effects of the stress of the game is to increase the secretion of norepinephrine in the active players. In two players who sat out the game because of injuries, however, there was a significant increase in epinephrine but not in norepinephrine. Both men reported being very worried about their injuries and their ability to play. One other player was involved in a fistfight, and he showed very large increases in both norepinephrine and epinephrine.

These results appear to support the conclusion that aggressive emotional displays are related to increased secretion of the adrenal medullary hormone norepinephrine. In contrast, tense, passive emotional responses are accompanied by increased excretion of epinephrine. These findings agree with those of Funkenstein et al.

One disease which is ascribed to psychosomatic causes is stomach ulcers. The ailment is of great concern because of its increasing prevalence among people whose occupations are stressful. There has been a good deal of research on stomach ulcers and their cause, and we will consider two studies which have related behavioral stress and the onset of the disease.

As early as 1943, using a patient whose stomach could be directly observed, Wolf and Wolf (1943) discussed the genesis of the peptic ulcer in man in terms of the psychological stresses to which the victim was exposed, and in 1956 a series of studies by William Sawrey and his coworkers appeared which demonstrated the induction of ulcers under controlled conditions in the laboratory.

Example 19–7 *Ulcers produced by psychological stress (Sawrey et al., 1956)*

We will consider two studies by Sawrey and his colleagues. In the first study, a special apparatus, illustrated in Figure 19–1, was used, consisting of a box with a wire-grid floor through which the animals could be given an electric shock to its paws. In the center of the floor there was a safe area. A receptacle for food was placed at one end of the box and a receptacle for water at the other end. During the periods when the shock was on, the animal could not eat or drink without exposing itself to a shock. For the nine experimental rats, the grids were charged for forty-seven hours, then uncharged for one hour. Thus the animal could obtain food for only one hour every two days without being shocked. Since the rat tends to feed and drink at more frequent intervals, the animal's moti-

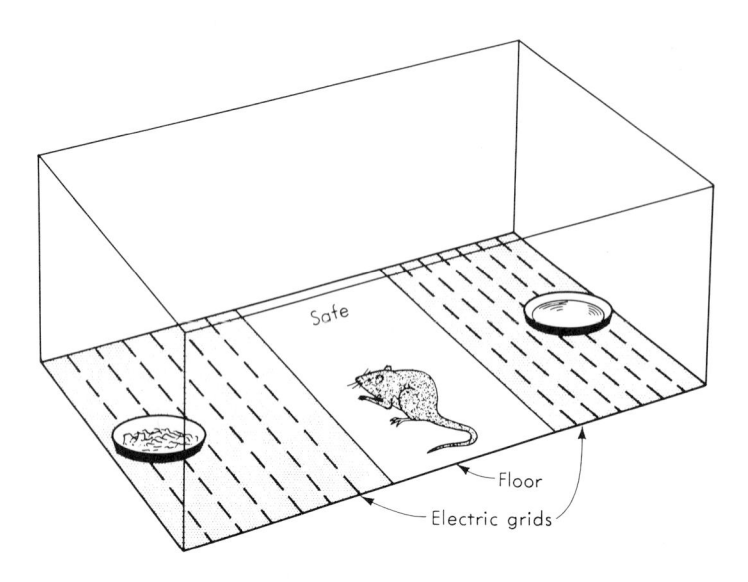

FIG. 19-1 Diagram of electric grid box.

vation to expose himself to the shock was increased over the period when the shock was on. A control group of rats was kept on the same deprivation schedule with no shock. After thirty days under this regimen, all the animals were sacrificed and examined for gastrointestinal ulcers. The results were clear: No control rats had ulcers. On the other hand, six of the nine experimental rats did have ulcers. Further, when the protocols of the three experimental animals which did not have ulcers were compared to those of the ulcerated rats, it was found that the healthy animals had not received as many shocks as the others.

This first study seemed to point to an interaction between stress and ulcers, but the design did not permit a definite conclusion, since it did not allow one to decide whether the effects were due to the electric shock, to the fact that the animals were hungry and thirsty, or to some combination of these two variables. Because of this lack of definition, the second study was designed, this time using a more complex apparatus.

The experiment controlled for the effects of shock itself in an ingenious manner: The same two-part grid box used for the experimental group was connected to a second, "yoked" box for controls. The grid in this was electrified whenever the rat in the first box stepped on his grid. The control rat in the second box, therefore, got a shock every time the first one did, except that the shocks were not contingent on its own behavior. Therefore, there was no conflict associated with the shocks for the second group of animals. Rats were run either hungry or thirsty, or both. Food and water were available to the animals in the yoked box only during the periods when the grid was safe in the conflict box. The results are shown in Table 19-2. The

Table 19-2 Results of Sawrey's experiment, showing conditions for his 8 groups

Group	Con-flict	Hun-ger	Shock	Thirst	No. of animals	Percent with ulcers
1	X	X	X	X	50	76
2		X	X	X	20	30
3		X	.	X	10	0
4			X	X	10	0
5		X			10	20
6			X		10	0
7				X	10	0
8					10	0

348 BIOLOGICAL MODELS

Table 19-3 Hunger, thirst, and shock versus ulcers in eighty animals which did not undergo conflict (groups 2 through 8 of Table 19-2)

	Ulcers	No ulcers
Hunger	11	29
No hunger	0	40
Thirst	5	35
No thirst	6	34
Shock	9	31
No shock	2	38

X's indicate the conditions to which the groups were subjected.

Without doubt, conflict is an important cause of ulceration in this experiment. But it is interesting to take a further look at the data and observe the incidence of ulcers in conjunction with shock, thirst, or hunger when no conflict was present. Table 19-3 shows this analysis. The data indicate that shock was about as effective as hunger in producing ulcers in rats who were not under conflict.

NEUROCHEMICAL BASIS OF INTELLIGENCE

Transmitter Substances

A second area of research in psychochemistry has been concerned with the transfer of information from cell to cell in the nervous system. One possible way in which experience is recorded in the nervous system is through changes in the junctions between nerve cells—the synapses.

When an impulse travels down a neuron to a synapse, it appears that the electrical charge does not simply jump the gap of the synapse. Rather, the arrival of the impulse results in the release of a chemical substance which travels across the gap and acts upon the postsynaptic membrane in such a way as to set up a local current which, if it builds up to a certain level, will result in a nerve impulse in the neuron. It should be understood, however, that all impulses which arrive at a nerve cell are not excitatory. Some impulses result in inhibitory processes at the postsynaptic sites. The activity of the postsynaptic neuron is a result of some combination of excitatory and inhibitory impulses.

The chemical which is thought to be the transmitter substance in parts of the nervous system is acetylcholine (ACh). ACh is thought to produce an electrical event in the nerve cells and thereby to create the generator potential. It is obvious that once ACh or some other transmitter substance has crossed the synapse and done its work, it is necessary to remove the transmitter in order to prevent continuous action which would destroy the discrete nature of informational transmission. The breakdown of ACh is accomplished by the enzyme cholinesterase (ChE). But not all parts of the brain appear to utilize ACh and ChE as the excitatory system. In some areas, ACh has an inhibitory function. Other substances appear to be the specific transmitters for different loci.

The Laboratory of Brain Chemistry and Behavior at the University of California at Berkeley has pioneered in this work, and we will consider an example of their research. As will be seen in Example 19-8, the work relates at least indirectly to the basic notions of the growth of structures in the nervous system expounded by D. O. Hebb. The work is interesting also because it represents work by a cross-disciplinary team—psychologists, biochemists, and neuroanatomists. It seems highly likely that we will see much more of such cooperative efforts in the future.

Example 19-8 *The psychochemical analysis of the brain: Early experience affects the chemistry of the brain (Rosenzweig et al., 1962)*

David Krech, Mark Rosenzweig, Edward Bennett, and Marion Diamond, working at Berkeley, have performed a highly interesting series of experiments designed to evaluate the hypothesis that differential early experience could modify the brain in measurable anatomical and chemical ways.

In retrospect, it appears that the decision to explore certain changes, such as the amounts of chemical transmission at the synapses follows logically from the work of Lashley and Hebb. Hebb suggested that the effects of experience change the way in which the units of the nervous system, that is, the neurons, are hooked up one to the other. As we mentioned earlier, he called these changes the development of cell assemblies. Taking the neuron as a unit of analysis, Krech and his coworkers decided to explore changes in the amount of transmitter substances. The particular chemical which they have concentrated on is the enzyme

ChE, which degrades the actual transmitter substance, ACh.

Since they believed that the changes which they would observe would turn out to be quite small and transient, they made every attempt to maximize the differences by a system of extremely precise control procedures.

The subjects used in these experiments were pigmented rats from the Berkeley animal colonies. Krech and his coworkers felt that it was important to use such rats in these studies because they have a good sense of sight, in contrast to albino rats, which have poor vision. Because they believed that the greatest changes in the brain occur during the first period of life, they worked with very young animals and decided to rear the animals under two markedly different conditions. The animals were weaned at twenty-five days of age. Then the animals were divided into two groups. One group was placed in a highly enriched environment. This consisted of a large cage in which ten to twelve animals lived in luxury, for rats. There was a complex system of shelves, ladders, tunnels, and swings designed to provide playthings and much variety in both visual and motor experiences. Each day these animals were also handled and run in a set of exploratory mazes and then given a series of problem mazes to solve. In general, the life experience of this group was characterized by rich environmental opportunities. Because this situation involves environmental complexity and training, the group was given the designation ECT.

For each ECT animal a littermate was assigned to a second group called the impoverished-condition (IC) group. Under this condition, the animals lived in individual cages with solid walls which prevented them from seeing each other. The colony of IC animals were kept in a quiet dimly lighted room, which contrasted with the ECT cages that were kept in the general colony with all its hustle and bustle. As a further control, there were some animals which lived in standard colony conditions (SC) of minimum isolation but also little enrichment.

In different experiments, different measures were made of the changes in the brain due to these manipulations. Included among the dependent measures were the weight of the cortex of the brain, the thickness of the cortex of the brain, the ChE activity in the cortex, and the number of neurons and glial cells in the cortex. The glia are the nonneuronal cells which surround the neurons of the brain. For a long time they were thought to be simply supporting structures, but recently it has been suggested that they have a role in the nutrition of neurons.

Table 19-4 Effects of various treatments on brain cholinesterase in twenty-five pairs of rats

Part of brain	Percent gain of experimental over control
Visual cortex	1.6
Somatic cortex	6.1
Subcortex	3.1
Brain weight	4.2

The first result showed the ECT rats consistently developed greater weight of cerebral cortex than their impoverished littermates. However, it was also found that the different regions of the cortex differed in the amount of this effect. Thus, the greater difference was found in the occipital, or visual, cortex. The results are given in Table 19-4. The biochemical results showed that there was a difference in the amount of ChE activity in the cortices of the ECT and IC groups with greater activity in the ECT group. Finally, the histological studies revealed that there was a significantly greater number of glial cells in the cortex of the ECT animals than in the IC animals.

Krech, Rosenzweig, Bennett, and Diamond concluded that the experience of the rat during the first stages of its life influenced the growth and chemistry of its brain in ways highly relevant to adult intellectual performance. In later studies, they also used adult rats and found that the effects of experience also changed the brains of adult rats. From these studies they suggest that the record of experience may consist in the development of neural structures and glial cells which act to mediate later behavior. Certainly the relevance of their findings for the rearing of the young appears to be direct and important.

A further interesting fact about the role of ACh in brain activity is that strains of animals have been selected which have differing amounts of ChE activity in their brains. In Example 19-9 we consider the work of the Berkeley laboratories on genetic transmission of ChE activity level.

Example 19–9 *Selective breeding of strains of rats for high and low ChE activity in the brain (Roderick, 1958)*

Roderick, working with the hypotheses that ACh is the mechanism of the storage of information in the brain, set out to select strains of rats for high or low ChE activity in the cortex. He began his work with two heterogeneous stocks of rats and carefully bred the animals so as to differentiate groups on the basis of the ChE activity they showed. In seven generations of selection, he was able to achieve two high-ChE and two low-ChE strains.

This area of research is a very lively one and much is being done to further explore the specific effects of ACh and other transmitter substances and the role which they play in the transmission of information as well as the storage of information in the brain. As we will see in the section which follows, there is a second type of theory of the storage of information, or memory, which places the mechanism for storage *within* the cell.

Chemical Coding Within the Cells of the Brain

In recent work on the biology of memory, some researchers have tended to concentrate their work on structural changes in the nervous system after learning. The area of research is an exciting one because a knowledge of the cellular effects of experience could possibly lead to a solution to some of the most pressing problems of mental health. Perhaps, we can learn the nature of the specific changes due to experience and then develop treatments which specifically remedy maladaptive changes. A recent experimental approach to the problem of the microbiology of experience is illustrated in Example 19–10.

Example 19–10 *The record of experience: Changes in the nervous system after learning (Hydén & Egyházi, 1962)*

Working at a remarkably microscopic level of analysis, Hydén and Egyházi have explored the biochemical changes within the nervous system which occur after experience. In one experiment, rats were trained to obtain food by climbing a tightrope which led to a platform high above their cage floor. After they were proficient, they were sacrificed, and a very small number of nerve cells were removed from the part of the brain which has to do with balancing: Deiters' cells in the first vestibular relay. The technique of teasing out the nerve cells is very difficult. In addition, the surrounding glial cells were removed and also examined. Hydén and Egyházi then examined the structure of the RNA contained in the nucleus of the cells. He found that there were changes in the base ratios, that is, in the way in which the RNA was put together. In a later study, Hydén reported that there seems to be a relationship of a feedback sort between the neurons and the glial cells which suggests that the glial cells are more than supporting structures.

Interpretation of Hydén's work is difficult. The situation he uses is stressful, and the effect may be due to internal conditions rather than learning. Also, since RNA is involved in the process whereby protein structures are built up, the effects may not be due to a recording of experience in the RNA itself but rather may reflect some growth process in which structures are being built up in the brain. Beyond such criticisms, it appears that an exploration of the effects of experience on the microstructure of the nervous system has begun to yield suggestive results.

Hydén's theory suggests that the effect of experience is to change the nature of the RNA in the cells of the brain, both the neurons and the glia, and thereby to change the proteins which are built up through the mechanisms of DNA–RNA. However, other workers have advanced different theories about the way in which memory is stored. Briggs and Kitto (1962) have suggested that the process of enzyme induction is the basic mechanism of memory storage. They point out that the action of the nervous system requires the transmission of impulses across synapses by the mediation of the transmitter substances. Therefore, it seems to them that the best explanation of the manner in which experience affects the nervous system might be in terms of a change in the amount of these enzymes which is produced at specific sites. The reader will recall that the work of the California Brain Chemistry Group which we have been discussing provides some support for this notion.

Beyond experiments of the direct kind which we have been discussing, there has also been an area of research dealing with what is called "transfer of memory." A number of workers have reported evidence that memory can be transferred from a trained animal to an untrained animal by extracting substances, usually RNA, from the brains of the donor animals and injecting it into the host animals. At the present writing, this area is highly controversial, and it remains for proponents of the transfer of learning hypotheses to pin down the conditions under which demonstration of an effect may be reliably accomplished in other laboratories. Grossman (1967) has reviewed the evidence in this area of research and suggests that the effects observed may be due to a nonspecific sensitization of the recipient animals, rather than any true transfer of memory. Since a number of laboratories are pursuing this work, the outcome of their work may settle the issue. Certainly, it is an exciting and sensational proposal. It appears, as yet, to be unproved.

EXOGENOUS CHEMICAL COMPOUNDS AND BEHAVIOR

With the increased usage by the medical profession of drugs which affect behavior, a new cross-disciplinary science has come into being: *psychopharmachology*. In general, three classes of psychotropic drugs have been of concern to this discipline: the stimulants, the tranquilizers, and the hallucinogens. We will consider each of these classes of drugs briefly and take up an example of the experiments which have explored the effects of these drugs on behavior.

The Stimulants

Stimulants are drugs which energize the psychic processes of the recipient. While this statement has a highly subjective flavor, it is intended only to imply that people who are given stimulants report, verbally, that they feel increased mental alertness and vigor, and heightened awareness. Also, their behavior becomes more active. They may exhibit hyperexcitability, and they may, if dosage is high, go into convulsions.

There are three groups of stimulants: The first group acts to antagonize the depressant agents in the central nervous system. This includes drugs such as amphetamine (Benzedrine). The second group inhibits the action of monoamine oxidase, an enzyme which is widely distributed in the central nervous system and which plays a part in metabolism of serotonin, and the catecholamines, which are thought to be involved in the transmission of information across synapses. The last group consists of ACh precursors which increase the amount of ACh in the brain. There is some evidence (Pfeiffer et al., 1957) that treatment with large doses of cholinergic agents produces remission in some cases of schizophrenia. This finding suggests that some cases of psychosis may be due to a lack of ACh in the brain. In Example 19-12, the work by H. J. Eysenck on the relationship of stimulants and behavior is explored.

Example 19-11 *The effects of stimulant drugs on behavior (Eysenck, 1960)*

Working at the University of London, Eysenck and his students have explored the action of stimulant drugs in terms of several behavioral changes. Here we will consider some of the research which his group has done to test predictions or deductions based on Eysenck's theories.

1. The first deduction is that eye-blink conditioning will be facilitated by stimulant drugs. Using dextroamphetamine, a stimulant, Laverty and Franks (1956) found this prediction to be true. It appears that the person under the influence of a stimulant learns faster to avoid the noxious stimulation which is used in this situation. The result may be due to a change in the rate of central nervous systems processes, increased sensitivity to the puff of air, or some process of focusing of attention. Eysenck favors the first of these possibilities.

2. Visual aftereffects, such as the Archimedes spiral, are lengthened by the administration of stimulant drugs. Eysenck believes this to reflect a change in such persons toward the type of behavior exhibited by introverted people.

3. Long-term continuous tasks, which involve muscular effort, such as pursuit-rotor performance, are better performed after administration of stimulant drugs. Eysenck (1960) and his students have shown that this is indeed the case. The pursuit-rotor performance is a task in which a subject is required to follow a whirling phonograph turntable with a baton in order to maintain contact at a particular point. The task is quite difficult, since it

requires muscular agility and effort. In ordinary situations, people improve greatly with practice but show a large decrement in performance within any one practice session. The stimulant drugs appear to reduce the rate of intrasession decrement, evidently reducing inhibition due to fatigue.

In general, other predictions about performances also hold. Eysenck makes the deduction that the stimulant drugs act to increase cortical excitation.

The Tranquilizers

With the widespread publicity of the tranquilizing drugs, it is hardly necessary to speak very much about their acceptance for use in the treatment of behavioral disturbance. Suffice it to say that a great number of prescriptions for these drugs are written every year, and their introduction has greatly changed the whole spectrum of treatment of mental illness. Perhaps because of the tranquilizers, mental hospitals today are a far cry from the snake pits of the past.

We will consider five classes of tranquilizing drugs, listing their general pattern of behavioral effects. Then we will examine one example of experimental analysis of the behavioral effect of a tranquilizing drug.

1. *The phenothiazine derivatives,* such as chlorpromazine, act to block the part of the nervous system in which epinephrine is the initiator of activity. They have an antihistiminic effect, and they are antiemetic. Further, they produce sedation, hypnosis, and anesthesia. In addition, they potentiate the action of anesthetics and other drugs. They also block learned responses.

These drugs have been much used in the treatment of psychosis, but they also appear to decrease motivation and increase suggestibility in patients.

2. *The* Rauwolfia *alkaloids,* such as reserpine, are derived from the root of the *Rauwolfia* plant, which has been used as a medicinal specific in India for centuries. The action of these drugs appears to be an inhibition of centers in the hypothalamus of the brain which control the sympathetic nervous system. This action results in increased activity of the gastrointestinal system and in sedation. These drugs do not cause anesthesia. The *Rauwolfia* compounds also block conditioned reflexes.

3. *The diphenylmethanes,* such as benactyzine, are best known for their effect in prolonging the action of other drugs, such as barbiturates and hypnotics. They do not block conditioning.

4. *The substituted propanediols,* such as meprobamate, are muscle relaxants, relieve anxiety and nervousness, and appear to raise the threshold for frustration, thereby permitting better performance under stress. In large doses they produce reversible paralysis of voluntary muscles. They do not appear to affect conditioned reflexes.

5. *The substituted amides,* such as pentobarbital, are sedatives and hypnotics. They produce sleep and anesthesia, and they are also anticonvulsants. They have been used in the treatment of hyperexcitable neurotic patients.

Clearly, usage of the tranquilizers by physicians depends on the belief that they reduce the anxiety of patients who are rendered unable to deal with the environment because of their anxious state. In Example 19-12, we consider an experiment in which findings were not supportive of the hypothesis that one of the commonly used tranquilizers, meprobamate, is a reducer of anxiety in normal persons.

Example 19-12 *The effect of meprobamate on laboratory-induced anxiety (Kenyon & Pronko, 1960)*

All too often, discussions of the effects of drugs on behavior make the assumption that effects observed in clinical situations may, with confidence, be extrapolated to normal subjects. Thus, the tranquilizing drugs which effectively reduce the hyperreactiveness of neurotic patients are discussed in terms of their general effect in reducing anxiety. In a very interesting study, Kenyon and Pronko (1960) asked whether meprobamate would improve the performance of college students when they were asked to perform a complex stress-producing manipulation task.

Fifty-one beginning psychology students were placed in a situation which required them to manipulate a set of dials while they were rapidly reading a text from a machine which exposed the material at a rate just a bit too rapidly for easy scanning. In addition, the subjects wore earphones and could hear their own speech, delayed 1.75 seconds. This was a very stressful situation because the subject had an electric-shock device strapped to his wrist which he was told would be used if he failed to read the instructions aloud or stopped adjusting the dials in accordance with the instructions.

The students were divided into two groups. Half underwent the task after administration of meprobamate; the remainder were given a placebo.

The results showed that there was no difference between the two groups. Evidently, in this extremely anxiety-producing task, the tranquilizing drug made no difference in the performance of the subjects. Of course, it is also true that the drug did not interfere with the highly complex motor task with which the subjects were faced. This finding appears to indicate that meprobamate does not interfere with motor performance.

Since several other investigators have reported similar findings, it seems that meprobamate does not improve performance in an anxiety-producing task.

The Hallucinogens

As everyone knows well, a class of drugs has recently been developed which have profound effects on the reported conscious states of those who use them. The most famous of these is LSD-25 (lysergic acid diethylamide). Ingestion of these compounds is reported to result in extreme changes in mood, perception, self-awareness, and a distortion of time sense. In Table 19–5, the most commonly used hallucinogens are listed.

The widespread use of the hallucinogens has resulted in a social turmoil of great proportion (cf. DeBold & Leaf, 1967). Their distribution has been made illegal, and they are no longer manufactured in the United States. However, the usage continues in spite of several reports that LSD-25 in particular may be a mutagenic agent (Alexander, Miles, Gold, & Alexander, 1967; Cohen, Marinelle & Back, 1967). In the first of these reports, administration of LSD was reported to result in chromosomal abnormalities. In the second study, the administration of LSD resulted in extreme incidences of abnormal births in rats. The implications appear very dangerous. The use of LSD may cause damage to the genetic material and result in the birth of abnormal offspring.

As a conclusion to our discussion of exogenous compounds and behavior, and as a way of returning to the consideration of memory processes with which we have been concerned earlier in this chapter, we will consider a phenomenon which has been of great interest to psychologists: drug dissociation.

It has been known for some time that there are certain drugs, such as curare, which affect subjects who learn a response under the drug so that they are not able to perform the response when the drug wears off. This phenomenon came to be called dissociation, because there seemed to be a separation of cognitive functions under the two states. As discussed in the following example, D. A. Overton (1964) performed a series of studies designed to document the phenomenon and to ensure that the effects were not an artifact of the experimental designs previously used.

Example 19–13 *Drug dissociation (Overton, 1964)*

In this study, Overton was concerned with avoiding the paralyzing effects of curare upon the subjects which might confound the results of the experiment. Therefore, he made two innovations in his experimental design. First, he used drugs such as sodium pentobarbital, which acts primarily on the central nervous system, and, second, he used a response which reliably appeared on every trial; escape from shock in a simple T-maze.

The subjects used were laboratory rats. The apparatus was a simple maze in the form of a T. In such an apparatus, the animal is started from the base of the stem of the T and must learn to choose the correct arm in order to escape shock, which is delivered through an electrified grid also serving as the floor of the entire apparatus. We will summarize all five of his experiments, since the results of the series form a unit. Beyond the basic design, the remainder of the experiments were actually controls to ensure that the results were in fact due to dissociation and not to other variables such as simply the administration of any drug.

In general, the procedure involved training animals to escape shock while under the influence of the drug, and then allowing the drug to wear off. Then the animals were tested to see if they had retained the response they had learned. Control animals were run with saline solution injections or with other drugs which were not central nervous system inhibitors.

As common sense would suggest, the first finding was that the drugged animals showed slower learning and generally less retention than rats which had

Table 19-5 Some hallucinogens used throughout the world

Substance	Active principle	Source	Major area of use	Purpose	How taken
Glue	Toluene	Commercial	U.S.	Euphoria	Sniffing
Gas vapor	Trichlorethylene, cyclohexanol, ethylene, dichloride, toluene	Commercial	U.S.	Euphoria, hedonism	Sniffing
Cannabis (marijuana, bhang, dagga, kif, hashish)	Cannabinol	*Cannabis sativa* (*C. indica*)	Worldwide	Pleasure	Smoking, drinking, in food
Peyote	Mescaline (epinephrine-like)	Cactus, *L. williamsii*	U.S., Mexico	Religious, ritual, hedonism	Chewing, drinking, mescaline can be injected
Psilocin, psilocybin	Serotonin derivatives	Basiodiomycete *Psilociba mexicana* (teonanactyl)	Mexico, U.S.	Religious, ritual	Orally
Ololiuqui	Lysergic acid	*Rivea corymbosa*	Mexico	Pleasure, ritual	Chewing seeds
Pituri	Scopolamine	Potato-like shrub *Dubiosia hopwoodii*	Australia	Relief from thirst, strength	Mixing with ashes or acacia wood and chewing
Caapi (yahee, ayahuasca)	Banisterine	Vine—*Banisteria caapi*	South America, (Columbia, Brazil)	Whipping ceremony, aphrodisiac, prophecy	Drinking
Datura	Stramonium, scopolamine, hyoscyamine	*Datura* species	Mexico, Ecuador, Peru, Columbia	Aphrodisiac, religious, magic	Drinking
Ibogaine	Harmine (banisterine)	Plant—iboga tabernanthe	Africa	Stimulant, ordeal ceremony	Chewing
Fly agaric	Muscarine, bufotenine	Basidiomycete, *Amanita muscaria*	Siberia	Pleasure, relief from environment	Drinking, chewing
Yakee epina	Myristicin, DMT, bufotenine	*Virola* species (nutmeg)	Venezuela, Brazil, Columbia	Religious, magic	As snuff
Vinho de juremena	Nigarine (dimethyl-tryptamine)	*Mimosa hestilis*	South America	Magic, religious	Drinking
Cohoba (yopo, niopo)	Bufotenine, DMT	*Piptadenia peregrina*	Columbia, Venezuela	Magic, warfare, orgiastic	As snuff
—	—	*Salvia divinarum*	Mexico	Religious, magic	Chewing leaves

not had treatment of any kind. But the crucial finding was that animals trained under the drug seemed to perform at random when the drug wore off. That is, there was clear evidence for dissociation of the drug and normal states. Somehow, the effect of the drug was to create a memory system which could not be used later when the drug wore off.

Overton, following previous researchers, has called this phenomenon *state-dependent learning*. He concluded from his results that he had demonstrated three salient features of dissociation: First, dissociation really does occur. This appears to be valid in view of the fact that he could find no evidence for transfer of training between the two states. Second, when drugs like sodium pentobarbital are used as control injections, there is some transfer between the two drug states, which indicates that dissociation is a continuous rather than an all-or-none phenomenon. The final finding is that the effect is not a sensory one in that Overton could not reproduce his results by selectively depriving the animals of sensory functions.

CONCLUSION

Our discussion of physiological psychology has been organized on the premise that the brain and its control of behavior can be divided into three structural divisions: the core, the old brain and the new brain. Further, these divisions were considered in terms of an external system which has to do with the processing of information about the external world and an internal system which is related to programs stored within the brain.

Starting with the external system, we traced the historical course of investigation of the processes of nerve conduction and the sensory systems by which the external environment is encoded into information within the organism. From this we proceeded to a consideration of studies of the role of the brain in learning and memory. This indicated that the relationship between structure and function was a useful one. Concern with the engram, or the locus of storage of memory, led us to the ideas of Karl Lashley and his principles of equipotentiality and mass action.

Then we turned to the internal systems of the brain. As an aid to organizing our study of this system, we introduced Stellar's theory of motivation, which placed emphasis on the hypothalamus as an integrative system which samples information from the external world, the internal environment, and other centers in the brain. To illustrate systems which involve internal programming, we considered sleep and wakefulness, hunger and thirst, and sexual behavior. All involve cyclic activity, and the latter two appear to have complex determinants, with both the internal and external systems playing a role.

We next considered those structures which underlie emotional behavior, in particular the work of James Olds which implicated the limbic system. Examination of studies on stress and on the genesis of stomach ulcers were put forward to illustrate the field of psychosomatics. This led to a consideration of the psychochemistry of the synapse, and in particular the work of the California Laboratory of Brain Chemistry. Finally, we looked at the emerging science of psychopharmacology, which has attempted to relate exogenous chemical agents to behavior. In conclusion, we considered the phenomenon of dissociation due to drugs, in which organisms show one behavior when under the drug and fail to behave in the same fashion when the drug effects wear off.

SECTION SIX: REFERENCES

ALEXANDER, G. J., MILES, B. E., GOLD, G. M., & ALEXANDER, R. B. LSD: Injection early in pregnancy produces abnormalities in offspring of rats. *Science,* 1967, **157** (3787), 459–460.

BEACH, F. A. Analysis of the stimuli adequate to elicit mating behavior in the sexually inexperienced male rat. *Journal of Comparative Physiological Psychology,* 1942, **33,** 163–207.

BEACH, F. A. Normal sexual behavior in male rats isolated at fourteen days of age. *Journal of Comparative Physiological Psychology,* 1958, **51,** 37–38.

BEACH, F. A. The snark was a Boojum. *American Psychologist,* 1959, **5,** 115–124.

BITTERMAN, M. E. Towards a comparative psychology of learning. *American Psychologist,* 1960, **15,** 704–712.

BRIGGS, M. H., & KITTO, G. B. The molecular basis of memory and learning. *Psychological Review,* **69** (6), 537–541, 1962.

BRUCKNER, G. H. Untersuchungen zur Tiersoziologie, inbesondre der Auflosung der Familie. *Zeitschrift fur Psychologie,* 1933, **128,** 1–120.

BULLOCK, T. H. The origins of patterned nervous discharge. *Behavior,* 1961, **17,** 48–59.

CANNON, W. B. *Bodily changes in pain, hunger, fear, and rage: An account of recent researches into the function of emotional excitement.* New York: Appleton, 1929.

CATTELL, R. B., STICE, G. F., & KRISTY, N. F. A first approximation to nature-nurture ratios for eleven primary personality factors in objective tests. *Journal of Abnormal and Social Psychology,* 1957, **54,** 143–159.

COHEN, M. M., MARINELLE, M. J., & BACK, N. *Science*, 1967, **155**, 1417.

COLBERT, E. H. Morphology and behavior. In A. Roe & G. G. Simpson (Eds.), *Behavior and evolution*. New Haven, Conn.: Yale University Press, 1958.

CRAIG, W. Appetites and aversions as constituents of instincts. *Biological Bulletin*, 1918, **34**, 91–107.

DARWIN, C. *Origin of species by means of natural selection*. (1859.) New York: Dolphin Books, n.d.

DEBOLD, R. C., & LEAF, R. C. *LSD, man and society*. Middletown, Conn: Wesleyan, 1967.

DELGADO, M. M. R., ROBERTS, W. W., & MILLER, N. E. Learning motivated by electrical stimulation of the brain. *American Journal of Physiology*, 1954, **179**, 587–593.

DEMENT, W. C. An essay of dreams: The role of physiology. In T. W. Newcomb (Ed.) *New directions in psychology, II*. New York: Holt, 1965.

DUNCAN, C. P. The retroactive effect of electroshock on learning. *Journal of Comparative Physiological Psychology*, 1949, **42**, 32–44.

ERLENMEYER-KIMLING, L., & JARVIK, L. F. Genetics and intelligence: A review. *Science*, 1963, **142**, 1477–1478.

EYSENCK, H. J. *Experiments in personality*. London: Routledge, 1960.

EYSENCK, H. J., & PRELL, D. B. The inheritance of neuroticism: An experimental study. *Journal of Mental Science*, 1951, **97**, 441–465.

FALCONER, D. S. *Introduction to quantitative genetics*. New York: Roland Publishing, 1960.

FORSMANN, H., & HAMBERT, A. Chromosomes and antisocial behavior. *Excerpta Criminologica*, 1967, **2**, 113, 117.

FRANZ, S. I. On the functions of the cerebrum: The frontal lobes in relation to the production and retention of simple sensory-motor habits. *American Journal of Physiology*, 1902, **8**, 1–22.

FULLER, J. L. Cross-sectional and longitudinal studies of adjustive behavior in dogs. *Annals of New York Academy of Sciences*, 1953, **56**, 214–224.

FULLER, J. L., & THOMPSON, W. R. *Behavior genetics*. New York: Wiley, 1960.

FUNKENSTEIN, D. H., KING, S. H., & DROLETTE, M. The direction of anger during a laboratory stress-inducing situation. *Psychosomatic Medicine*, 1954, **16**, 5, 404–413.

GALTON, SIR F. *Hereditary genius: An inquiry into its laws and consequences*. London: Macmillan, 1883.

GERARD, R. W. What is memory? *Scientific American*, **188**, 1953.

GOTTESMAN, I. Heritability of personality: A demonstration. *Psychological Monographs*, 1963, **77** (9, Whole No. 572), 1–21.

GREGORY, I. Genetic factors in schizophrenia. *American Journal of Psychiatry*, 1960, **116**, 961–972.

GRIFFIN, D. R. *Listening in the dark*. New Haven, Conn.: Yale University Press, 1958.

GROSSMAN, S. P. *A textbook of physiological psychology*. New York: Wiley, 1967.

HARRIMAN, H. E., & MacLEOD, R. B. Discriminative threshold for salt for normal and adrenalectomized rats. *American Journal of Psychology*, 1953, **66**, 465–471.

HASLER, A. D., & LARSEN, J. A. The homing salmon. *Scientific American*, 1955, **201**, 3–6.

HEBB, D. O. *The organization of behavior*. New York: Wiley, 1949.

HEINROTH, O. *Aus dem Leben der Vogel*. Berlin: Springer-Verlag, 1938.

HESS, E. H. Imprinting. *Science*, 1959, **130**, 133–141.

HESS, E. H. Ethology: An approach toward the complete analysis of behavior. In T. W. Newcomb (Ed.), *New directions in psychology*. New York: Holt, 1962.

HIRSCH, J. (Ed.) *Behavior-genetic analysis*. New York: McGraw-Hill, 1967.

HOAGLAND, H. Some endocrine stress responses in man. Paper presented at the conference on Research on Stress in Relation to Mental Health and Mental Illness, held by the Mental Health Research Fund, Oxford, July, 1958.

HONZIK, C. H. Maze learning in the absence of specific intra- and extra-maze stimuli. *University of California Publications in Psychology*, 1933, **6**, 99–144.

HUNTER, W. S. Conditioning and extinction in the rat. *British Journal of Psychology*, 1935, **26**, 135–148.

HYDÉN, H., & EGYHÁZI, E. Nuclear RNA changes in nerve cells during a learning experiment in rats. *Proceedings of the National Academy of Sciences of the United States of America*, 1962, **48**, 1366–1673.

IERSEL, J. J. A. VAN An analysis of the parental behavior of the male three-spined stickleback. *Behaviour,* 1953, Suppl. 3, 1–159.

JACOBSEN, C. F. The effects of extirpations on higher brain processes. *Physiological Review,* 1939, **19**, 303.

JENNINGS, H. S. *Behavior of the lower organisms.* New York: Macmillan, 1906.

KALLMAN, F. *Heredity in health and mental disorder.* New York: Norton, 1953.

KENYON, G. Y., & PRONKO, N. H. Meprobamate and laboratory-induced anxiety. In Leonard Uhr and James Miller (Eds.), *Drugs and behavior.* New York: Wiley, 1960.

KLEITMAN, N. *Sleep and wakefulness.* Chicago: University of Chicago Press, 1963.

LAMARCK, J. B. *Philosphie zoologisch.* Leipzig: Kröner, 1809.

LANSDELL, H. C. Effect of brain damage on intelligence in rats. *Journal of Comparative Physiological Psychology,* 1953, **46**, 461–464.

LASHLEY, K. S. *Brain mechanisms and intelligence.* Chicago: University of Chicago Press, 1929.

LASHLEY, K. S. Cerebral organization and behavior. *Proceedings of the Association for Research in Neurological and Mental Disease,* 1958, **36**, 1–18.

LAVERTY, S. G., & FRANKS, C. M. Sodium Amytal and behavior in neurotic subjects. *Journal of Neurology, Neurosurgery, and Psychiatry,* 1956, **19**, 137.

LOEB, J. *Comparative physiology of the brain and comparative psychology.* New York: Putnam, 1900.

LORENZ, K. The comparative method in studying innate behaviour patterns. *Symposia of the Society for Experimental Biology,* 1950, **4**, 221–268.

MacLEAN, P. D. Psychosomatic disease and the "visceral brain": Recent developments bearing on the Papez theory of emotion. *Psychosomatic Medicine,* 1950, **11**, 338–353.

MARLER, P. Developments in the study of animal communication. Ch. 7 In Bell, P. R. (Ed.), *Darwin's biological works: Some aspects reconsidered.* Chap. 7. London: Cambridge University Press, 1959.

MORUZZI, G., & MAGOUN, H. W. Brain stem reticular formation and activation of the EEG. *Electroencephalography and Clinical Neurophysiology.* 1949, 1, 1455–1473.

McCLEARN, G. E., & MEREDITH, W. Behavioral genetics. *Annual Review of Psychology,* 1966, **17**.

MOLTZ, H. Contemporary instinct theory and the fixed action pattern. *Psychological Review,* 1965, **72**, 27–47.

MYERS, R. E. Corpus callosum and visual gnosis. In J. F. Delefresnaye (Ed.), *Brain mechanisms and learning.* Oxford: Blackwell, 1961.

NEWMAN, H. H., FREEMAN, F. N., & HOLZINGER, K. J. *Twins: A study of heredity and environment.* Chicago: University of Chicago Press, 1937.

OLDS, J., & MILNER, P. Positive reinforcement produced by electrical stimulation of septal area and other regions of rat brain. *Journal of Comparative Physiological Psychology,* 1954, **47**, 419–427.

OVERTON, D. A. State-dependent of "dissociated" learning produced with pentobarbital. *Journal of Comparative Physiological Psychology,* 1964, **57**, 3–12.

PAPEZ, J. W. A proposed mechanism of emotion. *Archives of Neurology and Psychiatry,* 1937, **38**, 725–744.

PFAFFMAN, C., & BARE, J. K. Gustatory nerve discharges in normal and adrenalectomized rats. *Journal of Comparative Physiological Psychology,* 1950, **43**, 320–324.

PFEIFFER, C. C., JENNEY, E. H., GALLAGHER, W., SMITH, R. P., BEVAN, W., JR., KILLAM, K. F., KILLAM, E. K., & BLACKMORE, W. Stimulant effect of 2-dimethylaminoethanel: Possible precursor of brain acetylcholine. *Science,* 1957, **126**, 610–611.

PRIBRAM, K. H. A review of theory in physiological psychology. *Annual Review of Psychology,* 1960, **48**, 1–40.

RICHTER, C. P., & ECKERT, J. F. Mineral metabolism of adrenalectomized rats studied by the appetite method. *Endocrinology,* 1938, **22**, 214–224.

ROBERTS, W. W. Both rewarding and punishing effects from stimulation of posterior hypothalamus of cat with same electrode at same intensity. *Journal of Comparative Physiological Psychology,* 1958, **51**, 400–407.

RODERICK, T. H. The genetics of variation of cholinesterase activity in the cerebral cortex of the rat with reference to possible physiological and morphological correlates. Unpublished doctoral dissertation, University of California, 1958.

ROEDER, K. D., & TREAT, A. E. The detection and evasion of bats by moths. *American Scientist,* 1961, **49**, 135–148.

ROSENZWEIG, M. R., KRECH, D., BENNETT, E. L., & DIAMOND, M. C. Effects of environmental complexity and training on brain chemistry and anatomy: A replication and extension. *Journal of Comparative Physiological Psychology*, 1962, **55**, 429–437.

SAWREY, W., CANGER, J., & TURRELL, E. An experimental investigation of the role of psychological factors in the production of gastric ulcers in rats. *Journal of Comparative Physiological Psychology*, 1956, **49**, 269–270.

SCHNEIRLA, T. C., & ROSENBLATT, J. S. Behavioral organization and genesis of the social bond in insects and mammals. *American Journal of Orthopsychiatry*, 1961, **31**, 223–253.

SELYE, H. *The physiology and pathology of exposure to stress.* Montreal: Acta, 1950.

SHERRINGTON, C. *The integrative action of the nervous system.* London: Scribner's, 1906.

SMITH, C. J. Mass action and early environment in the rat. *Journal of Comparative Physiological Psychology*, 1959, **52**, 2, 154–156.

SNYDER, L. H. The inheritance of taste deficiency in man. *Ohio Journal of Science*, 1932, **32**, 436–440.

STELLAR, E. The physiology of motivation. *Psychological Review*, 1954, **61**, 5–22.

STELLAR, E., HYMAN, R., & SAMET, S. Gastric factors controlling water-and-salt solution drinking. *Journal of Comparative Physiological Psychology*, 1954, **47**, 220–226.

THOMPSON, W. R. Behavior genetics. In *McGraw-Hill yearbook of science and technology*. New York: McGraw-Hill, 1965.

TINBERGEN, N. An objectivistic study of the innate behaviour of animals. *Bibliotheca Biothea.*, 1942, **1**, 39–98.

TINBERGEN, N. *The study of instinct.* London: Oxford University Press, 1951.

UEXKULL, J. VON. *Umwelt und Innenwelt der Tiere.* Jena, 1909 (2d ed., Berlin, 1921.)

VALENSTEIN, E. S. V., RISS, W. R., & YOUNG, W. C. Y. Experimental and genetic factors in the organization of sexual behavior in male guinea pigs. *Journal of Comparative Physiological Psychology*, 1955, **48**, 397–403.

VON HOLST, E., and VON SAINT PAUL, U. On the functional organization of drives. *Animal Behavior*, 1963, **11**, 1–20.

WHITEHEAD, A. N. *Science and modern world.* New York: Macmillan, 1925.

WHITMAN, C. O. *Animal behavior.* Biology lectures, Marine Biological Laboratory, Woods Hole, Boston, Mass., 1899.

WODINSKY, J., & BITTERMAN, M. E. Resistance to extinction in the fish after extensive training with partial reinforcement. *Journal of Psychology*, 1960, **73**, 429–434.

WOLF, S., & WOLF, H. G. *Human gastric function.* New York: Oxford University Press, 1943.

SECTION SEVEN
INDIVIDUAL DIFFERENCES: THEIR MEASUREMENT AND MEANING

"The universe is made up of innumerable entities, each probably individual, each probably non-permanent; all man can achieve is to classify by measurement or observation of characteristics these entities into classes of like individuals. Within these classes, variation can be noted, and the fundamental problem of science is to discover how the variation in one class is correlated with or contingent on the variation in a second class. Consciously, or more often unconsciously, the man of science is forever making contingency tables."
(Pearson, 1911, p. 165)

"The correlational psychologist is in love with just those variables the experimenter left home to forget. He regards individual and group variations as important effects of biological and social causes. All organisms adapt to their environments, but not equally well. His question is: What present characteristics of the organism determine its mode and degree of adaptation."
(Cronbach, 1957, p. 674)

PROLOGUE

The material in this section will explore two central ideas contained in the quotations on the previous page by Karl Pearson and Lee Cronbach. Restated simply, these ideas are (1) that individuals tend to differ from each other in respect to virtually every measurable dimension, for example, height, weight, and intelligence and (2) that though we cannot observe directly cause-and-effect relations, we can describe exactly the degree of association between two or more variables. These two basic notions turn out to be intimately linked together. For the time being, however, they will be discussed separately.

The first idea, that there are individual differences, does not seem very startling to us today. Most of us have lived, at least until recently, in an individualistic age in which the success and achievement of a particular person have been highly valued. However, as a scientific idea, the notion of individual differences is of fairly recent origin. In medieval times, the individual was so much a part of some group that his individuality was eclipsed by it (Huizinga, 1956). In the eyes of the Church, all men were equal before God. In the eyes of a feudal lord, a serf was a serf, no more, no less. Without this group membership the individual was nothing. A knight who had violated his vows and as a result had been stripped of his knighthood was totally alienated from society. With no social role, he was less than human.

This attitude is strikingly reflected in medieval art, literature, and music. For example, it is characteristic of the Gregorian chant that its authorship was usually anonymous and that it had no part harmonies as we have in later music. All participants sang the same melody at the same tempo. There was no more room for individual virtuosity in music than there was in social behavior. This is not to say, of course, that people were blind to individuality. Undoubtedly, there were as many perceptible individual differences in character, personality, and intelligence as there are in contemporary society. But it seems likely that these were not salient enough in human experience to provide a basis for significant conceptualizations about human nature and society.

This point of view is nicely reflected in the following observations made by René Descartes, in the seventeenth century:

> Good sense is, of all things among men, the most equally distributed; for everyone thinks himself so abundantly provided with it, that those even who are the most difficult to satisfy in everything else, do not usually desire a larger measure of this quality than they already possess. And in this it is not likely that all are mistaken; the conviction is rather to be held as testifying that the power of judging aright and of distinguishing Truth from Error, which is properly what is called Good Sense or Reason, is by nature equal in all men; and that the diversity of our opinions, consequently, does not arise from some being endowed with a larger share of Reason than others, but solely from this, that we conduct our thoughts along different ways, and do not fix our attention on the same objects [Descartes, 1637].

Descartes modestly deprecated his own mind as no better than "those of the generality"—yet through his writings he profoundly influenced Western thought for the three centuries following him.

Gradually, with changes in the economic and political structure of society, with the rise of nationalism and of protestantism, and with a shift in emphasis in philosophy away from the relation of man to God and toward the relation of men to each other, the worth of individual enterprise began to be emphasized more and more, so that by the beginning of the nineteenth century the idea of individual differences was a major one in society and accordingly commenced to influence the course of science.

In the latter half of the nineteenth century, it will be recalled, experimental psychology in Germany studied the laws of consciousness without reference to individuals. Individual variation was recognized but regarded simply as an annoying source of error. In fact, much of psychology still takes this approach, as we have seen in other chapters. The psychology of learning, for example, is concerned not with the differences between individuals but rather with their conformity to the same basic laws.

What did emerge, however, in the late nineteenth and early twentieth century, was a formal branch of psychology devoted to the study of individual differences. Perhaps two main events set the stage for this. One was the founding of statistics, chiefly by Gauss and Quetelet. These mathematicians found that the scores of individuals in a population distributed themselves, in respect to most measurable traits, according to a typical function—the *normal curve function,* described in earlier chapters. Such an observation represented a major step in the exact study of individual differences. A second important event was the publication of Darwin's theory of natural selection. As any student who has taken courses in biology will know, the notion of individual variation is crucial to this theory, inasmuch as the diversity of organic forms supplies the basis on which selection can act. Followed as it was by the rediscovery of Mendelian genetics, such an idea gave tremendous impetus to the study of individual differences.

Sir Francis Galton, Darwin's half cousin, did much to further this point of view. With characteristic energy and inventiveness, he set about to construct tests that would accurately measure individual capacities in human psychological functions and to trace their hereditary causes. Compared to the instruments we now have available, his mental tests were primitive and arbitrarily constructed, but they did provide the ideas on which all modern psychometrics is based. It is for this reason that Galton has often been referred to as the "father of mental testing."

Against such a cultural and scientific background, the psychology of the individual emerged as a bona fide discipline with its special techniques and problems, to be discussed later. Let us first look at the second basic idea behind the material presented in the section, the idea of correlation.

Before Hume, the principle of causality had been basic to most philosophies and cosmologies. For every effect a cause was considered to exist, and for every cause, various effects. Such a notion was taken as being axiomatic. That is to say, it was held to be true a priori, and consequences were deduced from it. As we saw in Section Three, Hume's criticism of it was very simple but also cogent. He asked the question, Is it in fact true that we can really observe causal relations between two events rather than simply associations? His answer was in the negative. For him, causality was a mental construction and not immediately observable by us in the physical world. Thus we may observe that a red sunset is often followed by clear weather the next day, but it is certainly not correct to conclude that a red sunset *produces* good weather. The two events are associated, but their causal relationship is merely inferred.

Hume's point of view does not, of course, prove there is no such thing as a cause-and-effect relation. As one way of thinking, the principle of causality has proved to be immensely valuable. Nonetheless, it has limitations if we use it as an exclusive explanatory principle. From an empirical and scientific standpoint, it is often enough to observe simply that two events are associated or vary together. Thus it is useful to know that height and weight, for example, are associated and to what extent they vary together, or covary.

When the fact of relationship among events in the world is viewed in this way, it becomes one of contingency; that is to say, the degree to which some events are contingent on (etymologically, "touch on") other events. Quantitatively, contingency is expressed in terms of the *correlation coefficient,* a statistical expression developed by Karl Pearson. As indicated in Chapter 2, the correlation coefficient tells us the degree to which two or more measures taken on a number of individuals are related.

It will be noted that this second basic idea of correlation is closely related to the first idea of variation. Thus, it is only by virtue of the fact that individuals vary along certain dimensions that we can correlate these dimensions. We must be able to *measure* height and weight in a number of individuals before we can discover the degree of correlation between them. The same applies to psychological traits. Before we can correlate them we must be able to measure them.

Correlational statistics are absolutely basic to the whole problem of constructing and standardizing tests. They enable us first to estimate the degree to which a measure is liable to fluctuation when used on repeated occasions. This is called the *reliability* of a test. They also can tell us the extent to which the test predicts some criterion in which we may be interested, for example, whether an aptitude test, given before entrance to college, will predict good academic grades. This is the concept of *validity*. These two notions will be fully discussed later in this section.

Another way in which the Pearson correlation coefficient can be used is perhaps the most interesting and the most substantive. Once the measurement of mental abilities became possible, the question naturally arose as to the number of abilities possessed by human beings and the extent to which they were related. The first man to examine this problem thoroughly was Charles Spearman, an associate of Pearson and Galton. His basic point was that if two tests showed covariation between individuals, so that individuals scoring high or low on one scored high or low respectively on the other, then these tests must have something in common. This communality Spearman called a *factor,* and the technique he developed to educe factors he labeled *factor analysis*. The latter involved essentially the statistical analysis of a matrix of correlations between a large number of tests, so that the common factor or factors could be extracted. Through this method, it became theoretically possible to make exact statements about the nature of mental organization.

Spearman himself claimed he had evidence for a single general factor (at least, for intellectual performance), but many workers following him, particularly Godfrey Thomson in Scotland and L. L. Thurstone, J. P. Guilford, and Raymond Cattell in the United States found it necessary to think in terms of multiple factors. The notion they implied was that someone could be high in one ability, for example, deductive reasoning, but low, medium, or high in another, for example, mathematical ability. In Spearman's view, a person could be only *generally* intelligent: if he was good at one thing, he tended to be good at everything else. Though the reader may find one of these positions more attractive than the other, he should be warned that the problem is not one to be settled by opinion but by reference to empirical criteria.

The discussion above has dealt with two major ideas—variation and covariation, or correlation. The field of testing, or psychometrics, is devoted to an analysis of these ideas and, in this orientation, diverges somewhat the tradition of experimental psychology. The two disciplines, though not by any means exclusive of each other, do in fact concern themselves with different kinds of problems and tend to use rather different methodologies (Cronbach, 1957). Experimental psychology uses mainly inferential statistics as exemplified by the t test. It sets up studies in terms of an independent variable, or treatment, which it imposes, usually in a controlled laboratory setting, on a group of subjects and looks for effects in terms of some measurable dependent variable. Since it is concerned with closely specifying such treatment effects, the behavioral indices chosen for study by the experimentalist are usually simple ones, for example, activity level or bar pressing. Differences between individuals are not regarded as intrinsically interesting but are treated, instead, as nonrelevant variance against which is compared the average change in the experimental group produced by the main variable.

Psychometrics, on the other hand, uses mainly descriptive statistics, particularly the correlation coefficient. It is concerned with describing the individual in terms of his traits and abilities and comparing him with other individuals. It does not impose treatments and look for effects these may bring about but simply takes nature as it exists in an average environment. Whereas experimental psychology is closer to physiology, psychometrics is more akin to comparative anatomy. A paradigm case pertaining to the former discipline is the study of the nerve-muscle preparation. A nerve is electrically stimulated, and measurable changes in muscle contraction are recorded. In the latter field, a paradigm study would be the dissection of a mammalian spinal cord and the description of how the pairs of spinal nerves are arranged along its length.

This section will deal first with the meaning of measurement and scaling in psychology. Second, it will examine the tests we use to assess abilities, achievement, and personality and the ways in which we are able to make up standard tests. Third, it will discuss the dimensions of personality and intelligence and the methods we use to describe the relationships between mental functions and traits in an economical way. A final section of Chapter 22 will deal with the problem of creativity. It will probably become clear to the reader, as we proceed, that the subject of the present section is to a large extent concerned with methodology. That is to say, much of it will deal with the development of techniques of assessment and only part of it with basic findings about the makeup of man. To this extent, these chapters are somewhat different from the others in this book, which have focused on content rather than on method.

CHAPTER 20
SCALES AND THE MEASUREMENT OF INDIVIDUAL DIFFERENCES

SCALING

There is no question that today the measurement of psychological abilities and personality traits is very much in vogue. Magazines and papers are full of so-called tests that tell a person whether he is "adjusted," how "creative" he is, or whether he or she is a "good husband or wife." It should be emphasized immediately that most of these tests are almost meaningless. They are constructed quite arbitrarily and are completely unstandardized. It is perhaps because of these failings that much suspicion has recently been directed toward the use of all psychological tests, and in the United States a congressional committee was formed to investigate the charges that they not only represent an invasion of privacy but that they lack validity in any case (cf. "Testing and Public Policy," *American Psychologist,* 1965).

Whatever the truth of the claims made by the critics, even popular tests are, in a crude way, attempting to *measure* individual differences. To understand better why they fail and how they differ from standardized tests, we will look first at what the notion of measurement really means and how it can be applied to psychological functions. Only by specifying exactly what measuring really involves will we be able to see how it can be usefully and responsibly applied to human behavior.

In general, measurement can be defined as the assignment of a class of numerals to a class of objects (Lorge, 1951). In the usual case, this is simple enough. For example, the class of individual persons who reach the same point on a ruler may be called 6 feet tall. Those coming a certain distance below—5 feet 10 inches, and so on—are placed in a different class. The classes here are defined in terms of *height*. The numerals assigned to each class have certain relationships with each other that are crucial in speaking about height and that allow us to make certain statements, for example, to the effect that Jones is *twice as tall* as his son, or that he is taller than his wife by the same amount that she is taller than the boy. Obviously, such properties do not always apply in the case of measurement. Thus it does not make much sense to say that Jones' car registration number is twice as big as Smith's. Nor does it make sense, for reasons we will specify, to say that Green is twice as adjusted emotionally as Brown, or, for that matter, even twice as intelligent.

What we wish to discuss here is just what different kinds of measurements allow us to say about the relation of one individual to another and how much we can, in fact, say in respect to psychological tests. To measure anything, we have to perform two main operations: First, we have to be able to identify classes in respect to some property, and, second, we have to be able to make decisions as to the way in which the classes differ from each other. This twofold procedure is essentially what is meant by measurement, or *scaling*. We find that there are, in fact, four basic types of scale. These are called the nominal, ordinal, interval, and ratio scales. Each has certain properties that define it, and correspondingly each permits certain kinds of statements to be made about the individuals to which it applies and does not permit others to be made (cf. Stevens, 1949).

Nominal Scale

This is the simplest case. Here we classify individuals into groups on the possession or nonpossession of a property. For example, we can measure people in respect to the dimension "having a hunting rifle." Quite clearly, an individual either has a rifle or he does not. There are no degrees in between. Furthermore, even in cases where such degrees are possible, we may still group in this all-or-none fashion simply by arbitrarily setting some criterion point. Thus we may divide a group into such classes as bright or dull, heavy or light, even though the traits involved could be treated as continuous. Once we have made two or more such groupings, we can perform a number of simple statistical operations which give us useful information about the relative sizes of the groups. Looking at Table 20-1 (which is only hypothetical) makes it immediately clear that owning a rifle is modally a male trait in the sense that the class "males" includes more rifle owners than does the class "females." The definition of the *mode* is, in fact, that class which occurs most frequently in a distribution. In addition, we can also find out how two properties relate to each other in terms of frequency and can calculate by certain statistical procedures the degree of relationship.

Evidently a good deal of data can be handled by means of the nominal scale. The predictions of many political opinion polls, such as the Gallup Poll, are often made on the basis of *contingency tables* constructed in this way. The nominal scale is thus a useful type of measurement, although it is limited in comparison to the other scales.

Table 20-1 Owning a hunting rifle

	Yes	No
Male	40%	60%
Female	5%	95%

Ordinal Scale

One of the most commonly used scales in psychology and the behavioral sciences is the ordinal, or rank-order, scale. The empirical operation crucial to this type of measurement is the placement of classes in an order—greater than and less than. Thus a teacher may rate the pupils in her class on the basis of her judgment of their ability from highest to lowest. The same may be done with many physical properties of objects, for example, "quality" of cloth or "hardness" of metals. The only unchangeable feature of the scale is order. That is to say, the numbers assigned to each class retain the same meaning no matter how big or small the actual intervals between the different classes may be. The rank-order scale does not assume equality of intervals, only fixed ordinal positions. Consider the placement of five individuals on the two measures "impulsiveness" and "extroversion," as shown in Table 20-2.

In terms of the rank-order scale, the five persons are still absolutely equivalent in respect to the two dimensions. Clearly, then, the numbers we are using to designate these orders (i.e., 1, 2, 3, 4, 5) do *not* have the same meaning here that they have in most standard arithmetic computations. Thus the difference between 1 and 2 (Jones and Smith) on impulsiveness is *not* equal, in the example given, to the difference between 1 and 2 (Jones and Smith) on extroversion. Normally, of course, $1 - 2 = 1 - 2$, but not so here. As soon as we have operations to determine the truth of this equality, we have another type of scale, one which we will examine further on.

Formally, then, the rank-order scale has two properties *asymmetry* and *transitivity*. By asymmetry we mean that we can make the following types of statements:

   Jones = Brown
or Jones > Brown
or Brown < Jones

Table 20-2 In an ordinal scale, intervals between ranks may or may not be equal

	Extremely	Above average	Moderately	Below average	Very slight
Impulsiveness	Jones	Smith	Brown	Green	Robinson
Extroversion	Jones	Smith	Brown	Green	Robinson
Rank order	1	2	3	4	5

NOTE: The equality illustrated would hold true even though the *real* differences between the individuals (if we could estimate them) looked like this:

Impulsiveness (amount)

Jones		Smith	Brown	Green	Robinson
1		2	3	4	5

Extroversion (amount)

Jones	Smith	Brown		Green	Robinson
1	2	3		4	5

By transitivity we refer to the following relationship:

If   Jones > Brown
and   Brown > Green
then Jones > Green.

Note that transitivity does not always hold true. For example, a person may like Jones more than Brown and Brown more than Green, but still like Green more than Jones. In such a case, it is likely that several dimensions are involved in the judgment of liking.

Interval Scale

As indicated above, rank scores as such do not involve any operation for determining equality of intervals between them as far as the dimension on which the ordering is carried out is concerned. It is certainly true that one rank separates ranks 1 and 2 and likewise 1 rank separates ranks 2 and 3. But as far as the underlying dimension, whatever it may be, is concerned, we cannot say if the *amount* of the dimension separating ranks 1 and 2 is the same as that amount separating ranks 2 and 3. We can represent the situation in this manner.

	Jones	Smith	Brown
Actual rank	1	2	3
Hypothetical score on underlying dimension	100	80	40

Rank 1 − rank 2 = rank 2 − rank 3
Dimension score 100 − 80 ≠ 80 − 40

As soon as we have some way of determining the equality of the intervals between the numerals we assign, we have a third type of scale, the interval scale. Temperature or conventional time measures are such scales. Thus we can say, for example, that the difference in time between 1948 and 1952 is the same as the difference between 1962 and 1966. In this case, we have a concrete empirical operation that allows the statement, namely, the passage of the earth around the sun.

Clearly, most psychological scales and tests are not known to be additive. For example, three 10-year-olds may obtain IQ scores of 115, 120, and 125, respectively. We might think, then, that the difference of 5 IQ points between the first and the second is equal to the difference of 5 IQ points between the second and the third; and it might also be true that the first obtained 60 correct items, the second 75, and the third 90. But we still do not really know if these equal-appearing intervals of 5 IQ points and 15 items are really equal in terms of actual intelligence. Thus it is quite likely that it is much harder (intellectually speaking) to get from 120 to 125 than to get from 115 to 120. The same applies to most tests of personality, achievement, and attitudes. These are mainly only approximations to a true interval scale, by no means perfect, yet certainly useful.

We should note that the intervals between the numerals of our scale do not have to be equal to give us an interval scale. We need only know how many units fill each of our intervals, so that we can, if we wish, extrapolate to equality. Thus in the example below, either scale is as good as the other provided that B is derivable from A by some kind of transformation. Here, B is a logarithmic scale which can readily be transformed into scale A. In both, operations of addition and subtraction can be carried out equally readily.

```
Scale A      |              |              |
score       80            100            120
Scale B      |   |              |
score       80  90                         100
```

Ratio Scale

This is the most advanced type of scale we will consider here. In addition to the properties needed for the other scales, the ratio scale has the additional one of having a true or absolute zero point. If we have available the empirical operations for determining zero, then we can compute ratios. Consider the following example:

```
A. Equal interval           |        |  |  |  |  |
   (zero point unknown)    0(?)      4  6  8 10 12
B. Ratio scale              |     |  |  |  |  |
   (zero point known)       0     2  4  6  8 10 12
```

In case B, we can establish the identity $2/4 = 4/8 = 6/12$. But we cannot do this with the interval scale, since we do not know where the zero point is. Thus the first number of it, 4, does not mean 4 units above zero, but 4 plus some unknown quantity x. Thus instead of $4/8 = 6/12$, we would have $(4 + x)/8 \neq (6 + x)/12$, unless $x = 0$, in which case we do have a ratio scale. Thus, even supposing we had an interval scale for intelligence, we still could not say that Johnny, with an IQ of 80, is only half as bright as Jimmy, who has an IQ of 160, because we do not know what zero intelligence is. For that matter, it may be a meaningless concept, much as zero mass would be. The same applies to most psychological measures. Ratio scales are quite common for physical measures, however, size and weight being good examples.

To summarize what we have said so far about measurement, we have available to us in psychology four ways of measuring the differences between individuals in respect to any behavioral dimension. Most of the time, psychologists work with the first two, the nominal and ordinal scales, though they may assume the third—the interval scale. For most purposes of statistical analysis, these seem to be quite adequate. Thus if we wish to find out, for example, whether there are any differences between males and females in intelligence, we can proceed using some standard IQ test and perform the necessary statistical operations that yield some definite statement about sex differences.

We might ask, then, at this point, if we can do so much with such crude scales, just what advantages ensue from attempting to get more refined measurement? The answer to this question is that by getting real scales of measurement we gain, first, in precision—that is, we will be able to predict more exactly—and, secondly, through greater precision we may also gain *additional information* about the behavior we are attempting to measure. This second gain is without any doubt the more important one. In this regard, accurate measurement (that is, having empirical operations to meet the criteria of a proper scale) can help us in psychology as it has in other sciences.

Up to now we have been speaking of measurement in reference to the differences between individuals on some traits or ability, and we have delineated four scales by which variation may be ordered. It should be noted that these techniques of scaling can be used not only for this purpose but also for the purpose of ordering variations that are perceived to exist between stimuli of different kinds, for example, sounds of varying intensities, items of different degrees of excellence, or hues of different brightnesses. We have already seen an application of such methods in our discussion of attitude scale construction in Section Three. There are many others that have been made. For example, food preferences can be scaled, so that we may find out how much individuals in a certain population prefer roast beef to roast lamb. In institutional settings, this information can be of great importance in preparing menus that are satisfactory from the standpoint of maintaining good morale, health, and a reasonable outlay.

Psychophysics deals with this basic problem. Thus its purpose, according to one contemporary psychologist, Eugene Galanter (1962), derives from the classic problem of the relation between the mind and the physical world, and one of its major problems is that of scaling the response of the average person to variations in the physical stimuli that impinge on him.

It is fair to say that although testing and psychophysics often employ the same methods, their history and theoretical orientations are different. Our interest in this chapter is with differences between people and the measurement of these differences, rather than with the differences between stimuli as perceived by the typical person. Consequently, we will not discuss further the topic of psychophysics in this chapter.

PSYCHOLOGICAL TESTING

Background

As noted above, Galton has often been called the "father of mental testing." His keen interest in anthropology, his faithfulness to Darwin's emphasis on diversity of living forms, and his natural brilliance, all combined to produce in him a man who could suitably lay the groundwork for the development of psychological testing. But the fact of the matter is, though his contribution was great, he did not get very far with the problem of defining and measuring such complex functions as intelligence and personality, in which many psychologists were interested. For the most part, the measures Galton developed assessed only sensory abilities and vividness of imagery. For example, he designed a whistle capable of emitting variable frequencies of sound in order to measure the upper limits of auditory acuity. Again, he developed a kind of self-rating scale on which subjects were asked to estimate the clarity and detail of some image they were asked to generate, for example, a mental picture of their own breakfast table.

These were ingenious methods—even though they may seem naïve to us today—and coupled with Galton's statistical contributions represented a large step forward in the understanding of individual differences. But it was perhaps the French psychologist, Alfred Binet, more than anyone else, who was most responsible for formulating the approach to testing out of which modern psychometrics has grown.

Like many men in the nineteenth century who were interested in psychology, Binet brought to it a highly varied background and training in biology, philosophy, and clinical medicine. His major concern, like Wundt and the German psychologists, was the formulation of general laws of mind, and the philosophic framework within which he attempted to do this was supplied by British associationism. Unlike the structuralists, however, he had a strong preoccupation with the practical operations of mind in everyday life, not only with the normal but also with the abnormal mind, not only with the mind of the adult but also with the mind of the child.

These interests led him in three major theoretical directions: first, toward the study of such complex processes as intelligence and reasoning, rather than with the elements of consciousness; second, toward the study of individual differences; third, to an emphasis on studying the way in which mental functioning developed from childhood to maturity. These problems had for Binet immediate priority and had to be solved before psychology could turn to the ultimate task of laying down the general laws governing the operation of the human mind.

Note how these orientations differed not only from those of German psychology but also from those of Galton. Galton was a gentleman scientist of the British upper class and did not have behind him the tradition of the French Revolution that led men like Binet and, one hundred years before, the psychiatrist Philippe Pinel, to have a passionate concern for the welfare of every individual regardless of his station in life. We saw something of Pinel's contribution in Section Two. Similarly, Binet's humanism directed him to study the manner in which the individual mind expressed itself in its natural environment rather than in the artificial setting of the laboratory. In fact, one event that gave considerable impetus to his work was his appointment by the Minister of Public Instruction in Paris in 1904 to a commission charged with considering the problem of subnormal children in the schools.

The types of tests that Binet and his collaborator, Herbert Simon, constructed were specifically geared to this practical purpose. Galton, in his early attempts to measure intelligence, had used only tests of sensory acuity on the ground that ability in this sphere set the limits to intellectual capacity. This had also been the view of the American psychologist, James McKeen Cattell, who in 1890 put forward as measures of intelligence such tests as strength of grip, rate of hand movement, speed of reaction time, and accuracy of time estimation. Binet and Simon approached the problem less cautiously and used instead tasks commonly considered as reflecting intelligence, for example, comprehension of sentences, vocabulary, attention span, and memory ability—a simple enough idea, but still a very new one in psychology at the turn of the century.

Binet's interest in children and in the development of intelligence supplied him with an ingenious method of scaling ability. Initially, he and Simon chose items which discriminated between children who were bright and children who were dull according to a scholastic criterion. Even today, this is a common way of validating a test. It is a somewhat arbitrary one, however, in that school marks may depend on many other variables besides sheer intelligence, for example, effort and motivation, emotional stability, or bias of a teacher. What became more and more obvious to Binet was that developmental age could supply a criterion that was far more objective and that was, in a sense, biologically rooted. Accordingly, he started to search for test items according to whether they discriminated between the ability of average children of different ages. For example, at age twelve a child should be able to tell how "snake," "cow," and "sparrow" are alike, though the same task should be beyond the ability of the average eleven-year-old. However, if an eleven-year-old child is able to pass such an item, then one might infer that his *mental age* was greater than his *chronological age*. It is the ratio of these two ages that constitutes the measure we have come to know as the intelligence quotient, or IQ. Thus

$$IQ = 100 \times \frac{MA}{CA}$$

It is obvious, of course, that this way of scaling ability can be used only up to a certain age when intelligence stops developing any further. This is usually considered to be around sixteen, though it may well be later than this. After this time, it may still make sense to assign to a person a certain mental age when this happens to be lower than his chronological age, but it does not make logical sense to assign one that is higher. Thus at age eighteen an IQ of 80 may have the same developmental meaning that it has at age ten. But an IQ of 140 would not have the same meaning at the two ages. In the case of the ten-year-old, we could say his intelligence was like that of the average fourteen-year-old. We could not say, however, that the eighteen-year-old had the intelligence of an average twenty-five-year-old if we stick by the assumption that intelligence does not increase in the average person after sixteen years of age. For this reason, an age scale has its greatest usefulness with children rather than with adults.

Despite this qualification, there is no doubt that the Binet-Simon scale represents a landmark in the history of testing. It has been revised by several different groups, including, especially, Terman and his workers at Stanford University, and has been adapted to many different cultures. It is undoubtedly one of the most widely used tests of intelligence for children today. In a later section of the chapter, we will discuss its composition in more detail.

Aside from the early efforts of Galton and Pearson, England's main contribution to the testing movement was the method of factor analysis first put forward by Spearman and others, including Cyril Burt, Godfrey Thomson, and Raymond Cattell. Their attempt to find basic "purified" traits and abilities contrasts with the highly practical "shotgun" approach of Binet. Factor analysis was quickly taken up by American investigators, particularly by Thurstone, Guilford, Tryon, and Holzinger, and today represents a focus of great activity. Thanks to the development of computer methods, the laborious statistical operations involved no longer present a real problem.

The great interest in testing in America is perhaps natural in view of the orientation of this country toward the useful and the practical, and its emphasis on the value of the individual. In fact, one historian of psychology, E. G. Boring, has asserted that the whole testing movement, though not originating in America, is essentially American in style and character (Boring, 1929). Indeed, it was probably the entry of the United States into World War I in 1917 and therefore the practical necessity of identifying ability and leadership quickly and reliably that gave to research on testing its greatest impetus.

Today, psychological tests are used all over the world in almost every sector of society—hospitals, business and industry, government, and schools. Probably very few people reading this book have escaped being exposed, at one time or another, to a test of some kind. As we have already said, this popularity has been viewed with alarm in some quarters, and there have appeared several books severely criticizing tests in general and their too casual usage in particular. For this reason, it is of the utmost importance to discuss at this point the purposes, basic nature and mode of construction of psychological tests. Only by giving these points full consideration can we hope to arrive at a fair judgment about their practical usefulness as well as their scientific merit for understanding behavior.

Purposes

According to Cronbach (1960, p. 21) *a psychological test is a systematic procedure for comparing the behavior of two or more persons.* We have already indicated that the comparison of individuals—that is, the measurement of individual differences—is the major idea being articulated in this chapter, and we have also outlined something of the broad historical background out of which this idea emerged. Before examining the first part of Cronbach's definition, namely, what is meant by "systematic procedure," we will discuss the purposes of tests and some of the major concepts they embody.

The complexity of modern society demands that *decisions* continually be made concerning the abilities and personality traits of individuals and the extent to which these are appropriate for certain kinds of positions. Such decisions have to do mainly with (1) *selection*, that is, rejection or acceptance of an individual for a particular slot, for example, admission to a good "ivy-league" college, or (2) *classification*, that is, the placement of an individual in a slot most suited to his abilities or interests. Typically, the armed services attempt, by various screening devices, to fit each enlistee to the job for which he is best suited. Though many jokes are made about their ineptitude in achieving this goal, there is little doubt that their successes are more frequent than their failures.

Apart from these rather practical aims, tests also have the potentiality of telling us something about the psychological makeup of man, that is, the structure of abilities and personality. By factor analytic methods, to which we have already referred, we may eventually be able to decide whether it makes more sense to think in terms of general intelligence or in terms of particular specialized aptitudes instead. From the standpoint of psychology as a science, this is perhaps the most important purpose of test development. Great attention has been paid to improving the efficiency and precision of psychological tests, and numerous applications of them have been made to many practical problems; but these must be counted as secondary to the major purpose of furthering the progress of psychology as a science.

Basic Nature of Tests

A test attempts to sample performances that reflect the trait it is designed to measure. We cannot measure intelligence directly. But we can measure ability to solve problems considered to require intellectual ability. Thus a typical scale usually involves a large number of discrete items—perhaps a hundred or more—which a subject can pass or fail and which constitute a representative test of the domain under consideration. Often the latter is very well specified, in which case the test may be either a replica or a shortened version of the actual task being predicted. For example, ability to pilot an airplane may be tested by means of a "mock-up" training plane with simulated flying conditions. Again, ability to run a lathe may be assessed by actually getting the subject to perform such a task for a brief period. More often, however, the psychometrician distinguishes between *a potential achievement* and *an actual achievement* that is the result of both *aptitude* and training. With new, untrained personnel this is obviously critical, not only for selection but also for appropriate classification.

To assess aptitude, the tester must therefore make up items which he believes reflect the ability that the job involves. To do this calls for some initial guesswork, which is subject, of course, to empirical check later on. Item selection thus typically calls for a back-and-forth process between intuition and actual validation. In this way, the psychometrician hopefully ends up with a list of items which measure the basic potentialities that will be realized as a result of training.

A test then consists of a number of items that have some theoretical and empirical relation to a certain criterion. The degree of relationship is what is meant by the validity of the test. Another characteristic of tests is their reliability. This is the degree to which the performance of individuals remain constant over time when they are retested or the degree to which performance on one part of the test is equivalent to performance on another part. Though these notions seem simple, they are actually rather subtle and require a good deal of further elaboration. This we shall do in the section following.

Whatever kind of criterion a test is designed to predict, any score obtained on it by an individual must be interpretable. It is necessary to know just what a number assigned to an individual means in relation to the numbers obtained by other individuals. By itself, an obtained score of 100 might mean anything from poor to perfect performance. To specify its meaning, we must have a scale of some kind, and we must also know something about the group with whom the individual is being compared. This is, in fact, what is meant by the term *standardization*. More exactly, it may be defined as *the set of procedures that permit exact interpretation of a given score*. Consider these two examples:

A ten-year-old boy passes all items on the Stanford-Binet test up to the top of the twelve-year-old level. As the reader will recall, this gives him an IQ of 120. This means that he has exceeded approximately 80 percent of ten-year-old children and reflects relatively high intellectual capacity. Several qualifications may be in order, however, if we examine more closely the composition of the comparison group. We find that the norms for the Stanford-Binet have been standardized on predominantly white, urban, middle-class American children. Eells and his coworkers at the University of Chicago (Eells, 1951) have demonstrated distinct bias in the test against lower-class American children, this bias being expressed in several ways but chiefly in terms of the kind of language demands placed on a subject. For example, a child whose world does not encompass such phenomena as symphony orchestras is unlikely to solve the analogy "Symphony is to conductor as baseball is to umpire," not because he does not have the capacity to do so, but rather because the words in which the form of the analogy is couched are foreign to him.

Again, it is probably true that the score obtained by a Zuñi child would not properly reflect his ability in relation to the standardization group, even with a translated text, simply because of the noncompetitiveness of the Zuñi culture. Unlike white middle-class children, the Zuñi child tends deliberately to underachieve in a test situation in order to avoid the breach in politeness that doing better than his peers would entail.

Accordingly, we have to be very careful to interpret correctly the meaning that a test score has by being conversant with the *scale being used* and by knowing enough about the *nature of the standardization group* so that we do not make comparisons when these are not really proper.

We thus have two initial problems in standardizing a test. The first has to do with *scaling*; the second, with *norms*. They are closely related insofar as both involve the uniformity of meaning that a test score can have. Thus we aim, in the first case, at *uniformity of units,* in the sense that $a-b = b-c = c-d = \cdots = m-n$. We also wish, if possible, to obtain some means of establishing an absolute zero point to give equality of ratio as well. In respect to norms, we aim at obtaining *uniformity of interpretation* of a score, so that we can say that a particular score reflects the same trait in different tested groups. Every university runs into this problem when it attempts (if it does) to achieve some common standards of marking across different departments. We will now examine a number of techniques aimed at dealing with scaling and norms.

Problems of Scaling and Norms

STANDARD BY GENERAL AGREEMENT OR BY EXPERT JUDGMENT We often find scales of this type used, especially in education. For example, it is a common convention in most universities throughout the world to use a letter or a number division for broad classification: A, B, C or I, II, III. These correspond roughly to the verbal designations "excellent," "good," "fair." Finer distinctions are often made by dividing each grade into three: A+, A, A—. These in turn may correspond with arabic numerals, for example, A+ = 97.5, A = 95, A— = 92.5.

That this system has persisted for so long and is used so widely means it is a reasonably workable one. At the same time, as everyone who has used it or been subject to it knows, it is by no means foolproof. Often, a mark of A in one institution represents a much lower standard of work than the same mark in a different place. Even in the same institution, it may mean different things for different people or in different courses. Furthermore, the meaning a certain mark has must also be related to how many people in a class achieve it. An A can give little satisfaction to a student if everyone else in the class also gets an A. On the other hand, the individual who has obtained such a mark for the first time for three years in that course can be justly proud of it. By taking this point into consideration we can start to attach a little more meaning to a mark or score than we would otherwise be able to. Let us now turn to several methods that allow us to do this.

PERCENTILE SCORES We discussed percentile scores briefly in Chapter 2. They are obtained simply by finding out what percentage of the group is exceeded by individuals having a certain score level. A score of 75, which is relatively meaningless by itself, now acquires much more direct significance. Thus we may learn that in school 1 an individual getting a grade average of 75 has a percentile score of 98. This means that the mark is a very high one for that school, since it is a higher mark than obtained by 98 percent of students in the school. On the other hand, if we find that the same mark in school 2 corresponds with a percentile score of 65, we then know that in that school such a mark does not present particularly unusual performance. Regardless of this fact, however, notice that we still cannot say that 75 in school 1 is actually better than 75 in school 2. It might well be that in school 2 the standard of marking is very much higher than in school 1. On the other hand, it may mean that school 2 has a great many students of outstanding ability. It may also mean both these possibilities.

In other words, a percentile score as such gives us no additional information about the absolute meaning a score has, but it does make a score more meaningful in terms of the particular group to which it has reference. To obtain more generality, we must collect more information by having the same test given to many different groups of the same type, for example, American children in grade 9. We do not need to take all such children, of course, but only a representative sample of them. Even this is not so easy as it sounds, since many factors must be taken into account, such as race, religion, socioeconomic status. However, if we can obtain

Table 20-3 Percentile norms for numerical aptitude in grade 9 children (Psychological Corporation, 1952, Thorndike & Hagen, 1955)

Percentile score	Numerical aptitude
99	35
97	32–34
95	30–31
90	27–29
85	25–26
—	—
—	—
—	—
3	1–2
1	0

for our test the scores of such a standard group, we then have some basis for judging any individual who is subsequently given the test.

Consider the following example in Table 20-3. This shows the scores obtained on part of an aptitude test and the corresponding percentile norms. We find, for example, that a score between 27 and 29 on numerical ability corresponds with a percentile score of 90. Thus if we give our test to Johnny Smith, who scores 28, we know that, other things being equal, he has done better than 90 percent of children of his age level. The limits of our judgment about his performance are determined by the breadth of our standardization group. If it is very broad, for example, all children of that age in the world (if this were possible), then our judgment about Johnny can be very general. If the standardization group is very particular, for example, all children of that age in the East End of London, then our judgment about Johnny's ability must be correspondingly narrow.

Since interpretation can be so limited, it is always important for the test constructor to specify exactly the size and characteristics of his standardization group or groups. This is, of course, one important feature of a proper test that is almost never found in the psychoquizzes of popular magazines.

Though useful in a general way, percentile scores do not give us a very refined kind of scale. In other words, the distances between percentile scores are seldom equal. 90–85 is *not* equivalent to 55–50. The reason for this is contained in the way ability and, in fact, most biological and psychological traits

FIG. 20–1 A cumulative frequency distribution.

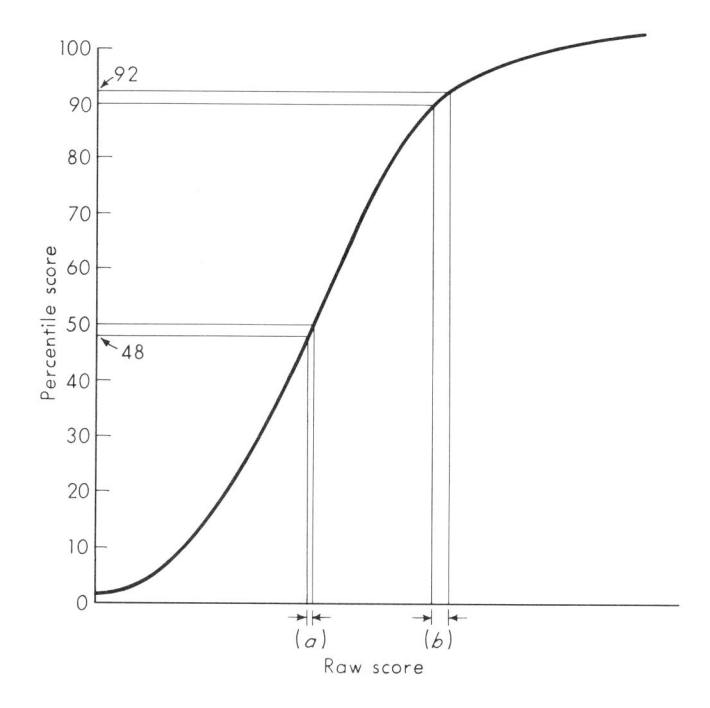

are distributed. Typically they follow the normal curve form. This means that most people get moderate scores and a few are very high or very low. Consequently, the actual distance between individuals at the high levels is much greater than between individuals at medium levels. This can readily be seen if we plot raw scores for some normally distributed trait against a cumulative frequency distribution, as in Figure 20–1. The two distances 48–50 and 90–92 on the y axis are equal. They represent equal differences between percentile scores, but at different levels, one at a high level, the other at a low level. The distances on the test scores to which these correspond on the x axis, however, are clearly very unequal.

STANDARD SCORES Scores for any test may be expressed in terms of a common unit, the standard deviation. The resulting scores are also sometimes called Z scores as well as standard scores. The basic transformation is very simple. It is

$$Z_{jk} = \frac{X_{jk} - \overline{X}_k}{\sigma_k}$$

where Z_{jk} = standard score of individual j on test k

X_{jk} = raw score of individual j on test k
$\overline{X}_k$ = mean of group on test k
σ_k = standard deviation of group on test k

The procedure is quite analogous to any other kind of transformation from one unit to another. In most physical units, we have an absolute zero and can use this as a reference point rather than the mean of group scores.

Thus to translate the height of an individual from inches to feet we would proceed as follows:

$$h'_j = \frac{h''_j - 0}{12}$$

where h'_j = height of individual j in feet
h''_j = height in inches
12 = number of inches in a foot

Notice that 12 is a constant. We have defined our units so that 12 inches always equals 1 foot. What does the standard deviation equal? Provided the distribution of scores with which we work is normal, it too represents a kind of constant, namely, the proportion of individuals falling between different scores. Thus about 68 percent of cases will lie between the mean and the mean plus or minus one standard deviation. If an individual's standard score is + 1.0, we know that he will be equal to or better than 84 percent of the group (50 percent below the mean plus 34 percent up to one standard deviation above the mean). Similarly, a score of −1.0 will mean that he will be equal to or better than only 16 percent of other individuals in the group. For a number of individuals, our standard scores will range roughly from −3 or −4 to +3 or +4. If we wish to expand this scale and make it positive, we can merely add a constant and multiply by a constant, as follows:

$Z' = aZ + b$
where Z' = new standard score
Z = regular standard score
a = multiplication constant
b = additive constant

Thus if $Z = 1.5$, a is set at 20, b at 100, we should get

$Z' = 20 (1.5) + 100 = 130$

Note, however, that in terms of percentiles the scale generated by a standard score transformation of this type is not an equal-interval one. The distance 0 to +1 does not equal the distance +2 to +3, the second one being really very much larger. Another difficulty is that with distributions that are not normal, standard scores will not have a constant meaning from one test to another.

It is possible by another kind of transformed score called the normalized standard score to remedy some of these difficulties. However, the complexity of this method is beyond the scope of this book.

AGE NORMS As we noted earlier, one of the first tests ever constructed, the Binet-Simon test of intelligence, used age norms. Individuals were scored in terms of the number of items they could get right in comparison with the number a child of a certain chronological age could get right. If we plotted mean number right obtained by groups of different ages against age levels, we might get a curve something like the one in Figure 20–2.

Provided these standardizing groups were large enough and representative enough of the whole population in a country, we might then score any individual subsequently tested in terms of these age norms. For example, individual X gets a score of

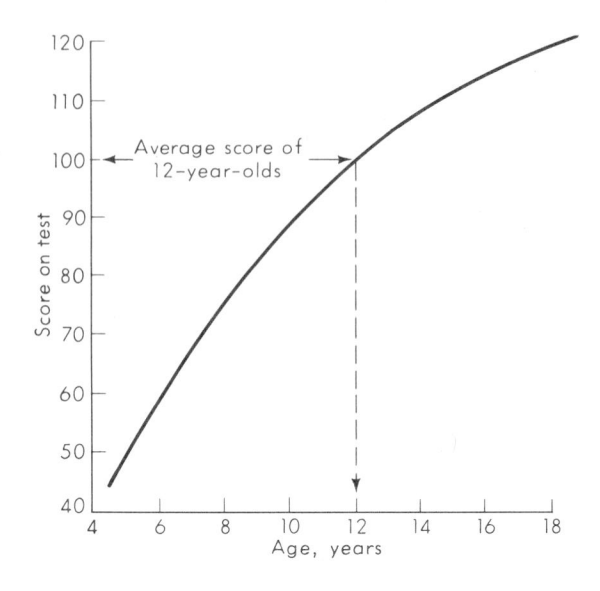

FIG. 20–2 Hypothetical relation between age and score on an intelligence test.

80. This is at the eight-year-old level, we see from the graph. If X is only six years old, he is then obviously doing very well. We may actually go a good deal farther than this qualitative kind of statement and talk quantitatively by using the IQ score as defined above. Certainly IQ scores are used very widely by testers everywhere to represent intellectual level. A classificatory scheme of grading intelligence (eight to twelve years) is shown in Table 20–4.

Although IQ scores have such wide usage, they do have many limitations, some of which we have already discussed. Let us look at them again more formally. In the first place, the score given to any individual can only have meaning in so far as that individual is like those in the standardization groups. That is, it must have *uniformity of interpretation*. An IQ score obtained for an African, for example, would be worthless if American norms were used. It has even been claimed (Havighurst, Eells et al., 1951) that the same is true even within the United States for children of different classes. Thus the Stanford University revision of the Binet test (Terman & Merrill, 1937) used for its standardization groups mostly middle-class children. The language employed in the test is consequently of a kind more

Table 20-4 Classification for grading intelligence

Grades of intelligence, or IQ grade	IQ range (Stanford-Binet)
Idiot	0–25
Imbecile	26–50
Moron	51–70
Borderline	71–79
Low average	80–91
Normal	92–115
High average	116–125
Superior	127–136
Very superior	137 and above

understandable to middle-class rather than lower-class children.

This is purely apart from the form of any particular problem. A test having such a bias would be giving an estimate, not of any basic intelligence, but rather of a cultural intelligence. In one way, of course, this would not matter. If the test correlated highly with success in school, then we could say that the child who did poorly on such a test would not be as likely to perform as well in school as the one who had a high test score. On the other hand, we could also argue that a deficiency due merely to such lack of cultural opportunity should be very easily remedied and therefore not a real deficiency. The underlying assumption here is that the test score, to the extent that it is reliable, is measuring something fairly stable and unchangeable.

A second difficulty with IQ scores is related to the one just discussed. In establishing a typical level of performance for a certain age group, *it is assumed that mental growth is constant*, that is to say, that it is linearly related to chronological age. This may not be true. In fact, there is reason to believe that mental growth is rapid at first and then gradually slows down and perhaps stops at maturity. This is so with height and weight. If it is also true for intellectual growth, then clearly the differences between early age levels are not equal to the differences between later age levels. The fact that the IQ (the *ratio* of mental to chronological age) tends to remain constant suggests that mental growth may tend to follow a negatively accelerated curve. Thus to get an IQ of 125 at chronological age 4 an individual only needs a mental age of 5; to get the same IQ score at age 8, he needs to have a mental age of 10; and at 12, a mental age of 15.

A related point, finally, is that variability of IQ at later ages must be greater than at earlier ages if the IQ is to have a constant meaning from age to age. Suppose that at age 6, the standard deviation in IQ is 10. This would mean that 68 percent of children should score between 90 and 110, representing a range between 5.4 and 6.6 years mental age. To have the same frequency of IQs between 90 and 110 at age 10, however, the range must be between 9 and 11, a range of 2 years rather than the 1.2 years as in the first case. Consequently, *variability of mental age must be inversely correlated with age, if IQ remains constant.*

Two outcomes of this change in variability of mental age as a function of chronological age are as follows: First, we can expect that intelligence tests of very young children will be unreliable. This is a direct derivation from the fact that if observed variance of test scores is low, reliability is also low. For the same reason, the predictive value of infant IQ tests is also bound to be low, unless suitable corrections are made. This is in fact the case. At a young age, IQ tests appear to be less efficient predictors of a child's later IQ than the IQ of the child's parents. The graph in Figure 20-3 illustrates this point.

A second outcome of diminishing variability of mental age with diminishing chronological age is that it enables us to extrapolate backward to a point where intelligence should be zero—that is, to where variability is zero. Thurstone (1928) has in fact done this, concluding that intelligence starts at a few months before birth.

We may conclude this discussion of scaling and norms with a few summarizing points: First, we do have available a number of ways of scaling data so that some meaning may attach to a particular score given both within a group and between different groups. Second, these methods, though giving us interpretable scores, do not, for the most part, give us very refined (i.e., equal-interval or ratio) scales. Third, the methodological problems involved in test scores and scaling raise many substantive problems regarding the nature of the trait, its development and modifiability under various conditions.

Problems of Reliability

Psychological measurement is obviously not much like physical measurement. If we measure the

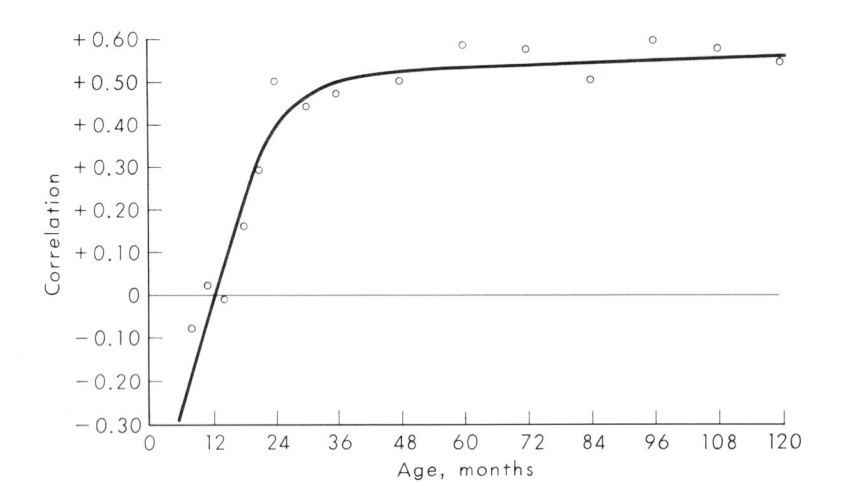

FIG. 20-3 Children's mental scores at successive ages as related to parents' education. (*Jones, 1946*)

height or weight of an adult with a ruler, we have no reason to suppose that a second measurement will give us a different result, provided our measurements are taken close together in time. It is still true, on the other hand, that if we weighed a person just before he ate a large meal and just after he had eaten it, our two measurements would probably not agree. In other words, the weight of an individual is subject to fluctuations, or variation. Now, if it happened that we were weighing three people who were all within 3 pounds of each other, the amount by which the weight of each one varied due to such factors as meals eaten or ill health would have a good deal of bearing in determining the real difference between them. The situation might be as follows:

Individual	First weighing Wt., lb	Rank	Interval	Second weighing Wt., lb	Rank
A	156	1	A gets sick.	150	3
B	154	2	B constant.	154	2
C	153	3	C has large meal just before second weighing.	156	1

Clearly we could not place much reliance on the scores obtained in either weighing so far as making statements about the order of the three individuals is concerned. We would say, in fact, that our test was unreliable, by which assertion we would mean that the *variation within* individuals (on the two testings) in respect to weight was about as great as the *average variation between* them. This is the essential problem of reliability. For psychological characters, we can expect to find a good deal more fluctuation than we do with weight. People vary greatly in their motivation, their moods, and their feelings. These factors may have a greater or lesser effect, depending on what trait the test is measuring. Some traits seem to be more stable than others. Thus it is of great importance that we have available some way of stating in precise quantitative form how much an estimate of the difference between individuals on a test is affected by these irrelevant, or *error*, factors and how far it represents real, or *true*, differences.

METHODS OF CALCULATING RELIABILITY The general method of making such a statement is by calculating a so-called reliability coefficient. This is simply a correlation computed between scores obtained by a number of individuals on one test, or sample of items reflecting a certain trait, with their scores on another equivalent test, or sample of items. To the extent that the ranks of the individuals remain constant from one sample to the next, we can say that our test is a reliable one and is not greatly subject to the influence of error factors.

Basically, there are three methods of assessing reliability, though there are a number of variations of these. They are parallel-forms, test-retest, and split-half methods. We may think of each of these as being subject, more or less, to different sources of variation that together account for the total error variance. There are three such sources: first, variations that arise within the measurement procedure itself; second, variations due to changes over time in the individuals taking the test; third, variations due to changes in the specific samples of items we choose as being equivalent to each other (Thorndike & Hagen, 1955). As we shall see, different methods of estimating reliability cope with these rather differently.

The notion of *parallel forms* of a test and the statistical definition of a parallel test underlies almost all the equations that can be derived about test theory. The main criteria for parallel tests are that they have equal means, equal variances, and equal intercorrelations with other tests. The item content of the forms will, of course, be different, but each should get at the same trait or ability. We may think of the latter as a domain, or area, comprised by innumerable bits of behavior. A test simply takes samples of this domain. If two or more tests sample the domain adequately and precisely, they should naturally resemble each other in certain respects. This sampling notion is represented graphically in Figure 20–4.

Tests A and B mostly cover the domain being measured. Consequently, they correlate highly. Test C, on the other hand, measures only a small part of the domain and therefore has a low correlation with test B. Thus the main task with this method is the construction of two tests that will meet the criterion of parallelism without allowing them to appear too much alike. The experimenter does not have a great deal to go on except his intuition. Fortunately, he does have the statistical criteria available to him afterward to check on the success of his judgment.

The forms chosen as parallel may be given successively without any time interval, or they may be given with an interval between them. If the domain being sampled is affected by time changes, there is obviously less chance in the second case that the two versions will turn out to be statistically parallel. This is especially true if opportunity for practice is allowed during testings. For example, a typing test given to individuals who have just started to learn typing would show a low variance at first, but the

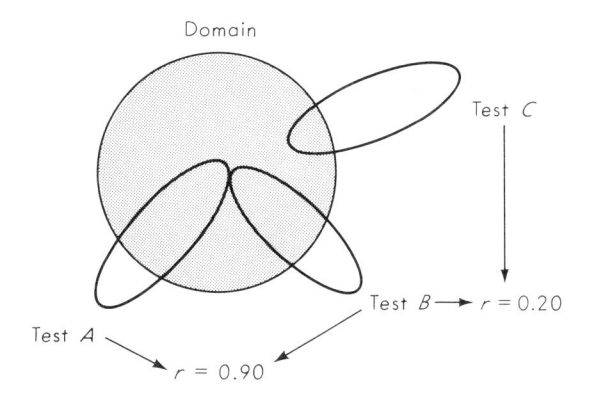

FIG. 20–4 The meaning of correlation.

variance would certainly increase as the individuals practiced. Then the two forms would, of course, not be parallel.

A commonly used method of obtaining reliability is to give the same test twice to the same subjects. This is known as the *test-retest method*. Usually an interval will separate the two administrations. This interval should be large enough so that no fatigue effects occur from having subjects do a great deal of work and that there is a minimal possibility of practice effects carrying over from the first to the second testing. For the most part, we can tell if there have been such effects by comparing the mean scores from the two testings. A rise in mean performance will indicate that there were practice effects. A drop will indicate probable fatigue effects. If these effects are uniform for all individuals, they will not affect the size of the reliability coefficient.

On the other hand, by giving the same test twice, the experimenter is liable to get an artificially high estimate, because variations which are really a function of that particular sample of items—and are therefore really part of the error variance—tend to be repeated the second time and thus become part of the true variance. This inflates the reliability. Individuals tend to remember their answers to items, whether these answers are correct or incorrect, and then repeat them, so that a correct answer on the first testing due merely to a lucky guess tends to be given again. The same applies to incorrect answers based on unlucky guesses. Aside from giving to the subjects specific instructions to avoid this kind of inertia in answering the retest items, not much can be done to avoid an artificially high reliability coefficient. For this reason, most test constructors prefer to use the other methods instead of, or at least in addition to, this one.

The *split-half method* involves simply splitting a test into two parallel parts and then correlating the parts. Thus a 100-item test is divided into two subtests of 50 items each. The main problems here lie in the method of splitting and in the effects of reduced length.

In regard to the first problem, several approaches are commonly used. One is to divide the test into odd against even items, 1, 3, 5, 7, ..., $n-1$ against 2, 4, 6, 8, ..., n. The correlation between the two subtests is then calculated in the usual way. The main difficulty here lies in the fact that the subtests may not be really equivalent statistically. If their variances are unequal, for example, the reliability coefficient will tend to be overestimated.

Another method, which involves taking the first half against the second half, may also be unsatisfactory, since the responses to successive items are not time-independent. Growing fatigue, loss of motivation, and other such factors will tend to reduce the individual's score on the second as compared to the first half of a test. The reduction will be even more drastic if the test is a speed test and has a time limit. In this case, many of the later items will not even be attempted by many individuals. Another complication lies in the fact that the items in many tests are arranged in order of difficulty with easier items at the beginning and harder ones at the end. This again reduces the equivalence of the two halves and lowers reliability. Again, the reduced length of each subtest makes for less reliability. This can be allowed for by special statistical procedures.

Gulliksen (1950) has evolved *matched random subtests*, a method for finding parallel subtests. Two main variables are considered important. One is the *difficulty* of each item. If we are to have really equivalent tests, they should obviously be of about the same degree of difficulty. The second dimension is the *degree to which each subtest predicts or mirrors or is a good example of the whole test*. If a subtest does measure what the whole test measures, then performance on items in the subtest should agree with performance on the whole test.

Table 20-5 Correlations between item and whole-test score

Item	(a) Test score, item j, high correlation		(b) Test score, item k, low correlation	
	Low	High	Low	High
Right	4	47	26	27
Wrong	46	3	24	23

That is, individuals who do well on item X should do well on the whole test, and individuals who do poorly on item X should do poorly on the whole test. Usually, of course, the response to an item does not admit a grading of individuals answering it. They either pass or fail. But we can still correlate each item with the whole test. In the two examples in Table 20–5, one (a) represents the case of a high correlation, the other (b) a low correlation.

In a whole test, some items will have a high and others a low correlation with the total test score. Consequently, to find equivalent subtests we must also take into account this factor of item-test correlation.

Let us suppose we have such a test made up of twenty items. We take an estimate first of the difficulty level of each item simply by finding out what proportion of people in the group pass it, or get it right. Secondly, we find out (as above) the correlation of each of the items with the whole test. We are now ready to plot these two dimensions against each other. We do this as indicated in Figure 20–5. For example, item 9 correlates with the test about .7 and has a difficulty level (p) of about .1. Item 50 is about the same. To construct our two subtests, we simply pick out pairs of items (like 9 and 50) which occur close to each other on the plot. Each member of a pair is then *randomly* (e.g., by tossing a coin) assigned to a subtest. In the example given we might have two subtests as follows:

Subtest A: Items 9, 2, 47, 11, 15, 35, 41, 20, 7, 39
Subtest B: Items 50, 33, 1, 48, 21, 13, 37, 42, 12, 5

The order in which the items are arranged should be the same for both subtests. That is, each member of a pair should occur at the same place in its respective test. If item 9 comes first in subtest A, then item 50 should come first in subtest B, and

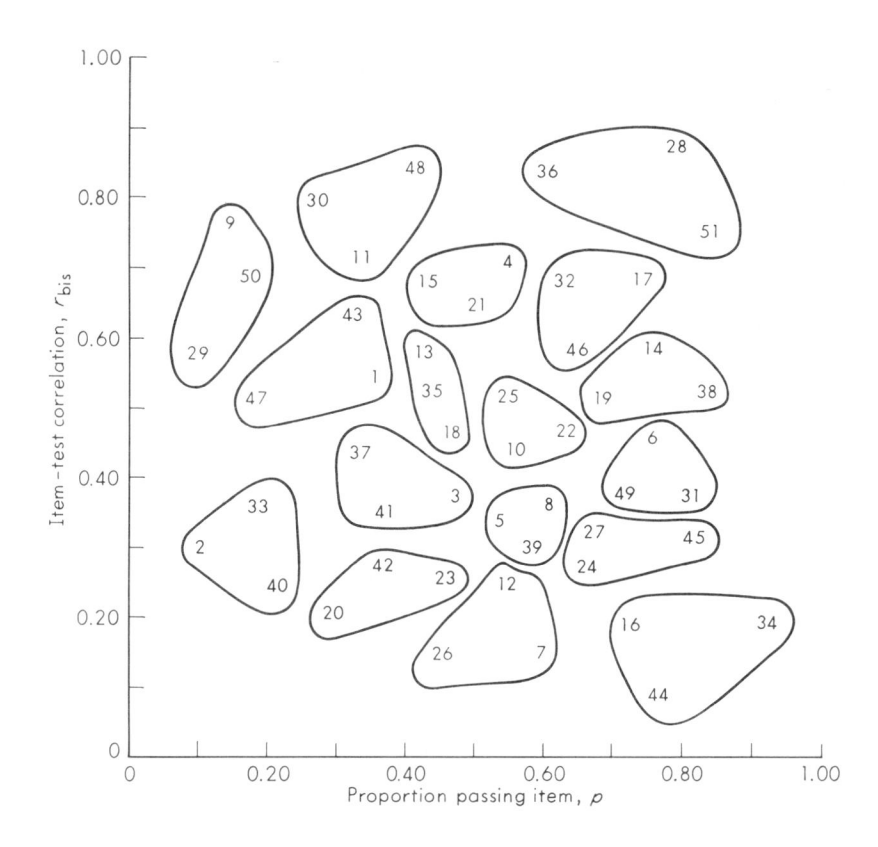

FIG. 20-5 Method of assessing reliability by means of matched random subtests. (*Gulliksen, 1950*)

so on. Gulliksen's procedure is laborious but does tend to give us an accurate estimate of reliability.

The next question that naturally occurs concerns what main factors affect test reliability. There are many obvious ones such as the clarity of instructions to the testees and the uniformity of the physical makeup of the test. Two more subtle but basically more important factors are the length of the test and the composition of the subjects taking it. Let us look at each of these briefly.

FACTORS AFFECTING RELIABILITY On the whole, as might be expected, it is true to say that as a test is made longer, its reliability increases. It is certainly obvious—and also happens to be true—that ten items will give us a better indication of, say, a person's intelligence than only one item. The general relation of *test length* and reliability can, in fact, be stated in exact mathematical terms. To spare the nonstatistically minded reader we will not attempt to derive the equations which relate reliability to length. What they demonstrate, granting certain assumptions such as we made before, is that the main effect of increasing test length is to increase the variance between subjects taking it. This hardly offends common sense. It is obvious enough, for example, that an examination with only one item in it would be less successful in discriminating between the abilities and knowledge of all the individuals in a class than an examination with many questions. However, it is comforting to know that it is also a fact that can be rigorously demonstrated mathematically.

There are two outcomes of the relation between length of test and reliability which are worth mentioning: In the first place, knowing the reliability of a short, preliminary test *we can estimate by how much* it should be lengthened to make it a more satisfactory (i.e., more reliable) instrument. For example, a test of 10 items with a reliability of only 0.30, if lengthened by a factor of 10, will yield a new reliability of .80, a satisfactory level. In the second place, given a test of sufficient length to have a fairly high reliability, we can calculate by means of an available formula what the reliability would be if the test were lengthened to an infinite number of items. This may seem a strange thing to do, but it does happen that the psychometrician may be interested in the characteristics of something not realizable in nature, namely, infinitely long tests, and particularly the extent to which they intercorrelate. We will return to this point when we discuss validity. Suffice it to remark at this point that the consideration of conditions beyond empirical inspection—for example, infinite spaces or infinite velocities—has yielded surprising kinds of information about the finite reality which we occupy in our everyday lives.

The second factor affecting reliability of a test is the *composition of the subjects* taking it. The subjects to whom we give a test may comprise a very homogeneous or a very heterogeneous group. If we gave an intelligence test to a group of men in a very selective college, we would expect to find that their scores did not vary a great deal. On the other hand, if we gave the same test to the same number of people representing a cross section of a large city, we would probably find a comparatively large variation in scores. We wish to establish that such a difference in subject variability, or homogeneity, can markedly affect the reliability of a test.

We suggested earlier that when the subjects are close together in their scores, minor fluctuations may result in shifts in ordinal position. Such shifts in rank order will lower reliability. We can illustrate this graphically by means of Figure 20–6. Here we see the score of each subject of a test plotted against his score on a parallel test or on the same test given again. It is clear that if we were to compute a reliability coefficient on the whole range of subjects, it would tend to be high, as shown by inspection of the scatter plot. The closer the ellipse approximates a straight line, the higher the correlation between the two variables. On the other hand, if we took only the middle section of subjects on each variable, we would have a circular scatter plot that would yield a very low correlation.

Reliability has to do with the accuracy of our measuring instrument and the separation of true or real differences between individuals from those that

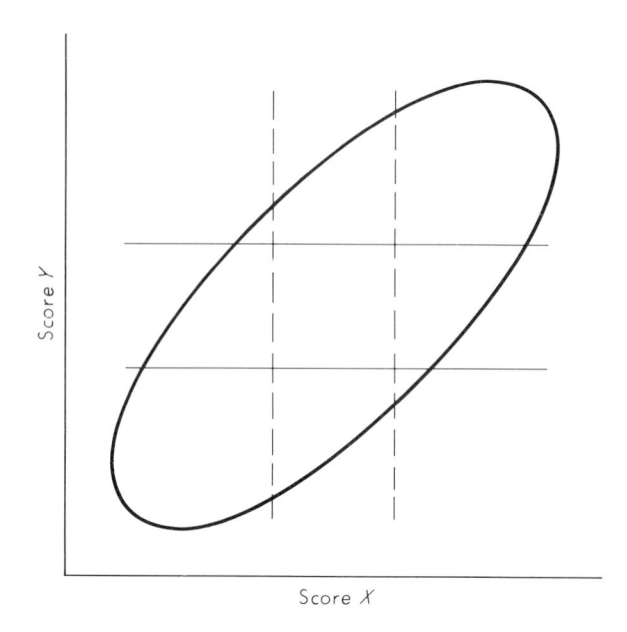

FIG. 20–6 Effect of subject heterogeneity of homogeneity on test reliability. (*Gulliksen, 1950*)

are due only to chance. Validity, the next concept to be discussed, has to do with the meaning that a test has and the extent to which it measures what it is supposed to measure.

Problems of Validity

The notion of validity covers the problem of finding out what a test really measures. This is not as simple as it sounds. Actually, the validity of any kind of measure, even a physical one, is defined in an arbitrary way. For example, a weighing scale is meant to tell us how much a person weighs. But if the scale is an old or crude one, it may also tell us many other things that are quite irrelevant, such as the extent to which the springs in it have lost their tension with usage. To guard against the operation of such factors, scales of this kind, when used in precise work, are calibrated against some exact and carefully preserved standards. Having such criteria, we may then expect uniformity of measurement from all scales that have been calibrated against these criteria. The validity of any weighing scale would then be the correlation between it and the standard in respect to the same objects.

The situation is the same with psychological tests, except that their definition and the definition of standards against which to calibrate them is much more arbitrary. We have no exact criterion or standard, for example, of intelligence. In fact, it is perhaps useless to look for one, at least, in any absolute sense. We can define intelligence as having something to do with solving problems and deduce from this that it must manifest itself in a great variety of life situations. But it may be fruitless to suppose that there is some ultimate reality that is pure intelligence and that this will eventually be grasped by psychology. This need not, however, stop inquiry into the composition of intellectual behavior at a theoretical level.

A more practical approach to the validity problem that is often taken is to decide what it is the test is to predict and then to find out if it does in fact do so. Thus if we wish to predict school achievement by means of an intelligence test, we try to find a test that is valid for that purpose, that is, a test that correlates highly with the criterion or standard of school marks. It is certainly true that performance on such a standard will depend on a great many other factors besides what we might think of as pure intelligence. Motivation, personality, and physical characteristics will all play some part. But from a practical standpoint this does not matter very much, so long as our prediction is a good one.

TYPES OF VALIDITY The discussion so far suggests that there are two main types of validity: rational validity and empirical validity. *Rational validity* involves the judgment by a professional of what kinds of items best represent a certain trait. He may, for example, consider that intelligence involves ability to solve problems in mathematics, verbal skills, or memory and therefore include in his test items which involve these processes. This is called *content validity*, since it involves comparison of the content of the criterion task with content of the test. He may also attempt to analyze rationally the process of problem solving into its components—into, say, abstracting, analogizing, deducing—and then make up items that involve these processes. This is *construct validity*. Usually, it is assessed by making a hypothesis about the nature of the measure and then testing some outcome of the hypothesis. For example, we may hypothesize that, because of early training influences, women in our culture have less mechanical skill than men. If our test in fact measures this aptitude, women should score lower on it than men. Verification of this prediction provides validation of the test in terms of the model. It goes considerably beyond content validity. In either case, the decision as to what items will be included on a particular test is made on an a priori basis alone. As we shall see later, we may also make up our test first and then analyze its composition later. The technical name for this approach is *factor analysis*.

The second main type of validity involves an empirical or statistical decision and is therefore called *empirical validity*. The question to be considered here is simply, How well does a test correlate with some other test or with a criterion? Here, the content does not matter so much provided good prediction is achieved. If it happened that ability to play poker was highly correlated with success as a business executive, then poker-playing ability would be an empirically valid test for selecting potential business executives. This is *predictive validity*. Of the same order is *concurrent validity*, which is the correlation between one test and another test designed to measure the same trait but in a different way, for example, the correlation between a test of emotional adjustment and rating of adjustment by a teacher.

The meanings of validity may then be classified as follows:

Type of validity	Method
Rational:	
Content	Inspection or theoretical model or
Construct	factor analysis
Empirical:	
Predictive	Statistical test theory
Concurrent	

Since we are mainly involved with test theory at this point, we will now consider in more detail the special problems relating to empirical validity, in particular, those factors that affect predictive validity of a given test. We will deal with three of them:

reliability, length of test, and composition of subjects.

FACTORS AFFECTING VALIDITY The alert reader may have already guessed that the *reliability* of a test has an important bearing on its predictive efficiency. The less the reliabilities, the lower the correlation between the tests. This can be expressed in an equational form as follows:

$$r_{xy} = r_{x_t y_t} \sqrt{r_{xx} r_{yy}}$$

where r_{xy} = observed correlation between scores of test *x* and *y*
$r_{x_t y_t}$ = correlation between *x* and *y* due to *true* scores only
r_{xx}, r_{yy} = reliability of *x* and *y*

This equation is known as the *Spearman-Brown correction for attenuation.* Besides showing how unreliability reduces validity, it can also tell us (by transposing $r_{x_t y_t}$ to the left side) what the real correlation between two variables is when we allow for unreliability, or fallibility, of our measuring instruments. This is of some theoretical interest in deriving common factors from a matrix of intercorrelations. In fact, Spearman educed his notion of general mental ability from consideration of correlations that had been so corrected for unreliability. In practical situations, however, where an actual empirical prediction is called for, the formula is not applicable, since it would result in an artificially high predictive validity.

If *test length* is related to reliability, then it is logical, on the basis of the preceding discussion, that it should also affect validity. Like other relationships, the one here can be stated in equational terms exact enough to predict what actual rise in the validity coefficient can be expected from increasing a test by a certain factor *k*. Interestingly enough, if *k* is set at infinity, the equation reduces to the Spearman-Brown formula—that is, the correlation of two variables when each has perfect reliability.

The *group composition,* or the variability of the group, it will be recalled, can alter reliability. The same is true for validity. On the whole, validity increases with increased heterogeneity of subject scores and decreases with increased homogeneity. This fact poses a problem that must often be faced when we use a test as a predictor. For example, a school psychologist may give an intelligence test to a group of entering freshmen in a college. He may then correlate their scores with their academic success in their final year. It will probably happen, however, that many of the poorer ones have been dropped before they even take final examinations in their last year. Consequently, the individuals for whom a correlation can be computed will be highly select and therefore constitute a homogeneous group. The validity of the test will then appear to be much lower than it really is.

There are available a number of equations that allow us to make predictions as to what the size of the correlation between the two variables would have been if selection had not occurred. Since a complete treatment of these would involve a rather lengthy discussion of some concepts of correlation in addition to those already dealt with, no attempt to derive these equations will be made here. The main points to remember are that selection does often occur, it does lower validity, and this can be remedied statistically.

We have now covered the most important features of validity. It is clear that it is intimately dependent on reliability, although the opposite is not true. That is to say, reliability of any test is not affected by the correlation of this test with another test.

VALUE OF A VALID TEST Before leaving the subject of validity, let us look at the gain we can expect from having a valid test. As already indicated, as validity increases, accuracy of prediction of the criteria from the test also improves. Table 20–6 illustrates this point numerically.

This table clearly shows how much is lost or gained by having certain cutoff points at different validity levels. For example, suppose it is desired to select individuals who will fall within the top half of the criterion measure. If the test has a validity of .40, a cutoff point can be set at the top quarter. Of the individuals so selected, 705 (428 + 277) will meet the criterion standard. However, 295 (191 + 104) will not. Furthermore, this will have eliminated a great many who would have passed the criterion if they had been selected, in fact, 1,295 individuals (277 + 191+ 104 + 277 + 255 + 191). This obviously represents considerable waste.

If the test has a validity of .80, on the other

Table 20-6 Validity and accuracy of prediction (Thorndike & Hagen, 1955)

(1,000 cases in each row or column)

Quarter on predictor	r = .00 Quarter on criterion				Quarter on predictor	r = .60 Quarter on criterion			
	4th	3d	2d	1st		4th	3d	2d	1st
1st	250	250	250	**250**	1st	45	141	277	**537**
2d	250	250	**250**	250	2d	141	264	**318**	277
3d	250	**250**	250	250	3d	277	**318**	264	141
4th	**250**	250	250	250	4th	**537**	277	141	45

Quarter on predictor	r = .40 Quarter on criterion				Quarter on predictor	r = .70 Quarter on criterion			
	4th	3d	2d	1st		4th	3d	2d	1st
1st	104	191	277	**428**	1st	22	107	270	**601**
2d	191	255	**277**	277	2d	107	270	**353**	270
3d	277	**277**	255	191	3d	270	**353**	270	107
4th	**428**	277	191	104	4th	**601**	270	107	22

Quarter on predictor	r = .50 Quarter on criterion				Quarter on predictor	r = .80 Quarter on criterion			
	4th	3d	2d	1st		4th	3d	2d	1st
1st	73	168	279	**480**	1st	6	66	253	**675**
2d	168	268	**295**	279	2d	66	271	**410**	253
3d	279	**295**	268	168	3d	253	**410**	271	66
4th	**480**	279	168	73	4th	**675**	253	66	6

hand, it does much better. Using the same cutoff point, there will be 928 (675 +253) individuals who will successfully pass the criterion, and only 72 (66 + 6) who will fail it. In addition, there will have been eliminated fewer individuals who would have passed had they been selected; in this case 1,072 (253 + 66 + 6 + 410 + 271 + 66). The gain in this last respect is not as great.

By setting a high level for selection, we get a group which will almost certainly do well, but, on the other hand, we will be turning away a large number who would have done equally well. The total number of persons wasted—the poor ones admitted plus the good ones turned away—is 1,144.

We can cut this number down considerably by lowering our selective standard to take all those scoring in the top half. With this arrangement, we will be admitting 1,591 (675 + 253 + 253 + 410)

who will pass the criterion, and 409 (66 + 6 + 271 + 66) who will fail. We will be rejecting 409 who would have passed (66 + 271 + 6 + 66). Thus the total wastage is now less—818 rather than 1,144. This is fairer, on the whole, to the individuals seeking admittance. But as far as the institution for which selection is being carried out is concerned, it is less desirable, since it can now expect a passing rate of less than 80 percent rather than over 90 percent with the higher cutoff point.

Clearly, decision on this point depends on many factors, some statistical, such as the reliability of the test, others economic, such as the resources of the institution and its ability to tolerate a certain amount of wastage.

As far as the individual who is rejected is concerned, he cannot really regard himself as having been unfairly dealt with. From a statistical standpoint, it is more likely he would fail the criterion than pass it if he fails the entrance test, though it is still true that he might have succeeded.

The three problems of test theory discussed above, namely, standardization, reliability, and validity, emerge directly from the basic ideas of individual variation and causation that were presented at the beginning of this chapter. Notice that they have figured predominantly as methodological rather than substantive issues. Thus we have been concerned mostly with techniques for scaling and for maximizing reliability and validity, and less with these concepts as they pertain to the understanding of behavior and personality. However, this is necessary in science. Many of the greatest breakthroughs have been achieved only by improvements in methods, for example, the measurement of nerve conduction, the invention of the telescope, the electron microscope, and many others. So, also, in the area of testing, work has been directed to the refinement of our methods of assessing the psychological differences between individuals in the hope of providing a firm basis for comparable breakthroughs. Since we have been dealing with testing at a rather abstract level, we will present in the next chapter some concrete examples of tests that are commonly used.

CHAPTER 21
EXAMPLES OF TESTS: THEIR USEFULNESS

TYPES OF TESTS

There are available an enormous number of tests which may be classified in a number of different ways. For example, they may be divided into *group tests* as against *individual tests,* according to whether a number of people can take the test simultaneously or whether only one person at a time can be tested. Again, they may be grouped by the *kind of trait* they attempt to assess, whether it is general intelligence, differential intellectual abilities, interests and values, mechanical skills, personality, and so forth. Another basis for classification is according to whether they assess *present achievement or proficiency* or attempt to predict *aptitude* as indicated by behavior on a criterion quite different from the test itself. We can measure typing ability, for example, simply by asking a person to type out a short passage in some time limit; on the other hand, it is also possible to assess the potential ability of a person who does not know how to type by giving him tests of manual dexterity, visual-motor coordination, and reading speed. In the first case, we would be measuring proficiency or achievement; in the second case, we would be assessing capacity or aptitude.

The second of these classifications is the one most commonly used, and it is the one we will employ here for the purpose of presenting examples of some of the most widely used tests. We will first consider the domain of intelligence.

Tests of Intelligence

THE STANFORD-BINET This individually administered test is probably the most widely used scale of intelligence today. The 1937 revision consists of two parallel forms, L and M, both of which provide a broad sampling of intellectual skills though verbal ability predominates. Ten years of research went into making up the revision of the test. Large numbers of children of different ages from many geographical areas and from different socioeconomic levels (though predominantly middle-class) were given preliminary sets of items. The percentage of children at each age level passing an item was plotted, and those items were picked out which best discriminated between different age levels. Thus an item which was failed by the majority of six-year-olds, passed by about 50 percent of seven-year-olds, and passed by most eight-year-olds would be placed at the seven-year-old level. In this way, there was gradually drawn up a list of items each having a certain developmental difficulty level.

This list was again given to new carefully chosen standardized groups for the purpose of further selecting among the items. The final test was settled on only after several more such revisions. It consists of two parallel forms which may be used interchangeably. Each is made up of items geared to about eighteen different age levels. Those for younger children involve mostly skill in manipulating or sorting objects, some hand-eye coordination, and simple drawing tasks, for example, stringing beads or copying a square or a circle. At older ages the items call for more abstract and verbal ability and may deal with vocabulary items, analogies, common-sense comprehension of the surrounding world, memory, spatial orientation, numerical aptitude, and understanding of concepts; for example, the subject may be asked to specify the difference between "laziness" and "idleness," to explain the proverb "You can't make a silk purse out of a sow's ear," to define such abstract terms as "courage," and so forth.

Since the test is individually administered, a good deal of skill is required on the part of the tester. He or she must be able to notice, for example, whether nervousness or motivation are affecting performance and be careful not to help the child in a way that would artificially raise his score. Many of the tests are speed tests which have to be timed with a stopwatch, and this must be done in as unobtrusive a manner as possible. Many subjects are disturbed by the sight of a stopwatch, and their performance will suffer accordingly. In general, then, it is important to realize that the Stanford-Binet involves more than a simple assessment of intellectual ability. Much information about personality and emotional adjustment can also be obtained from its judicious use by a well-trained administrator.

THE WECHSLER ADULT INTELLIGENCE SCALE

While the Stanford-Binet is perhaps the most useful test for children, it is less suitable for adults, partly because it does not assess very high intellectual levels and partly because many of the items are couched in rather childish language. To ask an Army sergeant to make up a sentence out of the words "boy," "ball," and "river," for example, hardly seems appropriate. For these kinds of reasons, David Wechsler at Bellevue Hospital in New York attempted to design a test like the Stanford-Binet but specifically geared to adult subjects. His first two scales, which appeared in 1939 and 1946 respectively, were never adequately standardized and are now not in use. The form currently in use—the Wechsler Adult Intelligence Scale (WAIS)—was designed in 1955. It is supplemented by a similar scale for children—the Wechsler Intelligence Scale for Children (WISC).

The adult scale is based on a model of intelligence like that used by Binet—that is, a general capacity to perform in many different areas. Thus it is a composite test, though unlike the Stanford-Binet test, it is divided up according to types of items into two main scales—*verbal* and *performance*. Each of these is further divided into subscales. Thus the Verbal Scale covers tests of Information, Comprehension, Digit Span, Similarities, Arithmetic, and Vocabulary. The Performance Scale takes in Picture Arrangement, Picture Completion, Block Design, Object Assembly, and Digit Symbol Tests. Some of these are speed tests; for example, the Digit Symbol Test requires the rapid substitution of abstract symbols for numbers according to a specified arrangement. If the subject can learn and memorize the substitutes quickly, he will be able, of course, to perform the task that much more quickly. Other items in the test are not timed and can be answered correctly or not, depending on the subject's intelligence or general knowledge. Three examples are shown in Figure 21–1.

Like the Stanford-Binet, the WAIS uses age norms and has conversion tables for translating raw scores at different ages into IQs. These are based on the assumption that mental age on performance tasks rises up to about age twenty-two and then declines rather rapidly, and that mental age on verbal skills rises up to about age thirty and then falls off more slowly.

The WAIS is a rather widely used test with adults. It has a concurrent validity—in this case, correlation with the Stanford-Binet—as high as .82, and a reliability of over .90 obtained by test-retest and split-half methods. Again, like the Stanford-Binet, it can be used by a trained administrator as a means of assessing personality and emotional adjustment as well as intellectual ability. Furthermore, because of its organization into subtests, it is able to provide clues as to particular types of mental disorder. For example, according to one psy-

(a) A picture arrangement item

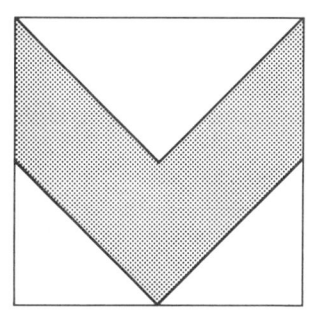

(b) A block design pattern

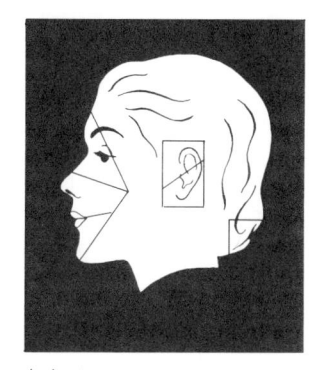

(c) An object assembly item

FIG. 21-1 Sample items from the Wechsler Adult Intelligence Scale. In (a), the three pictures are to be arranged in the correct sequence. In (b) and (c), the design and face must be constructed from a set of separate cubes. (*Wechsler, 1944*)

chologist, E. R. Schafer (1948), a pattern of high scores on the performance scale coupled with low scores on parts of the verbal scale is very suggestive of a psychopathic personality. Such "clues," we must emphasize, do not by themselves constitute firm evidence, but they may at least tell the tester where to look more closely.

Many other individual tests of general ability are available for assessing both child and adult subjects. The interested reader may find out more about these by consulting any of the general reference works we have listed at the end of the chapter.

GROUP TESTS OF GENERAL INTELLIGENCE Since the general principles underlying the construction of most group tests of intelligence are similar to those involved in individual tests, we will not discuss them in detail. For the most part, such tests are made up of a fairly large number of discrete items covering a range of types of problems arranged in order of difficulty. Time limits are usually imposed, of the order of half an hour to an hour. The tests can be administered to a large number of individuals simultaneously in a group and can usually be scored mechanically. Consequently they have the great advantage of economy of time and effort as compared to individual tests, though, of course, they cannot reveal the more subtle aspects of psychological functioning that are discoverable by an experienced tester working with a single subject.

The following list represents a small sample of some of the more widely used and better-standardized tests:

Kuhlmann-Anderson Intelligence Tests. This is a well-standardized series comprising nine separate tests for each three-grade level from kindergarten to adulthood. A variety of special abilities are tapped. Reliability is high, and validation against the Stanford-Binet is almost perfect.

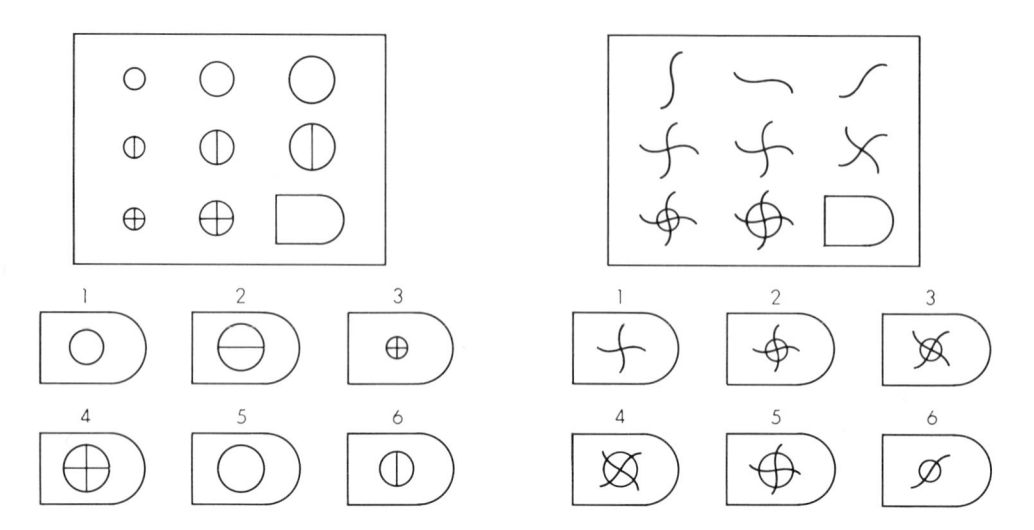

FIG. 21-2 Two examples (fictitious) of matrix problems.

Otis Quick-scoring Mental Ability Tests. This is a series going from grade 1 to college level. This was one of the first group tests of general intelligence and has been widely used since 1920.

American Council Psychological Examination (ACE). This was constructed originally in 1929 by two pioneers in the testing field, L. L. Thurstone and Thelma G. Thurstone. It is aimed mainly at college entrants and correlates about .45 with college grade averages. It has been used a great deal in research on predicting success in college.

Henmon-Nelson Tests of Mental Ability. This is a series comprising tests for each three grade-levels from grade 3 through college. It taps a number of special abilities and has a high reliability, of over .90.

Miller Analogies Test. This is distinctive in that it is a test designed to assess superior adults. It is composed entirely of analogies arranged in increasing order of difficulty. Many graduate schools require applicants to take this test, though there is some doubt as to its validity in predicting success at this level. This may be partly due to the restricted range of ability being covered.

Raven Progressive Matrix Test. This is intended to assess reasoning ability independently of cultural influences. All items use the same principle—that is, they require the subject to deduce from examining the given elements in the rows and columns of a matrix what a missing element should be. For example, in the simplest case, if all given elements in the matrix are identical, then it is reasonable that the missing ones should be the same. On the other hand, each element may vary systematically along several dimensions at once, making the solution a great deal more difficult. An easy item and a slightly more difficult one are illustrated in Figure 21-2. Neither one of the two examples shown is very close in difficulty level to the most difficult ones in the test. It is obvious that they can be complicated to a point well beyond the limit of all but very superior persons.

One great advantage of the test is the fact that instructions can be given in any language or even in pantomime if necessary, and no reading skills are required. This makes it a very flexible task indeed. Its homogeneity, however, makes its usefulness somewhat limited. It has proved not as good a predictor of success in various kinds of training programs as the more usual heterogeneous type of test. For the same reason it is likely that it could serve as a valuable research tool. The simplicity which makes it unsuitable to deal with the complexities of practical behavior may make it very suitable for increasing our understanding of unitary psychological processes in a laboratory setting.

The six examples we have just given will be sufficient to acquaint the reader with some of the major group tests of intelligence. As we have indicated already, there are a very large number that can be used. Choice of a suitable one for any particular purpose must be made on the basis of reliability, validity, and thoroughness of standardization procedures as well as on the basis of the goals envisaged in using it.

Tests of Personality

The accurate assessment of intelligence poses many problems. Measuring personality, however, is even more difficult. The items comprising any test of intellectual ability can be answered only correctly or incorrectly, and there is usually little room—if the test is properly constructed—for misinterpretation of the question. With items relating to personality, the situation is very different. In the first place, there are no right or wrong answers. Many subjects may mistakenly think that there are, particularly if they have some preconceptions about the criterion the test is attempting to predict. An applicant for a position of insurance salesman, for example, may have a strong and probably well-founded suspicion that his prospective employer will not hire someone who answers "yes" to the question "Do you feel a great lack of self-confidence?" From a practical point of view, this is clearly a "wrong" answer, though from a scientific point of view it is neutral.

Again, there is a relative uniformity of cultural influence on language dealing with intellectual tasks. Schools and textbooks take care of this, with the result that the range of interpretation that can be given to an intelligence-test item is usually rather small. But such a molding does not occur nearly so much in respect to language dealing with personality. The adjective "nervous" may conjure up, in one individual, visions of a screaming hysteric; in another individual, an image of a slightly high-strung and sensitive person. Even such adverbs—often used in personality tests—such as "frequently," "seldom," or "rarely" connote for different people a considerable range of incidence. One investigator, Simpson (1944), has, in fact, shown this empirically by asking groups of subjects just what percentage of all occasions are suggested by such words. He obtained a large spread in the percentages given. For example, "often" varied from 65 to 85 percent; "occasionally," from 10 to 33 percent. It must be remarked, parenthetically, that these ambiguities of interpretation have applied to most of the test makers as well.

It is obvious, then, that personality testing poses special problems. However, as we shall show shortly, some of these problems are more than methodological nuisances; they are of great interest and importance in themselves. This often happens in the progress of science. Some "bugs" in a piece of apparatus may yield data which have not been sought but which shed considerable light on the fundamental problem being studied.

We will now consider some actual tests of personality. There are a number of ways of classifying them, but the one we will use here, perhaps the most common, groups them into the following categories: (1) self-report tests, (2) performance tests, (3) situational tests.

SELF-REPORT TESTS *Bernreuter Personality Inventory*. This is one of the older self-report types of personality test. It is made up of over one hundred statements to which the subject has to answer "Yes," "No," or "Don't know." There are four scoring keys, and each response has been assigned a different weight in each key. The keys purport to measure four dimensions of personality: neuroticism, self-sufficiency, introversion, and dominance. These are, however, correlated so that according to another worker, Flanagan (1935), they are really reducible to two variables, namely, confidence and sociability. The validity of the test is probably not great, but norms are supplied for high school, college, and general adult populations, thus allowing an estimate to be made of how closely the answers of a subject approximate those of the average person.

Minnesota Multiphasic Personality Inventory (MMPI). Since its appearance in 1940, the MMPI has been widely used both for research and for practical clinical purposes. Unlike the Bernreuter, which deals with only mild abnormality, it sets out to assess those traits or behavior patterns that are characteristic of disabling psychological abnormalities. The test is made up of 550 items representing nine different scales. The scales are as follows:

1. Hs—hypochondriasis
2. Dp—depression
3. Hy—hysteria
4. Pd—psychopathic deviate
5. Mf—masculinity-femininity
6. Pa—Paranoid
7. Pt—psychasthenia
8. Sc—schizophrenia
9. Ma—hypomania

A noteworthy feature of the test is that those items have been chosen which are already known to distinguish actual groups of patients having these nine types of mental illness. This method has been called "criterion keying," and it is essentially a validation procedure. The basic assumption is that if a person answers, for example, "Yes" to the statement "I believe I am being plotted against," then he has something in common with the group of paranoids among whom the vast majority also answer in the affirmative. This inference may not, of course, be true, but it seems like a reasonable one. In this manner, any subject emerges with a profile of scores on the nine scales.

In addition to these nine scales, four other *control* scales, or keys, can also be scored. The first of these is the "?" or "question" score. It is given simply by the number of times the subject chooses to answer statements with the "Cannot say" category. When it is too heavily used, the subject cannot be compared with the standardization groups, and his test results are not used.

Second, there is the "L," or "Lie" score, which is based on a count of improbable answers. There have been inserted in the test a number of items of a type to which a certain reply, positive or negative, would most probably reflect either carelessness or lying. For example, an answer of "False" to the statement "I do not like everyone I know" might conceivably be truthful, but if we find other statements of the L key answered in the same manner, then we have reason to be suspicious.

The third scale is the "F," for "False," scale. This measures the extent to which a subject gives an excessive number of rare responses. It indicates probable malingering—that is, an attempt, on the person's part, to make himself out to be sick or to "fake bad" in order to avoid some responsibility.

The final scale, "K," is the most subtle and ingenious. It is essentially a correction for the tendency of some people to overestimate themselves or "defend" against their own symptoms and of others, on the other hand, to underestimate themselves and to deprecate unnecessarily the stability of their personalities. The criterion items are simply those commonly marked in a certain way by cases whose *overall* scores were *less* deviant than those of psychiatric groups. High score on these items, or high K, indicates defensiveness; low K designates excessive self-criticism. The correction is applied to five of the scales, so that the obtained score on each is weighted by a certain amount. Prediction has been claimed by some investigators to be more accurate using K but not by others. Consequently, its usefulness in practice is questionable whatever the merit of the logic behind it.

The MMPI has many uses, among which number general screening for psychological maladjustment in any group, diagnosis of particular kind of illness, general research.

PERFORMANCE TESTS Our personalities are revealed in almost everything we do. Two tennis players, closely matched in ability, may approach the sport in very different ways, one with a strong, aggressive power game, the other with a delicate precision that is equally effective in winning points. It is likely that these differences as they appear on the court will also find expression in many other phases of their lives, particularly those in which some task orientation or challenge is imposed by circumstances. In some situation, such intrusions of a personality style can actually militate against success. Poker is a good example of a game in which the ability of a player to uncover some general rules that dictate how his opponents play can be critical to his coming out on top. Equally, he must have the ability, by maintaining a so-called poker face, not to give himself away.

There is no question that all behavior in some of its aspects is highly idiosyncratic in that it reveals what we are really like. Freud, of course, saw this clearly and so laid the groundwork for the development of many of the performance tests of personality that we have today. We have already described one type, namely, projective tests. It may be well at this point to look at projective tests again in terms of the context of this chapter. We will also examine several other types of performance tests.

The *Rorschach*, the *Thematic Apperception Test* (TAT) of Henry Murray, the *Need-Achievement test* of David McClelland and the *Blacky test* of Gerald Blum are a few of the many kinds of projective techniques used by psychologists and psychiatrists for assessing personality. These have been found to be valuable tools in the hands of the trained clinician. They are definitely not for the amateur for at least two reasons: in the first place, their scoring is not well standardized but is highly interpretive. They are not at all like some of the tests we have discussed, such as the self-report tests, which can readily be scored by anyone. Proper interpretation and administration of projective tests require a good deal of supervised practice, in the same way that clinical medicine does. The practicing physician, in his everyday dealings with his patients, must rely heavily on experience as well as on his scientific knowledge. So also must the projective tester.

There have been a number of attempts made to work out objective scoring methods—for the TAT, for example—and these may eventually be successful, but, for the time being, a high premium must be placed on the interpretive skill of the person giving the test. This is dependent on experience and practice, certainly, but it is also dependent on a sensitivity in dealing with other people—a characteristic in which may be difficult to train people.

A second reason why projective tests should have restrictive usage is that they yield information that is most meaningful when taken in a broader context of information about the person. In isolation, the results of a TAT, for example, may supply only hunches, but coupled with what is already known about the subject—either through other tests he has taken or through clinical interviews with him—it may allow us to draw much firmer and more legitimate conclusions.

We will now describe briefly one of the first, and still one of the most popular, tests falling under this category. This is the so-called Rorschach test.

The Rorschach Ink Blot Test was initially published in 1921, many years before the TAT and its offshoots. It was first used as a way of diagnosing psychiatric conditions in terms of the different ways in which the patients perceived a set of ten

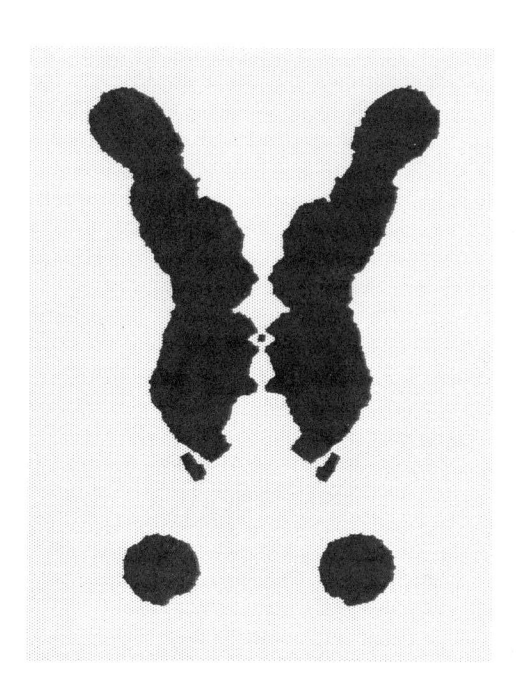

FIG. 21–3 Example (fictitious) of a Rorschach inkblot. (*Kendler, 1963*)

symmetrical inkblots. An example is shown in Figure 21–3. It soon came to be used, however, as a means of exploring the workings of normal or near-normal personality rather than merely a way of putting sick people into different diagnostic categories. Its rationale is basically the same as that of any projective test, inasmuch as the subject exposes his personality through the way he experiences certain situations—these being relatively well-structured pictures in the case of the TAT and unstructured and meaningless inkblots in the case of the Rorschach.

The subject is shown these one at a time and simply asked to say what he sees or, more exactly, what the blot makes him think of. His responses are scored according to three major categories, each of these being further subdivided. The first refers mainly to whether responses are made in terms of all or most of a blot or only parts of it; the second deals with the use of form, color, shading, the white spaces, and other such characteristics; and the third category refers simply to the *content* of the associations made by a subject, such as animal, human figures, inanimate objects, and so on. For example, the common response to one card, "Two witches dancing," involves these three categories. It uses the whole blot, in the first place; in the second place, it is in terms of definite forms, namely, quasi-human figures; and in the third place, it specifically involves witches, rather than ordinary objects or human persons.

These principles of scoring are explicated in the several Rorschach manuals in great detail. In spite of the ingenuity which has gone into them, however, a good deal of clinical insight is needed if they are to yield a valid description of personality. Most experts in the area agree on this point. The Rorschacher forms, on the basis of all that the subject says and does during the test, a global, clinical picture, and, so far, this is not easily expressible in objective, quantifiable terms.

Although the Rorschach was originally supposed to deal with *perception*, it really deals more with cognition—that is to say, the interpretations a subject places on his perception. After all, inkblots are immediately seen as inkblots and nothing more. To see one as an animal or a ruined castle requires some interpretations and cognitive associations. There are available, however, some tests that do deal directly with perception itself. And, as the reader might expect, the theoretical underpinnings of these relate closely to Gestalt psychology.

Let us look at one example, the *Bender-Gestalt Test*. This presents the subject with a number of simple figures which he is asked simply to copy. Observations are made as to how he goes about accomplishing this seemingly straightforward task. Examples of some of the figures are shown in Figure 21–4.

According to some researchers—for example, Gobetz (1953)—it is possible to distinguish neurotics from normals by a number of "signs," for example, the degree to which the copied figures are crowded rather than spread over a whole page, or the extent to which straight rows of figures such as dots are slanted when copied.

Curiously enough, in some brain-injured patients, simple copying became impossible unless the abstractness of the figure is reduced. Thus a triangle can be satisfactorily copied only if seen as a spade or a roof. Otherwise, the subject literally cannot

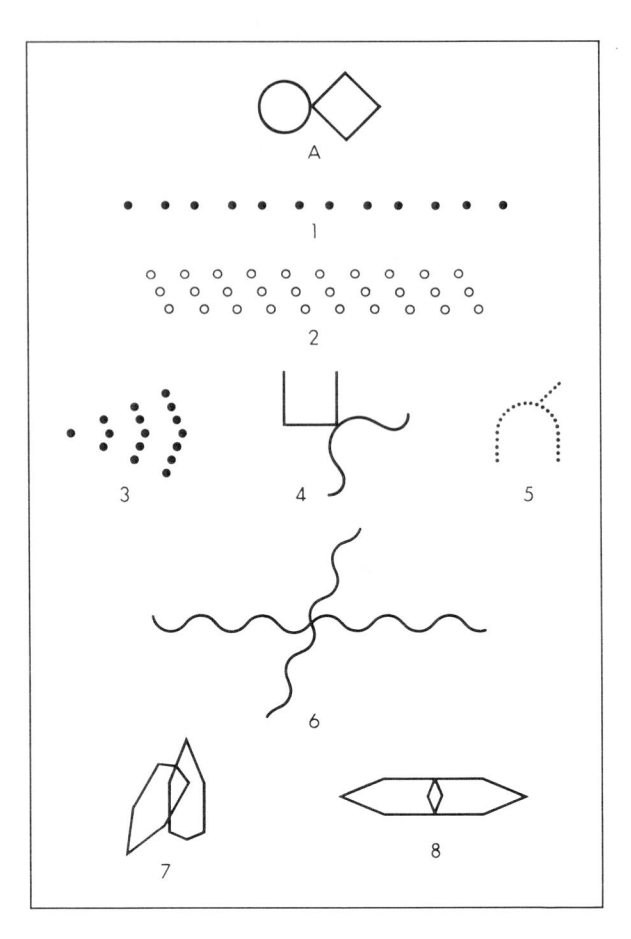

FIG. 21–4 Examples of items in the Bender-Gestalt test. (*Bender, 1938*)

perform this task at all. According to one worker in this area, Kurt Goldstein (1939), this is due to loss of an abstract attitude due to brain trauma. Such persons have become concrete and "stimulus-bound" in their thinking. They cannot rise above the most immediate properties of objects and inhibit these in favor of more general but less obvious characteristics. Nor can they pretend or behave in an "as if" way. Though perfectly able to drink real water from a real glass, many of them are, according to Goldstein, unable to pretend to drink if the glass is empty. The Bender tests and others of this series—such as the Goldstein-Scheerer—are useful for diagnosing such disabilities as well as the more subtle disorders associated with neurotic illness.

SITUATION TESTS The tests in this class are very much like those described in the preceding section. The main difference relates to a distinction made by Florence Goodenough (1949) between "sample" as against "sign" tests. The latter are those in which the behavior involved in the test does not directly relate to that involved in the criterion but does indirectly signify it. Telling a certain kind of story when presented with a TAT card is not the same as the behavior which this test is supposed to predict, but it is taken as a sign of it. If the subject gives to the hero of his story (a figure with whom he presumably identifies) highly aggressive characteristics, he may be suspected, according to theory, of possessing such characteristics himself in real-life situations.

Sample tests, on the other hand, simply involve observation of a part, or sample, of the total population of behaviors to be predicted. An applicant for a driving license is tested in this way. The examiner simply observes him during a ten- or fifteen-minute drive around the block. It is assumed (probably falsely) that this will yield a fair picture of how the would-be driver will behave when he is on his own under typical traffic conditions.

Obviously, there can be as many situation tests as there are situations that are of concern to people. Some excellent examples are given by Henry Murray and some of his colleagues in their book *Assessment of Men*. This is a description of an elaborate set of procedures used during World War II for screening OSS candidates. Since the conditions for which selection was being made were likely to be arduous to say the least, some of the tests used were equally difficult and unpleasant.

A similar technique is the *Leaderless Group Discussion* (LGD). This involves rating by trained observers, using certain predetermined categories, of subjects engaged in discussion of some problem. The topic is left relatively unstructured, and no one in the group is assigned any particular role—hence the name "Leaderless Group." Observers look for such qualities as ability to lead the discussion, negativity, creativity, ability to define the problem lucidly. It has been quite widely used for a variety of purposes, including selection of executives in business, rating of Army cadets' potential, and prediction of success in diplomatic service. The test-retest reliability is reasonably good provided the time interval between the testings is not much more than a week, and the predictive validity, using such criteria as those just mentioned, is reasonably good.

Besides intelligence and personality, many other behavioral domains can be assessed by means of tests. These include interest patterns, special aptitudes, values, achievement in various areas, and social ability. Descriptions of these can be found in specialized books devoted to the topic of psychological measurement. We cannot attempt such a summary here, since our main goal is merely to supply the reader with something of the rationale and style of the field. We will turn now to a consideration of a general question of great practical importance, namely, whether tests really work.

THE USEFULNESS OF PSYCHOMETRIC PROCEDURES: CRITICISMS

We have so far discussed the requirements for a good test and given some examples of those that are most widely used. Since most of these have reasonably satisfactory validity coefficients, we can say immediately that, to that extent, they are useful. Nevertheless, a number of criticisms can be and have been raised about them. We will now examine a few of these.

First, granting that the better tests have some statistical validity and therefore tend, on the whole, to select accurately, we can ask whether there is still a significant number of good people being rejected because of careless construction of test items. As was shown earlier, there is no question that this happens, to a greater or lesser extent, depending on the degree of validity the test possesses. The problem is, Can we afford to be so casual about letting go some of our potentially best candidates just for the sake of an overall statistical gain?

Furthermore, it may well be, as some critics have suggested, that some of those failing a test may be not only as good as those who pass it but actually far better and fail the test precisely for this reason. Banesh Hoffman, a professor of mathematics at Queens College in New York, has raised essentially this major criticism (plus many others) in a book called *The Tyranny of Testing*, published in 1962. As the several respondents to his criticism have pointed out, Hoffman has little real evidence on which to base his attack. The examples he cites are more hypothetical than real. But still, many who have taken tests—particularly of the so-called objective type—may have sometimes had the feeling that there is something to such a notion and that they fail some items not so much because they do not understand the problem but rather because they are perspicacious enough to see aspects of it that the person making it up did not. Hoffman gives the following question taken from an important test—The College Entrance Examination Board test—as an example illustrating this point:

Item 54 in *Science*

The burning of gasoline in an automobile cylinder involves all of the following except:
(*A*) reduction
(*B*) decomposition
(*C*) an exothermic reaction
(*D*) oxidation
(*E*) conversion of matter to energy

According to Hoffman, the *average* chemistry student will quickly choose E, since this alternative seems to relate to nuclear power rather than to internal-combustion engines. In this sense, he is certainly correct. However, a brighter student may reason that in both nuclear reactions and in the burning of gasoline, energy is released by the dissociation of chemical bonds and that both consequently involve the conversion of matter into energy. He would therefore conclude that all items are involved and that no answer is correct. For this extra subtlety and insight he would be penalized.

Now there is no question that this sometimes happens. Mistakes are inevitable. The only question is whether this is the rule rather than the exception. Is there prevalent, in modern culture, particularly in the United States, an unconscious though very general bias against the unusually creative person, this being expressed, in its most extreme form, in the way in which tests are used and constructed? Hoffman thinks there is. He concludes that tests

> ...are apt to be superficial and intellectually dishonest, with questions made artificially difficult by means of ambiguity... [that they] often degenerate into superficial guessing games in which the candidate does not pick what he considers the best answer out of a bad lot, but rather the one he considers the unknown examiner would consider the best... [and that, finally] they have, in sum, a pernicious effect on education and the recognition of merit [Hoffman, 1962].

Hoffman speaks from a sense of obvious exasperation and consequently perhaps overstates his case. As we said before, convincing evidence for his position seems to be lacking. At the same time, we must certainly concede that his criticisms have some cogency. The unusual and creative mind is difficult to assess on any conventional measure, and it is up to testers to improve their techniques. No one would dispute this. Whether there is abroad in twentieth-century society, however, a set of principles, represented by testing, that are abhorrent to all that is precious and noble about human nature is something else. This point has been taken up especially by another critic, John M. Schlein of the University of Chicago, and represents a second major criticism of testing.

The problem may be posed as follows: supposing tests are weak in validity (and perhaps reliability also), can it not be said that testers are attempting to control human beings and on grounds that are shaky at the best? The point can also be raised as to whether such control would be desirable even if the testing instruments were capable of yielding perfect predictions. Schlein (1964) does not include this second objection as part of his *formal* argument against tests. In fact, he specifically states otherwise. Nevertheless, it is obvious from the general tenor of his paper that he is at least intuitively sympathetic to it. Again, many readers will share his feelings. It is bad enough to be controlled by perfect tests, but it is even worse to be controlled by imperfect ones. Nobody cares to be cataloged in terms of a set of scores that is held to describe him completely and permanently. Most of us, rightly or wrongly, feel we have the freedom and the capacity to change and that these characteristics are not allowed for by tests.

As with the first criticism, so also with this the evidence is ambiguous. But, in a general sense, it does seem to be true—and, indeed, all psychotherapeutic techniques are based on this premise—that human personality, taken at any age level, is not something fixed and crystallized but is capable of change, often within fairly wide limits. Abilities, skills, and intelligence may be more resistant than personality to change, but even they are not considered by modern psychometricians to be as stable as they were once thought to be. It is well known, for example, that IQ score is rather unstable at very young age levels. Not until about the age of four years does it start to become a good predictor of subsequent performance (Cronbach, 1960). Furthermore, stability of intelligence is itself highly variable from one individual to another. In some cases, despite drastic environmental changes, it remains relatively constant; in others, it may fluctuate wildly even in fairly constant conditions (Honzik, Macfarlane, & Allen, 1948).

The upshot of the above discussion is that there are probably certain dimensions of personality and intelligence having to do with potentiality for changes that are, at present, not readily accessible to the tester. As a consequence, when the tester assesses an individual and draws up a profile of his scores on various measures, he should feel a strong sense of responsibility and caution before he allows himself to "play God" with another person's life.

A third criticism that has been directed against tests is that, granting they yield some information, they do not yield any more than we could obtain by simpler and perhaps cheaper methods, for example, by merely talking to the subject for a short time. Tests are often given favorable judgments too easily. Their predictive power is often implicitly contrasted with a hypothetical situation in which success of prediction is zero. But this very desperate case probably does not exist. So the question really relates to the increase in accuracy we can expect from using a test as against some other less sophisticated procedure. Example 21–1 presents some relevant evidence.

Example 21–1 *Predictive success of different types of assessment procedures (Kelly & Fiske, 1951)*

In 1947, in the United States, the Veterans Administration began systematic training programs for clinical psychologists to work in its hospitals. An important aspect of the program was the selection of personnel for this kind of job. To this end, a practical study was undertaken by Kelly and Fiske and by others to find out what kinds of assessment procedures would best predict candidates going successfully through the training program. A large number of tests were used, as well as many different ratings. A sampling of these and the extent to

Table 21-1 Validity coefficients of various predictors of success in a clinical training program (Kelly & Fiske, 1951; cf. Cronbach, 1960)

Predictor	Academic	Therapeutic	Diagnostic	Clinical competence
Miller analogies (verbal ability)	.47*	.02	.24*	.35*
Bender-Gestalt (ratings based on performance)	.15	.02	.33*	.32*
Ratings from pooled performance tests	.19	.19	.02	.24*
Self-ratings	.25*	−.20	.05	.00
Peer ratings	.13	.28*	.23*	.25*

*Statistically significant correlations.

which they served as good predictors of four aspects of the program are shown in Table 21–1.

Some interesting points emerge from the table. In the first place, it is clear that none of the tests does very well. Those coefficients that are statistically significant (i.e., not due to chance) are very small. Even the highest one of .47 represents only a 12 percent improvement over chance—some gain but not very much. Secondly, we find that the Bender-Gestalt, when used in a *clinical* way rather than as a simple performance test, yields quite good prediction coefficients. This must mean that the judgment of a trained person about the way a subject performs on a test—though rather intuitive and not readily quantifiable—can still give useful information. This point is further backed up by the validity coefficients for peer ratings. Although these assessments were carried out by relatively untrained persons, they still turned out rather well. Finally (not shown in the table), if trained judges are used and they pool together information on a subject including autobiographical data, his credentials file, and his objective-test scores, a fairly high validity coefficient can be obtained. This is not improved—in fact it goes down—if performance tests are added.

Since this study was done carefully on a large sample of subjects, its results must be taken seriously. And it must be said that these results do not give unqualified support to the use of tests—especially single ones—as against the judgment of trained assessors who are quite familiar with the job requirements.

Several other major validation studies involving such groups as OCS candidates, civil servants, and psychiatric residents have arrived at similar conclusions. Tests do not add a great deal provided that the persons doing the assessing have some degree of skill (not necessarily psychological training, however) and, most important of all, are very familiar with the nature of the criterion, or job for which prediction is being attempted. However, it must be strongly emphasized that such persons are not always very easy to find. Thus, for the run-of-the-mill situation, tests will provide useful data.

In spite of the three types of criticism against tests discussed above, we can still conclude on an optimistic note. If tests are at least as good as informed judgment, they also have at least two advantages: In the first place, they are usually more economical of time and can be administered in a routine way with a minimum of difficulty, and, second and more important, deficient as they are, tests have a great potentiality for being improved and refined to a degree that will give them not only more accuracy but also more scope in allowing for creative or highly qualified deviants who do not conform to usual norms. We should certainly think twice before casually dismissing them. The other questions—how we use them, whether they involve an invasion of privacy, whether they may carry an implication of control of society by an intellectual elite—these can be answered only in terms of working out careful prescriptions for their usage and maintaining high ethical standards. Indeed the American Psychological Association has already put a great deal of thought into just such considerations and has published a booklet, *Standards of Ethical Behavior for Psychologists,* which deals specifically with testing among other issues.

The problems we have just discussed are interesting ones, because they impinge on all of us in our immediate, everyday lives. From the standpoint of psychology as a science, however, they do not have so much relevance. As we stated above, tests do have the potentiality for being improved, and this potentiality ensues from the great amount of theorizing and experimentation that has gone into their construction. It is likewise true that, for the same reason, testing procedures may be able to tell us a great deal about behavior and the basic makeup of man. It would certainly be good, from a practical standpoint, if we had tests which could predict accurately; but technology is not science and there is still a need to ask about the usefulness of such instruments in furthering the progress of psychology. This is the problem to which we will now address ourselves.

CHAPTER 22
TESTS AND PSYCHOLOGICAL TRAITS

It should be obvious that much of the field of testing is highly empirical in orientation. The Binet test grew out of practical necessity to classify children in the Paris schools. Similarly, any number of tests have been constructed to predict success in business and industry, in the Armed Forces, and in the civil service. As we have already emphasized, if a test predicts accurately, to that extent it can be regarded as a success. But it may still help very little in our understanding of what capacities and traits are really like, and if the field of psychometrics is to be a real part of psychology, it must contribute to the progress of this subject matter as a science. We will now explore two major paths that seem fruitful in this respect. Both have been referred to earlier, though not discussed in detail. One relates to response sets and styles; the other, to factor analysis.

RESPONSE SETS AND RESPONSE STYLES

The answer a person gives to any question he is asked may be shaped by a number of factors, only one of which is a desire to be truthful. He may also wish to represent himself in a good light, or, on the other hand, he may wish simply to be "agreeable" or "disagreeable." Thus, an affirmative answer given to the hypothetical question (which perhaps many of us are often asked, in one form or another) "Do you for the most part like other people?" may reflect the following possibilities: (1) the respondent's true feeling about himself—whether what he answers is really true or not; (2) the respondent's wish to present himself as a friendly and likable person; (3) the respondent's tendency to say yes to almost any question that might be asked of him. The first of these three alternatives is obvious enough and is usually assumed to be the factor operating in psychological tests. However, consider these two illustrations, which dramatize the manner in which the other two factors can play a part:

Regarding alternative 2, it is obvious that many tests are used for selection purposes and that the way in which a job applicant answers will determine whether he is chosen for the job or not. If he has any sophistication at all, it will usually be clear to him what kinds of answers he should give in order to appear in the most favorable light possible from the standpoint of that situation. William H. Whyte, Jr., in his book *The Organization Man* (1956), has satirized this possibility by suggesting the kinds of responses most suitable for a prospective Madison Avenue business executive: He should not care too much for books or music. He should never worry about anything. He should love his wife and children but never let them get in the way of company work. He should love his father and mother, but his father a little bit more. On tests of value, he should be low on the aesthetic scale, fairly high on the economic (not too high), and moderate on all the others (theoretical, social, and political). Knowing something of the criterion, any person can thus adjust his answers to it. This kind of adjustment, which may be unconsciously as well as consciously motivated, is called in testing a *response set*. Note that it can also work in reverse, if the job for which the test is being given is not considered a desirable one—for example, induction into the Army.

The second illustration is drawn from an older source: Shakespeare's *Hamlet*. In act 3, scene 2, Ophelia's father, Polonius, wishing to humor Hamlet—by this time considered by all to be slightly dangerous—engages with him in the following conversation:

Hamlet: Do you see yonder cloud that's almost in shape of a camel?
Polonius: By the mass, and 'tis like a camel, indeed.
Hamlet: Methinks it is like a weasel.
Polonius: It is backed like a weasel.
Hamlet: Or like a whale?
Polonius: Very like a whale.

The manner in which Polonius is responding is obviously not dependent on the content of Hamlet's remarks or questions. Rather his replies are all governed by a single desire—to agree—and agreement is chosen even at the expense of near contradiction, a fact which Hamlet deliberately plays upon. The tendency so to respond in terms of the form of a question or the reason for it rather than in terms of its content has been called by psychometricians *response style*.

In any test, though most especially tests in which there are no right or wrong answers, for example, personality tests or interest inventories, the same factors will usually operate. We mentioned before that they were first seen as causing a methodological problem, which indeed they do. For this reason, various measures were taken to allow for them. The Lie Scale in the MMPI is such a check. However, it soon came to be realized that response sets and response styles are of interest in themselves and may tell us as much about the person as his "true" response to content. One of the first to suggest this was Lee Cronbach in a series of papers starting in 1941. Many other researchers quickly took up this hypothesis, and as a result, between this time and 1965, as many as a hundred papers exploring the issue were published. Their main concern was with the separation of the three response factors outlined above and the relating of these to other variables of personality. Although in 1966 a sharp critical review of these papers was published by Rorer, it can perhaps be said that the general idea of response sets and response styles is a good one, and whatever the methodological faults the studies on them may entail, they are well worth illustrating by means of two examples.

Example 22-1 *A test of the deviation hypothesis (Grigg & Thorpe, 1960)*

One of the first (after Cronbach) to see the potential interest of response sets or biases was Irwin Berg (1957). His so-called deviation hypothesis states essentially that the content of a test item is relatively unimportant but what is crucial is the extent to which it elicits normative or deviant responses. More specifically, in his own words:

a. Deviant response patterns tend to be general: hence those deviant behavior patterns which are significant for abnormality ... and thus regarded as symptoms ... are associated with other deviant response patterns which are in non-critical areas of behavior and which are not regarded as symptoms of personality aberration ... ; *b.* Stimulus patterns of any type and of any sense modality may be used to elicit deviant response patterns; thus particular stimulus content is unimportant for measuring behavior in terms of the Deviation Hypothesis [Berg, 1957, pp. 158, 160].

According to this view, we should expect to find that people who are odd, or different, in one area are odd also in other areas. A person who is so troubled as to seek psychiatric help, for example, would show his deviation not merely in this area of psychological adjustment but also in other areas, such as his speech, his dress, his use of language, or his bathroom habits.

Though the theoretical aspects of this notion are rather poorly developed, as an empirical hypothesis it is both interesting and testable. Grigg and Thorpe have attempted to test this in the following manner: They used a test known as the Adjective Check List developed by Gough (1952). This involves a list of 300 adjectives (e.g., "impulsive," "friendly") which a subject is asked to check or not depending on whether he thinks each applies to him or not. Starting with a sample of 181 males and 92 females, Grigg and Thorpe located, from the whole list, 33 adjectives which were most often checked and 39 which were least often checked by subjects in this group. These 72 items were then put together to form a single new list and administered to 1,400 entering freshmen at the University of Texas. Some time later, four groups were taken from this total sample: one whose members had sought psychiatric help during their first year, another whose members had gone to the counseling service to seek aid in solving personal problems, another also seeking aid of a vocational sort, and a randomly chosen "normal" control group. The percentages of deviant responses—that is, of uncommon adjectives checked—are shown for these four groups in Table 22–1. The mean number of deviant responses differ from each other at a statistically significant level of probability. Furthermore, the main difference occurs between the first two groups and the second two.

These results are taken by Grigg and Thorpe to be consistent with Berg's deviation hypothesis. Again, however, the methodology certainly does not rule out content as a determiner of response. To assert that a preference for the odd or the unusual is the only factor at work here may be going somewhat beyond the data. Nevertheless, the study is an interesting one that suggests some fruitful lines of research.

Example 22–2 *Yea-sayers and nay-sayers (Couch & Keniston, 1960)*

Another explication of the deviation hypothesis of Berg has been made by Couch and Keniston (1960). The rather interesting refinement made by these writers has been to further specify deviants into two classes—"yea-sayers" and "nay-sayers"—that is, persons who tend to agree and persons who tend to disagree with any statement confronting them. Since content is here assumed to be largely irrelevant, these tendencies would be called response styles rather than response sets.

Their research fell into two parts: the first was concerned with developing a general measure of the dimension under consideration—what they called an "overall agreement score" (OAS)—and the second with determining with what traits of personality this measure would correlate.

Table 22-1 Frequency of deviant responses in the four groups of college students

Type of problem	No. of students responding	Mean no. of deviant responses
Psychiatric	24	14.29
Personal	37	12.08
Vocational	186	9.98
Control	150	9.77

THE OAS Over sixty Harvard undergraduate subjects were used in this part of the experiment. They were asked to respond to 681 questionnaire items drawn from a number of personality scales. These were of the Likert type, that is to say (as the reader will recall from Section III), they required the subject to express degree of agreement on a seven-point scale going from strong agreement (scale value of 7) to strong disagreement (scale value of 1). An attempt was made to cancel out the effect of content by selecting, from all the items, 360 comprising an equal number that were balanced in content. A hypothetical example might be the item "I trust people" balanced by its opposite number "I do not trust people." Presumably, a person's answering yes to both or no to both would reveal yea-saying or nay-saying tendencies, respectively. Thus an overall-agreement score was computed for each subject by taking the average of his responses to the 360 items. Split-half reliability of this measure turned out to be .85. It also had a high stability over time.

CORRELATES OF THE OAS Couch and Keniston examined the relationship of the OAS to a number of personality scales. These included the MMPI, the Cattell and Thurstone personality tests, the Basic Disposition Scales developed to measure tendencies to orality, anality, alienation, and psychological inertia, the F scale measuring authoritarianism and a number of other traits. In addition, a clinical assessment was made of those scoring high or low on the OAS.

Results of this part of the study are highly detailed and can be summarized here only in the broadest terms. Couch and Keniston identified, as the major dimension operating, a bipolar factor—"stimulus acceptance" versus "stimulus rejection." Since this is a kind of abstraction from a great deal of data, it perhaps does not help us very much, apart from suggesting that we may be dealing with a very general basic trait involving a person's relationship vis-à-vis the external world. More concretely, yea-sayers tend to be impulsive, anxious, and dependent people with fixations at the anal level involving lack of internalization of impulse control. Thus they tend to express themselves freely but particularly in anally tinged ways and show fondness for such metaphors as "really splurging on something," "sitting surrounded by your possessions," or "sitting in the seats of the mighty." They are "Dionysian" in the sense that they are quick to act and unable to tolerate long delays in gratification even though the reward may be greater in the end.

By contrast, nay-sayers, according to the results, are controlled and resistant to change, slow to respond, and, in psychoanalytic terminology again, anally suppressive. Thus, they are strongly disinterested in "splurging," "messing around," or "blowing up." Their self-control surface calmness and distrust in immediate pleasures all add up to an Apollonian character structure.

This study, though carefully executed and producing interesting results, is nonetheless open to some ambiguities. Thus in spite of the method of balancing items it is not absolutely certain that content played no part. It is quite possible to answer in the same direction to some statements and their contraries. An example given by Rorer (1966) of a reversal permitting double rejection is the following:

> "Every person should have complete faith in some super-natural power whose decisions he obeys without question."

and

> "No person should have complete faith in some super-natural power whose decisions he obeys without question."

One could readily disagree with both of these statements. Likewise, one could agree with both of these:

> "Nowadays more and more people are prying into matters that should remain personal and private."

and

> "There are times when it is necessary to probe into even the most personal and private matters."

As a matter of fact, a subject could also disagree with both of these.

Consequently, though Couch and Keniston may be correct in their assumption that the content of the items of their OAS is not important, they have not definitively demonstrated this.

Additional criticisms have been made in regard to a number of other aspects of the study (cf. Rorer, 1966). Nonetheless, as we have indicated already, the general idea developed by Couch and Keniston seems a good one and has certainly been responsible for a good deal of subsequent research.

It is worth noting that Keniston has followed up one aspect of the work described above with an intensive study of a group of Harvard students whom he identified as "alienated." In his book *The Uncommitted* (1965), he designated these students as "rebels without causes," persons so dissatisfied with and negative about everything in the world around them that they hold to almost no affirmative values or definitive goals with perhaps the exception of the most basic and all-consuming one of self-definition. Thus this group is not composed necessarily of political activists, free-speech advocates, or civil libertarians. Rather they represent the psychological core from which such protests may emanate—a basic stance of characterological negation from which various affirmations may arise. That this may be so is perhaps indicated by the curious diversity of causes that were part of the so-called free-speech movement at the University of California at Berkeley—these causes having included sexual freedom, freedom to use four-letter words, freedom to use LSD, civil rights, university regulations, quality of teaching, Vietnam, and selective service.

The two studies presented above and the many others which they exemplify represent a substantive problem area that has emerged directly from consideration of a methodological difficulty. To be specific, out of Cronbach's initial concern with the effects of response biases on validity and reliability of tests has grown a point of view about human personality and its makeup that has far-reaching psychological and sociological implications. Whether alienation, nay-saying, and deviancy are equivalent has not by any means been established. Sometimes such traits turn out to have an unexpected particularity. Sometimes they turn out to be general. Intuition and guesswork cannot give us real answers to this important problem. Fortunately, as we shall show in the next section, we have available certain mathematical techniques that allow us to reach some more definite conclusions about this problem of generality. These come under the collective heading of factor-analytic methods. Let us now look at these methods.

FACTOR-ANALYTIC METHODS

As one of the great American proponents of factor analysis, the late L. L. Thurstone pointed out (1947) that one of the most fundamental tasks in any science is the parsimonious description of the data which it is attempting to study. Naïve, unaided observation may result in the formulation of separate laws for cases which may be regarded as specific but which in fact replicate each other. For example, we can measure intelligence by means of several hundred different tests. If we are interested in working out laws that govern, let us say, the development of intelligence, we should have some idea as to whether these tests are all measuring the same thing—in which case we need study the data from only one test—or whether some or all of them measure different aspects of intelligence—in which case data from a single test may not be adequate for the construction of general laws.

Personality presents a domain of even greater complexity. The number of trait names used in a language to describe personality is high. We must have some way of finding out the extent to which a small number will do as good a job of description as a very large number. Do "thorny" and "abrasive" mean the same thing? "Kind" and "warm"? "Impulsive" and "volatile"? We may be able to make intuitive guesses about such cases, but if we are to reach real agreements, more sophisticated techniques must be available to us for doing this. Factor analysis aims at doing exactly this. Basically it is a method for analyzing a large set of tests to find those factors or elements that they measure in common and then specifying exactly the nature of these factors. We will now discuss the way in which this is done.

The Correlation Coefficient

In psychometrics, one of the fundamental ideas, which was emphasized at the beginning of the section, was the notion of *covariation*. As Pearson pointed out, it is often difficult—perhaps impossible—to specify cause-and-effect relations; but when dealing with continuous characters we can examine their covariation and, by means of the correlation statistic, set a numerical value that describes the extent of this covariation. As the reader will remember, it is by this device that we are able to calculate the validity and reliability of a test, the first being the covariation of the test with a criterion, the second being the covariation of the test with itself. These are methodological uses of the correlation primarily. In the present context, however, we will be looking at the way it can be used to find out something about the underlying structure and basic makeup of personality and intelligence.

The basic assumption that lies behind factor analysis is that if two or more measures correlate, or covary, to that extent they are measuring the same trait. This is fairly easy to see in the case of, say, school marks. Most of us are not surprised to observe that a student who does well in one subject tends, on the whole, to do well in most others. We attribute this success to "brightness," a characteristic we tacitly assume to be so general as to pervade performance in any subject, no matter what its special content. At the same time, we are also usually ready to accept the idea of special abilities. Some people do seem to be better in certain areas than in others, for example, mathematics, literature, or the fine arts.

To express these notions in a more precise statistical fashion we need to go to the formula for the Pearson product-moment correlation and see how it may be broken up into parts—one which produces the covariation between measures, the other which limits their covariation.

Example 22–3 *The correlation coefficient in terms of common and specific factors.*

The general formula for the correlation coefficient is as follows:

$$r_{xy} = \frac{\Sigma xy}{N\sigma_x \sigma_y}$$

The meaning of the various terms has already

been designated in Chapter 2, which the reader may consult if necessary to refresh his memory.

Now let us suppose that any score X obtained by an individual on one test is made up of two parts: one part, C, which is also measured by the other test, and another part, A, which is measured only by the first test but not by the other. Algebraically, this will be expressed as follows:

$$X = C + A$$

or, in deviation scores (i.e., $x = X - \overline{X}$, $c = C - \overline{C}$, $a = A - \overline{A}$

$$x = c + a$$

Similarly for the other test:

$$Y = C + B$$

or, in deviation scores

$$y = c + b$$

Putting these into the formula for the correlation, we have

$$r_{xy} = \frac{\Sigma xy}{N\sigma_x \sigma_y} = \frac{\Sigma(c+a)(c+b)}{N\sigma_{C+A}\sigma_{C+B}}$$

$$= \frac{\Sigma c^2 + \Sigma cb + \Sigma ca + \Sigma ab}{N\sigma_{C+A}\sigma_{C+B}}$$

Now c and b, c and a, and a and b are all independent of, or uncorrelated with, each other. Consequently the sum of their products will equal zero. Thus the last equation given above may be rewritten as follows:

$$r_{xy} = \frac{\Sigma c^2}{N\sigma_{C+A}\sigma_{C+B}}$$

Now

$$\frac{\Sigma c^2}{N} = \sigma_C^2$$

Therefore

$$r_{xy} = \frac{\sigma_C^2}{\sigma_{C+A}\sigma_{C+B}}$$

This last term can be further simplified by means of a derivation which is a little more complicated and which we will only state:

$$\sigma_{C+A} = \sqrt{\sigma_C^2 + \sigma_A^2}$$

and

$$\sigma_{C+B} = \sqrt{\sigma_C^2 + \sigma_B^2}$$

Thus

$$r_{xy} = \frac{\sigma_C^2}{\sqrt{\sigma_C^2 + \sigma_A^2}\sqrt{\sigma_C^2 + \sigma_B^2}}$$

If we assume that $\sigma_A^2 = \sigma_B^2$, then we have

$$r_{xy} = \frac{\sigma_C^2}{\sqrt{\sigma_C^2 + \sigma_A^2}\sqrt{\sigma_C^2 + \sigma_A^2}}$$

Or

$$r_{xy} = \frac{\sigma_C^2}{\sigma_C^2 + \sigma_A^2} = \frac{\sigma_C^2}{\sigma_C^2 + \sigma_B^2}$$

Thus the correlation is simply the ratio of that part of the variance common to the two tests to the total variance of either one. In other words, we have to think of a hypothetical cause, or factor, partly measured by both tests which, if the specific qualities of each test (A and B) could be taken out, would produce identical rankings of individuals on the two tests. Indeed, the two tests would in fact be replicates of each other, and the correlation between them would be simply a reliability coefficient.

The derivation in the above example may seem to the reader to be rather trivial. But like many mathematical statements, its apparent triteness cloaks a hidden usefulness to which we will return shortly. For the moment, this fact will have to be taken on faith. All we need to be concerned with at this point is that we have a precise way of expressing the correlation between variables in terms of a common factor C which has a variation σ_C^2.

Spearman's General Intelligence

We have already discussed very briefly something of the background of Charles Spearman, who may be considered to be the founder of the factor-analytic movement. Binet, with Gallic practicality, was interested in developing a measure of intelligence that would work, one that would cover most aspects of this trait and would predict school achievement. In attaining these goals, he was very successful. However, he did little to advance our understanding of the basic makeup of intelligence, of whether it was a broad general trait or a set of abilities each highly specific to a certain subject matter. It was precisely to this problem that Spearman addressed himself.

In a number of articles that appeared early in the century and later in his classic work *The Abilities of Man*, published in 1927, Spearman put forward the theory, backed by empirical and statistical proof, that intelligence was a general factor which was expressed to a greater or lesser degree in every intellectual task. In addition to measuring g, any test also involved a unique specific ability s. Together, these determined the performance of an individual. This idea can be illustrated graphically as follows:

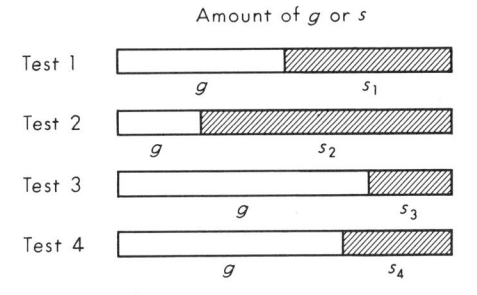

Amount of g or s

Test 1: g | s_1
Test 2: g | s_2
Test 3: g | s_3
Test 4: g | s_4

Test 3 has the most amount of g; test 2, the least. Another way of saying this is that test 3 and test 2 have, respectively, the highest and lowest *loadings on,* or *correlations with,* g. The latter Spearman defined as a kind of general mental energy having to do particularly with the educing of relationships.

This is an intuitively appealing idea, one that many of us hold implicitly. Certainly Binet had something of the sort in mind in constructing his global test of intelligence. Spearman, however, was not content to entertain such a notion merely on the basis of a hunch, no matter how correct it might seem to be. Rather he based it on actual data obtained from giving large numbers of tests to many subjects. Let us look now at his evidence.

To take the simplest case, suppose we give four tests purporting to measure intelligence to a hundred subjects. Correlations may then be computed between the tests to form the following *correlation matrix*.

Correlation matrix

Test	Test 1	2	3	4
1	r_{11}	r_{12}	r_{13}	r_{14}
2	r_{21}	r_{22}	r_{23}	r_{24}
3	r_{31}	r_{32}	r_{33}	r_{34}
4	r_{41}	r_{42}	r_{43}	r_{44}

The correlation elements in the diagonal (r_{11}, r_{22}, r_{33}, r_{44}) are reliability coefficients. The values above the diagonal simply replicate those below it; this is, for example, r_{12} is identical with r_{21}, and so on.

Observing matrices of this kind, though usually of a much larger size involving many more intelligence tests, Spearman noticed, in the first place, that the correlations all tended to be high and positive. Furthermore, if the reliabilities of the tests were corrected to make them perfect (i.e., $r_{xx} = 1.0$), the magnitude of the correlations was even higher, as might be expected. This immediately suggested to Spearman that there might be a common factor underlying all tests and hence responsible for such covariance. In the second place, it was clear that the elements were not all equal. That is to say, some correlations were higher than others. This suggested that the common factor might be more important in some tests, less important in others. This condition would generate such variability in size among the correlational elements in the matrix. As a rough test by inspection of this hypothesis, Spearman tried rearranging his correlational matrices in such a way that the test labeled number 1 was that with the highest average intercorrelation with all other tests; number 2, that with the second highest; and so on, as the following tables illustrate:

Original correlation matrix

	Test			
Test	1	2	3	4
1		.54	.43	.48
2	.54		.63	.72
3	.42	.63		.56
4	.48	.72	.56	
Sum	1.44	1.89	1.61	1.76

Rearrangement according to size of average r with other tests

	Test			
	1' (2)	2' (4)	3' (3)	4' (1)
1' (2)		.72	.63	.54
2' (4)	.72		.56	.48
3' (3)	.63	.56		.42
4' (1)	.54	.48	.42	
Sum	1.89	1.76	1.61	1.44

If the matrix is rearranged in this way, there emerges a new and interesting property which Spearman was the first to notice. The elements which form symmetric squares, which he called *tetrads,* show a constant proportionality between themselves. Take the following such square, or tetrad, drawn from the above matrix:

	Test	
Test	2	4
3	.63	.56
1	.54	.48

The coefficient .56 is 8/9 of the coefficient .63. The same ratio holds between .54 and .48. In other words .56/.63 = .48/.54, or

.56 × .54 = .48 × .63

or

(.56 × .54) − (.48 × .63) = 0

or

.3024 − .3024 = 0

These calculations can be represented in a more general algebraic form by the following equation, known as the *tetrad equation:*

$$r_{ab}r_{cd} - r_{ad}r_{bc} = 0$$

This is based on the matrix

	a	c
b	r_{ab}	r_{bc}
d	r_{ad}	r_{cd}

The same relation holds true if we take the other possible tetrads. For example,

	Test	
Test	4	1
2	.72	.54
3	.56	.42

Ratio = 3/4

and

	Test	
Test	2	3
4	.72	.56
1	.54	.42

Ratio = 7/9

and

	Test	
Test	2	1
4	.72	.48
3	.63	.42

Ratio = 2/3

From this hierarchical arrangement, Spearman inferred that each test in such a matrix has a certain amount of g. The more each has, the higher will be its correlations with other tests; hence the proportionality that exists between correlations of tests that have more or less g. This will be more easily understood if we make the reasoning concrete by assigning hypothetical g values to each of the four tests used in the example. Let us suppose that test 2 has .6g, test 4 has .5, test 3 has .4, and test 1 has .3. We will then set up the following tetrad:

	Test	
	2 (.6g)	4 (.5g)
Test		
3 (.4g)	.24	.20
1 (.3g)	.18	.15

The elements in the matrix are obtained simply by multiplying the g loadings. It will be immediately obvious that the tetrad equation holds. That is, (.24 × .15) − (.18 × .20) = 0. Thus the predictions generated by the assumption of a common factor on which the tests in the battery have loadings of varying extent hold true. This fact suggests that the assumptions are valid.

The reader may have wondered by now whether such a neat arrangement always holds in correlation matrices. Spearman initially felt that it did and that departures from it were due only to error. It soon became clear to other workers and eventually to Spearman himself, however, that more than random factors were operating, but rather systematic factors other than g. With this realization, a new chapter in factor-analytic theory was born. Since there was no reason to suppose that any new factors found had any less importance than g, it became reasonable to speak in terms of *multiple factors.* As we shall see, however, g was to return again though by a curiously devious route. First, let us have a look at the main theoretical developments involved in multiple-factor analysis.

Multiple-Factor Analysis

In a large correlation matrix, say, one consisting of twenty tests, there are obviously an enormous number of tetrads that have to be calculated—to be exact, 14,535. Spearman developed averaging procedures which simplify the calculations that would otherwise be involved, but it is still true that his method is unwieldy and furthermore that after g is taken out, there usually turns out to be left over a good deal of covariation which cannot be dismissed simply as error. Consequently, it is necessary, in such a case, to go back to the correlations now reduced in size by the removal of the first factor and take out another factor. Likewise, third, fourth, and fifth factors may have to be removed until what is left of the correlations can be regarded as statistical error.

It was L. L. Thurstone of the University of Chicago who saw how this could be done by essentially an ingenious extension of Spearman's tetrad method involving the application of *matrix algebra*. In the terminology of this branch of mathematics, a tetrad is called a *minor determinant of order 2*, and if all such minors in the matrix equal zero, or *vanish*, the rank of the matrix is said to be unity. This is another way of saying that the interdependency of the tests as represented by the elements in the cells—that is, the correlation coefficients—can be explained by a single common factor. However, if tetrads do not vanish, we can make tetrads of tetrads—that is, minors of order 3—and see if they vanish. For example, in the following matrix we have four tetrads which together form such a higher-order tetrad:

	Test		
Test	4	5	6
1	r_{14}	r_{15}	r_{16}
2	r_{24}	r_{25}	r_{26}
3	r_{34}	r_{35}	r_{36}
$(r_{14}r_{25} - r_{24}r_{15})$		$(r_{14}r_{26} - r_{24}r_{16})$	
$(r_{14}r_{35} - r_{34}r_{15})$		$(r_{14}r_{36} - r_{34}r_{16})$	

If this minor vanishes, we may then conclude that the rank of the matrix is 2—that is to say, two factors are needed to explain the correlations between tests. The principle then is this: that the rank of a correlation matrix is equal to the order of nonvanishing minors. Thus, in the matrix above, if the tetrads do not vanish but the tetrad of tetrads—a minor of order 3—does vanish, then we conclude that two factors are needed.

Thurstone's actual methods are far too complex to go into here. All we wish to make clear is that they represent an extension of Spearman's; or perhaps a fairer way of putting it is to say that the Spearman's common factor is a special case of the more general multiple-factor solution developed by Thurstone.

Today, most workers in the field of factor analysis favor multiple-factor solutions. In fact, the number of factors of personality and intelligence that have been uncovered runs into the hundreds. At the same time, it has turned out that, in the domain of intelligence, many of the factors making it up are themselves correlated. A matrix constituted by inter-factor, rather than inter-test correlations, can itself be factor analyzed. If this is done, as Thurstone (1947) showed, a second-order general factor emerges. Clearly this is much like Spearman's g.

THE FRUITS OF FACTOR ANALYSIS

Having explained something of the methodology of factor analysis, we will discuss what it has yielded in the way of helping us understand human abilities and personality. We will look first at intelligence and aptitudes.

Factorial Analyses of Intelligence

SPEARMAN AND THURSTONE As indicated in the discussion above, Spearman was the first to develop a theory about how intelligence worked in man, this being his notion of g plus specifics. Gradually, as Thurstone's multiple-factor method gained ascendancy, Spearman's view gave way to the notion that intelligence was made up of a number of specific, though somewhat related abilities. These Thurstone labeled the *primary mental abilities*. They include, among a number of others, numerical ability (N), memory (M), verbal fluency (W), verbal comprehension (V), spatial ability (S). Thurstone and his colleagues have constructed and standardized a test to measure them—the PMA test—composed of sections that are designed to measure the separate abilities in purified form.

In view of the correlation between the primary abilities and the second-order factor this generates, there seems to be no large conflict between the positions of Spearman and Thurstone. Certainly, neither point of view seems to be markedly favored over the other by authorities in the field, and tests both for general intelligence and for special abilities are widely used. However, the Thurstone solution is certainly backed by greater methodological sophistication and for at least this reason is perhaps to be preferred over that of Spearman. In addition, it has been much more productive of further research on the subject. The work of Guilford, whom we will consider next, can serve as an example of this.

GUILFORD'S STRUCTURE OF INTELLECT Both Spearman and Thurstone used a relatively narrow range of tests with which to assess intelligence. Guilford, in a program on selection of service personnel in World War II, extended this greatly to a large number of new tests aimed at studying many such a priori categories as reasoning, creativity, planning, associative ability, skill in classifying, foresight, and flexibility. Many of his tests were derived from different areas of experimental psychology, particularly those to do with perception, learning, and thinking. One major result of using such a wide range of tests was the obtaining of correlational data far too complex to be handled by any unitary theory of intelligence. A large number of primary abilities emerged, some of these new and some identical with those discovered previously by Thurstone and others. This led Guilford to look for some theoretical classifying principles by which the long list of specific abilities could be more readily understood. The model now to be described is his attempt to provide a complete picture of the structure of intellect. It is represented in Figure 22–1.

Some of the categories need a little explanation. First, the *content* of any test has obvious importance. Individuals will perform better or worse depending on whether they have to deal with figures, symbols (letters or numbers), semantic content (concepts or meanings), or behavior (as in empathy).

Secondly, given a certain content, a certain kind of *operation* will be called for. Guilford distinguishes five of these. Evaluation means making a judgment as to whether some material is right, correct, good, or adequate. Convergent thinking involves the capacity to proceed in a linear deductive way from one conclusion to another that logically follows the first. Divergent thinking, on the other hand, goes off in many directions in a kind of search pattern that allows the possibility of many correct answers. Memory speaks for itself, and, finally, cognition has to do simply with the comprehension of material or discovery of information.

The third major category relates to the *products* of operations applied to content. This has six subdivisions which describe the kinds of end products in which a particular application of intelligence can result. Most of these are self-explanatory, since they are the kinds of products we are required to generate in many intellectual tasks. Thus we are often required to classify objects into groups and recognize the principle of such classification, to be able to locate out of a confused array of data the most appropriate units to work with, to see what a certain kind of datum or event implies, and so on.

Such is Guilford's view of intelligence. It should be noted that it is supported only in part by actual evidence. Data from tests suggest the validity of the model but do not go so far as to verify it completely. Many of the cells are still unrepresented by existing tests or factors and as such, as Guilford points out, should challenge the psychometrician to further exploration.

Factorial Analysis of Personality

Perhaps the two researchers who have done most to develop theories of personality based on factor-analytic methods have been Raymond Cattell of the University of Illinois and Hans Eysenck of the Maudsley Hospital, University of London, England. Both of them are very eclectic theorists in that they have made use of the concepts of many other points of view, including psychoanalysis, behaviorism, Gestalt psychology, and need theory among others. In the end, in fact, it is a little difficult to specify that part of their contributions that stems uniquely from factor analysis. Bearing this in mind, let us now briefly discuss their models of personality.

CATTELL'S TRAIT THEORY The key unit in Cattell's system (1946, 1950, 1957) is the *trait*. He is by

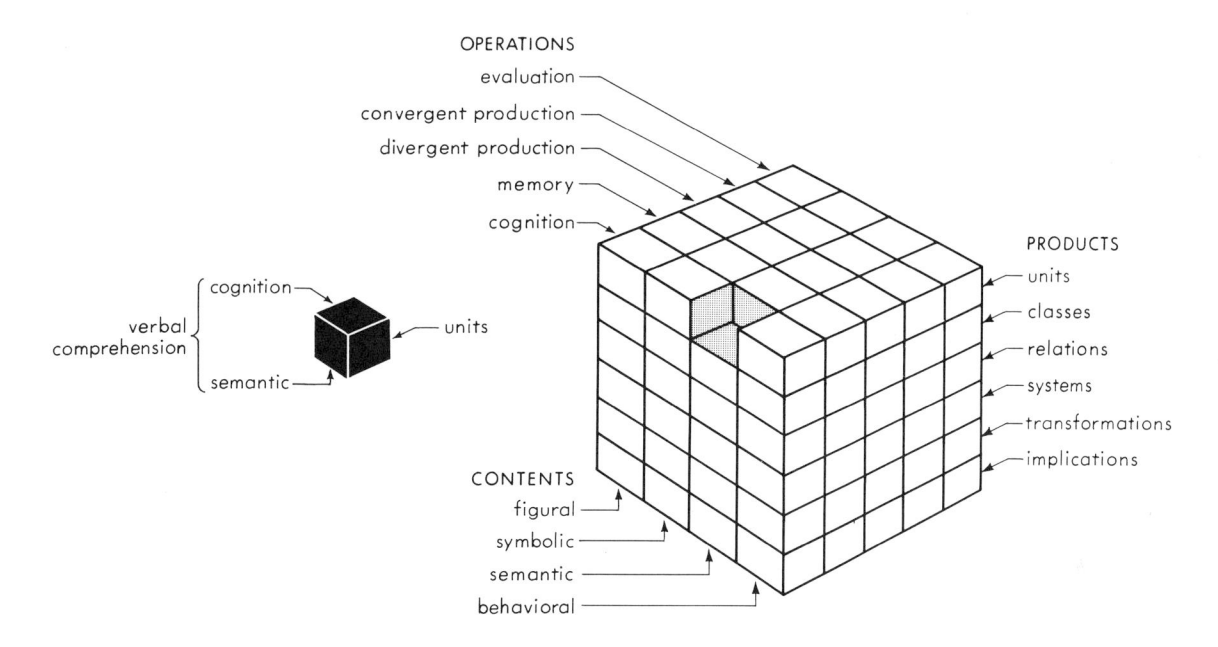

FIG. 22–1 Guilford's geometrical model of intellect. (*Guilford, 1959*)

no means alone in this respect, but he is certainly a thinker who has explicated this concept more fully and more deeply than most other trait theorists. One of his key distinctions, obviously drawn from the factor-analytic approach, is between *surface traits* and *source traits*. The former are those variables of personality that are immediately observable or testable and that seem to go together or correlate. For example, we may find that certain people who tend to be very outgoing also are talkative and impulsive, hate to be alone, like physical exercise, and tend to be cheerful. The analog in clinical medicine is the syndrome—that is, a collection of symptoms frequently found to occur together.

Underlying such surface traits and the structural cause of them are source traits. These, though more remote from common sense, are of greater and more basic scientific importance, according to Cattell, and it is with them that we should deal in attempting to study the dynamics of personality and the influence of genetics and environment on it. Source traits are discernible only by means of factor analysis, and they correspond, of course, to factors. By means of massive research effort, Cattell has claimed to have uncovered at least fifteen source traits, these having to do mostly with personality but also with general intelligence. Several of these (besides intelligence) which appear to be most convincing are cyclothymia (mood swings) versus schizothymia (tendency to be withdrawn); surgency versus desurgency (anxious melancholy); socialized and cultured tendency versus boorishness; Bohemian unconcernedness versus conventional practicality. The rather colorful names assigned to these source traits are of course provisional and may represent, as Cattell admits, simply approximations of their real nature.

Another basic source trait inferred by Cattell in the sphere of motivation is *ergic strength*. This he regards as innate. Besides relating to energy level, it also disposes its possessor to like or dislike certain classes of objects and to attend to these more or less closely. Some of his theorizing about ergs and their development are rather strongly influenced by the psychoanalytic model. He lists altogether ten ergs: sex, self-assertion, escape, protectiveness, gregariousness, rest seeking, exploration, narcissistic sex, appeal, and construction. The reader may recognize that, in addition to Freud, Cattell has drawn on Murray's need theory discussed in Section Two.

This brief resumé hardly does justice to Cattell, who has been one of the most prolific of contemporary psychologists in terms of publications. These include about twenty books and close to three hundred articles. However, in the present context, we are not so much concerned with presenting his complete theory as with illustrating one kind of explication of the factor-analytic method. The manner in which this has contributed to Cattell's views on personality is perhaps subtle but nonetheless real.

EYSENCK'S DIMENSIONS OF PERSONALITY Whereas Thurstone, Guilford, and Cattell have tended to proliferate the number of factors that are supposed to explain personality and intelligence, Eysenck (1952), on the other hand, has opted for using only a few dimensions, which are then studied in depth both clinically and experimentally. In fact, it has been one of the unique features of Eysenck's program at the Maudsley that it has involved parallel research at the animal, human-experimental, and human-clinical levels. Like Cattell, he has been a prolific producer and has published books on many subjects including political attitudes and susceptibility to cancer.

We referred in Section Two to some of Eysenck's work in connection with a discussion of the concept of normality. The reader may recall that he considered psychoticism and neuroticism to be two separate dimensions, though each was continuous with normal. It may be stated now that he arrived at these through extensive factor-analytic studies of large populations of normal and abnormal subjects. In addition, by the same procedures, he arrived at another basic dimension—introversion-extroversion. This is orthogonal to, or uncorrelated with, the other two factors. Thus personality is describable in terms of a three-dimensional space by these three traits. This is illustrated in Figure 22–2.

We may thus have introverted neurotics or extroverted neurotics, the two classes being very different from each other in many ways other than neuroticism, of course. Introverted neurotics tend to be anxious and depressed, obsessional, often irritable, and easily hurt. They daydream frequently, are moody, and are given to feelings of inferiority.

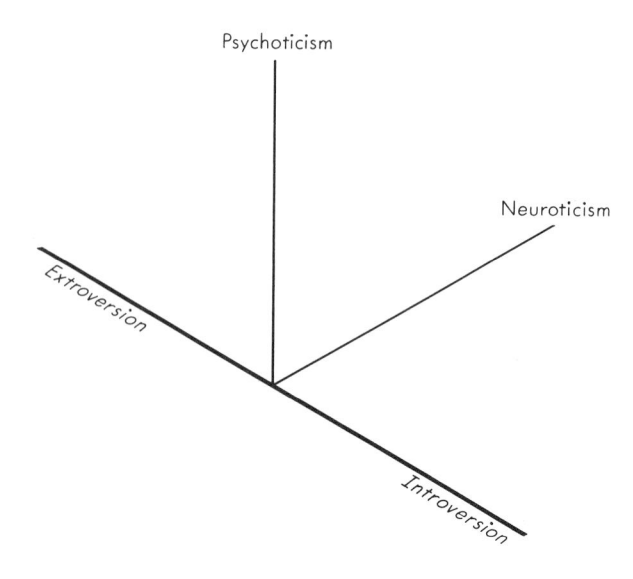

FIG. 22–2 Eysenck's basic dimensions of personality.

Extroverted neurotics, on the other hand, tend to show hysterical symptoms and hypochondria. Many of their psychological problems tend to become somatic and to be expressed in aches, pains, and accident proneness. They have little energy and rather narrow interests.

Eysenck has felt that all three of these dimensions are strongly influenced by heredity. Such evidence as there is available, in our opinion, does seem to favor his position, although it is admittedly not definitive. At the same time, Eysenck is not at all committed to the idea that neurotics or psychotics cannot be changed by treatment, and the kind he has advocated has been of the Skinnerian "behavior therapy" variety.

His interest in learning theory emerges also at other points—and this fact again marks him as rather different from most factor analysts. Taking Hull's notion of reactive inhibition (I_R, discussed in Section Five), he has hypothesized that extroverts possess a large amount of I_R, causing them to tire quickly of doing the same thing. This makes them appear impulsive, flighty, easily bored, and highly sociable—in the sense of preferring many friends. Introverts are thought to have a low amount of I_R, this in turn producing a personality rather resistant to change, able to concentrate on the same material for long periods of time, and preferring few friends. Though his reasoning is perhaps somewhat *post hoc*, Eysenck's hypothesis does have some experimental support. The following example will serve to illustrate this.

Example 22–4 *Personality factors and reactive inhibition (Franks, 1957)*

One of the first to investigate the relation between personality as defined factorially and Hullian inhibition was an associate of Eysenck's, Cyril M. Franks (1957). Eysenck had suggested a positive relationship between rate and strength of buildup and slowness of dissipation of I_R and extroversion, and also the propensity to develop "hystericopsychopathic" neurotic disorders. Introversion and a disposition to dysthymic neurotic disorders were postulated as being related to low rate and strength of buildup and rapid dissipation of I_R. From this hypothesis, it follows that neuroticism as such is unrelated to I_R but that both neurotic and normal extroverts should be distinguished from neurotic or normal introverts in respect to this variable.

This particular study of Frank's was only one in a series of researches but may be taken as illustrative of the kinds of methods he used and the general direction of results he obtained.

Testing sixty undergraduate subjects between eighteen and twenty-six years, he subjected them to an eyelid conditioning procedure as follows: The UCS was a puff of air to the eye, and the CS was a tone of 1,100 cps occurring 350 milliseconds prior to the onset of the UCS. The response was an eyelid blink elicited by the CS during a set number of conditioning and extinction trials. Subjects were tested on the Maudsley Personality Inventory developed by Eysenck to measure neuroticism and introversion-extroversion.

Results are summarized graphically in Figure 22–3. They indicate, in general, that conditionability is related strongly to the introversion-extroversion dimension but not to neuroticism. Introverts tend to be conditioned faster than extroverts. However, contrary to Eysenck's explicit hypothesis, their responses are extinguished faster than those of extroverts. At the same time, it is clear from a close inspection of the graphs that the extinction slope of extroverts is a good deal steeper than that of introverts. If this result is added to the fact that the base line for extinction for extroverts starts at a much higher level than for introverts, the data do not strongly deviate from Eysenck's hypothesis, though they do not necessarily make it a unique or necessary explanation.

This example is only one of many which support Eysenck's speculation about the personality dimension of introversion-extroversion. However, as often happens with rather bold theories in psychology (as the reader must by now realize), there are studies whose results are not fully in agreement with Eysenck's. Consequently, we can conclude that the idea has been only partly substantiated. It is, however, a very promising one which has led to a most interesting and variegated line of experimentation. Though his work has frequently been criticized, Eysenck deserves much credit for being one of the few in the area of factor analysis who has made a genuine attempt to relate his factors to empirical variables. This is a most important goal and is worth a little discussion by itself.

The Reality of Factors

The reader may recall that one original reason for dealing with the methods and findings of factor analysis was that it is one application of psychometrics which has produced substantive data about human personality and behavior. The different theories put forward above certainly have made such claims, but are we to believe them? In other words, if it is asserted, for example, as it is by Guilford, on the basis of his studies, that the mind is made up of 120 factors, are we to take this seriously? Are these factors real in some sense, or are they purely mathematical fictions?

The answer to this question hinges on what is meant by the term "real." To be "real" in science does not mean to be immediately available to sense observation. It was many years before Mendel's factors could be so explored. Before that happened they were simply constructions whose properties uniquely explained certain kinds of data, specifically, the distribution of morphological characters in offspring of certain mating types. In this sense, genetic factors were real. It is something of a question as to whether psychological factors so qualify. Certainly they are useful in describing in an economical way a great deal of test data, but whether

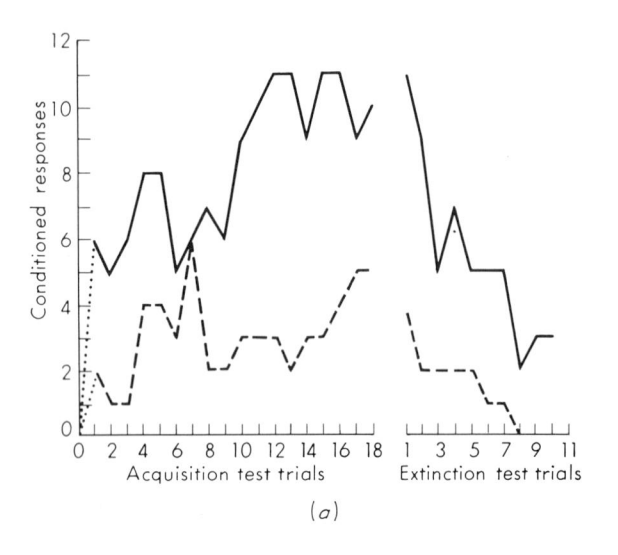

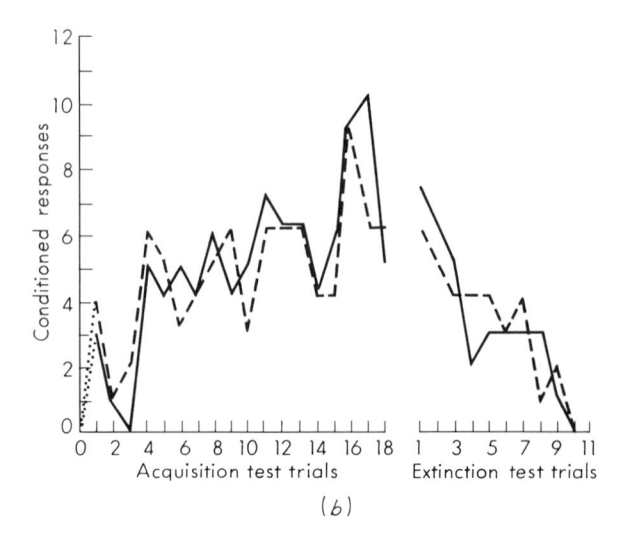

FIG. 22-3 Relation of conditionability to introversion-extroversion and to neuroticism. (*Franks, 1957*)

factors in general, and more especially any particular sets postulated by some workers, uniquely do so is another question. The kind of work being done by Eysenck, in which an attempt is made to tie factors more closely to certain experimental manipulations, seems to us to represent a step in the right direction. All too few factor analysts have done this, with the result that the number of factors (covering all behavior domains) that have been found in psychology must number in the thousands. This is more like stamp collecting than like science. Both are commendable pursuits, but at least in psychology it is only the second that is of importance.

It will be clear by now that work on response sets and styles and on factors lead directly into personality theory. It is equally true, however, that the kinds of theories that emerge are not uniquely determined by the constructs of testing but draw rather heavily on those of the kind reviewed in Section Two, especially Freud and the psychoanalytic writers. Even Hull has been drawn into the factorial frame of reference. This kind of merging of interests is undoubtedly a fruitful trend, since it indicates that the gap between the so-called "two disciplines of scientific psychology" designated by Cronbach is rapidly closing and that the techniques and theories of the experimentalist are starting to be used by the psychometrician as a way of validating his tests and factors.

In our final discussion that follows, we will consider a subject on which the kind of work done also demonstrates the same trend, namely, creativity. Since it is a topic about which relatively little is known but which holds great interest, we are discussing it last.

CREATIVITY

As two authorities on this subject, Getzels and Jackson (1962), of the University of Chicago, point out, creativity is one of the most highly valued of human characteristics and also one of the most difficult to deal with scientifically. It is very doubtful whether most intelligence tests come even close to measuring it, and though we may be able to recognize its presence retrospectively by seeing its products, we cannot really recognize it prospectively in process, as it were, before a concrete product appears. Furthermore, there are indications that our whole educational structure not only is unable to assess creativity but actually is biased against it. Most teachers do not care much for the unusual, "offbeat" child who gives answers that do not conform to some predetermined idea of what is "correct." Getzels and Jackson put the matter very aptly:

> There is ample evidence that the criteria of factualism and usefulness—if you will, of vocationalism, although it may seem silly to use this term at so early an age—are being insinuated into many childhood experiences once viewed as the happy hunting ground for "childish" play and imaginative activity. Rumpelstiltskin and Goldilocks on the child's bookshelf are being shouldered aside by Nurse Nancy and Mr. Fixit. Journeys to the Land of Oz and the World of Pooh are being displaced, even at the kindergarten level, by "real" educational visits—as they say—to the airport and the municipal sewage disposal plant. Even that last bastion of the child's private world—his box of toys—is being taken over by the press of practicality. Here, too, the key adjectives are "realistic" and "educational" or at the very least "readiness-producing" instead of "imaginative" or "exciting" or even just plain "enjoyable." The floppy rag doll that did nothing and yet everything as the malleable companion of the child's dreams has given way to the true-to-life human replica that leaves nothing to the imagination—it "really talks" and takes in and oozes at all the appropriate orifices. The ancient lead soldier in his frozen posture, which the child could transmute into anything his play required, is no match for the modern Transparent Man whose removable vital organs form an educational jigsaw puzzle for mother's little, successful doctor-to-be. And of course, the institutionalized and curriculumized activities of the kindergarten, to which the child once was introduced in his fifth year, has been moved to the institutionalized and curriculumized activities, let's not say lessons, of the nursery school to which the child arrives in his fourth year—if indeed the nursery school itself is not already a graduate institution of the pre-nursery school. Even the preverbal child's toys are now sold not just as playthings but as Playschool, the pitch being that these toys are not "just toys," but carefully designed to train the infant in "appropriate" motor, intellectual and problem-solving skills, presumably appropriate for gaining early admission to prenursery school [Getzels & Jackson, 1962, pp. 121–122].

The reader may recall from an earlier part of this chapter that one of the criticisms directed against tests such as the college boards is that they seem to penalize the creative person who is able to see in a question ambiguities that are not obvious to a more conventionally minded person and were perhaps not even obvious to the person who made up the test in the first place. Consequently, there is a great need to extend the concept we have of "giftedness" or "intellectual ability" so as to take in some factor of creativity whose fruits in art, literature, music, and science we know well and value but whose workings we do not know much about. Let us now discuss what information we do have.

The Nature of Creativity

Looking back through history, we can identify fairly readily the great creative geniuses. Such names as these readily spring to mind: Plato, Aristotle, St. Thomas, Kant, and Hegel in philosophy; Gallileo, Darwin, Kepler, Einstein, and Freud in the sciences; Shakespeare, Molière, Cervantes, Dostoievski, Kafka, and Hemingway in literature; Da Vinci, Rembrandt, Cezanne, Gainsborough, Picasso, and Andrew Wyeth in the visual arts; Bach, Beethoven, Mozart, Stravinsky, and Bartok in music; and in the world of political affairs, Alexander, Napoleon, Disraeli, Tallyrand, Jefferson, Churchill, and Ghandi. The works of such men have stood the test of time to an extent that permits little disagreement about their creativity. About contemporary figures however, there is usually less unanimity. Not everyone is ready to accept, for example, John Cage's now famous composition "3½," which consists simply of 3½ minutes of silence, or, for that matter, something less startling but still unconventional like the abstract expressionist painting of Jackson Pollock achieved by dripping paint on a horizontal canvas. We must rely, in the end, on critics, or on our own critical faculty if it is good enough, and on time. In the end, these, through some mysterious alchemy, tend to sort out what is really creative from what is repetitious and trivial.

If the products of creativity are hard to evaluate, the successful identification of this quality in an individual child or adult prior to their producing some distinguished piece of work is even more difficult. But this is the task faced by those working in this area.

Research on creativity started in a serious, programmatic way around the early 1950s. Guilford, with his dedication to the factorial analysis of mind, was one of the first to emphasize the importance of this trait. Another was Mackinnon, who came to Berkeley from the Harvard Clinic and the influence of Henry Murray. Since that time, many articles and a number of important books have been published on the subject.

In all these, one finds as a main concern the problem of defining creativity, or originality. In general, those working on it have adopted two kinds of strategy in starting out: One has been to start with judgments of experts in a certain sphere of activity, say, architecture, as to which of their peers are the most creative. Such a procedure has been used particularly by Mackinnon and his colleagues at the Institute of Personality Assessment in Berkeley, California. The other strategy has been to construct some a priori definition which is then translated into some test or set of tests. A good example of this is given by Getzels and Jackson (1962), who defined creativity, or creative potential, as "the ability to deal inventively with verbal and numerical symbol systems and with object-space relations [p. 17]." The operative word in this definition is "inventive," and this is left unspecified. In the end, it turns out to be a quality who presence is inferred by the experimenters from the subject's responses. So we are really back to where we started.

A more carefully constructed type of definition has been offered by Mednick (1962) and by Wallach and Kogan (1965). Starting with the introspections of creative people, they find these involve frequent use of phrases such as these: "combinatory play," "associative play," "ideas that rise in crowds," "flow of ideas," "springs of ideas bubbling up," and so on. Such data can be taken to imply an *associative theory of creativity*. Thus Mednick (1962, p. 221) defines creative thinking as "the forming of associative elements into new combinations which either meet specified requirements, or are in some way useful." Wallach and Kogan (1965, p. 14) suggest a basically similar notion: ". . . greater creativity should be indicated by the ability to produce more associations and to produce more that are unique."

A key qualification that is made by both Mednick and by Wallach and Kogan—and for that matter, most people working in this field—is that the above definitions hold only under a condition of relaxed time limits. Speed tests favor the intelligent person, perhaps, but not the creative individual. Certainly, the archetypal concept of creation dissociates it from time. In Genesis, the creation of the world precedes and, as it were, makes "time," but it starts outside it; and all the enclaves of artists around the world offer, in the way of life they endorse, a negation of time and the rules it imposes. Eastern religious thought, for example Buddhism or Taoism, whose main thrust is the identification of the individual with God as the Creator, also stresses an escape from, or transcendence over, the strictures of time.

This point of view is translated into more humble scientific terms by Mednick and Wallach and Kogan with the model shown in Figure 22–4. All the points discussed above are implied by it, and furthermore it offers a direct method of measuring creativity.

What the model deals with specifically is the number and uniqueness of free associations that can be made by a subject to a stimulus word and the speed with which these associations can be given (strength of associate on the ordinate axis). Obviously, this definition of creativity is a good deal more specific than most. Furthermore, as we mentioned above, it can be nicely explicated into a number of concrete hypotheses that predict how creative people as compared with noncreative persons should behave when given certain kinds of tests. Let us now see what kinds of tests these are.

Measures of Creativity

In the first place, unlike most tests of aptitude, those purporting to measure creativity are made up of items to which a great range of answers is possible. There are no right answers, though naturally some turn out to be better than others. Wallach and Kogan (1965) following their model use the following tests:

1. Instances: The subject is asked to give as many possible instances of some class concept as he can. For example, one such concept is "All the round things you can think of." A conventional answer to this might be "Ball"; an original answer, on the other hand, might be "Lifesaver."
2. Alternate uses: The subject is asked for alternative uses for each of a set of eight common objects, for example, a newspaper, a shoe, or a chair. Again, creativity is scored in terms of unique or very unusual responses. For example, "A shoe is to drink champagne out of."

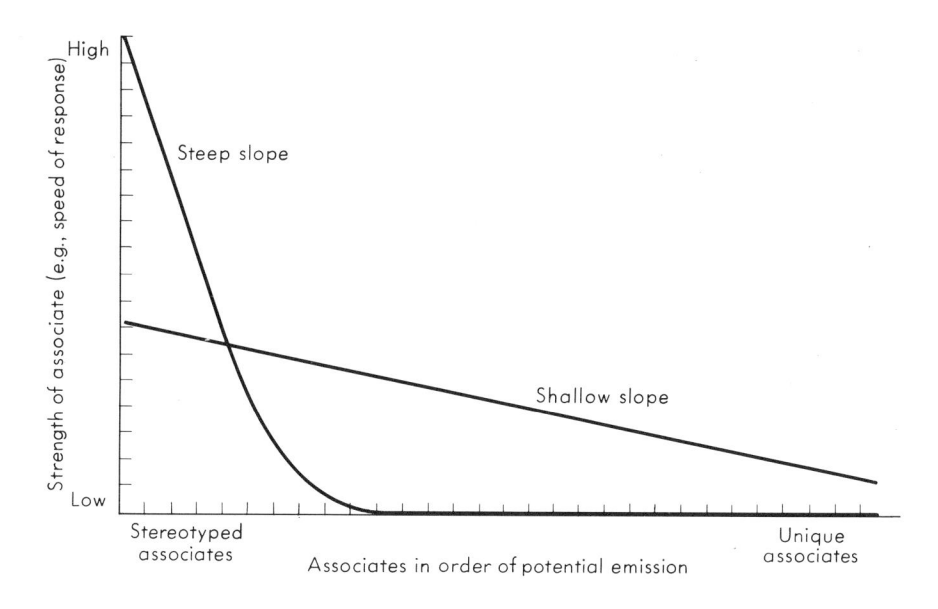

FIG. 22-4 The associative model of creativity. (*Mednick, 1962; Wallach & Kogan, 1965*)

3. Similarities: This test also occurs in the Stanford-Binet, except here interest lies not in the logicality but the inventiveness of the response. To say "cat" and "mouse" are "both animals" is not original. To say that "both could be eaten if you were starving" might well be.
4. Pattern Meanings: This uses visual materials to which the subject is asked to free-associate. The principle is the same as in test 3.
5. Line meanings: The same idea as in tests 3 and 4.

In all these tests, subjects are scored on unique responses and total number of responses. This allows the model in Figure 22-4 to be tested, as well as identifying creative individuals.

Tests used by the other major research groups studying creativity are basically similar to the above. Frank Barron (1957), of the Institute of Personality Assessment, for example, has put together a battery of eight tests to comprise a Composite Test of Originality. Again they all involve the assessment of novel reactions to conventional material. The same applies to the five tests used by Getzels and Jackson (1962).

It will be clear to the reader by now that no great scientific genius is required to make up a test of creativity. All one needs is a commonplace task in which many alternative modes of response are possible. The unique modes—as defined either by rating or by the statistical infrequency of their occurrence—are then used as the index of creativity. Having done this, however, one is still faced with several key problems that have plagued experimenters in this field. One is whether creativity or originality is a unitary trait extending over a wide variety of tests, comparable to general intelligence; the other is whether creativity and originality are mostly accounted for by intellectual ability—that is to say, whether, if the factor of intelligence is partialled out of the variation between individuals in creativity tests, any significant differences remain. We will discuss each of these two problems briefly.

Is Creativity a Unitary Trait?

Most researchers have tended to answer this question in the affirmative and have regarded creativity as a trait comparable to the Spearman g factor. Such an assumption is perhaps only partly in accord with commonsense experience. Most of the geniuses in history have been specialists. It is true that there are exceptions such as Leonardo Da Vinci, but by and large the great painters were not great musicians, the great literary figures were not great statesmen, and the great actors have not been great scientists. At the same time, one must also recognize that specialization is partly a necessity imposed by time and culture. It applies as much to intelligence, although this trait may have an underlying breadth and generality that is at odds with the narrow character which society may impose on it. Because of his professional commitments, a scientist, a university president, or a business executive must channel his capacities so much as to appear deficient and even stupid outside his area of specialization. And yet it is likely that on a variety of tests of intelligence each will perform well on all of them, thereby suggesting far greater scope than they are permitted to show.

So it may be with creativity. Furthermore, if we are dealing with creative *capacity* or *potential*, we might well expect to find, if our tests really get at capacity, that the content of each matters very little and that the original mind given any test content will still respond with novel and creative responses.

Whatever may be the bias of common sense—and no doubt each reader may have his own bias—some empirical data on the subject are available.

A cursory examination of the major researches in the field might lead one to believe that creativity is indeed a general trait. Many workers have so concluded. Yet a critical review of these by Wallach and Kogan (1965) suggests that such a conclusion usually does not follow from the data gathered. For example, Guilford's ten tests of creativity, which he identifies with "divergent thinking," yield an average intercorrelation of only .24. Likewise, the eight tests used by Frank Barron to form his composite test correlate, on the average, .18. Such low relationships are at variance with the conclusion of these workers that the trait they are attempting to measure is a general one.

Perhaps the researchers most successful in making a case for a unitary creative ability are Wallach and Kogan. The ten measures they use (five tests each with two scores) yield an average intercorrelation of .41. This is not extravagantly high, yet it is probably of sufficient magnitude to allow the conclusion that a general ability underlies performance in these tests. One might suspect that the intercorrelations of measures (unique responses and total responses) within each of the five tests serve to inflate the average intercorrelation for the whole matrix, but such is not the case. The correlations between measures are only slightly higher on the average (.48) than those between tests (.40).

Is Creativity Related to Intelligence?

The consensus among most experts is that there is a low positive correlation between intelligence and creativity. However, it is likely that this applies only at the upper end of the IQ scale. In other words, a person with an IQ below 100 is very unlikely to be creative, but one with an IQ of 120 may be creative or not. For this reason, most of the research done on creativity has been with subjects of well above average intelligence. For example, Getzels and Jackson (1962) used a class of children having a mean IQ of 132 (about in the upper 1 percent of the whole population). Likewise the work at the Institute of Personality Assessment dealt to a large extent with people of outstanding ability in some particular field such as architecture or science.

Since most IQ tests are constructed to cover a rather broad range and discriminate poorly at the extremes, it is not surprising that they show low correlations with creativity. As we saw earlier in the chapter, curtailment of range is one factor that will lower the correlation between two variables. Consequently, there is some doubt as to the true magnitude of relationship between intelligence and creativity. Generally, there are two ways to get around the problem: One, used by Barron (1965), has been to remove the influence of intelligence by means of a special statistical technique known as partial correlation. With this it is possible to find how creativity measures relate to other variables such as personality tests independently of any effect intelligence might have on such a relation. The other method, more commonly used, is to select from the population of subjects studied four groups representing the possible combinations of high and low intelligence with high and low creativity. Persons in these classes can then be studied in detail on any other measures of interest. We will now discuss some of the data obtained by these two methods.

What Are Creative People Like?

This is our final and perhaps most interesting question. So far we have dealt mainly with problems of a more methodological kind. What we would really like to know, however, is whether the creative persons are recognizable in any way. Are they unusual in their personality characteristics? Are they slightly mad, as the popular view has it? Do they fit as well into such institutional subcultures as the school, or the home, or the job as well as noncreative people? Do they have unusual or offbeat hobbies and interests? And a different but equally important kind of question: assuming we value creativity highly, can we train ordinary people to be creative? Is there a place in our educational curricula at all levels for courses in creativity? These are crucial questions. We will now illustrate by a couple of examples the many attempts that have been made to deal with some of these problems.

Example 22-5 *The personalities of creative people (Barron, 1965)*

This was one among the many attempts made at the Institute of Personality Assessment at Berkeley. The population to be evaluated consisted of 100 military officers. They were given a large number of tests, including the Originality Composite. They also took part in a three-day "living-in" session in the institute. "Living in" has been a special technique used by the Berkeley group, and it has consisted simply of the subjects and staff living casually together for a weekend in a friendly atmosphere of relaxation, reinforced by a "wine cellar and a fireplace." During this period, the experimenters attempted to form ratings of the subjects in terms of creativity. Let us look at some of the results obtained.

When a division of the subjects was made into high and low creative groups as judged by the Originality Composite and by staff ratings, the following differences between the two groups appeared on a personality test:

High scorers tended to:

1. Be verbally fluent and conversationally facile.
2. Have a high degree of intellect.
3. Be able to communicate ideas clearly.
4. Be highly sensitive to intellectual activity.
5. Be effective leaders.
6. Be persuasive and able to win others over to their point of view.

Low scorers tended to:

1. Conform.
2. Be stereotyped in their approach to problems.
3. Have a narrow range of interests.
4. Be reluctant to become involved in things.
5. Lack social poise and presence.
6. Be unaware of their own social stimulus value.

When intelligence, as measured by the Concept Mastery Test, is partialed out of the creativity tests with which it correlates, the following picture of the creative person emerges: He tends in the Rorschach inkblot test to give a large number of so-called whole (W) responses, these being categorizations using the whole blot rather than parts of it. He is judged by staff rating to be fluent with ideas and to have a high drive. He tends to be somewhat exhibitionistic and is good at charades and improvisations. In psychoanalytic terms these characteristics may be described as ego undercontrol of impulses and active phallicism. Likewise the creative person tends to prefer, at least initially, disorder, asymmetry, and messiness. Presumably these represent for him a challenging opportunity for the final imposition of an order of his own, something not furnished if the order has already been supplied by someone else. Such preferences reflect, according to Barron, an early rejection, during the anal stage of development, of external control of impulse.

The above data give us the wherewithal to measure and predict creativity even in the absence of any creative products. They further indicate something about the psychodynamics of originality and the kinds of events during development which promote it or suppress it. As we have already pointed out, the factor of sheer intelligence was removed by a statistical method. We can now ask, however, whether there would be differences between creative persons who are also intelligent and creative persons who are relatively unintelligent? Is it only the former combination that truly represents what might be called "giftedness" or genius? The monograph by Wallach and Kogan is one of the most thorough and careful attempts to examine these questions.

Example 22-6 *Modes of thinking in young children (Wallach & Kogan, 1965)*

The population Wallach and Kogan studied consisted of seventy boys and eighty-one girls—the entire fifth grade of a suburban New England public school system. Their average age was 10 years 7.60 months, and they came mostly from families of the professional and managerial class. As stated earlier, ten indicators of creativity were used, three with verbal materials and two using visual materials. Each provided two scores: unique responses and total number of responses. No time limits were imposed. Intelligence was assessed by ten standard indicators including the Wechsler Intelligence Scale for Children.

All creativity tests proved to be reliable, only one yielding a split-half coefficient under .75. The intercorrelations among creativity instruments and any intelligence tests were high, but the two domains turned out to be relatively independent of each other. This allowed the investigators to set up the following four-cell table:

Sample sizes*

Creativity	Intelligence	
	High	Low
High	39	36
Low	37	39

*Total number of children studied = 151.

The major question to be then explored was how these four categories of children differed psychologically, particularly in regard to their general behavior in the school environment, their conceptualizing activities, their sensitivity to the emotional significance of stimuli (physiognomic properties), their motivational states, and, finally, their individual personalities. We will give here only a few highlights of the findings of Wallach and Kogan.

In respect to behavior in the classroom, it was found that for girls, the highly creative and highly intelligent were the least hesitant and subdued. Those high in creativity but low in intelligence, on the other hand, showed the most of these kinds of behaviors. The data are shown in Table 22–2.

This interaction effect between intelligence and creativity is statistically significant. It was also found that among girls, those in the high-creativity–high-intelligence and low-creativity–low intelligence groups sought out others for companionship more than those in the two other groups. However, though the high-highs were sought after by others, the same did not apply to the low-lows. The highly intelligent but low-creativity individuals apparently were preferred over those in the other two categories. The general impression is that the group of girls who were highly creative but low in intelli-

Table 22–2 Ratings of hesitant and subdued behavior (girls)

Creativity	Intelligence	
	High	Low
High	3.86	6.06
Low	5.37	5.82

gence were the most isolated group in the classroom. They avoided others, and, in turn, were avoided by others. They tended to represent a negative and disruptive force in the classroom. Strangely enough, differences in creativity in boys contributed very little to the classroom behavior.

In regard to the emotional significance of stimuli, it was found that for boys, both creativity and intelligence tended to increase sensitivity to this dimension. For example, the ability of boys to correctly match abstract patterns and emotional states related to intelligence and creativity, as indicated in Table 22–3.

The low-low group evidently showed the least skill in making the jump between abstract line drawings and the emotional meaning these were judged to have by three independent adult judges. Wallach and Kogan suggested that intelligence increases physiognomic sensitivity through the person's ability to make inferences and see implications, whereas creativity augments it by providing a wealth and richness of "associational freedom."

The final dimensions to be considered were anxiety and defensiveness. Again, some interesting interactions were found. In general, highly intelligent, low-creativity boys turned out to be low in anxiety, whereas the low-low group showed the highest level of anxiety. Girls showed less systematic effects.

The summaries of the four groups given by Wallach and Kogan are:

High creativity–high intelligence: These children can exercise both control and freedom, both adultlike and childlike kinds of behavior.

High creativity–low intelligence: These children are in angry conflict with themselves and with their school environment and are beset by feelings of unworthiness and inadequacy. In a stress-free contest, however, they can blossom forth cognitively.

Low creativity–high intelligence: These children can be described as "addicted" to school achievement.

Table 22-3 Mean number of correct abstract-pattern choices by boys from the four groups

Creativity	Intelligence	
	High	Low
High	20.29	20.56
Low	20.06	17.76

Academic failure would be perceived by them as catastrophic, so that they must continually strive for academic excellence in order to avoid the possibility of pain.

Low creativity–low intelligence: Basically bewildered, these children engage in various defensive maneuvers ranging from useful adaptations such as intensive social activity to regressions such as passivity or psychosomatic symptoms.

This brief summary hardly does justice to the penetrating and detailed analysis that has been offered by Wallach and Kogan. Nonetheless, perhaps it will serve to introduce the reader to a mode of attack on a problem of first importance for basic psychology and for educational practice. The curricula of most schools are mainly geared to conventional intellectual skills and tolerate creativity apparently only so far as it is backed up by a high degree of intelligence. Yet surely we should value creativity and find some ways of aiding and encouraging it. This is perhaps the main point that Wallach and Kogan wished to emphasize.

The summary above by no means covers all the work on creativity. This is extensive. But it will perhaps suggest to the reader some of the questions that can be asked about it and the general modes of answering them. It is by no means inconceivable that when we know more about the nature and origins of creativity, we will be able to develop ways of deliberately training it. In fact, several research programs have been initiated at different centers with just this in mind (cf. Barron, 1965), and their success gives us some grounds for hope. Certainly there seems little doubt that creativity, intelligence, and knowledge are all different aspects of mind and hence require separate attention in our educational institutions.

With the topic of creativity we end this section, and with it we have, in a sense, turned full circle back to Section Two, where psychoanalysis was discussed. Freud and many who followed in his footsteps became deeply concerned with creativity and its wellsprings in the human unconscious. This interest is well reflected in Freud's studies of Da Vinci, Dostoievski, and other such creative geniuses, and any reader who wishes to glance through the pages of a psychoanalytic journal like *American Imago* will find that this tradition is still a strong one.

It certainly seems true that the process of creating is hidden from our consciousness and, for this reason, has a quality of mystery and transcendence about it that almost make our scientific attempts to dissect it seem sacreligious. Indeed, it is very common for artists to shy away from participation in such investigations, for fear that in being understood their gift will be destroyed. Whether the unconscious to which creativity pertains is the infantile and archaic Freudian unconscious is something else. Freud himself confessed to reservations about this, and many others have suggested that creativity emanates from another kind of unconscious. A well-known contemporary philosopher, Jacques Maritain, has suggested this be labeled "spiritual unconscious," or, in honor of Plato—one of the first to discuss it—"the musical unconscious." This, and the Freudian, or "deaf," unconscious—the "two great domains of psychological activity screened from the grasp of consciousness [Maritain, 1953]" —together represent aspects of the most mysterious side of man.

CONCLUSION

We started this section by emphasizing an idea that greatly impressed the founders of the field of psychometrics: the idea of variation between individuals. We ended up by stressing, on the other hand, a rather different notion, namely, the importance of variation within individuals. These two ideas are not, of course, mutually contradictory, but it is nevertheless true that their orientations point research and theorizing in dissimilar directions. It has thus been traditional in the field to have, as a major goal, the assessment of individuals in terms of fixed values on a set of scales, or tests, on the basis of which accurate predictions of some criterion performance might be made. Lately, workers such as Cronbach commenced to stress the potential for change that may be found in most individuals—

particularly those kinds of changes seen in situations where learning and, more especially, creative ability are demanded.

This seems to us to represent a healthy trend. As we pointed out, most people feel a strong antipathy to being permanently pigeonholed or classified in terms of a set of ability or personality test scores. They usually consider themselves capable of much more growth and improvement than conventional tests give them credit for. And they are probably right. This is not to say that we will ever be able to turn imbeciles into geniuses—though even this possibility is not so remote, as a result of our growing fund of information about brain biochemistry—but it must certainly be true that most psychological functions are capable of alteration within limits. Indeed, psychometrics must do a disservice to society to entertain any other position.

This is not to say that we must give up the notion of predictability, but rather that predictions must be made conditional on a set of environmental or organismic variables. Therefore instead of stating merely that Johnny has an IQ of 110 and therefore is probably not college material, a psychologist might say that this present score is liable to shift up, say, 10 points, if Johnny is put into a special educational program. He might also say that the same shift upward is less likely to occur with Jimmy, also scoring 110 at the same age, since the latter's intellectual ability, perhaps for genetic reasons, is less sensitive to environmental manipulation.

It is important to point out that such an orientation will do much to bridge the gap pointed up by Cronbach (1957) between the two disciplines of psychometrics and experimental psychology. The focus will come to be on how traits and abilities develop and the dependence of this development on maturational factors and variables to do with learning. Likewise, the converse problem of how undesirable traits are unlearned—until recently the major concern mainly of the clinical person—will now also come to be of interest to the psychometrician.

SECTION SEVEN: REFERENCES

BARRON, F. Originality in relation to personality and intellect. *Journal of Personality,* 1957, **25,** 730–742.

BARRON, F. The psychology of creativity. In T. W. Newcomb (Ed.), *New directions in psychology.* Vol. II. New York: Holt, 1965.

BENDER, L. A visual motor gestalt test and its clinical use. *American Journal of Orthopsychiatry Association Research Monograph,* 1938, No. 3.

BERG, I. A. Deviant responses and deviant people: The formulation of the deviation hypothesis. *Journal of Counseling Psychology,* 1957, **4,** 154–161.

BORING, E. G. *A history of experimental psychology.* New York: Century, 1929.

CATTELL, R. B. *Description and measurement of personality.* New York: World, 1946.

CATTELL, R. B. *Personality: A systematic theoretical and factual study.* New York: McGraw-Hill, 1950.

CATTELL, R. B. *Personality and motivation structure and measurement.* New York: World, 1957.

COUCH, A., & KENISTON, K. Yea-sayers and nay-sayers: Agreeing response set as a personality variable. *Journal of Abnormal and Social Psychology,* 1960, **60,** 151–174.

CRONBACH, L. The two disciplines of scientific psychology. *American Psychologist,* 1957, **12,** 671–684.

CRONBACH, L. *Essentials of psychological testing.* (2d ed.) New York: Harper, 1960.

DESCARTES, R. *Discourse on the method of rightly conducting the reason, and seeking truth in the sciences.* (1637). La Salle, Ill.: Court, 1945.

EELLS, K., et al. *Intelligence and cultural differences.* Chicago: University of Chicago Press, 1951.

EYSENCK, H. J. *The Scientific study of personality.* London: Routledge, 1952.

FLANAGAN, J. C. *Factor analysis in the study of personality.* Stanford, Calif.: Stanford University Press, 1935.

FRANKS, C. M. *Personality factors and the rate of conditioning. British Journal of Psychology,* 1957, **48,** 119–126.

GALANTER, E. Contemporary psychophysics. In T. W. Newcomb (Ed.), *New directions in psychology.* Vol. II. New York: Holt, 1962.

GETZELS, J. W., & JACKSON, P. W. *Creativity and intelligence; Explorations with gifted students.* London: Wiley, 1962.

GOBETZ, W. A quantification, standardization, and validation of the Bender-Gestalt test on normals and neurotic adults. *Psychological Monographs,* 1953, **67** (Whole No. 356).

GOODENOUGH, F. L. *Mental testing.* New York: Rinehart, 1949.

GOLDSTEIN, K. *The organism: A holistic approach to biology derived from pathological data in man.* New York: American Book, 1939.

GOUGH, H. G. *The adjective check list.* Berkeley, Calif.: University of California Press, 1952.

GRIGG, A. E., & THORPE, J. S. Deviant responses in college adjestment clients: A test of Berg's deviation hypothesis. *Journal of Consulting Psychology*, 1960, **24**, 92–94.

GUILFORD, J. P. *Personality.* New York: McGraw-Hill, 1959.

GULLICKSEN, H. *Theory of mental tests.* New York: Wiley, 1950.

HOFFMAN, B. *The tyranny of testing.* New York: Crowell-Collier, 1962.

HONZIK, M. P., MACFARLANE, J. W., & ALLEN, L. The stability of mental test performance between two and eighteen years. *Journal of Experimental Education*, 1948, **17**, 309–324.

HUIZINGA, J. *The waning of the middle ages.* (1934.) New York: Anchor Books, Doubleday, 1956.

JONES, H. E. *Manual of child psychology.* New York: Wiley, 1946.

KELLY, E. L., & FISKE, D. W. *The prediction of performance in clinical psychology.* Ann Arbor, Mich.: University of Michigan Press, 1951.

KENDLER, H. H. *Basic psychology.* New York: Appleton-Century-Crofts, 1963.

KENISTON, K. *The uncommitted: Alienated youth in American society.* New York: Harcourt, Brace, 1965.

LOEVINGER, J. A systematic approach to the construction and evaluation of tests of ability. *Psychological Monographs*, 1947, **61** (4).

LORGE, I. The fundamental nature of measurement. In E. F. Lindquist (Ed.), *Educational measurement.* Washington: American Council on Education, 1951.

MARITAIN, J. *Creative intuition in art and poetry.* New York: Pantheon, 1953.

MEDNICK, S. A. The associative basis of the creative process. *Psychological Review*, 1962, **69**, 220–232.

MURRAY, H., et al. *Assessment of men: Selection of personnel for the office of strategic services.* New York: Rinehart, 1948.

PEARSON, K. *Grammar of science.* (1911.) (3d. ed.) New York: Meridian, 1957.

RORER, L. G. The great response-style myth. *Psychological Bulletin*, 1965, **63**, 129–156.

SCHAFER, R. *The clinical application of psychological tests.* New York: International Universities Press, 1948.

SCHLEIN, J. M. Mental testing and modern society. In W. Leslie Barnette, Jr. (Ed.), *Readings in psychological tests and measurements.* Homewood, Ill.: Dorsey, 1964.

SIMPSON, R. H. The specific meanings of certain terms indicating different degrees of frequency. *Quarterly Journal of Speech*, 1944, **30**, 328–330.

SPEARMAN, C. E. *The abilities of man: Their nature and measurement.* London: Macmillan, 1927.

STEVENS, S. S. *Handbook of experimental psychology.* New York: Wiley, 1951.

TERMAN, L. M., & MERRILL, M. A. *Measuring intelligence: A guide to the administration of the new revised Stanford-Binet tests of intelligence.* Boston: Houghton Mifflin, 1937.

Testing and public policy. *American Psychologist*, 1965, **20** (11, Special Issue).

THORNDIKE, R. L., & HAGEN, E. P. *Measurement and evaluation in psychology and education.* New York: Wiley, 1955.

THURSTONE, L. L. The absolute zero in intelligence measurement. *Psychological Review*, 1928, **35**, 175–197.

THURSTONE, L. L. *Multiple-factor analysis.* Chicago: University of Chicago Press, 1947.

WALLACH, M. A., & KOGAN, N. *Modes of thinking in young children: A study of the creativity-intelligence distinction.* New York: Holt, 1965.

WECHSLER, D. *The measurement of adult intelligence.* Baltimore: Williams and Wilkins, 1944.

WHYTE, W. H. *The organization man.* New York: Simon and Schuster, 1956.

EPILOGUE
THE SEARCH FOR UNITY

"The acceptance of different kinds of articulate systems as mental dwelling places is arrived at by a process of gradual appreciation."
(Polanyi, 1958, p. 202)

THEORY BUILDING

In the final analysis, the kind of theory a scientist builds will depend on the way he has come to look at the world, that is, on his experience. The experiments he does, the concepts he uses, and the ways in which he relates these concepts to each other will depend on his view of reality. It is probably fair to say that there is no single or absolute view of the world, and the one the scientist selects will be a matter of his policy or belief as to which will be the most *fruitful*.

It is almost inevitable, then, that there are going to emerge a great many different views according to the definition of what is fruitful. We have already examined, in the preceding chapters, six broad views held in psychology, each of which has its own special outlook. At least in modern thought, all these ways should—and perhaps do—agree on a basic scientific methodology that allows them to make valid and communicable observations. However, we must be concerned not only with this common thread that binds them together but also with the differences in viewpoint that tend to divide them from each other. The question we must now ask is this: *What are the basic dimensions that can be used to describe any viewpoint or general theory in psychology?*

Obviously, many answers could be given to such a question. For example, at the broadest level, we can separate theories according to whether they deal with normal persons or abnormal persons or, again, whether they use animal subjects or only human beings. We can, however, use more basic dimensions. Let us look at some of these.

According to one psychologist, Kenneth Spence (1944), we may divide the dimensions of theory making into two types: (1) *variable characteristics* and (2) *laws*. Variable characteristics may be specified for *independent, dependent,* and *inferred* variables. Their main characteristics are set out in Table E–1. Independent variables, or stimuli, in the first place may be directly manipulated or not. Secondly, they may be past events or present events. In the third place, they may be gross (molar) or minute (molecular). Dependent variables—that is, behavior—may be described in terms of these dimensions: molar or molecular, and physiological or behavioral (including inferred experience). Naturally, it is always present behavior that we are concerned with measuring, though, of course, we may still make predictions about future behavior. Finally, inferred variables may be molar or molecular, physiological or psychological, central or peripheral. Let us now look at some applications of these dimensions to the theories we have studied, as shown in Table E–1.

Table E-1 Variable characteristics of different theories

Theory	Independent	Dependent	Inferred
Psychoanalytic	Nonmanipulated Past events Molar	Molar Behavioral Present	Molar Central Psychological
Social	Manipulated or nonmanipulated Present or past Molar	Molar Behavioral Present	Molar Central Psychological
Gestalt and phenomenological	Manipulated Present events Molar	Molar Behavioral Present	Molar Central Psychological
Physiological	Manipulated Present events Molecular	Molecular-molar Physiological or behavioral Present	Molecular-molar Central Physiological
Behavioristic	Manipulated Present events Molecular-molar	Molecular-molar Behavioral Present	Molecular-molar Central Psychological
Individual difference models	Manipulated or nonmanipulated Present Molar	Molar Behavioral Present	Molar Central Psychological

Clearly, the emphasis is rather different in each case. Thus psychoanalytic theory, for example, might study a problem like the effect of harsh parental treatment in early life on obsessional behavior later in life. In tying these two variables together, it would employ such inferred constructs as "instincts," "libido," or "superego," dealt with in Section Two. Behaviorism, on the other hand, might be interested in studying the effect of stimulus intensity on strength of performance. The construct so linking the physical energy of the stimulus to the measured performance is "V," or "stimulus-intensity-dynamism." All these variables are more molecular than molar and are psychological or behavioral rather than physiological. Many other examples may be found by going back over the previous chapters.

The second way in which theories vary is in respect to the kinds of laws they set up. Spence suggests that there are four types of empirical laws used in psychology and five types of hypothetical laws. These are as shown below. R stands for response, f for function, S for stimulus, and O for organism—meaning measurement of various physiological properties of the organism.

Empirical laws

Type	
1	$R = f(R)$
2	$R = f(S)$
3	$R = f(O)$
4	$O = f(S)$

Type 1 is characteristic of approaches using mainly the correlation coefficient of the kind described in Section Seven—e.g., factor analysis. Type 2 is characteristics of most behavioral approaches in psychology, and refers to the classical stimulus-response laws. Types 3 and 4 are used mainly in physiological psychology where a certain physiological property of the organism is treated either as an independent (type 3) or dependent (type 4) variable. The laws dealing with relationships involving hypotheticals are as follows, where I stands for any inferred construct or variable and S, R, and f have the same meanings as for empirical laws.

Hypothetical laws

Type	
5	I = f (S past)
6	I = f (S present)
7	I = f (time)
8	I = f (I)
9	R = f (I)

Type 5 refers to laws in which any construct is tied to some past events, for example, in Hullian theory, D (drive) is defined in terms of h (number of hours deprivation preceding some test). Type 6 could well describe the hypothetical process of "closure" in Gestalt psychology, this being partly a function of certain stimulation conditions present at the moment (e.g., low illumination). Type 7 refers to laws dealing with changes in the properties of certain constructs over time, for example, the decay of I_R (reactive inhibition) as a function of time, or changes in the memory trace toward simplicity and symmetry that supposedly occur with time according to Gestalt psychologists. Type 8 laws deal with relations between two constructs. Many Freudian "laws" fall in this category, for example, the relations hypothesized to occur between id, ego, and superego. Finally, type 9 laws are those relating certain responses to some construct, for example, in social psychology, some measured behavior such as resistance to group pressure being formally related to attitudinal structure.

The main value of specifying these different types of laws lies in the fact that it forces us to attend more closely to the job of theory construction. Furthermore, it can make us more clearly aware of the deficiencies of some theories which involve a preponderance of type 8 laws but very few of any of the others. These hardly can qualify as scientific theories, since they involve no observable variables. Among the theories we have examined, it certainly seems true that the behavioristic approach fares the best in this respect. The psychoanalytic model and its offshoots fare the worst in their present state, though we may hope they will improve as time goes on.

We can summarize the above discussion by stating that we have so far two main ways of defining theories and differentiating them from each other, namely, (1) the nature of the variables they study and (2) the types of laws they educe. Three more ways may be added, namely, (3) the explicitness and care of language and definitions, (4) the amount of actual supportive data, and (5) their fruitfulness in generating research. These criteria are not easily applied, since different people may not agree on what degree of precision and explicitness is desirable or obtainable, or on the extent to which data give support to some idea, or again on exactly what "fruitfulness" means. All six approaches we have discussed in this book have certainly been fruitful of research, but it is equally true that, within each, particular subtheories have generated more work than others, for example, the Freudian more than the Jungian, the Hullian more than the Tolmanian. In the final analysis, however, it is very difficult to lay down exact rules according to which our three dimensions may be applied, and we can probably make useful judgments only in fairly extreme cases.

The reader may find it a useful exercise to try to apply these criteria of excellence to the approaches we have presented in the main part of this book. This may be an aid in making a decision as to which he finds to be a comfortable intellectual "dwelling place." But many other factors will also play a part, most of them highly personal and perhaps intuitive. We have emphasized the criterion of "fruitfulness" as a basis of choice. This term has a slipperiness which makes it difficult to define; yet in the end it points to a general position which represents a major theme in this book.

How then do we judge, in any particular case, a theory's fruitfulness? There is no final answer to this problem. Apart from such qualities as its intellectual beauty, its validity, and its demonstrated heuristic value in generating useful data, a system may still appeal or not to any particular person. The ultimate reasons for these are quite analogous to those that determine whether we prefer Bach to Sibelius, Turner to Matisse, or, for that matter, football to baseball. In the end the decision is a highly personal one. Yet it is one that we must in some way, make. And such a commitment requires an expression of the beliefs we have and hold to be true and the comparison of them with those implied by the organized system of knowledge which we wish to examine. To do this effectively, we can only, at least for a time, suspend our judgment and accept provisionally the premise before us. In so doing we return, as Polanyi suggests (1958, p. 266), to a mode of thought espoused in the fourth century by Saint Augustine and best espoused by his famous imperative *Crede ut intelligas*—"Believe in order that you may understand."

Many readers may have been so thoroughly immersed in a tradition of rationalism and its handmaiden, skepticism, as to find little attraction to this point of view. Thus, to quote Polanyi again:

> It has been taken for granted throughout the critical period of philosophy that the acceptance of unproven beliefs was the broad road to darkness, while truth was approached by the straight and narrow path of doubt. We were warned that a host of unproven beliefs were instilled in us from early childhood. That religious dogma, the authority of the ancients, the teaching of the schools, the maxims of the nursery, all were limited to a body of tradition which we tended to accept merely because these beliefs had previously been held by others who wanted us to embrace them in our turn. We were urged to resist the pressure of this traditional indoctrination by pitting against it the principle of philosophic doubt. Descartes had declared that universal doubt should purge his mind of all opinions held merely on trust and open it to knowledge firmly grounded in reason. In its stricter formulations the principle of doubt forbids us altogether to indulge in any desire to believe and demands that we should keep our minds empty, rather than allow any but irrefutable beliefs to take possession of them [Polanyi 1958, p. 269].

It has been common in many of the sciences to attempt to imbue the student with just such an outlook by stripping the subject matter of its adornments of theory to leave only the corpus of valid and irreducible facts. The present book has been dedicated to the avoidance of such a point of view, for, while unassailable in some ways, this approach does not give a picture of psychology as it exists in the minds of those central figures who have developed it as an organic and vital enterprise.

Thus when we search for unity, we are not likely to find it except at the level of the general commitment of psychologists as scientists to an understanding of the mind and behavior of man. It is the diversity of approaches by which this basic commitment is explicated that constitutes the interest and beauty of the field. Freud, Hull, Hebb, Koffka, Spearman, and Lewin each has his unique intellectual style and subtlety. And our enjoyment of these need be no less than that of the art critic in viewing a set of paintings or of the historian in gazing over the panorama of the past. In this respect, science and the humanities can share a common experience and by doing so can move toward a bridging of the gulf that has grown up between them in the last century.

PSYCHOLOGY AND SOCIETY

We have considered many different approaches to the field of psychology and have presented different sets of experimental data that have a bearing on these. And, finally, we have suggested that a search for unity in psychology may be futile except in a very general sense. The different views of mankind espoused by the various systems we have discussed are very disparate in style and emphasis. There is little reason to suppose that any one of them supplies now or will ever supply the key that unlocks all doors behind which hide the answers to the mystery of man. Only the general commitment to truth and honesty in which they all participate furnishes a bond that holds them together. Though this does not imply our automatic acceptance of any particular position, this commitment we should respect and cherish.

As the famous proponent of Zen Buddhism D. T. Suzuki has said:

> Our minds are to be so matured as to be in tune with those of the masters. Let this be accomplished and when one string is struck, the other will inevitably respond. Harmonious notes always result from the sympathetic resonance of two or more chords. And what Zen does for us is to prepare our minds to be yielding and appreciative recipients of old masters. In other words, psychologically, Zen releases whatever energies we may have in store, of which we are not conscious in ordinary circumstances [Suzuki, 1956, p. 20].

This kind of viewpoint, this resonance with other minds and with reality is called, in Zen, *satori*, or enlightenment. While we are not here suggesting that our readers adopt this philosophical system of thought, we would urge that such an injunction applies as well in the present context. And it is through following it that we can most fruitfully develop links between psychology and society. Applied psychology is commonly thought to be a set of clever maxims which are handed to us by those "in the know" and which will automatically furnish us with direct power over various sectors of practical life. But nothing is farther from the truth. Such maxims are at best ways of asking questions rather than answering them. As William James said in one of his talks to teachers in reference to educational psychology (James, 1908, p. 7):

> I say, moreover, that you make a great, a very great mistake, if you think that psychology being the science of the mind's laws, is something for which you can deduce definite programmes and schemes and methods of instruction for immediate schoolroom use. Psychology is a science, and teaching is an art; and sciences never generate arts directly out of themselves. An intermediary inventive mind must make the application, by using its originality.

In a sense, all of psychology, since it starts with the person—how he lives, feels, thinks, and acts—is applied psychology. We all live and work with other people in many contexts, and the best way we can manage such an enterprise is by being aware of the various dimensions of man laid out for us by the great thinkers in psychology. At present, a psychologist cannot tell a mother how to raise her child in an optimal fashion. Bringing up children is by no means equivalent to building a bridge on the basis of a set of exact specifications. Yet he can supply her with a set of general strategies, or heuristics, which will aid her considerably in her task. Her awareness of the relevant aspects of the situation will be sharpened and extended, and she will begin to ask questions that did not exist for her previously. Answers to these questions will emerge or not, depending on her resourcefulness.

At least in its broadest sense, this is what applied psychology involves, whether the setting be a home, an industry, or a school. In all these a knowledge of psychology can have great usefulness in the way we have indicated. That psychology will inevitably intrude into all sectors, of life, no one can doubt. For today, we are in the midst of an upheaval in society, a revolution involving the transition from the consideration and management of things to the consideration and management of people. This is the challenge of tomorrow, and psychology must lead the way in meeting it.

REFERENCES

JAMES, W. *Talks to teachers on psychology and to students on some of life's ideals.* New York: Holt, 1908.

POLANYI, M. *Personal knowledge: Towards a post-critical philosophy.* London: Routledge, 1958.

SPENCE, K. W. The nature of theory construction in contemporary psychology. *Psychological Review,* 1944, **51**, 47–68.

SUZUKI, D. T. *Zen Buddhism: Selected Writings.* Garden City, N.Y.: Anchor Books, Doubleday, 1956.

NAME INDEX

NAME INDEX

Abelson, R. P., 129, 130, 152
Alexander, G. J., 354, 356
Allen, L., 397, 421
Allport, F. H., 158, 207
Allport, G. W., 33, 62, 87, 118, 151, 178, 207, 253, 275
Ambrose, J. A., 100, 101, 151
Ames, A., 159, 180, 181, 187, 196, 207
Angell, J. R., 214, 275
Archer, E. J., 267, 275
Asch, Solomon, 91, 92, 95, 96, 150, 151, 193
Attneave, F., 177, 207
Augustine, Saint, 425

Bacon, F., 213
Bales, R. F., 135, 136, 139, 140, 142, 143, 145, 146, 151
Bandura, A., 105, 106, 151
Bare, J. K., 342, 358
Barker, R., 71, 72, 87
Barron, Frank, 415–417, 419, 420
Bartley, S. H., 184, 207
Bateman, F., 206, 207
Beach, F. A., 304, 356

Bender, L., 394, 420
Benedict, R., 92, 148, 151
Bennett, E. L., 349, 358
Bentham, J., 157
Berg, Irwin A., 400, 401, 420
Berkeley, Bishop, 10, 158, 198, 200, 216
Binet, A., 370, 371, 405
Bitterman, M. E., 304, 356
Blake, William, 38
Blodgett, H. C., 251, 275
Blum, G. S., 83, 84, 86, 87, 393
Boas, Franz, 148
Bogardus, E. S., 120, 151
Boring, E. G., 188, 208, 371, 420
Brehm, J. W., 125, 126, 151
Briggs, M. H., 351, 356
Brill, A. A., 54, 87
Brooks, V., 174, 175, 208
Brown, J. F., 82, 87
Brown, N. O., 80, 87
Bruckner, G. H., 314, 356
Bruner, J. S., 191, 193–197, 207, 209
Bullock, T. H., 314, 356
Burt, Cyril, 371

Butler, J. M., 67, 87
Butler, R. A., 251, 275

Cannon, Walter B., 107, 344, 356
Cartwright, D., 129, 151
Cattell, James M., 370
Cattell, Raymond B., 291, 356, 364, 371, 408–410, 420
Chandler, K. A., 192, 209
Charlesworth, W. R., 75, 89
Chaucer, G., 80
Chave, E. J., 119, 152
Chomsky, N., 261, 275
Cline, V. B., 115, 116, 151
Cofer, C., 260, 276
Cohen, M. M., 354, 357
Cohen, W., 166, 167, 208
Colbert, E. H., 301, 357
Coleridge, S. T., 38
Comte, Auguste, 94, 151
Cooley, C. H., 135
Copernicus, 3, 38
Cotzin, M., 13, 14, 32
Couch, A., 401, 402, 420
Craig, W., 312, 357

429

Cronbach, L., 361, 362, 364, 372, 397, 400, 402, 412, 419, 420
Crutchfield, R. S., 95, 96, 111, 151, 168, 177, 178, 209

Dalbiez, R., 50, 87
Dale, L. A., 205, 208
Dallenbach, K. M., 13, 14, 32
Darwin, Charles, 19, 38, 94, 214, 217, 275, 279, 363, 370
Daumier, H., 178
DeBeauvoir, Simone, 82, 87
DeBold, Richard C., 354, 357
Delgado, J., 337, 357
deMaupassant, G., 37
Dember, W. N., 196, 208
Dembo, T., 71, 72, 87
Dement, W. C., 48, 49, 87
Denenberg, V. H., 77, 78, 87
Denney, Ray, 134, 152
DeSade, Marquis, 36
Descartes, René, 10, 319, 362, 420, 425
Dewey, J., 214, 275
Diamond, M., 349, 358
Diderot, C., 13
Dobzhansky, T., 19, 31
Dollard, J., 102–106
Dostoevski, F., 10
Duncan, C. P., 330, 357
Duncker, Karl, 150, 207, 208
Dunne, J. W., 204, 208
Durkheim, Emile, 93, 144

Ebbinghaus, H., 228, 275
Eckert, J. F., 341, 358
Eells, K., 373, 376, 420
Efron, D., 114, 151
Egyhazi, E., 351, 357
Einstein, Albert, 3, 11
Ellis, Havelock, 37
Engel, W., 166, 208
Eriksen, C. W., 196, 208
Erikson, E. H., 85–87

Erikson, M. H., 51, 87
Estes, W., 244, 275
Eysenck, Hans J., 43, 67, 87, 292, 352, 357, 408, 410–412, 420

Falconer, D. S., 297, 357
Fantz, R. L., 203, 208
Farber, L. H., 47, 87
Fechner, G., 228, 275
Feierabend, R. L., 132, 133, 151
Feleky, A. M., 113, 114, 151
Fenichel, O., 70, 84, 86, 87
Festinger, L., 124–127, 151
Fichte, J. G., 93
Field, P. B., 133, 134, 151
Fisher, C., 47, 87
Fisher, Ronald, 5, 31
Fiske, D. W., 397, 421
Flanagan, J. C., 391, 420
Fleming, Sir Alexander, 11
Flourens, P., 319
Fodor, N., 74, 87
Foley, J. P., Jr., 114, 151
Forel, A. H., 37
Forgus, R. H., 197, 207, 208
Forsmann, H., 287, 357
Franks, C. M., 411, 412, 420
Franz, S., 320, 357
Freeman, F. N., 290, 358
Freud, Anna, 62, 85, 87
Freud, Sigmund, 19, 31, 37–52, 54–62, 68, 74, 76–78, 81, 82, 84–88, 92, 105, 109, 114, 122, 162, 197, 392, 409, 412, 419, 425
Friedan, Betty, 82, 88
Frink, H. W., 50
Fromm, Erich, 86
Fuller, J. L., 290, 295, 357
Funkenstein, D. H., 345, 357

Galanter, E., 262, 276, 369, 420
Galton, Sir Francis, 280, 357, 363, 364, 370, 371

Ganz, L., 177, 208
Gardner, M., 205, 206, 208
Gauss, C. F., 363
Gerard, R. W., 330, 357
Getzels, J. W., 412–416, 420
Gibson, E. J., 201–203, 208, 209
Gibson, James J., 161, 162, 164, 166, 179, 182–187, 190, 191, 199, 208
Glaser, H., 134, 152
Glaze, J., 266, 275
Gobetz, W., 394, 420
Goldberg, I., 206
Goldstein, Kurt, 394, 421
Gombrich, E. H., 155, 178, 208
Goodenough, F. L., 395, 421
Goodman, C. C., 193–195, 207
Gottesman, I., 292, 357
Gough, H. G., 400, 421
Green, Samuel, 156, 208
Greenacre, P., 74, 75, 88
Gregory, I., 293, 357
Gregory, R. L., 201, 208
Griffin, Donald, 13, 14, 31, 302, 357
Grigg, A. E., 400, 401, 421
Grossman, S. P., 352, 357
Guilford, J. P., 364, 371, 408–411, 413, 416, 421
Gullicksen, H., 380, 381, 421
Guthrie, Edwin, 242, 275

Hagen, E. P., 374, 379, 421
Haigh, G. V., 67, 87
Hall, Calvin S., 45–47, 88
Hambert, A., 287, 357
Harary, F., 129, 151
Harlow, Harry F., 106, 107, 117, 254, 275
Hartmann, H., 38, 57, 62
Hasler, A. D., 303, 357
Havighurst, R. J., 376
Hebb, Donald O., 169–171, 199, 200, 208, 209, 328, 357, 425
Hegel, G. W. F., 5, 92, 93

Heider, F., 95, 97, 98, 110–113, 123, 124, 129, 151, 193
Heinroth, O., 312, 357
Helmholtz, H. von, 159, 179, 186, 199, 208
Helson, H., 188, 208
Henry, G. W., 37, 89
Hering, E., 188, 199, 208
Heron, W., 169–171, 209
Hess, E. H., 312, 316, 357
Heyer, A. W., Jr., 177, 209
Heyns, R. W., 143, 151
Hilgard, E. R., 220, 275
Himmelweit, H. T., 12, 31
Hirsch, J., 297, 357
Hitler, A., 93
Hoagland, H., 346, 357
Hobbes, J., 157, 216
Hochberg, J. E., 166, 173–175, 177, 199, 208
Hoedemaker, F. S., 49, 88
Hoffman, Banesh, 395, 396, 421
Hogarth, W., 178
Holway, A. H., 188, 189, 208
Holzinger, K. J., 290, 358, 371
Honzik, C. H., 327, 357
Honzik, M. P., 397, 421
Horney, Karen, 57, 86
Hovland, Carl I., 130–133, 151, 222, 275
Howes, D., 197, 198, 209
Huizinga, J., 362, 421
Hull, C. L., 102, 107, 222, 234, 275, 410, 412, 425
Hume, David, 10, 97, 151, 157, 198, 216, 363
Hunter, W. S., 327, 357
Hydén, H., 351, 357

Iersal, J. J. A. van, 313, 358
Isaacs, S., 80, 88
Ittleson, W. H., 159, 188, 196, 208

Jackson, P. W., 412–416, 420
Jacobi, J., 54, 55, 88

Jacobsen, A., 49, 88
Jacobsen, C. F., 334, 358
James, W., 100, 212, 213, 263, 275, 426
Janis, I. L., 131–134, 151
Jaynes, Julian, 3, 31
Jennings, H. S., 311, 358
Jones, H. E., 378, 421
Judson, A. J., 261, 276
Jung, Carl G., 54, 67, 68, 259

Kales, A., 49, 88
Kalish, D., 247, 276
Kallman, F., 293, 358
Kant, Immanuel, 97, 158, 160, 208
Karas, G. G., 77, 78, 87
Katona, G., 207, 208
Katz, D., 129, 151, 189, 208
Keet, C. D., 68, 88
Keller, Helen, 207
Kelley, H. H., 131, 132, 151
Kelly, E. L., 397, 421
Kelman, H. C., 129, 151
Kendler, H. H., 168, 176, 208, 393, 421
Keniston, K., 401, 402, 420, 421
Kenyon, G. Y., 353, 358
Kilpatrick, F. P., 159, 188, 208
Kitto, G. B., 351, 356
Klein, Melanie, 78, 85, 88
Kleitman, N., 48, 49
Klineberg, Otto, 114, 151
Klopfer, P., 316
Koch, Sigmund, 11, 32
Koffka, Kurt, 122, 154, 158, 166, 168, 169, 172, 173, 176, 183, 186, 187, 199, 208, 425
Kogan, N., 414–419, 421
Kohler, Wolfgang, 122, 144, 158, 160, 163, 172, 175–177, 199, 209
Kopfermann, H., 172, 209
Krafft-Ebing, R., 37

Krech, D., 95, 96, 111, 151, 168, 177, 178, 209, 349, 358
Kris, E., 62
Kristy, N. F., 291, 356
Kuleshova, Rosa, 206
Kutner, B., 120, 151

Lamarck, J. B., 279, 358
Lansdell, N. C., 328, 358
Larson, J. A., 303, 357
Lashley, K., 71, 88, 277, 325, 358
Leaf, R. C., 354, 357
Leavitt, H. J., 136, 152
LeBon, Gustav, 93
Levine, J., 53, 88
Levine, S., 77, 88
Levy, D., 79, 88
Lewin, K., 71, 72, 87, 98, 122, 138, 139, 151, 152, 425
Lichtenstein, E., 49, 88
Life magazine, 180
Likert, R., 120, 152
Lilienfeld, A. M., 75, 88
Lindner, Robert M., 34, 88
Lippitt, R., 138, 139, 152
Locke, John, 10, 159, 160, 198, 200, 209, 216, 276
Loeb, J., 310, 358
Lorenz, K., 312, 358
Lorge, I., 366, 421
Lotze, R. H., 199, 209
Lowenstein, R. M., 62
Lubetkin, B. S., 205, 209

McAlister, E. A., 173, 175, 177, 208
McClelland, David, 64–66, 88, 393
Maccoby, Eleanor, 12, 32
McDougall, William, 94, 100, 152
MacFarlane, J. W., 397, 420
McGinnies, E. M., 196, 197, 209
McGuire, W. J., 129, 130, 152

MacLean, P. D., 321, 358
Magoun, H. W., 337, 358
Maier, N. R. F., 71, 88
Mailloux, N., 58, 88
Malinowsky, B., 82, 88
Maritain, Jacques, 419, 421
Marler, P., 303, 358
Marquis, D., 220, 275
Maslow, A. H., 10, 32, 57
Mead, G. H., 144, 145, 147, 152
Mead, Margaret, 96, 152
Mednick, S. A., 414, 415, 421
Meehl, P. E., 29, 30, 32
Mendel, G., 19, 279, 411
Merrill, M. A., 376, 421
Mesmer, Franz Anton, 37
Metzger, W., 166, 209
Michotte, Albert E., 97, 98, 110–112, 152
Miles, Elaine, 110
Miles, T. R., 110
Mill, John Stuart, 5, 10, 32, 93, 152, 157, 198
Miller, G. A., 262, 276
Miller, N. E., 72, 88, 102–106, 123, 152, 253, 276
Milner, P., 335, 358
Mishler, E. G., 139, 141, 142, 152
Moltz, H., 313, 358
Monet, C., 155, 156, 158
Morant, R. B., 192, 193, 209
Moreno, J. L., 135, 152
Morgan, C. L., 102, 159, 181, 214, 276
Moruzzi, G., 337, 358
Mowrer, O. H., 39, 88
Munroe, R. L., 62, 68, 69, 72, 74, 86, 88
Murphy, G., 206, 209
Murray, H. A., 62, 63, 88, 393, 395, 421
Myers, R. E., 330, 358

Nagel, E., 31, 32

National Aeronautics and Space Administration, 182
Newcomb, Theodore, 123, 124, 144, 152
Newman, H. H., 290, 358
Newton, I., 3, 6
Nietzsche, F., 38
Noble, C. E., 267, 276

O'Connor, M., 77, 89
Olds, J., 335, 358
Oppenheim, A. N., 12
Orlansky, H., 79, 88
Osgood, C. E., 126–129, 152, 177, 209
Overton, D. A., 354, 358

Papez, J. W., 334, 358
Pasamanick, B., 75, 88
Pascal, Blaise, 34, 36, 88
Pavlov, I. P., 212, 213, 217, 276
Peak, H., 129, 152
Pearce, H., 204
Pearson, K., 361–364, 371, 403, 421
Perin, C. T., 237, 276
Pernau, Baron von, 310
Petrullo, L., 113
Pfaffman, C., 342, 358
Pfeiffer, C. C., 352, 358
Piaget, Jean, 97, 98, 152
Pinel, Philippe, 36, 37, 370
Pinneau, S., 77, 88
Plato, 3, 4, 154, 155, 209, 419
Poincaré, H., 11, 32
Polanyi, M., 1, 32, 422, 425, 426
Pope, Alexander, 3
Postman, L., 178, 191, 193, 196, 197, 207, 209
Prell, D. B., 292, 357
Pribram, K., 262, 276, 320
Pritchard, R. M., 169–171, 209
Pronko, N. H., 353, 358

Proust, Marcel, 37, 38

Quetelet, A., 363

Rachman, S., 43, 87
Ramsey, G. V., 44, 88
Rank, Otto, 76, 86
Rayner, R., 225, 276
Redlich, F. C., 53
Reyna, L. J., 43, 89
Rhine, J. B., 204–206, 209
Ribble, M. A., 76, 77, 88, 107
Rice, C. E., 14, 32
Richard, J. M., Jr., 115, 116, 151
Richter, C. P., 341, 358
Riesen, A. H., 201, 203, 209
Riesman, D., 134, 152
Riley, D. A., 178, 209
Riss, W. R., 307, 351
Ritchie, B. F., 247, 276
Roberts, W. W., 337, 357
Robespierre, J., 36
Roderick, T. H., 351, 358
Roeder, K. D., 302, 358
Rogers, Carl, 57, 62, 67, 68
Rogers, M. E., 75, 88
Romains, J., 206, 209
Romanes, George, 214
Rorer, L. G., 401, 402, 421
Rosenberg, M. J., 129, 130, 152
Rosenblatt, J. S., 308, 359
Rosenzweig, M. R., 349, 358
Rousseau, J. J., 36
Rubin, E., 167, 209
Ruskin, J., 161

Salter, A., 43, 89
Santayana, G., 3
Sarbin, T. R., 114, 116, 145, 147, 152
Sartre, J. P., 113
Sawrey, W., 347, 359
Schafer, E. F., 389, 421

Schlein, J. M., 396, 421
Schneider, B. H., 197, 209
Schneirla, T. C., 308, 359
Schulz, R., 268, 276
Seaman, G., 166, 208
Sears, R. R., 70, 88
Sechenov, I. M., 217, 276
Seeman, J., 57, 88
Selye, N., 345, 359
Shakespeare, W., 10, 31
Simmel, E., 112, 151, 193
Simon, Herbert, 370, 371
Simpson, R. H., 391, 421
Skinner, B. F., 30, 234, 239, 276
Smith, C. J., 329, 359
Snyder, L. H., 289, 359
Soal, S. G., 206, 207
Solomon, R. L., 197, 198, 209
Spallanzani, L., 13
Spearman, C. E., 364, 371, 384, 405–408, 415, 421
Spence, Kenneth W., 422, 423, 426
Spencer, H., 217, 276
Sperry, R. W., 330
Spitz, René A., 77, 101, 152
Sprinthall, R. C., 205, 209
Stafford, Jean, 2, 32
Stellar, E., 331, 342, 359
Stephan, F. F., 139, 141, 142, 152
Stephenson, W., 67, 88
Stevens, S. S., 367, 421
Stice, G. F., 291, 356
Stotland, E., 129, 151
Suchman, E. A., 121, 122, 152
Sullivan, Anne, 207
Sullivan, H. S., 57, 86
Sullivan, P. L., 114, 116
Sumner, W. G., 148
Supa, M., 13, 14, 32
Suzuki, D. T., 425, 426
Swift, J., 80
Szasz, Thomas S., 41, 89

Tagiuri, Renato, 113, 152
Tannenbaum, P. H., 126–129, 152
Tarde, Gabriel, 93, 102
Terman, L. M., 371, 376, 421
Thompson, W. R., 75, 89, 290, 357, 359
Thomson, Godfrey, 364, 371
Thomson, J. Arthur, 16
Thorndike, E. L., 100, 215, 225, 276, 374, 379, 421
Thorpe, J. S., 400, 401, 421
Thurstone, L. L., 119, 120, 152, 364, 371, 377, 390, 403, 407, 408, 410, 421
Thurstone, Thelma G., 390
Tichener, E. B., 186, 209
Tinbergen, Niko, 100, 312, 359
Tolman, G., 234, 245, 276
Topffer, R., 178
Treat, A. E., 302, 358
Triebel, W., 166, 208
Tryon, R. L., 371

Uexkull, J. von, 311, 359
Underwood, B. J., 268, 276

Valenstein, E. S., 307, 359
Vandwert, W., 202
Vince, M., 12
Von Holst, E., 317, 359
Von Saint Paul, V., 317, 359
Von Senden, M., 165, 200, 201, 203, 209

Waddell, D., 166, 208
Walk, R. D., 201–203, 209
Wallace, J. G., 38, 201, 208
Wallach, H., 176, 177, 209, 414–419, 421
Walters, R. H., 105, 106, 151
Wapner, S., 164, 191–193, 209

Warren, H. C., 100
Watson, J., 75, 89, 144, 224, 276
Wechsler, David, 388, 389, 421
Weininger, O., 77, 89
Werner, H., 164, 191–193, 209
Wertheimer, Max, 98, 122, 158, 163, 172, 173, 199, 207, 209
Wertheimer, Michael, 201, 209
Wheatstone, C., 183
Whistler, J. M., 155
White, R. K., 138, 139, 152
Whitehead, A. N., 6, 17, 32, 277, 359
Whitman, C. O., 312, 359
Whyte, William H., 399, 421
Wickens, D. D., 221, 276
Wilde, Oscar, 155
Wilkins, C., 120, 151
Williams, S. B., 237, 276
Wittreich, W. J., 195, 196, 209
Wodinsky, J., 306, 359
Wohlwill, J. F., 188, 210
Wolf, H. G., 347, 359
Wolf, K. M., 101, 152
Wolf, S., 347, 359
Wolpe, Joseph, 43, 89
Wolpert, E. A., 49, 87
Wolstenholm, G. E. W., 77, 89
Woodworth, Robert S., 114, 115, 152, 253, 276
Wulf, F., 178, 210
Wundt, Wilhelm, 14, 94, 122, 144, 160, 162, 370
Wyeth, Andrew, 156

Yarrow, P., 120, 151
Young, W. C., 307, 359
Youtz, Richard, 206, 210

Zeller, A. F., 68, 89
Zilboorg, Gregory, 37, 89
Zola, E., 37

SUBJECT INDEX

SUBJECT INDEX

Abasement, need for, 63
Abilities, testing of, 387–391
Ablation of brain, 319–320, 326–327
Abnormal behavior, 34–38, 40–41
Abnormal fixations, 70–71
Absolute threshold, 322
Acetylcholine (ACh), 349–352
Achievement, tests of, 372, 387
Achievement need, 64–66
   high versus low need achievers, 64
   relation to other variables, 65–66
Acquisition, need for, 63
Action potential of neuron, 323
Action-specific energy, 312
Adaptation, behavioral modes of, 300–304
Adequate stimulus, 161, 322
Adjective Check List, 400
Adrenal glands, 344, 346–347
Adrenalectomy, effects on salt intake in rats, 342–343
Adrenalin (see Epinephrine)
Afferent code (see Sensation)

Affiliation, need for, 63
Age norms in test construction, 376–377
Aggression, need for, 63
Aggressive behavior in stickleback, 314–315
Aggressive instinct, 62
Air, need for, 63
Alarm reaction, 345–346
Albedo in brightness constancy, 189–190
Alkaloids, effects on behavior, 353
Allport-Vernon Study of Values Test, 196–197
Ambiguity in perception, 159, 173
Ambivalence:
   and oral stage, 78
   in psychosexual development, 78
American Council Psychological Examination (ACE), 390
Anal personality, 79–80
Anal stage in psychological development, 80
Anality:
   components of, 80
   in literature, 80

Anger:
   effects of frontal ablation on, 334
   and hormones, 345
Animal behavior, systematic study of, 300–318
Animals, as subjects in psychology, 8, 214–215
Animism, 96
Ant, army, 308–310
Anthropology and social psychology, 94
Anxiety:
   as acquired drive, 253–254
   (See also Fear)
   effects of drugs on, 353–354
   effects of prenatal maternal, on offspring, 75
Apparent behavior, 112
Appearance and reality, 154–158
Aptitude tests, 372, 387
Archetypes, 55
Arithmetic mean, 21–22
Army ant, cyclic behavior in, 308–310
Arousal and brain stimulation, 337–338

437

Artificial populations, genetic study of, 294–298
Assertion constant in Osgood-Tannenbaum model, 128
Assimilation in perception, 177, 178
Association, stimulus-response (S-R), 244
Association theory and human learning, 259–261
Association value, as measure of meaningfulness, 266–267
Associationism, 216–217
Associations:
　directional, 260–261
　simple, 259–260
　types of, 231
Associative chaining, 267
Associative model of creativity, 415
Associative networks, 259–261
Associative processes in creativity, 414–415
Athletes, response of stress, 346–347
Attitude change and communication, 130–131
　"sleeper effect" in, 131–132
Attitude properties, studies of, 121
Attitude structure, 122–129
Attitudes:
　toward the Church, 119
　and cognitive organization, 117
　components of, 118, 120–121
　nature of, 117–119
　and overt behavior, 120–121
　properties of, 118, 121
　racial, 120–121
　scaling, 119, 120
Attitudinal bonds, associative and dissociative, 127–128
Attitudinal linkages, 127
Auditory reception, 324–325
Autochthonous components in perception, 193

Autocratic leadership in children's groups, 138–139
Autonomy, need for, 63
Autosomal trisomies, 287
Autosomes, 281–282
Average, statistical meaning, 21–22
Average deviation, 22

Balance concept:
　properties of, 107
　and social behavior, 107–108
　and symmetry, 107
Bales' interaction analysis, 136, 139–143
Basic statistics, 19–29
Basilar membrane, 324
Bats, echolocation in, 13, 302–303
Behavior:
　and functionalism, 214
　levels of, 6
　meaning of, 6
　and mind, 7
　and objectivism, 213
　overt and covert, 7
　as process, 7, 213
　types of, 7–8
Behavior disorders, as inherited, 293–294
Behavior genetics, 280–299
Behavior therapy, 43
Behavioral variables in perception, 193
Behaviorism, 15, 224–275
　basic ideas in, 212–215
　comparative, 304–310
　of E. Guthrie, 242–245
　of Clark Hull, 234–239
　of G. H. Mead, 144–145
　of B. F. Skinner, 239–242
　and social motives, 102–106
　of E. C. Tolman, 245–248
　variables in, 423–424
　of J. B. Watson, 224–225
Behavioristic models, 224–275

Belief and science, 425
Bender-Gestalt Test, 394, 397
Bernreuter Personality Inventory, 391
Bicêtre Hospital, 36
Binet-Simon scale, 371, 376, 399
　Stanford revision of, 376
Binocular cues in depth perception, 180–183
Binocular disparity in depth perception, 181, 182
　gradients of, 182
Biochemical systems:
　and behavior, 339–356
　in emotional behavior, 344–349
　and hormones, 339–340
　in hunger and thirst, 340–343
　in intelligence, 349–352
　in sexual behavior, 343
Biological models, 277–356
Biological psychology, basic orientations, 278–279
Biometrical genetics, 288–294
Blacky test, 83–84, 393
　and sex differences, 84
Blamavoidance, need for, 63
Blind, detection of obstacles in, 13, 14
Body tilt and perception of verticality, 192
Bogardus Social Distance Scale, 120
Boomerang effects in communication, 132
Brain:
　geography of, 320–321
　input and output systems, 321–322
　and instinctive behavior, 317–318
Brain damage and emotions, 332–335
Brain stimulation:
　and fixed action patterns (FAPs), 317–318

Brain stimulation:
   and motivation, 335–337
Brain waves, 48–49, 338
Breed comparisons in genetics, 259–260
Brightness and color constancy, 188
Brightness constancy and albedo, 189–190
British empiricist philosophers, 157, 159, 198–199
Brood-excitation theory of ant behavior, 309–310
Buffering, genetic, 298–299
Bulbar preparation and emotional behavior, 332

CA (see Chronological age)
Cannabis, 355
Carrier, genetic, 286
Case history and prediction, 29, 397
Castration complex in psychoanalytic theory, 80
Castration fear, 80
Cat:
   evolution of behavior in, 301–302
   puzzle-box learning, 226
Categories of mind, 97
Cathexes, 60
Cattell personality test, 401
Causality:
   in agents, 97
   as association, 97
   development of, 97–98
   perception of, 110–112
   in persons, 96–98
Causation and correlation, 363
Cell assemblies, 328, 349
Censor in psychoanalytic theory, 45–46, 50, 55
Centile scores (see Percentile scores)
Central nervous system, 319–338

Central tendency, 20–22
   and additivity of scores, 22
   measures of, 20–22
Centrality in small groups, 137
Centralization in small groups, 139
Cerebral cortex and emotion, 334–335
Character, as defense mechanism, 73
Chemical systems and behavior (see Biochemical systems)
Chicks:
   alarm response in, 314
   imprinting in, 316–317
Children, rearing of, 77, 106–107
Cholinesterase (ChE), 349–351
Chromosomal anomalies, 287–288
Chromosomes, 19, 281–285
Chronological age, 371
"Chunk," as informational unit in language, 272
Clairvoyance, 204
Classical conditioning, 218–225
   and discrimination, 223
   of eye blink, 220–221
   of finger withdrawal, 221
   generalization in, 222–223
   and neurosis in dog, 223–224
   relation between conditioned and unconditioned response, 221–222
   of salivation in dog, 218–219
   variables after learning, 221–223
   variables during learning, 219–221
Classical memory span, 270–271
Clinical method, validity of, 29, 39
Closure in perception, 170
Coalitions in social groups, 141–142
Cochlea, 324, 326
Cognition, 158

Cognitive dissonance, Festinger's theory of, 124–126
Cognitive elements, 124
   dissonance between, 124
   types of, 124
Cognitive maps in learning, 247
Cognitive psychology, 198
Cognitive structure, balance in, 122–129
Cognizance, need for, 63
Coldavoidance, need for, 63
Collective unconscious, 54–55
Comanche Indians, 79
Communication, 131–142
   attributes of, 131
   credibility of, 131
Communication networks, dimensions of, 137
Communicator, characteristics of, 131
Comparative behaviorism, 304
Comparative study:
   of learning, 305–306
   of sexual behavior, 306–308
   of social behavior, 308–310
Condensation in dreams, 46
Conditioned emotional reaction, 225
Conditioned neuroses, 223
Conditioned stimulus, 218
Cones of the retina, 325
Configurations in perception, 168
Conflict, 123
   and anxiety, 68
Congenital cataract and perception, 165, 200–201
Congruity model of Osgood and Tannenbaum, 126–129
   experimental test of, 129
Connectionism of E. L. Thorndike, 225–228
Conscience and superego, 58
Consciousness, stream of, 213
Conservance, need for, 63
Consolidation of memory trace, 328

Constancy:
   of brightness perception, 186–189
   in perception, 185–190
   of shape perception, 186–187
   of size perception, 187–188
Constant stimuli, method of, 271
Construction, need for, 63
Contact:
   need for, 77–78, 106–107
   and social behavior, 106
Contact need, 77–78, 106–107
   innateness of, 106
Contiguity, law of, 243
Contiguous conditioning, 242
Contingency and correlation, 363
Continuation, law of, in perception, 168, 170
Continuity of normal and abnormal personality, 40–41
Contrarience, need for, 63
Contrast effect in perception, 167, 178
Contrasts, method of, 223
Control groups in experimentation, 5–6
Convergence in depth perception, 180, 181
Copying and imitation, 102
Corpus callosum, 331
Correlation coefficient, 27–29, 363–364
   and factor analysis, 403–404
   meaning of, 379
   statistical formula, 27
   in terms of common and specific factors, 403–404
Corresponding points in retina, 181
Counteraction, need for, 63
Covariation and correlation, 27
Creative persons, personalities of, 417
Creativity:
   associative model of, 415
   and classroom behavior of children, 418

Creativity:
   correlation between measures of, 416
   definition of, 414
   and intelligence, 416, 418
   measures of, 414–415
   nature of, 413–414
   potential for, 416
   relation to other traits, 416
   sex differences in, 418
   and the unconscious, 419
   as unitary trait, 415–416
   in young children, 417
Credibility in communication, 131
Criterion keying in tests, 392
Critical periods:
   in imprinting, 316–317
   in psychosexual development, 74
Cultural relativity, 150
Culture:
   and individuals, 148
   and society, 148
Cummulative record in learning, 239
Curiosity drive, 251
Cyclic changes in behavior, 337–338

Darwinism, 214–215, 278–279, 363
Death instincts, 62
Decerebrate preparation, 332–333
Decerebrate rage, 332–333
Decision making and testing, 372
Deductions in science, 5–6
Deep structure in language, 262
Defecation, need for, 63
Defendance, need for, 63
Defense mechanisms, 59, 68–73
   and conflict, 68
Deference, need for, 63
Democratic leadership in children's groups, 138–139

Dependent variable, 422–423
Deprivation and perception, 201
   (See also Sensory deprivation)
Depth perception, 166, 169, 171, 174, 179–185
Dermooptical perception, 204, 206
Descriptive statistics, 364
Determinism, 39, 224
Development:
   early experience in, 74
   of perception, 198–204
   of personality, 74–89
   psychoanalytic theory of, 74–89
   psychosexual stages in, 74–85
Deviation hypothesis of I. Berg, 400–401
Differential accuracy in interpersonal perception, 116
Differential-cue error, 256
Differential threshold, 322
Direct experience, meaning of, 158
Discrimination in classical conditioning, 223
Disequilibrating stimulation, 192
Disequilibrium, effects on perception, 192, 193
Disinhibition, 238
Dispersion, statistical meaning of, 20
Displacement:
   of aggression, 72
   case study of, 72
   as defense mechanism, 72
   in dreams, 46
   experimental study of, 72
Dissonance:
   between cognitive elements, 124
   (See also Cognitive dissonance)
   postdecisional reduction of, 125–126
   ways of reducing, 124–125

Distance perception (see Depth perception)
Ditchburn-Riggs effect in perception, 169
Dizygotic twins, 290–294
DNA (deoxyribonucleic acid), 284, 351
Dobuans, 148–149
Docility of behavior, 246
Dogs:
 evolution of behavior in, 301–302
 genetics of behavior in, 295–296
Dominance:
 in genes, 286
 need for, 63
Dramatization in dreams, 46
Dream translation, 47
Dreams:
 case analyses of, 44
 censor in, 45
 children's, 44
 dramatization in, 46
 dynamic theory of, 45
 effects of deprivation on, 49
 experimental analysis of, 47
 experimental production of, 47
 and external stimuli, 43–44
 and hypnosis, 47
 of infanticide, 45
 manifest and latent content in, 43–44
 and physiological tensions, 44
 properties of manifest content, 44
 purposes of, 44
 recall of, 49
 regressive elements in, 46
 relation to depth of sleep, 49
 representability in, 46
 sexual elements in, 46
 symbols in, 47
Dreamwork, mechanisms of, 46
Drive for curiosity, 251–253

Drive-reduction hypothesis, 235
Drive-reduction principle of Hull, 248
Drives:
 and performance, 237–238, 249
 physiological basis of, 331–332, 340–344
Drug dissociation, 354
Dynamics:
 in perception, 163
 of personality, 59–73

Ear, structure of, 325
Early development, importance of, in psychoanalytic theory, 74
Early perceptual experience, importance of, 328
Early stimulation, effects of, on rats, 77
Eating compulsion, case study of, 35
Echolocation in bats, 14, 302–303
Eclecticism, as theoretical position in psychology, 15
Ecological behaviorism, 300–304
Economics in psychoanalytic theory, 59–73
Effect, law of, 227
Effectance, need for, 63
Ego:
 and instincts, 61
 motives of, 62–63
 and oral stage, 78
 in personality, 55, 56, 68, 79
Ego ideal, 58
Ego strength, 57
Electrical engineering and psychology, 9
Electroconvulsive shock (ECS), 330
Electroencephalogram (EEG), 48–49, 337–338

Emotional behavior:
 and hormones, 344–349
 physiological basis of, 332–335
Emotional expressions:
 accuracy of judgment of, 115
 cultural differences in, 114
 interpretation of, 113–114
Emotional reactivity, effects of prenatal maternal anxiety on, 75
Empathy, 82, 105, 145
Empirical laws in psychology, 423
Empiricism, 10, 215
 (See also British empiricist philosophers)
Empiricist theory of perception, 199–200
Endocrine glands, 339–340
Endocrine stress response in athletes, 346–347
Energy:
 and dynamics of personality, 59
 range to which receptors respond, 323–324
Engram and brain, 325–328
Environment versus heredity:
 in animal behavior, 295–299
 in intelligence and personality, 290–294
 in perceptual development, 203–204
Environment complexity training (ECT), 349–350
Enzyme induction and memory, 351
Enzymes in neural transmission, 349–352
Epinephrine and behavior, 344–347
Equilibrium:
 of attitude components, 127
 and sensory-tonic theory of perception, 192
 in small groups, 139–143

Equipotentiality of brain function, 325, 327
Erikson's theory of psychosexual development, 85–86
Eros (life instincts), 62
Error factors in learning, 254
Eskimos, 150
Esthesic system, 162
Ethogram, 311
Ethology, 100, 310–318
Evolution:
  of brain, 320–321
  of cats and dogs, 301
Excitatory nuclei of hypothalamus, 332
Exhaustion, stage of general adaptation syndrome, 346
Exhibition, need for, 63
Exogenous chemicals and behavior, 352–356
Experience:
  and behavior, 98
  categories of, 157
  direct, 158
  objective, 158
Experiment, definition of, 5
Experimental method in psychology, 5–6, 30–31, 39
Exploration, visual, 203
Exposition, need for, 63
External system of brain, 321
Extinction in learning, 221–222
Extirpation (see Ablation of brain)
Extrasensory perception (ESP), 204–206
  individual differences in, 205–206
Extroversion, 410
Eye, structure of retina, 185, 325
Eye fixations in human neonates, 203

Factor analysis:
  of abilities and traits, 8, 29, 364, 407–411

Factor analysis:
  basic methods, 403–407
  and correlation, 403–404
  matrix algebra in, 407
  of multiple-factor methods, 407
Factors:
  in psychological tests, 29, 364
  reality of, 411–412
Failed acts, 50
Faking in personality tests, 392, 399
Familiarization in verbal learning, 268
Family studies in genetics, 290
Fear:
  as conditioned reflex, 225
  and hormones, 345
  as a learned drive, 253–254
Fetus, effects of stress on, 74–76
Field theory, 98, 163–164
Figural aftereffects, 176–177
Figure-ground perception, properties of, 167–168
Figure perception:
  and ground orientation, 169
  simple line figures, 171
Figure reversal, 175–176
  in moving frames, 174
  and satiation, 174
Figures, goodness of, 176
Fixation:
  in children, 71
  as defense mechanism, 74
  and frustration in rats, 71
  oral, 79
  and psychosexual development, 70
  and regression, 70–71
Fixed action patterns (FAP), 312–318
Fixed-interval schedule, 240
Fixed-ratio schedule, 240
Follicle-stimulating hormone (FSH), 340
Food, need for, 63
Forebrain, 320

Forgetting, 230–231
  dynamic theory of, 50
Form preferences in human neonates, 203
Formalization of learning theory, 234
Framework in perception of figures, 168
Fraternal twins (see Dizygotic)
Free associations, 69, 259–260, 267
Free will, 38–39
French symbolists, 38
Frequency curves, 22, 23, 25
Frontal cortex, effects of ablation in monkeys, 334–335
"Fruitfulness," as criterion of scientific theory, 17, 422, 424
Frustration and abnormal fixations, 71–72
Functional equivalence of stimuli in perception, 192
Functionalism, 214

g, 364, 404–407
Galvanic skin response (GSR) in learning, 222–223
Gamete, 283
Gametogenesis, 287
Ganzfeld in perception, 165–167, 184
Gene, 284
Gene dominance, 286
General adaptation syndrome (GAS), 346
General intelligence of Spearman, 364, 404–407
Generalization gradient, 223
Generalized other, 116, 144–145
Generator potential, 323
Genes, physiological action, 284–285
Genetic homogeneity and inbreeding, 297

Genital stage:
  in psychosexual development, 82
  and sublimation, 82
German psychology, 10
Gestalt, meaning of, 163
Gestalt psychology:
  influence on G. H. Mead, 144
  and memory, 178
  and perception, 157–158, 162–163
  and social behavior, 97–98
Glands and behavior, 339–340
Glial cells, 350
Goal-directed nature of behavior, 245–246
God, as archetype, 55
Goldstein-Scheerer test, 394
Good figure:
  experimental approach to definition of, 173–174
  law of, 173
Grammar, analysis of, 262–265
Gregarious instincts, 100
Ground, relation of figure, 167–168
Group:
  reality of, 92–93
  roles in, 143–144
Group dynamics, 139–143
Group spirit, 92
Group tests, 387
Grouping, laws of, 168–169
GSR (galvanic skin response), 222–223
Guilt in personality development, 81

Habit, 211–212
Habit strength ($_sH_R$) in Hull's system, 235–237
Habituation of smiling response in infants, 100–101
Hair cells in auditory mechanism, 324–325
Hallucinogenic substances, 355
Hallucinogens, 354

Haptic perception, 207
Hardy-Weinberg law, 288–289
Harmavoidance, need for, 63
Hearing, physiological basis of, 324–325
Heatavoidance, need for, 63
Heider's concept of balance, 123
Henmon-Nelson Test of Mental Ability, 390
Heredity:
  and animal behavior, 294–299
  and chromosomal defects, 286–288
  and human behavior traits, 290–294
  physical basis of, 281–285
  population studies, 288–290
  transmission of characters, 285–286
Heritability, methods of estimation, 292, 295, 297
Heritable variability of behavior, 279
Heterozygous gene pairs, 286
Heuristic, 39, 424
Hierarchical organization of innate behaviors, 315
Higher-order conditioning, 249–250
Hindbrain, 320
Hippocampus of brain, 334
History, importance of, in psychology, 3
Hitler, Adolf, as archetype, 55
Homeostasis and social behavior, 107
Homeostatic mechanisms:
  physiological nature of, 339–346
  in small groups, 140–141
Homing behavior in salmon, 303–304
Homogeneous stimulation:
  and color perception, 166
  and depth perception, 166
  Ganzfeld experiments, 166
Homosexuality, case study of, 70
Homozygous gene pairs, 286

Honi phenomenon, 187, 195
Hormonal systems, 339–340
Hostility, 62
Humanities, relation to psychology, 10–11
Humor, psychoanalytic theory of, 51–54
Hunger, physiological mechanisms in, 340–343
Hypnosis:
  and experimental demonstration of psychopathology of everyday life, 51
  and experimental production of dreams, 47–48
Hypnotic subject, role of, 147
Hypnotism, schools of, 37
Hypothalamus, role of, in motivation, 331–332
Hypothetical laws in psychology, 424
Hypotheticodeductive method of C. Hull, 234

Id, 55, 56
Idealism, German, 158
Identical twins, 290–293
Identification in psychoanalytic theory, 76
Illusion, 155, 159
Imbalance in small-group activity, 140
Imitation, 102
  generalization of, 104
  learning of: in children, 103–105
    in rats, 103
  model in, 102
  vicarious reinforcement in, 105
Imitative behavior, experimental production of, 102–105
Immediate-memory span, 273–274
Imprinting, 316–317
Incentive motivation, 237

Incredulity, correction for, in Osgood-Tannenbaum model, 127, 128
Individual differences, 15, 362–421
   and correlation, 363–364
   and genetics, 363
   ideas and history of, 362–365
   and statistical variation, 363
Individual tests, 387
Infavoidance, need for, 63
Inference:
   statistical and clinical, 29–30
   statistical significance levels in statistics, 24–27
Inferential statistics, 364
Information storage in brain, 325–326
Informational analysis of memory, 271–272
Inhibition:
   in classical conditioning, 221
   in Hull's theory, 238
   in neurons, 349
Initial memory span, 272
Innate releasing mechanism (IRM), 314–316
Instinct:
   Freudian definition of, 60–62
   and higher motives, 62
   human versus animal, 60
   life and death, 62
   sex and ego, 60–61
   social, 99–101
   [See also Fixed action patterns (FAP)]
Instrumental behavior, 226
Intelligence:
   class and cultural differences in, 377
   and creativity, 416
   and factor analysis, 407–408
   grades of, 377
   Guilford's model of, 408
   inheritance of, 280, 290
   and parents' education, 378

Intelligence:
   primary mental abilities in, 407
   tests of, 387–391
Intention in language, 262
Interaction process analysis, 135
Interference theory of forgetting, 231
Internal system of brain, 321
Interpersonal perception, study of, 115–116
Interposition in depth perception, 180
Interval scale, 368
Intervening variables, 245
Introjection, as defense mechanism, 58
Introspection, 14, 15
Introversion, 410
Introversion-extroversion and classical conditioning, 411
In vacuo phenomenon, 318
Ion-exchange experiment, 342
IQ:
   constancy of, 377
   interpretation of, 376–377
   stability of, 397
Isogenic strains, 296
Isolation experiment, 313
Isomorphism, 160

J curve of social participation, 139
J.N.D. (just noticeable difference), 222
Jokes, scotomatization of, 53

K scale in MMPI, 392
Kantian idealism, 97, 158
Kennedy assassination, 2
Kernel strings in language, 264
Kinesthetic system, 191
Kinship studies, 280
Klinefelter's syndrome, 287
Knowing, 153

Kopfermann cubes, 171, 173
Kuhlmann-Anderson Intelligence Tests, 389–390
Kurtosis, 23
Kwakiutl Indians, 148–149

Lactation, need for, 63
Laissez faire, leadership in children's social groups, 138, 139
Language, analysis of, 261–265
Language machine, 264
Lapsus linguae, 50, 51
Lashley jumping stand, 71
Latency of response in learning, 235, 236
Latent content in dreams, 44
Latent learning, 250, 251
Latent period in psychosexual development, 82
Laughter in analysis of humor, 53
Law of effect, 227
Law of good figure in Gestalt psychology, 173
Laws in psychology, 422–424
Leader in imitation learning, 102–105
Leaderless group discussion, 395
Leadership in small groups, 138–140
Learnable drives, 253, 254
Learning and brain, 325–331
   definition of, 231, 232
   and emotion-arousing material, 69
   interproblem, 255
   of language, 262, 263
   perceptual, 198–200
   and performance, 232, 235
Learning sets, 254–258
Left-to-right model of the sentence planner, 262
Length-difficulty relationship in verbal learning, 229, 230
Leptokurtic distribution, 23

Libido, 59, 60, 423
  and anal stage, 79
  and Id, 59
  and instincts, 60
  investment of, 60
  narcissistic, 60
  object, 60
  and oral stage, 78, 79
Lie scale in MMPI, 392
Likert scale, 120
Limbic system of the brain, 334, 335
Limits, method of, 271
Linear perspective in depth perception, 180
Litter comparisons in behavior genetics, 295–298
Lobectomy, 334
Lobotomy, 334
Local excitatory potential, 323
Local signs in perceptual learning, 199
Localization of function in the brain, 320
Logical coherence of theory, 16
Love, emotion of, 99
Lysergic acid diethylamide (LSD-25), 354

MA (mental age), 371, 376, 377, 387
Man, as a machine, 212
Manic-depression, inheritance of, 294
Manifest content in dreams, 43, 44
Manipulative drive, 257
Manus culture, 96
Marasmus, 77
Marbe's law, 267, 269
Markov process in grammar, 262, 263
Marxism and I. P. Pavlov, 224
Masculine protest in psychoanalytic theory, 81

Masculinity-femininity, scale on MMPI, 392
Masochism, 62
Mass action in brain function, 325–327
MAT (Miller Analogies Test), 390, 397
Matched-dependent behavior, 102
Materialism, 319
Maternal behavior and instincts, 100
Maternal influences on offspring behavior, 75, 76
Maternal separation, effects of, in children, 77
Maternal stimulation, effects of lack of, 77
Maternal stress, effects on offspring, 75, 76
Mathematicodeductive model of C. Hull, 234–239
Mating behavior in stickleback, 312, 313
Matrix algebra in factor analysis, 407
Maudsley Personality Inventory, 411
MAVA (multiple abstract variance analysis) of R. B. Cattell, 291, 292
Mean, 21, 22
Meaningfulness in verbal learning, 228, 265–270
  measurement of, 266, 267
Measurement:
  definition of, 366
  operations in, 366, 367
  psychological, 362–421
  and psychophysics, 369
Median, 21, 22
Mediational chain, 259
Meiosis, 281–285
Memory:
  dynamic theory of, 178
  early studies of, 228–231
  racial, 54

Memory:
  short-term, 270–274
  of single items, 274
  unconscious, 68, 69
  units in, 271–274
Memory span, 270, 271
Memory trace in the brain, 329–331
Mendelian analysis, 285–286
Mental age (MA), 371, 376, 377, 387
Mental disorders, inheritance of, 293, 294
Mental growth, constancy of, 377
Meprobamate, effects on anxiety, 353
Messenger RNA (ribonucleic acid), 284
Metabolic errors, 288
Method of constant stimuli, 271
Method of limits, 271
Method of savings, 229
Migration in salmon, 303, 304
Miller Analogies Test (MAT), 390, 397
Mind, as inferred from behavior, 7
Mind-body problem, 277, 320
Minimax principle, 173, 175, 177, 188
  and binocular fusion, 183
  and memory, 178
  and surface perception, 177, 178
  and texture gradients, 177
Minnesota Multiphasic Personality Inventory, 391, 392, 400, 401
Mitosis, 281
MMPI, 391, 392, 400, 401
Modalities in Erikson's theory of development, 85
Mode, statistical definition of, 20, 22
Models in imitative behavior, 102, 105–106

Modes in Erikson's theory of development, 85
Molar behavior, 246
Mongolism, 287
Monocular cues in depth perception, 179, 180
Motion parallax in depth perception, 180
Motivation:
 and learning, 237, 250
 physiology of, 331, 332
 unconscious, 49–51
Motives, autonomous, 62, 63
Movement constancy, 190
Movement origin, attribution of, 112
Movement produced cues in learning, 242
Multiple abstract variance analysis (MAVA) of R. B. Cattell, 291, 292
Multiple-factor analysis, 407
"Musical unconscious," 419
Mutagenic agents, 354
Mutations, 296

Narcissism, primary and secondary, 61, 62
National differences, 149
Nativism versus empiricism, 199, 200
 in perception, 199, 200
Natural selection, 279, 300
Nature of social psychology, 95–108
Nature-nurture controversy, 100, 198, 203, 204
Navigation in animals, 304
Nay-sayers and yea-sayers, 401, 402
Necker cube, 175, 177
Need, 62
 for contact, 106, 107
 self-actualization, 67
Need achievement, 64–66
 in ancient Greece, 66

Need achievement:
 and economic development, 66
 experimental manipulation of, 64–66
 measurement of, 64
Need-Achievement Test, 393
Need-reduction in learning, 248–250
Needs:
 biological, 56
 classification of, 63
 conscious and unconscious, 64
 instinctual, 56
 manifestation of, 64
Nervous system, central, 320, 321
Neural changes in memory, 351, 352
Neurochemical basis of intelligence, 349
Neuron, transmission in, 323, 324
Neuroticism, 410
 and classical conditioning, 411
 inheritance of, 292
New look in perception, 193–198
Newcomb, balance model of, 123, 124
Nirvana principle, 54
Nomadic phase in army ant, 310
Nominal scale, 367
Nondirective therapy of C. Rogers, 67
Nonsense syllable in study of rote learning, 228
Norepinephrine, 344
Normal:
 continuity with abnormal, 40
 as relative to culture, 41
Normal curve, 22
 and standard deviation, 23, 24
Normal distributions, 23, 24
Normality in perceptual constancies, 187, 188
Norms in testing, 373–377

Noumenon in Kantian philosophy, 158
Novelty, as incentive in learning, 251, 252
Noxavoidance, need for, 63
Null hypothesis, 19, 26
Nurturance, need for, 63

Objective experience, 158, 160
Objectivism, 213, 217
Objectivity in science, 425
Objects, perception of, 179–185
Observation, significance of, 5
Odor discrimination in fish, 303, 304
Oedipal stage, 68, 81, 82
Old brain, 321
One-trial learning, 243
Operant conditioning, 239
Operational flexibility in small groups, 137
Opinion, measurement of (see Attitudes, scaling)
Optic chiasma, 331
Oral eroticism, 78, 79
Oral fixations and frustration in dogs, 79
Oral sadism, 84
Order:
 need for, 63
 of pro and con arguments in communication, 132
Ordinal scale, 367
Ordinal stimulation, 162, 184, 185
Organization, principles of, in perception, 172
Originality, composite test of, 415
 (See also Creativity)
Osgood-Tannenbaum congruity model, 126–129
OSS, selection tests for, 395
Other and self, 144
Otis Quick-scoring Mental Ability Tests, 390
Output systems in brain, 321

Oval window in ear, 324
Overconstancy in perception, 188

Pacinian corpuscle, 323
Paired-associate learning, 267–270
Panmixis, 288, 289
Paradoxical sleep, 48
Parallax in depth perception, 181, 182
Parallel forms in test reliability, 379
Paranatal stage of development, 74–76
Parapsychology, 204
Parsimony, principle of, 214, 215
Partial reinforcement, 239, 240
  in learning of fish, 306
Pattern flexibility in small groups, 137
Patterns of culture, 148–150
Penis envy, 81
Percentile scores, 374, 375
Percept, definition of, 158
Perception:
  autochthonous and behavioral variables in, 193, 194
  and balance, 109
  of causality, 110, 111
  in children, 194
  and conflict, 110
  in congenital cataract patients, 200, 201
  contrast effect in, 167
  demand qualities in, 193
  of depth, 171, 172, 201–203
  dermooptical, 204
  development of, 198
  differentiation learning in, 199
  dimensionality and amount of information, 173
  effects of attitudes and motives on, 193–198
  effects of body rotation on, 193
  effects of body tilt on, 192, 193
  effects of familiarity, 194–196

Perception:
  effects of light deprivation on, 201
  "entraining effect" in, 110, 111
  extensions in study of, 191–207
  extrasensory, 204–206
  and eye fixations, 203
  of figures, 171
  of form, 200
  haptic, 207
  heredity and environment in, 203, 204
  historical background in study of, 159–162
  and Honi phenomenon, 195, 196
  innate or acquired, 171
  internal and external forces in, 172, 173
  kinesthesia in, 191
  laws of organization in, 199
  and "local signs," 199
  in monkeys and apes, 201
  and needs, 110
  in neonates, 203
  new look in, 193–198
  organismic theory of, 164
  "outer limits" of, 204–207
  phenomena of, 165
  physiological mechanisms in, 200
  properties of, 109, 110
  satiation in, 176
  selective factors in, 196
  and sensation, 155, 159, 160, 161
  sensory-tonic theory of, 191–193
  of size, 193, 194
  spatial selectivity in, 196
  and stabilized retinal images, 169
  successes in, 179
  symmetrization in, 193
  temporal selectivity in, 196

Perception:
  of three-dimensional world, 179
  of tridimensionality, 172, 174
  and unconscious defense, 196, 197
  unities and identities in, 165, 199, 200
  and values, 110, 196, 197
  veridical, 155
  of "visual cliff," 201–203
  and visual exploration, 203
  of wholes, 109, 110
Perceptual constancy, 185–190
  brightness and color, 188–190
  innateness of, 186
  movement, 190
  shape, 186, 187
  size, 187, 188
Perceptual defense, 196
Perceptual grouping, laws of, 168–171
Performance tests of personality, 392–394
Person perception, 110–113
  accuracy in, 115
  and balance concept, 107, 108
  and causality, 112
  individual differences in, 113
  sex differences in accuracy of, 114
Personality:
  accuracy of judgment of, 116
  development of, 74–89
  dynamics of, 59–73
  economics of, 59–73
  effects of early experience on, 74
  factor analysis of, 408–411
  normal and abnormal, 40
  tests of, 392–395
  topography and structure in, 42–58
Personality dimensions, Eysenck's theory of, 410, 411

447 SUBJECT INDEX

Personality traits:
    ergic strength in, 409, 410
    and heredity, 292, 293, 410
    and reactive inhibition, 410, 411
    source and surface, 409
Persons, social attributes of, 96
Persuasibility and communication, 133–135
    personality correlates of, 134
Persuasibility tests, 133, 134
Phallic fixations, 80
Phallic personality, 80
Phallic stage, 80, 81
    and narcissism, 80
Phase sequences in brain, 328
Phenomena of perception, 165
Phenomenal field, 98
Phenomenal vertical and stimulation, 192
Phenomenological method and the categories of experience, 157
Phenomenology, definition of, 157
Phenotype, relation to genotype, 297–299
Phenylketonuria (PKU), 288
Phrenology, 320
Phylogeny and behavior, 305
Physiological needs and Id, 56
Physiology of motivation, 331, 332
Pitch, 322, 323
Pituitary gland, 346
Place learning, 247, 248
Platykurtic distribution, 23
Play, need for, 63
Play techniques, 85
Pleasure principle, 56
Pleasure sucking, 78
Polygenic inheritance of traits, 286
Polymorphous perverse stage, 76
Population studies in human genetics, 288, 289
Position-habit error in learning, 256

Postremity, principle of, 243
Postsynaptic neuron, 349
Pragmatism, 214
Prägnanz, law of, 173, 174
Precognition, 204
Predatory adaptations, 301–303
Pregnancy stress and offspring behavior, 75, 76
Prejudice, racial, 120
Prenatal influences, 74–76
Pressure in touch and audition, 323–325
Prestige of communicator, 131
Primary groups, 135
Primary identification, 76
Primary mental abilities, 407
Primary mental abilities test, 408
Primary process, 56
Primary reinforcement, 235
Primitivation in play, 72
Principle of least effort, 246
Probability value in statistics, 25
Proband method in genetics, 293
Problem-solving patterns in social communication nets, 136–138
Process, idea of, in psychology, 213
Product-moment correlation (see Correlation coefficient)
Projection, 64, 69
    case study of, 70
    experimental study of, 70
Projective tests, 64, 393
Propositus method in genetics, 293
Proximity, law of, 168, 170
Pseudoaffective emotion, 322
Psilocin, 355
Psychiatry in development of psychoanalysis, 37
Psychoanalysis:
    basic notions and method, 36–41
    case study in, 34
    and instincts, 60–62

Psychoanalysis:
    methodological postulates, 38–41
Psychoanalytic theory:
    assessment of, 86–87
    experimental study of, 83
Psychogenic needs, 62–64
Psychokinesis, 204, 205
Psychological scaling, 366–370
Psychological testing:
    history of, 370, 371
    purposes, 372
    and response sets, 399–403
    and response styles, 399–403
    scales and norms in, 373–377
Psychological tests:
    aptitude versus achievement, 372, 373
    classification of, 387
    criticisms of, 395–398
    culture and class differences, 373
    and decision-making, 372
    definition and nature of, 372, 373
    examples of, 387–398
    parallel forms of, 379
    of personality, 391–395
    as predictors of success in clinical training program, 397
    and "psychoquizzes," 374
    and reliability, 377–382
    standardization of, 373
    "Testing and Public Policy," 366
    and traits, 399–426
    usefulness of, 395–398
Psychological theories:
    comparisons of, 424
    relative fruitfulness of, 424, 425
Psychological theory:
    laws in, 422–424
    variables in, 422–424
Psychology:
    and common sense, 5, 6

Psychology:
   definition of science of, 4–8
   drawing conclusions in, 18
   and everyday life, 14
   history of, 14
   intellectual structure of, 16
   major approaches in, 30
   present status of, 14
   relation to life sciences, 9
   relation to other disciplines, 8–11
   relation to philosophy, 10
   as a science, 4–6
   and society, 11, 425
Psychometrics in contrast to experimental psychology, 364, 365
Psychopathology of everyday life, 49–51
   experimental demonstration of, 51
Psychopharmacology, 352–356
Psychophysics, 228, 369
Psychosexual development:
   anal stage, 79, 80
   Erikson's theory of, 85, 86
   genital stage, 82, 83
   Klein's theory, 85
   latent period, 82
   Oedipal stage, 81, 82
   oral stage, 78
   phallic stage, 80
   polymorphous perverse stage, 76–78
Psychosis, inheritance of, 293, 294
Psychosomatics, 344
Psychoticism, 410
Psychotropic drugs, 352
PTC (phenylthiocarbimide), inheritance of taste blindness of, 289
Pueblo Indians, 149
   (See also Zuni)
Purkinje effect, 325
Purposive behaviorism, 245

Q-technique, 67
Queen, as dream symbol, 47
Quiescence principle, 54

R (response to selection), 297
r (see Correlation coefficient)
Racial memory, 54
Racial prejudice, 120, 121
Rage reactions and subcortical lesions, 334
Random mating in human populations, 288–289
Rank-frequency function in measuring meaningfulness, 267
Rank-order scale, 367, 368
Rapid eye movements (REMs), 48, 49, 338
Ratio scale, 369
Ratio schedules of reinforcement, 239–241
Raven Progressive Matrix Test, 390
Reaction formation, case study, 69
Reaction potential (SER), 235, 236
Reactive inhibition, 238, 410
   and personality, 410, 411
Reality principle, 56
Receptors and central nervous system, 322–325
Recessive genes, 286
Recipient of communication, 133, 134
Reciprocal sensitivity in social relationships, 97
Recognition:
   need for, 63
   threshold in, 196, 197
Recognition memory, 273
Recognition threshold and word frequency, 197
Reductionism, 162, 163
Reflexology of I. P. Pavlov, 217–224

Regression, 61, 74
   clinical examples of, 70
   and frustration, 71
   in play behavior, 71
   and tics, 70
Reinforcement:
   by acquired fear, 253, 254
   brain stimulation as, 335, 336
   in imitation learning, 102–105
   in learning theory of C. Hull, 248–250
   secondary, 249, 250
   vicarious, 105, 106
Rejection, need for, 63
Relatives and inheritance of behavior traits, 281, 294
Reliability:
   definition of, 28, 364, 377, 378
   factors affecting, 381, 382
   methods of calculating, 378–381
   problems of, 377–382
   and test length, 381, 382
Remote associations in verbal learning, 231
REMs (see Rapid eye movements)
Repetition and learning, 229
Repetition compulsion, 62
Repression, 50, 68, 69, 79
   experimental demonstration of, 68, 69
Reproductive isolation, 301
Resistance:
   to extinction after partial reinforcement in fish, 305, 306
   of phenotype to environmental influence, 298, 299
   stage of, in general adaptation syndrome, 346
   to stress, and early stimulation, 77
   in therapy, 55
Respondent behavior, 239
Response decrement in classical conditioning, 221, 222

Response equivalence in classical conditioning, 221
Response fatigue and inhibition, 222
Response sets, 399–403
Response-shift error, 256
Response styles in testing, 399–403
Retention, need for, 63
Reticular activating system, 338
Retina, rods and cones in, 184, 185
Retinal disparity in depth perception (see Binocular disparity in depth perception)
Retinal mosaic, 162, 184, 185
Reversible figures, 174–176
Ribonucleic acid (RNA), 284, 351
RNA (ribonucleic acid), 284, 351
Rods of the retina, 325
Role, 99, 143–148
    and self, 147
    in small groups, 142, 143
Role expectations, 146
Role strain, 146
Role-taking, aptitude for, 147
Rorschach Test, 393, 394
Rote learning:
    acquisition processing, 265, 266
    study of, by H. Ebbinghaus, 228–231
Rules in language learning, 262–265
Rumor and minimax principle, 178

Sadism, 62
    case study of, 34
Salience of attitudes, 118
Salivation, conditioned, 218, 219
Salpêtrière, school of hypnotism, 37
Salt balance in adrenalectomized animals, 341, 342
Samples in basic statistics, 19

Satiation in perception, 175–177
Satori in Zen Buddhism, 425, 426
Savings, method of, 229, 230
Scaling:
    of attitudes, 119, 120
    in psychology, 366–370
    and test norms, 373–377
Scalloping effect in operant conditioning, 240
Scapegoat in small groups, 142
Schizophrenia, inheritance of, 293, 294
Schools of psychology, 15
Science:
    and belief, 425
    definition of, 4, 5
    inference in, 5, 425
Scientific theory, 16
Scotomatization of jokes, 53
Secondary elaboration, 41
Secondary processes, 56
Secondary reinforcement, 249, 250
Secretion, 340
Selection of behavior, 296, 297
Selection criteria in prediction of job success, 384, 385
Selection differential (S), 297
Selective sensitization, 196
Self, relation to role, 144–148
Self-actualization, 66
Self-determination, need for, 39
Self-perception, 67
Self-report tests, 391, 392
Sensation, 158, 159
    meanings of, 162
    and perception, 155, 162, 184
Sensitivity:
    dimensions of, 161
    to generalized other, 116
    interpersonal, 116
Sensitivity training, 150
Sensory deprivation, 201, 203
Sensory modalities in learning, 327, 328
Sensory stimulation, 158, 322–325

Sensory-tonic theory, 164, 191–193
Sentence generation in language, 262–265
Sentience, need for, 63
Septal area of brain and electrical self-stimulation, 335, 336
Sex, need for, 63
Sex chromosome anomalies, 287, 288
Sex chromosomes, 281–284
Sex differences in persuasibility, 134
Sexual behavior:
    in animals, 306–308
    and hormones, 343, 344
Sexuality:
    and instincts, 60, 61
    pregenital, 68
Shadow, as cue in depth perception, 180
Sham rage, 334, 335
Shame, 81
Shape constancy, 186, 187
Short-term memory, 270–274
Significance of a difference, statistical example of, 25
Significance levels, 25
Similance, need for, 63
Similarity, law of, 168, 170
Situation tests of personality, 395
Size constancy, 187, 188
Size cues in depth perception, 179
Size-estimation, effects of values and needs on, 193–196
Skin senses, 323, 324
Skinner box, 239
Sleep:
    and dreaming, 48, 49
    and wakefulness, physiology of, 337, 338
"Sleeper effect" in attitude change, 131, 132
Small group behavior, 135–143
Small groups, structure and roles in, 135–143

Smiling response in infants, 100, 101
Snow White, psychoanalytic interpretation of, 83
Social act, dimensions of, 98, 99
Social attitudes, balance in, 98
Social behavior:
   in animals, 308–310
   cognitive approach to, 98
   models of, 91
   and reinforcement, 102
Social behaviorism of G. H. Mead, 144, 145
Social climate and leadership, 138, 139
Social communication (see Communication)
Social education, 150
Social experience, perception and attitude, 109–129
Social influence:
   and communication, 130–151
   nature of, 130, 131
   (See also Communication)
Social instincts, 99–101
Social interactions:
   categories of, 136
   measurement of, in small groups, 135
   in "satisfied" and "dissatisfied" groups, 142
Social motivation, 99–108
   learning of, 101–106
Social networks, 137
Social participation, J curve in, 139
Social perception, 109–117
   and balance concept, 107, 108
Social position, 145
Social psychology, 94
   nature of, 108
Social reality, 95, 96
Social role (see Role)
Social value and perception, 194–196
Sociogram, 135, 136

Sociology and psychology, 9, 93, 94
Sociometry, 135
Sodium, internal sampling for, 342, 343
Solidarity in small groups, 141, 142
Sonar systems, 13, 14, 302, 303
Source traits, 409
Spearman-Brown formula for correction for attenuation, 384
Species-typical behavior, 308–310
Specific hungers, 341–343
Speech area of brain, 320
Split-brain preparation, 330, 331
Spontaneous recovery, 222
Stabilized images, effects on perception, 169, 170
Stages of psychosexual development, 74–82
Standard deviation, 22
Standard deviation scores, 28
Standard error:
   of correlation, 28
   of differences between means, 27
   of mean, 24, 25
Standard scores, 375–376
Standardization of tests, 373
Standards of ethical behavior for psychologists, 398
Stanford-Binet test of intelligence, 387, 388
Statary phase in behavior of army ant, 308–310
State-dependent learning, 355, 356
Statistical versus clinical prediction, 29, 30
Statistical parameters, estimates of, 20
Statistics, 19–29
Steady-state hypothesis, 240
Stereoscope, 183
Stereotype accuracy, 116

Stereotyped behavior and frustration, 71
Stereotypy of behavior, 244, 313
Stimulant drugs, 352
Stimulation:
   gradients of, 183–185
   homogeneous, 165–167
   ordinal, 162, 184, 185
   patterns in, 164
   proximal, 185
   units in, 162
Stimulus, adequate, 161, 322
Stimulus generalization, 222, 223
Stimulus intensity dynamism, 237
Stimulus perseveration error, 256
Stimulus reception, 322
Stimulus-response connectionism, 225
Stimulus substitution, theory of, 220
Stomach ulcers and stress, 347–349
Storage capacity in memory, 273
Storage load in memory, 273
Strains, use of, in genetics, 295
Stress, response to, 345, 346
Structuralism, 144, 160, 162, 214
Structure of personality, psychoanalytic theory of, 55–58
Sublimation, 72, 73
Succorance, need for, 63
Sum of neighbors in small groups, 137
Superego, 55–58, 423
Superiority, need for, 63
Supernormal stimulus, 100
Surface texture and depth perception, 184
Surface traits, 409
Surrogate mothers, effects on young monkeys, 107
Survival, law of, 214
Symbolization in dreams, 46
Symmetrization, 193
Symmetry and social behavior, 107, 108

Symptomatic acts, 50
Synapse, 349
Syntactic structures in language, 261

T groups, 150
t test, 27
Tanala of Madagascar, 79
Taste blindness, inheritance of, 289
TAT (Thematic Apperception Test), 64, 393, 394
Tchambuli, 5
Telepathy, 204
Television viewing, effects of, 12
Test length:
   and reliability, 381
   and validity, 384
Tests, types of, 387–398
     intelligence, 387–391
     personality, 391–395
Tetrad differences in factor analysis, 406, 407
Texture and judgment of depth, 184, 185
Thalamus, 332, 334
Thematic Apperception Test (TAT), 64, 393, 394
Theory in science, 5, 17, 424, 425
Theory building in psychology, 422–425
Therapy:
   self-perception in, 67
   Skinnerian, 410
Thirst, physiology, 340, 341
Threshold, psychophysical, 228, 322
Thurstone Attitude Scale, 119, 120
Tics, 70
Time and creativity, 414
Token rewards in learning, 250
Tonic system and perception, 164, 165
Topographical correspondence between retina and cortex, 181

Touch receptors, 323
Trait theory:
   of R. Cattell, 408–410
   of H. Eysenck, 410, 411
Traits, 408–411
   (See *also* Personality traits)
Tranquilizers, 353, 354
Transactionalist functionalism, 159, 164
Transformations, linguistic, 264
Transmitter substances, 349, 350
Trial-and-error learning, 226–228
Trigram in study of rote learning, 228
Trobriand Islanders, 82
Tropism, 310, 311
Twin method, 290, 291

Uncertainty in information theory, 271, 272
Unconditioned response, 219
Unconditioned stimulus, 218
Unconscious, 37, 42–55
   collective, 54
   evidence for, 43–55
   inference, 159
   irony, 151
   motivation, 51
   relation to conscious, 42, 43
   relation to preconscious, 42, 43
Uniqueness of personality, 33
Units:
   in memory, 271, 327, 328
   in perception, 162
   in psychological tests, 373
Universe, statistical concept of, 19
Urination, need for, 63
Useful and psychology, 11, 12
Utility dimension in behavior, 214

Valence of attitudes, 118, 123
Validity:
   concept of, 364, 382, 383

Validity:
   of the clinical method, 39
   factors affecting, 384
   types of, 383
   value of valid test, 384–386
Value orientation, test of, 196
Value resonance, 196
Variability, measures of, 22, 23
Variable-interval schedule, 240, 241
Variables, types of, in psychology, 422–424
Variation:
   and heritability, 292, 295
   in living organisms, 19, 279, 363
Verbal behavior:
   and associations, 259–261
   and meaningfulness, 265–270
   and memory, 270–274
   and syntactic structures, 261–265
Verbal scale in Wechsler tests, 388
Veridical perception, 155
Vicarious reinforcement in imitation learning, 105, 106
Vicarious trial and error (VTE) 245
Visceral brain, 321
Viscerogenic needs, 62–64
Visual cliff, 201–203
Visual field, 161
Visual perception (see Perception)
Visual reception, 325
Visual world, 161, 162, 167

Wakefulness, physiology of, 337, 338
Water, need for, 63
Weber's law, 323
Wechsler Adult Intelligence Scale, 388, 389
Wechsler Intelligence Scale for Children, 388, 389, 418

Wertheimer-Benussi effect, 167, 168
Wholes in perception, 162, 163, 168
Wish fulfillment:
   in dreams, 44, 45
   in psychopathology of everyday life, 50, 51
   in wit, 52
Wit:
   experimental analysis of, 53, 54

Wit:
   Freudian theory of, 51–54
   in mental patients, 53
   relation to dreams, 52
   and repression, 54
Word frequency and perception, 197, 198

X chromosome, 283, 284, 287

Y chromosome, 283, 284, 287

Yea-sayers and nay-sayers, 401, 402

Z score, 24
Zen Buddhism, 425
Zero point in ratio scale, 369
Zones of development in Erikson's theory, 85
Zuni, 148, 149, 273
Zygote, 288–290

112
173
1963

110
112
113